MOTION AND TIME STUDY
DESIGN AND MEASUREMENT OF WORK

MOTION AND TIME STUDY

DESIGN AND MEASUREMENT OF WORK

Seventh Edition

RALPH M. BARNES

Professor of Engineering and Production Management Emeritus
University of California, Los Angeles, California

John Wiley & Sons

New York • Chichester • Brisbane • Toronto • Singapore

Library of Congress Cataloging in Publication Data:

Barnes, Ralph Mosser, 1900–
  Motion and time study.

  Includes indexes.
  1. Motion study. 2. Time study. I. Title.
T60,4.B39 1980   658.5′42   80-173
ISBN 0-471-05905-6

Printed in the United States of America

10 9 8 7 6 5 4

PREFACE

The purpose of this book is to present the basic principles that underlie the successful application of motion and time study and to supplement each with illustrations and practical examples. The body of knowledge and the diversity of practices in this field have become very broad, and in this revision I have included those practices that are basic, practical, cost effective, and widely used.

The design and measurement of work and the problem-solving process are fundamental to the modern industrial organization. Here is a powerful tool for increasing productivity, improving equipment utilization, conserving materials and energy, reducing human effort, and advancing the goals of the organization on many fronts. Moreover, described in some detail are ways of organizing work so that people will be motivated to use the methods and tools presented here. Thus, work itself will be more meaningful and rewarding and each working day can contribute to life satisfactions.

The social climate in this country and in other industrialized nations is changing. People are better educated, have broader interests, are more affluent, have more leisure time, and their expectations regarding all aspects of life, including their work, are different than they were even a decade ago. Some are seeking more interesting jobs with greater challenge. Others satisfy their physiological needs through the wages they receive and turn to off-job activities for their social and egotistic needs—belonging, recognition, self-actualization. For the increasing number of people who have high-level needs and want jobs calling for creative effort and responsibility, industry can provide forms of work organization and job designs to enable them to achieve their personal goals and at the same time achieve the goals of the organization.

New knowledge coming from social and behavioral science research has been assimilated, interpreted, and applied by managers and industrial engineers with great success. It is recognized that although pay is a powerful stimulator, people are motivated by other things as well. The time-tested techniques described in this volume can be used by the industrial engineer, the supervisor, and the individual worker, and by teams or groups.

Research findings seem to indicate that the major factors which determine job satisfaction are achievement, recognition, work itself, responsibility, and advancement. If management can provide an environment in which these factors can operate, the employees will respond in a positive way.

Under this plan, industrial engineers spend less time performing professional duties in the usual sense; instead, more time is devoted to assisting management and non-management people. Engineers fully understand the motivation-maintenance theory. They have participated in a number of successful applications, and know the benefits that come to the organization and to the employees.

The requirements of this more effective work system will be new to many people and will require considerable time to understand and accept. Implementation can take many different forms. There is no set system or procedure that must be followed. It is the basic theory—the philosophy—that is important, not the mechanism.

Revisions have been made throughout the book and much new material has been added. A new first chapter, "Productivity," discusses the various interpretations of the term and shows the relationship of motion and time study to the many factors influencing the effectiveness of the entire organization. A major development is the use of the minicomputer. Although computers have been used in work methods design and work measurement, the advent of the small data collector and the desk-top computer provides a simple and convenient way to make time studies, monitor and measure machine and equipment performance, make work sampling studies, and perform other data-gathering activities. Predetermined time systems are more widely used and they have computer-aided versions. Computerized standard data are another effective way to measure work. New chapters have been added on computer aided time study, computerized monitoring of downtime of machines, and developing standard data from predetermined times. The computer, using these available data, determines the optimum method for performing the job, prepares a detailed instruction sheet which can be used by the operator, and determines the standard for the job and prints it all out.

New material is included on wage payment, wage incentives, and multi-factor wage payment plans. A new chapter describes a company-wide participative management program with a computer-based bonus plan for all management and non-management people. The chapter on "Human Factors" includes a description of the scope and activities of the Human Factors Laboratory of a consumer products manufacturer and of the Human Factors Engineering Division of a missile and space company.

There is no way to fully acknowledge my debt to the many people and organizations contributing to this book. In fact, this volume reflects my total professional training and experience. I was influenced and guided by the lectures and personal contact with Dexter S. Kimball, Professor of Industrial Engineering and Dean of the College of Engineering at Cornell University. I have learned much from my colleagues and students at the University of Iowa and the University of California. I acknowledge the many contributions from the staff and participants of the Iowa Management Course in which I had a part for 10 years, and from the UCLA Engineering and Management Program, which is now in its 26th year. Moreover, I am greatly indebted to those people and to the industries they represent (in this country and abroad) who have generously shared their knowledge and have provided much valuable material in this book. The suggestions from the users of this book through several editions over some 40 years have been most helpful. I have tried to give specific acknowledgments to those whose work is reported.

My special thanks for assistance received in connection with the present revision go to Leroy O. Gillette, Armstrong Cork Company; L. C. Boehringer, Harry L. Davis, O. J. Feorene and James A. Richardson, Eastman Kodak Company; John L. Larson and C. Michael Allen, Eli Lilly and Company; Richard L. Burdick, The Maytag Company; Walter B. Scott, Motorola Inc.; and Richard A. Forberg, The Procter and Gamble Company.

Los Angeles, California   **Ralph M. Barnes**

CONTENTS

MOTION AND TIME STUDY
DESIGN AND MEASUREMENT OF WORK

PRODUCTIVITY

Productivity is a term that has a number of different meanings although it is most commonly associated with labor effectiveness in industry. In a broad sense productivity is the ratio of output to some or all of the resources used to produce the output. Productivity = output ÷ input. *Labor productivity* may be defined as "output per unit of time" or "output per labor hour."

Labor productivity = units produced ÷ hours worked
Capital productivity = output ÷ capital input
Material productivity = output ÷ materials input

A model such as the one shown in Fig. 1 aids in illustrating the fact that for the company as a whole its productivity is a function of all of the inputs.[1] Six of these are shown in the model. They all contribute to the Total Productivity of the Firm. This model takes the form of a closed system which starts with the inputs and results in outputs which are purchased by the customer, producing revenues from the sales which are fed back into the system. The flow is affected by the prices, the demand, and of course the productivity of the different inputs. Although we are concerned with all factors affecting productivity, greatest emphasis will be placed on the effectiveness of labor, the efficient operation of machines, equipment, and facilities and the economical use of materials. All of these factors relate to the cost of the product.

Productivity Index

Labor productivity or "output per hour," as compiled by the U.S. Bureau of Labor Statistics for many parts of the economy, is recognized as one of the standard guidelines. Labor productivity is determined by taking the ratio of output to input and indexing this relationship over time. Using the Bureau of Labor Statistics methods, a company can determine its labor productivity or output per man hour by dividing its total annual labor output by the total hours worked. The output is the "real" annual sales, that is, net sales adjusted by a corporate price index. The labor input is the average number of employees multiplied by the average number of hours worked during the year. The annual adjusted net sales are divided by the man hours for the year to give the output per man hour. These figures obtained from year to year can be

---

[1] William A. Ruch and James C. Hershauer, *Factors Affecting Worker Productivity,* Bureau of Business and Economic Research, College of Business Administration, Arizona State University, Tempe, Ariz., p. 24, 1974.

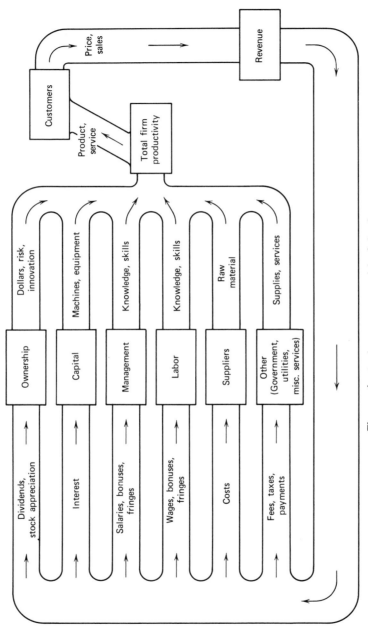

Figure 1 An input-output model of the firm.

indexed and can be related to a base year so that output per man-hour comparisons can be made.

Increased productivity makes it possible to pay good wages to employees, provide satisfactory dividends to stockholders and to sell products and services at low prices. Many companies compute their labor productivity index annually and keep a continuous record, making comparisons with other companies in their industry and with the national index. The ideal objective of an organization might be to provide adequately for employees and stockholders and to sell products at lower and lower prices. This would serve to increase the standard of living and reduce inflation. Although few companies can meet this objective, some have outstanding records.

Eli Lilly and Company, for example, a large pharmaceutical manufacturer, has a century-long record of increasing productivity and at the same time reducing the cost of its products. During the past ten years the annual increase in Lilly's labor productivity has been about four times as great as that for the average of other U.S. manufacturers. During the same ten-year period Lilly's U.S. prices compared with the U.S. Consumer Price Index increased only about one-fifth as much as did the average consumer prices. The customers have benefited from prices that have increased far less than they would have without the impact of greater productivity. Dr. John R. Virts, Corporate Staff Economist for Eli Lilly states:

There is no single cause or simple explanation of Lilly's record of strong productivity growth. Clearly, it is not just how hard people work or how fast machinery runs. It is these things *plus* the combination of technology, people, and their motivations; the blending of employees into successful teams; the use of effective management skills; and the generation of new solutions and innovative procedures in research, production, and marketing. Another vital ingredient, we believe, is our employees' pride in their work and desire to contribute their best.

Technological Innovation

Changes in technology are taking place at a rapid rate in many areas and with these changes an increase in productivity is expected. In many cases technological innovation has resulted in increased labor output, a reduction in costs, and a reduction in the price of the product or service.

Well-known examples are the dial telephone, which reduces the need for the telephone operator; hybrid seeds, fertilizer, and farm machinery, which increase the yield per acre and per hour of farm labor. Electronic technology has produced phenomenal productivity gains. Since the 1950s the speed of computer computations has increased 10,000 times and the cost of calculations has decreased drastically. The price of the hand-held calculator has been reduced from $1500 to less than $10 in a single decade. Texas Instruments, an electronic manufacturer, has increased its employees' average compensation about 9 percent a year for the last five years, yet its productivity gains have enabled it both to reduce prices 28 percent and increase profits 143 percent during the same period. Paul C. Ely, Jr., vice president and Computer Systems Group general manager at Hewlett-Packard, states that for his company the price/performance ratio has been decreasing since the early 1960s at a nearly constant 30 percent per year, and that improvement should continue into the foreseeable future. This results in part from the favorable impact of technology on cost and performance.

In many cases high technology requires an increase in capital investment and an increase in employees' skills. Heavy physical work and repetitive operations are performed by machines, the working environment is greatly improved, and the operator often becomes a manager directing and controlling complex machines and processes. With the coming of the computer, which is often an integral part of the machine, the operator may only need to take action when unusual conditions occur or when a changeover in the product or process takes place.

Measurement of Individual Worker Productivity

The productivity of the individual employee in a factory can be measured in a different way. If 100 employees produce 3000 units of a single product in one day, the average output might be stated as 30 units per person per day. In this illustration we merely have a record of what happened. We do not know anything about the condition of the equipment used, the methods employed, or the way the work was organized. However, there is a way to measure with precision the labor content of a job or operation and it can be expressed in standard minutes per unit.

By means of time study, predetermined time systems, or work sampling, the standard time for a specific task can be established. The number of pieces produced by a worker in one day multiplied by the standard time per piece represents the standard or expected output for the day. For example, if the standard time to assemble a bench grinder is 2.00 minutes per unit and if the operator assembles 275 grinders during the day, the output is 550 standard minutes ($275 \times 2.00 = 550$). If the operator works an 8-hour day or 480 minutes, the input would be 480 minutes. The operator's performance index would be 114.6 percent.

$$\text{Performance Index} = \frac{550}{480} \times 100 = 114.6\%$$

The average productivity index of a department or of a plant would be the total standard minutes or standard hours produced by all employees divided by the actual minutes or hours worked multiplied by 100. This assumes that all of the operations are covered by time standards. Thus a performance index can be used company wide as a labor productivity index. This form of performance measurement has been used regularly for many years and its use is growing.

Productivity of Capital

The productivity of capital as represented by tools, machines, and other operating facilities is of concern to many organizations. Factors such as energy consumption, maintenance, and obsolescence, as well as the utilization of the facilities may have a major affect on productivity and costs in capital-intensive industries. With a million-dollar investment in a single printing press or one paper-making machine and hundreds of millions invested in refineries, chemical plants, and steel mills, the factors mentioned above become very crucial. One element that is readily susceptible to improvement is the utilization of the equipment. Equipment may be scheduled to operate around the clock, seven days per week, but downtime is an ever-present problem.

For example, downtime is one of the most important factors affecting productivity of equipment in steel mills. In one modern high-speed slab mill a crew of eight people per shift operates the mill which has an operating cost of about $4500 per hour. A crew of 20 people is required for the hot strip mill and the cost is $8500 per hour. Assuming uniformity of the quality of the finished product, the speed of the mill and the downtime are the two most important factors controlling the productivity and costs. In these mills the crews are paid on a group incentive plan based on (1) amount of downtime and (2) their ability to operate the mill at optimum speed. The end result is the lowest cost per ton of steel produced and the highest earnings for the operators. In a case such as this the total wages paid to the operators are relatively small in comparison with the cost of capital invested in the rolling mills.

Motion and Time Study and Productivity

There is a body of knowledge which has evolved over the years that is designed to increase the productivity of an organization and of the individuals who make up the organization. Motion and time study has as its objective the elimination of unnecessary work, the design of methods and procedures which are most effective, which require the least effort, and which are suited to the person who uses them. Moreover, it provides methods of measuring work for determining a performance index or productivity index for an individual or for a group of workers, a department, or for an entire plant.

Although industrial engineers and staff specialists ordinarily perform work in this field, there is a trend toward developing forms of work organization in which motion and time study and the problem-solving process are used directly by the managers, supervisors, and the employees themselves. In the latter case they assume responsibilities for the design of jobs, determine work schedules, and verify the quality of the work they produce. It is the purpose of this book to present ways of increasing human effectiveness and improving life satisfactions through work itself.

2

DEFINITION AND SCOPE OF MOTION AND TIME STUDY

The terms *time study* and *motion study* have been given many interpretations since their origin. Time study, originated by Taylor, was used mainly for determining time standards, and motion study, developed by the Gilbreths, was employed largely for improving methods. Although Taylor and Gilbreth did their pioneering work about the same time, in the early days greater use was made of time study and wage incentive than of motion study. It was not until the 1930s that a general movement got under way to study work with the objective of finding better and simpler methods of getting the job done. Then there followed a period during which motion study and time study were used together, the two supplementing each other, and the combined term *motion and time study* came into use. Rapid changes are now taking place in this field. We are now concerned with the design of work systems and methods. Our objective is to find the ideal method or the method nearest to the ideal that can be practically used, whereas in the past the emphasis was too often on improving existing methods, rather than carefully defining the problem, formulating objectives, and then finding the preferred solution.

Originally motion and time study applications were made by industrial engineers and staff specialists, and this continues today. However, managers and line supervisors, and the workers themselves are to an increasing extent making direct use of the problem-solving process and motion and time study.

Some have suggested that the term *methods engineering, work design, work study,* or *job design* should be used in place of *motion and time study,* and it may be that eventually these terms will come into wider use. There is, however, at the present time a trend toward making *work methods design* synonymous with motion study and *work measurement* synonymous with time study. Therefore *motion and time study* and *work methods design and work measurement* will be used interchangeably in this book and will have the following broad meaning.

Definition of Motion and Time Study

Motion and time study is the systematic study of work systems with the purposes of (1) developing the preferred system and method—usually the one with the lowest cost; (2) standardizing this system and method; (3) determining the time required by a qualified and properly trained person working at a normal pace to do a specific task or operation; and (4) assisting in training the worker in the preferred method.

Motion and time study is composed of four parts, as this definition shows. However, the *two main parts* and those that will be given greatest emphasis in this book are:

Motion study or **work methods design**—for finding the preferred method of doing work. That is, the ideal method or the one nearest to it.

Time study or **work measurement**—for determining the standard time to perform a specific task.

1. Developing the Preferred Method—Work Methods Design. In the broadest sense, every business and industrial organization is concerned with the creation of goods and services in some form—utilizing workers, machines, and materials. In a manufacturing plant, for example, the production process might include the procurement of the raw materials, the machining and fabrication of the parts, and the delivery of the finished product. In designing such a manufacturing process, consideration would be given to the entire system and to each individual operation which would go to make up the system or process. The design of such a process employs the general problem-solving approach. People in the physical sciences and applied sciences refer to the problem-solving procedure as the systematic approach, scientific method, or engineering approach.[1]

Methods design therefore begins with the consideration of the purpose or goal—to manufacture a specific product, to operate a cash-and-carry cleaning and pressing establishment, or to produce milk on a dairy farm. The objective is to design a system, a sequence of operations and procedures that make up the preferred solution. Certain tools and techniques have evolved over the years to assist in developing preferred work methods, and these will be presented in detail on the following pages.

2. Standardizing the Operation—Written Standard Practice. After the best method for doing the work has been determined, this should be standardized. Ordinarily, the work is broken down into specific jobs or operations which are described in detail. The particular set of motions, the size, shape, and quality of material, the particular tools, jigs, fixtures, gauges, and the machine or piece of equipment should be definitely specified. All these factors, as well as the conditions should be definitely specified. All these factors, as well as the conditions surrounding the worker, must be maintained after they have been standardized. A written standard practice giving a detailed record of the operation and specifications for performing the work is the most common way of preserving the standard. A job can not be measured until it has first been defined.

3. Determining the Time Standard—Work Measurement. Motion and time study may be used to determine the standard number of minutes that a qualified, properly trained, and experienced person should take to perform a specific task or operation when working at a normal pace. This time standard may be used for planning and scheduling work, for cost estimating, or for labor cost control, or it may serve as the basis for a wage incentive plan.

---

[1] The general problem-solving process is described in Chapter 4.

Although standard data, predetermined time systems, and work sampling are widely used for establishing time standards, perhaps the most common method of measuring work is stop-watch time study or electronic time study. The operation to be studied is divided into small elements, each of which is timed with a stop watch. A selected or representative time value is found for each of these elements, and the times are added together to get the total selected time for performing the operation. The speed exhibited by the operator during the time study is rated or evaluated by the time study observer, and the selected time is adjusted by this rating factor so that a qualified operator, working at a normal pace, can easily do the work in the specified time. This adjusted time is called the normal time. To this normal time are added allowances for personal time, fatigue, and delay, the result being the standard time for the task.

   4.   Training the Operator. A carefully developed method of doing work is of little value unless it can be put into effect. It is necessary to train the operator to perform the work in the prescribed manner. Where but one or a few persons are employed on a given operation and where the work is relatively simple, it is customary to train the operator at the work place. The supervisor, the motion and time study analyst, a special instructor, or a skilled operator may act as the teacher. In most cases it is the supervisor who is responsible for training the operator, and the supervisor often depends upon the methods and standards department for assistance in this task. The written standard practice or the element breakdown sheet is a valuable aid to the supervisor in job training. When large numbers of employees must be trained for a single operation, the training is sometimes carried on in a separate training department. Charts, demonstration units, and motion pictures are frequently used to advantage in such a training program.

Scope

In order to gain perspective and to show relationships the tools and techniques of motion and time study are shown in Fig. 2. The *ways* in which motion and time study may be used can be divided into three *patterns* and Fig. 3 describes these in summary form. At one time, motion and time study was practiced almost exclusively by industrial engineers and specialists in this field. These staff members provided their services to the line managers and supervisors as shown in Fig. 3, Pattern A. By training the managers and supervisors in the problem-solving process and motion and time study, and with the encouragement and support of top management, these supervisors study their own problems and make applications in their own areas (Pattern B). More recently workers themselves in teams or groups have also received special training in this area and are participating directly in the design and management of their own jobs (Pattern C). They learn new skills and techniques and assume greater responsibilities. Industrial engineers still perform functions as professionals but they also serve as teachers and consultants to supervisors and to worker groups.

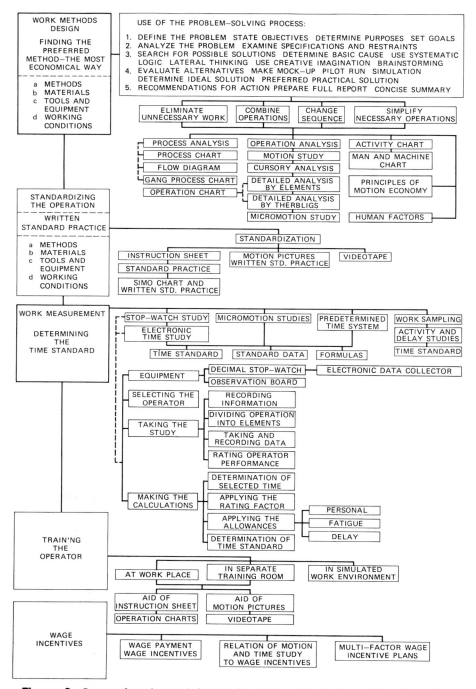

Figure 2 Scope of motion and time study—tools and techniques. Wage incentives.

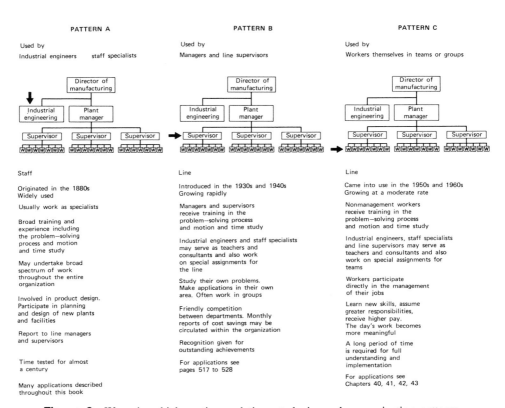

Figure 3   Ways in which motion and time study is used—organization patterns.

In the past greatest emphasis has been given to improving existing methods, and it has been customary to begin by making a detailed study of the method in effect. If an improved method is developed, it is put into operation, the worker is trained to use the new method, a written standard practice is prepared, and a time standard is established for the job. If a new product is to be manufactured or a new service is to be performed, however, then a fresh start can be made. There is no "old method" to improve. Here one has a free hand to design the ideal system and method. There is evidence to show that this same approach should be used even though an existing activity is being investigated. Of course, consideration would be given to the present method, but the approach would not be one of *improving* this current method, but rather of designing an ideal method. Work methods design then has as its purpose finding the ideal method, or the one nearest to the ideal that can actually be used. We call this the preferred method. Likewise, a systematic study of materials can bring about increased utilization, better quality, and lower costs. Thus, we have a systematic way of developing human resource effectiveness, providing high machine and equipment utilization, and making economical use of materials.

Originally motion and time study applications were mainly limited to direct factory labor. However, as more people learned about the objectives, methods, and techniques of motion and time study, new uses were found for it. People began to see that its principles are universal and may be equally effective wherever people and machines are employed. Attention is now being focused on the importance of increasing productivity per man-hour and reducing costs, for two main reasons: (1) the rapid increase in hourly wage rates tends to raise labor costs; (2) the rapid increase in capital invested and the increase in operating costs of machines, tools, and equipment tend to raise the "machine-hour rate" or the overhead cost. Moreover, the need for greater output of goods and services provides an additional incentive for increasing the productivity of people and machines. It is only natural that methods and techniques which have proved useful in increasing the effectiveness of direct factory labor should be applied in other areas.

Indirect Factory Labor

With the increasing use of mechanization and automation, the relative importance of direct labor will decrease and greater attention will be given to indirect labor. More factory operations will be performed by machines, and these machines will become more complex and will require more highly trained people to operate, service, and maintain them. The advent of the time-lapse camera, electronic data-processing equipment, work sampling, waiting-line theory, and other techniques for recording, analyzing, and measuring nonrepitive activities has made it profitable to study such work. Such studies have brought about increased labor effectiveness and increased machine utilization.

Nonmanufacturing Activities

Together with the rise in the importance of indirect factory labor, there has come a tremendous increase in office work. Some companies have expanded their motion and time study activities to include the office; others have established a separate department to study office methods and procedures. The use of paper work simplification, office work measurement, systems and procedures analysis, and office mechanization, and the installation of data-processing equipment are some of the approaches being utilized to increase productivity and reduce costs in offices.

Banks, mail-order houses, hospitals, department stores, and supermarkets are obtaining worthwhile results from the application of principles of motion and time study to their activities. Great strides are being made in simplifying work on farms, as well as in various branches of the government and the military.

HISTORY OF MOTION AND TIME STUDY

In order to understand how motion and time study has come to have the broad meaning presented in Chapter 2, it is necessary to go back and investigate the origin and examine the use that has been made of time study and motion study during the past 100 years.

TAYLOR'S USE OF TIME STUDY

It is generally agreed that time study had its beginning in the machine shop[1] of the Midvale Steel Company in 1881 and that Frederick W. Taylor was its originator. Taylor's employment with the Midvale Steel Company led him to the conclusion that the system under which the factory operated left much to be desired. Therefore, shortly after he became general foreman of the plant, he decided to make a determined effort to change the management system "so that the interests of the workmen and the management should become the same, instead of antagonistic." He further stated that "the greatest obstacle to harmonious cooperation between the workman and the management lay in the ignorance of management as to what really constitutes a proper day's work for a workman."[2] Taylor obtained persmission from the president of the Midvale Steel Company "to spend some money in a careful, scientific study of the time required to do various kinds of work."

A study of the literature in this general area revealed that two classes of experiments had been made; one by physiologists who were studying the endurance of workers, and the other by engineers who were attempting to measure physical work in terms of horsepower. These experiments had been made largely upon men who were lifting loads by means of turning the crank of a winch from which weights were suspended, and upon other men who were engaged in walking, running, and lifting weights in various ways.

Taylor started his study by employing two good steady workers who were physically strong. These men[3] were paid double wages and cooperated fully in the investigation. Taylor states that "in these experiments we were not trying to find the max-

---

[1] Subcommittee on Administration of the ASME, "The Present State of the Art of Industrial Management," *Transactions of the ASME*, Vol. 34, pp. 1197–1198, 1912.

[2] F. W. Taylor, *The Principles of Scientific Management*, Harper and Bros., New York, 1929, p. 52.

[3] The people employed in Taylor's studies were all men and the pronouns "he," "his," and "him" are used for accurate reporting. Other cases in this book involve female employees and the pronouns "she," "hers," and "her" are used. In some places the generic "man" and pronouns "he," "his," and "him" are used for grammatical simplicity.

imum work that a man could do on a short spurt or for a few days, but that our endeavor was to learn what really constituted a full day's work for a first class man; the best day's work that a man could properly do year in and year out, and still thrive."

In this study, Taylor hoped to determine what fraction of a horsepower a man could exert, that is, how many foot-pounds of work a man could do in a day. However, this study and other more carefully designed experiments carried out over a period of several years convinced Taylor that there was no direct relationship between the horseppower that a man exerts and the tiring effect of the work on the man.

However, Taylor did discover that, for very heavy work, the controlling factor in determining how much work a man could do in one day was the percentage of the day that the workman was under load, the percentage of the day he was resting, and the length and frequency of rest periods. As important as this was, Taylor's development and use of stop-watch time study was a far greater contribution. Taylor states, "Time study is the one element in scientific management beyond all others making possible the transfer of skill from management to men. . . .''

Important as is Taylor's contribution in originating time study, this is only one of his many achievements. To him also goes the credit for inventing high-speed steel, discovering and evaluating the variables affecting the cutting of metals, originating the functional type of organization, and developing a system or philosophy commonly referred to as scientific management. These achievements were not accidental, but the result of a systematic study of the factors affecting the problem in each instance. Taylor's real contribution to industry was his scientific method, his substitution of fact-finding for rule-of-thumb procedure. His questioning attitude and his constant search for the facts gave him the high place which he reached and still holds as a proponent of science in management. He was a pioneer in applying the systematic approach to that phase of industry which intimately affects the worker. He understood that he was dealing with a human problem as well as with materials and machines, and he approached the human side of his investigations with an understanding of its psychological aspects.[4]

So great has been Taylor's contribution to the whole problem of effective utilization of human effort in industry that we can profit from a review of some of his work in this field. Taylor came from a well-to-do Philadelphia family, was trained at Phillips Exeter Academy to enter Harvard, and after but a year and a half at Phillips Exeter passed the Harvard entrance examinations with honors but at the cost of seriously impaired eyesight. Forced to give up the idea of further study, at the age of eighteen

---

[4] Some maintain that Taylor merely tried to squeeze more work from the employees and that his methods were not scientific. For objections to Taylor's methods, see: R. F. Hoxie, *Scientific Management and Labor*, Appleton, New York, 1915. Symposium—"Stop-Watch Time Study, an Indictment and a Defense," *Bulletin of the Taylor Society*, Vol. 6, No. 3, pp. 99–135, June, 1921. E. Farmer, "Time and Motion Study," Industrial Fatigue Research Board, *Report* 14, H. M. Stationery Office, London, 1921.

he obtained a job in a machine shop where he served the apprenticeships of machinist and pattern-maker. In 1878, when he was twenty-two, he went to work at the Midvale Steel Works. Because business conditions were bad at that time, he took a job as an ordinary laborer. He was rapidly promoted to time clerk, journeyman, lathe operator, gang boss, and foreman of the machine shop, and at the age of thirty-one was made chief engineer of the works. During his early years at Midvale, Taylor studied at night and in 1883 obtained a degree in mechanical engineering from Stevens Institute.

Taylor's Principles of Management

It was as gang boss and foreman that Taylor first came face to face with such questions as "Which is the best way to do this job?" and "What should constitute a day's work?" Taylor, being very conscientious himself, expected the men under him to do a fair day's work. He set for himself the task of finding the proper method of doing a given piece of work, teaching the worker how to do it in this way, maintaining all conditions surrounding the work so that the worker could do the task properly, setting a definite time standard for accomplishing the work, and then paying the worker a premium in the form of extra wages for doing the task as specified. Many years later Taylor explained his objectives in the following way:

First. The development of a science for each element of a man's work, thereby replacing the old rule-of-thumb methods.

Second. The selection of the best worker for each particular task and then training, teaching, and developing the workman; in place of the former practice of allowing the worker to select his own task and train himself as best he could.

Third. The development of a spirit of hearty cooperation between the management and the men in the carrying on of the activities in accordance with the principles of the developed science.

Fourth. The division of the work into almost equal shares between the management and the workers, each department taking over the work for which it is the better fitted; instead of the former condition, in which almost all of the work and the greater part of the responsibility were thrown on the men.[5]

Taylor stated many times that scientific management required "a complete mental revolution on the part of the workman—and on the part of those on management's side."[6] "Both sides must recognize as essential the substitution of exact scientific investigation and knowledge for the old individual judgment or opinion."[7]

Although Taylor realized that there is more to the management of an industrial enterprise than conducting investigations on methods of doing work, he stated in no uncertain terms that one of the first duties of management was "to develop a science for

---

[5] F. W. Taylor, *The Principles of Scientific Management,* Harper & Bros., New York, 1929, p. 36.
[6] F. B. Copley, *Frederick W. Taylor,* Vol. I, Harper & Bros., New York, 1923, p. 10.
[7] *Ibid.,* p. 12.

each element of a man's work,'' and he used and advocated the scientific approach in the solution of every problem that arose in this connection.

Eric Farmer of Great Britain, in a most critical analysis of Taylor's work, states, "Taylor's greatest and lasting contribution to the science of industry is the method he adopted. He approached problems which had been thought either not to exist or to be easily solved by common sense, in the spirit of scientific enquiry."[8]

During his many years in industry Taylor carried on extended investigations in order to determine the best way to do work and to obtain specific data for standardizing the task. In order to illustrate his approach, one of his well-known studies will be briefly described here.

Taylor's Investigation of Shoveling

In 1898, when Taylor went to the Bethlehem Steel Works, he undertook to improve methods in various parts of the plant. One task that came to his attention was shoveling. Four hundred to 600 men were employed in the yard, and much of their work was shoveling. More iron ore was shoveled than any other material, and rice coal came next in tonnage. Taylor found that each good shoveler in that yard owned his own shovel; he preferred to do this rather than to have the company furnish it. A foreman supervised 50 to 60 men, and they shoveled a variety of material in the course of a day. The yard was approximately 2 miles long and a quarter of a mile wide, so that the gang moved about over a large area.

With little investigation Taylor found that shovelers were lifting loads of 3½ pounds when handling rice coal and up to 38 pounds to the shovel when moving ore. He immediately set about to determine what shovel load permitted a first-class shoveler to move the most material in a day. Taylor took two good shovelers, set them to work in different parts of the yard, and detailed two time study men with stop watches to study the work of these men. At first large shovels were used so that heavy loads were taken. Then the end of the shovel was cut off to permit a smaller shovel load, and again the tonnage handled was noted. This procedure was continued—from very heavy shovel loads to very light ones. The results of this study showed that with a load of 21½ pounds on the shovel, a man could handle a maximum tonnage of material in a day. Thus, a small spade shovel that would just hold 21½ pounds was provided for the worker when he handled ore, and a large scoop was provided for light material such as ashes.

A toolroom was established, and special shovels were purchased and issued to the workers as needed. In addition Taylor inaugurated a planning department to determine in advance the work to be done in the yard. This department issued orders to the foremen and the workers each morning, stating the nature of the work to be done, the tools needed, and the location of the work in the yard. Instead of the men work-

---

[8] E. Farmer, *op. cit.*

ing together in large gangs, the material handled by each man was measured or weighed at the end of the day, and each man was paid a bonus (60 percent above day wages) when he did the specified amount of work. If a man failed to earn the bonus, an instructor was sent out to show him how to do his job in the proper way and so earn the bonus.

After 3½ years at the Bethlehem plant Taylor was doing the same amount of work in the yards with 140 men as was formerly done by 400 to 600. He reduced the cost of handling material from 7 to 8 cents to 3 to 4 cents per ton. After paying for all added expenses, such as planning the work, measuring the output of the workers, determining and paying bonuses each day, and maintaining the toolroom, Taylor still showed a saving during the last 6-month period at the rate of $78,000 per year.[9]

One cannot read Taylor's experiments on the art of cutting metals,[10] his study of rest pauses in handling pig iron,[11] or his investigations in shoveling without at once realizing that he was a scientist of high order. With Taylor, as with managers today, time study was a tool to be used in increasing the over-all efficiency of the plant, making possible higher wages for labor and lower prices of the finished products to the consumer.

MOTION STUDY AS IT WAS DEVELOPED BY THE GILBRETHS

Motion study cannot be discussed without constant reference to the work of Frank B. Gilbreth and his wife, Lillian M. Gilbreth. Industry owes a great debt to them for their pioneering work in this field. The fundamental character of their work is indicated by the fact that the principles and techniques which they developed many years ago are being adopted by industry today at an increasingly rapid rate.

The story of the work of the Gilbreths is a long and fascinating one. Mrs. Gilbreth's training as a psychologist and Mr. Gilbreth's engineering background fitted them in a unique way to undertake work involving an understanding of the human factor as well as a knowledge of materials, tools, and equipment. Their activities cover a wide range, including noteworthy inventions and improvements in building and construction work,[12] study of fatigue,[13] monotony,[14] transfer of skill, and work for the handicapped,[15] and the development of such techniques as the process chart, micromotion study, and the chronocyclegraph.

[9] F. B. Copley, *op. cit.,* Vol. II, p. 56.

[10] F. W. Taylor, "On the Art of Cutting Metals," *Transactions of the ASME,* Vol. 28, Paper 1119, pp. 31–350, 1907.

[11] Copley, *op. cit.,* p. 37.

[12] F. B. Gilbreth, *Motion Study,* D. Van Nostrand Co., Princeton, N.J., 1911.

[13] F. B. and L. M. Gilbreth, *Fatigue Study,* Macmillan Co., New York, 1919.

[14] L. M. Gilbreth, "Monotony in Repetitive Operations," *Iron Age,* Vol. 118, No. 19, p. 1344, November 4, 1926.

[15] F. B. and L. M. Gilbreth, *Motion Study for the Handicapped,* George Routledge Sons, London, 1920.

In this book particular attention is given to their work dealing with the process chart, motion study, and micromotion study.

The Beginning of Motion Study

In 1885, Gilbreth, as a young man of seventeen, entered the employ of a building contractor. In those days brick construction constituted an important part of most structures, so Gilbreth began by learning the bricklayer's trade. Promotions came rapidly, and by the beginning of the century Gilbreth was in the contracting business for himself. From the very beginning of his connection with the building trades Gilbreth noted that each craftsman used his own peculiar methods in doing his work, and that no two men did their job in exactly the same way. Furthermore, he observed that the worker did not always use the same set of motions. The bricklayer, for example, used one set of motions when he worked rapidly, another set when he worked slowly, and still a third set when he taught someone else how to lay brick.[16] These observations led Gilbreth to begin investigations to find the "one best way" of performing a given task. His efforts were so fruitful and his enthusiasm for this sort of thing became so great that in later years he gave up his contracting business in order to devote his entire time to motion study investigations and applications.[17]

It was apparent from the beginning that Gilbreth had a knack for analyzing the motions used by his workmen. He readily saw how to make improvements in methods, substituting shorter and less fatiguing motions for longer and more tiring ones. He made photographs of bricklayers at work, and from a study of these photographs he continued to bring about increased output among his workers. For example, Gilbreth invented a scaffold which could quickly and easily be raised a short distance at a time, thus permitting it to be kept near the most convenient working level at all times. This scaffold was also equipped with a bench or shelf for holding the bricks and mortar at a convenient height for the workmen. This saved the bricklayer the tiring and unnecessary task of bending over to pick up a brick from the floor of the scaffold each time he laid one on the wall.

Formerly, bricks were dumped in a heap on the scaffold and the bricklayer selected the bricks as he used them. He turned or flipped each brick over in his hand in order to find the best side to place on the face of the wall. Gilbreth improved this procedure. As the bricks were unloaded from the freight car, Gilbreth had low-priced laborers sort them and place them on wooden frames or "packets" 3 feet long. Each packet held 90 pounds of brick. The bricks were inspected by these men as they unloaded them. They were then placed on the packet side by side, so that the best face and end were uniformly turned in a given direction. The packets were next

[16] L. M. Gilbreth, "The Quest of the One Best Way," p. 16, a sketch of the life of F. B. Gilbreth published by Mrs. Gilbreth, 1925.
[17] William R. Spriegel and Clarke E. Myers (eds.) *The Writings of the Gilbreths,* Richard D. Irwin, Homewood, Ill., 1953.

placed on the scaffolds in such a way that the bricklayer could pick up the bricks quickly without having to disentangle them from a heap. Gilbreth had the mortar box and the packets of bricks arranged on the scaffold in such relative positions that the bricklayer could pick up a brick with one hand and a trowel full of mortar with the other at the same time. Formerly, when the bricklayer reached down to the floor to pick up a brick with one hand, the other hand remained idle.

In addition, Gilbreth arranged for the mortar to be kept of the proper consistency so that the brick could be shoved into place on the wall with the hand. This eliminated the motion of tapping the brick into place with the trowel. These changes, along with others which Gilbreth developed, greatly increased the amount of work which a bricklayer could do in a day. For example, in exterior brickwork, using the ''pick and dip'' method, the number of motions required to lay a brick were reduced from 18 in the old method to 4½ in the new method.[18]

On a particular building near Boston, on a 12-inch brick wall with drawn joints on both sides and of two kinds of brick, which is a rather difficult wall to lay, bricklayers were trained in the new method. By the time the building was a quarter to a half of the way up, the average production was 350 bricks per man per hour. The record for this type of work previous to the adoption of the new system had been but 120 bricks per man per hour.[19]

Definition of Micromotion Study

Although Gilbreth was aided greatly in his motion study investigations by photographs which he made of his workers in motion, it was not until he adapted the motion picture camera to his work that he made his greatest contribution to industrial management. In fact, the technique of micromotion study as he and Mrs. Gilbreth developed it was made possible only through the use of motion pictures.

The term *micromotion study* was originated by the Gilbreths, and the technique was first made public[20] at a meeting of the American Society of Mechanical Engineers in 1912. A brief explanation of micromotion study might be given in this way: micromotion study is the study of the fundamental element or subdivisions of an operation by means of a motion picture camera and a timing device which accurately indicates the time intervals on the motion picture film. This in turn makes possible the analysis of the elementary motions recorded on the film, and the assignment of time values to each.

The Gilbreths made little use of time study. In fact, concentrating on finding the very best way for doing work, they wished to determine the shortest possible time in

---

[18] F. B. Gilbreth, *Motion Study*, D. Van Nostrand Co., Princeton, N.J., 1911.

[19] ''Taylor's Famous Testimony before the Special House Committee,'' *Bulletin of the Taylor Society*, Vol. 11, No. 3 and No. 4, p. 120, June–August, 1926.

[20] F. B. Gilbreth. See his discussion in ''The Present State of the Art of Industrial Management,'' *Transactions of the ASME*, Vol. 34, pp. 1224–1226, 1912.

which the work could be performed. They used timing devices of great precision and selected the best operators obtainable as subjects for their studies.

The Cyclegraph and the Chronocyclegraph

Gilbreth also developed two techniques, cyclegraphic and chronocyclegraphic analysis, for the study of the motion path of an operator.

It is possible to record the path of motion of an operator by attaching a small electric light bulb to the finger, hand, or other part of the body and photographing, with a still camera, the path of light as it moves through space. Such a record is called a cyclegraph[21] (Figs. 75 through 78).

If an interrupter is placed in the electric circuit with the bulb, and if the light is flashed on quickly and off slowly, the path of the bulb will appear as a dotted line with pear-shaped dots indicating the direction of the motion. The spots of light will be spaced according to the speed of the movement, being widely separated when the operator moves fast and close together when the movement is slow. From this graph it is possible to measure accurately time, speed, acceleration, and retardation, and to show direction and the path of motion in three dimensions. Such a record is called a chronocyclegraph. From the chronocyclegraph it is possible to construct accurate wire models of the motion paths. Gilbreth used these to aid in improving methods, to demonstrate correct motions, and to assist in teaching new operators.

Gilbreth's Work at the New England Butt Company

On May 13, 1912 Gilbreth started an important consulting assignment at the New England Butt Company in Providence, R.I.[22] This was a small, well-managed organization manufacturing machinery for making braids for wearing apparel and shoe laces, and coverings for insulated wires. John G. Aldrich, Vice President and General Manager of the company who had been making some use of scientific management, welcomed Gilbreth's arrival. Here Gilbreth made his first application of micromotion study in a manufacturing organization and eventually his work included the installation of the full Taylor system.

Gilbreth had the company build a special laboratory which he called the Betterment Room (Fig. 4)[23] Here problems were analyzed, mock-ups were constructed, and better methods developed. During his work at the Butt Company Gilbreth established a production planning department, improved the tool room, and studied the flow and handling of materials by constructing a scale model of the factory and mov-

[21] F. B. and L. M. Gilbreth, *Applied Motion Study,* Sturgis & Walton, New York, 1917, p. 73.

[22] Edna Yost, *Frank and Lillian Gilbreth: Partners for Life,* Rutgers University Press, New Brunswick, N.J., 1949, p. 214.

[23] J. T. Black, "IE's Have Roots, Too," *Industrial Engineering,* Vol. 10, No. 5, May 1978, p. 28. Reproduced by permission.

Figure 4 Gilbreth's laboratory, the Betterment Room, at the New England Butt Company. The operator, assembling a braiding machine, is being filmed by the camera at the right. Gilbreth, standing behind the microchronometer, is observing the making of the motion study, and John Aldrich is at his left.

able models of the machines. He first used the process flow chart in this connection. He also designed work tables of the proper height and provided chairs for the workers. He made use of the newly designed "skid and lift truck" method of material handling. His work and laboratory attracted much attention and many visitors.[24]

Gilbreth made some 200,000 feet of film during his professional career and many subjects were photographed in the laboratory at the Butt Company.[25]

[24] John G. Aldrich. See discussion of Gilbreth's work at the New England Butt Company. "The Present State of the Art of Industrial Management," *Transactions of the ASME,* Vol. 34, Paper 1378, pp. 1182–1187, 1912.

[25] Years later James S. Perkins reviewed, analyzed, and indexed these Gilbreth films with occasional assistance from Mrs. Gilbreth and this author. Some of these films were reduced from 35-mm to 16-mm and "The Original Films of Frank B. Gilbreth" was produced by Perkins. This sound film was shown for the first time at the "Frank Gilbreth Centennial" at the Winter Annual Meeting of the American Society of Mechanical Engineers in New York City in 1968.

National Organizations

The American Society of Mechanical Engineers (ASME) has played an important part in the development of scientific management, industrial engineering, motion and time study, and related fields. It should be remembered that Taylor's "Shop Management" was published under the auspices of the ASME in 1903, and his classic work on "The Art of Cutting Metals" occupied over 200 pages in the 1907 *Transactions*. From that time to this the ASME has been responsible for many outstanding publications in this general field, and the Management Division is one of the most active divisions of the Society.

In 1911 the Amos Tuck School of Dartmouth College sponsored a Conference of Scientific Management, and the following year the Efficiency Society, Inc., was organized in New York City. The Taylor Society came into existence in 1915, and this organization and the Society of Industrial Engineers, with headquarters in Chicago, joined forces in 1936 to form the Society for Advancement of Management (SAM). In 1971 SAM became an affiliated division of the American Management Association.

In 1922 the American Management Association was formed by people especially interested in industrial training programs. Over the years the objectives of the AMA have changed, and at the present time this organization is concerned mainly with broad management problems.

The Industrial Management Society was organized in the 1930s and holds Industrial Engineering and Management conferences and the annual *IMS Clinic*. Emphasis is placed on motion and time study, wage incentives, and related subjects. The published proceedings of the clinic and the bimonthly journal *Industrial Management* provide valuable additions to the literature in this field.

The American Institute of Industrial Engineers (AIIE), organized in 1948, has grown rapidly and now serves as the professional engineering society in this field. Although many groups have attempted to define industrial engineering, the AIIE Long Range Planning Committee has arrived at the following definition: "Industrial engineering is concerned with the design, improvement, and installation of integrated systems of men, materials, and equipment; drawing upon specialized knowledge and skill in the mathematical, physical, and social sciences, together with the principles and methods of engineering analysis and design, to specify, predict, and evaluate the results to be obtained from such systems."

The Human Factors Society, established in 1957, provides a forum for the interchange of information and ideas concerning the role of humans in complex systems, the design of organizations, equipment and facilities for effective use, and the development of environments for comfort and safety. The Society meets annually, publishes the bimonthly journal *Human Factors* and the monthly Human Factors Society *Bulletin*.

4

THE GENERAL PROBLEM-SOLVING PROCESS

The design of the method of performing an operation when a new product is being put into production, or the improvement of a method already in effect, is a very important part of motion and time study. Because methods design is a form of creative problem solving, it seems appropriate to present in some detail the general problem-solving process.[1] In fact, the five steps described here are useful in the logical and systematic approach to solving almost any problem.

1. Problem definition.
2. Analysis of problem.
3. Search for possible solutions.
4. Evaluation of alternatives.
5. Recommendation for action.

1. Problem Definition. Although we state that the definition or formulation of the problem is the first step in the problem-solving procedure, this is often preceded by the need to recognize that a problem exists. Sometimes such statements are made as, "Costs are too high," "Output must be increased," or "There is a bottleneck in order filling in the warehouse." In many cases, it is not easy to determine just what the real problem is. However, the problem must be isolated and clearly stated (Fig. 5). At the same time, one must ascertain whether the problem merits consideration, and, if so, whether this is the proper time to solve the problem. If it is decided to proceed with the formulation of the problem, then information should be obtained concerning the magnitude or the importance of the problem and the time available for its solution. Pareto's law, sometimes called the "80–20" rule, may help here. The Pareto distribution uses the concept that the *major* part of an activity is accomplished by a *minority*. For example, 80 percent of profits come from 20 percent of product items; 80 percent of total inventory value is in 20 percent of inventory items. Thus the problem presenting the greatest opportunity should receive the greatest attention.

[1] Edward de Bono, *Lateral Thinking for Management,* American Management Association, New York, 1971. Moshe F. Rubinstein, *Patterns of Problem Solving,* Prentice-Hall, Englewood Cliffs, N.J., 1975. Albert Rothenberg and Carl R. Hausman (eds.), *The Creative Question,* Duke University Press, Durham, N.C., 1976. Harold R. Buhl, *Creative Engineering Design,* The Iowa State University Press, Ames, Iowa, 1960. Alex F. Osborn, *Applied Imagination,* Scribners, New York, 1957. Eugene K. Von Fange, *Professional Creativity,* Prentice-Hall, Englewood Cliffs, N.J., 1959. Pareto's Law and ABC Curves: David Herron, "Industrial Engineering Applications of ABC Curves," *American Institute of Industrial Engineers Transactions,* Vol. 8, No. 2, June 1976, pp. 210–218.

METHODS DESIGN WORKSHEET

Problem Definition—Statement of purpose, goal or objective—Formulation of the problem

    a. Criteria—Means of judging successful solution of problem

    b. Output requirements—(1) Maximum daily output, (2) seasonal varia- tions, (3) annual volume, (4) expected life of product—shape of volume growth and decline curve

    c. Completion date—Time available (1) to design, (2) to install and try out facilities, and (3) to bring output up to full production

---

Figure 5 Methods design worksheet—problem definition.

At the outset it is best to define the problem broadly, and the constraints or restric-tions should be as few as possible at this stage. This gives greater freedom for the use of imagination and creativity in finding a solution. Moreover, in those cases where the task or operation is now being performed, undue attention should not be given to the "present method," and the problem should be defined independently of the way the task is currently being done. The following case illustrates this matter of problem definition.

Seabrook Farms in southern New Jersey operates some 20,000 acres, approxi-mately 7000 of which are planted to peas each year. Originally the company planted peas during the period from early March to the first of April, and then tried to cope with the harvesting problem as best it could. Sometimes during the harvest season so many acres of peas were ripe at the same time that the pickers, shellers, and quick-freeze crews had to work around the clock. Also, because of the delay in harvesting, some peas were overripe and poor in quality.

Dr. C. W. Thornthwaite, climatologist for Seabrook Farms, after considerable study and experimentation with the rate of growth for peas of different varieties dur-ing the different periods of the spring and summer, was able to predict when the crops would be ready for harvest.[2] For example, if a certain division of the farms was equipped to take care of 25 acres per day, Dr. Thornthwaite was able to schedule the planting so that just that number of acres would be ready during each of the six days of the week, with no crop maturing on Sunday. This not only made it unnecessary to operate on a crash basis at any time during the summer, but also resulted in a crop of more uniform quality with less waste due to overripe peas.

The problem might have been defined as that of finding a more effective method of harvesting peas during the night—using more and better floodlights and possibly selecting and training crews especially for harvesting peas at night. However, the basic problem was to find ways to have the peas ripen at a rate that would result in the desired loading for the personnel and equipment in the field and in the shelling and quick-freeze plants. In this case, the solution was not an improvement or a refinement of the present one. It was an original solution resulting from the logical problem-solving process.

Sometimes it is desirable to divide the problem into subproblems, or to determine whether the problem being considered is part of a larger problem. One may want to go back up the line and examine activities preceding the operation being considered, or possibly the activities that follow. Although a broad formulation of the problem in the early stages of the problem-solving process is desirable, it is usually more difficult to solve a complex problem than a simple one.

2. Analysis of the Problem. The formulation of the problem may have resulted in a broad statement or definition. Now it becomes necessary to obtain data—to sort out the facts and determine how they apply to the problem (Fig. 6). Of course, it is likely that the designer will already have considerable knowledge in the area and will seek additional information. Evaluation of the facts should not be made during the analysis stage. Critical judgment should be deferred until later in the problem-solving process.

At the outset, it is desirable to establish the criteria for the evaluation of alternative solutions to the problem. The preferred solution to a manufacturing problem might be the one that has the lowest labor cost, the lowest total cost, or the smallest capital investment, or the one that requires the least floor space or results in the greatest utilization of materials, or the one that permits the organization to get into full production in the shortest period of time.

The specifications or restrictions affecting the problem should also be known. In some cases, restrictions are flexible; in others, as one proceeds with the solution of the problem, he or she may be compelled to impose specific restraints. Consideration of restrictions is present at every stage in the problem-solving process. Restrictions should be examined with great care, however, for they sometimes are fictitious or imaginary. Only real restrictions merit consideration. The packing of citrus fruit in

---

[2] C. W. Thornthwaite, "Operations Research in Agriculture," *Journal of the Operations Research Society of America,* Vol. 1, No. 2, pp. 33–38.

METHODS DESIGN WORKSHEET

Analysis of Problem (No evaluation is to be made at this step)

a. Specifications or constraints, including any limits on original capital expenditures

b. Description of present method if operation is now in effect. This might include (1) process charts, (2) flow diagrams, (3) trip frequency diagrams, (4) man and machine charts, (5) operation charts, and (6) simo charts
LH, RH

c. Determination of activities that man probably can do best and those that the machine can do best and man-machine relationships

d. Re-examination of problems—Determination of subproblems

e. Re-examination of criteria

Figure 6 Methods design worksheet—analysis of problem.

cartons illustrates this point very well. For some time most citrus fruit shipped to market was packed in wood crates. People thought that citrus fruit had to be individually wrapped in tissue paper and packed in even layers in a well-ventilated wood crate, and that the fruit must be held tightly in place by a lid which was forced down under pressure and nailed and strapped at each end. The statements in the preceding sentence are all incorrect. Today nearly all oranges, lemons, and grapefruit are shipped in cardboard cartons. The fruit is not individually wrapped. It is not placed in the carton in layers. The cartons are not ventilated, and the fruit is not packed under pressure. A telescope-type carton holding only half as much as a wood create is easier to handle and costs less (Fig. 7). This better method of packing is saving the California lemon growers and packers over $5 million per year, and it is estimated that an equal amount in benefits accrues to those who transport the fruit and warehouse it, and to the grocer who sells it.[3]

Also the designer should have information as to the importance of the undertaking,

[3] Roy J. Smith, "Recent Developments in the Packing of Citrus Fruit," *Proceedings Sixth Industrial Engineering Institute,* University of California, Los Angeles-Berkeley, pp. 92–94.

Figure 7   Packing citrus fruit in cartons instead of wood crates saves the fruit growers over $5 million per year.

the volume of the product to be produced, the number of people to be employed in an activity, and the probable life of the project.

It is important to have a time schedule. The designer should know how much time is available for solving the problem, and if it is a production problem, should know the time available to put the process into operation, to "debug" it, and to get the specified output.

In the analysis of a problem, it may be desirable to divide it into small components, examining each of these separately. For example, if the problem is to drill a hole in a small metal plate for the manufacture of a television set, the operation might be broken down into three parts: (1) place part in fixture, (2) drill hole in piece, and (3) remove piece and dispose. The volume might consist of 500,000 parts per year with 60 days being available to develop the method and put it into operation. The first step could be performed manually, using a hand-operated fixture for holding the plate, or the plate could be manually placed in a cavity (with self-actuating clamp) in a dial feed, or the plates could be fed automatically from a magazine into the dial feed. The hole could be drilled manually, or a power-feed drill could be used. The finished part could be removed from the fixture manually, or it could be released automatically from the rotating table. If this operation had been considered at the time the television set was originally designed, consideration might have been given to eliminating this plate, punching the hole in the plate instead of drilling it, using a washer (which could be purchased) instead of the plate, or combining the plate with some other part. If a bolt were inserted through the hole in the plate to assemble it to other parts of the set, then consideration might have been given to spot-welding these parts together or perhaps using a die casting or a plastic molded piece instead of the metal plate.

3.   Search for Possible Solutions. The basic objective of course is to find the preferred solution that will meet the criteria and the specifications that have been established. This suggests that several alternative solutions be found and then the preferred solution can be selected from these.

Early in the problem-solving procedure one should ask the question, "What is the *basic cause* that has created this problem?" If the basic cause can be eliminated, then the problem no longer exists. For example, a company was considering the replacement of a roof over a row of open tanks containing liquid caustic soda. The present roof was badly corroded and replacement was suggested. When the question was asked, "What is the basic reason for having a roof over the tanks?," it was discovered that the only function for the roof was to keep the rain out—to prevent the dilution of the chemicals. However, an analysis showed that evaporation also affected the concentration of the chemicals, but that changes in the concentration were unimportant in the manufacturing process. Therefore, the old roof was removed and was not replaced. Of course the ideal solution to a problem is to remove the basic cause and thus eliminate the problem.[4]

If the problem cannot be completely solved by the elimination approach, perhaps part of the problem can be eliminated. If no way can be found to eliminate the problem, then one should explore the various avenues that may hold possible solutions. At the outset it is wise to take a broad and idealistic view in considering possible solutions to the problem.

Let us assume that the problem is to design and build a processing plant for grading and packaging eggs for distribution to grocery stores and supermarkets (Fig. 8). Eggs would be brought to the plant daily by trucks from farms and ranches located 5 to 25 miles from the plant. The usual process consists of (1) candling, determining quality; (2) sizing, determining weight; (3) packaging eggs in cartons; (4) placing cartons into cases and then into a cooler; and (5) delivering eggs to grocery stores and supermarkets.

In thinking of possible solutions, the eggs might be candled, sized, and packaged by hand; candled by hand but sized and packaged by machine; or the entire process of candling, sizing, packaging, and moving to the cooler might be automatic.

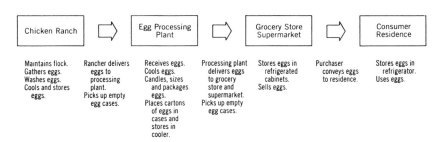

Figure 8   Egg production, processing, and distribution—from ranch to user.

[4] From "The Elimination Approach" by Procter and Gamble. See more complete discussion in Chapter 6.

By breeding and selection, one might raise chickens that would lay eggs of a given size. Through careful specification of feed and feed supplement and breed of chicken, the color of the yolk, the consistency of the white, and the color of the shell might be uniform. If the eggs were gathered and marketed each day, freshness would be assured. Eggs might be placed directly into the carton at the time they were gathered on the farm, thus eliminating the need for the candling, sizing, and packaging operations at the plant; or each egg might be removed from the shell and placed in an airtight cube-shaped plastic container automatically, further simplifying the packaging process.

If a small- or medium-sized egg processing plant were to be designed and constructed in the near future, it seems likely that the last two or three alternatives would be quickly dismissed. However, consideration certainly would be given to the manual method versus the automatic method of candling, of sizing, and of packaging the eggs.[5]

Here we are searching for ideas. Imagination, inventive ability, and creative talents are brought to bear on the problem. Some types of problems lend themselves to group effort. There are those who strongly advocate the use of systematic logic, whereas others believe that the problem-solving conference method often referred to as brainstorming can produce worthwhile ideas.[6] When this latter technique is used, it is essential that the individuals in the group suggest ideas rapidly, that no judgment evaluation whatsoever be made during the brainstorming session, and that the participants be urged to give free rein to ideas even though they may appear highly impractical.

Bernard S. Benson, a strong advocate of using systematic logic in solving problems, finds the following example useful in making his point:[7]

Once upon a time there were two men on an island, who had heard that during the war some soldiers in an army truck had driven to the end of one of the many roads and had buried a fabulous treasure. Both of them, being somewhat materialistically inclined, decided that it would be rather nice to get their hands on it. They decided this individually, however, and this created quite a competitive situation. The first man took a shovel and ran all over the island, digging and prodding at every likely spot. He explored under rocks, he dug at the foot of trees, he stopped at grassy patches and tried his luck. He did a lot of digging, but not much finding. The second man sat himself down and thought. He decided that he must first know of every road on the island; so he proceeded to make himself a map. He did not have the treasure, but at least he had a map of all the possible approaches. Next he inspected all of these possibilities against the relevant criteria and sealed off all of the roads which were too narrow for the truck's wheel base; then he sealed off all those where the overhanging rocks were too low to have allowed the truck to pass. Now he looked at every remaining possibility and sealed off all

[5] For a description of a modern egg-processing plant see Chapter 18.

[6] Alex F. Osborn, *Applied Imagination,* Scribners, New York, 1957.

[7] Bernard S. Benson, "In Search of a Solution—Cerebral Popcorn or Systematic Logic?" *Proceedings Tenth Industrial Engineering Institute,* University of California, Los Angeles-Berkeley, p. 14.

of the roads which ended in large granite areas, where the men could not have dug, and he was left with two roads open. Having first created all of the possibilities, he had eliminated all of those which did not meet the basic requirements. He dug at the end of the first road and found no treasure, but at the end of the second one, he had no trouble finding it; meanwhile, his friend . . . was still jumping around the island, trying here and trying there, frantically looking for the solution to his problem.

Electronic Thermometer

Sometimes a new technology can be used in the design of a new product to perform a desired function. An example of this is the IVAC electronic thermometer, which enables a nurse to take a patient's temperature in 15 to 25 seconds—a fraction of the time necessary with the glass thermometer.[8] (Fig. 9). A disposable probe cover is slipped over the thermometer probe and inserted under the patient's tongue. In seconds the read light and the audible signal indicate that the peak temperature has been reached. An illuminated digital temperature display stays on until the unit is turned off. The probe cover is ejected and the probe is reinserted in the storage position

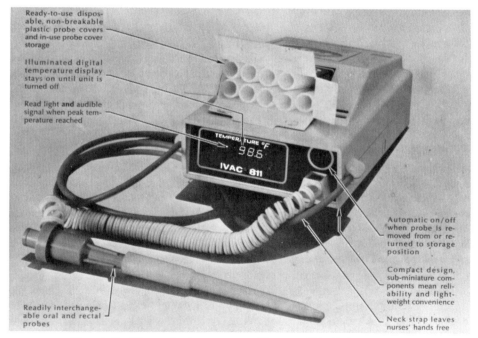

Figure 9 Electronic thermometer. (Courtesy IVAC Corporation)

[8] Reproduced by permission of IVAC Corporation.

which turns the unit off. The electronic thermometer has the advantages that the nonbreakable plastic probe cover eliminates the danger of cross-infection or exposure to mercury and broken glass which is present when using the conventional thermometer, and it also eliminates the need for costly sterilization and redistribution.

A System for Furniture Protection

The problem of protecting furniture during transporation and storage was solved by designing a new material and a system for using it. This has been most useful to furniture manufacturers.

A special polypropylene foam wrapping material[9] is now widely used for the protection of cartoned furniture in interstate shipping, and an economical system for applying the foam wrap in the factory is available. The foam wrap is superior to the conventional cellulosic blanket material in that it reduces the incidents of in-transit rub and abrasion damage to wood furniture and upholstery fabrics.

Foam wrap is available in jumbo untrimmed rolls 72 inches wide, 54-inch outside diameter, and containing 1500 square feet of material. This untrimmed roll is the most economical form in which to produce the material. It results in a substantial reduction in inventory of foam wrap over the many different cut-to-size paper pads. Specially designed equipment (Fig. 10) makes it possible to cut pieces of padding of the proper width and length from the big roll. Also, automatic equipment is available for lap heat-sealing leftover pieces together to form larger sheets and an automatic chair cap dispenser saves time on the production line (Fig. 11).

The pieces of padding are placed around the item being packed and special tape is used to hold the padding in place. A tape dispenser (Fig. 12), attached to the belt which each operator wears, makes the job easier. This pre-positions the tape and facilitates the operation of obtaining a piece of tape of the required length and applying it to the padding at the proper place.

The results are savings in cost, improved product protection, reduction in storage space requirements, and less inventory of wrapping material.

4.   Evaluation of Alternatives. We have now arrived at several solutions or partial solutions to the problem under consideration. In fact, we may have accumulated a large number of ideas bearing on the problem. Some of these can be eliminated rather quickly and the remaining solutions can be considered more carefully. An examination can be made to determine to what extent each solution meets the criteria and conforms to the original specifications.

In methods design, certainly there is no one "correct answer," but there are usually several possible solutions. Often judgment factors exist that must be considered over and above the quantitative evaluation in arriving at a preferred solution. Al-

---

[9] Microfoam Furniture Wrap manufactured by Du Pont. Reproduced by permission from "A Systems Approach to Furniture Protection," by Jack Murphy, *Du Pont Magazine,* Vol. 72, No. 1, January–*February, 1978.*

Figure 10   A special saw cuts the rolls of microfoam to the desired width. Automatic dispensers supply sheets of the proper length to the packing line.

Figure 11   Automatic chair cap dispenser.

31

Figure 12 Personal tape dispenser pre-positions the tape, makes the application easier, and saves time.

though each of several tentative solutions may satisfy the criteria, other solutions might be preferred if some restriction or specification could be changed. It frequently is desirable to select three solutions: (1) the ideal solution, (2) the one that is preferred for immediate use, and (3) possibly another that might be used at some future time—or under different conditions, such as a situation where the annual output might be increased substantially, or the quality of the raw material is more uniform, or more fully trained workers are available.

The evaluation of the preferred solution requires careful consideration of future difficulties that might be encountered, such as time and cost to maintain and repair the equipment, the adjustment to widely varying sizes or product mix, and the effects of wear and tear of equipment on quality of product and down time of equipment. One cannot overlook the human aspects in selecting the preferred solution. It may be that the success of the method selected depends upon getting the division superintendent or the department supervisor to approve it wholeheartedly, or it may be that the inspection department supervisor or the maintenance supervisor has the veto power over the proposed solution. Thus the recommended solution may be the one that is most likely to be accepted and put into effect rather than the ideal solution.

In certain types of problems an evaluation would center around the total capital that would be invested in each of the several proposed methods. In such an analysis we would want to know the initial cost, annual operating cost, expected life of equipment, and its scrap value. Another way to make a comparison is to compute the rate of return on the investment in percent per year, or the capital recovery period. That is, we determine the number of years that are required for the equipment to pay for itself. In certain types of problems, we may be concerned mainly with finding the method having the lowest direct labor cost. In such cases a comparative analysis could be made, using predetermined times to determine the total cycle time of each of the several methods. If there is a question as to whether a particular method actually can be performed, it may be necessary to construct a mock-up of the jig, fixture, or work place in the shop or laboratory and try out the method. Some companies have special laboratories and workshops for such projects.

5. Recommendation for Action. In many cases, the person who solves the problem is not the one who will either use the recommended solution or give final approval for its adoption. Therefore, after the preferred solution has been found, it must be communicated to other persons. The most common form of communication of course is the written or oral report. The written report or the oral presentation then becomes the final step in the problem-solving procedure. Circumstances determine whether the report is mainly a statement of recommendations with the supporting data, or whether an elaborate oral presentation before a group is called for. In some cases, a formal and carefully prepared presentation is needed, including the use of charts, diagrams, photographs, three-dimensional models, or working models. In any event, the presentation should be made in a logical and straightforward manner. It should be easy to follow and to understand. The source of all facts should be indicated, and any assumptions should be clearly stated. A concise written summary should be a part of every report.

Of course in the industrial situation the complete cycle might include a follow-up to ensure that the proposed solution has actually been put into effect. Then an audit or a check from time to time might be made to determine what difficulties were being encountered and to evaluate the over-all results of the installation. It is desirable to know whether the actual operating method is producing the results claimed for it in the proposal. To continue further, a re-evaluation or restudy of the method might be made with the purpose of finding further possibilities for improvement, and so the problem-solving cycle would be repeated. In most business and industrial operations there is no final solution to a problem. A given solution may be put into effect and used until a better one can be found.

5

WORK METHODS DESIGN—THE BROAD VIEW

In the early days, the production process consisted of a craftsman who possessed the skill, and who by means of simple tools converted materials into a usable product. Gradually, we learned how to transfer certain of the workers' skills to machines, and with the demand for large quantities of identical or similar products the factory system was developed. Division of labor took place, with the worker quickly learning to perform short, repetitive tasks with great speed. The use of jigs, fixtures, and machines further aided in increasing the productivity of the factory worker. Thus, today the production process consists of creating a product through the utilization of workers, machines, and materials.

When a new product is to be put on the market, it must be designed, materials for its manufacture must be specified, and the production methods, the tools, and machines must be designated. At an early stage in the design of the product, the materials to be used and the manufacturing process will be considered together with the quality standards and the cost to produce the product. There are almost an infinite number of ways to manufacture a particular product, harvest a crop, or mine coal. Methods designers have at their disposal the systematic problem-solving procedure to aid in determining the preferred processes and methods to be used.

The over-all process of putting a new product into production can be divided into three parts or phases:

1. Planning.
2. Pre-production.
3. Production.

The General Motors Corporation has shown this graphically in Fig. 13. In this illustration, emphasis is placed on work methods design, or "control of operator method," as it is called by General Motors.[1]

Planning

This is the first step in any production or manufacturing process. As Fig. 13 shows, there are six basic planning functions. (1) The *design of the product* results in drawings showing the size, shape, weight, material, and ultimate use. (2) The *design of the process* consists of determining the production system—the operations required

---

[1] Reproduced with permission of General Motors Corporation.

CONTROL OF OPERATOR METHOD

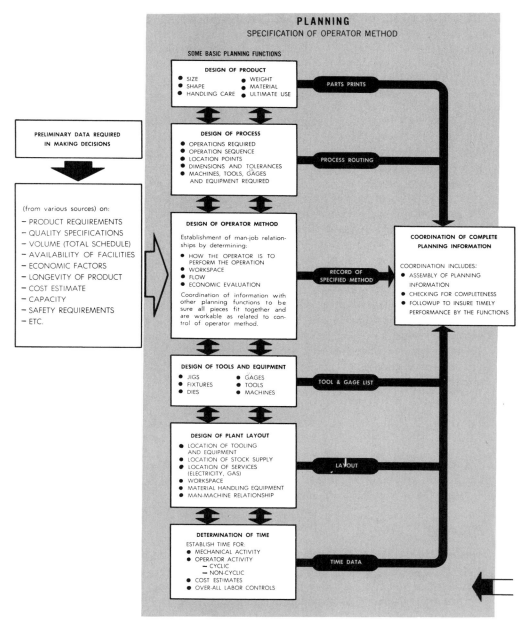

Figure 13 Factors to be considered in the control of operator method.

36

Developed by the General Motors Work Standards and
Methods Engineering Committees and the Work Standards
and Methods Engineering Section — Manufacturing Staff.

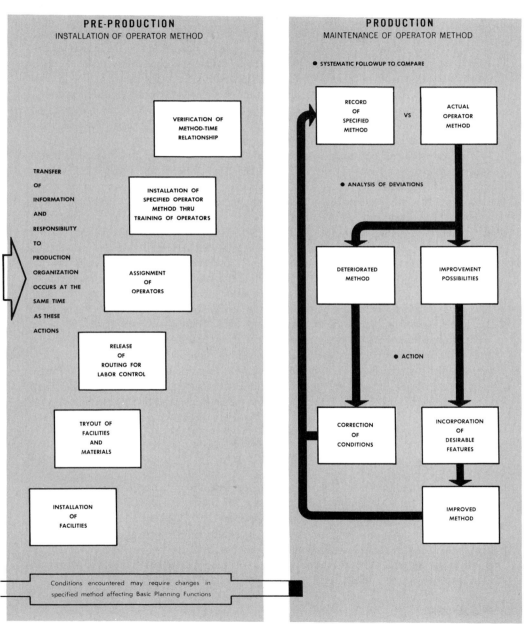

PRE-PRODUCTION
INSTALLATION OF OPERATOR METHOD

VERIFICATION OF
METHOD-TIME
RELATIONSHIP

TRANSFER
OF
INFORMATION
AND
RESPONSIBILITY
TO
PRODUCTION
ORGANIZATION
OCCURS AT THE
SAME TIME
AS THESE
ACTIONS

INSTALLATION OF
SPECIFIED OPERATOR
METHOD THRU
TRAINING OF OPERATORS

ASSIGNMENT
OF
OPERATORS

RELEASE
OF
ROUTING FOR
LABOR CONTROL

TRYOUT OF
FACILITIES
AND
MATERIALS

INSTALLATION
OF
FACILITIES

PRODUCTION
MAINTENANCE OF OPERATOR METHOD

● SYSTEMATIC FOLLOWUP TO COMPARE

RECORD
OF
SPECIFIED
METHOD

VS

ACTUAL
OPERATOR
METHOD

● ANALYSIS OF DEVIATIONS

DETERIORATED
METHOD

IMPROVEMENT
POSSIBILITIES

● ACTION

CORRECTION
OF
CONDITIONS

INCORPORATION
OF
DESIRABLE
FEATURES

IMPROVED
METHOD

Conditions encountered may require changes in
specified method affecting Basic Planning Functions

and their sequence; dimensions and tolerances, machines, tools, gauges, and equipment required. (3) The *design of work method* consists of the establishment of operator-job relationships by determining how the person is to perform the operation, the work place, flow, and economic evaluation. (4) The *design of tools and equipment* consists of determining the jigs, fixtures, dies, gauges, tools, and machines which will be needed to perform the operations. (5) The *design of the plant layout* consists of determining the total space required in terms of overall location of equipment, stock supply, service centers, work space, material-handling equipment, and the operator-machine relationship. (6) The *determination of the standard time* for the operation consists of measuring the work content of the job.

Planning is a decision-making process in that a goal or objective has been determined and a choice has been made from alternatives. The result is a specific product or part and specifications for its actual manufacture. For example, an electrical equipment manufacturer planned to produce and market a line of small electrical appliances. A team composed of a design engineer, an industrial engineer, and manufacturing staff personnel began the project by studying the design and production methods used to manufacture similar appliances already on the market. A product of original design with a minimum of components was finally developed, requiring the fewest operations and making the best possible use of raw materials. The direct labor hours required to produce this product were determined by predetermined time data. This enabled the team to compare alternative designs and to select the one that gave the lowest cost. After the best design had been determined and tested, detailed production and assembly methods and inspection procedures were developed, the equipment and facilities needed to manufacture the product were selected, and a factory layout was prepared. This included a three-dimensional layout showing arrangement of machines, inspection, and storage areas, as well as handling-equipment and service areas. It was possible to calculate the direct labor cost and to estimate the indirect labor cost and other overhead costs. Material costs were also determined as a part of the planning activity.

Pre-production

This is the transition phase. The planning information is transferred to the production organization. Tools, machines, and equipment are purchased, installed, and tried out. The routing for labor control is released. Operators are selected and trained for specific tasks. The planned operator method is carefully checked against the method being used, and the actual time taken is checked against the original estimate. This is a period during which the individual operations that go to make up the over-all manufacturing activity are tried out.

Production

This refers to the continuing operation of the manufacturing activity established in the planning and pre-production phases. It involves the use of operators, machines, and materials for the most effective manufacture of the part or product. Also, there is the ever-present necessity of (1) preventing the methods from deteriorating or deviating adversely from the planned methods, and (2) constantly examining the current methods for improvement and, when a better method is found, putting it into effect, in which case this then becomes the preferred method.

A SPECIFIC CASE—THE DESIGN OF A PLANT TO MANUFACTURE FIBERBOARD SHIPPING CARTONS

Assume that a large paper company wishes to construct a plant to manufacture fiberboard shipping cartons. The main objective might be to obtain an adequate return on the capital invested, or to have the plant serve as an outlet for kraft paper which the company makes and markets. Other objectives might be to keep the unit labor cost and the unit material cost as low as possible, and to get the best equipment utilization, that is, the lowest operating cost of the equipment.

At the outset, a market study would be made to determine the nature and extent of the present demand for fiberboard shipping cartons and to forecast future demands. This would be a factor in determining the capacity of the plant that would be constructed, and the provisions that would be made for future expansion. Together with this market survey would be studies to determine a geographic location, and also studies to select a local building site for the factory. A team consisting of an industrial engineer, a process engineer or mechanical engineer, and a market analyst would obtain the information that would be needed to make the decisions referred to above.

Procedure for Design of Manufacturing Process and Production Methods

The industrial engineer, working with a mechanical engineer and a production supervisor from one of the company's paper manufacturing plants, would determine the exact manufacturing process to be used, the general flow pattern, and the methods of handling the raw materials, the materials in process, and the finished product. The industrial engineer would assume the responsibility for designing the detailed operator method and the layout of the work place for each operation. This engineer would also fit this all together into a complete plant layout.

The industrial engineer might submit a detailed analysis of each of two or more methods of performing a specific operation when there appeared to be no clear-cut superiority of one method over another. For example, the finished cartons coming off the folding-gluing machine could be counted and tied into bundles manually, or this operation could be done by an automatic machine. The industrial engineer might submit a separate proposal for each method together with the recommendation as to the preferred method. As a result of the methods design a statement would be prepared showing the number of people required to operate each piece of equipment on each shift. This would include the power lift-truck operators as well as the people in the receiving and shipping departments and the human resources needed to operate the paper bailing machine. In a similar manner the number of supervisors on each shift would be determined.

The design of a manufacturing facility such as this one is very complex. For example, the operation of the combiner, which is over 200 feet long and represents an investment of some $1,400,000, is not a simple procedure—it is likely that specialists in various areas would be used in designing the plant. Moreover, it is to be expected that during the pre-production stage and during the "debugging" phase some changes and modifications would be made.

Detailed Statement of Problem

The problem is to build a new plant to manufacture corrugated fiberboard cartons and solid fiberboard cartons. All cartons are to be made to customers' orders and specifications. Carton sizes are to range from $4'' \times 4'' \times 4''$ to $45'' \times 45'' \times 40''$. The process will consist of (1) converting kraft paper into corrugated fiberboard or solid fiberboard and cutting to proper size for making cartons; (2) printing and slotting carton blanks; (3) folding and stitching seam, gluing seam, or taping seam, and counting and tying into bundles; and (4) receiving raw materials and shipping finished bundles of cartons (Fig. 14).

Specifications—Raw Materials

1. Kraft paper ranging in thickness from lightweight (18 pounds per 1000 square feet) to heavyweight (90 pounds per 1000 square feet). Roll size: Width 43 inches to 87 inches, diameter 54 inches, weight up to 5000 pounds.
2. Cornstarch adhesive.

Specifications—Equipment Requirements and Output Requirements

A. *Combiner* with a capacity up to 165,000 square feet per hour or 26,500 lineal feet per hour (Fig. 282). Time required to change any of the following is 1 minute each: change blank length or width, or change grade of paper.

Combiner should be capable of producing:

1. Two-, three-, or four-ply solid fiberboard.
2. Double-face corrugated fiberboard, and double-wall and triple-wall corrugated fiberboard.

Combiner should run three 8-hour shifts per day, 5 days per week, 52 weeks per year. Capacity of combiner is 19,800,000 square feet per week. Maximum expected down time is 5 percent. Fiberboard waste expected at combiner is 2 percent. Total waste expected for all operations in plant, including combiner, is 10 percent.

B. *Printer-slotter* (Fig. 15) is capable of handling blanks as shown in Table 1. Printing to be one or two colors. More than two colors requires rerun through printer.

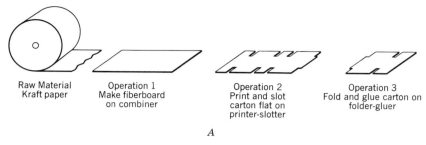

| Raw Material
Kraft paper | Operation 1
Make fiberboard
on combiner | Operation 2
Print and slot
carton flat on
printer-slotter | Operation 3
Fold and glue carton on
folder-gluer |

A

Loading Platform

Shipping   Receiving

Warehouse

Combiner ①

③ Folder-Gluer   ② Printer-Slotter

B

Figure 14 Manufacture of fiberboard shipping cartons. *A*, operations required to make carton; *B*, flow diagram for the manufacture of cartons.

Figure 15 Printer-slotter—machine for printing and slotting fiberboard blanks.

Table 1. Specifications for Printer-Slotter

Size of Printer-Slotter	Size of Carton Blank in Inches		Speed of Printer in Pieces per Hour
	Minimum	Maximum	
A	6 × 10	24 × 66	5000
B	20 × 25	35 × 78	5000
C	24 × 30	50 × 100	5000
D	30 × 40	80 × 180	1500

Printing ink and dies supplied from outside. Setup time for any size printer-slotter is 30 minutes.

C. *Folder-gluer* (Fig. 16) capable of handling blanks:

Size A, $10'' \times 30''$ minimum to $35'' \times 78''$ maximum.
Size B, $12'' \times 35''$ minimum to $50'' \times 103''$ maximum.
Speed of folder-gluer is 10,000 cartons per hour.

Cartons may be made by (*a*) stitching seam, (*b*) gluing seam, or (*c*) taping seam. Carton blanks must be stitched or taped if under $10'' \times 30''$ or over $50'' \times 103''$ in size. All other sizes may be stitched, glued, or taped. Setup time for either size folder-gluer is 20 minutes.

Estimated Cost of Equipment

Name of Equipment	*Cost per Unit Installed*
Combiner	$1,400,000
Printer-slotter	90,000
Folder-gluer	150,000
Steam boiler	16,000
Adhesive-mixing equipment	65,000
Fork lift trucks	15,000 each
Scrap fiberboard baler	65,000
Building to house equipment	3,500,000

Time Schedule

Activity	*Time in Months*
Design plant	3
Build building to house equipment	3
Install equipment	2
"Debug" equipment and get plant running to capacity	7
Total time	15

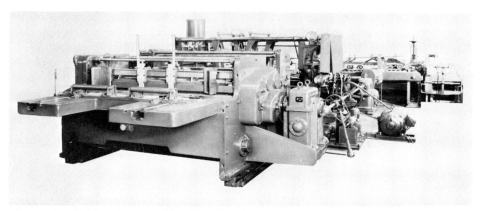

Figure 16   Folder-gluer, capable of handling folded cartons at the rate of 10,000 cartons per hour.

Work Methods Design

The relatively simple process of manufacturing a fiberboard shipping carton has been used to show how the person, the machine, the materials, and the methods must all be considered together in the design of the factory. The design must meet certain specifications as to volume, size of cartons, scrap, and cost of finished product. Because 15 months is the maximum time allowed to design, build, and put the plant into full operation, it is obvious that this does not permit extended research to determine new or original methods of making shipping containers, such as molding or blowing or forming out of plastic, Fiberglas, or rubber instead of making them out of fiberboard. Equipment and processes generally available would probably need to be used. Some novel features might be developed in the equipment and in the layout of the plant and certainly in the design of the operator methods. Although it is true that one has greater freedom in developing work methods when a new process or system is being designed than when improvements are being made in a going activity, numerous specifications and restrictions are always present, including those of time and development costs.

A SPECIFIC CASE—THE REDESIGN OF LIPSTICK MANUFACTURING METHODS IN A COSMETICS PLANT

An ongoing manufacturing process is often in a state of change. New and better materials are developed or become available, and changes in product models or changes in product parts design occur. New equipment and tools make existing facilities obsolete and there is a never ending opportunity to improve and redesign operator methods, to eliminate manual tasks, and make the job easier for the worker.

The following is an excellent example.[2] Elizabeth Arden, Inc., a cosmetics production firm, was acquired by Eli Lilly and Company, and its manufacturing facilities were moved from Long Island City, New York, to an existing Lilly plant in Roanoke, Virginia. Before the move was made Lilly industrial engineering personnel studied the operations and aided in the facilities transfer from New York to Virginia. Therefore, there is a well-documented and accurate description of the lipstick manufacturing process at the time of the acquisition. Changes have been made over a period of seven years resulting in a significant reduction in unit labor costs.

The lipstick unit consists of three parts: (a) a cap, (b) a base, and (c) the molded lipstick (Fig. 17). The base and cap are referred to as the lipstick case. The base contains a swivel or screw device and a metal cup into which the bottom end of the molded stick is inserted and held. (D in Fig. 17) Rotating the swivel device permits the stick to be raised for use or lowered for storage. In the recessed position the entire

A B C D

Figure 17 Parts of the lipstick. A, cap; B, base; C, molded stick; D, base with stick mounted in cup of base—swiveled in the "up" position.

[2] Appreciation is expressed to Eli Lilly and Company, and in particular, to Frank W. Sheffler and Gerard M. Van Vliet for the information on which this section is based.

stick is below the open end of the base and is protected. The cases are purchased from an outside supplier.

Lipstick cases are made in different sizes, designs, finishes, and styles. Also, the molded sticks are made in different colors and formulations and the shape of the tip may vary. However, the manufacturing process is essentially the same for all lipsticks.

First, the original lipstick manufacturing process will be described and then the changes that have been made will be presented.

Original Manufacturing Processes

The Arden lipstick manufacturing system consisted of the following processes:

1. Material dispensing and bulk manufacturing.
2. Molding of lipsticks.
3. Cooling of molded lipsticks.
4. Removal of lipsticks from molds.
5. Labeling bases and assembling lipsticks.

1. Material Dispensing and Bulk Manufacturing. The lipstick formulas consisted of mixtures of vegetable oils, waxes, preservatives, colors, antioxidants, and fragrances. The ingredients needed for a batch or lot were preweighed and placed in a steam-heated, jacketed kettle and mixed to form a homogeneous bulk mass (Fig. 18). This mix was checked and adjusted for color prior to the addition of the fragrance essence. Any of the bulk mix not used at the time of compounding was poured into 5 gallon cans, cooled and stored, to be remelted again and used when needed.

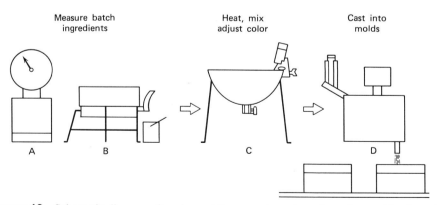

Figure 18 Schematic diagram of equipment for preparing mix and pouring molds. *A*, scales; *B*, supply tank for vegetable oils; *C*, steam heated, jacketed kettle with mixer (batch kettle); *D*, electrically heated dispensing pot with stirrer.

2.   Molding of Lipsticks. Lipsticks were formed by molding in multi-cavity aluminum molds which were split at the center line of the lipsticks. Seventy two or 90 cavity molds were used and each mold consisted of 4 or 5 sections or plates containing rows of cavities. The individual sections of the molds were held in position by dowels and were fastened together with swing bolts to facilitate assembly and disassembly.

The assembled molds were preheated in circulating air ovens to bring them to the temperature of the casting mix. Part of the premelted lipstick mix was transferred to the electrically heated dispensing pot which was equipped with a stirrer (Fig. 18 D). This bulk mix was dispensed into the preheated mold immediately after the mold was removed from the preheated oven. The dispensing pot valve was manually opened and the mix was dispensed by gravity into the header or reservoir section at the top of the mold from which it drained into the cavities. Excess material (above the cavity section of the mold) remained in the header section of the mold to assure that the cavities would be completely filled when cooled.

3.   Cooling of Molded Lipsticks. The filled mold was covered with a protective cover and placed on a conveyor which carried it through a water spray cooling tunnel. The mold was taken off the conveyor, the cover removed, and the moisture wiped off with a cloth. The excess material in the header was scraped off with a plastic scraper. This ''scag'' was remelted in the batch kettle and reused.

4.   Removal of Lipsticks from Molds. The mold was disassembled and the molded lipsticks were removed from the cavities (Fig. 19). Each plate or section of the mold was removed one at a time to permit the manual removal of all of the lipsticks from the section. After each section of the mold was stripped, the cavities were wiped clean with a silicone impregnated cloth and the sections were reassembled. The dowels in each section of the plate enabled them to be fitted together in the proper position. This procedure was followed, one section at a time, until the entire mold was reassembled and the swing bolts were put in place and the nuts tightened. At this time the assembled mold was placed in the oven for reheating. The removed sticks were inspected, placed in metal boxes, and stored prior to assembly. Rejected sticks were remelted in the batch kettle.

5.   Labeling Bases and Assembling Lipsticks. The lipstick case consisted of a base and a cap. The bases were labeled on a rotary label printing and affixing machine known as ''Print-A'Ply'' machine. Each base had a shade name as a part of the graphics. Labels were printed and affixed to the base in accordance with the particular order for lipsticks.

Premolded lipsticks and cases were drawn from inventory. The lipsticks were inspected and inserted into the cup end of the base (with the cup swiveled ''up,'' as purchased). Then the cup was swiveled ''down,'' the cap installed, the label was ink-stamped with an identity code, and the assembled lipsticks placed vertically in tote boxes prior to cartoning. All of the above operations were performed manually. The operators inserting lipsticks into bases wore finger cots to preserve the cleanliness of the product in handling.

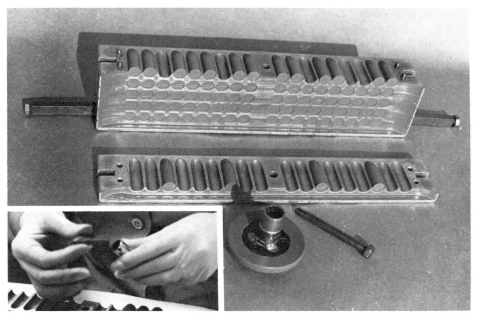

Figure 19   Original design of mold with five rows of cavities split at the centerline of the lipsticks. The top plate has been taken off so that the sticks can be removed. Closeup shows operator inserting molded stick in the lipstick base.

Present Manufacturing Processes

During the period since the manufacturing facilities were moved to the Lilly plant there has been a continuous stream of changes. Some of the most significant improvements occurred in the production processes associated with molding.

A. *De-aeration of the Product.* A recurring problem had been voids or "pin holes" in the surface of the lipsticks, resulting in rejected sticks after molding. This condition was greatly improved by casting the bulk mix into slabs which were then remelted on thermostatically controlled melting plates into the casting pots. The melting plates, with their large surface area, provided a means of allowing entrapped air bubbles to escape from the bulk material, resulting in fewer pin holes and higher yield.

B. *Improved Mold Heating Methods.* The mold oven heating process originally used had been time consuming and imprecise. A cored table through which hot water was pumped and circulated (with vertical clamping plates fastened to the table) replaced the oven providing more rapid heating and more accurate temperature control.

C. *Improved Mold Cooling.* The earlier method of spray cooling, although efficient from a heat transfer viewpoint, was undesirable because water would get on and into the molds requiring wiping after the sticks were removed from the mold. The improved method consisted of cooling the molds on a cooling table with vertical side clamps through which refrigerant was pumped. This method of cooling does not require mold wiping after the sticks have been removed.

D. *Improved Mold Cleaning and Lubrication.* Originally the mold cleaning and lubrication technique (wiping with a silicone impregnated cloth) was time consuming. Experimentation led to the use of ultrasonic cleaning with an aqueous solution of an alkaline detergent and subsequent rinsing. It was found that with this technique it was necessary to clean the molds once a day or less provided the molds were sprayed with a food-grade silicone after each unmolding. After about a year, however, it was found that the aluminum molds were becoming pitted by residual alkaline solution in the crevices and interfaces of the molds. Consequently, the ultrasonic cleaning was replaced with an ultrasonic vapor degreasing process utilizing a fluorocarbon azeotrope solution of methylene chloride. This compound was effective in cleaning the molds without attacking the aluminum mold surfaces. Moreover, the solution could be continually regenerated by evaporation from the sump containing the lipstick cleaned from the molds.

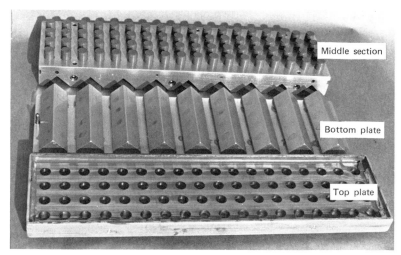

Figure 20 Current design of mold. After the mold is filled and cooled, the top plate is removed exposing the cup ends of the molded lipsticks. The stick is removed by placing the base cup over the end of the stick, pressing down to engage the stick, and then lifting the stick out of the cavity.

E. *Removing Sticks from Mold*. It was found that improved cleaning techniques combined with the silicone lubrication after each unmolding cycle permitted the removal of molded lipsticks from their cavities without disassembly of the mold. A mold of new design (Fig. 20) was constructed so that the cup end of the mold was a separate plate which, when removed from the rest of the mold, permitted the sticks to be transferred directly to the cups in the lipstick base. This was done by inverting the cup end of the base over the exposed end of the stick, pushing the base down to seat the stick in the cup, and then pulling the stick free from the cavity. This process (transfer of the stick directly from the mold cavity to the lipstick base) eliminated the inventory of molded sticks prior to assembly into cases. This resulted in less handling labor and less product damage and reduced the loss during storage.

Results

In addition to the changes that have been made in the lipstick molding processes as noted above, improvements in methods and equipment for handling and processing bulk raw materials and the finished mix, and in labeling and coding lipstick cases and finished product occurred. Quality assurance methods and quality specifications were changed resulting in a better product of a more uniform quality. Improvements were also made in planning and scheduling. As Table 2 shows, labor productivity more than doubled. The number of lipsticks produced per hour increased from 76 to 179 and this productivity increase more than offset the higher labor costs in the form of increased wages and fringe benefits.

Table 2. Labor Standards in Minutes per Unit and in Units Produced per Hour for Lipstick Manufacturing

| Year | Labor Standards in Minutes per Unit | | | Units Produced per Labor Hour |
	Bulk Mfg.	Molding, Unmolding, Assembling, Labeling	Total Labor	
0	.0800	.7079	.7879	76
1	.0755	.5412	.6167	97
2	.0704	.5012	.5716	105
3	.0671	.4732	.5403	111
4	.0658	.4732	.5390	111
5	.0455	.3912	.4417	136
6	.0337	.3410	.3747	160
7	.0337	.3008	.3345	179

6

WORK METHODS DESIGN—DEVELOPING
A BETTER METHOD

At the time a new product or service is being designed or developed, consideration is nearly always given to the system or process that will be required to manufacture the product or provide the service. It is at this stage that one has greatest opportunity to use the design process and to come up with the best production systems and methods. Experience shows, however, that there is no "perfect method." In fact, there are always opportunities for improvement. Also, conditions may change. Factors such as volume and quality of product, kind and price of raw material, and availability of machines and equipment may be different from those that were present when production first started. Therefore, one is always confronted with the opportunity to improve processes and methods. This may also include the redesign of the product itself, and its components (Figs. 21 and 22), as well as the standardization and better utilization of raw material (Fig. 23).

Because this improvement aspect of methods design is so important in every phase of human endeavor, considerable emphasis is given to it in this book. The same problem-solving approach should be used in designing a method for an activity already in operation as in designing a new one. This means the determination of the goal or objective—the formulation of the problem. Then follows the analysis of the problem, obtaining facts, determining specifications and restrictions, and obtaining information about the volume—potential savings per year and savings over the life of the product. However, one usually does not have the same freedom; more constraints are imposed simply because the activity is a going one. There is the added "cost to make a change" that must be considered.

In searching for a better method, the analyst should not be unduly influenced by the current one, but should look at all ways of achieving the objective rather than merely trying to make an improvement in the present method.

Search for Possible Solutions—Develop the Preferred Method

The following approaches should be considered in developing possible solutions from which the preferred work method will be selected:

> A. Eliminate all unnecessary work.
> B. Combine operations or elements.
> C. Change the sequence of operations.
> D. Simplify the necessary operations.

Figure 21 This product, redesigned for better appearance, has four components instead of six. (From Harold Van Doren, *Industrial Design,* 2nd ed., McGraw-Hill, New York. Photographs courtesy of Cushing & Nevell.)

Figure 22   Carburetor control lever used on Caterpillar tractor.

A, Original Design

Original material, malleable iron casting.

Machining operations required:

4 Drilling operations

2 Reaming operations

2 Tapping operations

1 Saw-cutting operation

B, Present Design

Present material, steel stamping.

Machining operations required:

1 Blanking and piercing operation

1 Burring operation

1 Forming operation

Note: The original method required a Woodruff keyway cut in both ends, as the shaft was keyed to the lever. The revised design requires a keyway at one end of the shaft only, as the other end is welded into the stamped lever.

Savings: The present cost is 66 percent of the original cost.

It is entirely possible that more than one method will be designed. As discussed in Chapter 4, it is usually desirable to design (1) an ideal system or method, (2) a practical method that can be put into immediate use, and (3) a method that might be used if certain restraints or restrictions could be removed.

A. Eliminate All Unnecessary Work

Far too much work is done today that is not necessary. In many instances the job or the process should not be a subject for simplification or improvement, but rather it should be eliminated entirely.

The Procter and Gamble Company has found this matter of work elimination and cost elimination so profitable that it has established a formal procedure which it calls "the elimination approach."[1] Although the company is constantly improving methods and simplifying work, it believes that the ideal solution is to eliminate the cost. Its approach to cost elimination is as follows:

[1] Arthur Spinanger, "The Elimination Approach—A Management Tool for Cost Elimination," paper presented at meeting of American Institute of Industrial Engineers, Cincinnati, Ohio, May 18, 1960. This material reproduced by the permission of the Procter and Gamble Company.

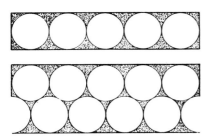

Figure 23 Savings in raw material. The Detroit Transmission Division of General Motors saved 567 tons of steel in one year by punching double rows of clutchplate blanks from steel stock, instead of single rows. In addition to saving the equivalent of 10 carloads of steel, there was a saving of $25,000 in freight and handling costs per year. (From Philip E. Cartwright, "Measured Day Work and Its Relationship to a Continuous Cost Reduction Program," *Proceedings Nineteenth Time and Motion Study Clinic,* IMS, Chicago.)

1. Select the cost for questioning. It is suggested that a major cost should be selected first in order to get the greatest money returns. If the major cost is eliminated, this will often lead to the elimination of many smaller operations as well. Labor costs, material costs, clerical costs, and overhead costs of all kinds are possible subjects for elimination. Efficient operations can be eliminated just as easily as those not as well done. The questioning procedure is easy to use. No paper work or calculations are necessary, and in fact complete knowledge of the job or activity is usually not required.

2. Identify the basic cause. A search should be made to determine the basic cause which makes the cost necessary. A basic cause is the reason, purpose, or intent on which the elimination of the cost depends. The basic cause is that factor which controls the elimination of the cost. The key question is, "This cost could be eliminated if it were not for what basic cause?" At *this stage* we do *not* ask such a question as "Why is this operation necessary?" or "How could this operation be done better?" These questions are avoided because they tend to justify and defend the job's continued existence. Instead the objective is to find the basic cause. Operations for which there is no basic cause, or for which a basic cause no longer exists, can be eliminated at once. When this is not the case and a basic cause has been identified, it is necessary to proceed to step 3.

3. Question the basic cause for elimination. If the basic cause has been identified, then it can be questioned in two ways.

a. Disregard the basic cause—consider what would happen if the operation were not done. If the same results or better results can be obtained without the operation, then consideration should be given to eliminating it at once. However, disregarding the basic cause can be dangerous. In this connection it is necessary to consider two points: (1) determine the area of influence of the basic cause— what else might happen if this basic cause were eliminated? and (2) determine the associated "price tag" of the basic cause—is there a proper return on the money spent to obtain the desired results? If the basic cause cannot be disregarded, the second opportunity for elimination is

b. Apply "why?" questioning. If the job under consideration seems to be necessary, can the job immediately preceding it be eliminated, thus perhaps making
all succeeding jobs unnecessary? If complete elimination is not possible, try for
partial elimination. Perhaps there are alternate possibilities—try to adopt the
lowest cost alternative. Identify the basic cause of each supporting factor and
question for elimination or change.

It is often desirable to undertake cost elimination on a department-wide or plantwide basis. Thus several qualified members of supervision working as a group can
help identify basic causes of specific costs selected for study.

Packing Lettuce in Cartons. Formerly lettuce was packed and shipped in large wood
crates holding a total of approximately 125 pounds. In packing, ice was interspersed
between the layers of lettuce. A better method of packing has been developed, using
a carton which holds approximately 50 pounds. The lettuce is selected, cut, and
packed directly into the carton in the field. Shortly thereafter, the packaged lettuce is
quickly cooled to 36 to 38° in a vacuum cooling plant, and it is not necessary to place
ice in the carton. Most of the lettuce grown in California is now packed in cartons instead of boxes. The result is a saving of approximately $3 per box, and some 60,000
carloads of lettuce are shipped out of California each year. The use of ice in packing
lettuce was eliminated, and the substitution of a fiberboard carton for a wood crate
further reduced the packing cost.

Code Dating Cartons. Originally four code dates were stamped on each carton of
soap coming off the packing line. The basic cause for these dates was the desire of
sales people in customers' stores to determine when the carton of soap was manufactured. This seemed necessary, but since one date was satisfactory the other three
dates were eliminated. In this case the cost was partially eliminated.

Splicing Insulated Wires.[2] Along the cable routes of the Bell System, wires are
spliced at a rate of 250,000,000 a year. Conventionally, connections are made by
"skinning" the insulation, twisting the bare wires together, and slipping on an
insulating sleeve. Now, with a special connector, splices can be made faster, yet are
even more reliable (Fig. 24). The craftsman slips the two wire ends, with insulation
intact, into the connector and then flattens the connector with a penumatic tool.
Springy phosphor-bronze tangs inside the connector bite through the insulation to
contact the copper wire. Here skinning the insulation and twisting the bare wires
together have been eliminated.

Benefits of Work Elimination. If a job can be eliminated, there is no need to spend
money on installing an improved method. No interruption or delay is caused while
the improved method is being developed, tested, and installed. It is not necessary to

---

[2] Reproduced by permission of Bell Telephone Laboratories.

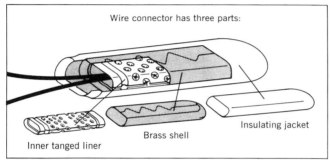

Figure 24 Splicing insulated wires without removing the insulation or twisting the wires.

train new operators on the new method. The problem of resistance to change is minimized when a job or activity that is found to be unnecessary is eliminated. The best way to simplify an operation is to devise some way to get the same or better results at no cost at all.

B. Combine Operations or Elements

Although it is customary to break down a process into many simple operations, in some instances the division of labor has been carried too far. It is possible to sub-divide a process into too many operations, causing excessive handling of materials, tools, and equipment. Also such problems as the following may be created: difficulty in balancing the many operations, accumulation of work between operations when improper planning exists, and delays when inexperienced operators are employed or when regular operators are off the job.[3] It is sometimes possible to make the work easier by simply combining two or more operations, or by making some changes in method permitting operations to be combined.

---

[3] For a more detailed discussion of division of labor and job enlargement see Chapter 40.

Figure 25 The two short belt conveyors eliminate the need for an off-bearer on this molding machine.

Figure 25 shows how two short conveyors installed at the end of a molding machine in a furniture factory replaced the off-bearer and made it possible for one person to do the work of two. The operator shown in the picture feeds the stock into the machine and places the finished molding strips in the truck as they come back to him on the conveyor. The truck shown is divided into four sections, only three of which are used to bring up raw stock; the fourth receives the finished strips as they come from the machine. This plan reduced the number of trucks needed and also saved floor space.[4]

C. Change the Sequence of Operations

When a new product goes into production it frequently is made in small quantities on an ''experimental'' basis. Production often increases gradually, and in time output becomes large, but the original sequence of operations may be kept the same as when production was small. For this and for other reasons it is desirable to question the order in which the various operations are performed.

For example, in one plant small assemblies were made on semiautomatic machines in Department A (Fig. 26). They were stored in Department B, inspected in Department C, and packed for shipment in Department D. The manufacturing methods were

---

[4] Martin S. Meyers, ''Evaluation of the Industrial Engineering Program in Small Plant Management,'' *Proceedings Sixth Industrial Engineering Institute,* University of California, Los Angeles-Berkeley, p. 37.

such that normally only 10 percent of the finished assemblies were inspected. When an excessive number of defects were found, however, all work was given a 100 percent inspection until the cause of the trouble was located and corrected.

Because there was always a bank of several days' work in Department B awaiting inspection, when trouble was encountered it was necessary to give this entire bank a 100 percent inspection; moreover, defective assemblies had to be repaired or scrapped. To correct this difficulty the inspectors were placed immediately adjacent to the assembly department, and the bank of finished assemblies awaiting inspection was eliminated, as shown in Fig. 27. Because each unit was inspected as it came from the assembly line, rejects were found within a few minutes after the units were completed, and the cause of the difficulty could be corrected before other "scrap" parts had been made. This simple rearrangement, which was easy and inexpensive to make, saved the company tens of thousands of dollars in inspection costs and greatly reduced the number of scrapped parts.

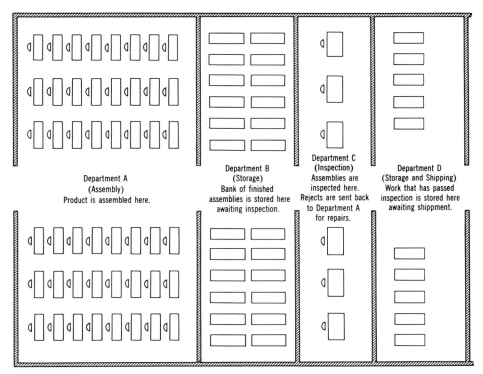

Figure 26 Layout of building for assembly and inspection of small parts produced on semiautomatic machines— old arrangement of departments. Notice that inspection was done in Department C.

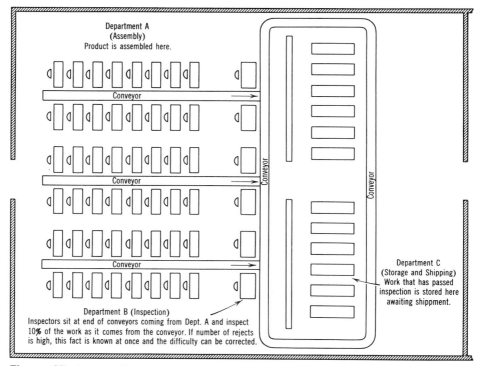

Figure 27 Layout of building for assembly and inspection of small parts—improved arrangement of departments. Inspection now takes place immediately adjacent to the assembly department.

The process chart and flow diagram described in Chapter 7 serve a useful purpose in pointing out the desirability of changing the sequence of operations to eliminate backtracking, to reduce transportation and handling, and to effect a smooth flow of work through the plant.

D. Simplify the Necessary Operations

After the process has been studied and all improvements that seem worthwhile have been made, the next step is to analyze each operation in the process and to try to simplify or improve it. In other words, the over-all picture is studied first and major changes are made; then the smaller details of the work are studied.

One of the best ways to approach the problem of methods improvement is to question everything about the job—the *way* the job is being done now, the *materials* that are being used, the *tools* and *equipment,* the *working conditions,* and the *design* of the product itself. Assume that nothing about the job is perfect. Begin by asking the questions: What? Who? Where? When? How? Why?

1. *What* is done? What is the purpose of the operation? *Why* should it be done? What would happen if it were not done? Is every part of the activity or detail necessary?
2. *Who* does the work? *Why* does this person do it? Who could do it better? Can changes be made to permit a person with less skill and training to do the work?
3. *Where* is the work done? *Why* is it done there? Could it be done somewhere else more economically?
4. *When* is the work done? *Why* should it be done then? Would it be better to do it at some other time?
5. *How* is the work done? *Why* is it done this way? This suggests a careful analysis and the application of principles of motion economy.

Question each element or hand motion. Just as in an analysis of the process we tried to eliminate, combine, and rearrange the sequence of operations, so in the single operation we try to eliminate motions, combine them, or rearrange the sequence of necessary motions in order to make the job easier.

Work Methods Design Laboratories

To an increasing extent business and industry are providing methods design laboratories with staff and facilities for the systematic study and improvement of production methods. The early methods laboratories were found mainly in industries having light assembly operations and short-cycle repetitive jobs. Here production methods were developed; temporary jigs and fixtures were designed, built, and tested; and in some cases a mock-up was made of the work place. Sometimes motion picture films were made for teaching the job to new operators, and in some instances the operators were brought into the laboratory for training.

In contrast to this, a large tractor manufacturing company established a methods laboratory and undertook as the initial project the determination of the best methods of performing welding operations as they pertained to the manufacture of the company's products. Twelve carefully selected men from the Industrial Engineering Department were assigned to this task. Approximately one year was needed to develop and standardize welding methods and procedures and to establish standard data for predetermining methods and time standards for such work. After this first investigation there has followed a continuous series of studies to increase productivity and decrease the cost of operating machine tools and production equipment of all kinds used by this company.

Tools for Methods Improvement

Before better and easier methods of doing a task can be developed, it is necessary to get all the facts pertaining to the job. This involves getting sufficient information to answer the what, who, where, when, how, and why questions, and to answer satisfactorily the four other questions already suggested. Most people find it useful to list the information in tabular or graphic form. Because several different methods of visualizing a process or an operation are widely used, each of them will be fully described in the next five chapters. Of course, not all of these different methods would be used on any one job. For example, it may be found that a process chart or flow diagram is all that is needed. If a single operation is the subject for study, then the operation chart may be used. The activity chart and the man and machine chart are also useful, and occasionally it may be worthwhile to make a micromotion analysis of the job, particularly if the cycle is short and a large number of people are employed on it.

It should be clearly understood, however, that the process chart, flow diagram, activity chart, man and machine chart, operation chart, and simo chart are merely tools to be used as needed.

7

PROCESS ANALYSIS

The entire system or process of doing work should be studied before undertaking a thorough investigation of a specific operation in the process. Such an over-all study will ordinarily include an anlysis of each step in the manufacturing process or system.

Process Charts

The process chart is a device for recording a process in a compact manner, as a means of better understanding it and improving it. The chart represents graphically the separate steps or events that occur during the performance of a task or during a series of actions. The chart usually begins with the raw material entering the factory and follows it through every step, such as transportation to storage, inspection, machining operations, and assembly, until it becomes either a finished unit itself or a part of a subassembly. The process chart might, of course, record the process through only one or a few departments.

A careful study of such a chart, giving a graphic picture of every step in the process through the factory, is almost certain to suggest improvements. It is frequently found that certain operations can be eliminated entirely or that a part of an operation can be eliminated, that one operation can be combined with another, that better routes for the parts can be found, more economical machines used, delays between operations eliminated, and other improvements made, all of which serve to produce a better product at a lower cost. The process chart assists in showing the effects that changes in one part of the process will have on other parts or elements. Moreover, the chart may aid in discovering particular operations in the process which should be subjected to more careful analysis.

The process chart, like other methods of graphic representation, should be modified to meet the particular situation. For example, it may show in sequence the activities of a person, or the steps that the material goes through. The chart should be either the *man type* or the *material type,* and the two types should *not* be combined.

◯ Operation

◯ Transportation

☐ Inspection

▽ Storage or Delay   **Figure 28**   The Gilbreth process chart symbols.

Figure 29 These process chart symbols save time in recording the steps used in doing work.

The process chart may profitably be made by almost anyone in an organization. The supervisor, and the process and layout engineers should be as familiar with the process chart as the industrial engineer and should be able to use it.

Many years ago the Gilbreths devised a set of 40 symbols which they used in making process charts.[1] The abbreviated set of four symbols shown in Fig. 28 has been

[1] F. B. and L. M. Gilbreth, "Process Charts," *Transactions of the ASME*, Vol. 43, Paper 1818, pp. 1029–1050, 1921.

widely used, and they are all that are needed for many kinds of work. These symbols serve as a special kind of shorthand to aid in listing quickly the steps or activities in a process.

The American Society of Mechanical Engineers has established as standard the five symbols[2] shown in Fig. 29. This set of symbols is a modification of the abbreviated set of Gilbreth symbols in that the arrow replaces the small circle and a new symbol has been added to denote a delay.

Perhaps it is not too important which symbols are used in making process charts and flow diagrams. In fact, an organization may find that it requires a special set of symbols for its particular needs. Experience shows, however, that where supervisors are expected to take an active part in developing better methods it is desirable to use as few process chart symbols as possible and charts that are simple to construct and easy to understand.

The process chart symbols used in the illustrations in this volume are those shown in Fig. 29, and are described as follows:

○ *Operation.* An operation occurs when an object is intentionally changed in one or more of its characteristics. An operation represents a major step in the process and usually occurs at a machine or work station.

⇨ *Transportation.* A transportation occurs when an object is moved from one place to another, except when the movement is an integral part of an operation or an inspection.

☐ *Inspection.* An inspection occurs when an object is examined for identification or is compared with a standard as to quantity or quality.

◗ *Delay.* A delay occurs when the immediate performance of the next planned action does not take place.

▽ *Storage.* A storage occurs when an object is kept under control such that its withdrawal requires authorization.

Combined Symbols. Two symbols may be combined when activities are performed at the same work place or when they are performed concurrently as one activity. For example, the large circle within the square ⬕ represents a combined operation and inspection.

Steps Used in Watering Garden

In order to illustrate how these symbols may be used, the process chart shown in Fig. 30 gives the steps followed by Mr. Smith in getting ready to water his garden. Mr. Smith, sitting on his porch, decides to water the garden. He leaves the porch, walks to the garage at the other end of the house, opens the garage door, and walks to the

[2] *Operation and Flow Process Charts, ASME Standard* 101, published by the American Society of Mechanical Engineers, New York, 1947.

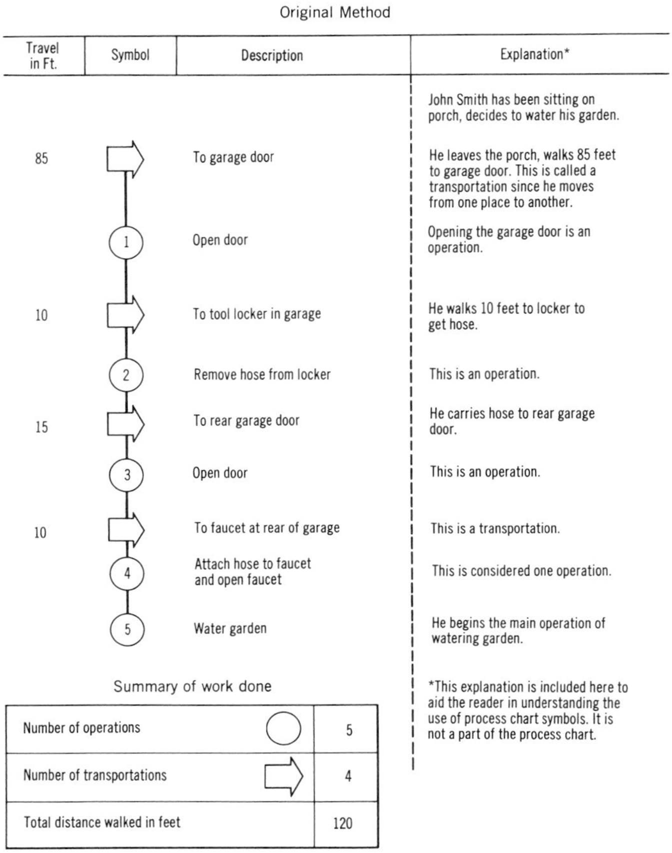

Original Method

Travel in Ft.	Symbol	Description	Explanation*
			John Smith has been sitting on porch, decides to water his garden.
85	⇨	To garage door	He leaves the porch, walks 85 feet to garage door. This is called a transportation since he moves from one place to another.
	①	Open door	Opening the garage door is an operation.
10	⇨	To tool locker in garage	He walks 10 feet to locker to get hose.
	②	Remove hose from locker	This is an operation.
15	⇨	To rear garage door	He carries hose to rear garage door.
	③	Open door	This is an operation.
10	⇨	To faucet at rear of garage	This is a transportation.
	④	Attach hose to faucet and open faucet	This is considered one operation.
	⑤	Water garden	He begins the main operation of watering garden.

Summary of work done

Number of operations	◯	5
Number of transportations	⇨	4
Total distance walked in feet		120

*This explanation is included here to aid the reader in understanding the use of process chart symbols. It is not a part of the process chart.

Figure 30   Process chart of watering garden.

tool locker. There he lifts the reel of garden hose from the locker, carries it to the rear garage door, opens the door, and carries the hose to the faucet at the rear of the garage. He attaches the hose to the faucet, turns on the faucet, and begins to water the garden. An examination of the process chart on the left-hand side of Fig. 30 will show that the nine symbols, five numbers, and nine phrases are all that are needed to describe the entire process.

Flow Diagram of Watering Garden

Sometimes a better picture of the process can be obtained by putting flow lines on a plan drawing of the building or area in which the activity takes place. A sketch of the plan view of the house, lawn, and garden is shown in Fig. 31. Lines are drawn on

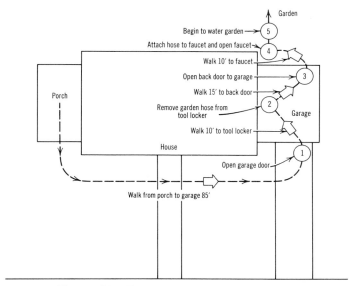

Figure 31 Flow diagram of watering garden.

this sketch to show the path of travel, and the process chart symbols are inserted in the lines to indicate what is taking place. Brief notations are included to amplify the symbols. This is called a flow diagram. Sometimes both a process chart and a flow diagram are needed to show clearly the steps in a manufacturing process, office procedure, or other activity.

Recoating Buffing Wheels with Emery

In large factories where heavy polishing and buffing operations are required, it is customary to recoat buffing wheels (Fig. 32) with emery in the plant, thus keeping a supply of fresh wheels always available. The wheels are made of layers of fabric

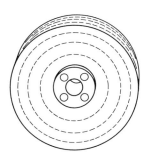

Figure 32 Buffing wheel.

sewed together, and their average weight is 40 pounds. They vary in diameter from 18 to 24 inches, and in width of face from 3 to 5 inches. The circumference or face of the wheel is coated with glue and emery dust. The first coat of glue is allowed to set approximately one-half hour before the second coat is applied. The temperature in the room where the wheels are cured is maintained between 80 and 90°, and the humidity is also controlled.

Original Method

The circumference of the worn wheel was coated with glue (Fig. 33) and then rolled by hand through a shallow trough filled with emery dust, thus coating the wheel (Fig. 34). After the glue had dried, a second coat of glue and emery dust was applied in a similar manner. The wheels were then hauled to a drying oven, and hung on racks in the oven until the glue was thoroughly dry. Figure 35 shows the flow diagram and Fig. 36 the process chart.

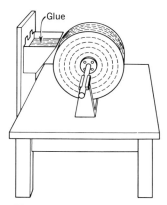

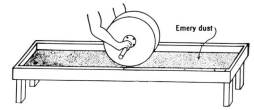

Figure 34   Old method of recoating wheel. Operator rolls glue-covered wheel back and forth in trough containing emery dust.

Figure 33 Operator applies glue to circumference of worn wheel by means of a brush.

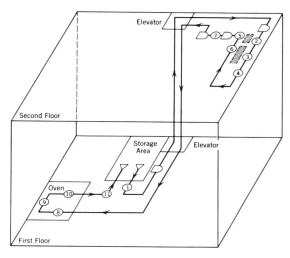

Figure 35   Flow diagram of old method of recoating buffing wheels with emery.

Travel, feet	Symbol	Description
	▽	Worn wheels on floor (to be recoated)
	①	Load wheels onto truck
40	Ⓗ	To elevator
	▽	Wait for elevator
20	Ⓔ	To second floor by elevator
35	Ⓗ	To coating bench
	▽	At coating bench
	②	Coat with glue
	③	Coat with emery (1st coat)
	④	On floor to dry
	⑤	Coat with glue
	⑥	Coat with emery (2nd coat)
	▽	On floor at coating table
	⑦	Load onto truck
15	Ⓗ	To elevator
	▽	Wait for elevator
20	Ⓔ	To first floor by elevator
75	Ⓗ	To drying oven
	⑧	Unload coated wheels onto racks in oven
	⑨	Dry in oven
	⑩	Load wheels onto truck
35	Ⓗ	To storage area
	⑪	Unload wheels onto floor
	▽	Storage

Summary

Number of operations _ _ _ _ _ _ _ _ _ ◯	11
Number of storages and delays _ _ _ _ _▽	6
Number of inspections _ _ _ _ _ _ _ _ _□	1
Number of transportations _ _ _ _ _ _ _◯	7
Total travel, in feet _ _ _ _ _ _ _ _	240

Figure 36 Process chart of old method of recoating buffing wheels with emery.

67

The following questions might be asked about this job: *Why* coat the wheels by hand? *Why* handle the wheels so often? Could the wheels be coated on the first floor instead of on the second? These questions were answered in the following way.

Improved Method

A special coating machine (Fig. 37) was built, making it possible to apply the glue and emery to the wheel in one operation with much less time and effort than by the old method. Because this machine was located on the first floor between the storage area and the drying oven (Fig. 38), it was unnecessary to move the wheels to the second floor. Special truck racks (Fig. 40) were used instead of regular platform trucks, eliminating much unnecessary handling of wheels. The coated wheels remained on the truck racks while in the drying oven. Figure 39 shows the process chart for the improved method, and a summary of the savings.

Results. The new coating machine, the special truck rack for handling wheels, and the better location of the coating machine reduced the number of *operations* needed

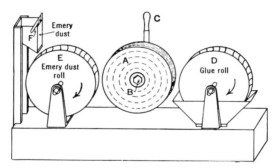

Figure 37 Schematic drawing showing coating machine. The wheel A to be coated is mounted on shaft B, which is attached to lever C. Swinging the lever to right makes contact with glue roll D, which coats circumference of wheel. Lever C is then swung to left, making contact with roll E, which coats wheel with emery. Rolls D and E are both power-driven. The lever at F controls the amount of emery dust fed onto roll E.

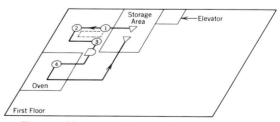

Figure 38 Flow diagram of improved method of recoating buffing wheels with emery.

Travel, feet	Symbol	Description
	▽	Worn wheels on special truck racks according to grit size
10	Ⓗ	To coating machine
	①	Coat with glue and emery (1st coat) and place on truck rack
	②	On truck rack for glue to dry
	▣③	Coat with glue and emery (2nd coat)
	▽	On rack at coating machine
25	Ⓗ	Rack into drying oven
	④	Dry in oven
35	Ⓗ	Truck rack to storage
	▽	Storage of finished coated wheels on truck rack

Summary

	Old Method		Improved Method		Difference	
Number of operations _ _ _ _ _ _ _ _ ◯	11		4		7	
Number of storages and delays _ _ _ _ ▽	6		3		3	
Number of inspections _ _ _ _ _ _ _ _ ☐	1		1		0	
Transportations	No.	Dist.	No.	Dist.	No.	Dist.
By truck _ _ _ _ _ _ _ _ _ _ Ⓗ	5	200	3	70	2	130
By elevator _ _ _ _ _ _ _ _ Ⓔ	2	40	0	0	2	40
Total _ _ _ _ _ _ _ _ _ _ _ _ _	7	240	3	70	4	170

Figure 39 Process chart of improved method of recoating buffing wheels with emery.

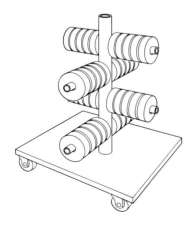

Figure 40 Special truck rack for holding buffing wheels. Racks are used for wheel storage between operations and also hold wheels while they are in drying oven.

69

to coat the wheels from 11 to 4, the number of *delays* from 4 to 1, and the *length of travel* from 240 to 70 feet. By the old method a crew of four men applied two coats of emery, and their average production was 20 wheels per hour. At the present time a two-man crew applies two coats of emery, producing 45 wheels per hour. Also, the new method of recoating wheels and a new type of synthetic glue seemed to improve the quality of the finished wheels; in fact, the operators using the wheels to grind and polish plowshares have increased their production approximately 25 percent. The wheels seem to cut faster and make the work easier for the operators.[3]

Flow Diagram of Feeding Silage on Small Dairy Farm

Farmers in increasing numbers are finding it profitable to use work methods design. Real savings are being made on small one-person farms as well as on larger ones. For example, on a 22-cow dairy farm in Vermont a systematic study was made of all the farm chores, and changes were designed to make the work easier and to save time. These changes were of four general types:

1. Rearrangement of the stables.
2. Improvement of work routines.
3. Provision of adequate and suitable equipment.
4. Convenient location of tools and supplies.

As a result, the time spent on chores was reduced from 5 hours and 44 minutes to 3 hours and 39 minutes daily, a saving of 2 hours and 5 minutes; the travel was

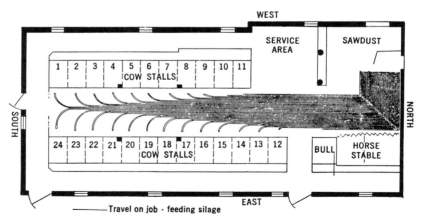

Figure 41 Flow diagram of feeding silage to cows on small dairy farm—old method. Distance traveled, 2070 feet.

[3] This project courtesy of James D. Shevlin.

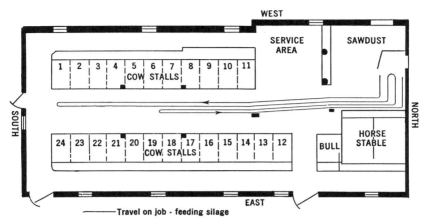

Figure 42 Flow diagram of feeding silage to cows on small dairy farm—improved method. Distance traveled, 199 feet.

reduced from 3¼ to 1¼ miles per day, a saving of 2 miles. Two hours a day is equivalent to more than 90 eight-hour working days in a year; 2 miles daily is equivalent to 730 miles yearly.

The lines in Fig. 41 show the amount of walking required to feed silage to the cows when the silage was carried from the silo in a bushel basket. Figure 42 shows the travel required when a two-wheel cart was used for hauling the silage. The total time to throw down the silage and feed 22 cows was reduced from 26.4 minutes to 14.8 minutes, and the travel was reduced from 2070 feet to 199 feet.[4]

Process Chart for an Office Procedure

In the office the process chart might show the flow of a time card, a material requisition, a purchase order, or any other form, through the various steps. The chart might begin with the first entry on the form and show all the steps until the form is permanently filed or destroyed (Fig. 43–46).

Assembly Process Charts

A special type of process chart, sometimes called an assembly process chart, is useful for showing such situations as the following: when several parts are processed separately and are then assembled and processed together; when a product is disassembled and the component parts are further processed, such as an animal in the packing

[4] R. M. Carter, "Labor Saving through Job Analysis," University of Vermont and State Agricultural College, *Bulletin* 503, p. 36.

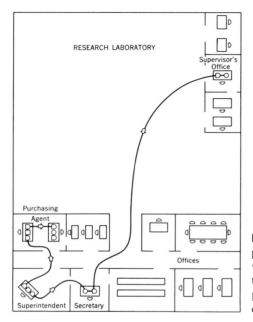

Figure 43 Flow diagram of an office procedure—present method. Requisition is written by supervisor, typewritten by secretary, approved by superintendent, and approved by purchasing agent; then a purchase order is typewritten by typist.

house; and when it is necessary to show a division in the flow of work, such as separate action on different copies of an office form.

Figure 47 shows a longer and more complicated process, that of baking soda crackers. Figure 48 shows the process chart of making, painting, filling, and closing a rectangular tin can for the export shipment of instruments. The raw material goes into stores and then through the various can-making operations. The two parts of the can are sprayed, the product is inserted into the can, the can is soldered shut, and the spraying is completed.

A study of the process chart shows several long moves that should be eliminated. Also, from general observation of the spraying operations it is apparent that some improvement might be possible. The can cover is sprayed on the outside, with the exception of a strip around the edge where it will be soldered to the bottom. In like manner the bottom of the can is sprayed on the outside, with the exception of a strip around the edge for soldering it to the cover. After these spraying operations, the two parts are assembled and moved 2500 feet to a storeroom, and then 570 feet to the packing department to be filled. The filled cans are moved 3000 feet to be soldered shut, and then moved to still another building where the unpainted portion of the outside of the filled can is painted.

As a result of a careful study of this entire process, the three spraying operations were eliminated entirely and one dipping operation was substituted for them. Clean-

	PROCESS CHART	

Present Method ☒
Proposed Method ☐

SUBJECT CHARTED ___Requisition for small tools___
Chart begins at supervisor's desk and ends at typist's desk in
purchasing department

DEPARTMENT ___Research laboratory___

DATE _____
CHART BY ___J. C. H.___
CHART NO. ___R 136___
SHEET NO. ___1___ OF ___1___

DIST. IN FEET	TIME IN MINS.	CHART SYMBOLS	PROCESS DESCRIPTION
		●⇨☐D▽	Requisition written by supervisor (one copy)
		○⇨☐D▽	On supervisor's desk (awaiting messenger)
65		○⇨☐D▽	By messenger to superintendent's secretary
		○⇨☐D▽	On secretary's desk (awaiting typing)
		●⇨☐D▽	Requisition typed (original requisition copied)
15		○⇨☐D▽	By secretary to superintendent
		○⇨☐D▽	On superintendent's desk (awaiting approval)
		○⇨■D▽	Examined and approved by superintendent
		○⇨☐D▽	On superintendent's desk (awaiting messenger)
20		○⇨☐D▽	To purchasing department
		○⇨☐D▽	On purchasing agent's desk (awaiting approval)
		○⇨■D▽	Examined and approved
		○⇨☐D▽	On purchasing agent's desk (awaiting messenger)
5		○⇨☐D▽	To typist's desk
		○⇨☐D▽	On typist's desk (awaiting typing of purchase order)
		●⇨☐D▽	Purchase order typed
		○⇨☐D▽	On typist's desk (awaiting transfer to main office)
		○⇨☐D▽	
		○⇨☐D▽	
		○⇨☐D▽	
		○⇨☐D▽	
		○⇨☐D▽	
		○⇨☐D▽	
		○⇨☐D▽	
105		3 4 2 8	Total

Figure 44   Process chart of an office procedure—present method.

73

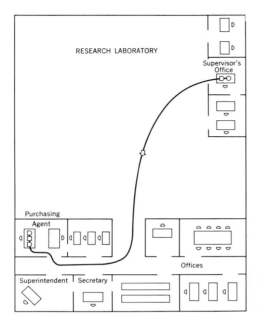

Figure 45 Flow diagram of an office procedure—proposed method. Requisition is written in triplicate by supervisor and approved by purchasing agent.

ing the cans before dipping them in lacquer was also found to be unnecessary—a procedure required in the spraying operations.

The process chart of the improved method is shown in the lower right-hand corner of Fig. 48. A summary gives the savings resulting from the improved method.

An over-all investigation should be the first one made, because entire operations or series of operations may be eliminated in this way. For the cans, it would have been a waste of time to make a detailed study of the cleaning and spraying operations with the idea of improving them, only to find later that all of them could be eliminated.

No matter how complicated or intricate the manufacturing process may be, a process chart can be constructed in the same manner and serves the same purpose as those in the examples given. It is sometimes desirable to insert photographs of the work place or of a key set of motions at the appropriate point on the chart. Occasionally time values are placed opposite each operation.

Utilization of Space in a Warehouse

A new addition to a factory warehouse was being proposed in order to provide additional storage space. Cases of product were stacked three skids high, and aisles were arranged as shown in *A* of Fig. 49. As the result of a careful study of this problem utilization of the present warehouse space was increased from 4.3 to 7.9 cases per

		PROCESS CHART		

Present Method ☐
Proposed Method ☒

SUBJECT CHARTED ___Requisition for small tools___
Chart begins at supervisor's desk and ends at purchasing agent's desk

DATE _____
CHART BY _J. C. H._
CHART NO. _R 149_
SHEET NO. _1_ OF _1_

DEPARTMENT ___Research laboratory___

DIST. IN FEET	TIME IN MINS.	CHART SYMBOLS	PROCESS DESCRIPTION
		●⇨☐D▽	Purchase order written in triplicate by supervisor
		○⇨☐D▽	On supervisor's desk (awaiting messenger)
75		○⇨☐D▽	By messenger to purchasing agent
		○⇨☐D▽	On purchasing agent's desk (awaiting approval)
		○⇨■D▽	Examined and approved by purchasing agent
		○⇨☐D▽	On purchasing agent's desk (awaiting transfer to main office)
		○⇨☐D▽	
		○⇨☐D▽	
		○⇨☐D▽	
		○⇨☐D▽	
		○⇨☐D▽	
		○⇨☐D▽	
		○⇨☐D▽	
		○⇨☐D▽	
		○⇨☐D▽	
		○⇨☐D▽	
		○⇨☐D▽	
		○⇨☐D▽	

	SUMMARY		
	PRESENT METHOD	PROPOSED METHOD	DIFFER-ENCE
Operations ○	3	1	2
Transportations ⇨	4	1	3
Inspections ☐	2	1	1
Delays D	8	3	5
Distance Traveled in Feet	105	75	30

75		1 1 1 3	Total

Figure 46 Process chart of an office procedure—proposed method.

75

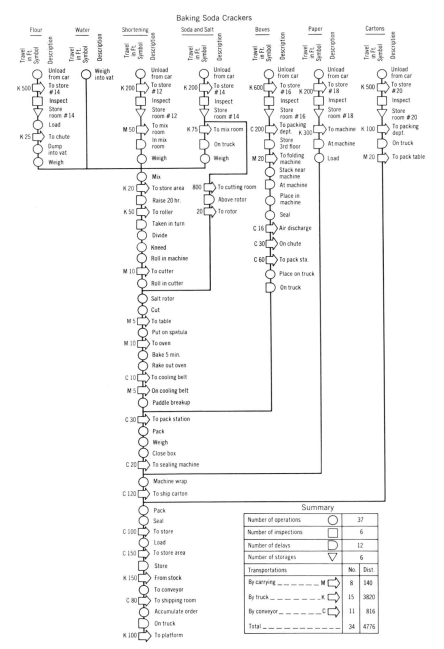

Figure 47 Assembly process chart—baking soda crackers.

76

square foot by the changes shown in *B, C,* and *D* of Fig. 49. This made the proposed addition to the warehouse unnecessary.

Gang Process Charts

The gang process chart is an aid in studying the activities of a group of people working together.[5] This chart is a composite of individual member process charts, arranged to permit thorough analysis. Those operations which are performed simultaneously by gang members are indicated side by side. The basic purpose of the chart is to analyze the activities of the group and then compose the group so as to reduce to a minimum all waiting time and delays.

Construction

1. The same symbols are used as for ordinary process charts.
2. A process chart covers the cycle or routing followed by each member of the gang. Member charts are placed side by side, with steps that are performed simultaneously shown on the same horizontal line. Figure 50 shows the form used for gang charts. The dots aid in chart construction, symbols being centered around the dots.
3. So that symbols of member charts may be placed close together, the various steps are given code numbers rather than entering descriptions beside each symbol. Numbers are entered in the center of each symbol and corresponding explanations are placed at the side of the chart. This eliminates repetition of the description when similar steps are repeated, and at the same time permits the member charts to be placed close together.
4. Attention must be paid to entering simultaneous steps side by side. It may be found that an operation performed by one member of the group continues while another is performing more than one operation. In such instances, the symbol is repeated at each step for the operation which occupies the larger number of steps. On the chart in Fig. 50 it will be noted that the transportation distance was broken down to intervals of 20 feet, as movement over this distance was accomplished while one step of another worker was started and completed. Such divisions of transportation distances are approximate, but for the purpose of analysis are sufficient.
5. The chart should cover a complete cycle for the member performing the largest number of steps. Other gang members usually repeat their cycles during the largest member cycle.
6. Elements which do not occur in every cycle may be omitted from the chart. This includes preparatory work which is done before a cycle is started, such as obtaining supplies for an entire shop. On the other hand, if an operational step occurs

---

[5] The gang process chart was originated by John A. Aldridge, and the description of chart and illustrations presented here were developed by him.

Lacquer

Travel in ft.	Symbol	Description
	◯	Unload from car
H 600	⇨	To stock #70
	☐	Inspect
	▽	In stock room #70
H 350	⇨	To spray room

Key and solder

Travel in ft.	Symbol	Description
	◯	Unload from car
H 400	⇨	To stock #53
	☐	Inspect
	▽	In stock room #53
H 525	⇨	To solder bench

Top and bottom of can

Travel in ft.	Symbol	Description
	◯	Unload from car
H 250	⇨	To stores #96
	☐	Inspect
	▽	In stores #96
H 50	⇨	To slitter in bldg. 42B
	☐	Store on skid
	◯	Slit to length and width
	☐	Store on skid
H 20	⇨	To bar folder
	☐	Store on skid
	◯	Make 4 breaks on bar folder
	☐	Store in truck
H 25	⇨	To bench
	☐	Store in truck
	◯	Solder side seam
	☐	Store at solder bench
	◯	Assemble parts and solder
	☐	Store in truck at bench
H 150	⇨	To bench for cleaning
	☐	Store at bench
	◖	Inspect, wash and dry
	☐	Store in truck at bench
H 200	⇨	To spray room
	☐	Store in truck in spray room
	◯	Disassemble cover from body, spray part of outside of cover and body
H 45	⇨	To oven
	◯	Bake lacquer
H 30	⇨	To bench
	◖	Inspect and assemble cover and body
	☐	Store in truck at bench
K 2500	⇨	To stores room in bldg. 10B
	▽	In finished stores
H 570	⇨	To packing room
	☐	Store in truck in packing room
	◯	Open can, insert product, close can
	☐	Store on skid in packing room
K 3000	⇨	To bench in bldg. 13A
	☐	Store on skid at bench
	◯	Solder cover to body
	☐	Store on skid at bench
K 3300	⇨	To spray booth in bldg. 31B
	☐	Store on skid at booth
	◯	Spray over soldered seam
	☐	Store while lacquer dries
H 2500	⇨	To shipping dept. in bldg. 19A

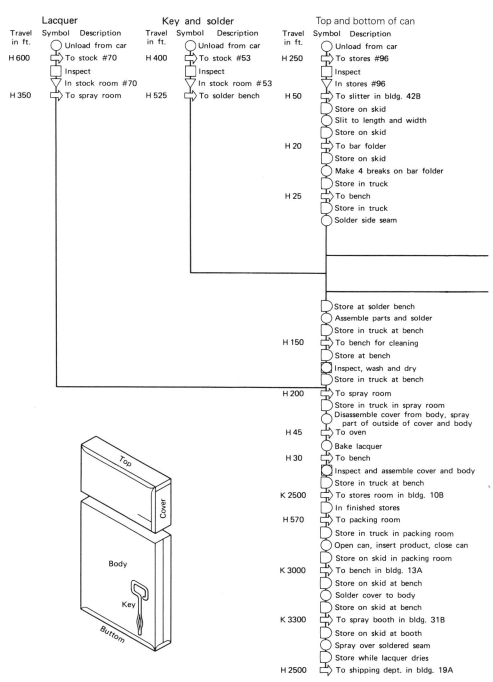

Figure 48 Process chart for making, filling, and sealing rectangular can for export shipment of instruments.

Top and bottom of can

Travel in ft.	Symbol	Description
	◯	Unload from car
H 250	⇨	To stores #96
	☐	Inspect
	D	In stores #96
H 50	⇨	To slitter in bldg. 42B
	D	Store on skid
	◯	Slit to length and width
	D	Store on skid
H 40	⇨	To foot press
	D	Store on skid at press
	◯	Mitre four corners
	D	Store on skid at press
H 30	⇨	To foot press
	D	Store on skid at press
	◯	Fold four sides
	D	Store on skid
H 20	⇨	To solder bench

Cover of can

Travel in ft.	Symbol	Description
	◯	Unload from car
H 250	⇨	To stores #96
	☐	Inspect
	▽	To stores #96
H 50	⇨	To slitter in bldg. 42B
	▽	Store on skid
	◯	Slit to length and width
	D	Store on skid
H 50	⇨	To foot press
	D	Store on skid at press
	◯	Punch hole in rip strip tab
	D	Store on skid at press
H 20	⇨	To bench
	D	Store on skid at bench
	◯	Mark and cut, fold back tab
	D	Store on skid at bench
H 25	⇨	To bar folder
	D	Store on skid at bar folder
	◯	Make first break on bar folder
H 40	⇨	To bench

Improved method of lacquering cans

Travel in ft.	Symbol	Description
	D	Store at solder bench
	◯	Assemble parts and solder
	D	Store in truck at bench
K 2500	⇨	To packing room in bldg. 10B
	D	Store on truck in packing room
	◯	Open can, inspect cover and body, insert product, close can
	D	Store on skid in packing room
H 50	⇨	To bench
	D	Store on skid at bench
	◯	Solder can, dip in lacquer, place on rack to dry
	D	Store on hangers while lacquer dries
K 2500	⇨	To shipping dept. in bldg. 19A

Summary for lacquering cans		Old method	Improved method	Difference		
Number of operations	◯	8	3	5		
Number of inspections	☐	2	1	1		
Number of delays	D	13	6	7		
Number of storages	▽	0	0	0		
Transportations		No.	Dist.	No.	Dist.	No.	Dist.
By motor truck - - - - - - K ⇨		4	11,300	2	5000	2	6300
By hand truck - - - - - - - H ⇨		5	995	1	50	4	945
Total - - - - - - - - - - - - - - - - -		9	12,295	3	5050	6	7245

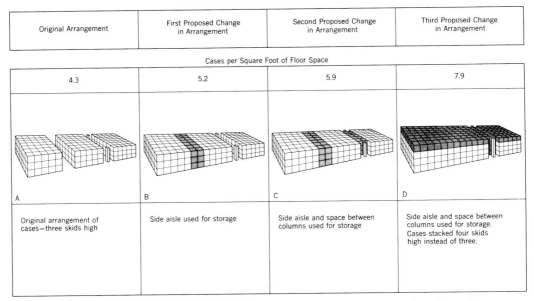

Original Arrangement	First Proposed Change in Arrangement	Second Proposed Change in Arrangement	Third Proposed Change in Arrangement
Cases per Square Foot of Floor Space			
4.3	5.2	5.9	7.9
A	B	C	D
Original arrangement of cases—three skids high	Side aisle used for storage	Side aisle and space between columns used for storage	Side aisle and space between columns used for storage. Cases stacked four skids high instead of three.

Figure 49 Four different methods of stacking cases of finished product in a factory warehouse.

at periodic intervals within the cycle, such as the moving of empty pallets as shown under operation 6 in Fig. 51, it should be included on the chart. If such an operation occurs every two or three cycles, enough cycles should be shown to include the operation.

7. The summary usually takes a different form from that described in the first part of this chapter. Steps per unit before and after study are used in gang chart summaries. This ratio is obtained by dividing the total steps on the chart by the total units handled for the cycles represented on the chart. On the chart illustrated in Fig. 50 the total steps are 120 and the total units (cases) handled are 24. Four cases are loaded on a truck and 6 trucks are loaded in the cycle shown on the chart. One hundred and twenty divided by 24 equals 5 steps per unit. Table 3.

Table 3. Summary of Savings from Proposed Method of Unloading Freight Cars

	Present Method	Proposed Method	Difference
Total steps	120	50	
Total units	24	40	
Steps per unit	5	1.25	75%

GANG PROCESS CHART

OPERATION Unload canned goods from freight car by 2-wheel hand truck.   **OPERATION NO.** T10

SUBJECT Warehouse operation   **PART NO.** 45

DATE

DEPARTMENT Shipping & Receiving   **LOCATION** B14-A7   **PRESENT** ☒ **PROPOSED** ☐

PLANT 643   **CHARTED BY** J. H. S.   **SHEET** 1 **OF** 1

Columns: Unloader, Unloader, Trucker, Trucker, Trucker, Trucker, Trucker, Trucker, Stacker, Stacker

NO. OF GROUP 10

NO.	DESCRIPTION
1	Load 2 cases on truck
1a	Load 2 cases on truck
2	Move 2 cases forward in car
3	Receive load - 4 cases
4	20 ft. loaded
5	Release load
6	20 ft. unloaded
7 & 7a	Unload truck
8 & 8a	Stack on pallets
9	Wait for work

Chart rows (Unloader, Unloader, Trucker, Trucker, Trucker, Trucker, Trucker, Trucker, Stacker, Stacker):

	Unl	Unl	Tr	Tr	Tr	Tr	Tr	Tr	St	St
1	1	1a	3	9	9	9	6	4	8	8a
1a	2	2	4	9	9	9	6	5	7	7a
2	1	1a	4	3	9	9	9	6	8	8a
3	2	2	5	4	9	9	9	6	7	7a
4	1	1a	6	4	3	9	9	9	8	8a
5	2	2	6	5	4	9	9	9	7	7a
6	1	1a	9	6	4	3	9	9	8	8a
7	2	2	9	6	5	4	9	9	7	7a
8	1	1a	9	9	6	4	3	9	8	8a
9	2	2	9	9	6	5	4	9	7	7a
10	1	1a	9	9	9	6	4	3	8	8a
11	2	2	9	9	9	6	5	4	7	7a

REMARKS

SUMMARY

Total Units	24
Steps per Unit	5

Figure 50 Gang process chart of unloading canned goods from freight car—present method.

81

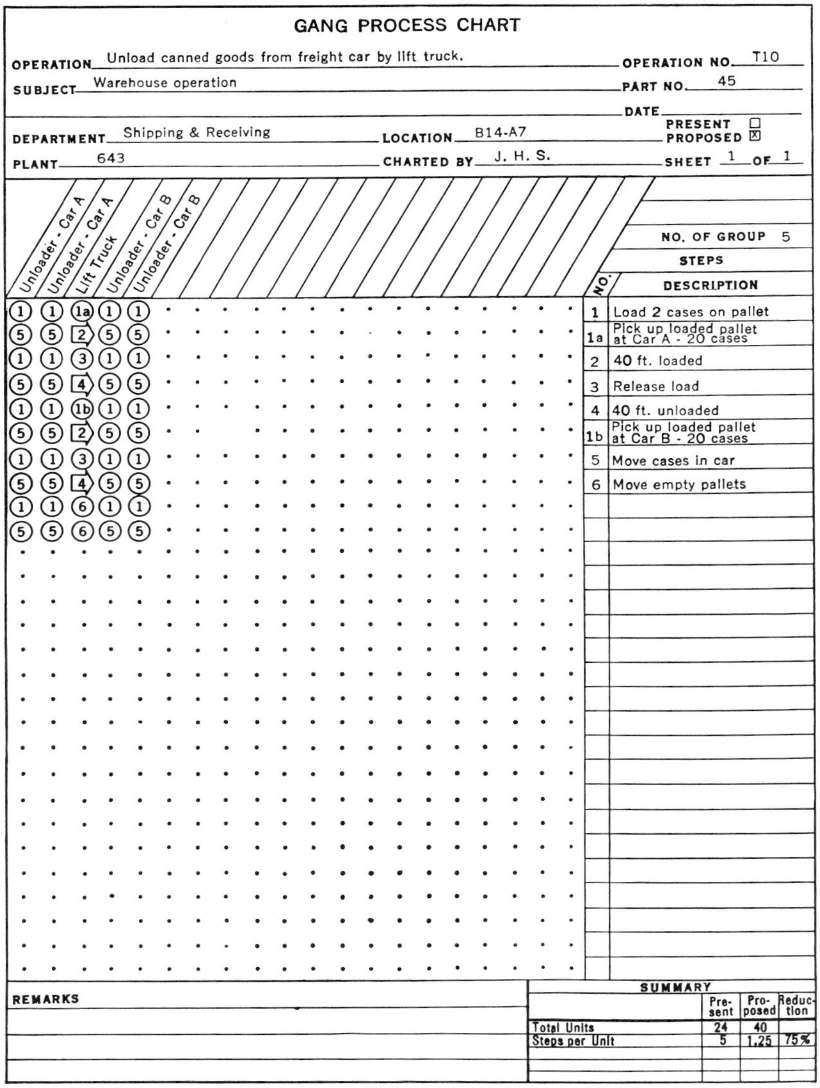

GANG PROCESS CHART

OPERATION Unload canned goods from freight car by lift truck. **OPERATION NO.** T10

SUBJECT Warehouse operation **PART NO.** 45

DATE

DEPARTMENT Shipping & Receiving **LOCATION** B14-A7 PRESENT ☐ PROPOSED ☒

PLANT 643 **CHARTED BY** J. H. S. **SHEET** 1 **OF** 1

Columns: Unloader - Car A, Unloader - Car A, Lift Truck, Unloader - Car B, Unloader - Car B

NO. OF GROUP 5

STEPS

NO.	DESCRIPTION
1	Load 2 cases on pallet
1a	Pick up loaded pallet at Car A - 20 cases
2	40 ft. loaded
3	Release load
4	40 ft. unloaded
1b	Pick up loaded pallet at Car B - 20 cases
5	Move cases in car
6	Move empty pallets

Step rows (Unloader A, Unloader A, Lift Truck, Unloader B, Unloader B):

- ① ① ①a ① ①
- ⑤ ⑤ ②̲ ⑤ ⑤
- ① ① ③ ① ①
- ⑤ ⑤ ④̲ ⑤ ⑤
- ① ① ①b ① ①
- ⑤ ⑤ ②̲ ⑤ ⑤
- ① ① ③ ① ①
- ⑤ ⑤ ④̲ ⑤ ⑤
- ① ① ⑥ ① ①
- ⑤ ⑤ ⑥ ⑤ ⑤

REMARKS

SUMMARY

	Present	Proposed	Reduction
Total Units	24	40	
Steps per Unit	5	1.25	75%

Figure 51 Gang process chart of unloading canned goods from freight car—proposed method.

82

8. A chart should not be constructed from observation of a single cycle. A number of cycles should be observed, as the amount of waiting time may vary from cycle to cycle. The average condition should be reflected by the chart.

Analysis. Four steps are followed in analyzing a gang process chart. First, the six questions what, who, where, when, how, and why are asked of the entire process. Next, each operation and inspection is analyzed by utilizing the same six questions. Third, the remaining transportations and storages are studied. These three steps are the same as those used in analyzing individual process charts. The fourth step consists of applying the "how" question in a new way after refinements have been completed under steps 1, 2, and 3. This question is asked: "How should the gang be composed to reduce waiting time to the minimum?" The following will assist the analyst to "balance" the gang under step 4:

1. Determine the class of operator having the largest amount of waiting time per cycle, and the class having the least.
2. Adjust the gang by decreasing number of operators least busy and increasing number of operators most busy. Generally, it is preferable to work toward a smaller rather than a larger gang.

A Specific Case

The activity to be considered is unloading a car of canned goods (Figs. 50 and 51). In answer to the "how" question it was decided that the work could be performed better if a lift truck were used to transport the material and if pallets were loaded in the car. It was determined that one lift truck could service two cars. These questions resulted in a radical change in the entire procedure. The substitution of the lift truck eliminated all truckers and stackers.

Installation of a Pipe Bridge in a Factory Building

The Procter and Gamble Company makes extensive use of methods design in the construction of its factory buildings. A careful analysis of the method of constructing a pipe bridge and of installing the pipe and conduit in it resulted in substantial savings in time and cost. The bridge shown in Figs. 52 and 53 was installed at the company's plant in Florida.[6] The bridge was built in a steel fabricating shop and delivered to the site in one piece. The normal procedure for erecting a bridge of this kind would be to pick it up with a crane, fasten it in place, and then install the pipe and conduit. A better method was developed which consisted of installing the pipe and conduit inside the bridge while it was still on the ground. In fact, the insulation and painting were also done in this position. Then the bridge, with the pipe in place, was

[6] Gunnar C. Carlson, "A Cost Reduction Program for Construction," *Proceedings Eighth Industrial Engineering Institute,* University of California, Los Angeles-Berkeley, p. 21.

Figure 52 Pipe bridge, outside view.

Figure 53 Pipe bridge, inside view.

raised into position with the same crane that would have been required to lift the empty bridge. This better method saved $2800 over the normal method.

Careful Process Analysis Is Required for Mechanized Production Lines

When a factory is laid out for the production of a specific product in quantity, the process of manufacture is studied with great care, and the machinery, equipment, and work stations are located so that the product will flow through the plant with the least amount of backtracking and lost motion. The path of travel for each part and subassembly is worked out before the equipment is installed in the plant.

The layout (Fig. 54) showing one department in the Ford plant illustrates this type of manufacture. Most factories, however, are not laid out in this manner. Rather, the material moves from work station to work station intermittently by truck, and in

Figure 54 Model of mechanized production line at the Ford Motor Company. Careful analysis of the process was made, including the use of three-dimensional models of machines and operators, before the actual machinery and equipment were installed. (Courtesy of Ford Motor Company.)

many cases little thought has been given to the sequence of operations or to the path of travel through the plant. Because of this fact there are usually many opportunities to save time and money through an analysis of the process.

Steps to Be Followed in Making a Process Chart and Flow Diagram

1. Determine the activity to be studied. Decide whether the subject to be followed is a person, product, part, material, or printed form. Do not change subjects during the construction of the process chart.
2. Choose a definite starting point and ending point in order to make certain that you will cover the activity that you want to study.
3. Draw the process chart on a sheet of paper of sufficient size to allow space for (a) the heading, (b) the description, and (c) the summary. The heading should identify the process being studied. The body of the process chart should contain a column for *Travel* (distance in feet), *Symbol, Description,* and possibly *Time.* The five process chart symbols should be used. Every step in the process should be shown if the analysis is to be of real value. Unnecessary steps and inefficiencies in the work must first be "seen" before they can be eliminated.
4. Include on the process chart a tabular summary showing the number of operations, number of moves of each kind, distance the part was moved, number of inspections, and number of storages and delays. After improvements have been made, a combined summary should be compiled giving this information for the old method, the proposed method, and the difference.
5. Obtain floor plans of the department or the plant, showing location of machines and equipment used in making the part. If these are not available, draw floor plans to scale. It is frequently desirable to mount the floor plans on a drawing board or table, cut out cardboard templates the size of the machines (scale ¼ inch = 1 foot), and use these when new arrangements for the equipment are suggested. Sometimes three-dimensional scale models of machines and equipment are used instead of templates (Fig. 54).
6. Draw on the floor plans in pencil the path of the part through the plant, noting the direction of travel by means of arrows. The flow diagram should be made on location and not from memory at a desk. Distances should be measured or paced off.

8

ACTIVITY CHARTS;
MAN AND MACHINE CHARTS

ACTIVITY CHARTS

Although the process chart and the flow diagram give a picture of the various steps in the process, it is often desirable to have a breakdown of the process or of a series of operations plotted against a time scale. Such a picture is called an activity chart. Figure 56 shows an activity chart for the operation of picking up castings from a tote box, carrying them 10 feet, and placing them in a sandblast. The sketch shown in Fig. 55 was made to emphasize the fact that the operator carried the castings 10 feet and returned empty handed the same distance.

The chart suggests the obvious fact that walking could be eliminated by placing the tote box beside the sandblast. This was not done originally because the sandblast was located on a 4-inch concrete platform. When an inclined plank runway was built, the power-lift truck was able to move the tote box of castings up to the sandblast, as shown in Fig. 57. Figure 58 shows how this eliminated the walking and enabled the

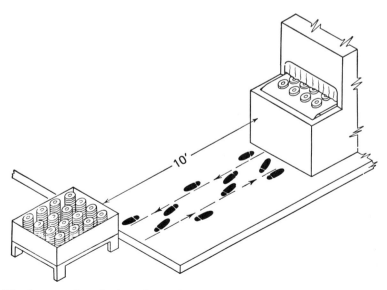

Figure 55 Layout of work place for sandblasting castings—old method. Notice excessive walking.

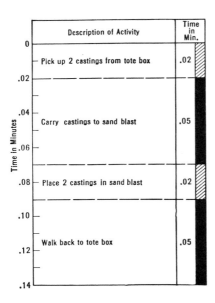

Description of Activity	Time in Min.
Pick up 2 castings from tote box	.02
Carry castings to sand blast	.05
Place 2 castings in sand blast	.02
Walk back to tote box	.05

Figure 56 Activity chart for sandblasting castings—old method.

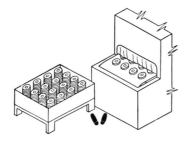

Figure 57 Layout of work place for sandblasting castings—improved method. Unnecessary walking has been eliminated. One person does the work of two.

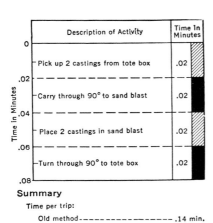

Description of Activity	Time In Minutes
Pick up 2 castings from tote box	.02
Carry through 90° to sand blast	.02
Place 2 castings in sand blast	.02
Turn through 90° to tote box	.02

Summary

Time per trip:

Old method ------------------- .14 min.

Improved method -------------- .08 min.

Savings --------------------- .06 min.

.06 ÷ .14 = 43 per cent saving in time

Figure 58 Activity chart for sandblasting castings—improved method.

88

operator to sandblast 75 percent more castings per hour. One person can now feed this sandblast, whereas it originally required two.

The activity chart is of special value for analyzing maintenance work, jobs involving people working in groups, and operations where the work is unbalanced and where there is "necessary" idle time.

MAN AND MACHINE CHARTS

The operator and the machine work intermittently on some types of work. That is, the machine is idle while the operator loads it and while he or she removes the finished work from it, and the worker is idle while the machine is in operation. It is

Drill Hole in Casting

Man	Machine
1. Pick up piece, place in jig, clamp, lower drill, throw in feed. Time, ½ minute. **(GET READY)**	Idle
Idle	2. Drill ½-inch hole in piece. Power feed. Time, 2.5 minutes. **(DO)**
3. Raise drill, remove piece, dispose, blow chips out of jig. Time, ¾ minute. **(PUT AWAY OR CLEAN UP)**	Idle

SUMMARY

	Man	Machine
Idle time	2.50 minutes	1.25 minutes
Working time	1.25	2.50
Total cycle time	3.75	3.75
Utilization in per cent	Operator utilization $= \dfrac{1.25}{3.75} = 33\%$	Machine utilization $= \dfrac{2.50}{3.75} = 67\%$

Figure 59 Man and machine chart (simple form). It required a total of 3.75 minutes to drill the hole in the casting. During this time the operator worked 1¼ minutes and the machine was in operation 2½ minutes. The operator working time was 33% of the cycle, and the machine working time was 67% of the cycle.

desirable to eliminate idle time for the worker, but it is equally important that the machine be kept operating as near capacity as possible.

The first step in eliminating unnecessary waiting time for the operator and for the machine is to record exactly when each works and what each does. Many operations consist of three main steps: (1) GET READY, such as putting material in the machine; (2) DO (doing the work), such as drilling a hole; and (3) PUT AWAY or clean up, such as removing the finished piece from the machine.

In Fig. 59, which shows the drilling of a hole in a steel casting with a power-feed drill, the steps performed by the operator are listed on the left-hand side and the operation performed by the machine is listed on the right-hand side. This is a man and machine chart in its simplest form.

Very often a clearer picture of the relationship of the operator's working time and the machine time can be obtained by showing the information graphically to scale.

Slitting Coated Fabric

Special fabric is coated with adhesive on continuous coating machines, and the finished material is taken off the drying racks in rolls approximately 3 feet wide and 2 feet in diameter. These rolls go to storage and later are removed and slit into narrower rolls to customers' orders.

Original Method

The material is slit on machines similar to the one shown in Fig. 60. The roll is placed on the shaft A at the back of the machine. The material is passed under rotating cutters B, which press against a rotating cylinder C, thus slitting the material into the desired width. The material is then rolled onto cardboard cores held in place on a shaft at D. After the desired length of fabric has been spooled, the machine is stopped and the cloth is cut parallel to shaft D. The operator, with the assistance of a helper, then places wrapping paper around the spooled material, attaches a label to each roll, and marks the grade, roll length, and other information on the label. The rolls are then removed from shaft D and placed on a skid. During this time the slitting machine is idle.

Improved Method

The following change was made in the method, increasing the capacity of the slitting machines 44 percent. A shaft was mounted on a pedestal shown in Fig. 61. After the desired length of coated fabric had been slit, spooled, and cut off, the rolls were slid from shaft D of the slitting machine onto shaft A of the pedestal. This is a short and simple operation. The helper then wraps, labels, and marks the rolls while the machine operator immediately starts the slitting machine, eliminating much of the idle machine time. Because of the design of the machine it is necessary for the operator to

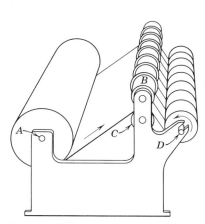

Figure 60 Slitting machine. Coated fabric is drawn under slitting knives *B* onto the "wind up" shaft *D*.

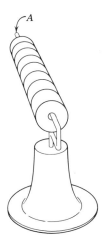

Figure 61 Special pedestal. The rolls of fabric are transferred onto arm *A* to be wrapped and labeled.

manipulate the slitting machine controls while the fabric is being slit. The man and machine charts, Figs. 62 and 63, show the idle time and the working time before and after the new method was developed.

Results. The total cycle time was 5.2 minutes using the old method, or 11.5 cuts were made per hour. The new method reduced the cycle time to 3.6 minutes, which increased the output to 16.6 cuts per hour. This increase of 5.1 cuts per hour represents a gain of 44 percent. As the man and machine charts show, the machine utilization was increased from 42 to 61 percent. This was especially important in this case, as these slitting machines were operating 24 hours per day 7 days per week and were still unable to supply the demand for the product.

Design of Machines and Equipment

Manufacturers of machines and equipment are confronted with the problem of designing machines that will do better work at a lower cost. In approaching this problem they should study the process and the individual operations from the point of view of the person who is doing the work, and design the machine or equipment to save the operator's time and energy.

The fact that new equipment saves time by eliminating some operations is often used in advertising the equipment. Figure 64 is a reproduction of part of an advertisement used by a commercial laundry machinery manufacturer to show that an extractor of improved design eliminates several hand operations and does in 8 minutes the

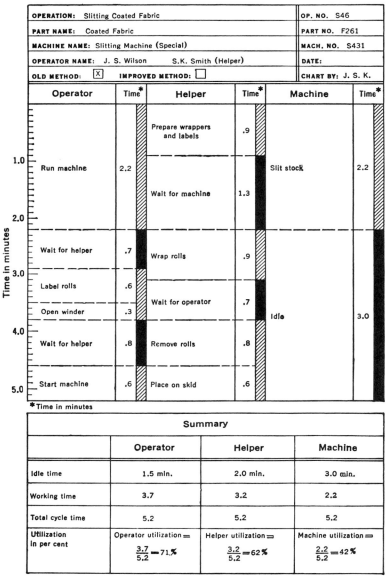

OPERATION: Slitting Coated Fabric				OP. NO. S46	
PART NAME: Coated Fabric				PART NO. F261	
MACHINE NAME: Slitting Machine (Special)				MACH. NO. S431	
OPERATOR NAME: J. S. Wilson S.K. Smith (Helper)				DATE:	
OLD METHOD: [X] IMPROVED METHOD: [ ]				CHART BY: J. S. K.	

Operator	Time*	Helper	Time*	Machine	Time*
Run machine	2.2	Prepare wrappers and labels	.9	Slit stock	2.2
		Wait for machine	1.3		
Wait for helper	.7	Wrap rolls	.9		
Label rolls	.6				
Open winder	.3	Wait for operator	.7	Idle	3.0
Wait for helper	.8	Remove rolls	.8		
Start machine	.6	Place on skid	.6		

*Time in minutes

Summary			
	Operator	Helper	Machine
Idle time	1.5 min.	2.0 min.	3.0 min.
Working time	3.7	3.2	2.2
Total cycle time	5.2	5.2	5.2
Utilization in per cent	Operator utilization = $\frac{3.7}{5.2}$ = 71.%	Helper utilization = $\frac{3.2}{5.2}$ = 62%	Machine utilization = $\frac{2.2}{5.2}$ = 42%

Figure 62 Man and machine chart for slitting coated fabric—old method. Total cycle time, 5.2 minutes. Total number of cuts per hour, 11.5.

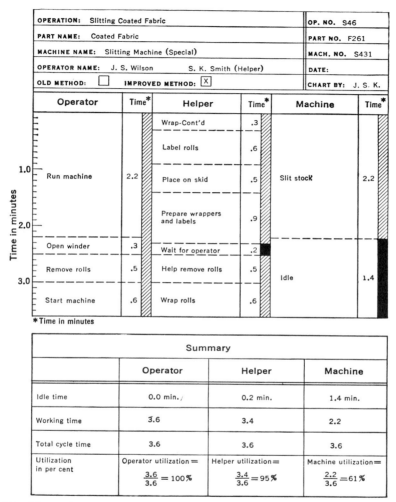

OPERATION: Slitting Coated Fabric					OP. NO. S46	
PART NAME: Coated Fabric					PART NO. F261	
MACHINE NAME: Slitting Machine (Special)					MACH. NO. S431	
OPERATOR NAME: J. S. Wilson S. K. Smith (Helper)					DATE:	
OLD METHOD: ☐ IMPROVED METHOD: ☒					CHART BY: J. S. K.	

Operator	Time*	Helper	Time*	Machine	Time*
		Wrap-Cont'd	.3		
		Label rolls	.6		
Run machine	2.2	Place on skid	.5	Slit stock	2.2
		Prepare wrappers and labels	.9		
Open winder	.3	Wait for operator	.2		
Remove rolls	.5	Help remove rolls	.5	Idle	1.4
Start machine	.6	Wrap rolls	.6		

*Time in minutes

Summary			
	Operator	Helper	Machine
Idle time	0.0 min.	0.2 min.	1.4 min.
Working time	3.6	3.4	2.2
Total cycle time	3.6	3.6	3.6
Utilization in per cent	Operator utilization = $\frac{3.6}{3.6} = 100\%$	Helper utilization = $\frac{3.4}{3.6} = 95\%$	Machine utilization = $\frac{2.2}{3.6} = 61\%$

Figure 63 Man and machine chart for slitting coated fabric—improved method. Total cycle time, 3.6 minutes. Total number of cuts per hour, 16.6.

work that formerly took 29½ minutes. A more complete description of this work is given here.

Extracting Water from Clothes in a Commercial Laundry—Ordinary Method

After clothes are washed in a commercial laundry, they are removed from the washing machine by hand, placed in a truck, moved to an extractor, and unloaded by hand

Figure 64 Chart used by laundry machinery manufacturer to show how extractor is designed to eliminate hand operations and save time.

from the truck into the extractor. The extractor lid is then closed, and the extractor is run at high speed 10 to 15 minutes, during which time the water is thrown out of the clothes by centrifugal force.

The extractor is then stopped, the lid opened, and the clothes removed by hand and placed in a truck. The truck is moved to a "shake-out" table, where the clothes are removed from the truck by hand and placed on the table.

Extractor with Removable Containers

The extractor shown in Fig. 65 has a removable container or spinner basket, made in two parts or halves. Each of the two parts of the container is fitted with casters, and the bottom is hinged on one side and opens downward.

With this extractor the operation of extracting water from clothes is as follows. The halves of the container are moved to the washing machine, and the clothes are removed from the washing machine by hand and placed in them. The container halves are then shoved together to form a cylinder (Fig. 65). By means of a power hoist mounted on a monorail, the container is lifted up and moved over the extractor, balanced, and lowered in place. The extractor is run for 15 minutes. After the water

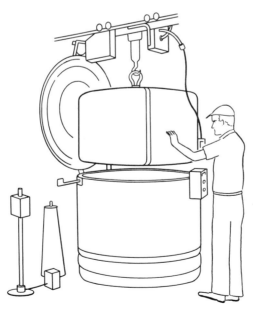

Figure 65   Extractor used in commercial laundry to remove water from clothes by centrifugal force. The removable extractor container is made in halves, each of which is fitted with casters and a hinged bottom.

is removed from the clothes, the extractor is stopped, the lid opened, and the container lifted out of the extractor with the hoist. It is then moved over the "shake-out" table, the hinged bottom of each half of the container opened downward, and the clothes are allowed to drop onto the "shake-out" table by gravity. The bottom of each container is then closed, and the extractor is returned to the washing machine for another load of clothes.

Mechanization and Automation

The extractor with removable containers is a decided improvement. Also a combination washer-extractor is available in sizes from 135-pound (dry weight) to 350-pound capacity. Both are widely used in commercial laundries. A few automated laundry units which wash, rinse, dry, and polish flatwork as a continuous process have been installed.

9

OPERATION ANALYSIS

The over-all study of the process should result in a reduction in the amount of travel of the operator, materials, and tools, and should bring about orderly and systematic procedures. The man and machine chart often suggests ways of eliminating idle machine time and promotes a better balancing of the work of the operator and the machine.

After such studies have been completed, it is time to investigate specific operations in order to improve them. The purpose of motion study is to analyze the motions used by the worker in performing an operation, in order to find the preferred method. A systematic attempt is made to eliminate all unnecessary motions and to arrange the remaining necessary motions in the best sequence. It is when we come to the analysis of specific operations that motion study principles and techniques become most useful.

The extent to which motion study, as well as the other phases of motion and time study, should be carried will depend largely upon the anticipated savings in cost. Motion study may vary in extent from a cursory analysis followed by a general application of motion economy principles, to a detailed study of individual motions of each hand followed by a careful and extensive application of motion economy principles. The most elaborate analysis is possible, of course, only by means of full micromotion study, which will be explained in the chapters to follow.

Operation Charts

For those who are trained in the micromotion study technique—that is, those who are able to visualize work in terms of elemental motions of the hands—the operation chart, or the left- and right-hand chart, is a very simple and effective aid for analyzing an operation. No timing device is needed, and on most kinds of work the analyst is able to construct such a chart from observations of the operator at work. The principal purpose of such a chart is to assist in finding a better way of performing the task, but this chart also has definite value in training operators.

Two symbols are commonly used in making operation charts. The small circle indicates a transportation, such as moving the hand to grasp an article, and the large circle denotes such actions as grasping, positioning, using, or releasing the article. In signing a letter with a fountain pen the left hand holds the paper while the right hand performs the various movements indicated in Fig. 66.

The first step in making an operation chart or a left- and right-hand chart is to draw a sketch of the work place, indicating the contents of the bins and the location of

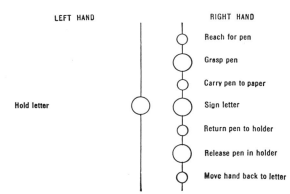

LEFT HAND   RIGHT HAND

                             Reach for pen

                             Grasp pen

                             Carry pen to paper

Hold letter   Sign letter

                             Return pen to holder

                             Release pen in holder

                             Move hand back to letter

Figure 66   Operation chart showing the movements of the two hands in signing a letter.

tools and materials. Then watch the operator and make a mental note of his or her motions, observing one hand at a time. Record the motions or elements for the left hand on the left-hand side of a sheet of paper, and then in a similar manner record the motions for the right hand on the right-hand side of the sheet. Because it is seldom possible to get the motions of the two hands in proper relationship on the first draft, it is usually necessary to redraw the chart.

Bolt and Washer Assembly

A left- and right-hand chart of the operation of assembling a lock washer, a steel washer, and a rubber washer onto a bolt is shown in Fig. 67. This operation is described fully on page 175. A glance at the chart shows that the left hand is holding the bolt while the right hand is doing useful work, assembling the washers. It is obvious that the motions of the two hands are unbalanced. The chart in Fig. 68 shows how the operation would appear if an assembly fixture were used and if the two hands worked together simultaneously.

When one has a detailed breakdown of the operation before him, he is in a much better position to question each element of the job and work out an easier and better method.

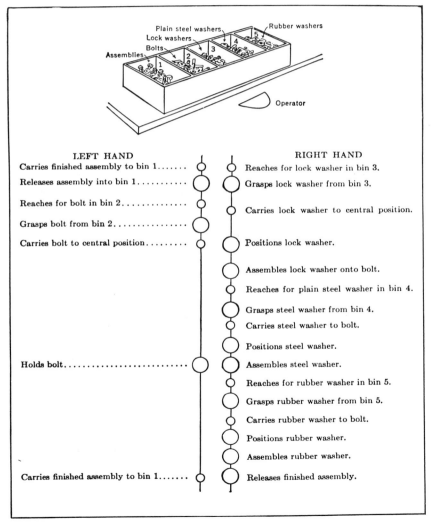

Figure 67 Operation chart of bolt and washer assembly—old method.

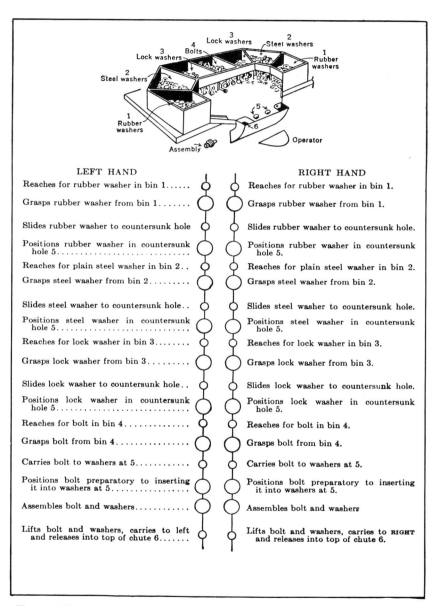

Reaches for rubber washer in bin 1......

LEFT HAND			RIGHT HAND

<table>
</table>

LEFT HAND

Reaches for rubber washer in bin 1......

Grasps rubber washer from bin 1.......

Slides rubber washer to countersunk hole

Positions rubber washer in countersunk hole 5.........................

Reaches for plain steel washer in bin 2..

Grasps steel washer from bin 2.........

Slides steel washer to countersunk hole..

Positions steel washer in countersunk hole 5...........................

Reaches for lock washer in bin 3........

Grasps lock washer from bin 3.........

Slides lock washer to countersunk hole..

Positions lock washer in countersunk hole 5...........................

Reaches for bolt in bin 4..............

Grasps bolt from bin 4................

Carries bolt to washers at 5...........

Positions bolt preparatory to inserting it into washers at 5................

Assembles bolt and washers...........

Lifts bolt and washers, carries to left and releases into top of chute 6.......

RIGHT HAND

Reaches for rubber washer in bin 1.

Grasps rubber washer from bin 1.

Slides rubber washer to countersunk hole.

Positions rubber washer in countersunk hole 5.

Reaches for plain steel washer in bin 2.

Grasps steel washer from bin 2.

Slides steel washer to countersunk hole.

Positions steel washer in countersunk hole 5.

Reaches for lock washer in bin 3.

Grasps lock washer from bin 3.

Slides lock washer to countersunk hole.

Positions lock washer in countersunk hole 5.

Reaches for bolt in bin 4.

Grasps bolt from bin 4.

Carries bolt to washers at 5.

Positions bolt preparatory to inserting it into washers at 5.

Assembles bolt and washers

Lifts bolt and washers, carries to RIGHT and releases into top of chute 6.

Figure 68 Operation chart of bolt and washer assembly—improved method.

100

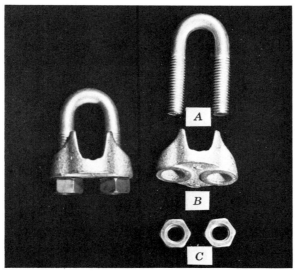

Figure 69 Rope clip assembly: *A*, U bolt; *B*, casting; *C*, nuts.

Assembling Rope Clips

The rope clip shown in Fig. 69 consists of three different parts: *A*, the U bolt; *B*, the casting; *C*, the hexagonal nuts. The rope clips were originally assembled in the following manner. The operator grasped a U bolt from bin 1 (Fig. 70) with her left hand and carried it up in front of her. Then she grasped a casting from bin 3 with her right hand and assembled it onto the bolt; and in a similar manner she grasped (from bin 2) and assembled in succession the two nuts onto the threaded ends of the bolt. She then disposed of the assembly with her right hand into bin 4 at her right. The operation chart for this operation is shown in Fig. 70.

Check Sheet for Operation Analysis

One approach to the problem of finding a better way of doing the work is to subject the operation to specific and detailed questions. If the several persons interested in the job consider these questions together, a more satisfactory solution is likely to result. In addition to studying the motions used in performing an operation, it is also desirable to give consideration to materials, tools, jigs, fixtures, handling equipment, working conditions, and other factors affecting the job. Finding the best way is not always easy, and considerable imagination, ingenuity, and inventive ability are required. Therefore, the cooperation of such persons as the supervisor, the tool designer, and the operator is of decided value to the analyst.

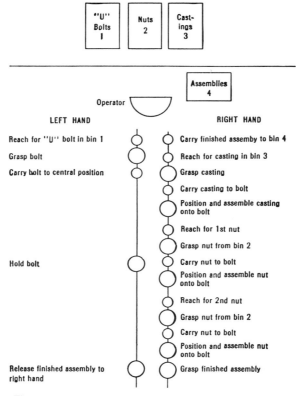

Figure 70 Operation chart of assembling rope clips.

After recording all that is known about the job, the various phases of the operation should be considered:

I. *Materials*
   1. Can cheaper material be substituted?
   2. Is the material uniform and in proper condition when brought to the operator?
   3. Is the material of proper size, weight, and finish for most economical use?
   4. Is the material utilized to the fullest extent?
   5. Can some use be found for scrap and rejected parts?
   6. Can the number of storages of material and of parts in process be reduced?
II. *Materials Handling*
   1. Can the number of times the material is handled be reduced?
   2. Can the distance moved be shortened?
   3. Is the material received, moved, and stored in suitable containers? Are the containers kept clean?

4. Are there delays in the delivery of material to the operator?
5. Can the operator be relieved of handling materials by the use of conveyors?
6. Can backtracking be reduced or eliminated?
7. Will a rearrangement of the layout or combining of operations make it unnecessary to move the material?

III. *Tools, Jigs, and Fixtures*
1. Are the tools the best kind for this work?
2. Are the tools in good condition?
3. If metal-cutting tools, are the cutting angles of the tools correct, and are they ground in a centralized tool-grinding department?
4. Can tools or fixtures be changed so that less skill is required to perform the operation?
5. Are both hands occupied by productive work in using the tools or fixtures?
6. Can slide feeds, ejectors, holding devices, etc., be used?
7. Can an engineering change be made to simplify the design?

IV. *Machine*
A. Setup
1. Should the operator set up his or her own machine?
2. Can the number of setups be reduced by proper lot sizes?
3. Are drawings, tools, and gauges obtained without delay?
4. Are there delays in making inspection of first pieces produced?
B. Operation
1. Can the operation be eliminated?
2. Can the work be done in multiple?
3. Can the machine speed or feed be increased?
4. Can an automatic feed be used?
5. Can the operation be divided into two or more short operations?
6. Can two or more operations be combined into one? Consider the effect of combinations on the training period.
7. Can the sequence of the operation be changed?
8. Can the amount of scrap and spoiled work be reduced?
9. Can the part be pre-positioned for the next operation?
10. Can interruptions be reduced or eliminated?
11. Can an inspection be combined with an operation?
12. Is the machine in good working condition?
13. Can structural adhesives be used?

V. *Operator*
1. Is the operator qualified to perform this operation?
2. Can unnecessary fatigue be eliminated by a change in tools, fixtures, layout, or working conditions?
3. Is supervision satisfactory?
4. Can the operator's performance be improved by further instruction?

VI. *Working Conditions*
1. Are the light, heat, and ventilation satisfactory on the job?
2. Are washrooms, lockers, restrooms, and dressing facilities adequate?
3. Are there any unnecessary hazards involved in the operation?

4. Is provision made for the operator to work in either a sitting or a standing position? Do they meet the needs of the employees?
5. Are the length of the working day and the rest periods set for maximum economy?
6. Is good housekeeping maintained throughout the plant?

This list of questions, although by no means complete, shows some of the elements that enter into a thorough consideration of the problem of finding the best way of doing work. The list is typical of a check sheet that can be prepared for use in a specific plant.

Another approach to the problem is to divide the job into the three phases: (1) get ready; (2) do the work (or use); and (3) put away or clean up, as has already been mentioned. The second phase is the primary object of the work, and the first and the third phases are auxiliary to it. Often the get-ready and the cleanup can be shortened and simplified without impairing the do or use phase of the operation.

Spray Inside and Outside of Metal Box Covers and Bottoms

This example shows the steps that were taken to improve the method of spray-painting black enamel on the two parts of a small metal box. Of the questions listed in the preceding section, the one that seemed to give the greatest promise in this case was IV-B-6—"Can two or more operations be combined into one?"—referring to the possibility of spraying the inside and the outside of the container in a single operation.

When a systematic attempt is made to find a better method, it is seldom that the first one tried proves to be the best. Finding the preferred method for doing a given task is usually a process of development and invention. The following case illustrates this in an excellent manner.

The boxes (Fig. 71), made in slightly different sizes and shapes, are used for such products as surgical instruments and sewing machine attachments. The container is composed of a cover and a bottom, which fit together (Figs. 72 and 73). The containers are manufactured in lots of 5000 to 10,000.

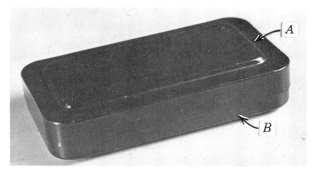

Figure 71   Metal box: *A,* box cover; *B,* box bottom.

 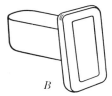

Figure 72 Clamps for holding box covers and bottoms for spraying by the original method: *A,* for spraying inside; *B,* for spraying outside.

Original Method

The operator, standing in front of the spray booth, procured an unsprayed box cover or bottom with the right hand from a tote box at her right and placed it on the metal fixture *A* shown in Fig. 72, which she held in her left hand. Grasping the spray gun in her right hand and holding the part inside the spray booth, she sprayed the inside surface, then disposed of the part on a screen tray. When the screen tray was filled (35 covers or bottoms), it was placed on an oven rack and an empty screen was positioned at the left of the spray booth.

When an oven rack was full, the oven operator moved it into the oven on the other side of the room, where it was baked for 1½ hours. The rack was then removed and cooled, and the outside of the parts were sprayed, using fixture *B* shown in Fig. 72. The sequence of motions used in spraying the outside was similar to that for spraying the inside. The box parts were again baked in the oven for 1½ hours. When removed and cooled, they were ready for the final inspection.

Improved Methods

The following methods were tried in the order indicated.

1. *Steel Spring Hooks*. It was apparent that considerable savings would result if a way could be devised that would permit the operator to spray both the inside and the outside of the box cover or bottom in a single operation.

    Several designs of spring hooks were tried, similar to those used for another type of container, which held the piece from the inside.
    Results. It was found that the blast from the air gun would blow the piece from the hook. Hooks made from stiffer spring made hooking too difficult for the operators. This method was discarded as impractical.
2. *Dipping in Enamel*. Since some products were being satisfactorily dipped in enamel and baked in a continuous oven, it was suggested that an attempt be made to dip the boxes. Wire hangers, *A* in Fig. 73, were made and dipping was tried.
    Results. An air pocket formed in the upper corner of the box covers, which

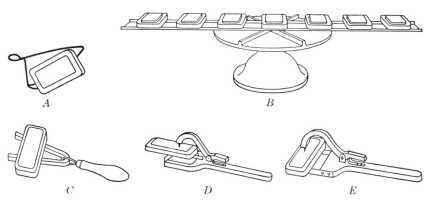

Figure 73 Devices for use in spray-painting box covers and bottoms by "improved" methods: *A*, steel spring hook for dipping; *B*, rack and turntable; *C*, magnetic fixture; *D*, mechanical fixture; *E*, improved mechanical fixture—the one finally adopted.

prevented the enamel from making contact with the metal. Also, the enamel failed to drain out of the lower corner properly. The device for dipping the boxes was discarded.

3. *Spray Outside on Turntable.* The box covers were sprayed on the inside in the original manner and placed on a narrow tray, *B* in Fig. 73. When seven box covers had been placed on the tray the outsides of all of them were sprayed and the trayful then sent to the oven for baking.

   Results. The air from the spray gun blew the boxes off the rack. If heavy corrugations or teeth were cut in the edges of the tray, they disfigured the enamel finish on the boxes. This method was discarded.

4. *Magnetic Fixture.* A permanent magnet, *C* in Fig. 73, was used to hold the box cover while the operator sprayed both the inside and the outside in one operation.

   Results. This proved to be a satisfactory method for holding the cover, but it was difficult to get the sprayed pieces off the magnet to the screen tray. The suggestion was not used.

5. *Mechanical Fixture.* A fixture, *D* in Fig. 73, was made so that the cover rested on two knife-edges and was held mechanically in place with a needle point.

   Results. This device was satisfactory in that it permitted the inside and outside of the cover to be sprayed at one operation and it was easy to release the piece and dispose of it on the screen tray. However, the two knife-edges tended to scrape the enamel off the edges of the cover as it slid off the holder and onto the screen tray.

6. *Improved Mechanical Fixture.* A holder, *E* in Fig. 73, was built with two parallel knife-edges that did not scrape off the enamel in disposing of the sprayed part.

Results. This fixture proved to be entirely satisfactory, and several were made of aluminum and immediately put into use on production work. Each operator is supplied with two fixtures, allowing one to soak in solvent while the other is being used.

The improved method, using this fixture, proved to be superior to the old method in the following ways:

1. The operator now sprays both the inside and the outside of the box cover or bottom at one operation. This effects a saving of approximately 25 percent in direct labor.
2. The covers and bottoms are baked only once instead of twice. This reduces the use of the baking ovens 50 percent, and also reduces the indirect labor for handling racks and trays 50 percent.
3. An additional saving results because the investigation showed that the insides of the box covers and bottoms were being sprayed with a dull-finish enamel and the outsides with a glossy-finish enamel. There is no need for the dull finish on the inside, and it is more expensive than glossy. Use of the dull has been discontinued; the entire box is now sprayed with glossy enamel. This alone has saved in one year more than enough to pay for all the experimental fixtures that were used in the development work.

Cleanup Work

Custodial or cleanup work represents a sizable part of office and factory payroll. In some organizations such work accounts for as much as 10 to 15 percent of total wages. Some of the results of a careful study of cleaning tools and equipment and of cleanup methods made by one organization are given here. They show what may be accomplished by setting out to answer such a single question as "Are the tools the best kind for this work?" (III-1, page 103). Although these findings apply to conditions in this particular organization, many of the results of this investigation are basic and have wide application.

The first step was to find the best equipment. Because the cost of tools that the janitor uses represent less than two tenths of 1 percent of the total cleanup costs, it is false economy to purchase any but the most efficient tools.

Cleaning with Mop

Mopping of floors is one of the important classes of janitor work. Of the 700 people on cleanup work in this plant the equivalent of 215 spend their full time mopping floors. Factory tests made of more than 40 different styles and kinds of mops resulted in the following specifications for a good mop:

1. Mops should be of wide tape type to be used with detachable handles.
2. The mop should be made of a good grade of 4-ply, soft roving, long staple yarn free from linters and foreign material.

3. The length of the mop strands should be 38 to 42 inches, taped in the middle with good cotton duck at least 5 inches wide. The completed mop should be 6¼ to 6¾ inches in width after sewing on the tape with at least three rows of double stitching. The mop is not to be sewed in the folded shape, in order that both sides may be used to equalize wear.
4. The average dry weight of the cotton should be 23½ to 24½ ounces for wet mopping and 31½ to 32½ ounces for dry mopping.
5. The mop handle should be 60 inches long, 1¼ inches in diameter, and should have an aluminum knob at the end.
6. The mop attachment device should be of the claw or clamp type, wherein the mop is folded, placed in the open clamp, and the wing nut tightened. The hardware on the mop should be light in weight and made of rust-resisting material.

The ordinary "ferrule" mop is unsatisfactory for factory work. The mop is too small, the handle is too short, and the ferrule where the mop is attached to the handle prevents the mop from lying flat on the floor.

The "head" mop is preferred. The handle is long, with a knob on the end. Because the head mop lies flat on the floor, there is 30 percent more cotton in contact with the floor than with a ferrule mop of equal weight. In addition, the head mop fits the wringer better and 10 percent more water can be removed, making for faster pickup of dirty water from the floor, less dead weight for the janitor to handle, and fewer wringing operations.

Recommended Method of Mopping

The recommended method for mopping is the use of the "side to side" stroke rather than the "push or pull" stroke. The janitor positions himself in the middle of the stroke length, with his feet spread well apart and at right angles to the direction of the stroke (Fig. 74). The mop handle is grasped over the end with one hand and approximately 15 inches down the handle with the other hand. The mop is placed flat on the floor and passed from side to side in front of the janitor, in the form of an arc. The arc should be slight, as too wide an arc will greatly increase the effort required in that the arms are extended in front of the body at a lower muscular efficiency. The mop should pass in front of the janitor and within about 3 inches of his feet. At the ends of the stroke the mop is slightly looped to reverse the direction. Centrifugal force in describing the arc spreads the mop strands to increase the area covered in the stroke.

Much time is lost in transporting water in small buckets. A specially designed mop truck has been developed, with three large water compartments having a 42-gallon capacity for clean water and a 37-gallon capacity for dirty water. The temperature of the clean water should not fall below 130° F. for effective use.

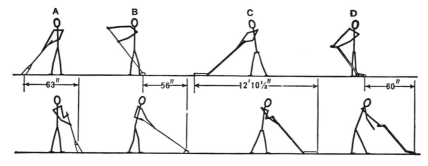

A. CLEANING WITH SWEEP BROOM

Length of Broom Handle, 54 Inches

At start of stroke: Shoulder is normal, feet normal and in a position for a forward step. Right arm is straight.

At end of stroke: Shoulder is turned 45 degrees, broom is just past vertical.

B. CLEANING WITH PUSH BRUSH

Length of Brush Handle, 68 Inches

At start of stroke: Shoulder is turned 45 degrees, right arm is horizontal.

At end of stroke: Shoulder is normal, feet positioned for normal step forward on return stroke. Left arm is straight at 45 degrees with vertical. Back is turned 45 degrees at hip.

C. CLEANING WITH MOP

Length of Mop Handle, 60 Inches

At start of stroke: Shoulder is turned 90 degrees to right, with right arm at 45 degrees and down 14 inches on the handle. Weight is shifted to right foot, with back inclined 4 inches to right. Left hand is grasping end of handle.

At end of stroke: Shoulder is turned 90 degrees to left, with right arm at 45 degrees and down 14 inches on the handle. Weight is shifted to left foot, with back inclined 4 inches to left. Left hand is grasping end of handle.

D. CLEANING WITH VACUUM TOOL

Height of Tool above Floor, 29 Inches
Length of Tool, 56 Inches

At start of stroke: Shoulder is turned 90 degrees, right arm is at 45 degrees to back, and feet are together.

At end of stroke: Shoulder is normal, right arm is 45 degrees to front, and a forward step is taken.

Figure 74 Description of recommended method for using broom, brush, mop, and vacuum cleaner.

With all the improvements of mopping methods and equipment, the coverage is now 2000 square feet per man-hour, in comparison with slightly less than 1000 square feet per man-hour before the installation of the improvements.

Although space does not permit detailed analysis and recommendations for each of the other tools that the janitor uses, a brief description of some of them is given in Fig. 74.

10

MICROMOTION STUDY

Micromotion study proviodes a technique for recording and timing an activity. It consists of taking motion pictures of the operation with a clock in the picture or with a motion picture camera or video camera operating at a constant and known speed. The film becomes a permanent record of both method and time and may be re-examined whenever desired.

Purposes of Micromotion Study

Micromotion study was originally employed for job analysis work, but new uses have been found for this valuable tool. Micromotion study may be used for the following purposes: as an aid in studying the activities of two or more persons on group work, as an aid in studying the relationship of the activities of the operator and the machine, as a means of timing operations (instead of time study), as an aid in obtaining motion-time data for time standards, as a permanent record of the method and time of activities of the operator and the machine, and for research in the field of motion and time study.

As valuable as micromotion study is for these purposes, however, its two most important uses are: (1) to assist in finding the preferred method of doing work, and (2) to assist in training individuals to understand the meaning of motion study and, when the training is carried out with sufficient thoroughness, to enable them to become profiocient in applying motion economy principles.

Micromotion Study as an Aid in Improving Methods

Micromotion study provides a technique that is unique for making a minute analysis of an operation. As will be explained in detail later, the procedure consists of (1) filming the operation to be studied, (2) analyzing the film, (3) charting the results of the analysis, and (4) developing an improved method through the problem-solving process.

Micromotion study is usually associated with camera speeds of 960 or 1000 frames per minute, but faster speeds may be used to study very fast hand motions or complex operations. When the film is projected on the screen, the pictures are enlarged many times to facilitate the analysis of the motions. Each movement of the worker can be timed to any degree of accuracy desired.

Although micromotion study provides a convenient, accurate, and positive means of studying work, it is used only to a limited extent for improving methods. In fact, micromotion analysis is not necessary for studying a large majority of the operations to be improved. One who understands the technique and the principles of motion study can, in most cases, visualize the operation completely and, by applying the principles that comprise good motion economy, determine methods that should be used. Motion study may be carried out without taking a motion picture and making the full analysis that micromotion study requires. Moreover, a micromotion study, although not prohibitive in cost, does require special motion picture equipment, film, and considerable time for the analysis. This is the less valuable of the two main purposes of micromotion study.

Micromotion study should be treated like any tool, that is, to be used when it is economical to do so. It might profitably be utilized in the investigation of short-cycle operations that are highly repetitive or largely manual in character, of work produced in large volume, or of operations performed by large numbers of workers. These factors alone do not always determine whether a micromotion study should be made. In fact, a micromotion study is often the last resort. Sometimes in a complex operation it is difficult to get the motions of the two hands balanced without the aid of the simo chart, which is a graphic picture of the motions on paper.

Micromotion Study as an Aid in Teaching

Industry has been slow to realize the fact that micromotion study is of greatest value in aiding one in understanding motion study. From its definition motion study would appear to be very simple and easily understood. There is a knack to getting at the real meaning of it, however, and to being able to understand it fully.

The observer must become proficient in detecting and following the motions used by the worker in performing the task. The observer must *see* the motions made by the operator's right hand, and by the left hand, even noting what the fingers of each hand do. It is necessary to be able to detect where one motion ends and another begins. As the Gilbreths state, ". . . one must have studied motions and measured them until his eye can follow paths of motions and judge lengths of motions, and his timing sense, aided by silent rhythmic counting, can estimate times of motion with surprising accuracy. Sight, hearing, touch, and kinesthetic sensations must all be keenly developed."[1]

The term *motion-minded* has been used to describe this ability of persons who have trained themselves to follow unconsciously the motions of the worker and check them against the principles of motion economy with which they are familiar. Micromotion study is of great assistance in training individuals to become motion-minded.

R. M. Blackelock once said:

. . . the greatest value of micromotion training comes through the ability to visualize industrial operations in terms of motions . . . the ability to visualize the motions that are necessary to perform each step of an operation, and to recognize which are and which are not good

---

[1] F. B. and L. M. Gilbreth, *Applied Motion Study,* Sturgis & Walton, New York, 1917, p. 61.

motion practice, rather than think in such terms as describe steps in the operation itself.

Most time study observers, as they record steps in the operation, think in terms of elemental operations, such as "drills one hole," "faces off side," "rivets end," or "assembles part 2 to part 3," making no analysis of the motions of the operator, and giving little thought to them unless there is a glaring case of bad motions that is quite obvious.[2]

Blakelock, while in charge of the motion study division at the Schenectady plant of the General Electric Company, seldom found it necessary to make a micromotion study to determine proper methods for doing work. He applied the principles of motion study without resorting to the motion picture camera. However, he did make extensive use of this technique for training members of the organization.

For information concerning the use of micromotion study by the Fort Wayne works of the General Electric Company and by other companies, see Chapter 37.

Memomotion Study

Motion pictures must be made and projected at approximately normal speed if one wants a fairly accurate reproduction of motion of people and objects. But for certain types of worker and machine activities, motion pictures made at 60 or 100 frames per minute are quite satisfactory. The term *memomotion study*[3] has been suggested to designate this form of micromotion study.

The Gilbreths, using a hand-cranked camera, took pictures at very slow speeds to study group activities,[4] and time-lapse photography using a motor-drive camera has long been employed for studying the growth of plants and flowers. In recent years many new uses have been found for this valuable technique. In addition to its applications in the factory and office, memomotion study serves in studying such activities as check-in operations at airline counters, the manner in which customers select items in a self-serve store, and the flow of traffic on highways and in stores and banks.

The major advantage of slow-speed pictures over those made at normal speed is the great savings in film cost and in the time required for film analysis. With the film exposed at 60 frames per minute instead of 960, film cost is only about 6 percent as great.

---

[2] R. M. Blakelock, "Micromotion Study Applied to the Manufacture of Small Parts," *Factory and Industrial Management,* Vol. 80, No. 4, pp. 730–732.

[3] M. E. Mundel, *Motion and Time Study,* 3rd ed., Prentice-Hall, Englewood Cliffs, N.J., 1960, p. 301; *Motion and Time Study,* 5th ed., 1978, p. 287.

[4] "Our methods and devices have been criticized as being specially adapted to problems involving the minutia of motions, but too expensive for the general time study purposes. A moment's consideration will show that the turning of the crank of the cinematograph may be done as slowly as the requirements of the particular case of time study demand. In fact, we have made films that were taken at the rate of one picture every ten minutes. With the sixteen pictures to the foot, a foot will last 160 minutes, or two hours and forty minutes, at a total maximum cost of six cents." From *Fatigue Study,* by Frank B. Gilbreth, Sturgis and Walton Co., New York, 1916, p. 126.

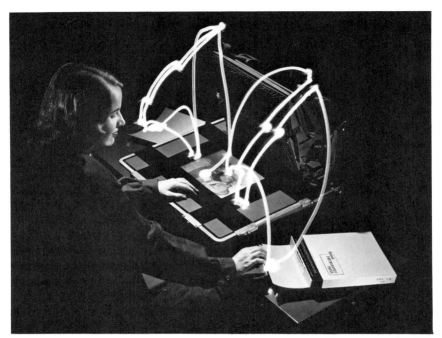

Figure 75 Motions needed to make a print with hand-operated photoprinter.

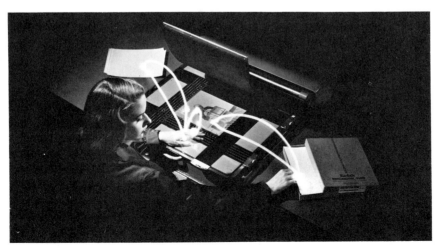

Figure 76 Motions needed to make a print with power printer of improved design.

113

Figure 77 Motions needed to wrap rolls of cellophane—old method.

Figure 78 Motions needed to wrap rolls of cellophane—improved method.

CYCLEGRAPHIC AND CHRONOCYCLEGRAPHIC ANALYSIS

The cylegraphic and the chronocyclegraphic methods of analysis developed and used by the Gilbreths are described on page 19. These techniques have had limited use in this country as a means of improving methods, although they seem to have met with greater favor in Great Britain.[5] We have used the cyclegraph to some extent for training purposes, as an aid in describing a motion pattern used in performing a task, and to dramatize the superiority of one method of motion pattern over another.

The improved power printer developed by Eastman Kodak Company, shown in Fig 76 requires many fewer motions than the hand-operated printer in Fig. 75. These two illustrations were included in the annual report of this company, under the caption "An Improved Professional Product Resulting from Development Work."

The illustrations in Figs. 77 and 78 show the old method and the improved method of wrapping rolls of cellophane. Originally the rolls were wrapped in two layers of cellophane and placed in an inner box and an outer box; then the 52-pound package was lifted onto a pallet for shipment. The method shown in Fig. 78 has been greatly simplified, as the motion pattern shows. Now rolls are wrapped in a single layer of cellophane and shipped on a pallet that is loaded with the aid of a small elevator. These two illustrations are from a publication, *This is Du Pont,* of the E. I. du Pont Company. Under the caption "Modern Technology Spurs New Advances" the following statement is made:

The contrasting pictures [Figs. 77 and 78] show a simple improvement in the method of doing a day-to-day job. Hundreds of these are effected in du Pont operations every year. In sum total, such improvements are as significant a part of modern technology as the discovery of a new product, the development of a new process, or the creation of intricate and costly new tools.

When Slit Roll Packer Irvin Coleman can handle cellophane more quickly and easily, then he can accomplish more in a day's time. Economists call that "increased productivity." And there has been no more important element in the rise of America's industrial economy than the steady rise in the individual's productivity due to technological improvements.

Three things happen when an employee of industry can turn out more in less time. Cost of product drops, enabling more people to buy it. The operator does not have to work as long to make the product, which in time leads to shorter hours and higher earnings. Finally, as the nation, which is the sum of its people, produces more, its material well-being is enhanced.

---

[5] A. G. Shaw, *The Purpose and Practice of Motion Study,* Columbine Press, London, 1960, pp. 92–121.

11

FUNDAMENTAL HAND MOTIONS

Most work is done with the two hands, and all manual work consists of a relatively few fundamental motions that are performed over and over again. *Get* or *pick up* and *place* or *put down* are two of the most frequently used groups of motions. In most cases *get* is followed by some use or process element, such as driving a nail with a hammer, using a wrench to tighten a bolt, or writing with a pen. In using a pen the sequence of motions would be *get* pen, write—that is, *use* pen, *place* pen in holder. Although *get* and *place* represent two very common groups of motions, they are not fundamental motions in themselves.

Frank B. Gilbreth, in his early work in motion study, developed certain subdivisions or events which he thought common to all kinds of manual work. He coined the word *therblig* (Gilbreth spelled backwards) in order to have a short word with which to refer to any of these 17 elementary subdivisions of a cycle of motions.[1] Not all of these 17 therbligs are pure of fundamental elements in the sense that they cannot be further subdivided. The experienced analyst has no difficulty in using the therbligs in industrial applications.

The term *therblig* is more convenient to use than "hand motion" or "motion element," and perhaps carries a more precise meaning than "motion." Although the word *therblig* is familiar to industrial engineers, the term *motion* or *hand motion* is preferred when discussing the subject of micromotion study with factory and office personnel. Uncommon terms and symbols (such as the mnemonic therblig symbols) may be a handicap in a training program and are to be avoided whenever possible.

The fundamental hand motions, together with their letter symbols, mnemonic symbols, and color designations,[2] are shown in Fig. 79. The definitions of these motions are given on the following pages.

Definitions of Fundamental Hand Motions

1. *Search* (Sh): that part of the cycle during which the eyes or the hands are hunting or groping for the object. Search begins when the eyes or hands begin to hunt for the object, and ends when the object has been found.

   The original list of the Gilbreth motions contained the therblig *find*. Because

---

[1] F. B. and L. M. Gilbreth, "Classifying the Elements of Work," *Management and Administration,* Vol. 8, No. 2, p. 151, August, 1924.

[2] The color symbols are included in order to indicate color on the printed simo charts in this book. These color symbols should *not* be used in the actual construction of simo charts. Colored pencils should be used instead.

Name of Symbol	Therblig Symbol		Explanation-suggested by	Color	Color Symbol	Dixon Pencil Number	Eagle Pencil Number
Search	Sh	◯	Eye turned as if searching	Black		331	747
Select	St	→	Reaching for object	Gray, light		399	734½
Grasp	G	∩	Hand open for grasping object	Lake red		369	744
Transport empty	T E	◡	Empty hand	Olive green		391	739½
Transport loaded	T L	◡	A hand with something in it	Green		375	738
Hold	H	◠	Magnet holding iron bar	Gold ochre		388	736½
Release load	RL	◠	Dropping content out of hand	Carmine red		370	745
Position	P	9	Object being placed by hand	Blue		376	741
Pre-position	P P	◊	A nine-pin which is set up in a bowling alley	Sky-blue		394	740½
Inspect	I	◯	Magnifying lens	Burnt ochre		398	745½
Assemble	A	‡	Several things put together	Violet, heavy		377	742
Disassemble	D A	‡	One part of an assembly removed	Violet, light		377	742
Use	U	U	Word "Use"	Purple		396	742½
Unavoidable delay	U D	↷	Man bumping his nose, unintentionally	Yellow ochre		373	736
Avoidable delay	A D	↵	Man lying down on job voluntarily	Lemon yellow		374	735
Plan	Pn	℘	Man with his fingers at his brow thinking	Brown		378	746
Rest for over-coming fatigue	R	ℇ	Man seated as if resting	Orange		372	737

Figure 79   Standard symbols and colors for fundamental hand motions.

find occurs at the end of the therblig search, and because it is a mental reaction rather than a physical movement, it is seldom used in micromotion analysis work. Therefore find is omitted from the list of fundamental hand motions here.

2. *Select* (St): the choice of one object from among several. In many cases it is difficult if not impossible to determine where the boundaries lie between search and select. For this reason it is often the practice to combine them, referring to both as the one therblig *select*.

Using this broader definition, select then refers to the hunting and locating of one object from among several. Select begins when the eyes or hands begin to hunt for the object, and ends when the desired object has been located.

EXAMPLE   Locating a particular pencil in a box containing pencils, pens, and miscellaneous articles.

3. *Grasp* (G): taking hold of an object, closing the fingers around it preparatory to picking it up, holding it or manipulating it. Grasp begins when the hand or fingers first make contact with the object, and ends when the hand has obtained control of it.

EXAMPLE   Closing the fingers around the pen on the desk.

4. *Transport empty* (TE): moving the empty hand in reaching for an object. It is assumed that the hand moves without resistance toward or away from the object. Transport empty begins when the hand begins to move without load or resistance, and ends when the hand stops moving.

EXAMPLE   Moving the empty hand to grasp a pen on the desk.

5. *Transport loaded* (TL): moving an object from one place to another. The object may be carried in the hands or fingers, or it may be moved from one place to another by sliding, dragging, or pushing it along. Transport loaded also refers to moving the empty hand against resistance. Transport loaded begins when the hand begins to move an object or encounter resistance, and ends when the hand stops moving.

EXAMPLE   Carrying the pen from the desk to the letter to be signed.

6. *Hold* (H): retention of an object after it has been grasped, no movement of the object taking place.[3] Hold begins when the movement of the object stops, and ends with the start of the next therblig.

EXAMPLE   Holding bolt in one hand while assembling a washer onto it with the other.

7. *Release load* (RL): letting go of the object. Release load begins when the object starts to leave the hand, and ends when the object has been completely separated from the hand or fingers.

EXAMPLE   Letting go of the pen after it has been placed on the desk.

8. *Position* (P): turning or locating an object in such a way that it will be properly oriented to fit into the location for which it is intended. It is possible to position an object during the motion *transport loaded*. The carpenter, for example, may turn the nail into position for using while carrying it to the board into which it will be driven. Position begins when the hand begins to turn or locate the object, and ends when the object has been placed in the desired position or location.

---

[3] Gilbreth did not classify hold as a separate therblig but considered it a form of grasp.

EXAMPLE   Lining up a door key preparatory to inserting it in the keyhole.

9. *Pre-position* (PP): locating an object in a predetermined place, or locating it in the correct position for some subsequent motion. Pre-position is the same as *position* except that the object is located in the approximate position that will be needed later. Usually a holder, bracket, or special container of some kind holds the object in a way that permits it to be grasped easily in the position in which it will be used. Pre-position is the abbreviated term used for *pre-position for the next operation.*

EXAMPLE   Locating or lining up the pen above the desk-set holder before releasing it. The pen may then be grasped in approximately the correct position for writing. This eliminates the therblig position that would be required to turn the pen to the correct writing position if it were resting flat on the desk when grasped.

10. *Inspect* (I): examining an object to determine whether or not it complies with standard size, shape, color, or other qualities previously determined. The inspection may employ sight, hearing, touch, odor, or taste. Inspect is predominantly a mental reaction and may occur simultaneously with other therbligs. Inspect begins when the eyes or other parts of the body begin to examine the object, and ends when the examination has been completed.

EXAMPLE   Visual examination of pearl buttons in the final sorting operation.

11. *Assemble* (A): placing one object into or on another object with which it becomes an integral part. Assemble begins as the hand starts to move the part into its place in the assembly, and ends when the hand has completed the assembly.

EXAMPLE   Placing cap on pen.

12. *Disassemble* (DA): separating one object from another object of which it is an integral part. Disassemble begins when the hand starts to remove one part from the assembly, and ends when the hand has separated the part completely from the remainder of the assembly.

EXAMPLE   Removing cap from pen.

13. *Use* (U): manipulating a tool, device, or piece of apparatus for the purpose for which it was intended. Use may refer to an almost infinite number of particular cases. It represents the motion for which the preceding motions have been more or less preparatory and for which the ones that follow are supplementary. Use begins when the hand starts to manipulate the tool or device, and ends when the hand ceases the application.

EXAMPLE   Writing one's signature in signing a letter (use pen), or painting an object with spray gun (use spray gun).

14. *Unavoidable delay* (UD): a delay beyond the control of the operator. Unavoidable delay may result from either of the following causes: (*a*) a failure or inter-

ruption in the process; (*b*) an arrangement of the operation that prevents one part of the body from working while other body members are busy. Unavoidable delay begins when the hand stops its activity, and ends when activity is resumed.

EXAMPLE   If the left hand made a long transport motion to the left and the right hand simultaneously made a very short transport motion to the right, an unavoidable delay would occur at the end of the right-hand transport in order to bring the two hands into balance.

15. *Avoidable delay* (AD): any delay of the operator for which he or she is responsible and over which he or she has control. It refers to delays which the operator may avoid if desired. Avoidable delay begins when the prescribed sequence of motions is interrupted, and ends when the standard work method is resumed.

EXAMPLE   The operator stops all hand motions.

16. *Plan* (Pn): a mental reaction which precedes the physical movement, that is, deciding how to proceed with the job. Plan begins at the point where the operator begins to work out the next step of the operation, and ends when the procedure to be followed has been determined.

EXAMPLE   An operator assembling a complex mechanism, deciding which part should be assembled next.

17. *Rest for overcoming fatigue* (R): a fatigue or delay factor or allowance provided to permit the worker to recover from the fatigue incurred by the work. Rest begins when the operator stops working, and ends when work is resumed.

Motions Used in Signing a Letter

It is a relatively easy matter to learn the names of these fundamental motions. For example, in signing a letter, the sequence of motions is *transport empty* (reach for pen), *grasp* (take hold of pen), *transport loaded* (carry pen to paper), *position* (place pen on paper at correct position for writing), *use* (sign letter), *transport loaded* (return pen to holder), *pre-position* (position pen in holder), *release load* (let go of pen), and *transport empty* (move hand back to letter). These motions are fully defined and illustrated in Fig. 80.

Pinboard

It seems natural for most people, when observing another person at work, to notice the material being handled or the tools being used rather than the motions made in performing the task. After one becomes "motion-minded," that is, after one has learned the classification of hand motion, this situation is changed. The observer then notices the motions made with the right hand and those made with the left hand, and then proceeds to use those motions which are easy and effective and to discard

	Name and Definition of Motion	Symbol	Description of Motion	Illustration
1	**TRANSPORT EMPTY** (Transport Empty refers to moving the empty hand in reaching for an object. It is assumed that the hand moves without resistance toward or away from the object. Transport empty begins when the hand begins to move without load or resistance and ends when the hand stops moving.)	TE	Reach for pen.	
2	**GRASP** (Grasp refers to taking hold of an object, closing the fingers around it preparatory to picking it up, holding it or manipulating it. Grasp begins when the hand or fingers first make contact with the object and ends when the hand has obtained control of it.)	G	Take hold of pen – close thumb and fingers around pen.	
3	**TRANSPORT LOADED** (Transport Loaded refers to moving an object from one place to another. The object may be carried in the hands or fingers or it may be moved from one place to another by sliding, dragging, or pushing it along. Transport loaded also refers to moving the empty hand against resistance. Transport loaded begins when the hand begins to move an object or encounter resistance and ends when the hand stops moving.)	TL	Carry pen to paper.	

Figure 80 Fundamental hand motions of the right hand in signing a letter.

(Continued)

121

	Name and Definition of Motion	Symbol	Description of Motion	Illustration
4	**POSITION** (Position consists of turning or locating an object in such a way that it will be properly oriented to fit into the location for which it is intended. It is possible to position an object during the motion transport loaded. The carpenter, for example, may turn the nail into position for using while he is carrying it to the board into which it will be driven. Position begins when the hand begins to turn or locate the object and ends when the object has been placed in the desired position or location.)	P	Position pen on paper for writing.	
5	**USE** (Use consists of manipulating a tool, device, or piece of apparatus for the purpose for which it was intended. Use may refer to an almost infinite number of particular cases. It represents the motion for which preceding motions have been more or less preparatory and for which the ones that follow are supplementary. Use begins when the hand starts to manipulate the tool or device and ends when the hand ceases the application.)	U	Sign letter.	
6	**TRANSPORT LOADED**	TL	Return pen to holder.	

	Name and Definition of Motion	Symbol	Description of Motion	Illustration
7	**PRE - POSITION** (Pre-position refers to locating an object in a predetermined place or locating it in the correct position for some subsequent motion. Pre-position is the same as position except that the object is located in the approximate position that it will be needed later. Usually a holder, bracket, or special container of some kind is used for holding the object in a way that permits it to be grasped easily in the position in which it will be used. Pre-position is the abbreviated term used for pre-position for the next operation.)	PP	Position pen in holder.	
8	**RELEASE LOAD** (Release Load refers to letting go of the object. Release load begins when the object starts to leave the hand and ends when the object has been completely separated from the hand or fingers.)	RL	Let go of pen.	
9	**TRANSPORT EMPTY**	TE	Move hand back to letter.	

123

awkward, fatiguing, and ineffective motions. People who accomplish the most do not necessarily work hardest. Rather, they make every motion count—they use good work methods. We are not at all interested in the "speed-up" or "stretch-out." We are interested in getting more quality work done with less expenditure of energy. Excessive speed is no substitute for good work methods.

To illustrate what is meant by developing a better method through the analysis of

Figure 81 Inserting pins in board, using the one-handed method. Left hand *holds* pins; right hand works productively. It takes 0.62 minute to fill the board.

hand motions and the application of principles of motion economy, let us consider the task of filling a board containing 30 holes with 30 wooden pins (Fig. 81). You will notice that there are five rows of six holes to a row in the board. The pins are square on one end and bullet-shaped on the other. The job is to fill the board with the pins as quickly as possible, inserting the pin in the hole with the bullet nose down.

Most people would fill the board by the method shown in Fig. 81. The left hand

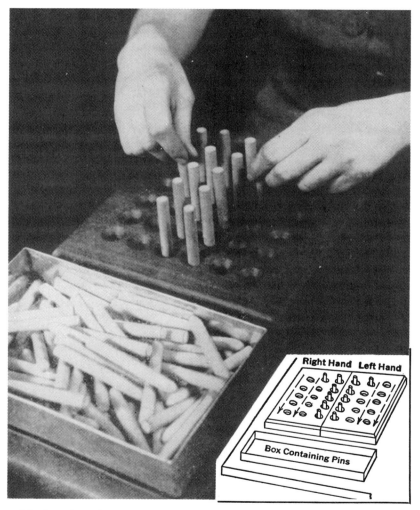

Figure 82 Inserting pins in board, using simultaneous motions, both hands working together. It takes only 0.41 minute to fill the board using this method.

grasps a handful of pins from the box and holds them while the right hand gets pins from the left, one at a time, and places them in the board. The right hand is working in a very effective manner inasmuch as it is performing the desired task, that is, filling the board with pins. Notice that the left hand is doing very little productive work; most of the time it is merely holding the pins.

If both hands were to work simultaneously at getting and placing the pins in the holes, the operator's efforts would be much more effective. We are now applying one of the "principles of motion economy" which will be presented later. We are having a preview of one of these principles now.

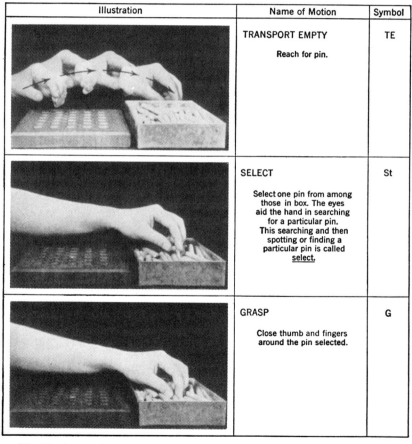

Illustration	Name of Motion	Symbol
	TRANSPORT EMPTY **Reach for pin.**	TE
	SELECT Select one pin from among those in box. The eyes aid the hand in searching for a particular pin. This searching and then spotting or finding a particular pin is called <u>select</u>.	St
	GRASP Close thumb and fingers around the pin selected.	G

Figure 83 Fundamental motions used in inserting pin in pinboard. The operator is using simultaneous symmetrical motions in filling the pinboard (Fig. 82). Because the motions of the left hand and the right hand are the same, those of the left hand only are shown here.

Illustration	Name of Motion	Symbol
	TRANSPORT LOADED Carry pin from tray to hole in board into which it will be inserted. Also: POSITION (in transit) Pin is turned into vertical position as it is transported to board.	TL P
	POSITION Pin is lined up directly over the hole in the board into which it is to be inserted.	P
	ASSEMBLE Insert pin into hole in board.	A
	RELEASE LOAD Open fingers — let go of pin.	RL

127

Using this improved method (Fig. 82)) it is obvious that the lefthand *hold* has been eliminated, and the left hand, like the right, now performs useful motions. The two hands work together in a symmetrical manner, getting the pins and placing them in the holes in the board.

Results. One study showed that it requires 0.62 minute to fill the board using the one-handed method, whereas but 0.41 minute is required with the two-handed method. This is a saving of 34 percent in time.

The fundamental motions of the left hand in filling the pinboard are shown in Fig. 83.

Pinboard Demonstration. It is suggested that the pinboard be used as a demonstration in introducing the subject of motion study to an individual or a group. Let each person try various methods of filling the pinboard, timing himself with each method. It is convincing indeed to discover that there is an easier and a far faster way to fill the board than the conventional one-handed method. Specifications for the pinboard and pins are given in Fig. 332.

12

MOTION STUDY AND MICROMOTION STUDY EQUIPMENT

MAKING THE MOTION PICTURES

Motion study and micromotion study are concerned with the analysis of the motions of workers performing manual tasks. These may be the motions of a person using tools, handling materials, or operating machines. Motion study is facilitated by the use of photographic and electronic data-recording aids, whereas micromotion study requires the use of such equipment. The motion picture camera and the video camera and recorder are the most important pieces of equipment for micromotion study work. Both perform similar functions; both use cameras and produce similar results. The motion picture camera uses photographic film, whereas the video equipment uses magnetic tape.

Motion Picture Cameras

Motion picture cameras using 16-mm or Super 8-mm film are (1) spring driven, (2) motor driven by a self-contained battery, or (3) electric-motor driven (Fig. 84). Although the 8-mm camera and film are of high quality and produce excellent results, the 16-mm camera is more widely used for micromotion study work. The typical spring-driven camera is compact and light in weight with a motor that runs approximately ½ minute with one winding. Some cameras take either a 50-foot or a 100-foot roll of film. At the normal speed of 16 exposures per second a 100-foot roll of film will last approximately 4 minutes. Because there are a number of excellent cameras on the market suitable for this work, no attempt will be made to describe them.

A motion picture camera should have the following features if it is to be used for micromotion study work:

1. Lens—f.2.4 or faster; f.1.9 is preferred.
2. Focus—adjustable from 4 feet or closer to infinity.
3. Film capacity—100 feet.

The following additional features are desirable:

4. Variable speed spring motor which operates from one-half normal speed (8 frames per second) to four times normal speed (64 frames per second).
5. Interchangeable lenses or zoom lens.
6. Electric motor drive attachment.

Figure 84 Electric motor driven 16-mm motion picture camera with 400 foot film magazine. The spring-driven camera may be detached from the electric motor—camera speeds from 8 to 64 frames per second. (Courtesy Alan Gordon Enterprises Inc.)

Electric Motor-Driven Camera

Considerable use is being made of motion picture cameras driven by a constant-speed electric motor. The most common speed for this camera is 1000 frames per minute (Fig. 249). This speed is slightly faster than normal speed, which is 16 frames per second or 960 per minute. Camera speeds other than 1000 frames per minute may be obtained by changing the gear ratio between the motor and the camera or by a separate motor drive.

Because the camera operates at a constant and known speed, the microchronometer (Fig. 85) is not needed to indicate time on the film. Consequently, it does not occupy valuable space in the picture or shut out motions of the operator being studied. It is easy to assign time values to the motions, because no study need be made of the position of the clock's hands. If the film is projected on a screen, it is possible to know the exact projection speed by means of a tachometer attached to the projector. In other words, one can project the film on the screen at exactly the same speed at which it was made, or at a faster or slower speed of known value.

Although the electric motor-driven camera has certain advantages, a good amateur motion picture camera is satisfactory for most ordinary motion study and micromotion study work.

Camera Speeds

The camera shutter makes one complete revolution each time an exposure is made. Therefore, if the camera is operating at the normal speed of 16 exposures per second, and has a shutter with an open segment of 180 degrees, the time that the lens will be open during one revolution is $1/16 \times 180/360$ or $1/32$ of a second.

The motion picture camera photographs intermittent scenes. In photographing moving subjects there is an instant ($1/32$ of a second in the preceding case) between successive exposures during which no record of action that has been taking place is made on the film. It is for this reason that successive frames on the film show the moving object at different points along its line of motion (see enlarged print in Fig. 91). The hand reaching for an object is shown first a foot away from the object, then 10 inches, then 8 inches, etc. Where the movement of the subject is relatively rapid, the moving object appears to be blurred. The right hand in Fig. 97 appears blurred in exposures 2, 7, and 8; during the short instant when the shutter was open, the hand moved a sufficient distance to cause the blur. These blurs are eliminated by exposing the film at a more rapid rate. Had the picture been made at 32 instead of 16 exposures per second, the time during which the shutter remained open would have been $1/64$ of a second, and the hand would have moved but one half the distance. This would have reduced or entirely eliminated the blur.

Although the camera normally operates at a speed of 16 exposures per second, amateur spring-driven cameras are available which operate at speeds as high as eight times normal. For ordinary micromotion study work the normal camera speed is satisfactory. For studying rapid hand motions it may become necessary to use twice normal speed, and in evaluating very short and fast motions under laboratory conditions, speeds of 5000 exposures per minute or higher may be required.

Microchronometer

Because the number of exposures made on the film in any given time interval will depend upon the speed of the camera, and because the speed of a spring-driven camera is not constant, it is necessary to place some accurate timing device in the picture so that the time interval from the exposure of one frame to the exposure of the next will be indicated on the film. The clock shown in Fig. 85 is driven by a small syn-

Figure 85 Electric motor-driven microchronometer.

chronous motor. It has 100 divisions on the dial. The large hand makes 20 revolutions per minute, and the small hand 2 revolutions per minute. Each division on the dial indicates $1/2000$ of a minute. The clock reading in Fig. 85 is 652.

When the electric motor-driven camera is used, the microchronometer is not needed unless it is wanted for the purpose of quickly identifying particular motions or places in a cycle. It is sometimes so used.

Time-Lapse Cameras

For memomotion study analysis a motion picture camera may be equipped with an electric-motor drive or with a solenoid operated attachment to take a single frame of film at regular intervals. Figure 86 shows a Super 8-mm camera and a drive system with solid state intervalometer with single frame drive intervals of 1, 2, 4, 6, 8, 12, 20, 60, 120, and 180 seconds. Also included are external contacts for activating the camera via switch closures such as photo-cells, pneumatic tubes, and mercury switches. The camera may be removed from the drive and used independently.

Laboratory

At times it may be desirable to make the motion pictures in a special laboratory apart from the main production floor. This requires that the tools and equipment be moved into the laboratory and the operators be brought in from the factory. Studies of the

Figure 86 Super 8-mm motion picture camera. Drive system with solid state intervalometer with intervals of 1 to 180 seconds. Spring-driven camera may be detached from the drive. (Courtesy Lafayette Instrument Company.)

operation can then be made without disturbing production. Although this procedure has many advantages, it is now common practice to take the pictures at the work place in the factory. This practice is less costly, and may aid in securing the cooperation of the workers. Where the work is of such a nature that the laboratory setup is possible, and where an extended study is warranted, it is not unusual to make the investigation in the laboratory. The laboratory also may be used for storing motion picture equipment, for analyzing the film, and for showing film to those concerned with improving methods. The motion study laboratory may be used as a classroom by members of the organization who are interested in learning the micromotion study technique. It frequently serves as a conference room for supervisor and operator training programs.

Motion Picture Projector

The motion picture projector is indispensable for analyzing film because the film must be studied frame by frame in minute detail. Frequently the motions of several members of the body, such as the fingers, arms, and feet, must be analyzed. This study requires that the same film be analyzed a number of times, once for each member of the body studied.

The projector shown in Fig. 87 is designed for film analysis and for showing performances rating films. There is a hand-held remote control box which provides control of all projector functions. It is available in 16-mm and 8-mm models and is equipped with a digital electronic resettable frame counter that adds and subtracts.

Figure 87   Motion picture projector (16-mm, also available in 8-mm). Designed for film analysis and for projecting film at speeds from 800 to 1800 frames per minute. (Courtesy Lafayette Instrument Company.)

The projector has a variable-speed motor which operates at from 800 to 1800 frames per minute with an indicator showing the speed in frames per minute. Special filters and an auxiliary blower protect the film even when a 750 or 1000 watt lamp is used in the projector.

List of Equipment for Motion Study Work

To summarize, the following equipment is recommended where a fairly extensive program is to be carried on:

1. Motion picture camera, preferably with f.1.9 lens, adjustable focus from 4 feet to infinity, or zoom lens, and film capacity of 100 feet.
2. Metal tripod with tilting and panoraming head.
3. Exposure meter.
4. Three or four lamps with reflectors.
5. Two tripods for lamps.
6. Microchronometer.
7. Motion picture projector for film analysis and calibrated for showing film at a known speed.

8. Portable screen.
9. Cabinets for storage of film and equipment.
10. Tilting outfit, rewind, editor, and film splicer.

MAKING THE MOTION PICTURES

Motion pictures can be used for numerous purposes in motion and time study work. They are frequently made (1) for micromotion study and memomotion study, (2) for obtaining work sampling data, (3) for training factory operators, (4) for showing the current method of doing a particular job, (5) for performance rating in time study and work sampling, and (6) for motion study research.

Because films for micromotion study are perhaps the most difficult to make, an explanation is given here of the procedure to be followed. It will be assumed that a particular operation has been selected for study.

Operator to Be Studied

The first step is to select one or more operators as subjects for making the motion picture. It is of greatest value to make the pictures of those operators who are the most highly skilled and who perform the work in the most satisfactory manner. Every operator who gives promise of contributing something to the establishment of the improved method should be studied.

It is very important and necessary that the workers and the supervisor understand what is going to be done. Their cooperation should be obtained from the very beginning. In most cases the workers will give their very best performance while the motion pictures are being made, because they know that a permanent record is being made and that their fellow workers and perhaps others may review their work on the screen.

It should be emphasized that motion study makes no effort to force the worker to "move faster," but studies his motions to find the shortest and best ones to use. Motion study aids in finding the easiest and least fatiguing way of doing work. If the best operators are used as subjects for the study, the analyst is likely to progress more rapidly on the solution of the problem than if he or she selects inexperienced workers. The motions that the operators use are the things being studied, not the speed that they exhibit.

As stated at the beginning of Chapter 2, motion and time study has several objectives. It is the purpose of time study to determine a time value in minutes or hours which permits the qualified operator to work day after day and week after week without harm or undue fatigue, always being able to perform the task in this standard or specified time. In making micromotion studies, however, it is expected that the superior workers who act as subjects may perform at a faster speed than the "standard" calls for. No one can object to this, for in motion study the discovery of the very best possible *way* of doing the work is the object. Those operators who will aid most in determining this method are the ones who should be studied.

Placing the Camera

Assuming that the operator or operators to be studied have been selected and understand that a micromotion study is to be made, the motion study analyst is ready to set up the equipment and make the picture.

Although it is not necessary to have pictures of a quality equal to that of professional movies, it is essential that the pictures be sufficiently clear when projected to give all necessary details. They should be sharply focused, and they should be taken from an angle which gives a satisfactory picture of all motions of the operator.

The camera should be placed as close to the subject as possible without omitting anything necessary from the picture. Both the work place and the actions of the operator should be considered in positioning the camera. The motions of the operator may occur in two directions—those made perpendicular to the line of sight and those made parallel to the line of sight. The camera should be placed at such an angle, relative to the operator and the work place, that a majority of the motions will be perpendicular to the line of sight. Not only does such an arrangement tend to permit a sharp focus throughout the cycle, but it also makes the analysis of the film easier. It is less difficult to judge the nature and extent of movements made at right angles to the line of sight than it is to judge movements made toward or away from the line of sight. The view finder on most cameras is sufficiently accurate even at close range to show what will be included in the picture.

The camera should preferably be placed to include the entire range of the worker's motions for the cycle. Seldom is it desirable to follow the movements of the operator by moving the camera as the cycle progresses. It is difficult to anticipate the movements of the operator and almost impossible to keep all the motions in the picture at all times.

In some cases motion pictures may profitably be made from more than one position, although this is by no means required on every operation. It is desirable, however, to make a few pictures of the operator and the work place from a distance in order to have a complete record of the job, and incidentally a good picture of the operator.

The camera should be mounted on a tripod, which should be placed securely on the floor or on top of a solid table or bench so that the camera will be free of vibration while it is in operation.

Lighting

Daylight is preferable to artificial light for making pictures; however, it is sometimes necessary to supplement daylight with some artificial light. Photoflood lamps can supply this additional illumination. These lamps should be located to light properly the darkest places in the picture. With the development of fast motion picture film the need for artificial light has been greatly reduced.

Making the Motion Picture

If a microchronometer is used, it should be placed so that its entire face will appear in the picture and yet not hide any of the motions of the operator or any part of the work place that should be included in the picture. Neither should motions of the operator interfere with the clock's being in full view at all times. The microchonometer should be in focus if it is to be easily read when photographed.

The camera is loaded with film, the film-footage meter set to zero, and the diaphragm opening adjusted for the lighting conditions present and for the speed at which the camera is to operate. The distance from the center of action of the operator to the lens of the camera should be carefully measured with a tape measure and the camera focused accurately. This is particularly important when the camera is placed near the work to be photographed.

To identify the film a card bearing such information as operation name, part number, date of study, department number, and film number is often placed in front of the camera and photographed on the first few frames of film. Another method is to place a single number or symbol so that it shows in the picture during the entire "run." A different number is used for each setup or run. This number is referred to as the "film number." A special motion picture data sheet bearing the film, number, such as the one shown in Fig. 88, may be used to list all data pertaining to the particular study. This sheet forms a permanent record of the information about the work being filmed, as well as of data pertaining to the mechanics of making the picture. Because the same symbol appears on each frame of the film in a given run, it is always possible to refer to the data sheet in order to identify any piece of film.

The analyst should estimate or measure with a watch the time required for a cycle if this is not already available. There should be plenty of material ahead of the operator, and everything should be in readiness so that there will be no unnecessary interruptions while the pictures are being made. The film is then exposed, making pictures of as many cycles of the operation as desired.

Outline of Procedure for Making Motion Pictures

1. Secure the cooperation of the supervisor and the operators before making the motion picture. Explain why the picture is being made.
2. Determine whether electricity is available for the lamps, microchronometer, and camera if an electric motor-driven camera is to be used.
3. Locate the camera to give the best picture of the operation. Use the view finder to ascertain whether the entire cycle is covered.
4. Locate the lamps to give adequate intensity of illumination without deep shadows. See that the darkest places are properly lighted.
5. Place the microchronometer so that it will be in the picture and in focus. See that it does not obscure any part of the operation.

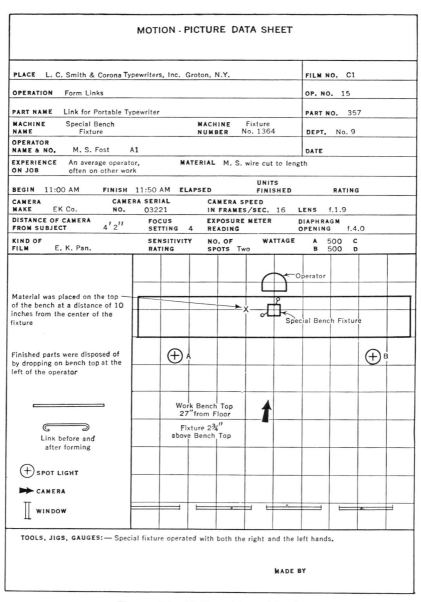

MOTION - PICTURE DATA SHEET

PLACE L. C. Smith & Corona Typewriters, Inc. Groton, N.Y.	**FILM NO.** C1
OPERATION Form Links	**OP. NO.** 15
PART NAME Link for Portable Typewriter	**PART NO.** 357

MACHINE NAME Special Bench Fixture	**MACHINE NUMBER** Fixture No. 1364	**DEPT.** No. 9
OPERATOR NAME & NO. M. S. Fost A1		**DATE**

EXPERIENCE ON JOB   An average operator, often on other work   **MATERIAL**   M. S. wire cut to length

BEGIN   11:00 AM   **FINISH** 11:50 AM   **ELAPSED**   **UNITS FINISHED**   **RATING**

CAMERA MAKE   EK Co.   **CAMERA SERIAL NO.** 03221   **CAMERA SPEED IN FRAMES/SEC.** 16   **LENS**   f.1.9

DISTANCE OF CAMERA FROM SUBJECT 4'2"   **FOCUS SETTING** 4   **EXPOSURE METER READING**   **DIAPHRAGM OPENING**   f.4.0

KIND OF FILM   E. K. Pan.   **SENSITIVITY RATING**   **NO. OF SPOTS** Two   **WATTAGE**   **A** 500 **C**   **B** 500 **D**

Operator

Material was placed on the top of the bench at a distance of 10 inches from the center of the fixture

X — Special Bench Fixture

Finished parts were disposed of by dropping on bench top at the left of the operator

⊕ A   ⊕ B

Work Bench Top 27" from Floor

Fixture 2¾" above Bench Top

Link before and after forming

⊕ SPOT LIGHT

➤ CAMERA

‖ WINDOW

TOOLS, JIGS, GAUGES: — Special fixture operated with both the right and the left hands.

MADE BY

Figure 88 Motion picture data sheet.

6. Place the card bearing the film number or other identification in the picture, preferably near the microchronometer.
7. Have sufficient film in the camera for the number of cycles to be photographed.
8. Determine the proper diaphragm opening by means of an exposure meter and adjust the diaphragm setting on the camera.
9. Measure the distance of the subject from the camera lens and adjust the focus setting on the camera to correspond.
10. Fill in the motion picture data sheet.
11. Turn on the lights, start the microchronometer, and make the picture.

13

FILM ANALYSIS

After the motion picture has been made and the film processed, it is placed in the projector and shown on the screen, where it may be examined. Because the film contains an exact record of the activities photographed, a process chart, activity chart, man and machine chart, or an operation chart can be made from the film as well as from the actual activity. If the film is projected at the same speed at which it was made, a time study can also be made from the film. In this chapter, however, an explanation will be made of the method of analyzing the film for simo (simultaneous-motion-cycle) chart construction. Before starting the analysis it is customary for the analyst to run the films through the projector several times in order to become familiar with the entire operation. A particular cycle is then selected to be analyzed in detail.

The extent to which the movements of the hands, arms, legs, head, and trunk will be analyzed depends largely upon the nature of the work. Most operations selected for micromotion study analysis involve either benchwork or short-cycle machine work requiring motions of the hands only. It is usually satisfactory to consider the hand as a unit in making the analysis. That is, it is not necessary to analyze the motions of each finger independently. However, an operation may be studied in which several body movements take place. When such detailed analysis is required, it is entirely possible to adapt the technique to this use, although much more time is required when all the members of the body must be considered separately.

In the bolt and washer assembly, which is to be an example, the simplest form of analysis will be used, that is, analysis of hand motions. When the thumb and index finger of the right hand grasp a washer, it will be assumed that the right hand grasps the washer, and so on.

Forms for Recording Motion Analysis Data

As the film is analyzed, the data are transferred to a data sheet, commonly called an analysis sheet. Various forms have been devised for this, and the one used will depend upon the type of work studied and the extent to which the analysis is to be carried. The forms in Figs. 89 and 92 are very satisfactory for right-hand and left-hand analysis. The extra column on the form in Fig. 89 provides space for the analysis of a third member of the body, such as the foot in punch-press work or the knee in knee-controlled sewing machine operation. The analysis sheet in Fig. 90 was designed for use by Macy's Department Store when a complete analysis was to be made.

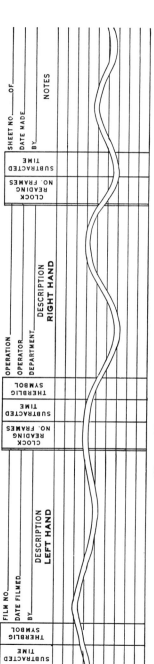

Figure 89 Micromotion study analysis sheet.

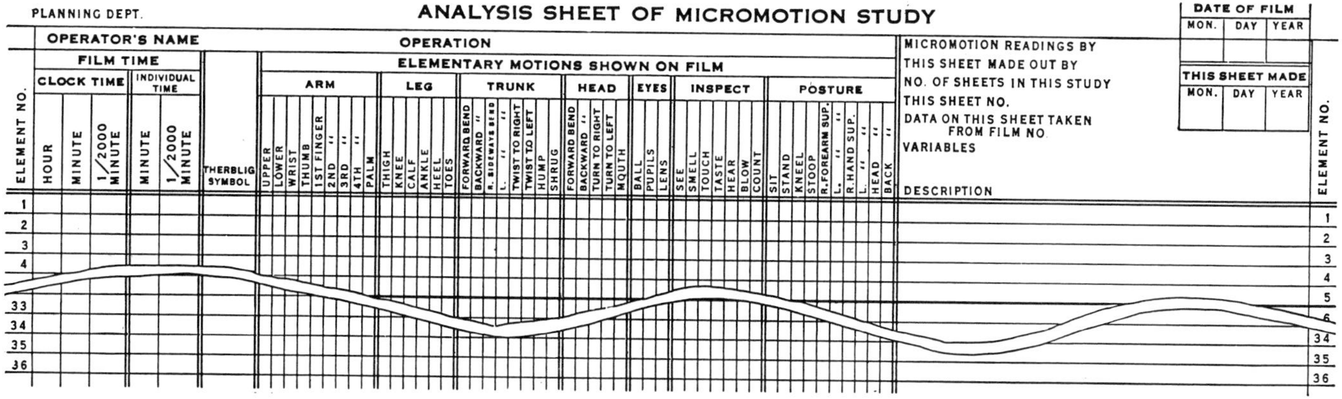

Figure 90 Form for complete micromotion study analysis.

141

Film Analysis of the Bolt and Washer Assembly

The enlarged print of one cycle of the film showing the operation "Assemble Three Washers on Bolt" is reproduced in Fig. 91. The pictures were taken at normal speed of 16 exposures per second, and the microchronometer speed was 20 revolutions per minute. The operation is described in detail on page 175. The enlarged print in Fig. 91 will be analyzed in the same manner as if the analyst had the actual film before him. In that case, however, the task would be easier because the film would be in a projector and could be greatly enlarged on the screen.

Analysis of the Left-Hand Motions

The motions of the left hand of the operator are usually analyzed first. The film is then run back to the beginning of the cycle and analyzed for the motions of the right hand.

To begin the analysis, the film is run through the projector until the beginning of a cycle is found. This is usually the point where the hand begins its first *transport empty* therblig. Sometimes it is best to begin the analysis at a point where both the right and the left hands begin or end their therbligs together. If the enlarged print of film in Fig. 91 is examined, it will be noted that the microchronometer is located at the left of the operator, the card bearing the film number (B21) appears above the clock, and the material to be assembled is located in small bins directly in front of the operator. The exact arrangement of the material is shown in Fig. 67. The large clock hand makes 20 revolutions per minute; the small hand makes 2. There are 100 equal divisions on the dial of the clock; therefore, time is indicated directly in $1/2000$ of a minute by the large hand. This time interval of $1/2000$ of a minute was called a "wink" by Gilbreth.

The first frame of film in the upper left-hand corner of Fig. 91 shows the operator holding the head of the bolt with her left hand and completing the assembly of the last washer on the bolt with her right hand. The second frame shows the operator in the act of beginning to carry the finished assembly (with her left hand) to the bin nearest the clock, where she will dispose of it. This frame is an excellent place to begin the analysis, because it shows the two hands at the instant they are beginning to separate. The clock reads 595, meaning $595/2000$ of a minute from zero.

The motions of the left hand are recorded on the analysis sheet (Fig. 92) in the column "Description Left Hand." The clock reading is recorded in the first column, 595 being the time at which the motion *transport loaded* begins. The symbol for this motion is placed in the third column and the motion is described, "Carries assembly to bin."[1] The film is then examined frame by frame until this therblig (for the left

---

[1] The best practice is to let the therblig symbol indicate the action, thus making it unnecessary to include the verb in the description. The description of the first therblig would therefore have been "Assembly to bin" instead of "Carries assembly to bin." The verbs have been included on the analysis sheets and simo charts in this book in order to aid the reader in learning the meanings of the therblig symbols.

hand) ends. The frame of film showing the left hand in the act of releasing the assembly also shows the clock to read 602. Therefore, 602 is recorded in the second horizontal line and in the first vertical column. Because the operator's left hand is now beginning the therblig *release load,* the symbol for this therblig is placed in the third vertical column, and the description of the therblig, "Releases assembly," is recorded in the fourth column. The analyst now turns to the film and examines it further, looking for the end of the *release load* and for the beginning of the next motion, *transport empty.* The very next frame of film shows the operator's left hand in the act of moving empty to the bin of bolts; consequently the *release load* therblig has ended, and the *transport empty* motion has begun. The clock is read 604, and this reading is recorded in the third horizontal line and in the first vertical column. The symbol for *transport empty* is placed in the third column, and the description of the therblig is noted in the fourth column. In a like manner the film is examined through the entire cycle, the analyst noting where one motion ends and the next one begins and recording the data on the analysis sheet. After the analysis has been made for both hands, the clock readings are subtracted to get the elapsed time for each motion. These subtracted times are recorded in the second vertical column.

Analysis of the Right-Hand Motions

After the motions of the left hand have been analyzed, the film is run back to the starting place and the motions made by the right hand are analyzed and recorded on the right side of the analysis sheet in Fig. 92. In the second frame of film in the upper left-hand corner of Fig. 91, the operator's right hand is beginning the motion *transport empty,* the hand moving to the bin of lock washers. Therefore, the clock reading 595 is recorded in the first vertical column, "Clock Reading," for the right hand in Fig. 92. The therblig symbol for *transport empty* is placed in the third vertical column, and the description of the motion is recorded. The film is then studied frame by frame until the point is found where the motion *transport empty* for the right hand ends and the next one begins. This motion is a long one because the hand moves very slowly in order to allow time for the left hand to dispose of the assembly and procure a bolt. It is not until the frame in the middle of the second row of pictures of Fig. 91 that the operator begins to *select* and *grasp* a lock washer from the bin on the bench. The clock is read 621, and the data are recorded on the analysis sheet; the analysis is continued in this manner for the remainder of the cycle. After the analysis has been made for both hands and the subtracted time obtained, it is possible to picture the entire cycle easily and accurately. The left hand is analyzed independently of the right hand except that the cycle must begin and end at approximately the same point for the two hands. It must be remembered that the subtracted time shown in Fig. 92 is in 2000ths of a minute.

As many cycles of the operation may be analyzed as seem necessary. Usually one or two are all that are required if care is used in their selection.

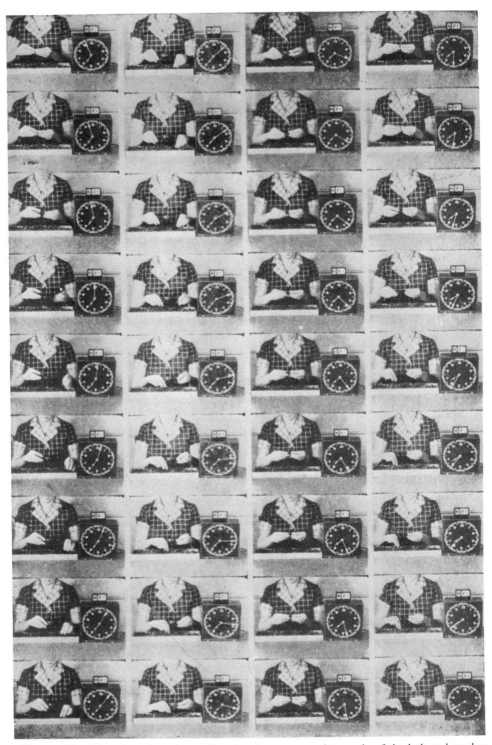

Figure 91 Print of motion picture film showing one complete cycle of the bolt and washer assembly—old method.

144

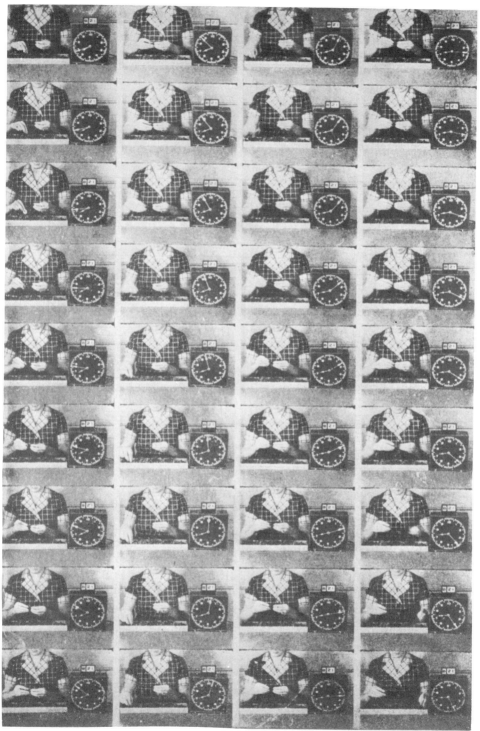

145

			MICROMOTION STUDY ANALYSIS SHEET				

PART   Bolt and washer assembly - Old Method   DEPARTMENT   AY16   FILM NO. B21

OPERATION   Assemble 3 washers on bolt   OP. NO. A32

OPERATOR   M. Smith 1C634   DATE   ANALYSED BY M.E.R.   SHEET NO. 1 OF 1

CLOCK READING	SUBTRACTED TIME	THERBLIG SYMBOL	DESCRIPTION LEFT HAND	CLOCK READING	SUBTRACTED TIME	THERBLIG SYMBOL	DESCRIPTION RIGHT HAND
595	7	TL	Carries assembly to bin	595	26	TE	Reaches for lock washer
602	2	RL	Releases assembly	621	6	St+G	Selects and grasps washer
604	4	TE	Reaches for bolt	627	7	TL	Carries washer to bolt
608	2	St+G	Selects and grasps bolt	634	6	P	Positions washer
610	17	TL	Carries bolt to working position	640	12	A+RL	Assembles washer onto bolt and releases
627	5	P	Positions bolt	652	8	TE	Reaches for steel washer
632	104	H	Holds bolt	660	8	St+G	Selects and grasps washer
736	7	TL	Carries assembly to bin	668	9	TL	Carries washer to bolt
743	2	RL	Releases assembly	677	3	P	Positions washer
745				680	10	A+RL	Assembles steel washer and releases
				690	6	TE	Reaches for rubber washer
				696	10	St+G	Selects and grasps rubber washer
				706	9	TL	Carries washer to bolt
				715	5	P	Positions washer
				720	16	A+RL	Assembles washer and releases
				736			
			Time in 2000ths of a minute				

Figure 92   Analysis sheet for the bolt and washer assembly—old method.

CONSTRUCTION OF SIMULTANEOUS-MOTION-CYCLE CHARTS

The time for each therblig recorded on the analysis sheet may be shown to scale by means of a simultaneous-motion-cycle chart, commonly called a *simo chart*. Either the analysis sheet or the simo chart may be made independently, or the simo chart may be constructed from the data on the analysis sheet.

When a full simo chart showing every moving member of the body is made, it is customary to use a sheet of cross-section paper 22 inches wide with lines ruled 10 to the inch. For operations longer than ½ minute some analysts use paper with lines ruled 10 to the half inch, or paper ruled in millimeters in order to condense the chart. Headings containing information such as that shown at the top of Fig. 90 are often printed in quantities and are pasted across the top of the cross-section paper.

For many operations, however, it is not necessary to construct a complete chart of all the moving members of the body. A simo chart of the two hands for the bolt and washer assembly is shown in Fig. 93. Exactly the same procedure would be used to construct a chart showing the motions of the arms, legs, head, trunk, and other parts of the body.

The vertical scale shown in the center of the chart in Fig. 93 represents time in 2000ths of a minute. The therblig description, symbol, color, and relative position in the cycle all appear on the chart. The time required for each motion is drawn to scale

MICROMOTION STUDY
SIMO CHART

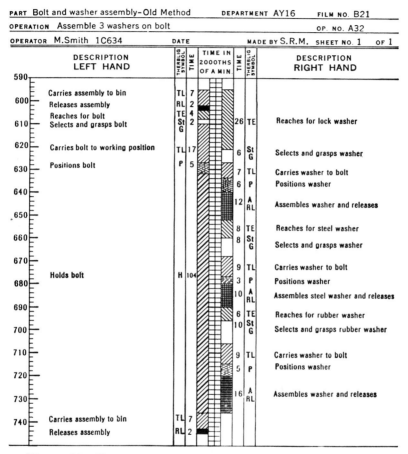

PART Bolt and washer assembly–Old Method	DEPARTMENT AY16	FILM NO. B21
OPERATION Assemble 3 washers on bolt		OP. NO. A32
OPERATOR M.Smith 1C634	DATE	MADE BY S.R.M. SHEET NO. 1 OF 1

Figure 93 Simo chart for bolt and washer assembly—old method.

in the vertical column and colored to represent the particular motion. The sheet is arranged much like the analysis sheet. The clock read 595 at the beginning of the motion *transport loaded* for the left hand; therefore this point is located on the vertical scale by a heavy black horizontal line at the top of the column. The first motion, *transport loaded,* required seven winks ($7/2000$ of a minute); therefore, seven divisions are marked off on the vertical column for the left hand and a heavy black line is

PART Bolt and Washer Assembly–Improved Method   DEPARTMENT AY16   FILM NO. X75

OPERATION Assemble 3 washers on bolt   OP. NO. A32

OPERATOR M.S. Bowen   1C4327   DATE   MADE BY S.R.M.   SHEET NO. 1   OF 1

DESCRIPTION LEFT HAND	THERBLIG SYMBOL	TIME	TIME IN 2000THS OF A MIN.	TIME	THERBLIG SYMBOL	DESCRIPTION RIGHT HAND
Reaches for rubber washer	TE	10		10	TE	Reaches for rubber washer
Selects and grasps washer	St G	1		1	St G	Selects and grasps washer
Slides washer to fixture	TL	13	20	13	TL	Slides washer to fixture
Positions washer in fixture and releases	P RL	14	40	14	P RL	Positions washer in fixture and releases
Reaches for steel washer	TE	12		12	TE	Reaches for steel washer
Selects and grasps washer	St G	1		1	St G	Selects and grasps washer
Slides washer to fixture	TL	17	60	17	TL	Slides washer to fixture
Positions washer in fixture and releases	P RL	13	80	13	P RL	Positions washer in fixture and releases
Reaches for lock washer	TE	12		12	TE	Reaches for lock washer
Selects and grasps washer	St G	1	100	1	St G	Selects and grasps washer
Slides washer to fixture	TL	14		14	TL	Slides washer to fixture
Positions washer in fixture and releases	P RL	8	120	8	P RL	Positions washer in fixture and releases
Reaches for bolt	TE	10		10	TE	Reaches for bolt
Selects and grasps bolt	St G	10	140	10	St G	Selects and grasps bolt
Carries bolt to fixture	TL	12		12	TL	Carries bolt to fixture
Positions bolt	P	8	160	8	P	Positions bolt
Inserts bolt through washer	A	48	180 200	48	A	Inserts bolt through washer
Withdraws assembly	DA	3		3	DA	Withdraws assembly
Carries assembly to top of chute	TL	10		10	TL	Carries assembly to top of chute
Releases assembly	RL	1	220	1	RL	Releases assembly

Figure 94 Simo chart for bolt and washer assembly—improved method.

148

drawn in. The space above this horizontal black line is then colored solidly in green[2] with a pencil, No. 375. The next therblig for the left hand is *release load,* which required two winks. In a similar manner this elapsed time is marked off on the vertical scale immediately below the heavy black line, and another horizontal line is drawn in. The area for this therblig is colored red. And so for the remainder of the cycle the motions are marked off to scale and each area is colored with the standard therblig color. The motions made by the right hand are charted on the right-hand side of the sheet in exactly the same way as those for the left hand.

Figure 94 shows the simo chart for one cycle of the *improved method* of bolt and washer assembly as described on page 175.

Analysis of the Link-Forming Operation

The simple operation of bending a "hook" on each end of a short piece of wire to form a link (Fig. 95) for a portable typewriter was the subject of a number of studies. Because this operation involves the use of a fixture and because it is short in length, it will serve as an example.

The camera used for making the motion pictures of this operation was driven by a synchronous motor and operated at a constant speed of 1000 exposures per minute. Therefore, no microchronometer was needed, and the time interval from one frame of film to the next was exactly $1/1000$ of a minute. (See Figure 97.)

Description of the Link-Forming Operation

The material from which the link was formed consisted of soft steel wire cut from wire stock 0.045 inch in diameter to uniform length of 1¼ inches. The material was supplied in metal containers to the operator, who emptied the stock of cut wire on the linoleum-topped bench at the right of the fixture as she needed it. The link was formed in the following manner.

The pictures in Fig. 97 give a reproduction of each element of one complete cycle. The fixture was mounted securely on the bench so that its top surface was 2¾ inches above the top of the bench. The top of the bench was 27 inches above the floor. The material was spread out over the surface of the bench top so that it could be grasped

A   B   C

Figure 95   Link for portable typewriter: *A,* soft steel wire; *B,* link with one end formed; *C,* finished link.

[2] Because color cannot be reproduced in this book, color symbols are used instead. For standard therblig colors see Fig. 79.

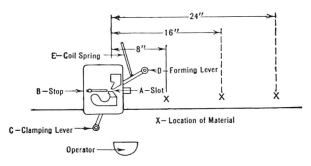

Figure 96 Fixture and layout of the work place for forming link.

more easily. The operator, seated behind the bench, picked up one piece of material with the thumb and index finger of her right hand, carried it to the left, and inserted it into the slot A in the fixture (Fig. 96). The operator pressed the piece of material against a stop B in the fixture, and at the same time she clamped the piece into place by moving lever C to the left with her left hand. Then with the right hand she grasped the knob of the forming lever D, which extended to the right of the fixture and was about 3 inches above the top of the bench. The right hand rotated the forming lever in the clockwise direction about the center of the fixture as an axis, through approximately 180 degrees, the radius of rotation being 8 inches. The lever was moved in a plane parallel to the top of the bench. This movement of the lever formed the "hook" on one end of the link. The operator then returned the lever in the counterclockwise direction toward its original position. A coil spring E, fastened to the forming lever and to the bench, assisted the operator in returning the lever to its original position. This spring made it possible for the operator to release the forming lever after she had returned it through about one-half its return travel, the spring pulling the lever back the remainder of the distance.

After the operator had released the knob of the lever, she moved her hand slightly to her right and into a position about 4 inches in front of her, and waited an instant while her left hand removed the half-formed link from the slot in the fixture. Then the two hands together turned the link end for end and placed it back into the slot. Care was taken to ensure that the "hook" was turned in the proper direction so that after the link had been completely formed the two hooks would be on the same side. As the right hand held the link in place in the fixture, the left hand moved the lever C to the left, clamping the link in the slot as in the first part of the cycle. The right hand then grasped the knob of the forming lever and, as before, moved it through 180 degrees in the clockwise direction, forming the second end of the link. While the right hand was forming the end of the link, the left hand continued to hold lever C in its position as far to the left as it would go, clamping the link in the fixture while it was being formed. After the link was formed, the right hand returned the forming lever toward its original position, releasing the knob of this lever directly in front of

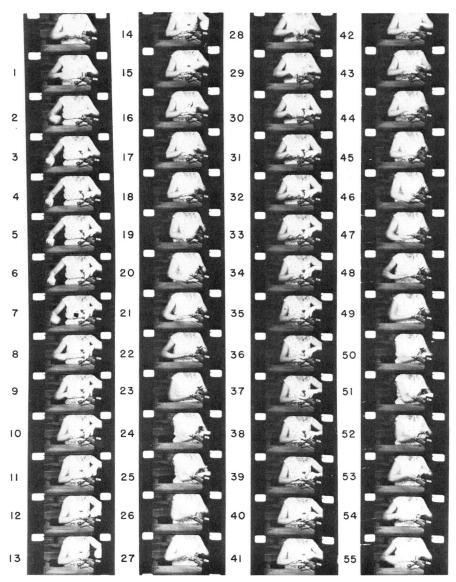

Figure 97 Print of motion picture film showing one complete cycle of the link-forming operation.

151

PART	Link for typewriter	DEPARTMENT 9	FILM NO. C18
OPERATION	Form link for typewriter		OP. NO. G11
OPERATOR	A.S.Sanders A2	DATE	MADE BY S.A.R. SHEET NO. 1 OF 1

DESCRIPTION LEFT HAND	THERBLIG SYMBOL	TIME	TIME IN 1000THS OF A MIN.	TIME	THERBLIG SYMBOL	DESCRIPTION RIGHT HAND
Returns clamping lever and releases it	TL RL	2				
				4	TE	Reaches for material
Moves hand to fixture	TE	3				
				2	St G	Selects and grasps one piece
Grasps formed link in fixture	G	6				
				6	TL	Carries piece to fixture
Carries formed link to left and releases it	TL RL	3				
				6	P RL	Inserts piece in fixture and releases it
Moves to clamping lever and grasps knob	TE G	3				
Moves lever to extreme left	TL	3				
				2	TE G	Reaches for forming lever and grasps knob
Holds lever in this position	H	6		5	U	Forms 1st end of link
Returns lever to original position and releases it	TL RL	3		3	TL RL	Returns forming lever and releases it
Moves hand to fixture	TE	3		4	TE UD	Moves hand toward fixture and waits for left hand
				4	TE	Moves hand to fixture
Grasps piece, turns it end for end in fixture and releases it	G P RL	8				
Moves to clamping lever and grasps knob	TE G	3		8	P	Assists left hand in turning piece end for end in fixture
Moves lever to extreme left	TL	3				
				2	TE G	Reaches for forming lever and grasps knob
Holds lever in this position	H	8		5	U	Forms 2nd end of link
				3	TL RL	Returns forming lever and releases it
Returns clamping lever and releases it						

Figure 98 Simo chart of link-forming operation.

152

the operator. She then moved her hand to her right to pick up a piece of material from the bench for the beginning of the next cycle. In the meantime the left hand released the knob of lever C and reached forward to remove the finished formed link from the slot in the fixture. The left hand then carried the link to the left, where it was dropped on top of the bench. During this time the operator was looking to her right, where the right hand was grasping a piece of material from the top of the bench for the next cycle.

Figure 98 shows the simo chart for the link-forming operation.

Complete Analysis of Hand Motions

Confusion sometimes occurs when making a left- and right-hand motion analysis because some members of the arm are performing certain motions while other members are performing other motions. The first motion on the simo chart in Fig. 99, for example, shows the thumb and the first and second fingers of the right hand performing a grasp while the palm and the third and fourth fingers of the same hand are holding a smooth piece of bone. The operation is folding and creasing sheets of paper by the improved method described on page 191. The right hand carries the bone at all times, although it is used during only a small part of the cycle.

When a complete analysis of an operation is made, each member of the arm and hand is analyzed separately—the upper arm, lower arm, wrist, first finger, second finger, and so forth. The film is run back to the starting place after the analysis of each member, and a separate vertical column on the simo chart is required for recording the motions of each. Although Fig. 99 does not show the movements of the head, trunk, and legs, it does show all motions of the arms, hands, and fingers.

Had a simple left- and right-hand simo chart been made of the paper-folding operation, it would have shown only those therbligs performed by the thumb and the first and second fingers. A note would have been included on the chart to show that the bone was carried in the right hand throughout the entire cycle.

Using the Simo Chart

When the simo chart of the operation has been made, the task of finding a better way of doing the work has just begun. A thorough study of the chart is ordinarily the first step in this task.

The simo chart aids one in grasping a picture of the complete cycle in all its details, and assists in working out better combinations of the most desirable motions. The simo chart of Fig. 93 shows in a very clear way that the left hand is used during most of the cycle for holding the bolt. This at once suggests that some mechanical device be substituted which will permit the left hand as well as the right to do more useful work.

It is often found that the sequence of motions in one kind of work may be used in other kinds, or a particularly good sequence in one operation may suggest a more ef-

MICROMOTION STUDY

SIMO CHART

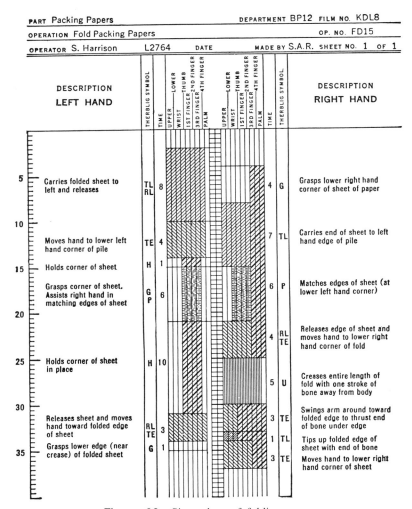

PART Packing Papers   DEPARTMENT BP12 FILM NO. KDL8

OPERATION Fold Packing Papers   OP. NO. FD15

OPERATOR S. Harrison   L2764   DATE   MADE BY S.A.R. SHEET NO. 1 OF 1

Figure 99 Simo chart of folding paper.

MICROMOTION STUDY
SIMO CHART

PART: ½ lb. and 1 lb. Cheddar Cheese			**FILM NO.:** S1486
OPERATION: Crimp Foil Liner over Top, Press Cheese in Cup,			**OP. NO.:**
Code Date, Move to Wrapper			**DATE:**
OPERATOR: M. Sanderson	**MADE BY:** M.G.S.		**SHEET NO.:** 1 of 1
NO. UNITS PER CYCLE: 2-Cup Cycle	**ORIGINAL METHOD:** X		**IMPROVED METHOD:**

FOOT	LEFT HAND	1000THS OF A MINUTE		RIGHT HAND
	T.E. to cup and aid right hand	10	10	T.E. to cup and move to position
	Crimp foil liner over cheese	28	26	Crimp foil liner over cheese
		—25—		
	Aid right hand	5	7	Aside cup
	T.E. to cup and grasp	8	17	Hold lever up
	Place cup in position to press	15	—50—	
			17	Lower lever pressing cheese to cup, raise
	Hold cup	11	—75—	
	Aside cup to table	7	7	Hold lever up
	T.E. pick up inserts, hold while right hand places, aside (6 at a time)	18	18	T.E. to instruction inserts in left hand, grasp and place on top of cheese in cup
		—100—		
	Aid place cover	13	32	Place cover and T.E. for next cover
	Shove cup aside	5		
	Move next cup in position	14	—125—	
	Turn cups upside down (1 in each hand)	10	10	Same as left
	T.E. for stamp pad, hold while right stamps, aside pad	13	—150—13	T.E. for stamp-stamp cover-aside stamp-avg. 12 per time
	Shove to wrapper (1 each hand)	5	5	Same as left
	T.E. to cup and aid right hand	10	10	T.E. to cup and move to position
	Crimp foil liner over cheese	28	—175—26	Crimp foil liner over cheese
		—200—		
	Aid right hand	5	7	T.L. and R.L. cup
	T.E. to cup and grasp	8	17	Hold lever up
	T.L. cup in position to press	15	—225—17	Lower lever pressing cheese in cup, raise
	Hold cup	11		
	T.L. cup to table	7	7	Hold lever up
	T.E. pick up inserts, hold while right hand places, aside (6 at a time)	18	—250—18	T.E. to instruction inserts in left hand, grasp and place on top of cheese in cup
	Aid place cover	13	32	Place cover and T.E. for next cover
		—275—		
	Shove cup aside	5		
	Move next cup in position	14		
	Turn cups upside down (1 in each hand)	10	—300—10	Same as left
	Reach for stamp pad, hold while right stamps, aside pad	13	13	T.E. for stamp-stamp cover-aside stamp-avg. 12 per time
	Shove to wrapper (1 each hand)	5	**324** 5	Same as left
	NOTE: In order to compare Old and New Methods a one-cup cycle of Old Method has been shown twice.			_____Indicates that element probably could be completely eliminated.
				▬ ▬ ▬ ▬ Indicates element probably could be reduced.

Figure 100 Modified simo chart of one operation in the process of packing Cheddar cheese in paper cups by the old method.

155

MICROMOTION STUDY
SIMO CHART

PART: ½ lb. and 1 lb. Cheddar Cheese		FILM NO.: S1347
OPERATION: Crimp Foil Liner over Top, Press Cheese in Cup,		OP. NO.: c-27
Code Date, Move to Wrapper		DATE:
OPERATOR: M. Sanderson	MADE BY: M.G.S.	SHEET NO. 1 OF 1
NO. UNITS PER CYCLE: 2 Cup Cycle	ORIGINAL METHOD:	IMPROVED METHOD: X

FOOT	LEFT HAND	1000THS OF A MINUTE			RIGHT HAND
	T.E. and G. cup	7		8	T.E. and G. cup
	T.L. and R.L. cup	9		10	T.L. and R.L. cup
	Fold over tinfoil liner on first cup	28	25	26	Aid left hand to fold over tinfoil liner on first cup
	R.L. and T.E.	6	50	6	Slide forward into depression
	G. and T.L. to position	6		6	T.E. to next cup
	Fold over tinfoil liner on second cup	28	75	28	Aid left hand to fold over tinfoil liner on second cup
	Grasp cup	5		4	T.E. and G. first cup
	Slide into position to press	9		10	Idle
	Hold while press	7	100	7	Hold while press
	T.E. to insert	4		5	Idle
	Grasp insert	22		7	T.E. to insert
			125	14	Grasp insert
	T.L. to cover	5		8	T.L. to cover
	Position insert and G. cover	7		8	Position insert and G. cover
	T.L. to cup	10	150	6	T.L. to cup
	Position	6		6	Position
	Slide out 3"-4"	4		4	Slide out 3"-4"
	PRESS COVER DOWN	3		3	PRESS COVER DOWN
	Grasp	4		4	Grasp
	Turn over and R.L.	11	175	11	Turn over and R.L.
				3	T.E. TO STAMP
	Idle	29		5	G. and T.L. stamp to cup
				13	Stamp 2 cups
			200	8	T.L. and R.L. stamp
			210		
			225		
			250		
			275		Net reduction 35%
			300		
			324		
					Last 40 frames of this operation could be eliminated by stamping from bottom at the time of pressing.

Figure 101 Modified simo chart of one operation in the process of packing Cheddar cheese in paper cups by the improved method.

156

ficient sequence in another. The simo chart shows very distinctly where delays occur in the cycle, and it aids in finding an effective way of eliminating these delays.

The next four chapters give some methods of attack that may be useful in this problem of improving the way of doing a given task.

Possibility Charts

After the suggestions for the improvement of the method have been obtained and when worthwhile changes seem feasible, a possibility chart may be constructed. This is a simultaneous-motion-cycle chart showing the proposed method. A competent analyst will be able to draw such a chart listing the necessary motions in order and indicating the time for each. Possibility charts can be made with a surprising degree of accuracy by one trained in the micromotion study technique and experienced in making them.

Modified Simo Chart

Some organizations find it satisfactory to list the motions and the motion times on the simo chart, plotting the motion time values on a graduated scale, as shown in Figs. 100 and 101. The colored therblig identifications are not used. Moreover, such charts may be prepared with a typewriter. The simo charts for one operation in the process of packing Cheddar cheese in paper cups, shown in Figs. 100 and 101, were made in this manner.

In this case the company had several branch plants packing cheese, and the charts together with films of the original method and of the improved method were sent to each plant so that the plants could benefit from this work.

14

THE USE OF FUNDAMENTAL HAND MOTIONS

Although the definition of each therblig was given in Chapter 11, further explanation is needed in certain cases. Because each motion requires, for its performance, time and energy on the part of the worker, the elimination or the better arrangement of motions constitutes part of the regular technique of work design. Information that will aid in making better use of the therbligs is included in this chapter, and a check list follows the discussion of each therblig.

Select

The time for select is frequently so short in duration that it is impossible to measure it with the camera at ordinary speeds. When this is the case, it is advisable to combine it with either the preceding or the following motion. Because select usually precedes grasp, it is good practice to combine these two. The symbols for both motions should be included on the analysis sheet, and the color for the more important or the pedominating motion should be used in making the simo chart. Usually it will be the motion other than select.

Check List for Select
1. Is the layout such as to eliminate searching for articles?
2. Can tools and materials be standardized?
3. Are parts and materials properly labeled?
4. Can better arrangements be made to facilitate or eliminate select—such as a bin with a long lip, a tray that pre-positions parts, and a transparent container?
5. Are common parts interchangeable?
6. Are parts and materials mixed?
7. Is the lighting satisfactory?
8. Can parts be pre-positioned during preceding operation?
9. Can color be used to facilitate selecting parts?

Grasp

There are two main types of grasp: (1) *pressure grasp,* as in grasping a pencil lying flat on a table top; and (2) *full-hook grasp,* as in grasping a pencil lying on a table top with one end raised an inch or so, so that the thumb and fingers are able to grasp by reaching around it (hook) instead of grasping by pinching.

An investigation[1] of grasping small pieces of wire used in making a link for a portable typewriter (page 149) showed that it required twice as long to grasp a piece using a pressure grasp as it did using a full-hook grasp. The same investigation revealed that the time for the grasp was not greatly affected by the distance through which the hand moved in either the motion preceding or the one following the grasp, other conditions being constant.

The results of a study[1] of the time required to grasp washers from a flat surface using a hook grasp and a pressure (pinch) grasp are given in Table 4. The operator merely picked up a washer from one flat surface, carried it through a distance of 5 inches, and disposed of it onto another flat surface. Circular washers ½ inch in diameter, with a ⅛-inch hole in the center, and $1/32$, ⅛, ¼, and ½ inch thick were used.

Table 4. Time Required to Grasp, Carry, and Dispose of Washers from a Flat Surface, Using a Hook Grasp and a Pressure Grasp

Thickness in Inches	1/32		1/8		1/4		1/2	
	Hook	Pressure	Hook	Pressure	Hook	Pressure	Hook	Pressure
Time in Minutes	0.01527	0.01960	0.01524	0.01590	0.01630	0.01450	0.01750	0.01428
Time in Percent (Shortest Time = 100%)	100	138	100	112	107	102	115	100

The time for grasp using the hook grasp tended to increase slightly as the washer thickness increased, whereas the time for grasp using the pressure grasp decreased markedly as the washer thickness increased. The time for grasping the thinnest washer ($1/32$ inch thick) using a pressure grasp was 38 percent greater than that for grasping the thickest washer (½ inch thick).

It is usually quicker and easier to transport small objects by sliding than by carrying. In grasping a small object such as a coin or a washer preparatory to transporting it by sliding, the grasp consists merely of touching the ball of the index finger to the

[1] Ralph M. Barnes, "An Investigation of Some Hand Motions Used in Factory Work," *University of Iowa Studies in Engineering, Bulletin* 6, p. 29. For results of other similar motion study investigations see Ralph M. Barnes and Marvin E. Mundel, "Studies of Hand Motions and Rhythm Appearing in Factory Work," *Bulletin* 12; "A Study of Hand Motions Used in Small Assembly Work," *Bulletin* 16; "A Study of Simultaneous Symmetrical Hand Motions," *Bulletin* 17; and Ralph M. Barnes, M. E. Mundel, and John M. MacKenzie, "Studies of One- and Two-Handed Work," *Bulletin* 21. 1940.

top surface of the object; whereas in grasping the same object preparatory to transporting it by carrying, the grasp consists of closing the thumb and index finger around the piece. A study [2] showed that the grasp preceding the slide required as little as $1/30$ as long as the grasp preceding the carry.

Check List for Grasp

1. Is it possible to grasp more than one object at a time?
2. Can objects be slid instead of carried?
3. Will a lip on the front of the bin simplify grasp of small parts?
4. Can tools or parts be pre-positioned for easy grasp?
5. Can a special screwdriver, socket wrench, or combination tool be used?
6. Can a vacuum, magnet, rubber finger tip, or other device be used to advantage?
7. Is the article transferred from one hand to another?
8. Does the design of the jig or fixture permit an easy grasp in removing the part?

Transport Empty and Transport Loaded

Investigations show (1) that it requires a greater period of time to move the hand through a long distance than through a short distance, other conditions being constant; (2) that the average velocity of the hand is greater for long motions than for short ones; and (3) that in such motions as transport empty and transport loaded an experienced operator moves the hand through almost identically the same path in going from one point to another in consecutive cycles of a repetitive operation. The particular study relating to this last point was made by projecting the film, one frame at a time, on a sheet of paper and marking the position of the tip of the index finger. Connecting these points by pencil lines gave the path of the motion in two dimensions. By placing the camera perpendicular to the path of motion it was possible to secure a close approach to a true record of the motion path.

A movement of the hand, such as transport empty or transport loaded, is ordinarily composed of three phases: (1) starting from a still position the hand accelerates until it reaches a maximum velocity; (2) it then proceeds at a uniform velocity; and (3) finally it slows down until it comes to a dead stop. If the hand changes direction and returns over the same path, as in making a mark back and forth across a sheet of paper, there will be an appreciable length of time at the end of the stroke during which the hand is motionless, that is, while it is changing direction. [3]

For example, in a simple hand motion 10 inches in length, one study [4] showed the distribution of these events to be as follows: 38 percent of the cycle time for acceleration, 18 percent for movement at uniform velocity, 27 percent for retardation, and 17 percent for stop and change direction (Fig. 123).

[2] *University of Iowa Studies in Engineering, Bulletin* 6, p. 32.
[3] *Ibid.*, pp. 37–51.
[4] *Ibid.*, p. 48.

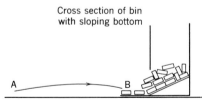

Cross section of bin
with sloping bottom

A → B

Figure 102 Straight-line motion of the hand. The hand moves from A to B to pick up a washer which rests on the lip of the bin. The cross-section of the bin shows sloping bottom which feeds washers forward.

Cross section
of tote box

C → D

Figure 103 A longer hand motion is required because the hand must reach down into box to get washer. The side of the box forms a barrier, making it necessary for the hand to change direction in going from C to D.

The time required to move the hand is affected by the nature of the motions which precede and which follow the transport. For example, when a delicate or fragile object is transported and placed carefully in a small receptacle, the time for the transport will be longer than when the transport is followed by an ordinary disposal such as tossing a bolt into a box. The manner in which an object is grasped and the way that it must be carried and positioned may also affect the time for the transport.[5]

The path of the hand in reaching for a small washer is shown in Figs. 102 and 103. The time to move the hand from A to B is less than that required to move the same distance from C to D because of the change in direction of the hand in the latter case. Barriers and obstructions that retard free hand motion or that require a change in direction should be eliminated whenever possible.

Gauging Hard-Rubber Washers

Mention has already been made of the fact that it is usually quicker and easier to transport small objects by sliding than by carrying. That a "grasp and slide" is definitely faster than a "grasp and carry" apparently results from the shorter grasp rather than from a saving in time in the transportation.

The inspection of small hard-rubber washers for thickness is another illustration of the use of a sliding transport. The purpose of this operation is to reject all washers that are too thick or too thin, as well as those having burrs on the edges. The washers have the following dimensions: outside diameter 0.280 ± 0.002 inch, inside diameter 0.188 ± 0.002 inch, and thickness 0.085 ± 0.005 inch. The gauge used for this operation (Fig. 104) was developed by W. R. Mullee while at the American Hard Rubber Company.

The metal bar A forms a "go" gauge and the bar B a "no-go" gauge with the base C, which is a heavy metal plate set at an angle with the bench top. The washers to be

[5] *University of Iowa Studies in Engineering, Bulletin* 16, p. 20.

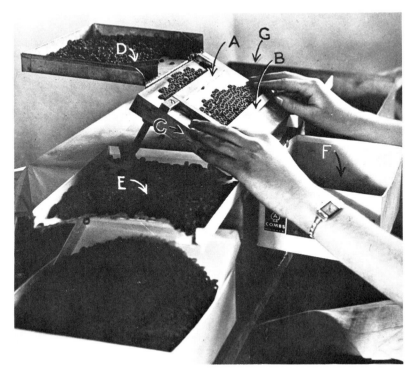

Figure 104 Special gauge for inspecting hard-rubber washers for thickness: *A*, go gauge; *B*, no-go gauge; *C*, base plate of gauge; *D*, supply of washers; *E*, rejected washers (oversize); *F*, rejected washers (undersize); *G*, good washers.

inspected are drawn from the hopper *D* by hand into the upper section of the inclined go gauge. Those washers that do not slide underneath the bar *A* are too thick and are slid in multiple to the chute *E* at the left of the gauge. The pieces that go through the gauge *A* drop down into the middle compartment. If they are too small, they slide under the gauge *B* and drop into the box *F* directly in front of the operator. Washers that are the correct size are slid off into the chute *G* at the right.

All movements of the washers in this operation are sliding transports. The washers are not picked up at any place in the cycle. They are not handled individually but are shuffled back and forth in groups across the metal plate and against the bar gauges so that gravity is able to act as the force which tends to pull them through the gauge. The height and angle at which the gauge is mounted above the bench are such as to make the task as easy and comfortable as possible. With this arrangement one operator inspects 30,000 washers per day.

Effect of Eye Movements on Transport Time

In any activity where the eyes must direct the hands, the eye movements and eye fixations often control the operation. In such work it is necessary to study the relationship of the eye movements to the hand motions.

A study[6] was made to obtain information bearing on the question "How are eye and hand movements coordinated when simultaneous symmetrical motions are performed?" A simple operation of picking up a washer in each hand and placing them, bright side up, on two vertical pins in the center of the work place (Fig. 105) was used for the investigation. Nine different operators did the job, and careful records were made of eye and hand movements by means of an eye-movement camera. Figure 106 is an eye-hand simo chart of one cycle of the operation. The results of this study showed that, in reaching for the washers in the two bins, the eyes went first to the right bin, then to the left bin, and finally to the center pins. In most cases the eyes led the hands to the bins and also to the pins. In this operation it seemed to make no difference whether the eyes were focused on the right pin or the left pin. Apparently the eyes could direct the hands equally well when focused on either pin.

Check List for Transport Empty and Transport Loaded

1. Can either of these motions be eliminated entirely?
2. Is the distance traveled the best one?
3. Are the proper means used—hand, tweezers, conveyors, etc.?
4. Are the correct members (and muscles) of the body used—fingers, forearm, shoulder, etc.?
5. Can a chute or conveyor be used?

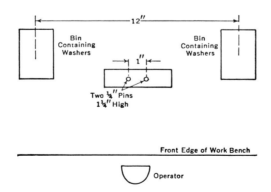

Figure 105   Layout of work place for the assembly of washers onto pins.

[6] Study made by Dr. D. U. Greenwald at the University of Iowa.

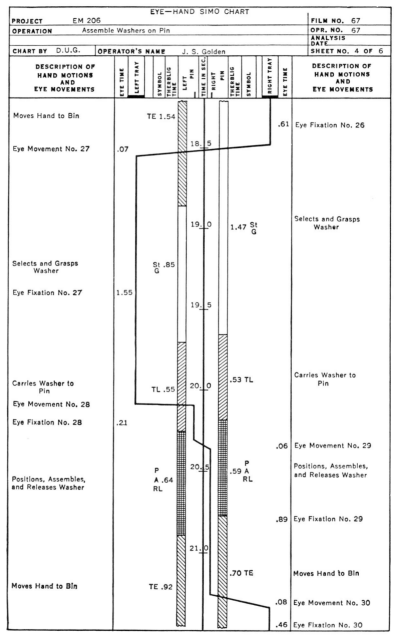

Figure 106 Eye-hand simo chart for one cycle of an assembly operation.

164

6. Can "transports" be effected more satisfactorily in larger units?
7. Can transport be performed with foot-operated devices?
8. Is transport slowed up because of a delicate position following it?
9. Can transports be eliminated by providing additional small tools and locating them near the point of use?
10. Are parts that are used most frequently located near the point of use?
11. Are proper trays or bins used, and is the operation laid out correctly?
12. Are the preceding and following operations properly related to this one?
13. Is it possible to eliminate abrupt changes in direction? Can barriers be eliminated?
14. For the weight of material moved, is the fastest member of the body used?
15. Are there any body movements that can be eliminated?
16. Can arm movements be made simultaneously, symmetrically, and in opposite directions?
17. Can the object be slid instead of carried?
18. Are the eye movements properly coordinated with the hand motions?

Hold

Hold is a therblig that frequently occurs in assembly work and in hand-manipulated machine operations. It is one of the easiest therbligs to eliminate, and disposing of it often leads to substantial increases in output. The elimination of the hold therblig in the bolt and washer assembly (page 175), for example, was largely responsible for the 50 percent increase in output.

The hand should not be used for a "vise"—a mechanical device of some kind is usually much more economical for holding. In fact, when one hand is used for holding, the operator has reduced his or her capacity for productive handwork by 50 percent. Although not every hold therblig can be eliminated, certainly all such therbligs in a cycle are vulnerable points of attack for improving the method.

Check List for Hold
1. Can a vise, clamp, clip, vacuum, hook, rack, fixture, or other mechanical device be used?
2. Can an adhesive or friction be used?
3. Can a stop be used to eliminate hold?
4. When hold cannot be eliminated, can arm rests be provided?

Release Load

Although release load is often of very short duration, it should always be included in the analysis. In the operation "Assemble Three Washers on Bolt" (page 175) the operator released the washer after having assembled it onto the bolt. This motion required such a short time that it could not be measured with the camera at ordinary speeds, and consequently this motion was combined with the preceding one, as shown in Fig. 93.

Release load should be short. If it is of long duration, some change should be made in the operation to shorten it. The discussion of drop delivery on page 210 suggests some possible changes.

Check List for Release Load

1. Can this motion be eliminated?
2. Can a drop delivery be used?
3. Can the release be made in transit?
4. Is a careful release load necessary? Can this be avoided?
5. Can an ejector (mechanical, air, gravity) be used?
6. Are the material bins of proper design?
7. At the end of the release load, is the hand or the transportation means in the most advantageous position for the next motion?
8. Can a conveyor be used?

Position and Pre-position

The difference between position and pre-position may be illustrated by the simple operation of picking up a pen, writing, and returning it to its holder.[7] The motions involved in this operation are shown in Table 5.

After the pen is carried to the paper it is necessary to *position* it, that is, to bring the pen down on the sheet of paper at the correct place on the line to begin writing. This is a *position* motion. The writing completed, the pen is returned to the holder.

Table 5. Motions Used in Writing

Steps Used in Writing	Name of Motion		Time in Thousandths of a Minute
1. Reaches for pen	Transport empty	TE	10
2. Grasps pen	Grasp	G	3
3. Carries pen to paper	Transport loaded	TL	8
4. Positions pen for writing	Position	P	3
5. Writes	Use	U	44
6. Returns pen to holder	Transport loaded	TL	9
7. Inserts pen in holder	Pre-position	PP	6
8. Lets go of pen	Release	RL	1
9. Moves hand to paper	Transport empty	TE	9

[7] This refers to the usual form of desk-set pen.

The motion *transport loaded* is followed by *pre-position* (rather than by position), because the pen rests in the holder in such a way that it can be grasped in the position in which it will be used the next time. Had the pen been placed in a horizontal pen holder on the desk top, the motion sequence would then have been *transport loaded* and *position* (rather than pre-position), because the pen would have been resting in such a way that it could not have been grasped in the correct position for using. Had the pen merely been dropped on the desk top, however, the motion sequence would have been *transport loaded* and *release load,* because no positioning or pre-positioning would have occurred.

Positioning Pins in Bushings with Beveled Holes

Beveled holes in bushings, funnel-shaped openings in fixtures, and bullet-nosed pins all tend to reduce positioning time.

The results of a study[8] of the time required to position and insert pins in bushings with beveled holes are given in Table 6. The operation consisted of grasping a quarter-inch brass pin 1¼ inches long from a magazine, carrying it through a distance of 5 inches, positioning and inserting it in the hole in the bushing, withdrawing the pin, and disposing of it in a tray on the table top. The time for the motions transport loaded, position, and assemble and disassemble was measured.

The study was conducted in two parts, one where the clearance between the pin and the hole in the bushing was 0.002 inch, and the other where the clearance was 0.010 inch.

Table 6.   Time Required to Position Pins in Bushings with Beveled Holes

	1		2		3		4		5	
	Clearance Between the Pin and the Hole in the Bushing in Inches									
	0.002	0.010	0.002	0.010	0.002	0.010	0.002	0.010	0.002	0.010
Time in Minutes	0.0047	0.0027	0.0054	0.0029	0.0048	0.0039	0.0049	0.0038	0.0081	0.0067
Time in Percent (Shortest Time = 100%)	100	100	115	107	102	144	104	141	172	248

[8] *University of Iowa Studies in Engineering, Bulletin* 12, p. 19.

Least time was required to position the pin in the bushing with the 45-degree bevel, (1) in Table 6. Seventy-two percent more time was required to position the pin in the bushing with no bevel (5) when the clearance was 0.002 inch.

Check List for Position

1. Is positioning necessary?
2. Can tolerances be increased?
3. Can square edges be eliminated?
4. Can a guide, funnel, bushing, gauge, stop, swinging bracket, locating pin, spring, drift, recess, key, pilot on screw, or chamfer be used?
5. Can arm rests be used to steady the hands and reduce the positioning time?
6. Has the object been grasped for easiest positioning?
7. Can a foot-operated collet be used?

Check List for Pre-position [9]

1. Can the object be pre-positioned in transit?
2. Can tool be balanced so as to keep handle in upright position?
3. Can a holding device be made to keep tool handle in proper position?
4. Can tools be suspended?
5. Can tools be stored in proper location to work?
6. Can a guide be used?
7. Can design of article be made so that all sides are alike?
8. Can a magazine feed be used?
9. Can a stacking device be used?
10. Can a rotating fixture be used?

Inspect

In inspection work the time for the therblig inspect is usually proportional to the reaction time of the individual and the type of the stimulus used. Only an individual with fast reaction time should be employed on inspection operations. Good eyesight is a second essential requirement for success on this kind of work.

As to the type of stimulus, the data in Table 7 show that, other conditions being equal, a person reacts more quickly to sound than to light, the time being 0.185 second for the former and 0.225 second for the latter. Reaction to touch is the quickest of all, being 0.175 second.[10]

---

[9] Pre-position is discussed on page 231.

[10] A slight difference in reaction time results from different attitudes of mind on the part of the operator. For example, if the operator's mind is concentrated primarily on the *stimulus,* the reaction times are likely to be a little slower than those indicated. However, if the operator's attention is directed primarily to the *muscular sensations* involved in reacting, the reactions will be a little faster.

Table 7. Average Speed of Reaction

(Thousandths of a second)

Type of Stimulus	Reaction Time
Simple reaction—visual stimulus. Subject was instructed to press telegraph key as quickly as possible after light flashed.	225
Simple reaction—auditory stimulus. Subject was instructed to press telegraph key as quickly as possible after electric buzzer sounded.	185
Simple reaction—touch stimulus. Subject was instructed to press telegraph key as quickly as possible after feeling bar touch hand.	175
Simple reaction—electric shock stimulus. Subject was instructed to press telegraph key as quickly as possible after receiving electric shock on hand.	140
Choice reaction—visual stimulus. Subject could react to two lights. If the right light flashed, the subject pressed the right key. If the left light flashed, the subject pressed the left key.	325
Timed action stimulus—touch stimulus. Subject is given notice of the approaching stimulus. The subject watched the operator's descending hand and was instructed to react as soon as the operator's hand touched the key.	50

Inspection of Printed Labels

The manufacturer of pharmaceutical products has the important task of making certain that the proper label is applied to the bottle or container of the products produced. For most products the bottles are filled, capped, labeled, and inserted in cartons on automatic machines. Some labels are printed in two or three different colors, and each label must be correct and complete in every respect. Because labels are printed on offset presses and there must be a separate run for each color, there is the possibility that the press may misprint a sheet and consequently produce a label that is imperfect. In order to make certain that all labels are acceptable, they are individually inspected.

To facilitate the first step in the inspection of labels, Eli Lilly and Company has small rectangular bars printed on one edge of the sheet at the time the label is printed (Fig. 107). There is a bar for each color, and the bars are located side by side on one edge of the sheet. The sheets are riffled or fanned out and placed flat on the inspection table. If all sheets are properly printed, there will be an uninterrupted line across the edges of the sheets for each color as shown in Fig. 108. If there is a blank sheet or if there is a sheet with one color printing missing, it is easy to detect this, remove the sheet, and scrap it. This procedure has not only been a great time-saver but has also made it possible to detect and remove imperfect labels at the source rather than later in the process after the labels have been cut to size.

Figure 107 Small bars are printed on the edge of the sheet at the time the label is printed. There is a bar for each color, and these bars are located side by side to facilitate inspection.

Figure 108 The printed sheets of labels are fanned out for inspection. Blank sheets or sheets with one color missing will show up as a break in the line and can be removed and scrapped.

Check List for Inspect

1. Can inspect be eliminated or overlapped with another operation?
2. Can multiple gauges or tests be used?
3. Can a pressure, vibration, hardness, or flash test be used?
4. Can the intensity of illumination be increased or the light sources rearranged to reduce the inspection time?
5. Can a machine inspection replace a visual inspection?
6. Can the operator use spectacles to advantage?

Assemble, Disassemble, and Use

The following explanation is included here to clarify the meaning of assemble and use. *Use* always refers to the use of a tool or device for the purpose for which it was intended. Thus, in Table 5 the actual writing was a use therblig. Similarly, painting, drilling, and sawing are all use therbligs. If a nut is assembled onto a bolt by hand, this motion is *assemble;* whereas if a wrench is used for this operation, the sequence is assemble (fit wrench to nut), use (turn nut down), and disassemble (remove wrench from nut).

Frequently a tool will be held in the palm of the hand when not in use. For example, the clerk checking boxes in a shipping department may place a crayon mark on certain items as they pass by on a conveyor. The use therblig would not include the entire cycle, but only that part during which the crayon is actually used for marking. The use of the bone in folding paper (Fig. 124) presents another example of this.

Some analysts advocate limiting use to ultimate objectives and restricting assemble to such temporary acts as fitting a tool to its work. Thus, any permanent assembly of two or more parts would be use even when no tool is involved. Because this interpretation is likely to result in some confusion to the beginner, and in view of the fact that the former interpretation is more widely accepted, use will, in this book, always refer to the use of a tool or device for the purpose for which it was intended; and assemble will be understood to consist of placing one object into or onto another object with which it becomes an integral part.

Painting with Spray Gun. The scope of the *use* therblig is so wide that it is impossible to cite representative cases. However, one illustration will be included because it gives an interpretation of this therblig that is often overlooked. The operation is painting the motor unit of an electric refrigerator with a spray gun.

From observation of the operation it was apparent that the operator was wasting paint, because he was missing the surface, "spraying air" by spraying past corners, and making sweeping flourishes during which little or none of the paint was being directed at the motor unit. In this operation the use motion involved not only time but material as well. Therefore, shortening the use motion meant saving both time and paint.

A micromotion study of this operation, made of a skilled operator, showed that during 23 percent of the time the spray gun was in use the paint was not hitting the surface of the unit being sprayed, but was being wasted "spraying air."

By careful training of the operator, and by some changes in the work place, including a power-driven, foot-controlled turntable for the work and three fixed spray guns mounted above the turntable, the following results were obtained:

Savings in time	50%
Reduction in rejects	60%
Direct labor savings per year	$3750.00
Savings in paint per year	$5940.00
Cost to develop and install new method	$1040.00

Not only did the total savings in direct labor and paint resulting from the improved method amount to a substantial sum, but also of importance was the great reduction in rejects.

Check List for Assemble, Disassemble, and Use

1. Can a jig or fixture be used?
2. Can an automatic device or machine be used?
3. Can the assembly be made in multiple? Or can the processing be done in multiple?
4. Can a more efficient tool be used?
5. Can stops be used?
6. Can other work be done while machine is making cut?
7. Should a power tool be used?
8. Can a cam or air-operated fixture be used?

Principles of Motion Economy

A Check Sheet for Motion Economy and Fatigue Reduction

These 22 rules or principles of motion economy may be profitably applied to many kinds of work. Although not all are applicable to every operation, they do form a basis or a code for improving the efficiency and reducing fatigue in manual work.

Use of the Human Body

1. The two hands should begin as well as complete their motions at the same time. (Page 175.)

2. The two hands should not be idle at the same time except during rest periods. (Page 175.)

3. Motions of the arms should be made in opposite and symmetrical directions, and should be made simultaneously. (Page 175.)

4. Hand and body motions should be confined to the lowest classification with which it is possible to perform the work satisfactorily. (Page 186.)

5. Momentum should be employed to assist the worker wherever possible, and it should be reduced to a minimum if it must be overcome by muscular effort. (Page 189.)

6. Smooth continuous curved motions of the hands are preferable to straight-line motions involving sudden and sharp changes in direction. (Page 190.)

7. Ballistic movements are faster, easier, and more accurate than restricted (fixation) or "controlled" movements. (Page 194.)

8. Work should be arranged to permit easy and natural rhythm wherever possible. (Page 195.)

9. Eye fixations should be as few and as close together as possible. (Page 197.)

Arrangement of the Work Place

10. There should be a definite and fixed place for all tools and materials. (Page 202.)

11. Tools, materials, and controls should be located close to the point of use. (Page 202.)

12. Gravity feed bins and containers should be used to deliver material close to the point of use. (Page 207.)

13. Drop deliveries should be used wherever possible. (Page 210.)

14. Materials and tools should be located to permit the best sequence of motions. (Page 211.)

15. Provisions should be made for adequate conditions for seeing. Good illumination is the first requirement for satisfactory visual perception. (Page 211.)

16. The height of the work place and the chair should preferably be arranged so that alternate sitting and standing at work are easily possible. (Page 219.)

17. A chair of the type and height to permit good posture should be provided for every worker. (Page 220.)

Design of Tools and Equipment

18. The hands should be relieved of all work that can be done more advantageously by a jig, a fixture, or a foot-operated device. (Page 223.)

19. Two or more tools should be combined wherever possible. (Page 228.)

20. Tools and materials should be pre-positioned whenever possible. (Page 231.)

21. Where each finger performs some specific movement, such as in typewriting, the load should be distributed in accordance with the inherent capacities of the fingers. (Page 231.)

22. Levers, hand wheels and other controls should be located in such positions that the operator can manipulate them with the least change in body position and with the greatest speed and ease. (Page 233.)

173

15

PRINCIPLES OF MOTION ECONOMY AS RELATED TO THE USE OF THE HUMAN BODY

In the general problem-solving process the search for possible solutions to the problem of designing better work methods can often be aided by considering the relationship of the worker to the job, the environment, and the organization of which the worker is a part. The person may perform work which is entirely manual or may be aided by tools, machines, and equipment. A body of knowledge commonly referred to as principles of motion economy has been in use for many years. Gilbreth listed certain "rules for motion economy and efficiency"[1] which govern hand motions, and from time to time other investigators in the field have added to the list. These principles of motion economy can be helpful in work design.

There is a second body of knowledge resulting from controlled research conducted by psychologists, sociologists, biologists, physiologists, and engineers. This general area, known as human factors or human factors engineering, will be described in Chapter 33.

It should be pointed out that in many cases the principles of motion economy have not resulted from research or scientific investigation. Rather they have been distilled from years of practice and are empirical in nature and might more accurately be called "some rules for motion economy and fatigue reduction."

In attempting to collect and codify the information which is already available as a guide in determining methods of greatest economy, one is confronted with a number of difficulties. If general principles are stated, they are likely to be abstract and of little practical use; whereas if narrower rules with specific illustrations are presented, they may lack universality of application.

It is the purpose of this and the following two chapters to state and interpret by means of specific illustrations some of the general rules or principles of motion economy which have been and are now being successfully used. Not all the principles presented in these chapters are of equal importance, nor does this discussion include all the factors that enter into the determination of better methods for doing work. These principles do, however, form a basis—a code or a body of rules —which, if applied by one trained in the technique of motion study and the problem-solving process, will make it possible to increase the output of manual labor with a minimum of fatigue.

---

[1] F. B. and L. M. Gilbreth, "A Fourth Dimension for Measuring Skill for Obtaining the One Best Way," *Society of Industrial Engineering Bulletin,* Vol. 5, No. 11, November, 1923.

These principles will be presented under the following three subdivisions:

I.   Principles of motion economy as realted to the use of the human body.
II. Principles of motion economy as related to the arrangement of the place.
III. Principles of motion economy as related to the design of tools and equipment.

PRINCIPLES OF MOTION ECONOMY AS RELATED TO THE USE OF THE HUMAN BODY

1. **The two hands should begin as well as complete their motions at the same time.**
2. **The two hands should not be idle at the same time except during rest periods.**
3. **Motions of the arms should be made in opposite and symmetrical directions and should be made simultaneously.**

These three principles are closely related and can best be considered together. It seems natural for most people to work productively with one hand while holding the object being worked on with the other hand. This is usually undesirable. The two hands should work together, each beginning a motion and completing a motion at the same time. Motions of the two hands should be simultaneous and symmetrical.

It is obvious that in many kinds of work more can be accomplished by using both hands than by using one hand. For most people it is advantageous to arrange similar work on the left- and right-hand sides of the work place, thus enabling the left and right hands to move together, each performing the same motions. The symmetrical movements of the arms tend to balance each other, reducing the shock and jar on the body and enabling the worker to perform the task with less mental and physical effort. There is apparently less body strain when the hands move symmetrically than when they make nonsymmetrical motions, because of this matter of balance.

Some examples will be cited to show how better methods were developed through the analysis of the hand motions with which you are now familiar, and through the application of the first three principles of motion economy.

Bolt and Washer Assembly

A manufacturing company uses eight bolts ⅜ inch by 1 inch, fitted with three washers each (Figs. 109 and 110), in the final assembly of one of its products. This operation was facilitated by having the three washers previously assembled onto the bolt; consequently the bolt and washers were assembled by operators at benches in another department.

Old Method

The bolt and washer assembly was originally made in the following manner. Containers with the bolts, lock washers, steel washers, and rubber washers were arranged

Figure 109   Bolt and washer assembly: *A*, special rubber washer; *B*, flat steel washer; *C*, lock washer; *D*, ⅜-inch × 1-inch bolt.

Figure 110   The hole in the rubber washer is slightly smaller than the outside diameter of the bolt so that when the bolt is forced through the hole it is gripped, thus preventing the washers from falling off the bolt.

on the top of the bench as shown in Fig. 67. The operator reached over to the container of bolts, picked up a bolt with her left hand, and brought it up to position in front of her. Then with the right hand she picked up a lock washer from the container on the bench and placed it on the bolt, then a flat steel washer, and then a rubber washer. This completed the assembly, and with the left hand the operator disposed of it in the container to her left. Figure 92 gives the analysis sheet for this operation, and Fig. 91 shows the pictures of one cycle.

It is readily seen that every one of the three principles named above was violated when the operation was performed in this way, although it is the customary method of doing such work. The left hand *held* the bolt during most of the time while the right hand worked productively. The motions of the two hands were neither simultaneous nor symmetrical.

Improved Method

A simple fixture was made of wood and surrounded by metal bins of the gravity-feed type, as shown in Figs. 111, 112, and 113. The bins containing the washers are arranged in duplicate so that both hands can move simultaneously, assembling washers for two bolts at the same time. As seen from Fig. 111, bins 1 contain the rubber washers, bins 2 the flat steel washers, bins 3 the lock washers, and bin 4, located in the center of the fixture, contains the bolts. The bottoms of the bins slope toward the front at a 30-degree angle so that the materials are fed out onto the fixture board by gravity as the parts are used in assembly.

Figure 111   Bins, fixture, and chute for bolt and washer assembly.

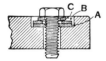

Figure 112   Enlarged view of recess in wood fixture for assembling bolt and washers: *A*, rubber washer; *B*, steel washer; *C*, lock washer.

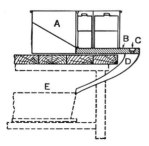

Figure 113   Cross-section of bins showing chute for drop delivery: *A*, bins with sloping bottom; *B*, top of fixture; *C*, countersunk holes in top of fixture; *D*, chute; *E*, container for finished assemblies.

Two countersunk holes or recesses were made in the front of the fixture (Fig. 112) into which the three washers fitted loosely, the rubber washer on the bottom, the flat steel washer next, and the lock washer on top. A hole slightly larger than the diameter of the bolt went through the fixture, as shown in Fig. 112. A metal chute was placed around the front of the wood fixture, with openings to the right and to the left of the two recesses so that assembled bolts and washers might be dropped into the top of this chute and carried down under the bench to a container (Fig. 113).

In assembling the bolt and washers, as the chart in Fig. 94 shows, the two hands move simultaneously toward the duplicate bins 1, grasp rubber washers which rest on the wood fixture in front of the bins, and slide the rubber washers into place in the two recesses in the fixture. The two hands then, in a similar way, slide the steel washers into place on top of the rubber washers, and then the lock washers are slid into place on top of these. Each hand then grasps a bolt and slips them through the washers which are lined up so that holes are concentric. The hole in the rubber washer is slightly smaller than the outside diameter of the threads on the bolt so that when the bolt is forced through the hole it is gripped and thus permitted, with the three washers, to be withdrawn vertically upward without losing the washers (Fig. 110). The two hands release the assemblies simultaneously over the metal chute. As the operator begins the next cycle with the hands in this position, the first and second fingers of each hand are in position to grasp the rubber washer, which is almost at the tip of the fingers.

A detailed study of the old and the improved methods of assembling the bolt and washers shows:

Average time per assembly, old method	0.084 minute
Average time per assembly, improved method	<u>0.055</u> minute
Time saved	0.029 minute

Increase in output = 53%[3]

---

[3] The results of an improved method are sometimes expressed in "increase in output in percent," and sometimes in "time saved in percent." These two percentages do not mean the same thing. Perhaps the following computations may serve to clarify this point.

Increase in Output in Percent

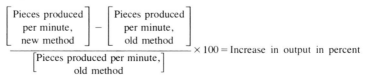

EXAMPLE

Time for assembly, old method = 0.084 minute
Number of assemblies per minute, old method = 1 ÷ 0.084 = 11.9
Time per assembly, new method = 0.055 minute

The improved method as opposed to the old method of assembling the bolt and washers conforms to each of the three principles of motion economy already mentioned. The two hands begin and end their motions at the same instant, and they move simultaneously in opposite directions. There is no idle time, and neither hand is used as a vise for holding material while the other does the work, as in the old method.

Filling Mailing Envelope with Advertising Material

This operation involved inserting four sheets of advertising material in a mailing envelope and tucking in the envelope flap. The job consisted of picking up the sheets one at a time with the right hand, transferring them to the left hand, jogging them, and then inserting them in the envelope (Fig. 114). It is obvious that the *left* hand was idle part of the time, held the sheets part of the time, and worked in an inefficient manner during the rest of the cycle. Also, the *right* hand was idle part of the time.

Improved Method

Two small triangular pieces made from cardboard and tape were fastened to flat sheets of cardboard (Fig. 115). The advertising material was stacked against the two sides of the triangular pieces, which served as fixtures, enabling the operator to pick up two sheets at a time with each hand. Rubber finger stalls facilitated the grasping. Because sheets of the particular size shown in Fig. 116 were mailed out at frequent intervals, the work place to handle this job was set up permanently. Triangular wood blocks are shown at *A*. The operation now consists of grasping two sheets of paper at a time with each hand, drawing them together, jogging them on block *B*, and inserting them in the envelope.

Number of assemblies per minute, new method $= 1 \div 0.055 = 18.2$

$\dfrac{18.2 - 11.9}{11.9} \times 100 = 53\%$ increase in output

Savings in Time in Percent

$$\frac{\left[\begin{array}{c}\text{Time per piece,} \\ \text{old method}\end{array}\right] - \left[\begin{array}{c}\text{Time per piece,} \\ \text{new method}\end{array}\right]}{[\text{Time per piece, old method}]} \times 100 = \text{Savings in time in percent}$$

EXAMPLE

Time per piece, old method $= 0.084$ minute

Time per piece, improved method $= 0.055$ minute

$\dfrac{0.084 - 0.055}{0.084} \times 100 = 35\%$ savings in time

Figure 114 Arrangement of work place—old method. Filling mailing envelope with sheets of advertising material.

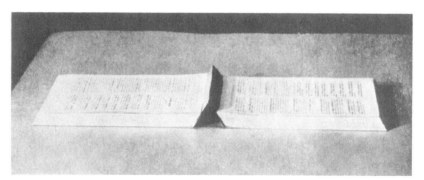

Figure 115 Temporary fixture for assembling two sheets of advertising material.

When the operator used the old method of filling envelopes, picking up the sheets one at a time, her production was 350 per hour. Using the improved work-place layout and the better method, she was able to fill 750 envelopes per hour. The new method is so much easier than the old that she has more than doubled her output.

Folding Paper Cartons

Frankfurters are usually packed in cardboard cartons for shipment to the retail store. The cartons are delivered to the packing house in flat bundles, and these flat cartons

Figure 116 Arrangement of work place—improved method. Filling mailing envelope with four sheets of advertising material. *A*, triangular blocks; *B*, block on which sheets are jogged.

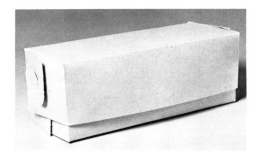

Figure 117 Carton for packing frankfurters.

must be formed and the end flaps folded over and locked together before they can be filled with frankfurters. A cover slightly larger than the bottom is placed over the filled carton bottom; telescope fashion (Fig. 117). The shape and design of the cover and bottom of the carton are alike; that is, both the cover and the bottom are folded the same way.

Old Method

The operator walked 10 feet, got bundle of 50 carton "flats," and carried them to carton-folding table. Using both hands, she grasped a group of 8 flat cartons, broke all seams or scored lines to facilitate forming, and placed flats on table with ends toward her. She then grasped sides of carton flap and simultaneously bent bottom and side flaps toward center of carton (Fig. 118). Holding left side flap in position, she inserted tongue of right flap into retaining groove of left flap. She then pushed the partly formed carton forward approximately 4 inches to nest. The above procedure was repeated until four cartons were folded at one end.

The operator took the group of partly formed cartons from position on table and turned them end for end so the unfolded ends were toward her. She then repeated the folding operation on the second end of the carton flat and placed the completely formed carton on the conveyor, to be filled with frankfurters.

Improved Method

A simple wood fixture, shown in Fig. 119, was designed by Eugene J. Smith. Bundles of flat cartons are now delivered by truck near the packing table. The operator gets a bundle of 50 flats, carries them to the table, and places them in holder *A* in Fig. 119. With her left hand she reaches to lower end of pile of carton flats, grasps end of middle flap, brings flap to position over forming fixture *B*. With her right hand she disposes of previously formed carton to conveyor. Then with her right hand she grasps middle flap on right end of carton, which is already positioned in fixture. Holding both middle end flaps, one in each hand, she bends flaps upward and pushes

Figure 118 Old method of folding cartons. Left hand holds one carton flap while right hand locks the other flap to the first.

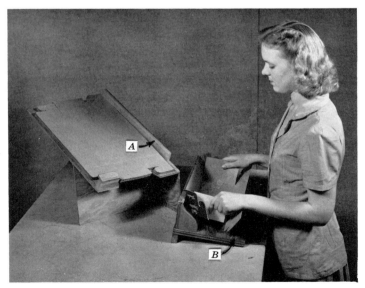

Figure 119 Improved method of folding cartons. Fixture aids in forming carton and holds it while both hands lock the flaps. Flaps on both ends of carton are assembled at the same time. Operator doubled her output.

carton into fixture. The fixture forces rear side flap up 90 degrees, folds two rear end flaps forward 90 degrees, and folds front side and end flaps up approximately 45 degrees. With both hands simultaneously, the operator then reaches to front end flaps and folds end flaps to rear and toward center of carton until ends of tongues on front flaps are inside notches of rear end flaps. While holding end flaps in position with fingers, the operator reaches with thumbs to front corners of carton, pushes front of carton to rear in order to lock tongues of front end flaps into notches of rear end flaps, and thus completes forming carton. The operator then disposes of finished carton onto conveyor.

Results. The improved method enabled the operator to double her output. The fixture was simple and inexpensive to make. The improved was superior to the old for two reasons: (1) elimination of the operation of breaking "seams" or scored lines of fold on carton flats before forming; (2) elimination of holding one flap in position with one hand while assembling the second flap with the other.

One- and Two-Handed Work

The results of a study[2] of the time to select and grasp, transport, and dispose of machine-screw nuts from two types of bins with the right hand alone, with the left hand alone, and with both hands working together are shown in Table 8.

The operation consisted of selecting and grasping machine-screw nuts (Nos. 2 and 8) from a bin, carrying them through a distance of 5 inches, and disposing of them in a hole in the table top. The study was made using a rectangular bin, and was then repeated using a bin with tray. These bins are shown in Table 10 in the next chapter. The operator worked first with the right hand alone, then with the left hand alone, and finally with both hands.

Least time was required for a total cycle when only the right hand was used. A cycle for the left hand required 6 percent more time with the rectangular bin, and 12 percent more time with the bin with tray; and a cycle with both hands required 30 to 40 percent more time. However, because two cycles were performed simultaneously when the two hands were used, the time chargeable to each cycle was considerably less than when only the right hand was used.

Under the conditions observed in this investigation and with the operators studied, there was considerable evidence to indicate that a good one-handed operator was also a good two-handed operator, and a relatively poor one-handed operator was also a relatively poor two-handed operator. This suggests that the introduction of two-handed simultaneous work in place of less efficient one-handed work will not inconvenience any one operator very much more than another operator.

[2] *University of Iowa Studies in Engineering, Bulletin* 21.

Table 8. Study of One- and Two-Handed Work

		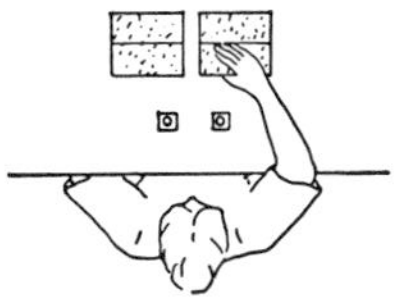 Right Hand Working Alone		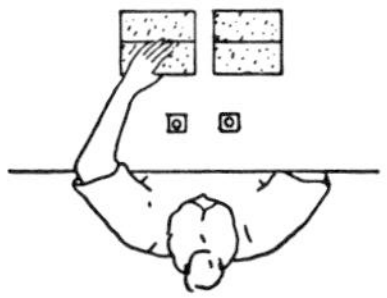 Left Hand Working Alone		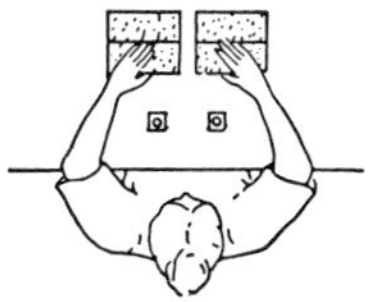 Both Hands Working Together	
		Rectangular Bin	Bin with Tray	Rectangular Bin	Bin with Tray	Rectangular Bin	Bin with Tray
SELECT AND GRASP Nut from Bin at A (see figure above).	Time in Minutes	0.00723	0.00438	0.00822	0.00520	0.01307	0.00674
	Time in Percent (Shortest Time = 100%)	100	100	114	118	181	154
TRANSPORT LOADED Carry nut through distance of 5 inches —from A to A.	Time in Minutes	0.00292	0.00235	0.00347	0.00234	0.00380	0.00270
	Time in Percent (Shortest Time = 100%)	100	100	119	100	130	115
RELEASE LOAD Drop nut into 1-inch hole in table top at B.	Time in Minutes	0.00403	0.00403	0.00380	0.00453	0.00463	0.00500
	Time in Percent (Shortest Time = 100%)	106	100	100	112	122	124
TRANSPORT EMPTY Move hand to bin at A for nut.	Time in Minutes	0.00314	0.00277	0.00282	0.00304	0.00308	0.00337
	Time in Percent (Shortest Time = 100%)	111	100	100	110	110	122
TOTAL CYCLE	Time in Minutes	0.01730	0.01351	0.01832	0.01510	0.02459	0.01778
	Time in Percent (Shortest Time = 100%)	100	100	106	112	142	131

4. Hand and body motions should be confined to the lowest classification with which it is possible to perform the work satisfactorily.

The five general classes of hand motions are listed here because they emphasize that material and tools should be located as close as possible to the point of use, and that motions of the hands should be as short as the work permits. The lowest classification, which is shown first, usually requires the least amount of time and effort.

General Classification of Hand Motions

1. Finger motions
2. Motions involving fingers and wrist.
3. Motions involving fingers, wrist, and forearm.
4. Motions involving fingers, wrist, forearem, and upper arm.
5. Motions involving fingers, wrist, forearm, upper arm, and shoulder. This class necessitates disturbance of the posture.

The operator shown in Fig. 120 is manually operating a swing saw for rough-cutting lumber to length in a furniture factory. A better method was devised (Fig. 121), and the operator now operates the saw by means of a motor control switch with his right hand while feeding the stock with his left hand. A guard directly in front of the

Figure 120   Manual method of operating swing saw in furniture factory—old method.

Figure 121   Swing saw is now operated by a control button at the operator's right hand —improved method.

saw protects the operator. In addition to this saving of time and effort on the part of the operator, belt conveyors were installed which carry the lumber to the off-bearer and the scrap directly to the incinerator. Originally each operator needed a helper; now one helper serves three operators.[3]

As desirable as it may be to keep hand motions as short as possible, it is incorrect to assume that finger motions are less fatiguing than motions of the forearm.

In one investigation it was found that finger motions were more fatiguing, less accurate, and slower than motions of the forearm. All evidence seems to show that the forearm is the most desirable member to use for light work, and that in highly repetitive work, motions about the wrist and elbow are superior to those of the fingers or shoulders.

Physiological Cost of Body Bending

Body movements are time-consuming and result in high physiological costs as well. We made a systematic study of an operation consisting of picking up 5-pound bricks under various conditions.[4] Change in energy expenditure and change in heart rate were measured, and the results pertaining to a party of the study are shown in Table 9

[3] Martin S. Meyers, "Evaluation of the Industrial Engineering Program in Small Plant Management," *Proceedings Sixth Industrial Engineering Institute,* University of California, Los Angeles-Berkeley, p. 37.
[4] Study made by Ralph M. Barnes, Robert B. Andrews, James I. Williams, and B. J. Hamilton.

Table 9. Physiological Costs of Two Different Methods of Handling Brick

Operator	Method A Major Body Bending							
	Energy Expenditure in Calories per Minute				Heart Rate in Beats per Minute			
	Number of Bricks Moved per Minute				Number of Bricks Moved per Minute			
	16	22	28	34	16	22	28	34
1	5.4	5.7	6.8	8.5	102	104	109	131
2	5.4	6.8	7.9	10.2	110	126	134	155
3	5.3	6.8	8.5	11.7	102	113	126	159
Average	5.4	6.4	7.7	10.1	105	114	123	148
	Method B Minor Body Movements							
1	2.8	3.1	3.3	5.8	92	92	92	113
2	2.3	2.6	3.3	3.8	100	97	107	109
3	2.5	2.7	3.0	3.8	90	97	97	95
Average	2.5	2.8	3.2	4.5	94	95	99	106

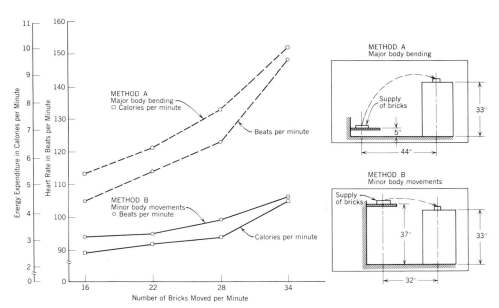

Figure 122 Physiological cost of two different methods of handling brick. Method A, major body bending; Method B, minor body bending.

188

and Fig. 122. In Method A, the operator picked up the brick from a platform 5 inches above the floor and placed it on a bench 33 inches high; this involved major body bending. In Method B the bricks were moved from a platform 37 inches high to a bench 33 inches high, which called for minor body movements. The operators worked at four different speeds. At the slowest speed, there was an increase in heart rate from 94 beats per minute to 105, and at the highest speed an increase from 106 to 148 beats per minute. Similarly, the energy expenditure increased from 2.5 calories (abbreviation for kilocalories) per minute to 5.4 at the low speed and from 4.5 to 10.1 at the high speed. These data give a quantitative evaluation of the physiological cost of work involving extreme body bending.

5. Momentum should be employed to assist the worker wherever possible, and it should be reduced to a minimum if it must be overcome by muscular effort.

The momentum of an object is its mass multiplied by its velocity. In most kinds of factory work the total weight moved by the operator may consist of three components: the weight of the material moved, the weight of the tools or devices moved, and the weight of the part of the body moved. It is often possible to employ momentum of the hand, the material, or the tool to do useful work. When a forcible stroke is required, the motions of the worker should be so arranged that the stroke is delivered when it reaches its greatest momentum. In laying a brick wall, for example, "If the bricks are conveyed from the stock platform to the wall with no stops, the mementum can be made to do valuable work by assisting to shove the joints full of mortar. If, instead of being utilized, the momentum must be overcome by the muscles of the bricklayer, fatigue . . . will result.

"The ideal case is to move the brick in a straight path and make the contact with the wall overcome the momentum."[5]

The improved method of candy dipping explained on page 193 is another illustration of the utilization of momentum for the performance of useful work. The piece to be dipped was submerged under the surface of the melted sugar by the right hand at the end of a long return stroke of the hand. The momentum developed in this movement of the hand and the empty dipping fork was employed in doing useful work instead of being dissipated by the muscles of the dipper's arm.

There are many times when momentum has no productive value, and its presence is undesirable in that the muscles must always counteract the momentum developed. When such is the case, the three classes of weight named previously should be studied for the purpose of reducing each to the minimum. In addition, the velocity of the motions should be kept low by using the shortest motions possible. A number of tools are most effective when they are made as light in weight as possible. Such tools do not depend upon momentum or the use of a blow to function properly. For many

[5] F. B. Gilbreth, *Motion Study*, Van Nostrand Co., Princeton, N.J., 1911, p. 78.

kinds of work a heavy shovel or a heavy trowel is more fatiguing to use than a light one of the same dimensions and rigidity.

Many additional considerations enter into the determination of the proper size and weight of materials and tools to produce maximum efficiency. Unfortunately, the accumulated data are of little value here. Each case, as a rule, is surrounded by circumstances and conditions peculiar to itself. Consequently each problem must be the subject for special investigation.

6.   Smooth continuous curved motions of the hands are preferable to straight-line motions involving sudden and sharp changes in direction.

The simple operation of moving a pencil back and forth across a sheet of paper consists of two phases, the movement and the stop and change direction. The results

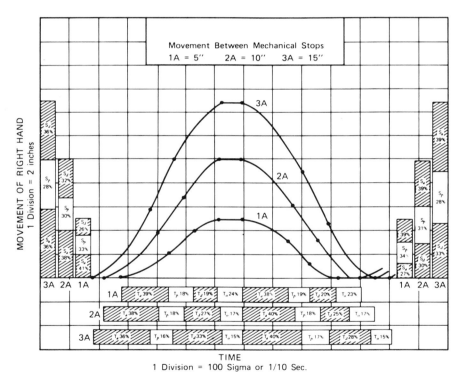

Figure 123 Curves showing movement of right hand through varying distances between mechanical stops. Results of 15″ hand motion away from the body are shown at the bottom of the figure. (3A) T_a 36% acceleration of the hand; T_p 16% movement at uniform velocity; T_d 33% deceleration; T_o 15% stop and change direction.

of a study[6] of the simple hand motions *transport loaded* (away from the body), *stop and change direction,* and *transport loaded* (toward the body) are given in Fig. 123. This figure shows that 75 to 85 percent of the time to make a complete back and forth movement is used in actually moving the hand, and the remaining 15 to 25 percent of the time in changing direction of the hand; that is, during 15 to 25 percent of the time the hand and the pencil are motionless. Further studies show that continuous curved motions are preferable to straight-line motions involving sudden and sharp changes in direction. Such abrupt changes in direction are both time consuming and fatiguing to the operator. In many jobs in the shop and office it is possible to use these smooth curved motions. Some examples will be given here.

Folding Paper

The first illustration is folding rectangular sheets of paper used in packing X-ray films. The sheets vary in size from 3 inches by 5 inches to 12 inches by 15 inches folded. Although several million of these sheets of paper are folded per year, it was found to be more economical to fold them by hand than by machine because of the many different sizes used.

Old Method

The worker, holding a smooth piece of bone in the palm of her right hand (Fig. 124), grasped the lower right-hand corner *A* of the sheet of paper to be folded. She folded this end of the sheet over to point *B,* where the two hands matched or lined up the two corners of the sheet of paper. Then, swinging the right hand away from the body and using the bone as a creasing tool, she struck the folded sheet of paper about midpoint at *C,* creasing the fold from *C* to *D.* At *D* she stopped, changed direction abruptly, and doubled back, creasing the entire length of the fold from *D* to *E.* At *E* the hand again changed direction and swung around to *F,* where the end of the bone was inserted under the edge of the creased sheet to assist the left hand in disposing of it on the pile of folded sheets at *G.*

Improved Method

In the improved method (Fig. 125) the worker grasps the lower right-hand corner *A* of the sheet of paper to be folded. She folds this end of the sheet over to point *B,* where the two hands match or line up the two corners of the sheet of paper. She then moves the right hand through a smooth S curve, the bone striking the paper and beginning to crease at *X* and ending at *Y.* The entire crease is completed with the single stroke of the bone. The hand then swings around in a curved motion from *Y* to

---

[6] Investigation by J. Wayne Deegan, *University of Iowa Studies in Engineering, Bulletin* 6, pp. 37–51. Also see results of study by A. B Cummins, *University of Iowa Studies in Engineering, Bulletin* 12, pp. 8–18.

Figure 124 Path of hand in creasing folded sheet of paper—old method. There is an abrupt change in direction at D and also at E. Two strokes of the bone are used to crease the fold.

Figure 125 Path of hand in creasing folded sheet of paper—improved method. The hand makes a smooth S curve, creasing the fold with one stroke of the bone. Output was increased 43%.

Z, where, as in the old method, the end of the bone is inserted under the creased sheet to assist the left hand in disposing of it on the pile of folded sheets at G.

Results. Using the improved method only one creasing motion was required to complete the cycle instead of the two (one short and one long one) in the old method. Moreover, in the improved method two curved motions of the hand were used instead of two complete change directions and one 90-degree change direction.

A micromotion study of these two methods shows that 0.009 minute was required to crease the fold by the old method and 0.005 minute by the improved method. The improved method of creasing the fold, plus some other changes in the cycle, reduced the total time from 0.058 to 0.033 minute per cycle, enabling the operator to increase her output 43 percent.

Dipping Candy

Another illustration of the value of curved motions over straight-line motions with sudden changes in direction is a candy-dipping operation.[7]

Old Method

The dipping process was carried out in the following manner. A "center" (an almond, walnut, Brazil nut, or caramel) was placed in a pot of melted sugar by using the left hand, and was covered with melted sugar by working it with a fork held in the right hand. The finished piece of candy was then placed on the tray to the right of the operator. Approximately 2 seconds were required to dip each piece.

While the left hand was placing a center in the container of melted sugar, the right hand carried the empty fork from the tray to the container, and took up some of the thick melted sugar and pulled it over the center. Then the hand moved to the left side of the container, the center being carried along with the end of the fork under it. The center was picked up and carried to the tray where it was deposited. The objections to this method of dipping were that the hand stopped and changed direction sharply, and then the direction was almost reversed. This stopping and sudden changing of direction placed unnecessary strain on the muscles of the arm.

Improved Method

Using the improved method the center is dipped by a smooth sweeping motion of the hand instead of by a number of short zigzagging motions as in the old method. In the improved method the hand, after disposing of the finished piece of candy on the tray, moves to the pot as before, but reaches the melted sugar in the middle of an inward and downward curve with the hand in its strongest position for doing work. This

[7] E. Farmer, "Time and Motion Study," Industrial Fatigue Research Board, *Report* 14, pp. 36–41.

makes it possible to utilize the momentum developed in the movement in doing the most fatiguing part of the work, the dipping being the part of the process that offers the greatest resistance to the hand. In the old process this dipping motion was made by a short backward movement just after the hand had stopped and changed its direction. Furthermore, the momentum developed during the motion was wasted in the old method, because the hand motion was checked in order to change its direction. In the new method the hand takes easy smooth movements with all changes in direction effected by curves.

Results. The improved method was taught to a group of workers in the factory, and after a short period of training an average increase in production of 27 percent resulted. However, because many workers had used the old method for years, it was difficult to persuade some of them to give the new method a fair trial. A new dipping room equipped with new-style tables and trays was opened, and new operators were trained in the proper method of dipping. After 3 months' work in this new room, these new workers were producing an average of 88 percent more than the workers in the original room.

7. Ballistic movements are faster, easier, and more accurate than restricted (fixation) or "controlled" movements.

Voluntary movements of the members of the human body may be divided into two general classes or groups. In the *fixation* or controlled movements, opposing groups of muscles are contracted, one group against the other. For example, in bringing the pencil down to the paper preparatory to writing, two or more sets of muscles are in action. The positive sets of muscles propel the hand, and the antagonistic sets oppose the movement. When the two sets of muscles act in an uneven or unbalanced manner, motion of the hand results. When the two sets of muscles exactly balance each other, the hand remains in a fixed position, although it is ready to act in any direction at any instant. The finger-and-thumb method of writing is an excellent illustration of fixation movements.

The *ballistic* movement is a fast, easy motion caused by a single contraction of a positive muscle group with no antagonistic muscle group contracting to oppose it. The contraction of the muscles throws the member of the body into motion, and because these muscles act only through the first part of the movement, the member sweeps through the remainder of the movement with its muscles relaxed. The ballistic movement is controlled by the initial impulse, and once under way its course cannot be changed.[8] A ballistic stroke may terminate (1) by the contraction of the opposing muscles, (2) by an obstacle, or (3) by dissipation of the momentum of the movement, as in swinging a golf club.

The ballistic movement is preferable to the fixation movement and should be used

---

[8] L. D. Hartson, "Analysis of Skilled Movements," *Personnel Journal,* Vol. 11, No. 1, pp. 28–43.

whenever possible. It is less fatiguing, for the muscles contract only at the beginning of the movement and are relaxed during the remainder of the movement. The ballistic movement is more powerful, faster, more accurate, and less likely to cause muscle cramp. It is smoother than the fixation movement, which is caused by the contraction of two sets of muscles, one acting against the other continuously. The skilled carpenter swinging a hammer in driving a nail illustrates a ballistic movement. The carpenter aims his hammer, then throws or swings it. The muscles are contracted only during the first part of the movement; they idle along the rest of the way. The swinging curves of an orchestra conductor's baton are another illustration of ballistic movement.

It is not difficult to develop the free, loose, easy movements of the wrist and forearm. The hand should move about the wrist for the shorter motions, and the forearm about the elbow for the longer motions. Experiments show that wrist and elbow movements are faster than finger or shoulder movements.

8.   Work should be arranged to permit an easy and natural rhythm wherever possible.

Rhythm is essential to the smooth and automatic performance of an operation. Rhythm may be interpreted in two different ways. Perhaps it is most frequently understood to mean the speed or the rapidity with which repeated motions are made. Reference is commonly made to the thythm of walking or breathing. The operator feeding material into a machine is said to work with a rhythm depending upon the speed of the machine. Rhythm, then, in this sense, refers to the regular repetition of a certain cycle of motions by an individual.

Rhythm may be interpreted in a second way:

A movement may be perfectly regular, uniform, and recurrent and yet not give the impression of rhythm. If one moves the hand or the arm in a circle, the hand may be made to pass a point in a circle much oftener per second than the tempo of the slower rhythms requires, and yet there will be no feeling of rhythm *so long as the hand moves uniformly and in a circle*. In order to become rhythmic in the psychological sense, the following change in the movement is necessary. The path of the hand must be elongated to an ellipse; the velocity of the movement in a part of the orbit must be much faster than in the rest of the orbit; just as the hand comes to the end of the arc through which it passes with increased velocity, there is a feeling of tension, of muscular strain; at this point the movement is retarded, almost stopped; then the hand goes on more slowly until it reaches the arc of increased velocity. The rapid movement through the arc of velocity and the sudden feeling of strain and retarding at the end of this rapid movement constitute the beat. In consciousness they represent one event, and a series of such events connected in such a movement cycle may be said provisionally to constitute a rhythm. Every rhythmic beat is a *blow*. . . . In all forms of activity where a rhythm is required, the stroke, the blow, the impact, is the thing; all the rest is but connection and preparation.[9]

[9] R. H. Stetson, "A Motor Theory of Rhythm and Discrete Succession," *Psychology Review,* Vol. 12, No. 4, p. 258.

Rhythm, either in the sense of a regular sequence of uniform motions, or in the sense of a regular sequence of accented motions, is of value to the worker. Uniformity, ease, and even speed of work are promoted by the proper arrangement of the work place, tools, and materials. The proper sequence of motions enables the worker to estabish a rhythm which assists in making the operation practically an automatic performance—the operator does the work with little or no mental effort.

In many kinds of work there is an opportunity for the operator to accent certain points in a cycle of motions. For example, every punch-press operator, feeding the press by hand, tends to feed the sheet of material forward with a sudden thrust which constitutes an accented point in the cycle. Where the work permits, it is most natural for the worker to fall into a rhythm in this second sense.

Individual Rhythm

Some have suggested that each individual has a "natural" rhythm or speed of movement that permits him or her to work with least effort. Some have urged that individuals be permitted to work at this natural speed and that no outside force, such as a wage incentive, should be exerted to cause the individual to work faster than his or her natural rhythm. Because it seems difficult to determine what the natural rhythm is for any person and because most workers can be taught to change their rhythm in performing the same work (to work at different speeds or use different sets of motions), it seems that too much emphasis should not be placed on this so-called natural rhythm. Habit acts in a powerful way to affect the speed and the sequence of motions which a worker uses in performing a task. Once the habit is formed, it *does* require real effort on the part of the worker to change or modify this habit.

To illustrate this point, a typewriter company had several polishers of long experience who had for several years been polishing a particular part of the typewriter. These polishers had been accustomed to take a definite number of strokes across the polishing wheel, and they knew the finish that the piece should have to pass inspection. In a new design of the typewriter this particular piece was located in a more obscure position than formerly and did not need such a high polish. The polishers were told just how the piece was to be polished for the new typewriter, and they were carefully instructed as to the finish that would now be required to pass inspection. The operators, however, found it difficult to change their habits. They "forgot" to take fewer strokes; as a result they were turning out work that was of higher quality than needed and their output was lower than it should have been. With constant and persistent attention, after 4 days these polishers were able to produce parts having just the finish desired and at a proportionately faster speed in pieces per hour.

Nearly every worker finds that a conscious effort and some persistence are required to do a new task or to perform an old one in a new way. For most people, change is by no means impossible and usually can be readily made. There are cases where a certain sequence of motions has been made by a person for such a long period of time that it is unwise to try to change it. This can, perhaps, also be said about the speed at which some people work.

9.   Eye fixations should be as few and as close together as possible.

Eye Movements

Although some kinds of work can be performed with little or no eye direction, where visual perception is required it is desirable to arrange the task so that the eyes can direct the work effectively; that is, the work place should be so laid out that the eye fixations are as few and as close together as possible.

Figure 126 shows head, eye, and hand motions of the operator performing a simple assembly operation. Small steel washers enameled green on one side and black on the other were to be assembled with green side up in the fixture directly in front of the operator. Duplicate bins containing the washers were located on each side of the fixture. As the figure shows, it was necessary for the operator to look first to the right and then to the left before grasping the washers. The first strip of film in Fig. 126 shows the operator looking to her right preparatory to grasping a washer from the bin at her right. The second and third strips of film show her looking to her left and grasping a washer from the bin at her left. The fourth strip of film shows the two hands moving simultaneously, carrying washers to the fixture. The 36 consecutive frames of film were made at 1000 exposures per minute.

The distance that the eyes and the hands have to move and the nature of the operation will determine whether the hands must wait for the eyes, thus increasing the time to perform the task. In this case, had the containers been placed directly in front of the operator, the head movements would have been eliminated entirely and the eye movements would have been greatly reduced.

Eye-Hand Coordination

In a study [10] of the effect of practice on individual motions of a punch-press operation, one of the observations involved eye movements.

The operation was the forming of a relay contact bar. The fixture and work-place arrangements show in Figs. 127 and 128 were designed to duplicate the mechanical movements and hand motions of the actual factory operation.

The eye movements and the hand motions of the beginner (Figs. 127 and 128-I) are as follows.

As the tweezers start to open when releasing the part in the die, the eyes shift to the part in the left hand to direct the tweezer grasping of the next part. The first fixation of the eyes occurs at A in Fig. 127-I.

[10] Ralph M. Barnes, James S. Perkins, and J. M. Juran, "A Study of the Effect of Practice on the Elements of a Factory Operation," *University of Iowa Studies in Engineering, Bulletin 22.*

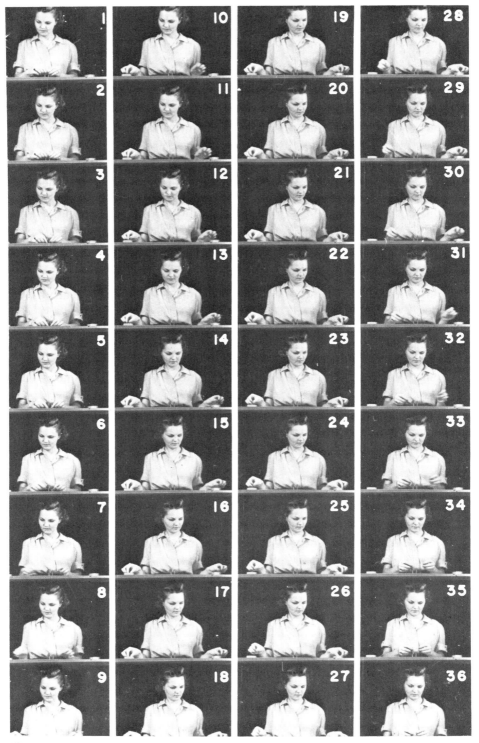

Figure 126 Print of motion picture film showing eye and hand motions of the operator assembling small parts.

I. As the tweezers start to open when releasing the part in the die, the eyes shift to the part in the left hand to direct the tweezer–grasping of the next part. First fixation at A.

II. Before the right hand releases the part in the tweezers, the eyes shift to the supply tray to select the next part. Second fixation at B.

III. After the left hand is sufficiently well directed towards the part on the supply tray, the eyes shift to the die to direct the right hand in locating the part over the pilot pins. Third fixation at C.

IV. The eyes remain fixed on the die until the part is properly located. The part is ejected by a foot pedal as the right reaches for the next part.

Figure 127 Punch-press operation, showing eye fixations and hand motions of a beginner. Three fixations were used per cycle.

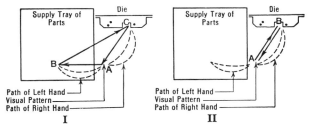

Figure 128 Punch-press operation. Schematic drawings, showing eye fixations and hand motions. I, three eye fixations; II, two eye fixations.

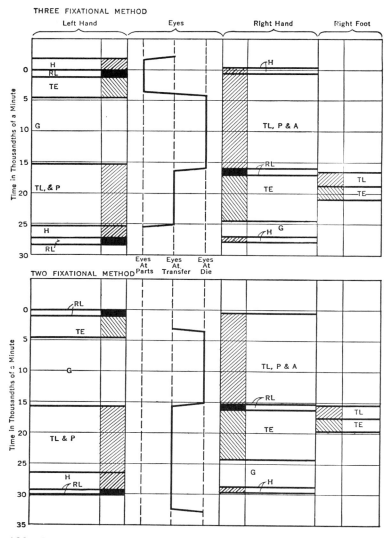

Figure 129 Eye-hand simo chart of punch-press operation, showing the three-fixation method and the two-fixation method.

Before the right hand releases the part into the tweezers, the eyes shift to the supply tray to select the next part. The second fixation occurs at B in Fig. 127-II.

If the left hand is sufficiently well directed toward the part on the supply tray, the eyes shift to the die to direct the right hand in locating the part over the pilot pins. The third fixation occurs at C in Fig. 127-III.

The eyes remain fixed on the die until the part is properly located. The part is ejected by a foot pedal as the right hand reaches for the next part.

After 10,000 cycles of practice, however, 56 percent of the cycles had three fixations and the remaining 44 percent had two fixations. At first the cycle time averaged 0.0584 minute; after 10,000 cycles of practice the average time was 0.0258 minute. When only two fixations occurred, the hand movements were the same but the eyes did not fixate on the supply of parts. The eyes would fixate on the part as it was transferred from the left hand to the right hand at A in Fig. 128-II, and then would move to the fixture to direct in locating the part over the pilot pins at B in Fig. 128-II. Although at first it was necessary to look at the parts in the tray to facilitate the grasping, after practicing a less-defined picture was required (Fig. 129). It is believed that attention was directed to the parts and to the hand in grasping them, but that it was not essential for the eyes to see the parts so clearly.

It seems that the better coordination resulting from practice not only enabled the operator to perform each of the motions in less time (although they were not all affected in the same way with practice) but also reduced the number of fixations required.

16

PRINCIPLES OF MOTION ECONOMY AS RELATED TO THE WORK PLACE

10. There should be a definite and fixed place for all tools and materials.

The operator should always be able to find the tools and materials in the same location. Similarly, finished parts and assembled units should be disposed of in fixed places. For example, in the assembly of the bolt and washers, the hand should move without mental direction to the bin containing the rubber washers, then to the bin containing the steel washers, then to the lock washers, and finally to the bolts. (Fig. 111). It should be unnecessary for the operator to have to think where the materials are located.

Definite stations for materials and tools aid the worker in habit formation, permitting the rapid development of automaticity. It cannot be emphasized too strongly that it is greatly to the worker's advantage to be able to perform the operation with the least conscious mental direction. Frequently, materials and tools are scattered over the work place in such a disorderly fashion that the operator must not only exert mental effort, but must also hunt around in order to locate the part or tool needed at a given instant. The workers are very much in favor of having stations for materials and tools, because this reduces fatigue and saves time.

When the eyes must direct the hand in reaching for an object, the eyes ordinarily precede the hand. However, if materials or tools are located in a definite place and if they are always grasped from the same place, the hand automatically finds the right location and in many cases the eyes may be kept fixed on the point where the tools or materials are used.

11. Tools, materials, and controls should be located close to the point of use.

Very frequently the work place, such as a bench, machine, desk, or table, is laid out with tools and materials in straight lines. This is incorrect, for a person naturally works in areas bounded by lines which are arcs of circles.

Normal Working Area

Considering the horizontal plane, there is a very definite and limited area which the worker can use with a normal expenditure of effort. There is a normal working area for the right hand and for the left hand, working separately, and for both hands working together (Figs. 130 and 131). The normal working area for the right hand is determined by an arc drawn with a sweep of the right hand across the table. The forearm only is extended, and the upper arm hangs at the side of the body in a natural

Figure 130   Normal and maximum working areas in the horizontal plane.

position until it tends to swing away as the hand moves toward the outer part of the work place. The normal working area for the left hand is determined in a similar manner. The normal arcs drawn with the right and left hands will cross each other at a point in front of the worker. The overlapping area constitutes a zone in which two-handed work may be done most conveniently.

Maximum Working Area

There is a maximum working area for the right hand and for the left hand, working separately, and for both hands working together (Figs. 130 and 131). The maximum working area for the right hand is determined by an arc drawn with a sweep of the right hand across the table, with the arm pivoted at the right shoulder. The maximum working area for the left hand is determined in a similar manner by an arc drawn with a sweep of the left hand. The overlapping area formed by these two maximum arcs

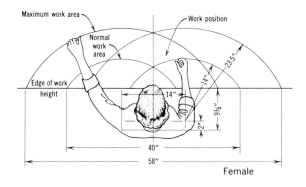

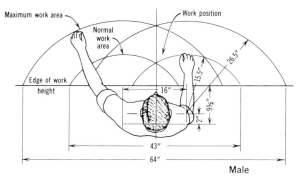

Figure 131 Dimensions of normal and maximum working areas in the horizontal plane as developed and used by the Process Development Section of the General Motors Manufacturing Staff. (From Richard R. Farley, "Some Principles of Methods and Motion Study as Used in Development Work," *General Motors Engineering Journal,* Vol. 2, No. 6, pp. 20–25.)

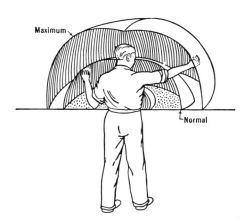

Figure 132 Normal and maximum working space in three dimensions.

constitutes a zone beyond which two-handed work cannot be performed without causing considerable disturbance of posture, accompanied by excessive fatigue.

Each hand has its normal working space in the vertical plane as well as in the horizontal plane, in which work may be done with the least time and effort (Fig. 132). A maximum work space in the vertical plane may also be determined, beyond which work cannot be performed without disturbing the posture. In locating materials or tools above the work place, consideration should be given to these facts.

Figures 133 and 134 emphasize the importance of arranging the material *around* the work place and as close in as possible. In Fig. 133 the five bins containing materials are outside the maximum working area, necessitating bending the body to reach them. In Fig. 134 the bins have been located within the normal working area, permitting a third-class motion which requires no movement of the body. The use of a duplicate fixture and duplicate bins arranged symmetrically on each side of the fixture permits the two hands to make simultaneous motions in opposite directions in performing the operation. Such an arrangement facilitates natural, easy, rhythmical movements of the arms.

Those tools and parts that must be handled several times during an operation should be located closer to the fixture or working position than tools or parts that are handled but once. For example, if an operation consists of assembling a number of screws into a metal switch plate, the containers for the screws should be placed closer to the fixture than the containers for the plates. This is done because only one plate must be transported from the container to the fixture per cycle, whereas several screws have to be transported from their containers to the fixture.

In considering this point it is equally important to remember that the parts must be arranged in such a way as to permit the shortest eye movements, the fewest eye fixa-

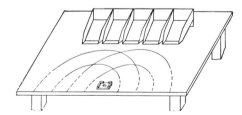

Figure 133 Incorrect work-place layout. Bins are located too far from the assembly fixture. The operator must bend forward to get the parts from bins.

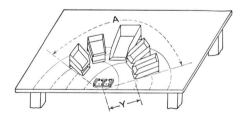

Figure 134 Correct work-place layout. Bins are located close to the fixture. In many kinds of work the eyes must direct the hands. In such cases the work area should be located directly in front of the operator so that eye fixations will be as few and as close together as possible. Angle *A* should be as small as possible, and distance *Y* should be as short as the nature of the work will permit.

tions, and the best sequence of motions, and to aid the operator in rapidly developing automatic and rhythmical movements.

Results of Moving Parts Closer to Fixture

The production of one model of a radio requires the assembly of 260 separate parts or subassemblies. Two hand movements are required to pick up each part from the supply bin and process or assemble it—one movement of the hand to the bin and one from the bin. By shortening the distance 6 inches for reaching each of these parts, there is a saving time of 34,000 hours per year.

Number of parts moved	260
Movements (motion of hand to and from bin)	2
Average saving in time to move hand 6 inches	
shorter distance, minute	0.002

or

$$260 \times \frac{2 \times 0.002}{60} = 0.017 \text{ hour per radio set}$$

This saving of 0.017 hour or 62 seconds per radio set per day is extremely small. However, because this company makes 8000 sets per day, the savings per day are

$$8000 \times 0.017 = 136 \text{ hours per day}$$

Consider this production to run 250 working days per year:

$$250 \text{ days} \times 136 \text{ hours per day} = 34,000 \text{ hours saved per year}$$

Another way to look at this is in total distance saved. If 6 inches is saved in the movement of the hand to the bin and another 6 inches from the bin, the total savings are 12 inches, or 1 foot per piece.

$$260 \text{ pieces} \times 1 \text{ foot} = 260 \text{ feet saved per set}$$

8000 sets × 260 feet per set = 2,080,000 feet or 394 miles saved per day. 250 working days × 394 miles per day = 98,500 miles saved per year.[1]

Arrangement of Machines

The following statement might be considered as a corollary to rule 11: *In the continuous type of manufacturing, machines, process apparatus, and equipment should be arranged so as to require the least movement on the part of the operator.*

When one worker operates several machines and when they are located in line

---

[1] This case developed for use in RCA training course by G. A. Godwin while industrial engineer for RCA.

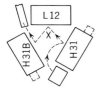

Figure 135 Machines arranged in groups. Machine time and handling time are so balanced that one operator can keep the three machines running.

along an aisle, considerable walking between machines is required. If a conveyor is used to bring parts to be machined and to take away finished parts, walking and handling time is reduced. A still better arrangement is to have those machines that can be operated by one person located close together in a group so the operator can load and unload each of the machines with little or no travel (Fig. 135).

12. Gravity feed bins and containers should be used to deliver material close to the point of use.

A bin with sloping bottom permits the material to be fed to the front by gravity and so relieves the operator of having to dip down into the container to grasp parts (Figs. 111 and 113). However, it is not always possible to slide material into position as in the bolt and washer assembly. More frequently bins such as those shown in Fig. 136 are used. Where many different parts are required, it becomes necessary to nest the bins one above the other in order to have the material within convenient reach of the operator.

Bins of standard sizes, such as those shown in Fig. 136, are standard equipment in many plants. The bins are interchangeable and are made in three heights and three

Figure 136 Standard bins of the gravity-feed type.

widths. By the use of these standard-unit bins, any combination can be made to suit a particular job. It is difficult to give a general rule as to the proper size of bins for a particular operation. Some companies try to have their bins large enough to hold material for 4 hours' work, which probably is an economical size for many kinds of material.

Figure 137 shows standard work-place equipment used by the RCA Manufacturing Methods Division.[2] Bins, tool holders, flat trays, solder iron holders, etc., are in-

Figure 137 Standard work-place equipment: *A,* lip tray, length (from back to lip) 5½ inches, width 2⅛ inches, 4¼ inches, or 8½ inches; *B,* edge tray, length (from back to lip) 4¼ inches or 8½ inches, width 5½ inches; *C,* open bin—bench type, length (from back to front) 8 inches, width 5 inches, 8 inches, or 10 inches, depth 8 inches; *D,* open bin—rack type, length (from back to front) 8 inches, width at back 8½ inches, width at front 5½ inches, depth 3 inches; *E,* curved rack to support trays, depth 5⅜ inches, height 4⅞ inches; *F,* universal brackets for mounting fixtures; *G,* tote-box dolly designed to hold tote boxes of material or finished work.

[2] Illustration and data courtesy of RCA.

terchangeable and may be mounted with equal facility on a workbench, drill press, or riveting machine, or hung on any standard rack in any position. This standard equipment is entirely flexible and can be readily adapted for the manufacture of new apparatus. When a new product is to be put into production, it is a simple matter to disassemble the standard bins and equipment and set them up again for the new job. The workbench itself is made in standard sections and is fitted with pipe to carry compressed air and conduit for electric power. When a long bench is needed, several standard bench sections are bolted together, electric lines being coupled together and plugged into the main power circuit. The regular setup operator is able to complete the job, making it unnecessary to have an electrician or a pipe fitter.

A Study of Three Types of Bins

The results of a study[3] of the time to grasp machine screws and machine-screw nuts from various types of bing are shown in Table 10.

The operation consisted of selecting and grasping with the right hand a machine screw or nut from a bin, carrying it through a distance of 5 inches, and releasing it into a hole in the table top. The time for each of the motions select and grasp, transport loaded, release load, and transport empty was accurately measured. The bin with tray (3) required the least time; the hopper-type bin (1) required 19 percent more time; and the rectangular bin (2) required 28 percent more time, than did bin 3 for handling the nuts.

Table 10. Time Required to Grasp, Carry, and Dispose of Machine-Screw Nuts and Machine Screws from Various Types of Bins

	1—Hopper Type Bin		2—Rectangular Bin		3—Bin with Tray	
	Nuts	Screws	Nuts	Screws	Nuts	Screws
Time in Minutes	0.0138	0.0157	0.0148	0.0161	0.0116	0.0143
Time in Percent (Shortest Time = 100%)	119	110	128	113	100	100

[3]*University of Iowa Studies in Engineering, Bulletin* 16, p. 28; also, *Iron Age* Vol. 19, No. 13, pp. 32–37.

13.   Drop deliveries should be used wherever possible.

The work should be arranged so that the finished units may be disposed of by releasing them in the position in which they are completed, thus delivering them to their destination by gravity. This saves time, and moreover the disposal of the objects by simply releasing them frees the two hands so that they may begin the next cycle simultaneously without breaking the rhythm. If a chute is used to carry the finished parts away, it should be located so that the parts can be released in the position in which they are finished, or as close to this point as possible.

A good example of this is shown in Fig. 138. The operation is burring a hole in the end of a small angle plate. The drill is fed by means of a foot pedal, and the angle plate is held in position for burring by means of a fixture. The fixture is mounted on the drill-press table and extends up through a plywood board mounted 6 inches above the table. This board serves as an auxiliary work place, making it unnecessary to cut disposal holes through the drill-press table itself. Holes cut in the board on either side of the fixture lead to a disposal chute underneath.

The part to be burred is placed in the fixture, and the drill is brought down against it. This holds the part in position while it is being burred, and when the burring is completed and the drill is raised, the burred plate drops out of the jig by gravity into the top of the disposal chute. It was economical to equip the drill press as described here because of the large quantity of burring to be done.

In the bolt and washer assembly (Fig. 111) it was necessary to lift the finished assemblies out of the fixture and move them a few inches to one side before releasing

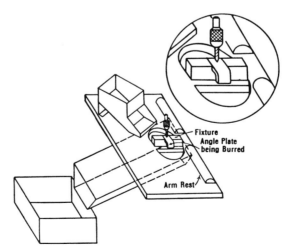

Figure 138   Foot-operated drill press for burring small parts. Finished parts drop out of the fixture into disposal chute by gravity.

them into the chute. A still better arrangement would have been to have the assemblies drop through the fixture by moving some sort of a trip on the bottom of the fixture which could have been actuated by a foot pedal. This arrangement, however, would have added to the cost of the fixture and was not justified in the factory where this fixture was used.

Many people do not appreciate the amount of time that may be used in disposing of finished parts. A study was made of gauging small pins in a fixture mounted on the front edge of the table and disposing of them by tossing them into a tote box located first at a distance of 3 inches behind the fixture, then at a distance of 10 inches, and finally at a distance of 20 inches. The time required for the motions transport loaded and release load was least when the pins were tossed into the bin nearest the fixture. Eighteen percent more time was required for the bin at 10 inches and 34 percent more at 20 inches.

14. Materials and tools should be located to permit the best sequence of motions.

The material required at the beginning of a cycle should be placed next to the point of release of the finished piece in the preceding cycle. In the assembly of the bolt and washers (Fig. 111) the rubber washers were in bins located next to the chute into which the assemblies were disposed as the last motion of the previous cycle. This arrangement permitted the use of the two hands to best advantage at the beginning of the new cycle.

The position of the motion in the cycle may affect the time for its performance. For example, the time for the motion transport empty is likely to be longer when it is followed by the motion select than when it is followed by a well-defined motion such as a grasp of a pre-positioned part. The reason for this is that the mind begins to select during the transport empty. When the motion transport loaded is followed by a position motion, it is slowed down by the mental preparation for the position. The time for the motion grasp is affected by the hand velocity preceding the grasp. A satisfactory sequence of motions in one kind of work may aid in determining the proper sequence in other types of work.

15. Provisions should be made for adequate conditions for seeing. Good illumination is the first requirement for satisfactory visual perception.

Visual perception may take place under such widely varying conditions that adequate provisions for seeing in one kind of work are not always most suitable for another. For example, the provisions for seeing on such very fine work as watch making would be different from those recommended for inspecting sheet plastic or tin plate for surface defects. If adequate illumination is provided, however, seeing is made easier in every case, although this may not be the complete solution to the problem. By adequate illumination is meant (1) light of sufficient intensity for the particular task, (2) light of the proper color and without glare, and (3) light coming from the right direction.

It should be borne in mind that the visibility of an object is determined by the following variables:[4] brightness of the object, its contrast with its background, the size of the object, the time available for seeing, the distance of the object from the eye, and other factors such as distractions, fatigue, reaction time, and glare. These variables are so related that a deficiency in one may be compensated by an augmentation of one or more of the others, provided all factors are above certain limiting values.

The intensity of illumination falling on an object and the reflection factor of the object or that of its background should be considered together in providing adequate illumination. For example, the pages of a telephone directory are dark in color, and the contrast between the printed letter and the page is not so great as that of printing on good book paper. The paper of the directory reflects only 57 percent of the incident light, whereas book paper reflects about 80 percent. Two or three times as much light is required to read a telephone directory as is required to read with equal facility the same critical details of names and numbers printed with blacker ink on white book paper. The task of sewing on very dark cloth is difficult even under the best conditions of lighting. For example, dark cloth of 4 percent reflection factor would require 200 foot-candles to produce the same brightness as 10 foot-candles on white cloth. A knowledge of this point suggests the use of greater intensity of illumination or lighter background for work with objects with a low reflection factor or for very fine work.

Relief of Eyestrain on Fine Assembly Work

The following case[5] shows the changes that may be made to improve the seeing on fine assembly work. The operation was assembling and adjusting the parts of a delicate electric meter mechanism. The task was performed by men, and about three quarters of an hour was required for each unit. Eyestrain and fatigue were excessive, owing to the fact that on certain parts of the operation the illumination was so inadequate in relation to the smallness of the parts that the work had to be held close to the eyes.

To remedy this condition a rest period was introduced and improvements were made in the illumination of the work place. Figure 139 shows the improved lighting units. Because certain parts of the operation could be done best by silhouetting the mechanism against an illuminated background, a background light was placed on the work bench and was kept ''on'' all the time. When it was necessary to view the assembly under direct light, the foot pedal was depressed, turning on the upper lamp.

---

[4] M. Luckiesh and F. K. Moss, ''The Applied Science of Seeing,'' *Transactions of the Illuminating Engineering Society,* Vol. 28, p. 846.
[5] J. H. Mitchell, ''The Relief of Eyestrain on a Fine Assembly Process,'' *The Human Factor,* Vol. 10, No. 10, p. 341.

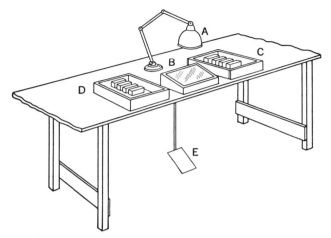

Figure 139 Improved lighting unit: *A*, adjustable lamp for direct light; *B*, background light; *C*, finished work; *D*, work awaiting adjustment; *E*, foot-operated switch for adjustable lamp.

Tests showed that the best color for the background light was white or pale yellow, and that it should be free of glare.

The effects of the rest period and of the improved illumination on six men in the experimental group over the period of the test were an improvement in the quality of the work and also an increase in output of 20 percent. The rest period was included as working time in calculating hourly output.

INSPECTION WORK

Inspection tasks are among the most difficult of all industrial work and ordinarily require special-purpose lighting. The demands are so varied that each poses a unique problem. The literature contains many reports of research in the field of illumination and some companies have compiled extensive guidelines to aid in providing proper illumination for their inspection operations.

The Eastman Kodak Human Factors Group has developed a "lighting library" with descriptions of more than 20 types of lighting systems.[6] This library contains examples of all of the basically different types of special-purpose lighting. For some years they have worked with these lighting systems for different inspection situations and find that low-level general illumination should be used in the areas where difficult visual work is being done and that the specific characteristics of a task should

[6] Terrence W. Faulkner and Thomas J. Murphy, "Lighting for Difficult Visual Tasks," *Human Factors*, Vol. 15, No. 2, pp. 149–162, April, 1973. Seventeen types of lighting systems are described.

be considered in determining the special type of lighting which is optimal. The designer can select from the 20 different types those that will be best for a special task.

A Specific Case

Constant attention and almost continuous use of the eyes are required in many kinds of inspection work. Perception of a defect must be followed by instant action on the part of the inspector to reject the defective part. Some individuals are able to see smaller differences than others and to perceive the same differences with greater speed. Because reaction time and visual acuity are important elements in most inspection work, it is essential that persons be selected by means of suitable tests before being employed for such work.

Inspection of Metal Spools

Some practical applications are included here to show how provisions were made for adequate conditions for seeing. The first case is the inspection of metal bobbin spools for dents, scratches, heavy paint, light paint, and bent flanges. The flange on one end of the spool had a pinhole in the center and the flange on the other end had a keyslot. The good spools were positioned in the tote box with the slot ends in the same direction. Because the improved method of inspection employs a number of principles of motion economy in addition to those for adequate seeing, this operation is presented in some detail.

Original Method

The inspector was seated at a table, as shown in Fig. 140. The spools to be inspected were placed at her left in a large steel tote box *A*. The good spools were arranged in order in the small metal tray *B* at her right. Defective spools were tossed into trays at

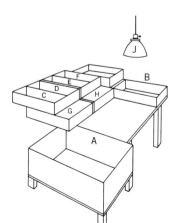

Figure 140 Layout of work place for inspection of metal spools—*A*, supply of good spools to be inspected; old method: *B*, good spools; *C-D-E-F-G-H*, rejected spools. Light was supplied from lamp at *J*.

the back of the table and directly in front of the inspector. They were classified as C, bent ends; D, light paint; E, overlap barrels; F, off-center flanges; G, culls; H, heavy paint.

Elements of the Operation. The inspector, turning to the tote box (previously positioned by the supply man) at her left, grasped spools with both hands and carried them to the table in front of her, where she deposited them. This was repeated until a pile had been accumulated. The inspector procured an empty tray for the good spools from a pile at her right. She also positioned empty trays for various kinds of defects.

The inspector then proceeded with the inspection of the spools in the following manner.

1. She picked up one spool from the pile with the thumb and index finger of each hand, inspected the outside of flanges by looking straight down on them, tipped spools slightly, and then by turning spools inspected them for bent ends. She turned spools end-for-end and repeated the above elements for the other flanges. Then she tipped spools back horizontally, and by turning spools around inspected for defects on the inside of flanges. If the spools were good, she flipped them back into the palm of her hand; if a defect was found, she disposed of the spool in the proper reject tray. These elements were repeated until three or four spools (depending upon the size of the spools) had been accumulated in each hand.
2. The inspector placed the spools held in her right hand in the tray of good spools at her right. She then transferred the spools accumulated in the left hand to the right hand, and placed these in the tray with her right hand. During this time the left hand was idle. The inspector then moved both hands to the pile in front of her and repeated the elements in 1.
3. As tiers of good spools were built up in the tray, the operator jogged the spools into position, pushing the tier against the preceding one; or if it was the first tier, she pushed it against the side of the tray.
4. When a tray was filled, the inspector made out a ticket and placed it in the end of the tray. She then placed the tray on the back of the table, where it was picked up by the supply man.

First Improved Method

The inspector was seated at a table, as shown in Fig. 141. The spools to be inspected were placed in the hopper A, by the supply man and were fed by gravity down on the inspection table. The good spools were placed in order in the tray B at the inspector's right. This tray was tipped up at an angle and was placed at the correct height for disposing of the spools with least effort. When a defective spool was found, it was placed by the left hand into one of the four openings in the top of the table at the inspector's left. These spools went by chute to trays on the floor. Defective spools were classified as C, bent ends; D, light paint; E, heavy paint; or F, culls.

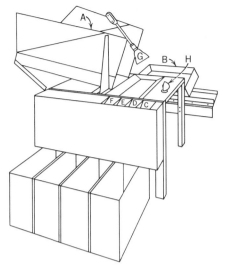

Figure 141 Layout of work place for inspection of metal spools—first improved method: *A*, supply hopper, spools to be inspected; *B*, good spools; *C-D-E-F*, rejected spools. Note the location of lamps at *G* and *H*.

Elements of the Operation

ELEMENTS FOR GOOD SPOOLS

Left Hand	*Right Hand*
1. Pick up two spools.	1. Pack good spools in tray.
2. Transfer one spool to right hand.	2. Receive one spool from left hand.
3. Inspect upper flange under upper light.	3. Inspect upper flange under upper light.
4. Turn spool 60 degrees.	4. Turn spool 60 degrees.
5. Inspect other flange in front of lower light.	5. Inspect other flange in front of lower light.
6. Inspect barrel while spool is rotated between thumb and index finger, under upper light.	6. Inspect barrel while spool is rotated between thumb and index finger, under upper light.
7. Flip spool to palm of hand.	7. Flip spool to palm of hand.
8. Pick up one spool.	8. Pick up one spool.

Repeat elements 3, 4, 5, 6, 7, and 8 until there are three or four spools in each hand.

9. Transfer spools to right hand.	9. Grasp spools from left hand.

ELEMENTS FOR DEFECTIVE SPOOLS

1. When heavy paint, bent ends, or ''jams'' are found in elements 3, 5, or 6, reject spools to disposal chute. When light paint is found in element 3, inspect spool (elements 5 and 6) for other defects before rejecting.	1. Pick up another spool.

2. Grasp spool from right hand and reject it.

2. When a defective spool is found in right hand, transfer it to left hand and get new spool.

AUXILIARY ELEMENTS

1. Procure empty tray from pile behind inspector and position tray on table at right.
2. When tray is full make out ticket and place in end of tray.
3. Push finished tray of work to back of table ready for collection by the supply man.

Comparison of the Two Methods of Inspection. The first improved method of inspection was superior to the old method in the following ways:

1. Two lights on the new table furnished illumination for inspection, so that it was necessary only to turn the spools 60 degrees to inspect both ends. In the old method, using but one light, it was necessary to turn the spools end-for-end or 180 degrees. In the first improved method the intensity of illumination was greatly increased so that at the point of inspection there was 150 foot-candles. The bulbs were completely shielded to prevent glare.
2. The work of the two hands was so arranged that there was practically no idle time during the cycle.
3. The supply of spools was placed in the hopper by the supply man, and they were fed by gravity (occasionally pulled down by the inspector with a hook) to the inspection table. This saved the time of lifting the spools from the tote box to the table as required in the old method.
4. The rejected spools were dropped in openings located conveniently near the working position of the hands. In the old method the inspector had to toss the spools into trays piled in front of her.
5. The tray for receiving good spools was located at the proper height and was tipped up at a convenient angle.
6. The tray of finished work rested on a metal track and could be easily shoved to the back of the table, from which the supply man removed it. The inspector was not required to lift full trays of work.
7. Inspectors were given a 5-minute rest period at the end of each hour, and they were enthusiastic about this. Formerly one 5-minute rest period was provided in the morning and one in the afternoon.
8. Arm rests on the front of the table tended to steady the hands and reduce fatigue. Chairs were carefully adjusted to fit the individual inspector.

Training Inspectors. Considerable study was required in designing the new table and in determining the proper procedure for the inspection elements themselves. After the most satisfactory method was worked out, the inspectors were carefully trained. Slow-motion pictures were used to show the sequence of motions, and only after very careful and persistent training were the inspectors able to do the work in the proper manner and thus accomplish the expected amount of work per day.

Savings. Using the first improved method, the inspectors were able to inspect *twice* as many spools per day as formerly, and apparently with less eyestrain and fatigue. Less than half the floor space was required for the inspection work, and the department had a neater appearance than formerly. The quality of inspection did not suffer by the increased output per inspector.

Second Improved Method

The first improvement in the method of inspecting spools was put into effect without requiring any change in the design of the spool itself and without the use of mechanical equipment, precision gauges, or other apparatus beyond a worktable of special design equipped with two ordinary 60-watt lamps located at a definite place and angle on the worktable. With the increasing volume of spools manufactured and with the increasing hourly wages paid to the operators, however, the whole matter of inspection of the spools was again carefully studied. It was concluded from this study that equipment could eventually be designed that would perform the inspection operation automatically. Rather than attempt to design a fully automatic machine at the outset, it was decided to make improvements in the method one step at a time. First, the spools were redesigned so that both ends were identical, each end having a keyslot in the center of the flange. This made it unnecessary to stack the good spools in order in

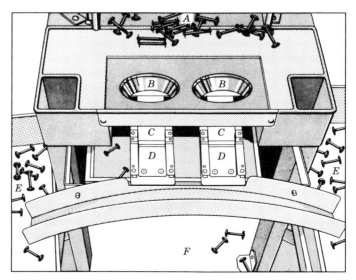

Figure 142 Layout of work place for inspection of metal spools—second improved method: *A*, supply of spools to be inspected; *B*, holes for feeding spools to be inspected to gauges; *C*, lead-in segment of gauge; *D*, inclined track gauge; *E*, good spools; *F*, rejected spools.

the trays. Because the limiting factor of the inspection operation was the operator's ability to handle the spools, a track gauge was designed. As the spools rolled down the two inclined track gauges (*D* in Fig. 142), the spools were gauged to their inside and outside tolerances simultaneously. If the spool rolled through the gauge, it passed inspection; if not, it was removed by the operator as a reject. In order to reduce positioning time in feeding spools to the gauges, two elliptical holes were cut in the table top (*B* in Fig. 142). A funnel of special shape placed below the holes allowed the operator to drop the spools with only minor alignment. The funnels or guides deposited the spools onto the lead-in segments (*C* in Fig. 142) of the gauge.

This second improvement in method eliminated visual inspection entirely and resulted in an increase of 108 percent over the first improved method.

With further increase in volume, it became economical to design a vibratory bowl feeder to supply reels to the track gauges, and the operator than needed only to remove rejects from the four track gauges which made up one working unit. This method resulted in a further increase of 125 percent over the second improved method. For a summary of the several improvements on this operation see Fig. 169.

Inspection by Transmitted Light

Products made of transparent or translucent material may be inspected by transmitting the light through the product. Broken fibers, knots, and other defects in cloth are easily detected; bubbles, cracks, and foreign material in glass and cellulose show up when transmitted light is used for inspection.

In one plant transmitted light was used for inspecting bottles for dirt, cracks, grease, and pieces of broken glass. In a trough just above the moving belt on which the washed bottles passed on their way to the bottling machines, 200-watt bulbs were installed base to base. Approximately 150 foot-candles of light was present on the belt surface. The back portion of the inspection surface was painted white to reveal black defects, and the conveyor belt was black to aid in detecting pieces of broken glass that might be resting on the bottom of the bottle. An operator could inspect bottles at the rate of 128 per minute as they passed by on the conveyor.

16.   The height of the work place and the chair should perferably be arranged so that alternate sitting and standing at work are easily possible.

Workers should be permitted to vary their positions by either sitting or standing as they prefer. Such an arrangement enables an individual to rest certain sets of muscles, and a change of position tends to improve the circulation. Either sitting or standing for long periods of time produces more fatigue than alternately sitting or standing. In many kinds of work provision can easily be made for this sitting-standing combination.

The height of the work place and the chair should fit the particular operator who uses them, but this is not always possible. It may be necessary to make the work sur-

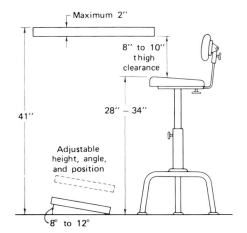

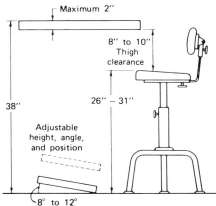

Figure 143 Sitting-standing work place for males.

Figure 144 Sitting-standing work place for females.

face of a height most suitable for the average worker (Fig. 143, 144). The height of the worker's elbow above the standing surface is commonly taken as the starting place for determining the proper height of the work place. For most manual tasks the surface should be 1 to 3 inches below elbow height. For fine detail the surface should be higher. If a sit-stand work place can be adjustable in height, the top of the working surface should be 40 to 45 inches for males and 35 to 43 inches for females.

The work place should be constructed to permit plenty of leg room for the worker. Braces, drawers, and other obstructions under the work place should not interfere with the natural position of the worker. The work bench should not be over 2 inches thick, and there should be a minimum of 8 inches between the top of the chair seat and the underside of the bench or table.

In some kinds of work it is necessary to have fixtures, equipment, or material containers mounted on top of the workbench. This has the effect of adding to the "thickness" of the bench. A work place more than 5 inches thick cannot ordinarily provide a comfortable sitting-standing position for the worker. In some plants small lathes have been cut in half (Fig. 145) and mounted on the bench with the axis of the spindle perpendicular to the front edge of the bench. This arrangement permits sitting-standing and facilitates working with both hands.[7]

17. A chair of the type and height to permit good posture should be provided for every worker.

When a person is standing properly, the different segments of the body—head, neck, chest, and abdomen—are balanced vertically one upon the other so that the

[7] W. R. Mullee, "Motion Study Is Safety's Partner," *National Safety News,* Vol. 34, No. 5. p. 23.

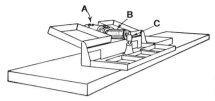

Figure 145 Bench lathe cut in half to permit sitting or standing at work. The lathe is used for the assembly of hard-rubber syringe parts.

weight is borne mainly by the bony framework and a minimum of effort and strain is placed upon the muscles and ligaments. In this posture, under normal conditions the organic functions—respiration, circulation, digestion, etc.—are performed with least mechanical obstruction and with greatest efficiency.

When the worker is seated, the chair should aid and not hinder in maintaining good posture. A good chair should have the following features. The chair should be adjustable in height so that it may be readily fitted to the particular individual who is to use it (Figs. 146 and 147). It should be rigidly built, preferably of steel frame with a lightly padded set and back rest. The edges of the seat and back should be rounded so that no sharp edges can cause discomfort and impede the circulation. Swivel chairs and chairs with casters are ordinarily not recommended for factory work unless the operator needs to work through an arc or move about. The easy movement of such chairs tends to cause unsteadiness in use. This is particularly noticeable if the task requires some muscular effort. The chair may be provided with smooth metal gliders which permit the operator to move it back out of the way.

The seat should be of sufficient width to accommodate the body—at least 17 inches. A wider seat permits the body to readily shift position. The seat should not be over 15 or 16 inches deep. A deep seat tends to cut off the circulation of the blood through the underside of the thighs. For normal work the front edge of the chair should be approximately 1 inch higher than the back edge. When the person works leaning forward, the seat of the chair should be approximately flat.

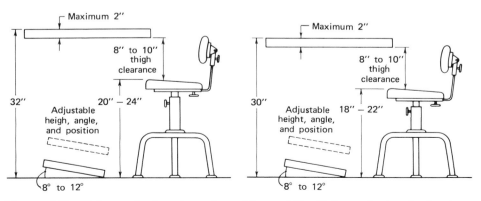

Figure 146 Sitting work place for males. **Figure 147** Sitting work place for females.

A back rest should be provided to support the lower part of the spine and should be adjustable up and down and in and out. It should be 6 to 8 inches high and 10 to 12 inches wide. It may be small and yet give satisfactory support. It can be so designed that it will not interfere with the movements of the individual's arms while working. It is important that the back rest be adjustable and that it be fitted to the worker's body. When the worker leans forward while working, the chair back is of no use; however, the worker can use it while resting and it serves a valuable purpose for momentary relaxation.

Foot Rest

An adjustable foot rest should be provided wherever possible. It may be attached to the floor or to the work table. The foot rest should be of ample width and depth to permit the entire bottoms of both feet to rest on it and allow for some movement. It requires a depth of 12 inches or more and should be inclined 8 to 12 degrees.

Arm Rest

Often the work is of such a nature that it is desirable to provide arm rests at the work place. Arm rests are most effective on work that requires little movement of the forearms, with the hands working at approximately the same position, often at some distance from the body, for long periods of time. Light drilling, tapping, and reaming operations are frequently of this type. On such work it is restful to have padded arm rests placed on top of or at the edge of the workbench, in a position to support the forearm. The arm rests need not interfere with the necessary working movements of the arms or hands. Figure 138 shows such an arm rest.

17

PRINCIPLES OF MOTION ECONOMY
AS RELATED TO THE DESIGN OF TOOLS
AND EQUIPMENT

18. The hands should be relieved of all work that can be done more advantageously by a jig, a fixture, or a foot-operated device.

From observation of the tools and fixtures found in factories, it is obvious that many tool designers often do not give enough thought to the principles of motion economy when they design them. In many cases the fixtures are made for hand operation only, whereas foot-operated equipment would permit the operator to have both hands free to perform other motions.

Foot-Operated Tools and Fixtures

A hand tool can often be attached to or incorporated with a simple foot press or a modified arbor press in such a way that the tool is manipulated entirely by the foot. The electric soldering iron *A* in Fig. 148 is raised and lowered by the foot pedal *B*. After the soldered joint is made and as the iron is raised, valve *C* on the compressed air line opens and a stream of air cools the soldered joint. One company saved 50 percent in time on the operation of soldering a wire to the end of a flat metal electric static shield by the use of this foot-operated soldering iron.

The operation of cutting and welding pipe is an important activity in the maintenance and construction department of many process industries. To make this job easier and to permit the welder to work more effectively, the Procter and Gamble Company designed and built foot-controlled units (Fig. 149) which rotate the pipe or tube while the welder works in a comfortable position.

It is sometimes possible to use two foot pedals to actuate different parts of a jig, fixture, or machine. Such a setup should cause no difficulty for the operator. We are all familiar with the fact that the automobile has several pedals which the driver manipulates with ease, often while traveling at high speed.

Design of Foot Pedals

Pedal design requirements are affected by such factors as; whether they are leg-operated or ankle-operated, the force required to actuate the pedal, the speed and travel distance, the location of the fulcrum if the pedal is hinged, and the precision required. The pedal should be wide enough to accommodate either foot if the opera-

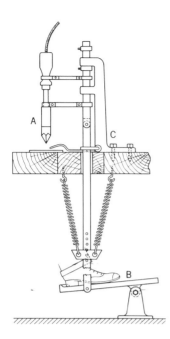

Figure 148 Foot-operated soldering iron.

Figure 149 Foot-controlled motor-driven unit rotates pipe for welder.

tor is to use it while standing. The displacement for a leg-operated pedal should be 2 to 4 inches. If ankle-operated, the displacement should be 2 inches. If the leg rests on the pedal, resistance to counteract this weight should be provided. If the operator is seated, the height of the pedal above the floor is determined by the height of the chair and the kind of pedal.

Studies show that there are optimal and maximum vertical and forward pedal spaces.[1] Figs. 150 and 151 present the results of studies for toe-operated and heel-operated controls for a seated operator.

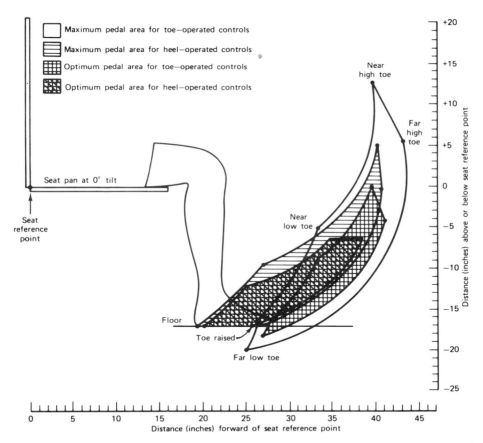

Figure 150 Optimum and maximum pedal space for seated operators. Vertical and forward dimensions.

[1] USAF, *AFSC Design Handbook 1-3, Human Factors Engineering,* 3d ed., AFSC DH 1-3, January 1, 1977, Headquarters AFSC, Andrews AFB, DC.

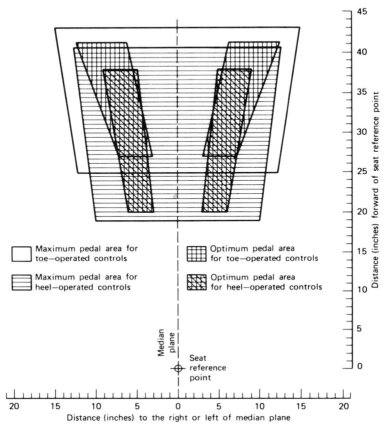

Figure 151　Optimum and maximum pedal space for seated operators. Lateral and forward dimensions.

Study of Five Types of Pedals

Figure 152 shows the results of a study[2] made to determine the relative effectiveness of five different types of pedals based on the time required to depress the pedal. Each pedal was depressed against a tension spring requiring 20 inch-pounds for one complete stroke. For example, pedal 1 had the fulcrum under the heel, and the ball of the foot moved through a distance of 2 inches against a resistance of 10 pounds. All the pedals were operated as trip type, such as would be found on a punch press. That is,

[2] Ralph M. Barnes, Henry Hardaway, and Odif Podolsky, "Which Pedal Is Best?" *Factory Management and Maintenance,* Vol. 100, No. 1, p. 98.

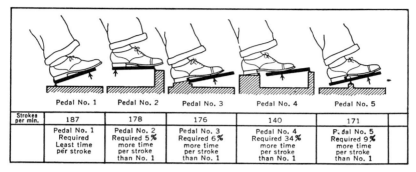

Strokes per min.	187	178	176	140	171	
	Pedal No. 1 Required Least time per stroke	Pedal No. 2 Required 5% more time per stroke than No. 1	Pedal No. 3 Required 6% more time per stroke than No. 1	Pedal No. 4 Required 34% more time per stroke than No. 1	Pedal No. 5 Required 9% more time per stroke than No. 1	

Figure 152   Results of a study of five types of pedals.

the operator was asked to depress the pedal as rapidly as possible, and the time for each pedal stroke was measured. The results of the study (Fig. 152) show that the operator using pedal 1 took the least time per stroke. Pedal 4 required the longest time—34 percent more than pedal 1.

Opening a Shipping Carton

The operation shown in Fig. 153 consists of opening a flat shipping carton and folding over the bottom flaps preparatory to filling it with boxes of breakfast cereal in the packing room of the cereal factory. Cartons are delivered to the packing table and are stacked horizontally as shown in Fig. 153

Improved Method

This operation is the same as the one described above. However, the cartons are stacked on the table vertically (Fig. 154) instead of horizontally. A simple fixture made of heavy wire, designed by E. H. Hollen, is used to aid the operator in folding in the two end flaps and the two side flaps.

Because the time required to open the carton and fold in bottom flaps is so short with this improved method, the same operator who does this also fills the carton with boxes of cereal (D of Fig. 154). The carton is then moved onto the automatic sealing machine, which applies glue and seals both ends.

Notice that the fixture contains no moving parts. It was made from 20 feet of No. 9 gauge wire and a piece of board, at a total cost of a few dollars. Using this fixture, the operator can open cartons in less than half the time required by the original method. The actual increase in output was 112 percent. The fixture saves many hand motions. Also as a result of this study, the carton was redesigned, saving over $20,000 per year in carton cost.

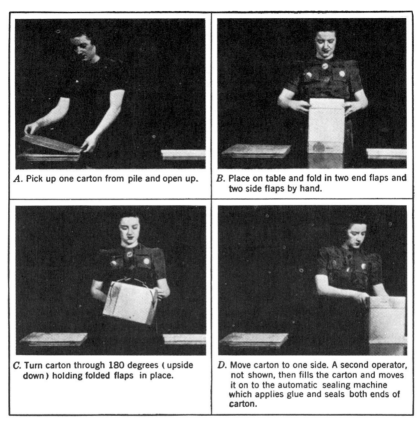

A. Pick up one carton from pile and open up.

B. Place on table and fold in two end flaps and two side flaps by hand.

C. Turn carton through 180 degrees (upside down) holding folded flaps in place.

D. Move carton to one side. A second operator, not shown, then fills the carton and moves it on to the automatic sealing machine which applies glue and seals both ends of carton.

Figure 153 Opening shipping cartons—old method.

19. Two or more tools should be combined whenever possible.

It is usually quicker to turn a small two-ended tool end-for-end than it is to lay one tool down and pick up another. There are many examples of two-tool combinations—tack hammer and tack puller, two-ended wrench, pencil and eraser—and the designer of the "handset" telephone used this idea when he incorporated the transmitter and the receiver in one unit.

Two very convenient tools which have been developed at a mid-western electrical equipment company are illustrated in Figs. 155 and 156. The first one replaces the screwdriver and tweezers—it holds the screw while it is being assembled. The second tool replaces a wrench and a screwdriver. This device permits the bolt to be set to the

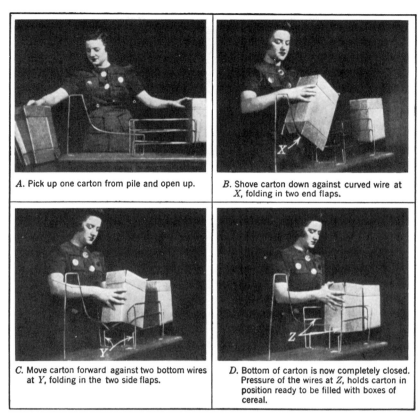

A. Pick up one carton from pile and open up.

B. Shove carton down against curved wire at X, folding in two end flaps.

C. Move carton forward against two bottom wires at Y, folding in the two side flaps.

D. Bottom of carton is now completely closed. Pressure of the wires at Z, holds carton in position ready to be filled with boxes of cereal.

Figure 154   Opening shipping cartons—improved method. Output was increased 112%. Also as a result of this study the carton was redesigned, saving over $20,000 per year in carton cost.

proper position and at the same time allows the operator to lock the nut in place by means of the ''sleeve wrench'' which slips over the screwdriver.

The practice of using only the thumb and first and second fingers is so common that attention is called to the fact that the third and fourth fingers and the palm should also be employed wherever possible. The combination screwdriver and wrench shown in Fig. 156, for example, permits the entire hand to be used. The thumb and first and second fingers manipulate the wrench while the palm and third and fourth fingers manipulate the screwdriver.

The multiple-spindle air-operated nut runner shown in Fig. 157 is used to tighten all five wheel nuts at once. The cable suspends the wrench in a convenient position and makes the job easier.

Figure 155 Combination screwdriver and tweezers.

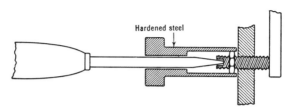

Figure 156 Combination screwdriver and wrench.

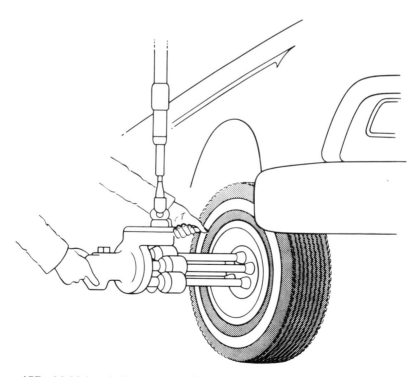

Figure 157 Multiple-spindle air-operated nut runner can tighten all five wheel nuts at once. (Courtesy Ford Motor Company.)

230

20. Tools and materials should be pre-positioned whenever possible.

Pre-positioning refers to placing an object in a predetermined place in such a way that when next needed it may be grasped in the position in which it will be used. For pre-positioning tools, a holder in the form of a socket, compartment, bracket, or hanger should be provided, into which or by which the tool may be returned after it is used, and where it remains in position for the next operation (Fig. 211). The tool is always returned to the same place. The holder should be of such design that the tool may be quickly released into its place from the hand. Moreover, the holder should permit the tool to be grasped in the same manner in which it will be held while being used.

21. Where each finger performs some specific movement, such as in typewriting, the load should be distributed in accordance with the inherent capacities of the fingers.

The normally right-handed person performs work with less fatigue and greater dexterity with the right hand than with the left. Although most people can be trained to work equally well with either hand on most factory operations, the fingers have unequal inherent capacities for doing work. The first and second fingers of the two hands are ordinarily superior in their performance to the third and fourth fingers.

Arrangement of Typewriter Keys

A study made to determine the ideal arrangement of the keys of the typewriter for maximum efficiency[3] also illustrates this difference in the capacities of the fingers (Fig. 158). That part of the study which is of most interest here revealed that the ability of the right hand as compared with that of the left was as 100 to 88.87, or approximately as 10 to 9. This agrees with the findings of another investigator already cited.[4] The data in Table 11 show the ideal load in strokes based on the abilities of the fingers. The finger loads required by the present typewriter keyboard are shown for comparison.

Table 11. Relative Finger Loads on the "Ideal" and on the Present Keyboard

	Left Hand				Right Hand			
Finger	4	3	2	1	1	2	3	4
Ideal load	855	900	975	1028	1097	1096	991	968
Standard keyboard load	803	658	1492	1535	1490	640	996	296

[3] R. E. Hoke, "Improvement of Speed and Accuracy in Typewriting," *Johns Hopkins Studies in Education,* No. 7, pp. 1–42.
[4] Wm. L. Bryan, "On the Development of Voluntary Motor Ability," *American Journal of Psychology,* Vol. 5, No. 2, p. 123.

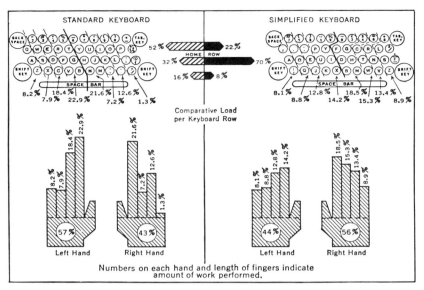

Figure 158 Comparison of standard typewriter keyboard with simplified keyboard. Figures indicate comparative loads for each row, hand, and finger. The new keyboard at the right has the letters rearranged so that the right hand carries its share of the load. Seventy percent of the commonly used words are written on the "home row" where the fingers are placed.

These data indicate that the first and second fingers of the right hand should carry the greatest load, whereas the fourth finger of the left hand should carry the smallest. They also show that the total load of the right hand using the present typewriter is 3422, and of the left hand 4488, or a ratio of 100 to 131.25, when it should be as 100 to 88.87. Thus there is an overload of the left hand of 47.7 percent as compared with the load of the right hand.

It was suggested from the analysis of the data secured in this investigation that the keys of the typewriter should be so arranged that the letters occuring most frequently would by typed with the fingers capable of carrying the greatest load. In fact, many investigators in this field have proposed new keyboards. The one shown on the right in Fig. 158 is the Dvorak-Dealey "simplified" keyboard[5] tested over a period of years at the University of Washington. Research conducted under a grant from the Carnegie Foundaiton for the Advancement of Teaching indicates that the simplified typewriter keyboard eliminates many of the defects of the standard keyboard, and that it is:

[5] A. Dvorak, N. I. Merrick, W. L. Dealey, and G. C. Ford, *Typewriting Behavior*, American Book Co., New York, 1936, p. 219. Reproduced by permission.

1. Easier to master in that it requires less time to attain any particular level of typing speed.
2. Faster, since it makes higher net rates possible for average typists.
3. More accurate, since fewer typing errors are made.
4. Less fatiguing through simplifying the stroking patterns and through adapting the hand and finger loads to the relative hand and finger abilities.[6]

Despite the advantages listed above, two practical problems have prevented any wide use of the simplified keyboard thus far. First, typewriters with the simplified keyboard are not generally available in offices and schools, and people learning to type hesitate to use a keyboard that is not in general use. Second, tests[7] seem to show that it is not economical to retrain experienced typists to use the simplified keyboard. Although there is still no widespread use of the simplified keyboard, typewriters with this keyboard are reaidly available. Because of its superiority there is a move to promote its use by noncommercial students and for data processing, and in other areas where the problems mentioned above are less important.

Also, the growing use of computers, office equipment, cash registers and mail sorters has renewed interest in the design of typewriters, keyboards, and other data entry devices. Studies are being made of such factors as key size and shape, key feedback, key grouping, keyboard size and slope, as well as the arrangement of the keys.[8] The ideal keyboard design is one that facilitates learning, and permits fast, error-free operation with the least possible strain on the operator.

22. Levers, hand wheels, and other controls should be located in such positions that the operator can manipulate them with the least change in body position and with the greatest speed and ease.

Some machine-tool manufacturers understand that it is possible to build a machine that will perform its functions satisfactorily and at the same time will be easy to operate. Unless a machine is fully automatic, the amount of work that it will produce depends to some extent upon the performance of the operator. The more convenient the machine is to operate, the greater the production is likely to be.

The operator should not be required to leave his normal working position to operate his machine. The controls should be placed in such a way that he need not bend over or twist his body in an uncomfortable manner when manipulating them

[6] Dwight D. W. Davis, "An Evaluation of the Simplified Typewriter Keyboard," *Journal of Business Education,* Vol. 11, No. 2, p. 21, October, 1935; A. Dvorak, "There Is a Better Typewriter Keyboard," *National Business Education Quarterly,* Vol. 12, No. 2, pp. 51–58, December, 1943.

[7] Earl P. Strong, *A Comparative Experiment in Simplified Keyboard Retraining and Standard Keyboard Supplementary Training,* General Services Administration, Washington, D.C., 1956.

[8] K. H. E. Kroemer, "Human Engineering the Keyboard," *Human Factors,* Vol. 14, No. 1, pp. 51–63. David G. Alden, Richard W. Daniels, and Arnold F. Kanarick, "Keyboard Design and Operation: A Review of the Major Issues," *Human Factors,* Vol. 14, No. 4, pp. 272–293.

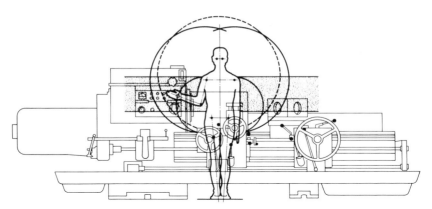

Figure 159   Controls are grouped near normal operating area. Major control panel is within easy reach of operator's left hand. (From Robert H. Hose, "Designing the Product to Suit Human Dimensions," *Product Engineering,* Vol. 26, No. 9, p. 171.)

(Fig. 159). Where this ideal condition cannot be provided, the nearest approach to it should be adopted.

It is well known that levers can be operated more effectively in certain positions and at certain heights than at others. A very exhaustive study was made to determine the effectiveness of levers and hand wheels located in both horizontal and vertical planes, and at three different heights from the floor.[9] These devices were arranged so that the force of the push or pull was indicated in kilograms by means of a dynamometer. The object in these tests was to determine the maximum strength that could be exerted in each case. Each of the devices was tested in the several positions shown in Figs. 160 and 161.

The vertical scale represents the force in kilograms exerted by the subject, and the horizontal scale shows the particular position of the device being tested. The three sets of curves on each chart represent the three different heights at which the devices were tested, namely, 580 mm. (22.8) inches), 780 mm. (30.7 inches), and 1080 mm. (42.5 inches). For example, in Fig. 160 the lever was most effective at the medium height, 780 mm. above the floor, and position II on the horizontal scale, which represents the position where the lever was horizontal and the operator pulled up on it.

The hand wheel was most effective when placed at the 1080-mm. height and in the vertical plane, position IV in Fig. 161. The operator, standing to one side of the wheel, pushed with the right hand and pulled with the left.

[9] W. P. Kühne, "Studien zur optimalen Kraftreaktion an Maschinenbedienungs elementen" (Studies on the Optimum Force Exerted on Machine Controls), *Industrielle Psychotechnik,* Vol. 3, No. 6, pp. 167–172.

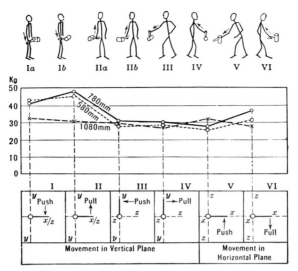

Figure 160 Results of the study of levers.

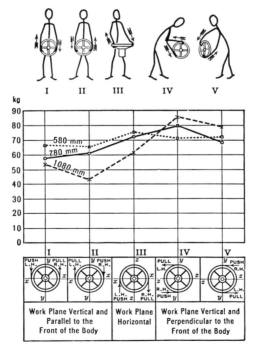

Figure 161 Results of the study of hand wheels.

235

Lathe with Compact Computer Controls

Jones and Lamson has a line of lathes with a compact computer numerical control with magnetic disc program storage built into the machine (Fig. 162). A small control center, located at the front of the machine, contains an alphanumeric keyboard for instant on-line commands and editing, plus a cathode ray tube (CRT) display. This allows the operator to have two-way communication with the lathe. The lathe, computer, and controls are a self-contained unit, occupying a minimum of floor space and permitting greater operator access to all working areas. The lathe has built-in skids and three-point support which makes the unit easy to move from one shop location to another without time-consuming wiring and leveling procedures.

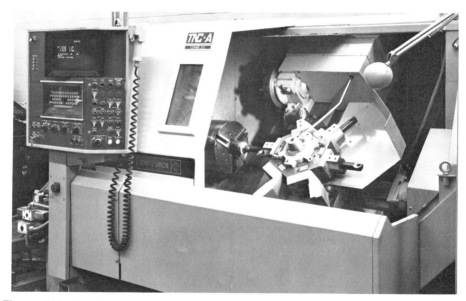

Figure 162 Lathe with control center conveniently located on machine. Computer numerical control with magnetic disc storage built into machine. (Courtesy of Jone & Lamson TEXTRON.)

18

MOTION STUDY, MECHANIZATION, AND AUTOMATION

Over the centuries, man has been finding easier and better ways to produce the goods and services he needs and wants. Work originally consisted of activities performed with the bare hands; then simple tools were devised, and later power-driven machines. Now fully automatic equipment makes it possible to remove much of the burden of manual work from the man and transfer it to machines. We have long recognized that an increase in productivity per man-hour was a major factor in bringing about improvement in our standard of living. Few people advocate using human labor to do work that can be done better and cheaper by machines. The day is far distant, however, when manual work in industry will disappear. Some activities are too complex to be mechanized and must therefore be performed manually. Some tasks occur so seldom that it is not economical to use machines. Moreover, other factors may affect the extent to which mechanization should be used in a given situation—factors such as quality, yield, material utilization, safety, availability of qualified workers, availability of capital, and the probable life of the product being made.

Because work methods design often calls for a relatively small capital investment and a minimum of design cost, it is suggested that the best manual method or the best combination of manual and machine method be developed and used as a basis for evaluating a proposed mechanized or automated process. For example, one company makes it a practice to determine and evaluate alternative methods. If a large-volume fairly complex job is to be considered, a comparison would be made of the estimated cost to do each element or each suboperation manually and also automatically. For example, in a punch-press operation the parts could be manually or automatically fed, the press could be actuated manually or automatically, and the finished parts could be removed by hand or ejected automatically. The cost to install and maintain each of the automatic components would be evaluated against the costs of the manual method. However, an efficient manual method should be used as the basis for comparison.

In the hypothetical case shown in Fig. 163 the operation has three elements, any one of which can be done manually or automatically. There are eight possible combinations, and the cost can be estimated for each. The lowest cost combination is the one that would be recommended, others things being equal.

The first two cases to be described in this chapter show how output per man-hour was affected by changes in method from purely manual operation, to partial mechanization, to completely automatic production. In the third case, that of warehouse han-

Combination	Elements of the Operation		
	1	2	3
A	Manual	Manual	Manual
B	Automatic	Manual	Manual
C	Automatic	Automatic	Manual
D	Automatic	Manual	Automatic
E	Manual	Automatic	Manual
F	Manual	Manual	Automatic
G	Manual	Automatic	Automatic
H	Automatic	Automatic	Automatic

Figure 163 Eight possible combinations of manual and automatic performance of a three-element operation.

dling of the finished product, the cost of the pallet was an additional factor that affected the total warehouse handling cost.

GRADING AND PACKAGING EGGS FOR DISTRIBUTION

A careful study of the method of candling, sizing, and packaging eggs for distribution in one plant[1] in California resulted in a substantial increase in the output and a reduction in labor costs. Basically the process consists of three parts: (1) candling, determining quality; (2) sizing, determining weight; (3) packaging eggs into cartons. Originally the method was as follows. The operator, called a candler, picked up two eggs in each hand and held the eggs, one at a time, directly in front of an intense light. She examined the eggs for exterior appearance (color, texture, and thickness of shell) and interior quality (size and mobility of the yoke and position and size of the air cell, and other characteristics which indicate the quality of the egg). She then placed the egg in the proper carton on her work place. In this particular plant eggs were classified into eight different quality grades and seven different sizes.

Four major changes have been made in methods.

First Improved Method

The first improvement was made by applying principles of motion economy to the job. A short belt conveyor, actuated by a motor drive controlled by a foot-operated switch, moved the eggs to be inspected into a convenient position for the operator. Semicircular shelves at several different levels were located above the conveyor to facilitate the packing of the eggs of various grades and sizes into the cartons. An air-

[1] Michel Brothers Edgemar Egg Company, Santa Monica, CA.

cooled candling lamp of special design further added to the effectiveness of the work place. As a result of these improvements output increased approximately 20 percent.

Second Improved Method—Mechanized Sizing and Packaging

In order to further increase productivity a machine [2] was installed which performed automatically two of the three parts of the job. The operator and the machine then worked together in the following manner. The operator, working at the head of the machine, candled the eggs much as in the first improved method. However, she took the eggs directly from the cases in which they were received from the egg producer. She merely inspected the eggs in front of the light as in the old method and graded them for quality, placing the candled egg in one of eight short conveyors located directly in front of her, a conveyor for each quality grade. From this point on, the machine took over and the balance of the process was automatic. Each egg was automatically weighed and code-marked with invisible ink, and by means of a memory device and electronic controls the egg was conveyed to one of 22 carton-filling stations on the machine, where it was deposited in the proper carton. After the carton containing one dozen eggs was filled, the lid was closed and the carton was code-dated, and conveyed to the operator who placed the carton in a case. The cases were then moved by conveyor to storage. Six candlers, two machine attendants, and the supervisor were able to process approximately 1620 dozen eggs per hour. This is as many eggs as were formerly processed by 12 operators.

Third Improved Method—Mechanical Candling, Sizing, and Packaging

Additional changes were made in the egg-processing plant which further increased the efficiency and improved the quality and uniformity of the eggs. First, a plan was devised that would pay a bonus to the egg producer in the form of a higher price per dozen if the eggs would meet a specified quality standard. To meet this quality standard, the rancher was required to remove from his flock those chickens that produced eggs of inferior quality—usually the older hens. Random samples of each rancher's eggs were inspected over the week, and the "quality level" was based on the inspection records. This quality level was in effect the following week.

The process was as follows. Eggs were gathered by the rancher and placed directly in special "egg flats" holding 30 eggs and then in cases holding a total of 30 dozen (Fig. 164). The cases were placed in a cooler until they were picked up by a truck for delivery to the processing plant. When the eggs were received at the processing plant, they were placed in a cooler, each rancher's eggs being kept separate. When the eggs were to be processed, the egg cases were moved to the front end of the processing machine (Figs. 165 and 166) and an operator called a loader placed the

[2] Designed and built by The FMC Corporation, Riverside, CA.

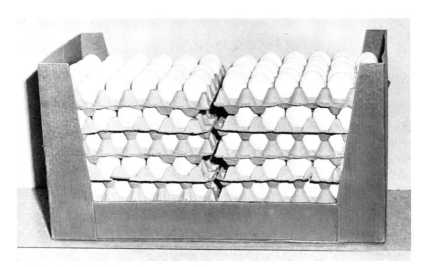

Figure 164 Special design of egg case. Fiberboard case holds 12 filler flats or trays, each containing 30 eggs.

Figure 165 Mechanized egg-processing equipment used in the "Third Improved Method." Filler flats containing 30 eggs are transferred from egg cases to conveyor by the "loader." The "scanner" removes cracked and soiled eggs as they pass over a bank of spotlights. The eggs are dropped into cartons which are automatically closed, and code dated.

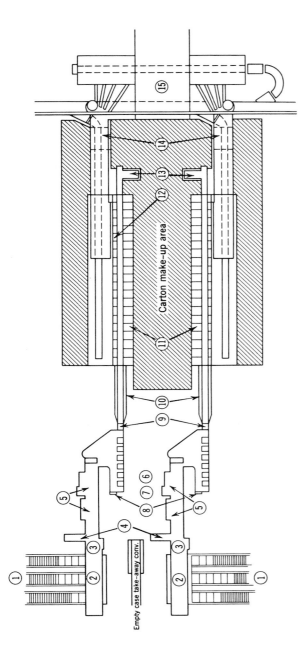

Figure 166 Layout of mechanized egg-processing equipment shown in Fig. 165. (*1*) Incoming producer case set on conveyor. (*2*) Case unloading conveyor. (*3*) Automatic egg transfer. (*4*) Automatic empty filler flat stacker. (*5*) Automatic egg cleaner—dryer (optional). (*6*) Semiautomatic mass candling unit. (*7*) Six automatic weighing stations. (*8*) Automatic printing and recording unit. (*9*) Automatic blood spot detector (optional). (*10*) Automatic processing unit (optional). (*11*) Carton and filler flat magazines. (*12*) Automatic packaging stations. (*13*) Memory control unit. (*14*) Conveying equipment through carton closing and code dating machines. (*15*) Outgoing case packing area.

241

flats on a conveyor which automatically distributed them evenly onto a rubber roll conveyor. The eggs were washed and dried automatically. They then passed over a bank of six 1000-watt lamps, and an operator called a scanner examined the eggs as they passed by and removed any cracked eggs or eggs with soiled spots which had not been removed by the washing process.

Next, each egg was automatically weighed and was classified into one of six different sizes: jumbo, extra-large, large, medium, small, and peewee. The eggs then passed into a blood detector and all eggs containing even the smallest bloodspot were discarded. Eggs of acceptable quality were dropped automatically from the conveyor into the proper carton. When a carton was full, it was automatically closed, code-dated, and conveyed to the operator, who placed it in a rectangular wire basket holding 15 dozen eggs. The baskets were moved by conveyor to the cooler and were later delivered to the grocer or supermarket and placed directly in refrigerated self-service display cases, thus eliminating a handling operation. A crew consisting of a loader, a scanner, and three packers, together with an inspector and a supervisor, was able to process approximately 1800 dozen eggs per hour.

Fourth Improved Method—High Capacity, Eight Lane, Mechanized Candling, Sizing, and Packaging

The egg processing plant performed very efficiently and eventually was fully depreciated. The decision was made to close the plant and purchase processed eggs from a

Figure 167 High capacity mechanized egg-processing equipment.

new facility[3] using faster and more sophisticated electronically controlled processing equipment.[4] Eggs are now processed by a machine occupying a space 33' by 39' having a processing capacity of 3600 dozen eggs per hour with six operators—that is, 600 dozen eggs per hour per person (Fig. 167).

In general, the machine functions much like the earlier one. However, this machine uses solid-state logic systems which eliminates many moving parts thus reducing maintenance and improving reliability. A candling booth is provided with "backspin" and high intensity sodium lamps with safety baffles against eye fatigue.

Plastic flats are used at the ranch for gathering and shipping eggs to the processing plant. There the plant washes, sanitizes, and dries the empty flats. This reduces the possibility of disease transmission between various ranches. It should be added that many processing plants are highly integrated. Pullet rearing and egg laying facilities, feed mills, egg processing plants, and truck fleets are owned and operated by the same company.

Table 12 and the curves in Fig. 168 show that the "number of eggs processed in

Table 12. Capital Invested in Building and Equipment—Five Different Methods of Grading and Packaging Eggs for Distribution

Method	Total Size of Work Force (Operators)	Total Number of Eggs Processed in Dozens		Capital Invested in Dollars (Equipment and Building)		
		Per Hour	Per Operator per Hour	Total	Per Operator	Per Dozen Eggs Processed per Hour
Original method of hand candling	10	1120	112	80,000	8,000	70
Improved method of hand candling	12	1620	135	80,000	6,667	41
*⎰ Hand candling, mechanized sizing and packaging	9	1620	180	140,000	15,555	86
Mechanized washing, sizing and packaging	7	1800	257	140,000	20,000	78
†⎰ High Capacity Mechanized washing, sizing and packaging	6	3600	600	350,000	58,333	100

*Michel Brothers Edgemar Egg Company.
†Embly Ranch.

[3] Embly Ranch, Chino, CA.
[4] Designed and built by Staalka of America, Inc., Lancaster, Pa.

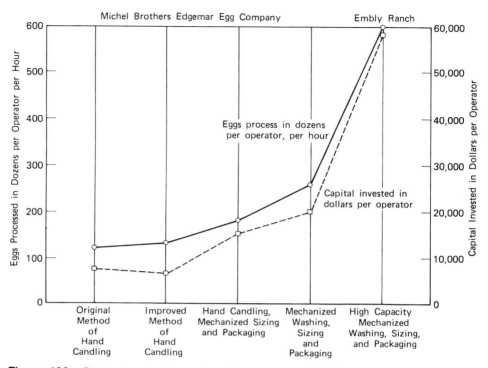

Figure 168 Curves showing the number of eggs processed in dozens per operator per hour and the capital invested in equipment in dollars per operator for each of the five different methods of processing and packaging eggs.

dozens per operator per hour'' increased from 112 by the original method to 600 by the present method. However, the ''total capital invested in equipment and building per operator'' increased from $6,667 for the first improved method to $58,333 for the present method. One is nearly always confronted with the problem of evaluating both unit labor cost and initial capital invested in determining the preferred method. In this case each advance in mechanization reduced labor cost and also reduced the total cost of processing eggs.

New Design of Egg Case

The fiberboard egg case (Fig. 164) consists of a pallet section or bottom part with handholds in each end to facilitate lifting the case; the two sides are cut out to make it easy to load and unload the pallet. A fiberboard top telescopes over the pallet and also has handholds cut out in the ends to match those in the bottom. The case holds 12 filler flats, or trays of 30 eggs each, or a total of 30 dozen. Eggs are gathered and placed directly into the flats and then into the pallet at the ranch, thus eliminating one handling. The cutout design of the pallet facilitates air circulation and permits the eggs to be cooled quickly in the refrigerator at the ranch. The new egg case was developed by the University of California, Department of Agriculture, and has been widely adopted by ranchers and egg processors.

INSPECTION OF METAL SPOOLS

Over a period of some 25 years, four major improvements have been made in the inspection of metal spools (Fig. 169). The first improvement, Method II, resulted from a better work-place layout and the use of two light sources which made it unnecessary to turn the spools end-for-end to inspect them. For a complete description of this method see page 215. Although output was doubled, this method still required 100 percent inspection on the part of the operator. Some years later the spools were redesigned so that both ends were alike. This design change permitted the use of two track gauges which eliminated visual inspection of the spools. All acceptable spools rolled down the two tracks into trays. Any rejects were caught in the track gauge itself, and these spools were removed by the operator. This method, Method III, resulted in an improvement of 108 percent in output over the previous method. Method IV, made use of a mechanical vibrating bowl feeder which fed the spools onto the track gauge instead of the operator's doing this by hand. This mechanical feeder, supplying spools to four track gauges, resulted in an increase in output of 125 percent over Method III.

A mechanical device was then designed to remove rejects from the track gauges, thus making the operation completely automatic. Spools to be inspected are brought to the vibrating bowl feeders by a belt conveyor from the preceding operation; they are inspected automatically, and then the good spools are moved by conveyor to the next operation.

COMPARISON OF FINISHED-PRODUCT WAREHOUSE HANDLING METHODS

There may be situations where the controlling factor is something other than labor. Fig. 170 shows four different finished-product warehouse handling methods which have been used at one time or another by the Procter & Gamble Company. Originally a flat-top hand truck was used, resulting in a total handling cost of $2.34 per 100 boxes. The substitution of a fork-lift truck and wood pallets brought about a reduction in the handling costs to $1.87 per 100 boxes. A Pul Pac pallet was designed, which reduced the pallet costs and also saved vertical space in the warehouse. This method gave a cost of $1.85 per 100 boxes. The Pul Pac method used a heavy, tough paperboard pallet instead of the heavy wood pallet previously used. The Pul Pac pallet cost approximately 50 cents in comparison with $4.50 for the wood pallet.

	I	**II**
Brief statement of method used	Original method. Inspection of spools from pile on top of worktable	Improved work-place layout. Use of two light sources make it unnecessary to turn spools end-for-end to inspect them
Equipment used	Ordinary worktable	Special worktable
Method of supplying spools to be inspected	Spools to be inspected are in tote box on floor beside worktable	Spools to be inspected are fed onto work place from hopper on back of bench
Location of light source for inspection of spools	Ordinary light source above worktable	Two light sources mounted at special locations on work place
Inspection procedure	Spools inspected from one end and then turned through 180 degrees and inspected from other end	Two light sources make it unnecessary to turn spools end–for–end for inspection
Disposal of good spools	Good spools are placed in order in tray to right of operator	Good spools are placed in order in tray to right of operator
Disposal of defective spools	Rejects disposed by operator into any one of six trays on back of table for six different classes of rejects	Rejects disposed by operator into any one of four openings on left side of work place for four different classes of rejects
Increase in output of operator per hour in comparison to previous method	Original method	100% of method I

Figure 169   Summary of five methods of inspection of metal spools.

246

M E T H O D

III	IV	V
		To be inspected Good spools Rejects
Spool was redesigned so both ends were alike. Use of two track gauges eliminated visual inspection of spools	Mechanical vibrating bowl feeder supplies spools to four track gauges, eliminates manual feeding and visual inspection	Rejects are removed from the track gauges by mechanical means, thus making the operation completely automatic
Special worktable. Funnel-shaped openings in table top lead to track gauges under table	Belt conveyor, mechanical vibrating bowl feeder, four track gauges	Completely automatic equipment
Spools to be inspected are fed onto work place from hopper on back of bench (Hopper not shown in above sketch)	Spools to be inspected are brought to vibrating bowl feeders by belt conveyor from preceeding operation	Spools to be inspected are brought to vibrating bowl feeders by belt conveyor from preceding operation
General lighting	General lighting	General lighting
No visual inspection. Good spools roll through track gauges; defective spools will not pass through gauges and are removed by operator	No visual inspection. Good spools roll through track gauges; defective spools will not pass through gauges and are removed by operator	No visual inspection. Good spools roll through track gauges; defective spools will not pass through gauges and are removed by mechanical means
Good spools roll from track gauge into tray under table. Spools are the same on both ends, need not be placed in order	Good spools roll from track gauge into a chute and are carried to tray	Good spools go by conveyor directly to next operation
Rejects disposed by operator into opening on either side of work place.	Rejects disposed by operator into opening in center of working area	Rejects disposed into chute by mechanical device
108% of method II	125% of method III	Equipment automatic, no operator required. One person attend several units. One maintenance person required for battery of machines

Load Clamp

$1.68

Pul Pac

$1.85

Fork Lift

$1.87

Hand Truck

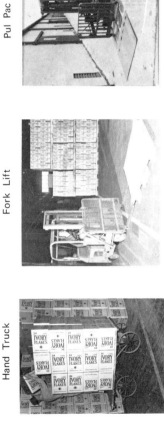

$2.34

Total handling cost per 100 boxes

Figure 170 Comparison of finished-product warehouse handling methods for a 30,000-case-per-day factory. Assume: (1) 15,000 cases per day direct to shipment, 15,000 cases per day to storage; (2) time in storage, 4 weeks; (3) product manually handled from slide to pallet or truck, and from pallet or truck into car.

Figure 171 Load clamp attached to power-lift truck makes it unnecessary to use pallets.

Later a load clamp attachment for the lift truck was developed, which eliminated the pallet entirely (Fig. 171). This method of handling boxes reduced the cost to $1.68 per 100 boxes. The cost of each of the four methods is given at the bottom of Fig. 170.

The Automated Factory

Machines and process operations are highly automated in many factories where volume is large and the product is standardized. Assembly work is also being automated to an increasing extent. Mechanical equipment, electronic controls, and the computer are taking over to relieve the operator of much of the repetitive work. Electric clocks and razors, watches, automobile batteries, and spark plugs are examples of products that are now being manufactured in fully or largely automated factories.

In some cases the major problem is not only to be able to automate a manufacturing process but to provide enough flexibility to adapt it readily to new product designs or modifications in design. There is some evidence to show that an organization which devotes its entire efforts to mechanization and automation over a considerable period of time may not have flexibility to meet customer demands for new products.[5]

[5] William J. Abernathy and Kenneth Wayne, "Limits of the Learning Curve," *Harvard Business Review,* Vol. 52, No. 5, pp. 109–119, September–October, 1974.

STANDARDIZATION—WRITTEN STANDARD PRACTICE

After finding the most economical way of performing an operation, it is essential that a permanent record be made of it. This record is frequently called a "standard practice." In addition to serving as a permanent record of the operation, the standard practice is often used as an instruction sheet for the operator or as an aid for the supervisor or instructor in training the operator.

The Standard Practice as a Permanent Record

Once the improved method is standardized and put into effect, constant vigilance on the part of management is necessary in order to maintain this standard. Often tools and equipment get out of adjustment, and materials vary from specifications. When such conditions exist, standard performance cannot be expected from the operator. Only by rigid maintenance of standard conditions can there be reasonable assurance of standard performance in output and quality.

Very often time standards are used as the basis for wage incentives, and most incentive plans either imply or specifically state that time standards will not be changed unless there is a change in the method of performing the work. It is therefore essential that an accurate and complete record be made of the method at the time it is put into effect or at the time the standard is set for the operation. If no such record is kept, it will be almost impossible in the future to tell whether the method then being used is the same as that in effect at the time the standard was originally established.

One company uses the forms shown in Figs. 172 and 173 as a permanent record of each operation. This standard practice is ordinarily perpared by the person making the time study, or by the person in charge of the investigation if several persons are engaged in the work. These two forms are prepared after the correct method has been established and put into effect. The "Standard Job Conditions" and the "General Job Conditions" forms used by this company are printed on bond paper. The original is placed in the folder with the original time studies of the operation and filed in the Wage Standards Department office. A copy is filed in a loose-leaf binder in the office of the supervisor of the department in which the operation is performed. This is used by the operator, supervisor, and timekeeper.

The "Standard Job Conditions" form contains complete details of the specific operation; "General Job Conditions" form, as the name indicates, contains more general information about the operation and the location of the work place relative to the rest of the department or building, information about the flow of material to and

STANDARD JOB CONDITIONS

BASE RATE NO. 27112 **CODE NO.** —

DATE _____ **STUDY NOS.** 32906-32909 **SYM. NO.** — **BINDER NO.** 27

BLDG. 148A **DEPT.** No. 17 **DIVISION** Eastern **OBSERVER** Davis, W.T.

OPERATION Label 4-oz. Bottles   Hardening Solution

SKETCH OF WORK PLACE

Brush for Moistening Pad

Supply Tray

Tray for Finished Bottles

Supply of Labels

Pressing Cloth

Labeling Jig

Moistening Pad

Operator in Sitting Position

SPECIAL TOOLS, JIGS OR FIXTURES Labeling Jig

JOB ELEMENTS

JOB ELEMENTS	AUXILIARY
1. Moisten pad with brush.	
2. Insert labels in jig.	
3. Procure bottle from supply tray, moisten bottle on moistening pad, label, using jig, press smooth on pressing cloth.	**AUXILIARY** Set up and clean up by handler or operator. No allowance in standard.
4. Dispose bottle to wooden tray.	
5. Upon completion of tray, make out ticket and place in tray as check against quality of labeling. Foreman can determine responsibility if labels are not up to standard.	Handler supplies bottles and disposes of finished tray.

AUDIT   Production can be checked by order number. Foreman checks time turned in.

B118

Figure 172 Standard job conditions form.

GENERAL JOB CONDITIONS

DATE OF ISSUE_____ BASE RATE NO. ___27112_____ CODE NO._____

BLDG.____148A____ DEPT. ____No. 17____ DIVISION ____Eastern____ OBSERVER _____Davis, W.T.____

TYPE OF OPERATION_____Fill and Pack Bottles of Liquid

LAYOUT OF OPERATION OR LOCALITY

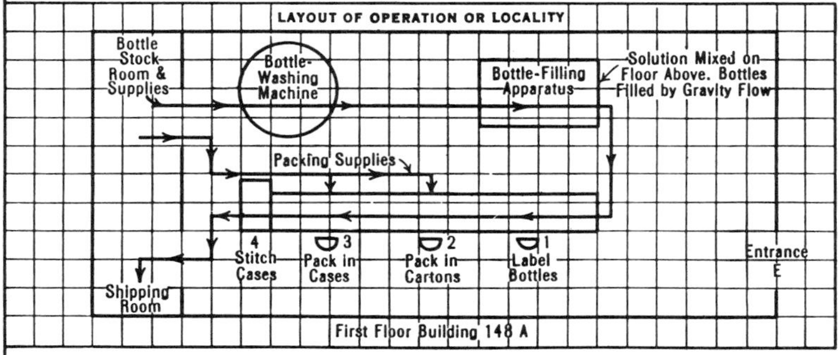

Bottle Stock Room & Supplies — Bottle-Washing Machine — Bottle-Filling Apparatus — Solution Mixed on Floor Above. Bottles Filled by Gravity Flow

Packing Supplies

4 Stitch Cases | 3 Pack in Cases | 2 Pack in Cartons | 1 Label Bottles | Entrance E

Shipping Room

First Floor Building 148 A

RANGE OF APPLICATION Unit designed for handling bottles of liquid product from 4-oz. to 32-oz. size.

DESCRIPTION OF STANDARD EQUIPMENT Balanced production line from supply room through to finished product in shipping room. Equipment consists of: bottle-washing machine No. 3712-A, bottle-filling apparatus No. 2192-O, battery of work places on long bench for labeling, packaging, and packing, and stitching machine No. 3127-C. Bottles handled in wooden trays to prevent accidents due to broken glass.

DESCRIPTION OF WORKING CONDITIONS Regular working hours 8-12, 1-5. Jobs performed in large airy room under daylight conditions. Artificial light available if necessary. Bottle washer wears rubber apron and gloves. Filling operator wears goggles, rubber apron and gloves, and cloth sleeves.

FLOW OF MATERIAL OR SUPPLIES Bottles supplied to washing machine from stock room. Washed bottles then moved to filling apparatus. Moved by truck from filling apparatus to labeling work place. Labeled bottles are then packed in cartons, cartons are packed in cases. Finished case is stitched on stitching machine, and then flows to shipping room. Packing supplies and labels are sent from supply room to position on work place.

B117

Figure 173 General job conditions form.

252

The Warner & Swasey Co.

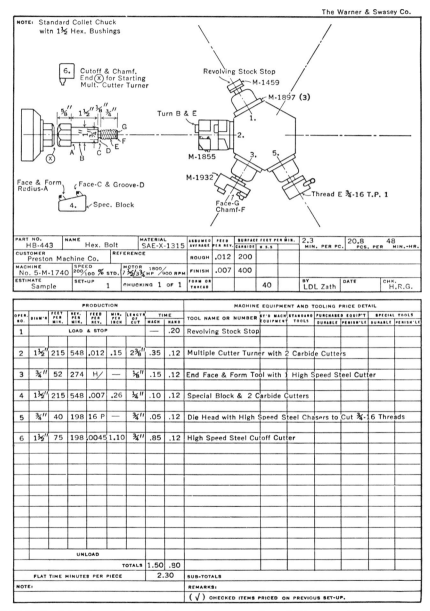

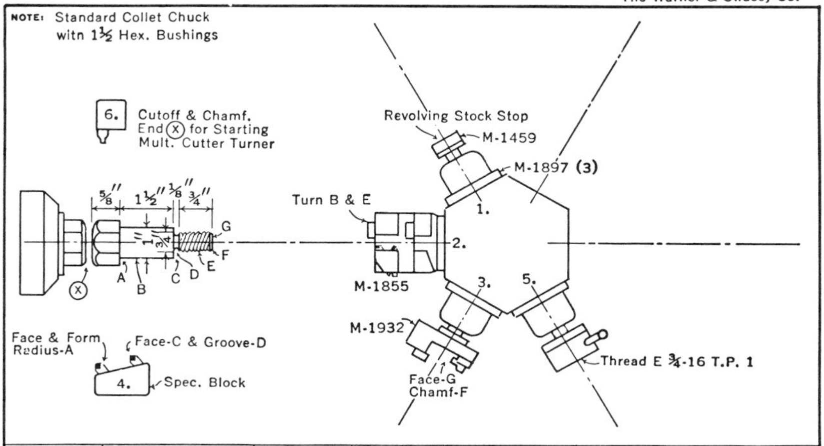
NOTE: Standard Collet Chuck
with 1½ Hex. Bushings
6.
Cutoff & Chamf.
End (X) for Starting
Mult. Cutter Turner
5/8" 1½" 1/8" 3/4"
G
F
E
A B C D
(X)
Face & Form Radius-A
Face-C & Groove-D
4.
Spec. Block
Revolving Stock Stop
M-1459
M-1897 (3)
Turn B & E
1.
2.
3.
5.
M-1855
M-1932
Face-G
Chamf-F
Thread E ¾-16 T.P. 1

PART NO.	NAME	MATERIAL	ASSUMED AVERAGE	FEED PER REV.	SURFACE FEET PER MIN. CARBIDE	H.S.S		2.3 MIN. PER PC.	20.8 PCS. PER 48 MIN.-HR.	
HB-443	Hex. Bolt	SAE-X-1315	ROUGH	.012	200					
CUSTOMER: Preston Machine Co.	REFERENCE		FINISH	.007	400					
MACHINE: No. 5-M-1740	SPEED: 200/100 % STD.	MOTOR: 7½/3¾ HP 1800/900 RPM	FORM OR THREAD			40		BY: LDL Zath	DATE	CHK.: H.R.G.
ESTIMATE: Sample	SET-UP: 1	CHUCKING 1 OF 1								

PRODUCTION									MACHINE EQUIPMENT AND TOOLING PRICE DETAIL						
OPER. NO.	DIAM'R	FEET PER MIN.	REV. PER MIN.	FEED PER REV.	MIN. PER INCH	LENGTH OF CUT	TIME MACH	TIME HAND	TOOL NAME OR NUMBER	ST'D MACH EQUIPMENT	STANDARD TOOLS	PURCHASED EQUIP'T DURABLE	PURCHASED EQUIP'T PERISH'LE	SPECIAL TOOLS DURABLE	SPECIAL TOOLS PERISH'LE
1	LOAD & STOP						—	.20	Revolving Stock Stop						
2	1½"	215	548	.012	.15	2⅜"	.35	.12	Multiple Cutter Turner with 2 Carbide Cutters						
3	¾"	52	274	H/	—	⅛"	.15	.12	End Face & Form Tool with 1 High Speed Steel Cutter						
4	1½"	215	548	.007	.26	¼"	.10	.12	Special Block & 2 Carbide Cutters						
5	¾"	40	198	16 P	—	¾"	.05	.12	Die Head with High Speed Steel Chasers to Cut ¾-16 Threads						
6	1½"	75	198	.0045	1.10	¾"	.85	.12	High Speed Steel Cutoff Cutter						
	UNLOAD														
						TOTALS	1.50	.80							
FLAT TIME MINUTES PER PIECE							2.30		SUB-TOTALS						
NOTE:									REMARKS:						
									(✓) CHECKED ITEMS PRICED ON PREVIOUS SET-UP.						

Figure 174 Job setup and standard practice for operation of Warner and Swasey turret lathe. Size of sheet 11 × 16½ inches.

from the work place, working conditions, and similar matters. Figure 174 shows a job setup and standard practice for an operation on a Warner and Swasey turret lathe.

Some classes of work are relatively simple, and written standard practices can be quickly prepared. On machine-tool work, for example, the speed and feed, shape and size of tools, coolant used, and method of chucking the piece are the important factors. The form in Fig. 293, developed by one company primarily as instructions for the operator, also serves as the basis for their permanent record of the operation.

In some plants where many operations are similar, methods are frequently developed for a whole class of work, and time standards are determined from tables of standard data or forumlas. In such cases similar operations can be grouped into classes for which one master standard practice can be prepared. For example (Fig. 293), all sizes of gear blanks turned on turret lathe JL58 (Operation 5TR, Case D) follow the same sequence of motions of the operator and machine although the speeds, feeds, and sizes of the tools vary with the size of the blank.

Combination Computation Sheet, Instruction Sheet, and Written Standard Practice

The Jones & Lamson Machine Company uses the form shown in Fig. 175 as a combination computation sheet, instruction sheet, and standard practice. The operation referred to is that of machining a sliding gear (Fig. 176) on a No. 5 J & L universal turret lathe. This part is made in the Jones & Lamson plant.

This is the way the time standard is determined and the way the instruction sheet (Fig. 175) is used. That portion of the sheet which appears above the dotted line *A–B* goes to the operator. It shows the standard setup time and standard operation time per piece. This information appears at the top left of the sheet. For Operation 2 (first operation on the turret lathe) the operator is allowed 96 minutes or 1.6 hours to set up his machine, and 7.10 minutes or 0.118 hour to machine each piece. Next follow instructions for machining the piece. Underneath these instructions are instructions in diagram form numbered for sequence of operation. For instance, 1/ is the first operation on the turret lathe, 2/ is the second, etc. These instructions also give the operator the part number of the tool that is to be used. For example, 525 TO is the number of the tool to be used in the first position of the square turret. The speeds and feeds to be used are also given. For example, in the third position of the square turret, the operator is to use a spindle speed of 340 rpm and a feed of 0.011 inch per rpm.

The lower half of the sheet shows exactly how the standard time for the operation is computed. This portion of the sheet, which is kept in the Time Study Department, is available for reference in case of possible complaint or error. In the left-hand corner of this section the setup time for each operation is shown. The general setup time is 16 minutes, this being an average setup. Underneath this figure the time is given for various operations incidental to the complete setup. In the column adjacent to this, time is given for setting stops. The fourth, fifth, and sixth columns show the

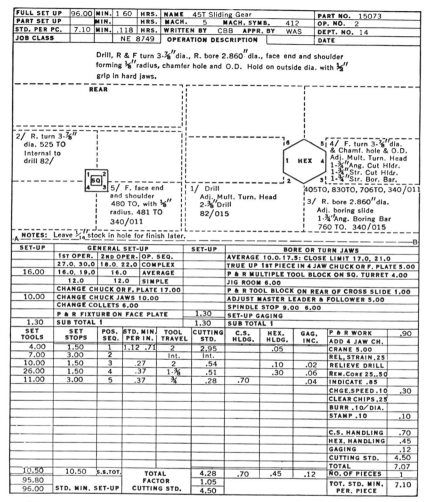

Figure 175 Combination computation sheet, instruction sheet, and written standard practice.

computation of the actual cutting time. This computation includes the actual cutting time plus an incentive allowance. The next three columns give time allowed for miscellaneous handling and gauging. All handling and gauging time contains 15 percent allowance for rest and personal time. The last two columns summarize the cutting and handling times, which total 7.10 minutes. The 1.05 factor by which the cutting time in column six is multiplied to get the final time of 4.50 minutes is an allowance for resharpening dull tools.

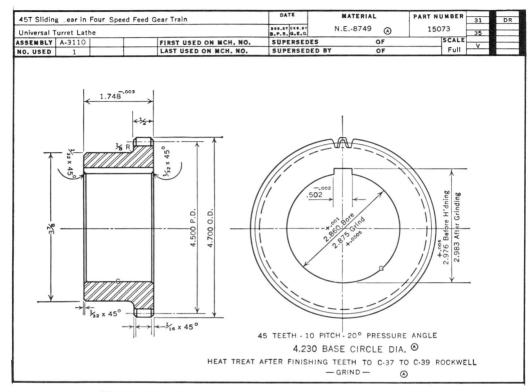

Figure 176 Detail drawing of sliding gear, part number 15073.

Motion Picture or Videotape Records

Some complicated manual operations can be recorded best by motion pictures or videotape. In fact, it may be more economical in certain cases to make the record in this manner than to rely entirely on a written description of the job. On important operations, "before" and "after" motion pictures are frequently made for other purposes and may also serve, of course, as a supplement to the written standard practice. Few companies, however, have seen fit to use motion pictures for standard-practice records in a general way.

20

TIME STUDY: TIME STUDY EQUIPMENT; MAKING THE TIME STUDY

Time study, predetermined time systems, standard data, and work sampling are used for measuring work in industry. Time study is the most versatile and the most widely used. Although work sampling has limited use for determining time standards, it is very effective for obtaining information about activities of operators and machines. Figure 177 shows in condensed form the several methods and devices used for measuring work.

Each of the different methods of determining the standard time required to do a given task will be presented in this and the following chapters. This chapter describes the equipment used and explains how a time study is made. Chapters 21 and 22 show how the rating factor, allowances, and time standard are determined. Chapter 25 describes computerized time study using an electronic data collector. Chapters 27 and 28 give detailed information about predetermined time systems, and Chapter 29 presents the development and use of computerized operational data obtained from predetermined times. Time standards obtained from these data are used as the basis for company-wide wage incentives.

Definition of Time Study

Time study is used to determine the time required by a qualified and well-trained person working at a normal pace to do a specified task. This is the third part of the definition of motion and time study which appears on page 6. It should be noted that, whereas motion study is largely design, time study involves measurement. Time study is used to measure work. The result of time study is the time that a person suited to the job and fully trained in the specified method will need to perform the job if he or she works at a normal or standard tempo. This time is called the *standard time* for the operation.

Uses for Time Study

Although time study originally had its greatest application in connection with wage incentives, it and the other methods of measuring work are now used for many other purposes including:

1. Determining schedules and planning work.
2. Determining standard costs and as an aid in preparing budgets.

Not Measurement	ESTIMATE*	Usually by an experienced estimator
	PAST PERFORMANCE*	From company records

Methods and Devices for Measuring Work	TIME STUDY	Data obtained by means of
		
		(a) Stop watch — electronic timer
		  1. Decimal—minute stop watch
		  2. Decimal—hour stop watch
		  3. Decimal—minute electronic timer
		(b) Electroning data collector — computer—aided
		  1. Datamyte
		(c) Motion picture cameras 16—mm. and 8—mm.
		  1. Spring—driven or battery—driven — normal speed 960 frames per minute.
		  2. Electric motor—driven — 1000 frames per minute
		  3. Time—lapse — 1 to 180 frames per minute
		(d) Video cameras and recorders
		  1. Portable camera and recorder — $\frac{1}{2}$ inch or $\frac{3}{4}$ inch tape
		
		(e) Machines using moving tape or disc
		  1. Operation recorder — tape
		  2. Productolog recorder — disc
		  3. Servis recorder — disc
		(f) Odometer—type counters

	STANDARD DATA	Information obtained from time study or predetermined time systems

	PREDETERMINED TIME SYSTEMS	Nine systems shown in Fig. 231 (listed chronologically by date system was first used or published). Two systems described in detail
		  (a) The Work—Factor System
		  (b) Methods—Time Measurement

	WORK SAMPLING	Measurement by sampling methods
		
		(a) Observer obtains and records data
		  1. Record and analyze data manually
		
		(b) Motion picture camera records information
		(c) Video camera and recorder
		(d) Electronic data collector — computer aided
		  1. Datamyte

*Often used for cost estimating and budget purposes but not recommended for establishing time standards for direct labor for wage incentive purposes.

Figure 177 Methods and devices for measuring work.

3. Estimating the cost of a product before manufacturing it. Such information is of value in preparing bids and in determining selling price.
4. Determining machine effectiveness, the number of machines which one person can operate, and as an aid in balancing assembly lines and work done on a conveyor.
5. Determining time standards to be used as a basis for the payment of a wage incentive to direct labor and indirect labor.
6. Determining time standards to be used as a basis for labor cost control.

TIME STUDY EQUIPMENT

The equipment needed for time study work consists of a timing device and an observation board. The devices most commonly used for measuring work are (1) stop watch or electronic timer, (2) motion picture camera (with constant-speed motor drive or with a microchronometer in the picture to indicate time), and (3) electronic data collector and computer.

Decimal Stop Watches and Electronic Timers

The stop watch (Fig. 178) and the electronic timer are the most widely used timing devices for time study. The electronic timer (Fig. 179), which performs the same function as the stop watch, is sometimes referred to as an electronic stop watch. The

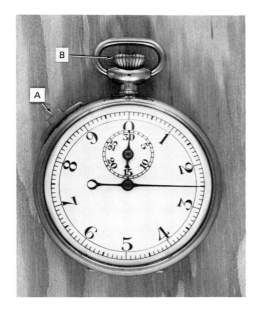

Figure 178   Decimal-minute stop watch.

Figure 179 Decimal-minute electronic timer. Conventional split action: Start timing with left button, then press and release right button for elapsed time of first element. Read time which is locked-in-place as time continues—invisibly. Press right button to restore moving figures. (Courtesy Meylan Stopwatch Corporation.)

electronic data collector and the computer provide an entirely different system for making time studies as will be described later.

The decimal-minute stop watch (Fig. 178) has the dial divided into 100 equal spaces, each of which represents 0.01 minute, the hand making one complete revolution per minute. A smaller dial on the watch is divided into 30 spaces, each of which represents 1 minute, the hand making one complete revolution in 30 minutes. The hands of the watch are controlled by the slide *A* and the winding stem *B* in Fig. 178. The starting and stopping of the watch are controlled by the slide. It is possible to stop the hand at any point and then start it again from that position. Pressure on the top of the stem *B* returns the hand to zero, but it starts off immediately upon releasing the stem. The hand may be held at zero either by holding the stem down or by pushing the slide *A* away from the stem.

The decimal-hour stop watch is like the decimal-minute watch in design and operation, but it has the dial divided into 100 spaces, each of which represents 0.0001 hour, the hand making 100 revolutions per hour. The small dial on the watch is divided into 30 spaces, each of which represents 0.01 hour, the hand making 3⅓ revolutions per hour. The principal advantage of this watch is that the readings are made directly in fractions of an hour, which is the common unit of time measurement in industry. The chief disadvantage of the decimal-hour watch is that it is more difficult to handle four decimal places than two decimal places. This is particularly true in recording stop-watch data on the observation sheet. The split-second stop watch is not recommended and is seldom used for this work.

The Motion Picture Camera and Video Equipment

The time for the elements of an operation can be obtained from motion pictures of the operation made with synchronous motor-driven motion picture camera (Fig. 180) of known speed, or by placing a microchronometer in the picture when the operation is filmed. The method of making such pictures has been explained in Chapter 12.

The camera speed most frequently used is 1000 frames per minute, which permits the measurement of time in thousandths of a minute. A motion picture of an operation forms a permanent record of the method used as well as the time taken for each element of the operation. Moreover, the film may be projected at the exact speed at

Figure 180 Motion picture camera with synchronous motor drive gives a constant speed of 1000 frames per minute.

which the picture was made, and a check may be made of the operator's performance. In other words, the operator's speed or tempo may be rated—that is, related to standard performance. Camera speeds greater than 1000 frames per minute may of course be used.

The video camera and recorder operate at a constant speed of 30 frames per second and identification numbers indicating the scene, the hour, minute, second and frame, appear at the top or bottom edge of the frame. The frame number begins with zero and each frame is numbered consecutively. Thus there is a positive and direct way of identifying each frame and of measuring time.

Electronic Data Collector and Computer

An electronic data collector (Fig. 181) and computer which simplify the making of time studies are available. The analyst using the hand-held unit collects the data and the computer performs the clerical work—makes the computations, analyses, and summarizes the data and computes the time standard. This equipment may also be used for work sampling, downtime studies, production studies, and other event recording. Electronic time study is fully described in Chapter 25.

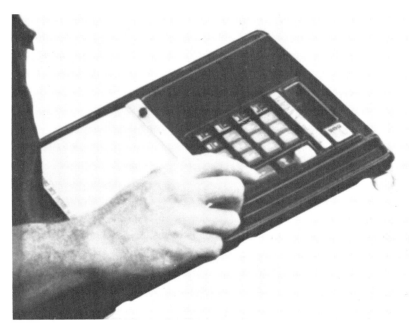

Figure 181 Datamyte data collector showing keyboard and display. (Courtesy Electro General Corporation.)

Electrical and Mechanical Time Recorders

Several different devices are available for recording machine downtime and running time and may also serve for obtaining information in connection with time studies.

The Servis recorder is a spring-driven instrument which records time on a wax-coated paper disc by means of a stylus attached to a small pendulum within the instrument. The recorder is fastened to a machine or piece of equipment, and the vibration of the machine causes the stylus to record running on the disc. When the machine stops, the pendulum stops vibrating and the instrument records downtime on the disc. The disc, divided into hours and minutes, indicates the length of running time or downtime and also the time of day when each occurs.

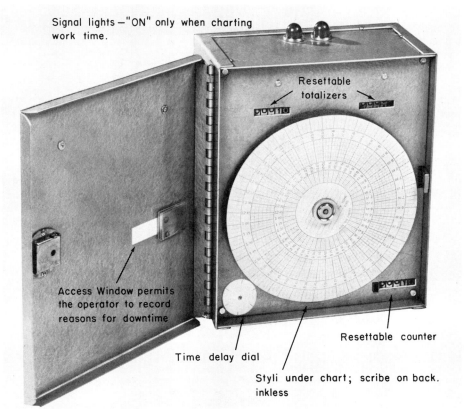

Signal lights —"ON" only when charting work time.

Resettable totalizers

Access Window permits the operator to record reasons for downtime

Time delay dial

Resettable counter

Styli under chart; scribe on back. inkless

Figure 182 Productolog. Electric motor driven time recorder. (Courtesy Meylan Stopwatch Corporation.)

The Productlog (Fig. 182) is an electric motor-driven device which records on a disc chart by means of a single or double stylus the downtime and running time of a machine. An access window permits the operator to record reasons for downtime. A device using moving paper tape performs similar functions. Odometer-type counters are also used for measuring downtime and running time of machines and equipment.

Observation Board

A lightweight board, slightly larger than the observation sheet, is used to hold the paper and the stop watch. There are many different arrangements, but it seems best to have the watch mounted rigidly somewhere near the upper right-hand corner of the board and observation sheets held in place by some form of clamp at the side or top of the board. The observation board shown in Fig. 183 is a type commonly used. Because the analyst, in most cases, must record the data while standing, it is desirable to have the watch and paper arranged as conveniently as possible.

While taking a time study the observer should hold the board against the body and

Figure 183 Observation board with observation sheet for recording data by the repetitive method.

the upper left arm in such a way that the watch can be operated by the thumb and index finger of the left hand. The observer holds the board with the left hand and arm, leaving the right hand free to record the data.

By standing in the proper position relative to the work being observed, and by holding the board so that the dial of the watch falls in the line of vision, the observer can concentrate more easily on the three things that demand attention, namely, the operator, the watch, and the observation sheet.

The observation sheet is a printed form with spaces provided for recording information about the operation being studied. This information usually includes a detailed description of the operation, the name of the operator, the name of the time study observer, and the date and place of study. The form also provides spaces for recording stop-watch readings for each element of the operation, performance ratings of the operator, and computations. Space may be provided for a sketch of the work place, a drawing of the part, and specifications of the material, jigs, gauges, and tools.

Observation sheets differ in size and design but a sheet 8½ inches by 11 inches is widely used, mainly because it fits the standard file or binder. The observation sheets shown in Figs. 184, 203, and 207 have proved to be satisfactory in industries manufacturing a diversified line of products. Some organizations find it convenient to supplement the observation sheet with a separate computation sheet (Fig. 209) and a sheet containing a more complete description of each element (Fig. 212).

Other Equipment

A speed indicator, or tachometer, is needed where machine-tool operations are studied. The analyst should check speeds and feeds in making a time study, even though the machine has a table attached which gives this information for each setting of the speed and feed-control levers.

MAKING THE TIME STUDY

The exact procedure used in making time studies may vary somewhat, depending upon the type of operation being studied and the application that is to be made of the data obtained. These eight steps, however, are usually required:

1. Secure and record information about the operation and operator being studied.
2. Divide the operation into elements and record a complete description of the method.
3. Observe and record the time taken by the operator.
4. Determine the number of cycles to be timed.
5. Rate the operator's performance.
6. Check to make certain that a sufficient number of cycles have been timed.
7. Determine the allowances.
8. Determine the time standard for the operation.

OBSERVATION SHEET

DATE

OPERATION Drill ¼" Hole

OP. NO. D-20

PART NAME Motor Shaft

PART NO. MS-267

MACHINE NAME Avey

MACH. NO. 2174

MALE ☑
FEMALE ☐

OPERATOR'S NAME & NO. S.K. Adams 1347

EXPERIENCE ON JOB 18 Mo. on Sens. Drill

MATERIAL S.A.E. 2315

FOREMAN H. Miller

DEPT. NO. DL 21

BEGIN 10:15	FINISH 10:38	ELAPSED 23	UNITS FINISHED 20	ACTUAL TIME PER 100 115	NO. MACHINES OPERATED 1

ELEMENTS	SPEED	FEED		1	2	3	4	5	6	7	8	9	10	SELECTED TIME
1. Pick Up Piece and Place in Jig			T	.12	.11	.12	.13	.12	.10	.12	.12	.14	.12	
			R	.12	.29	.39	.54	.66	.77	.92	8.01	14	.32	
2. Tighten Set Screw			T	.13	.12	.12	.14	.11	.12	.12	.13	.12	.11	
			R	.25	.41	.51	.68	.77	.89	7.04	.14	.26	.43	
3. Advance Drill to Work			T	.05	.04	.04	.04	.05	.04	.04	.04	.03	.04	
			R	.30	.45	.55	.72	.82	.93	.08	.18	.29	.47	
4. DRILL ¼" HOLE	980	H	T	.57	.54	.56	.51	.54	.58	.52	.53	.59	.56	
			R	.87	.99	3.11	4.23	5.36	6.51	.60	.71	.88	11.03	
5. Raise Drill from Hole			T	.04	.03	.03	.03	.03	.03	.03	.03	.04	.03	
			R	.91	2.02	.14	.26	.39	.54	.63	.74	.92	.06	
6. Loosen Set Screw			T	.06	.06	.07	.06	.06	.06	.06	.06	.07	.08	
			R	.97	.08	.21	.32	.45	.60	.69	.80	.99	.14	
7. Remove Piece from Jig			T	.08	.09	.08	.08	.09	.08	.07	.08	.09	.07	
			R	1.05	.17	.29	.40	.54	.68	.76	.88	10.08	.21	
8. Blow Out Chips			T	.13	.10	.12	.14	.13	.12	.13	.12	.12	.11	
			R	.18	.27	.41	.54	.67	.80	.89	9.00	.20	.32	
9.			T											
			R											
10. (1)			T	.12	.11	.13	.14	.12	.12	.11	.13	.12	.12	.12
			R	11.44	.56	.69	.82	.87	17.01	18.09	.21	.31	.42	
11. (2)			T	.12	.14	.12	.11	.12	.10	.13	.15	.12	.11	.12
			R	.56	.70	.81	.93	.99	.11	.22	.36	.43	.53	
12. (3)			T	.04	.04	.04	.03	.04	.04	.04	.04	.04	.04	.04
			R	.60	.74	.85	.96	16.03	.15	.26	.40	.47	.57	
13. (4)			T	.54	.53	.55	.52	.57	.54	.50	.53	.55	.64	.54
			R	12.14	13.27	14.40	15.48	.60	.69	.76	.93	21.02	22.11	
14. (5)			T	.03	.03	.03	.03	.03	.03	.03	.03	.03	.03	.03
			R	.17	.30	.43	.51	.63	.72	.79	.96	.05	.14	
15. (6)			T	.06	.06	.06	.07	.06	.05	.06	.06	.05	.06	.06
			R	.23	.36	.49	.58	.69	.77	.85	20.02	.10	.20	
16. (7)			T	.08	.08	.09	.08	.08	.07	.08	.06	.08	.08	.08
			R	.31	.44	.58	.66	.77	.84	.93	.08	.18	.28	
17. (8)			T	.14	.12	.10	.09	.12	.14	.15	.11	.12	12	.12
			R	.45	.56	.68	.75	.89	.98	19.08	.19	.30	22.40	
18.			T											1.11
			R											

SELECTED TIME 1.11	RATING 100%	NORMAL TIME 1.11	TOTAL ALLOWANCES 5%	STANDARD TIME 1.17

Overall Length 12" Drill ¼" Hole

TOOLS, JIGS, GAUGES: Jig No. D-12-33
Use H.S. Drill ¼" Diam.
Hand Feed
Use Oil - S4

TIMED BY *J.B.M.*

Figure 184 Stop-watch time study of a drilling operation made by the continuous method.

Request for a Time Study

A time study is not made unless an authorized person requests it. Usually it is the supervisor who requests that a study be made, but the plant manager, chief engineer, production control supervisor, cost accountant, or other member of the organization may make such a request.

If a time standard is to be established on a new job for wage incentive purposes, in most plants it is the supervisor's responsibility to make certain that the operation is running satisfactorily before requesting the study. The supervisor should also see that the operators have thoroughly learned the job and that they are following the pre-scribed method. The supervisor should inform the operators in advance that a time study is to be made, stating the purpose of the study.

Is the Job Ready for Time Study?

After a request for a time study has been received by the time study department and an analyst has been assigned to make the study, he or she should go over the job with the supervisor of the department. As they discuss each element of the operation, the analyst asks the question, "Is this operation ready for a time study?"

The time standard established for a job will not be correct if the method of doing the job has changed, if the materials do not meet specifications, if the machine speed has changed, or if other conditions of work are different from those that were present when the time study was originally made. The time study analyst therefore examines the operation with the purpose of suggesting any changes that he or she thinks should be effected before the time study is made.

Although the supervisor may have set up the job originally or may have checked the method with the process engineer who set it up, the time study analyst should question each phase of the work, asking such questions as:

1. Can the speed or feed of the machine be increased without affecting optimum tool life or without adversely affecting the quality of the product?
2. Can changes in tooling be made to reduce the cycle time?
3. Can materials be moved closer to the work area to reduce handling time?
4. Is the equipment operating correctly, and is a quality product being produced?
5. Is the operation being performed safely?

It is expected that the time study analyst will be trained in motion study and will bring all possible knowledge in this field to bear on the operation about to be studied. Any suggested changes that the supervisor wishes to adopt should be made before the study is started. The supervisor of course makes the decision as to the way the job is to be done, but the analyst and the supervisor should discuss each element of the operation and should agree that the operation is ready for a time study. Standard-ization of the work has been discussed at length in the preceding chapters, and it has been emphasized that all standardization should precede the actual setting of the time standard.

If a major change in the operation is to be made and if considerable time will be required to put the new method into effect, it might be wise to make a time study of the present method and then, after the improvements are installed, restudy the job and set a new time standard. If only minor changes are contemplated, it is usually advisable to complete such changes before making a time study of the job.

Making the Time Study

Those phases of time study that can be carried out at the time and place of the performance of the operation will be described in this and the following chapter. They are obtaining and recording necessary information, dividing the operation into subdivisions or elements, listing these elements in proper sequence, timing them with the stop watch and recording the readings, determining the number of cycles to be timed, noting and recording the operator's tempo or performance level, and making a sketch of the part and of the work place.

Recording Information

All information requested in the heading of the observation sheet should be carefully recorded. This is important because time studies hastily and incompletely made are of little value. The first place to practice thoroughness is in filling in all necessary information for identification. Unless this is done, a study may be practically worthless as a record or as a source of information for standard data and formula construction a few months after it has been made, because the person who made the study has forgotten the circumstances surrounding it. Ordinarily, the necessary information concerning the operation, part, material, customer, order number, lot size, etc., can be obtained from the route sheet, bill of material, or drawing of the part.

A sketch of the part should be drawn at the bottom or on the back of the sheet if a special place is not provided. A sketch of the work place should also be included, showing the working position of the operator and the location of the tools, fixtures, and materials. Specifications of the materials being worked on should be given, and a description of the equipment being used should be recorded. Ordinarily the trade name, class, type, and size of the machine are sufficient description. If the machine has an identification number assigned to it, the number should be included. Accurate record should be made of the number, size, and description of tools, fixtures, gauges, and templets. The name and number of the operator should be recorded, and the time study should be signed by the time study analyst.

Dividing the Operation into Elements and Recording a Description of the Method

The standard time for an operation applies only to that particular operation; therefore, a complete and detailed description of the method must be recorded on the observation sheet or on auxiliary sheets to be attached to the observation sheet. The importance of this description cannot be overemphasized. At any time after the standard has been established for a job, the time study department may be asked to determine whether the operator is performing the job in the same way it was being performed when the time study was originally made. The information contained on the observation sheet is the most complete description of the method that the time study department has available for such a check.

Reasons for Element Breakdown

Timing an entire operation as one element is seldom satisfactory, and an over-all study is no substitute for a time study. Breaking the operation down into short elements and timing each of them separately are essential parts of time study, for the following reasons:

1. One of the best ways to describe an operation is to break it down into definite and measurable elements and describe each of these separately. Those elements of the operation that occur regularly are usually listed first, and then all other elements that are a necessary part of the job are described. It is sometimes desirable to prepare a detailed description of the elements of an operation on a separate sheet and attach it to the observation sheet. The beginning and end points for each element may be specifically indicated (see page 312, also Fig. 212). Very often the elements taken from the time study can serve as the "standard practice" for the operation (Fig. 293). Such a list of elements also may be used for training new operators on the job.

2. Standard time values may be determined for the elements of the job. Such element time standards or standard data make it possible to determine the total standard time for an operation (see Chapter 23).

3. A time study may show that excessive time is being taken to perform certain elements of the job or that too little time is being spent on other elements. This latter condition sometimes occurs on inspection elements. Also the analysis of an operation by elements may show slight variations in method that could not be detected so easily from an over-all study.

4. An operator may not work at the same tempo throughout the cycle. A time study permits separate performance ratings to be applied to each element of the job.

When time studies are to be made of a new product or a new type of work, a careful analysis should be made of all variables of the work that are likely to occur. It is desirable to establish standard data as soon as possible, and such standards can be developed more quickly if the general framework of the standards is prepared before any time studies are made. It is especially important to prepare a definition of elements so that these same elements may be used in all time studies.

Rules for Dividing an Operation into Elements

All manual work may be divided into fundamental hand motions or therbligs, as has already been explained. These subdivisions are too short in duration to be timed with a stop watch. A number of them, therefore, must be grouped together into elements of sufficient length to be conveniently timed. Three rules should be followed in dividing an operation into elements:

1. The elements should be as short in duration as can be accurately timed.
2. Handling time should be separated from machine time.
3. Constant elements should be separated from variable elements.

To be of value a time study must be a study of the elements of the operation, not merely a record of the total time required per cycle to do work. If elements are too short, however, it is impossible to time them accurately.

In machine work it is desirable to separate the machine time, that is, the time that the machine is doing work, from the time during which the operator is working. There are several reasons for this. Where power feeds and speeds are used on the machine, it is possible to calculate the time required for the "cut" and thus check the actual stop-watch data when the machine time is kept separately. Also, the beginning and end of a cut are excellent beginning and ending points for an element. Where standard data and formulas are to be developed, it is essential that machine time be separated from handling time. The reasons for this separation will be explained in Chapter 23.

The elements of a cycle that are constant should be separated from those that are variable. The term *constant elements* refers to those elements that are independent of the size, weight, length, and shape of the piece. For example, in soldering seams of tin cans made by hand, the time to touch the iron to the bar of solder is a constant, whereas the time to solder the side seam on the can is a variable, varying directly with the length of the seam.

The analyst trained in the mecromotion study technique or in the use of predetermined times will find it relatively easy to decide upon the elements of the operation, because they are merely combinations of fundamental motions. The analyst without such training should see that the elements begin and end at well-defined points in the cycle. These points will have to be memorized so that the analyst will always read his watch at exactly the same place in the cycle; otherwise the time for the elements will be incorrect.

Each element should be concisely recorded in the space provided on the sheet. It is sometimes advisable to use symbols to represent elements that are often repeated. In some industries a standard code of symbols is used by all time study observers. When symbols are used, their meaning should appear on each observation sheet.

Taking and Recording the Data

The three most common methods of reading and stop watch are (1) continuous timing, (2) repetitive timing, and (3) accumulative timing. The first two methods have wider use than the last.

Continuous Timing. In the continuous method of timing the observer starts the watch at the beginning of the first element and permits it to run continuously during the period of the study (Fig. 184). The observer notes the reading of the watch at the end of each element and records this reading on the observation sheet, opposite its name or symbol. Fig. 203 illustrates the continuous method of timing. The operation "Make Core for Crank Frame" was divided into four elements. The observer started his watch at the beginning of the first element, read it at the end of the first element, and recorded the reading in vertical column 1 on the lower line. In a similar manner the watch was read at the end of each element, and the readings for the first cycle were recorded in column 1. The second cycle was then timed and the data recorded in the second vertical column, and so on.

STUDY NO. 8765

ELEMENTS	SPEED	FEED	1
1. Fill core box with 3 handfuls of sand. Press sand down each time.			*.09*
			0.9
2. Press sand down with one trowel stroke. Strike off with one trowel stroke.			*.06*
			.15
3. Get and place plate on core box, turn over, rap, and remove box.			*.13*
			.28
4. Carry plate with core 4 feet. Dispose on oven truck.			*.04*
			.32

Figure 185 Part of observation sheet for operation "Make Core for Crank Frame." The watch readings and the subtracted times for the first cycle are shown. See Fig. 203 for complete study.

The time for each element was later determined by subtraction (Fig. 185). Thus, for the first element, .09 (.09 − 0 = .09) minute was placed in the upper line opposite element 1. In a similar way for the second element, .06 (.15 − .09 = .06) minute was placed in the first vertical column opposite the second element.

Repetitive Timing. In the repetitive or snap-back method the hands of the watch are snapped back to zero at the end of each element. At the beginning of the first element the observer snaps the hand back to zero by pressing the stem of the watch. The hand moving forward instantly begins to measure the time for the first element. At the end of the first element the observer reads the watch, snaps the hand back to zero, and then records this reading. In a like manner the observer times the rest of the elements. This method of timing gives the direct time without subtractions, and the data are recorded on the observation sheet as read from the watch (Fig. 207).

Some people think that there is a tendency for the observer to neglect to time and record delays, foreign elements, or false motions of the operator by simply holding down the stem of the watch. This is not a valid criticism of repetitive timing, because the observer should be taught to time and record *all elements* that occur during the study. The main advantage of the repetitive method over the continuous method is that the time for each element is visible on the observation sheet and the time study analyst can see the variations in time values as the study is made.

Accumulative Timing. The accumulative method of timing permits the direct reading of the time for each element by the use of two stop watches. These watches are mounted close together on the observation board and are connected by a lever mechanism in such a way that when the first watch is started the second watch is automatically stopped, and when the second watch is started the first is stopped. The watch may be snapped back to zero immediately after it is read, thus making subtractions unnecessary. The watch is read with greater ease and accuracy because its hands are not in motion at the time it is read.

Recording the Stop-Watch Readings

To the uninitiated it may seem difficult for the observer to do the several things required in such quick succession, namely, observe the operator, read the watch, and record the data on the observation sheet; but it is easily possible after some practice. A distinctive sound frequently accompanies the beginning and the ending of the element. In the study of the drilling operation (Fig. 184), as the shaft is dropped into place in the jig, there is a metallic click which denotes the end of the first element. Such sounds aid the observer in taking the readings, and he or she soon learns to make use of them.

The general policy of carefully timing every part of the operation should be a requirement. If, for example, every fifth or every tenth piece is gauged, such information should be included on the observation sheet and a sufficient number of readings of this element should be made to include it in the time for the operation. The time for the element would, of course, be divided by 5 or 10, as the case might be, in order to prorate the gauging time.

Such elements as "change tools," "blow chips out of jig," "move finished parts," "replace empty tote box," "lubricate die," and the like should be considered specific parts of the operation and should be timed as such. In timing elements that occur infrequently, it is necessary to get a sufficient number of watch readings and also to obtain data as to the frequency of occurrence of such elements so that the time can be prorated.

When foreign elements occur, they should be timed and recorded on the observation sheet. These elements may or may not be included in the time standard, depending upon their nature. By foreign elements is meant elements that do not occur regularly in the cycle, such as accidentally dropping a wrench or piece of material on the floor, or placing oil on a tight screw in a jig.

Number of Cycles to Be Timed

The time required to perform the elements of an operation may be expected to vary slightly from cycle to cycle. Even if the operator worked at a uniform pace, each element of consecutive cycles would not always be performed in exactly the same time. Variations in time may result from such things as a difference in the exact position of the parts and tools used by the operator, or from possible differences in determining the exact end point at which the watch reading is made. With highly standardized raw materials, good tools and equipment, good working conditions, and a qualified and well-trained operator, the variation in readings for an element would not be great, but there would still be some variation.

Time study is a sampling process; consequently the greater the number of cycles timed, the more nearly the results will be representative of the activity being measured. Consistency of watch readings is of major interest to the analyst. For example, 20 cycles of the operation shown in Fig. 184 were studied, and the time for element 1 of the study varied from 0.10 to 0.14 minute. Had all of the 20 readings been 0.10 minute, then the consistency would have been perfect, and 0.10 would obviously have been selected as the time value for this element. The greater the variability of the readings for an element, the larger the number of observations will have to be for a desired accuracy.

Formula for Determining Number of Observations

Formulas 1 and 2 of this section provide a simple means of evaluating the error in the average time value of an element for a given number of readings. It is assumed that variations in the time from observation to observation are due to chance, and this seems to be a reasonable assumption.

The standard error of the average for each element (standard error of the mean) is expressed by the formula: [1]

$$\sigma \bar{x} = \frac{\sigma'}{\sqrt{N}} \tag{1}$$

where $\sigma \bar{x}$ = standard deviation of the distribution of averages

σ' = standard deviation of the universe for a given element

N = actual number of observations of the element

Standard deviation is denoted by σ (sigma). By definition, it is the root-mean-square deviation of the observed readings from their average.[2] That is,

$$\sigma = \sqrt{\frac{(X_1 - \overline{X})^2 + (X_2 - \overline{X})^2 + \cdots + (X_n - \overline{X})^2}{N}} \tag{2}$$

$$= \sqrt{\frac{\Sigma(X - \overline{X})^2}{N}} = \sqrt{\frac{\Sigma X^2}{N} - \overline{X}^2}$$

---

[1] Eugene L. Grant and Richard S. Leavenworth, *Statistical Quality Control,* 4th ed., McGraw-Hill, New York, p. 84, 1972.
[2] Ibid., pp. 50–51.

where X = each stop-watch reading or individual observation.
   $\bar{X}$ = (read "X-bar") average or mean of all readings of an element
   Σ = (read "sigma") sum of individual readings

Because $\bar{X} = \dfrac{\Sigma X}{N}$,

$$\sigma = \sqrt{\frac{\Sigma X^2}{N} - \left(\frac{\Sigma X}{N}\right)^2} = \frac{1}{N}\sqrt{N\Sigma X^2 - (\Sigma X)^2} \tag{3}$$

Combining formulas 1 and 3,

$$\sigma\bar{x} = \frac{\dfrac{1}{N}\sqrt{N\Sigma X^2 - (\Sigma X)^2}}{\sqrt{N'}} \tag{4}$$

A decision must be made as to the confidence level and the desired accuracy that are to be used in determining the number of observations to make. A 95 percent confidence level and ±5 percent precision are commonly used in time study. This means that the chances are at least 95 out of 100 that the sample mean or the average value for the element will not be in error more than ±5 percent of the true element time. Then

$$0.05\bar{X} = 2\sigma\bar{x} \quad \text{or} \quad 0.05\frac{\Sigma X}{N} = 2\sigma\bar{x}$$

$$0.05\frac{\Sigma X}{N} = 2\frac{\dfrac{1}{N}\sqrt{N\Sigma X^2 - (\Sigma X)^2}}{\sqrt{N'}}$$

$$N' = \left(\frac{40\sqrt{N\Sigma X^2 - (\Sigma X)^2}}{\Sigma X}\right)^2 \tag{5}$$

where N' is the required number of observations to predict the true time within ±5 percent precision and 95 percent confidence level.

If a 95 percent confidence level and a precision of ±10 percent are used as the criteria, then the formula will be

$$N' = \left(\frac{20\sqrt{N\Sigma X^2 - (\Sigma X)^2}}{\Sigma X}\right)^2 \tag{6}$$

EXAMPLE   Assume that 30 observations have been made of an element, as shown in the first column of Fig. 186, and the observer wants to know whether he has taken a sufficient number of observations for a 95 percent confidence level and a precision of ±5 percent. Formula 5 is the one to use for this. Figure 186 shows the sum of the 30 observations and the sum of the squares of the 30 observations. Substituting these data in formula 5, the computations would be as follows:

$$N' = \left(\frac{40\sqrt{30 \times 967 - 169^2}}{169}\right)^2 = \left(\frac{40\sqrt{29010 - 28561}}{169}\right)^2$$

$$= \left(\frac{40 \times 21.2}{169}\right)^2 = \left(\frac{848}{169}\right)^2 = 25 \text{ observations}$$

Another formula for determining the number of cycles to be timed is

$$N' = \left[\frac{40N}{\Sigma X} \sqrt{\frac{\Sigma X^2 - (\Sigma X)^2/N}{N - 1}}\right]^2 \tag{7}$$

Operation:	Make core for Crank Frame No. 7253.
Element No. 2:	Press sand down with one trowel stroke. Strike off with one trowel stroke.

Individual Watch Readings in 0.01 Min. X	Individual Watch Readings Squared X^2
6	36
5	25
8	64
6	36
5	25
5	25
6	36
5	25
5	25
6	36
6	36
5	25
5	25
6	36
6	36
5	25
5	25
5	25
5	25
6	36
6	36
6	36
6	36
5	25
6	36
6	36
7	49
6	36
5	25
5	25
$\Sigma X = 169$	$\Sigma X^2 = 967$

Figure 186   Values for X and X^2 for element 2 of the time study shown in Fig. 203.

This formula results from using the following formula instead of formula 3:

$$\sigma = \sqrt{\frac{\Sigma X^2 - (\Sigma X)^2 / N}{N - 1}}$$

Formula 7 tends to be more accurate as the number of cycles timed decreases.

Estimating the Number of Observations to Make

The Maytag Company uses the following procedure for estimating the number of observations to make.

1. Take readings: (a) ten good readings for cycles of 2 minutes or less; (b) five good readings for cycles of more than 2 minutes.
2. Determine the range R. This is the high time study value H minus the low time study value L ($H - L = R$).
3. Determine the average X. This is the sum of the readings divided by the number of readings (either 5 or 10). This average may be approximated by high value plus low value divided by 2. That is, $(H + L)/2$.
4. Determine $R/\bar{X}$. This is the range divided by the average.
5. Determine the number of readings necessary[3] from Table 13. Read down the

---

[3] The values shown in Table 13 were determined in the following way. It can be shown (see Grant, *op. cit.*, p. 72) that:

$$\sigma' = \frac{\bar{R}}{d_2}$$

where $\bar{R}$ = average range, the average of the difference between the high and low observed value of
     subgroups of same number of readings

d_2 = factor based on the number of readings in the subgroup (see Grant, *op. cit.*, p. 644.)

From formula 1,

$$\sigma\bar{x} = \frac{\sigma'}{\sqrt{N}} \quad \text{or} \quad \sigma' = \sigma\bar{x}\sqrt{N}$$

Then

$$\sigma\bar{x} = \frac{\bar{R}}{d_2\sqrt{N}} = \quad \text{or} \quad 2\sigma\bar{x} = 2\frac{\bar{R}}{d_2\sqrt{N}}$$

For a 95% confidence level and a precision of ±5%, then $0.05X = 2\sigma\bar{x}$.

$$0.05\bar{X} = \frac{2\bar{R}}{d_2\sqrt{N}}$$

$$0.025 d_2 \sqrt{N} = \frac{\bar{R}}{\bar{X}}$$

When the number of observations in the subgroup is 5, then $d_2 = 2.326$. When the number is 10, then $d_2 = 3.078$. (See Grant, *op. cit.*, p. 644.)

Table 13. Number of Time Study Readings N' Required for $\pm 5\%$ Precision and 95% Confidence Level

$\dfrac{R}{X}$	Data from Sample of		$\dfrac{R}{X}$	Data from Sample of		$\dfrac{R}{X}$	Data from Sample of	
	5	10		5	10		5	10
.10	3	2	.42	52	30	.74	162	93
.12	4	2	.44	57	33	.76	171	98
.14	6	3	.46	63	36	.78	180	103
.16	8	4	.48	68	39	.80	190	108
.18	10	6	.50	74	42	.82	199	113
.20	12	7	.52	80	46	.84	209	119
.22	14	8	.54	86	49	.86	218	125
.24	17	10	.56	93	53	.88	229	131
.26	20	11	.58	100	57	.90	239	138
.28	23	13	.60	107	61	.92	250	143
.30	27	15	.62	114	65	.94	261	149
.32	30	17	.64	121	69	.96	273	156
.34	34	20	.66	129	74	.98	284	162
.36	38	22	.68	137	78	1.00	296	169
.38	43	24	.70	145	83			
.40	47	27	.72	153	88			

R = range of time for sample, which is equal to high time study elemental value minus low time study elemental value.

X = average time value of element for sample. (For $\pm 10\%$ precision and 95% confidence level, divide answer by 4.)

first column until the value of R/X is found; then read across to column for sample size taken (5 or 10); and then to the total number of readings required. (For 95 percent confidence level and ± 10 percent precision divide the required number found by 4.)

6. Continue to take readings until the total of the indicated number required is obtained.

A copy of Table 13 is attached to the time study observation board so that the observer may determine on the job the approximate number of readings necessary.

EXAMPLE   Figure 187 is a time study of ten consecutive cycles of an operation consisting of three elements. The following is the procedure used to determine the number of readings needed for a 95 percent confidence level and a precision of ± 5 percent.

1. Take readings: Ten good readings for each element are shown in Fig. 187. Element 1 will be used for this example.

Element 1	.07	.09	.06	.07	.08	.08	.07	.08	.09	.07
Element 2	.12	.13	.12	.12	.11	.13	.12	.11	.13	.12
Element 3	.56	.57	.55	.56	.57	.56	.54	.56	.56	.55

Figure 187   Time study of ten cycles of an operation. The average of the ten observations for element 1 is 0.076 minute.

2.   Determine the range R for element 1.

$$R = H - L = 0.09 = 0.06 = 0.03 \text{ minute}$$

3.   Determine the average $\overline{X}$.

$$\overline{X} = \frac{0.76}{10} = 0.076 \text{ minute}$$

4.   Determine the value of $R/\overline{X}$.

$$\frac{\overline{R}}{\overline{X}} = \frac{0.03}{0.076} = 0.395$$

5.   Determine the number of readings necessary from Table 13. Since 0.395 is closer to 0.40 than 0.38, the number of readings corresponding to 40 is 27.
6.   Continue the study until a total of 27 readings is obtained.

Final Check as to Number of Observations

Table 13 was used at the beginning of the study to determine the approximate number of observations required. After the study was completed (Fig. 188), the time study observer at Maytag made a check to determine whether enough readings had been made, using the following procedure.[4]

Element 1	.07 .09 .06 .07	.08 .08 .07 .08	.09 .07 .08 .08	.07 .09 .08 .08
	.03	.01	.02	.02
Element 1	.06 .07 .08 .08	.08 .09 .09 .06	.07 .08 .08 .09	.10 .10 .07 .08
	.02	.03	.02	.03

Figure 188   Time study data for element 1, showing subgroups of 4 observations. Average of the 32 observations is 0.0787 minute. $\overline{X} = 0.0787$.

[4] For an explanation of a similar procedure, see John M. Allderige, "Statistical Procedures in Stop Watch Work Measurement," *Journal of Industrial Engineering*, Vol. VII, No. 4, pp. 154–163.

1. Divide the readings for the element into subgroups of 4 (Fig. 188).
2. Determine the range R for each subgroup. This is the high time study value minus the low time study value.
3. Determine the average range $\bar{R}$ of the subgroups. This is found by averaging all the ranges of the subgroups.
4. Determine the average $\bar{X}$. This is the unrated average value that is normally found in working up the time study.
5. Determine the number of readings necessary from Fig. 189. Read across on the vertical scale using average range $\bar{R}$, and up from the bottom scale using average

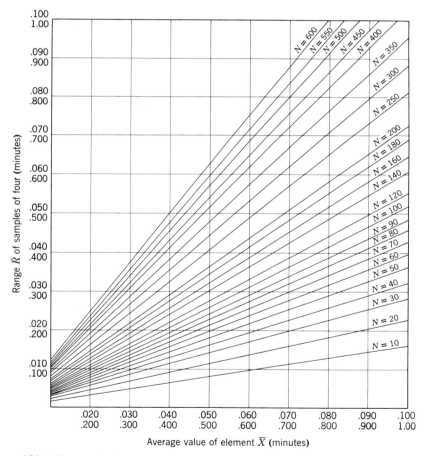

Figure 189   Curves showing relationship between average range of samples of four observations and average value of the element being timed. All readings are in minutes.

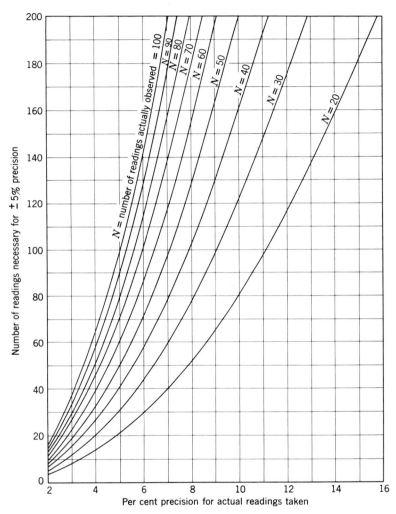

Figure 190 Curves showing the relationship between number of readings necessary for ±5% precision, number of readings actually observed, and precision in percent for readings actually taken.

value of element $\overline{X}$; where intersection occurs, note location with respect to diagonal lines running across graph.

6. Determine precision actually obtained from Fig. 190. Read across on the vertical scale, using the number of readings that would be necessary for ±5 percent precision, until the line intersects the number of readings actually taken; a vertical line running straight down from this intersection will fall on the actual precision obtained.

EXAMPLE   From the study shown in Fig. 188, determine (a) the number of readings necessary for a 95 percent confidence level and ±5 percent precision, and (b) the precision obtained from the actual number of readings observed if less than the number called for in (a).

Solution for a (number of readings necessary for ±5 percent precision):

1. Divide the readings for this element into subgroups of 4 (Fig. 188).
2. Determine the range R for each subgroup.

$$.03 + .01 + .02 + .02 + .02 + .03 + .02 + .03 = .18$$

3. Determine the average range $\overline{R}$ of the subgroups.

$$\overline{R} = \frac{0.18}{8} = 0.0225 \text{ minute}$$

4. Determine the average $\overline{X}$. The unrated average value for element 1, as shown on the study, is 0.0787 minute.
5. Determine the number of readings necessary for a 95 percent confidence level and ±5 percent precision from Fig. 189. (Solution for $\overline{R} = 0.0225$ and $\overline{X} = 0.0787$ is $N =$ approximately 30 observations.)

Solution for b (precision obtained from the actual number of readings observed): To illustrate the use of Fig. 190, let us assume that the time study observer makes only 20 observations, as indicated in Fig. 191, and that the number of observations required is 30. The precision of the 20 observations can be determined from the curves in Fig. 190 as follows. Locate 30 on the vertical scale and read across to the point where this line intersects the curve $N = 20$. Then drop straight down to the bottom scale and read precision. In this case

---

Element 1

.09 .08 .08 .07	.08 .07 .09 .07	.08 .07 .09 .07	.06 .07 .09 .07	.09 .10 .08 .08
.02	.02	.02	.03	.02

$\overline{R} = \frac{0.11}{5} = 0.022$ $\overline{X} = \frac{0.158}{20} = 0.0790$

Figure 191   Time study data for element 1, showing subgroups of 4 observations. Average of the 20 observations is 0.079 minute. $X = 0.079$.

it is ±6 percent. This means that with 20 observations, the precision is only ±6 percent, whereas it would be ±5 percent with 30 readings.

Use of Alignment Chart for Determining Number of Observations

One large organization uses the form shown in Fig. 192 and the alignment chart in Fig. 193 for determining the number of observations. The time study analyst makes the number of observations thought necessary, and while still on the job, determines for each element the range for each group of four observations and the average of all observations. Then, referring to the alignment chart which is attached to the time

SHEET 1 OF 1 SHEETS

OPERATION Drill 1/16" hole in control lever						OP. NO. DR 12				
PART NAME Control Lever						PART NO. CL 28				
MACHINE NAME & NO. Special Drill #249					OBSERVER: T.S. Wilson					
OPERATOR NAME & NO. John Williams #16432					MALE ☑ FEMALE ☐	DATE:				
ELEMENT	EXT.	SUM (S)	AVG. (x̄)	RANGE (R)	ELEMENT		EXT.	SUM (S)	AVG. (x̄)	RANGE (R)
Element No. 4: Drill 1/16" hole in control	1.02						1.17			
lever. Hand feed. Drilling time only.	1.32						.92			
	1.08						.90			
	.99	4.41	1.10	.33			1.05	4.04	1.01	.27
	1.04									
	.96									
	1.18									
	.90	4.08	1.02	.28						
	1.01									
	.94									
	.96									
	1.24	4.15	1.04	.30						
	1.28									
	1.13									
	.98				TOTALS			25.27		1.79
	.96	4.35	1.09	.32	NUMBER OF READINGS TAKEN 24					
	1.08				TOTAL (S) ÷ NUM- ⎱ AVERAGE TIME (x̄) BER OF READINGS ⎰ 25.27 ÷ 24				1.05	
	1.22				NUMBER OF GROUPS OF 4					6
	1.01				TOTAL (R) ÷ NUM- ⎱ AVERAGE RANGE (R̄) BER OF GROUPS ⎰ 1.79 ÷ 6					.30
	.93	4.24	1.06	.29	FROM PRECISION ⎱ READINGS REQUIRED FOR ±5% PRECISION				36	
					CHART ⎰ PRECISION FROM READINGS TAKEN				±5.5%	
								RATING		105%

Figure 192 Recap sheet for time study data.

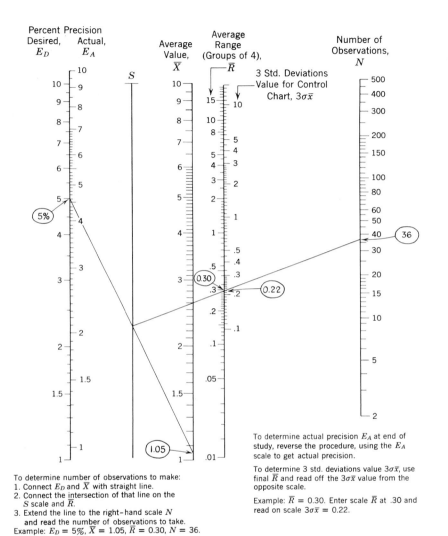

Percent Precision
Desired, Actual,
E_D E_A

S

Average Value, $\overline{X}$

Average Range (Groups of 4), $\overline{R}$

3 Std. Deviations Value for Control Chart, $3\sigma\overline{x}$

Number of Observations, N

To determine number of observations to make:
1. Connect E_D and $\overline{X}$ with straight line.
2. Connect the intersection of that line on the S scale and $\overline{R}$.
3. Extend the line to the right-hand scale N and read the number of observations to take.
Example: $E_D = 5\%$, $\overline{X} = 1.05$, $\overline{R} = 0.30$, $N = 36$.

To determine actual precision E_A at end of study, reverse the procedure, using the E_A scale to get actual precision.

To determine 3 std. deviations value $3\sigma\overline{x}$, use final $\overline{R}$ and read off the $3\sigma\overline{x}$ value from the opposite scale.

Example: $\overline{R} = 0.30$. Enter scale $\overline{R}$ at .30 and read on scale $3\sigma\overline{x} = 0.22$.

Figure 193 Alignment chart for determining the number of observations required for 95% confidence level and ±5% precision, and also for determining the control limits for control chart.

study observation board, the operator checks the required number of observations for ±5 percent precision and a 95 percent confidence level. He or she also determines the precision for the number of observations already taken.

For example, 24 observations were made of the element "Drill $^1/_{16}$ Hole in Control Lever," as shown in Fig. 192. The average range $\bar{R} = 0.30$ minute, and the average time $\bar{X} = 1.05$ minutes. As indicated in Fig. 193, the number of observations required is 36.

Figure 193 also shows that the 24 observations actually made gave a precision of ±5.6 percent.

Control Chart Analysis of Time Study Data

The control chart is an excellent device to test the consistency of the time study data. The average values $\bar{X}$ (average of group 4) of the time study readings are plotted in sequence on the control chart in Fig. 194. The upper and lower control limits are determined as follows. Using the alignment chart in Fig. 193, find the value of $\bar{R}$ on the scale and read the corresponding value of $3\sigma\bar{x}$. When $\bar{R} = 0.30$, then $3\sigma\bar{x} = ±0.22$. Because $\bar{x} = 1.05$, then the upper control limit $= 1.05 + 0.22 = 1.27$. The lower control limit is $1.05 - 0.22 = 0.83$.

As Fig. 194 shows, all points are within the control limits; the data are consistent, and the time value of 1.05 minutes for this element is acceptable.

Rating

As the time study analyst records the data, the analyst is also evaluating the operator's speed in relation to his opinion of normal speed for such an operation. The observer wants enough readings for each element to give a representative sample against which to apply the speed rating. Later the rating factor will be applied to this "representative time" to obtain the normal time for the element.

There are a number of different "systems" or methods of arriving at this rating factor, all of which depend upon the judgment of the time study analyst. A common method is for the analyst to determine a rating factor for the operation as a whole. At the beginning and at the end, and perhaps at intervals throughout the study, the observer concentrates on making ratings of the speed of the operator. It is the analyst's object to determine the average level of performance at which the operator was working while the study was being made. Such a rating is recorded on the observation sheet in the form of a rating factor (Fig. 184).

Another method is for the analyst to determine a rating factor for each element of the operation.[5] This is the plan most widely used today.[6] A still more refined rating

---

[5] A survey of 7444 time study analysts showed that 34 percent rated the over-all study, 53 percent rated each element, and 13 percent rated each stop-watch reading.

[6] R. B. Andrews and Ralph M. Barnes, "The Influence of the Duration of Observation Times on Performance Rating," *The Journal of Industrial Engineering,* Vol. 18, No. 4, pp. 243–247.

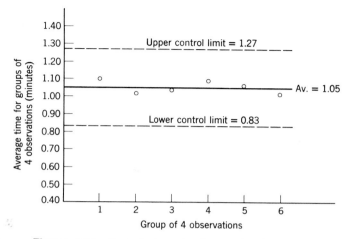

Figure 194 Control chart for time study observations.

plan requires the analyst to rate each element when it is timed, recording the rating for the element on the observation sheet when the stop-watch reading is recorded. Using this method, there would be a rating recorded for each stop-watch reading. Although this method is sound, it is very difficult for the time study analyst to rate each stop-watch reading unless the elements are fairly long.

The use of the rating factor will be explained more fully in the next chapter.

Selecting the Operator to Be Timed

If more than one person is performing the same operation, the time study analyst may time one or more of the operators. If all the operators are using exactly the same method, that is, the one prescribed for the job, and if there is a difference in the tempo at which the operators work, it is customary to time the operator working at nearest to normal pace. Because a rating factor is used to evaluate the operator's speed, theoretically it makes no difference whether the slowest or fastest operator is timed. However, it is admittedly more difficult to rate correctly the performance of a very slow operator. It is not desirable to time a beginner, because the method is seldom the same as it will be when this person has attained greater proficiency through experience on the job (see Chapter 38).

Because full micromotion studies are not generally used in industry for improving methods, the improvement of the job will in most cases tie in with the time study, so that the same operator will serve as the subject for the entire procedure. Frequently there is only one person on the job; consequently, there is no choice of operator.

Steps in Making Time Study Observations

1. Discuss the operation to be timed with the supervisor of the department.
2. Make certain that the operator has been informed that a time study is to be made.
3. Secure the cooperation of the operator. Explain what you are going to do.
4. Make certain that the operation is ready for time study.
5. Obtain all necessary information and record it on the observation sheet.
6. Make a sketch of the piece and of the work place.
7. Divide the operation into its elements and list these on the observation sheet. If necessary, describe the method more fully on a separate sheet, listing the beginning and ending points for each element.
8. Estimate the number of cycles to be timed.
9. Record the time of day as the study is begun.
10. Start the stop watch at the beginning of the first element of the cycle. Read and record the time for each element of the cycle.
11. When the study is completed and when the stop watch is read at the end of the last element, read and record the time of day on the sheet.
12. Rate the operator and record these ratings on the observation sheet.
13. Sign and date the study.
14. Check to make certain that a sufficient number of cycles have been timed.
15. Plot data on control chart.

21

TIME STUDY: DETERMINING THE RATING FACTOR

After the time study has been taken the next step is to subtract successive watch readings in order to get the time for each element.

Selecting Time Values

As the study in Fig. 203 shows, there are 45 time values for each of the four elements. It now becomes necessary to select from these data a time value for each of these four elements that will be representative.

Occasionally there may be an abnormally high or low time value which may require special attention. The fact that there is considerable variation in successive times for certain elements, however, does not mean that all high and low elements should be thrown out. In many cases there are good reasons for such data. An occasional hard casting may require longer drilling time, or a piece with a fin or a burr may take longer to place in the jig. If such time values are typical or representative of what may be expected on the job, they should not be eliminated from the study even though they happen to be abnormal. It is good policy not to eliminate any readings unless there is a definite reason for doing so.

Many organizations use the arithmetical *average* of the stop-watch readings in determining the representative time for the element. Because this is the most common method of handling data and because it is easy to explain to the worker, it is gaining in favor among time study analysts.

The *modal method* consists of taking the time that occurs most frequently for the element. High and low time values will have less effect upon the selected time by this method than by the average method. The selected time values in the time study shown in Fig. 184 were determined by the modal method.

After the time value for each element is selected, the next step in establishing the time standard is to determine and apply the rating factor.

DETERMINING THE RATING FACTOR

Perhaps the most important and the most difficult part of time study is to evaluate the speed [1] or the tempo at which the person is working while the study is being made.

---

[1] The terms *speed, effort, tempo, pace,* and *performance* all refer to the rate of speed of the operator's motions. In this volume these terms will be used synonymously, and they will *all have but a single meaning*—speed of movement.

The time study analyst must judge the operator's speed while making the time study. This is called rating.

Definition of Rating

Rating is that process during which the time study analyst compares the performance (speed or tempo) of the operator under observation with the observer's own concept of normal performance.[2] Later this rating factor will be applied to the selected time value to obtain the normal time for the job.

Rating is a matter of judgment on the part of the time study analyst, and unfortunately there is no way to establish a time standard for an operation without having the judgment of the analyst enter into the process.

We all know that there is a wide difference in the speed at which different people naturally work. For example, some people walk at a slow pace, others at a fast pace. The time required for a person to walk a given distance will of course vary directly with his walking speed. Speed or tempo can be rated. If walking at a speed of 3 miles per hour is considered normal performance or 100 percent, we have a definite standard or base to be used in rating the task of walking. Then walking at 2 miles per hour would equal 66⅔ percent of normal, and walking at 4 miles per hour would equal 133⅓ percent. We are measuring accomplishment. If the task is to go from one place to another, and if walking 3 miles per hour is normal or 100 percent, then without question we can use a percentage rating factor with precision in measuring performance.

Systems of Rating

Although performance rating, the system of rating described in detail in this chapter, is most widely used today, five other systems should be mentioned. However, several of these systems are little used.

1. Skill and Effort Rating. Around 1916 Charles E. Bedaux introduced the Bedaux system of wage payment and labor control in this country. His plan was based on time study, and his time standards were expressed in points or "Bs." A point or B was simply another name for what we now call a standard minute. His time study procedure included the rating of the operator's skill and effort and the use of a standard table of fatigue allowances. Bedaux used 60 points equal to standard performance. In other words, an operator working at a normal pace was expected to produce 60 Bs per hour, and it was expected that the average incentive pace would be around 70 to 85 points per hour.

Before Bedaux, performance rating had been done mainly by selecting stop-watch readings from the time study data. Thus, if the operator was judged to be working at a fast tempo, a watch reading considerably above average would be selected as the

[2] SAM Committee on Rating of Time Studies, *Advanced Management,* Vol. 6, No. 3, p. 110, July–September 1941.

	Skill			Effort	
+0.15	A1	Superskill	+0.13	A1	Excessive
+0.13	A2		+0.12	A2	
+0.11	B1	Excellent	+0.10	B1	Excellent
+0.08	B2		+0.08	B2	
+0.06	C1	Good	+0.05	C1	Good
+0.03	C2		+0.02	C2	
0.00	D	Average	0.00	D	Average
−0.05	E1	Fair	−0.04	E1	Fair
−0.10	E2		−0.08	E2	
−0.16	F1	Poor	−0.12	F1	Poor
−0.22	F2		−0.17	F2	
	Conditions			Consistency	
+0.06	A	Ideal	+0.04	A	Perfect
+0.04	B	Excellent	+0.03	B	Excellent
+0.02	C	Good	+0.01	C	Good
0.00	D	Average	0.00	D	Average
−0.03	E	Fair	−0.02	E	Fair
−0.07	F	Poor	−0.04	F	Poor

Figure 195 Performance rating table.

representative time for the element; if the operator was judged to be working at a slow tempo, then a watch reading below average would be selected. The Bedaux system was a definite improvement over this informal method of rating operator performance.

2. Westinghouse System of Rating.
A four-factor system[3] for rating operator performance was developed at Westinghouse and was originally published in 1927. These four factors are (1) skill, (2) effort, (3) conditions, and (4) consistency. A scale of numerical values for each factor was supplied in tabular form (Fig. 195), and the selected time obtained from time study was normalized or leveled by applying the sum of the ratings of the four factors.

For example, if the selected time for an operation was 0.50 minute and if the ratings were as follows:

Excellent skill, B2	+0.08
Good effort, C2	+0.02
Good condition, C	+0.02
Good consistency, C	+0.01
Total	+0.13

then the normal time for this operation would be 0.565 minute ($0.50 \times 1.13 = 0.565$).

[3] Described in *Time and Motion Study,* 3rd ed., by S. M. Lowry, H. B. Maynard, and G. J. Stegemerten, McGraw-Hill, New York, 1940, p. 233.

3. Synthetic Rating. Synthetic rating[4] is the name given to a method of evaluating an operator's speed from predetermined time values. The procedure is to make a time study in the usual manner, and then compare the actual time for as many elements as possible with predetermined time values for the same elements. A ratio can be established between the predetermined time value for the element and the actual time value for that element. This ratio is the performance index or rating factor for the operator insofar as that one element is concerned. The formula for computing the performance rating factor is

$$R = \frac{P}{A}$$

where R = performance rating factor

P = predetermined time for the element, expressed in minutes

A = average actual time value (selected time) for the same element P expressed in minutes

Table 14 illustrates the method of making the calculation. The selected times for elements 1 and 3 were 0.12 and 0.17 minute, respectively. The time values for these two elements as determined from a table of predetermined time values were 0.13 and 0.19 minute, respectively. In the first case the rating factor was 108 percent $(0.13 \div 0.12 \times 100 = 108\%)$, and in the second case it was 112 percent $(0.19 \div 0.17 \times 100 = 112\%)$. The average rating factor was the average of 108 and 112, or 110 percent. This average rating factor was then applied to all elements in this study. The rating factor, of course, is applied only to manually controlled elements.

Table 14.   Comparison of Average Actual Times and Times Determined from Predetermined Time Data

Time Study Element	Average Actual Time (Selected Time) in Minutes	Time as Determined from Predetermined Time Data in Minutes	Calculated Performance Rating Factor, $R = \frac{P}{A}$	Average Performance Rating Factor
1	0.12	0.13	108	110
2	0.09			*110*
3	0.17	0.19	112	110
4	0.26			*110*
5	0.32			*110*
6	0.07			*110*

[4] R. L. Morrow, *Motion Economy and Work Measurement*, Ronald Press Co., New York, 1957, p. 443.

4. "Objective Rating." Another method of rating performance has been given the name objective rating.[5] First, the operator's speed is rated against a single standard pace which is independent of job difficulty. The observer merely rates speed of movement or rate of activity, paying no attention to the job itself. After the pace rating is made, an allowance or a secondary adjustment is added to the pace rating to take care of the job difficulty. Job difficulty is divided into six classes, and a table of percentages is provided for each of these factors. The six factors or categories are (1) amount of body used, (2) foot pedals, (3) bimanualness, (4) eye-hand coordination, (5) handling requirements, and (6) weight. The following example illustrates how the normal time for an element is determined using this system of rating.

EXAMPLE   If the selected time for an element is 0.26 minute, the pace rating is 95 percent, and if the sum of all secondary adjustments amounts to 20 percent, then the normal time will be 0.297 minute $(0.26 \times 0.95 \times 1.20)$.

5. Physiological Evaluation of Performance Level. Heart rate in beats per minute and oxygen consumption in calories per minute can be used to measure physical work. Moreover, electronic equipment is available for monitoring and recording such information with a minimum of interference with the activity of the person. The increase in the heart rate and the increase in oxygen consumption above the resting level is an indicator of the physiological cost of the work performed.

Assume that an operator works on a job for which there is a time standard and that the number of pieces produced shows that his or her performance level is 100 percent. During this same time the operator's heart rate in beats per minute and oxygen consumption in calories per minute are measured. Then, if the same operator worked on another job at a speed that resulted in heart rate and oxygen consumption levels equal to those above, this person would have a performance index the same as that above or 100 percent. This approach to performance evaluation has not been widely used but it has possibilities for medium and heavy physical tasks. Measuring work by physiological methods is discussed in detail in Chapter 31.

6. Performance Rating. By far the most widely used system of rating in this country is that of rating a single factor—operator speed, pace, or tempo. This system is called "performance rating." The rating factor may be expressed in percentage, in points per hour, or in other units.[6] Here we shall use the percentage system, with normal performance equal to 100 percent. Because this system is so commonly used, it will be discussed more fully in the remaining pages of this chapter.

[5] M. E. Mundel, *Motion and Time Study,* 3rd ed., Prentice-Hall, Englewood Cliffs, N.J., 1960, p. 406; *Motion and Time Study,* 5th ed., 1978, p. 367.
[6] An investigation of time study practices among 72 companies showed that 90 percent used the 100 percent system, 12 percent used the point system, 7 percent used the Westinghouse system, and 1 percent used other systems. The reason the total of the percentages is greater than 100 percent is because some multi-plant companies use more than one plan.

The Range of Human Capacities

From our own observations and experience we know that there are wide differences in capacities and abilities of individuals in every activity of life. We have seen champion athletes run the mile in 3 minutes and 49.4 seconds, and the 10,000-meter race in 27 minutes and 30.8 seconds, and we have heard of such physical feats as one man's lifting 6270 pounds unaided. These, however, are rare exceptions. Wechsler shows that the range of most physical and mental activities varies as 2 to 1, if the rare exceptions are not considered.[7] That is, the best has roughly twice the capacity of the poorest.

In the factory this means that if a large group of people did exactly the same manual task using the same method, the fastest operator would produce approximately twice as much in a given time as the slowest operator. Table 15 shows the average performance for one day of 121 workers operating semiautomatic lathes, the work being identical for all operators.[8] All were experienced operators. They worked under a wage incentive plan and were paid a premium for all work produced above 60 pieces per hour, this being the normal performance level established by time study. As the table shows, the poorest operator produced 51 pieces per hour and the best 104 pieces per hour, or a ratio of 1 to 2.04.

T. R. Turnball conducted an experiment in his plant by having 500 employees toss 32 blocks ⅜ inch by ⅜ inch by 2 inches (pre-positioned in 4 rows on a work table) into a 2-inch by 4-inch hole 4½ inches from the edge of the table. The exact method of doing the task was first explained to each "operator." The operator then watched the person ahead of him perform the task, and finally he was asked to toss the 32 blocks into the hole as fast as he could. An observer recorded the time taken to perform the operation. As Table 16 shows, the slowest operator took 0.60 minute (100 cycles per hour), whereas the fastest took only 0.28 minute (214 cycles per hour), or a ratio of 1 to 2.14.

This range of 1 to 2 would be expected only if we considered a large sample of people just as they would be found in the factory. In any large group it is expected that an occasional misfit or an occasional star performer might fall outside the range.

---

[7] David Wechsler, *The Range of Human Capacities,* 2nd ed., Williams & Wilkins, Baltimore, 1952, p. 94.

[8] The 121 operators employed on this work were part of a large, well-managed organization that had an excellent reputation over a long period of years. This particular job paid a guaranteed hourly base rate equal to that in the community, and the operators also had an opportunity to earn a bonus. Time standards were carefully and accurately set by time study, and they were guaranteed against change. At the time the production record shown in Table 15 was taken, this operation had been in existence many years, and the time standard had also been in effect for a long time. The operators working on this job had been selected and trained with considerable care, and they seemed to be convinced that there was no "top on earnings." That is, there was no evidence that the operators were pegging production because of fear that the rate on the job would be cut if an operator earned "too much." Therefore, the output of these 121 operators presents a cross section of performance that might be expected of a group of people employed on a job for which they were reasonably well fitted.

Table 15. Difference in the Performance of Operators Working on Semiautomatic Lathes

(*Average performance of operators for one day*)

Number of Operators	Average Output in Pieces Per Hour for the Day	Distribution		
		No.	Percent	Range
1	104	1	1	100 to 109
2	98			
1	91	5	4	90 to 99
2	90			
2	89			
2	87			
1	86			
2	85			
6	84	25	21	80 to 89
2	83			
1	82			
1	81			
8	80			
4	79			
1	78			
3	77			
4	76			
4	75			
1	74	40	33	70 to 79
2	73			
4	72			
3	71			
14	70			
3	69			
2	68			
3	67			
4	66			
3	64	45	37	60 to 69
6	63			
4	62			
6	61			
14	60			
1	58			
1	55			
1	54	5	4	50 to 59
1	52			
1	51			
Total 121	Average 72	121	100	

293

Table 16. Performance of People Placing Wood Blocks in a Hole

(32 blocks ⅜ inch by ⅜ inch by 2 inches, pre-positioned in 4 rows on worktable; hole, 2 inches by 4 inches, 4½ inches from edge of table)

Number of People	Time for Cycle in Minutes	Distribution	
		Number in Interval	Percent in Interval
1	0.28		
5	0.30		
4	0.31	30	6
20	0.32		
20	0.33		
27	0.34		
33	0.35		
33	0.36	150	30
17	0.365		
20	0.37		
16	0.375		
31	0.38		
5	0.385		
35	0.39		
47	0.40	199	40
24	0.41		
25	0.42		
16	0.425		
13	0.43		
11	0.435		
18	0.44		
27	0.45		
10	0.46	109	22
15	0.47		
11	0.48		
4	0.49		
1	0.495		
2	0.50		
2	0.52	12	2
6	0.54		
1	0.60		
Total 500	Average 0.395	500	100

Frequency Distribution

With the range of working speeds or operator tempo now established, we are interested in knowing what the distribution would be for a group of factory workers all doing the same job.

Figure 196 shows one way to arrange the average hourly output data for the 121 semiautomatic lathe operators. Those operators who averaged between 50 and 59 pieces per hour for this particular day were tallied in the top horizontal line. There were 5 people in this group. Those who averaged between 60 and 69 pieces per hour were tallied in the second line. There were 45 people in this group. In a similar manner the operators in each of the six ranges from the slowest to the fastest were tallied, the total being 121 people. Such a graphical tally is called a frequency distribution.

Range Average Hourly Output In Pieces		Number
50 to 59	ШІ	5
60 to 69	ЈИ ЈИ ЈИ ЈИ ЈИ ЈИ ЈИ ЈИ ЈИ	45
70 to 79	ЈИ ЈИ ЈИ ЈИ ЈИ ЈИ ЈИ ЈИ	40
80 to 89	ЈИ ЈИ ЈИ ЈИ ЈИ	25
90 to 99	ЈИ	5
100 to 109	I	1

Figure 196 Tally showing number of operations in each rank. Average output in pieces per hour of 121 operators working on semiautomatic lathes.

Figure 197 presents a more convenient way to show the frequency distribution. The total range (on the X-axis) is the interval between the lowest hourly production (51) and the highest hourly production (104). The production records were kept to the nearest whole unit completed each day. The range on the X-axis is divided into six convenient intervals. The smooth curve shown in Fig. 197 is called a frequency distribution curve.

Figure 198 shows a normal curve fitted to the time taken by 500 people who performed the block-tossing operation.

Establishing a Standard as the Basis for Rating

The data obtained by a time study show the actual time taken by the operator to perform a series of consecutive elements of work. They tell nothing of the pace at which the operator worked while the study was being made. The operator might have been working at a level similar to that of the operator at the top of the column in Table 15, or at a level similar to that of the operator at the bottom of the column. It is necessary to consider the operator's speed in order to determine a standard that will permit an operator working at a normal pace to do the task in the time set for the job.

The need for rating has been pointed out, and the way the rating factor is used has been indicated. It is obvious, however, that some bench mark or some standard of comparison is required if rating is to be used as a measuring device. We must define our normal or standard. To say that normal speed is that speed expected of a qualified

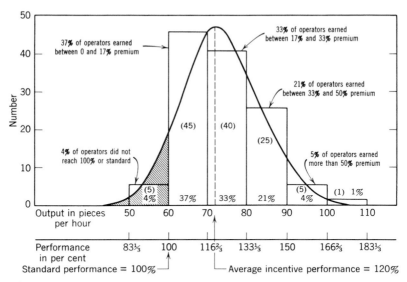

Figure 197 Normal curve fitted to the distribution of output in pieces per hour of 121 operators working on semiautomatic lathes. Data taken from Table 15.

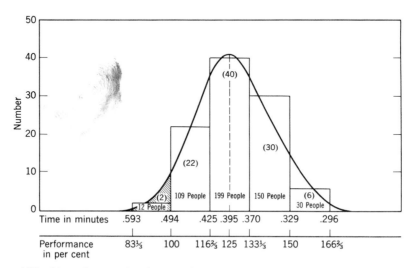

Figure 198 Normal curve fitted to the distribution·of time taken by 500 people who performed block-tossing operation. Data taken from Table 16.

296

person working without incentive, or at a day-work pace, using a standardized method, does not define the term adequately. In fact, there seems to be no written definition that is entirely satisfactory. However, normal speed or normal rate of movement can be demonstrated; motion pictures can be made of typical factory jobs with the operator working at a normal tempo or at a known level above or below normal. Almost any person can be taught to rate operator tempo in terms of the established standard.

Walking on the level at 3 miles per hour[9] is frequently used to represent normal tempo. A person dealing a deck of cards into 4 equal piles in 0.50 minute is often considered to be exhibiting normal pace.[10] Filling a standard pinboard with 30 pins, using the two-handed method, in 0.41 minute is also said to represent normal speed.[11]

One large company has made a set of 11 films, each containing a different sequence of body and arm motions commonly found in factory work. The operator in each of these films is shown working at ten different speeds from 75 percent to 150 percent, with 100 percent as the normal speed. This set of films is used in connection with training programs for time study analysts and as a means of acquainting managers and supervisors with time study technique.[12]

The Society for Advancement of Management (SAM) has made three sets of "Time Study Rating Films" consisting of office, laboratory, and manufacturing operations which have been rated by experienced time study analysts.

Some companies have made community time study surveys so that each participating company will know the position of its performance standard with relation to the average for the community.

Rating Film

Perhaps the most common form of rating film is made by having experienced operators, performing the same operation, work at a number of different speeds. Then the several sections of film are spliced together, separated from each other by a few feet of blank film, and each section is identified by a code number. Thus, the *film* of one

---

[9] Ralph Presgrave, *Dynamics of Time Study,* 2nd ed., McGraw-Hill Book Co., New York, 1945, p. 154.

[10] A standard deck of 52 cards is dealt in the following way by a person seated at a table. The deck is held in the left hand, and the top card is positioned with the thumb and index finger of the left hand. The right hand grasps the positioned card, carries and tosses it onto the table. The four piles of cards are arranged on the four corners of a 1-foot square. The only requirements are that the cards shall all be face down and that each of the four piles shall be separate from the others.

[11] For specifications of the pinboard and for a description of the method, see Chapter 11 and Fig. 81.

[12] The author has produced 11 silent films (Unit I Work Measurement Films—5 reels, and Unit II Work Measurement Films—6 reels) and 3 sound films showing 25 different operators working at a total of 80 different speeds. The silent films have been rated by some 5000 people from over 350 different companies in the United States and Canada, and a standard rating factor has been established for each operation shown in these films.

operation might consist of 10 and 12 different sections representing 10 or 12 different working speeds.

Another common form of rating film is the *film loop*. Each section of the film just described is formed into a loop by cementing the front end to the back end. This permits the film to be placed in the projector and shown as long as the viewer wants to see it. The film loops, of course, can be shown in any order desired.

The film may take still another form. Four images, 6 images, or 12 images, for example, may be printed on one frame of the film. That is, the area of one frame may be subdivided into rectangular sections and the film for each different speed printed in one of these areas. They would be arranged in order according to speed, from slowest to fastest. It would thus be possible to have 12 operators working at 12 different speeds simultaneously on the screen. Such a film is called a *multi-image film*.

Film in any of the three forms may be used for training people in performance rating, and it may also be shown as a refresher. Either the loop film or the multi-image film can be used for comparison purposes. If a film has been made of the operation under study, it can be projected on a screen beside the multi-image film. The analyst can refer to the multi-image film in rating the "unknown" film.

The Relation of "Normal Pace" to "Average Incentive Pace"

Because time standards are often used as the basis for some form of wage incentive plan, we are interested in the relationship between normal pace and the average pace expected of those on incentive. Most incentive earnings in this country fall between 15 percent and 45 percent, with the average around 25 percent to 35 percent.

The following explanation will show how the relationship between normal pace and average incentive pace may be established in a plant. It will also serve to emphasize the point that the performance of the great majority of workers on incentive should be fairly close to the average for the group. If the average incentive pace is 125 percent, it is expected that the average hourly output of approximately two-thirds of all workers would fall in a range extending from 15 percent below this point to 15 percent above this point. Only 3 or 4 percent of the group would be expected to exceed the 150 percent performance level, and only rarely would an operator exceed the 160 to 165 percent level. Similarly, only 3 or 4 percent would not reach the 100 percent performance level.

Reference will be made to the normal distribution curve (Fig. 199) for data to support the above statements. There is considerable evidence to show that if the working speed of each member of a large group of people, such as would be found in a factory, were arranged along the base line according to magnitude in percent of normal, and if the vertical scale indicated frequency, the shape of the curve would fit fairly closely the normal bell curve.

This assumption having been made, a normal distribution curve can be drawn (Fig. 199), with five intervals covering a total speed range of 200 percent. The pace of the

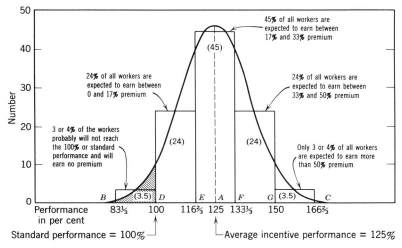

Figure 199 Chart showing the number of workers in each class interval through entire performance range, as determined from the normal distribution curve. Ratio of slowest worker (83⅓%) to fastest worker (166⅔%) is 1 to 2. A 100% premium plan of wage payment is used. It is assumed that a premium is paid for all production above standard. That is, for each 1% increase in production above standard, the worker is paid 1% additional wage above his hourly base rate. The base rate is the guaranteed wage paid to all workers whether they reach 100% performance or not. This hourly base rate is established by job evaluation.

slowest operator is one-half that of the fastest operator, which gives a ratio of 1 to 2. The next step is to establish the point on the curve that will represent normal speed.[13] If we assume that this group of people is already working on incentive, and if their average incentive pace is 25 percent above normal, than point *A* in Fig. 199 can be called 125 percent. This point would represent the average for the group. If the length of the line *B–C* represents a speed range from 83⅓ to 166⅔ percent, point *D* represents 100 percent or normal speed. In a similar manner, point *B* represents 83⅓ percent, *E* represents 116⅔ percent, *F* represents 133⅓ percent, *G* represents 150 percent, and *C* represents 166⅔ percent. Thus there is a range between 83⅓ percent and 166⅔ percent of 1 to 2. The number in each of the vertical bars represents the number of people per hundred who would fall in each of the five intervals.[14]

It is not expected, of course, that any group of workers would exactly fit the normal curve, although an examination of Fig. 197 will show that the output of this

[13] This method of determining the relationship between normal performance and average incentive performance, suggested by Ralph Presgrave, seems to be the most logical of any yet presented. See *Dynamics of Time Study,* 2nd ed., by Ralph Presgrave, McGraw-Hill, New York, 1945, Chapter 10.

[14] For information concerning the normal distribution curve see any book on statistics.

group of 121 operators tends to fit the normal curve. It should be noted that the standard established by time study was 60 pieces per hour; that is, 60 pieces per hour was equal to normal performance or 100 percent. The average output for the entire group was 72 pieces per hour, which is 20 percent above the standard. Thus 120 percent was the average incentive performance for this group of workers for this particular day. There were five operators who worked at such a slow pace that they did not reach the 100 percent or normal performance level. Incidentally, these slow operators were paid their guaranteed day rate, even though they did not earn it. The very fastest operator turned out 104 pieces per hour, which was 73 percent above normal. In other words, this operator worked at a pace equal to 173 percent and earned a bonus of 73 percent for the day.

Figure 200 shows the distribution and earnings curve for 121 semiautomatic lathe operators. Figure 198 shows a normal curve fitted to the time taken by 500 people who performed the block-tossing operation.

Establishing a Company Standard

After the basic reasoning back of rating is fully understood, each company should establish a standard for its own use. Agreement should be reached as to what the normal or standard tempo, or performance level, should be in the plant. The first step would be to establish a standard for walking, card dealing, and other similar operations used generally throughout the country. The standards given on page 297 are widely used.

Then some simple operations from the plant, which can be performed by anyone, should be selected for demonstration. The method should be standardized, and the time for each job, with the operator working at normal pace, should be established. Motion pictures at 1000 frames per minute should be made of typical factory jobs, and the operator's tempo in percent of normal should be established for each of them. Thus a library of standard rating films can be built up over a period of time for use as a bench mark for rating in the plant. Not only can time study analysts be taught to rate, but also managers, supervisors, and the operators themselves can do this; and they are doing it in many plants today.

Rating Scales

There are several different rating scales in general use, and undoubtedly a competent and well-trained time study analyst can obtain satisfactory results with any one of them. A survey shows that the percentage system (Scale A, Fig. 201) has greatest use and the point system comes next.

An examination of the four different rating scales shown in Fig. 201 may help to show the difference between these systems. Just as we can read temperature on both Fahrenheit and centigrade thermometers although there is a difference in their scale, so we can rate operator speed whether we use percentage, points, or some other unit

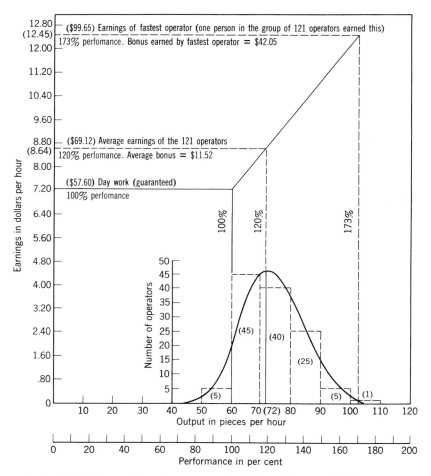

Figure 200 Distribution and earnings curve for 121 semiautomatic lathe operators. The average output is 72 pieces per hour, and the average earnings for the group are 20% above the guaranteed hourly rate.

of measure. Because the percentage system is the plan having widest use, it would be used in most of the illustrations in this book.

Scale A—100 Percent Equals Normal Performance. Normal performance (i.e., normal speed, tempo, or pace) equals 100 percent on rating Scale A. When this scale is used, it is expected that the average incentive pace will fall in the range of 115 to 145, and the average for the entire group will be around 130 percent. This

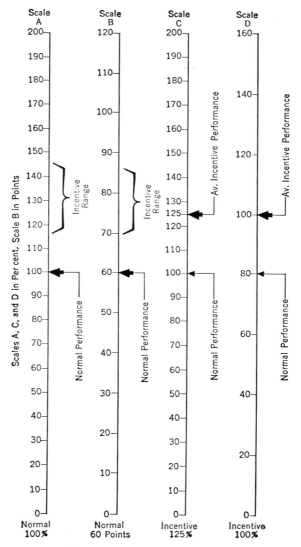

Figure 201 Four rating scales.

means that those operators who produce between 15 and 45 percent per day more than normal will earn 15 to 45 percent extra pay for this extra performance. It is also expected that an occasional person might work at a pace twice as fast as normal. This person's performance rating would thus be 200 percent, and consequently he or she would earn twice the hourly base rate. This would be a rare exception.

Scale B—60 Points Equals Normal Performance. Scale B illustrates the point system, with 60 points equal to normal performance and with the average incentive pace around 70 to 85 points. The maximum expected performance is around 100 to 120 points. This scale is similar to Scale A, 60 points being equal to 100 percent performance rating.

Scale C—125 Percent Equals Incentive Performance. Some time study analysts use the "average incentive pace" as their bench mark. A company might adopt 125 percent as the point at which it would like to have the average output fall. Therefore, it tries to determine this point, at which to set its "incentive time standard," and then adds 25 percent to the hourly base rate in computing the amount of earnings that a person should receive at this point. Although this plan is perhaps as sound as any other, some people think it is not as easy to explain to the operators and that it has no advantages over a plan using Scale A.

Scale D—100 Percent Equals Incentive Performance. A few organizations use a scale having 100 percent equal to "average incentive pace," and this point is usually set 25 percent above normal performance. Therefore, 80 percent equals normal performance on this scale.

Speed and Method as They Affect Output

To summarize, there are two main factors that affect the number of units of work that a person on manual operations can produce in a given time. They are (1) speed of muscular movements, and (2) method of doing the task.

Speed or tempo, which refers to the rate of physical activity of the worker, can be measured by the rating factor, as has already been described. Method is ordinarily defined as the specified motion pattern required to perform a given operation. From the practical point of view, the method for a particular operation must be one which can be maintained in the shop day in and day out, and it must be one that the worker can be trained to follow. With this definition of method it is obvious that different individuals working on a job will, with practice, develop some refinements. Some would say that they have become more highly skilled. If a careful analysis were made of the operation, however, it generally would be found that a skilled person uses a different method from the one used when he or she was less skilled on the job. Evidence to support this point is presented in Chapter 38.

Because there is neither a bench mark nor a unit for measuring differences in method, the only satisfactory way to handle this factor is to standardize the method and establish a standard time for this specified method. The time standard would not apply if a method other than the standard one were used.

Although some variation in method is expected in the average factory, if care is used in developing the proper method of doing the job and if the operators are trained to do the work in the specified manner before the time study is made, the problem of variations in output due to variations in method can be minimized.

Applying the Rating Factor

The rating factor is applied to the selected time to give the normal time. Assume that in a particular operation of assembling an electric switch the operator gave a consistent performance throughout the cycle and throughout the study, and that the total selected time was 0.80 minute. With a rating factor for the study of 110 percent, the normal time would be as follows:

$$\text{Normal time} = \text{selected time} \times \frac{\text{rating in percent}}{100}$$

$$= 0.80 \times \frac{110}{100} = 0.88 \text{ minute}$$

This value of 0.88 represents the time that a qualified and well-trained operator working at a normal pace would need to complete one cycle of the operation. This value is not the standard time for the job, because allowances must be added to the normal time to give the standard time. The determination and the application of allowances will be explained in the next chapter.

22

TIME STUDY: DETERMINING ALLOWANCES AND TIME STANDARD

DETERMINING ALLOWANCES

The *normal time* for an operation does not contain any allowances. It is merely the time that a qualified operator would need to perform the job if he or she worked at a normal tempo. However, it is not expected that a person will work all day without some interruptions. The operator may take time out for personal needs, for rest, and for reasons beyond his or her control. Allowances for such interruptions to production may be classified as follows: (1) personal allowance, (2) fatigue allowance, or (3) delay allowance.

The standard time must include time for all the elements in the operation, and in addition it must contain time for all necessary allowances. Standard time is equal to the normal time plus the allowances. Allowances are not a part of the rating factor, and best results are obtained if they are applied separately.

Personal Allowance

Personal allowance will be considered first because every worker must be allowed time for personal needs. The amount of this allowance can be determined by making all-day time studies or work sampling studies of various classes of work. For light work, where the operator works 8 hours per day without organized rest periods, 2 to 5 percent (10 to 24 minutes) per day is about all that the average worker will use for personal time.

Although the amount of personal time required will vary with the individual more than with the kind of work, it is a fact that employees need more personal time when the work is heavy and done under unfavorable conditions, particularly in a hot humid atmosphere. Under such conditions studies might possibly show that more than 5 percent allowance should be made for personal time.

Fatigue Allowance

In the modern well-managed plant so many steps have been taken to eliminate fatigue that it is not of as great concern as formerly. In fact, fatigue is of such little consequence in some kinds of work that no allowance is required at all. There are many reasons for this. The length of the working day and the length of the working week have been shortened; machinery, mechanical handling equipment, tools, and fixtures have been improved so that the day's work is more easily done and the employee works in greater physical comfort than formerly. There are, of course, some kinds of work that still involve heavy physical exertion and are performed under adverse conditions of heat and humidity, and therefore require rest for the operator. Fatigue results from a large number of causes, some of which are mental as well as physical.

At the present time there is no fully satisfactory way of measuring fatigue. Physiological measurements are the most objective means of determining the time and duration of periods of work and rest during the day.

We know from experience that a person needs time for rest when the work is arduous. The problem of determining the amount of time to be allowed for rest is very complex. Time needed for rest varies with the individual, with the length of the interval in the cycle during which the person is under load, with the conditions under which the work is done, and with many other factors. Some companies have from long experience arrived at fatigue allowances which seem to be satisfactory (Fig. 202). Some organizations having arduous physical work, such as stacking heavy boxes in warehouses or in freight cars, have tried various combinations of periods of rest and work until they have arrived at satisfactory allowances.

Organized rest periods during which time all employees in a department are not permitted to work provide one solution to the problem. The optimum length and number of rest periods should be determined. Perhaps the most common plan is to provide one rest period during the middle of the morning and one during the middle of the afternoon. The length of these periods ordinarily varies from 5 to 15 minutes each.[1]

If no wage incentive plan is used, employees are paid for the rest periods at their regular hourly base rate. If a wage incentive plan is used and if fatigue allowances have been incorporated in the time standard, employees are not paid for the rest periods as such. Workers merely take their fatigue allowance during the specified rest period rather than at intervals during the day at their own choosing.

It should be repeated that a fatigue allowance does not need to be made for much light factory work, and organized rest periods during the day provide sufficient rest for another group of factory operations. The amount of heavy work in factories is gradually decreasing because of the greater use of machinery and power-handling equipment; consequently the problem of fatigue allowances becomes one of decreasing importance to the time study analyst.

Delay Allowance

Delays may be avoidable or unavoidable. Intentional delays will not be considered in determining the time standard. Unavoidable delays do occur from time to time, caused by the machine, the operator, or some outside force.

It is expected that machines and equipment will be kept in good repair. When there

[1] For a more complete discussion of rest periods see Chapter 32.

Per cent

30 — Handle 70-pound containers from skid waist-high to shoulder-high stack.

29 —

28 — Handle 60-pound containers from skid waist-high to shoulder-high stack.
Pull loaded 4-wheel truck under normal conditions. (Gross weight, 2500 pounds.
    wheel diameter, 11 inches.)

27 —

26 — Up-end rosin barrel weighing 500 pounds gross. (Two men.)
Shovel salt from open-end box truck to kettle 40 inches high. (Shovel weight, 6 pounds.
    salt weight, 20 pounds.)

25 — Walking on level carrying 75 pounds on shoulder.
Push loaded wheelbarrow. (Weight of material, 350 pounds.)

24 — Push loaded 4-wheel truck. (Gross weight, 2000 pounds; wheel diameter, 11 inches.)
Handle 65-pound containers from skid waist-high to R.R. car knee-high.

23 — Handle 40-pound containers from skid waist-high to shoulder-high stack.

22 — Handle 65-pound containers from skid waist-high to knee-high stack.
Use pick weighing 9 pounds to loosen new salt in R.R. car.
Paint smooth ceiling from step-ladder using a 4-inch brush.

21 — Handle 50-pound containers from waist-high slide to skid.

20 — Pull loaded 4-wheel truck. (Gross weight, 1500 pounds; wheel diameter, 11 inches.)

19 — Wet-mop rough concrete floor.

18 — Dry-mop rough concrete floor.
Saw a yellow pine 2″ x 4″ across grain.
Handle 30-pound containers from waist-high slide to skid.

17 — Pull loaded 4-wheel truck. (Gross weight, 1000 pounds; wheel diameter, 11 inches.)
Wet-mop wooden floor in good condition.
Dry-mop wooden floor in good condition.

16 — Scrape dirt from wooden floor in good condition. (Handle of scraper 60 inches long,
    blade 6½ inches wide.)

15 — Walking on level carrying 25 pounds.
Sweep rough concrete floor.
Handle 20-pound containers from waist-high slide to skid.

14 — Dry and polish window with rag, working from inside.
Form and stitch fiber containers.

13 — Sweep a wooden floor in good condition.
Wash window with wet rag or sponge, working from inside.
Pull empty 4-wheel truck. (Weight, 400 pounds; wheel diameter, 11 inches.)

12 — Operate typewriter.
Wipe top of desk or table to remove dust.

11 — Cut strings on bundles of containers.
Walk down steps.
Stamp sample tags.

10 — Walking on level unobstructed.
Record data.

9 —

8 — Make phone call.

7 — Visual inspection and maintaining register for printed labels.

6 —

5 — { Personal allowance for women.
   { Personal allowance for men.

4 —

Figure 202 Personal and fatigue allowances used by one company. The allowances given include personal time.

307

is a breakdown or when repairs are necessary, the operator is usually taken off the job and such delays do not enter into the time standard. In such cases the operator is usually paid for waiting time at the hourly base rate. Sometimes there are minor adjustments, breakage of tools such as drills and taps, or lost time due to occasional variation in material and interruptions by supervisors, and these must be included in the standard. Each unavoidable delay should be considered as a challenge by the analyst, and the supervisor, and every effort should be made to eliminate these delays. The kind and amount of delays for a given class of work can best be determined from all-day time studies or work sampling studies made over a sufficient period of time to give reliable data. Noncyclic elements that occur as a part of the job are not to be treated as delays but should be timed as a part of the operation.

Applying the Allowances

Personal allowance is applied as a percentage of the normal time, and affects both handling time and machine time alike. For convenience, fatigue allowance is sometimes applied in the same way, although some believe that this allowance should apply only to those elements during which the operator works, and not to the machine time during which the machine works. Delays are applied as a percentage of the normal time, or if entirely a machine-delay allowance, then on the machine elements only. If these three allowances are applied uniformly to all elements, they may be added together and applied together, necessitating but a single computation.

Although allowances have traditionally been applied as a percentage of the normal time to be added to the normal time to obtain the standard time, there is a trend toward considering allowances in terms of minutes allowed per working day. Thus, instead of referring to personal allowance as 5 percent, it would be referred to as 24 minutes per 8-hour day ($480 \times 5 \% = 24$). If this were the only allowance made, the working time in this case would be 456 minutes per day ($480 - 24 = 456$).

If an allowance of 5 percent for personal time were made on the assembly operation referred to on page 304, 5 percent would be added to the normal time for this operation in the following way:

Standard time = normal time + (normal time × allowances in percent)
$$= 0.88 + (0.88 \times 0.05) = 0.88 + 0.044 = 0.924 \text{ minute}$$

To summarize:

$$
\begin{aligned}
\text{Selected time} &= 0.80 \text{ minute} \\
\text{Rating factor} &= 110\% \\
\text{Personal allowance} &= 5\% \\
\text{Normal time} &= 0.80 \times \frac{110}{100} = 0.88 \text{ minute} \\
\text{Standard time} &= 0.88 + (0.88 \times 0.05) = 0.924 \text{ minute}
\end{aligned}
$$

Another way to compute this is:

$$\text{Standard time} = 0.88 \times 1.05 = 0.924 \text{ minute}$$

Although this method of applying the personal allowance is often used it is not absolutely correct. If by a 5 percent allowance it is understood that 24 minutes per 8-hour day are to be available to the worker for personal needs, and if the normal time for one assembly of the electric switch is 0.88 minute, then during the 456 minutes available for work $(480 - 24 = 456)$ the operator could produce 518 pieces $(456 \div 0.88 = 518)$. Because the 8-hour day consists of 480 minutes, the standard time per piece would be 0.926 minute $(480 \div 518 = 0.926)$. Another way to state this is:

$$\text{Standard time} = \text{normal time} \times \frac{100}{100 - \text{allowance in percent}}$$

$$= 0.88 \times \frac{100}{100 - 5}$$

$$= 0.88 \times \frac{100}{95} = 0.926 \text{ minute}$$

Not only is this method of incorporating allowances into the time standard correct, but also there is considerable value in stating the total time in minutes per 8-hour day for each type of allowance. To the supervisor or operator the statement that 24 minutes per day is allowed for personal time means more than merely to say that 5 percent has been added to the normal cycle time for personal needs.

DETERMINING TIME STANDARDS

Stop-Watch Time Study of a Core-Making Operation

The study shown in Fig. 184 is a very common type of stop-watch time study used today, although many organizations have the policy of rating each element separately instead of making an over-all rating for the study, and they also determine and apply a fatigue and personal allowance factor for each element. Figures 203 and 204 show such a study.

The operation studied was the making of a dry sand core in a wood core box. The core was 7½ inches long and $1^3/_{16}$ inches in diameter, taking the general shape of half a cylinder.

A full description of the operation is given in the left-hand column of Table 17, and the abbreviated description recorded on the observation sheet is given in the right-hand column. The end points used in reading the watch are also given.

Before recording stop-watch readings the back of the observation sheet (Fig. 204) was filled out, a drawing of the layout of the work place was made, and a sketch of the core was placed in the lower right-hand corner of the sheet.

ELEMENTS

1. Fill core box with 3 handfuls of sand. Press sand down each time.
2. Press sand down with one trowel stroke. Strike off with one trowel stroke.
3. Get and place plate on core box, turn over, rap, and remove box.
4. Carry plate with core 4 feet. Dispose on oven truck.

Element	Line	1	2	3	4	5	6	7	8	9	10	11	12	13	14	15
1	Upper (subtracted)	.09	.09	.09	.08	.08	.08	.10	.07	.08	.08	.09	.07	.08	.09	.06
1	Lower (reading)	.09	.41	.71	1.07	.38	.67	.98	.28	.57	.87	.18	.46	.76	4.05	.32
2	Upper	.06	.05	.08	.06	.05	.05	.06	.05	.05	.06	.06	.05	.05	.06	.06
2	Lower	.15	.46	.79	.13	.43	.72	2.04	.33	.62	.93	.24	.51	.81	.11	.38
3	Upper	.13	.13	.15	.14	.13	.13	.14	.13	.14	.13	.12	.14	.12	.13	.13
3	Lower	.28	.59	.94	.27	.56	.85	.18	.46	.76	3.06	.36	.65	.93	.24	.51
4	Upper	.04	.03	.04	.03	.03	.03	.03	.03	.03	.03	.03	.03	.03	.02	.03
4	Lower	.32	.62	.98	.30	.59	.88	.21	.49	.79	.09	.39	.68	.96	.26	.54
(1)	Upper	.07	.10	.08	.08	.08	.08	.07	.08	.08	.08	.07	.07	.08	.09	.09
(1)	Lower	.61	.95	.25	.53	.83	.12	.41	.71	7.01	.28	.55	.84	.16	.48	.77
(2)	Upper	.05	.05	.05	.05	.06	.06	.06	.06	.05	.06	.06	.07	.06	.05	.05
(2)	Lower	.66	5.00	.30	.58	.89	.18	.47	.77	.06	.34	.61	.91	.22	.53	.82
(3)	Upper	.14	.13	.12	.13	.12	.13	.13	.12	.11	.12	.13	.13	.14	.13	.13
(3)	Lower	.80	.13	.42	.71	6.01	.31	.60	.89	.17	.46	.74	8.04	.36	.66	.95
(4)	Upper	.05	.04	.03	.04	.03	.03	.03	.04	.03	.03	.02	.03	.04	.02	.03
(4)	Lower	.85	.17	.45	.75	.04	.34	.63	.93	.20	.48	.77	.08	.39	.68	.98
(1)	Upper	.07	.07	.08	.08	.07	.08	.07	.08	.09	.09	.08	.08	.08	.08	.09
(1)	Lower	9.05	.34	.64	.93	.21	.50	.78	11.07	.39	.69	.99	.29	.59	.89	.19
(2)	Upper	.05	.06	.05	.06	.06	.06	.07	.07	.08	.07	.06	.06	.07	.06	.08
(2)	Lower	.10	.40	.69	.99	.27	.57	.84	.14	.47	.76	12.05	.35	.66	.95	.27
(3)	Upper	.14	.13	.13	.12	.11	.11	.11	.12	.10	.12	.12	.13	.12	.12	.11
(3)	Lower	.24	.53	.82	10.10	.39	.68	.95	.26	.57	.88	.17	.48	.78	13.07	.38
(4)	Upper	.03	.03	.03	.04	.03	.04	.04	.04	.04	.04	.03	.03	.03	.03	.03
(4)	Lower	.27	.56	.85	.14	.42	.71	.99	.30	.61	.20	.51	.81	.10	.41	

Summary (right-side columns):

Element	MIN. TIME	AV. TIME	SELECTED TIME	OCC. PER CYCLE	RATING	NORMAL TIME
1	.06	.081	.081	1	115	.093
2	.05	.059	.059	1	125	.074
3	.10	.126	.126	1	135	.170
4	.02	.032	.032	1	125	.040

FOREIGN ELEMENTS:

Tally-by elements

	No. 1	No. 2	No. 3	No. 4
	.06⌐	.05▪▪▪⌐	.10⌐	.02▪▪▪
	.07▪▪	.06▪▪▪⌐.11▪	.03▪▪▪⌐	.03▪▪▪⌐
	.08▪▪▪▪⌐	.07▪	.12▪▪▪	.04▪▪▪
	.09▪▪⌐	.08▪⌐	.13▪▪▪▪⌐	.05⌐
	.10⌐		.14▪▪⌐	
			.15⌐	

TOOLS, JIGS, GAUGES, PATTERNS, ETC.
Core box No. C-1D-7253, Size 1⅞ x 3½ x 8½", Wt. 1 lb.; 5" Molder's trowel.
Plates 4 x 9"; weight with core 3½ lb. Core sand No. A16

OVERALL RATING	BEGIN	END	ELAPSED	UNITS FINISHED	ACTUAL TIME PER PIECE
125	9:18	9:32	14:00	45	0.31 Min.

Figure 203   Front of observation sheet—core making operation. Size of form 8½ × 11 inches.

SUMMARY

NO.	ELEMENTS	NORMAL TIME	FATG & PERL ALLOW.	OTHER ALLOW.	TOTAL ALLOW.	STD. TIME
1.	Fill core box with 3 handfuls of sand. Press sand down each time.	.093	12	—	12	.106
2.	Press sand down with one trowel stroke. Strike off with one trowel stroke.	.074	15	—	15	.087
3.	Get and place plate on core box, turn over, rap, and remove box.	.170	15	—	15	.200
4.	Carry plate with core 4 feet. Dispose on oven truck.	.040	12	—	12	.046
						.439

TOTAL STD. TIME PER CYCLE: .439

NO. PIECES PER CYCLE: 1   STD. TIME PER PIECE: Use .44

DRAWING OF PART:

Core:

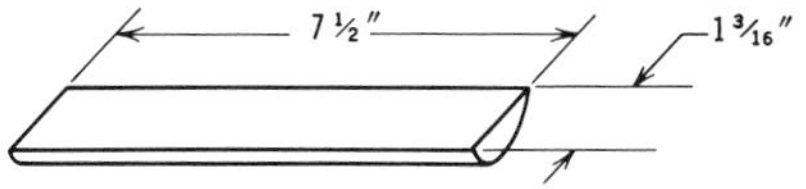

7 1/2"   1 3/16"

One half of cylinder 1 3/16" x 7 1/2"

Wt. of core before baking = 1/4 lb.

OPERATION: Make core for crank frame No. 7253

OP. NO.: C-10-A

PART NAME: Core for crank frame No. 7253   PART NO.: —

MACH. NAME: Bench No. 62   MACH. NO.: —

OPERATOR'S NAME & NO.: S.R. Martin   MALE ☑ FEMALE ☐

EXPERIENCE ON JOB: Six months   FOREMAN: M.L. Ray

NO. MACHINES OPER'D: —   MACH. SPEED —   DEPT. NO.: 17

MATERIAL: Dry core sand-specification No. A16

SKETCH OF WORK PLACE   SCALE: One square = 4 inches

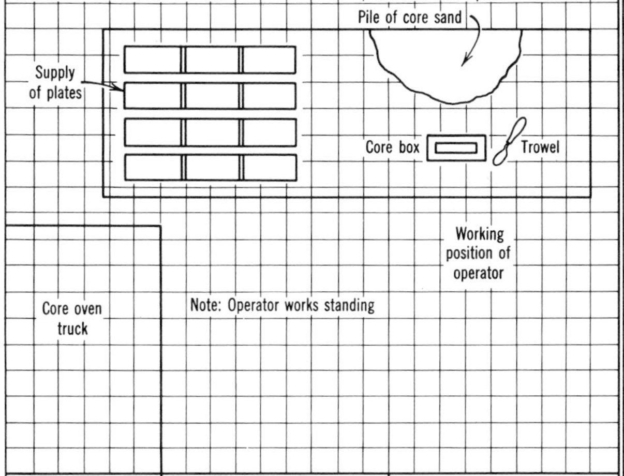

Pile of core sand

Trowel

Core box

Working position of operator

Supply of plates

Core oven truck

Note: Operator works standing

DATE OF STUDY | OBSERVER C.A. Clark | APPROVED J.S.R.

Figure 204 Back of observation sheet—core making operation.

311

Table 17. Elements of Core-Making Operation

Detailed Description	Condensed Description Recorded on Observation Sheet, with End Points for Reading Stop Watch
1. Walk 4 feet from core-oven truck to bench, pick up core box with both hands, push loose sand on front edge of bench back against pile with edge of core box. Hold core box with left hand and fill core box with three handfuls of sand, pressing sand down in core box each time.	1. Fill core box with 3 handfuls of sand. Press sand down each time. *End of element* as right hand begins to grasp trowel.
2. Pick up trowel with right hand, press sand down with one stroke of trowel across top of box, strike off (draw edge of trowel across top of box), removing excess sand with edge of trowel. Dispose of trowel on bench at right of core box.	2. Press sand down with one trowel stroke. Strike off with one trowel stroke. *End of element* as trowel is dropped on bench (hits bench).
3. Get plate and carry from pile on bench 3 feet to left of core box, turn plate upside down, and place on top of core box. Turn plate and core box over. Pick up trowel with right hand and rap core box twice with handle of trowel, and dispose of trowel on bench to right of core box. Using both hands, carefully lift core box upward from plate, allowing core to remain on plate. Place core box on bench to right of plate.	3. Get and place plate on core box, turn over, rap, and remove box. *End of element* as core box is placed on bench (hits bench).
4. Walk, carrying plate and core, 4 feet to left, and place on shelf of core-oven truck.	4. Carry plate with core 4 feet. Dispose on oven truck. *End of element* as plate is placed on (touches) shelf of core-oven truck.

The continuous method of timing and a decimal-minute stop watch were used. As the analyst made the study, he evaluated the speed of the operator for each element of the operation. In making studies such as this one the analyst may occasionally record a rating factor above the stop-watch reading as the study progresses. Then, after the study is completed, he will record the rating for each element of the study. These values are recorded on the front of the observation sheet (Fig. 203) in the vertical column headed ''Rating.'' An over-all rating factor for the entire study is also recorded in the space provided in the lower right-hand section of the observation sheet. It may be used in connection with the elapsed time and the number of pieces finished, to check the time standard after it has finally been determined.

The selected time value for each element is determined by tallying the data as shown on the bottom of the observation sheet. If there is no space on this sheet, the tally is made on a plain sheet of paper and attached to the observation sheet. The tally shows that for element 1 the minimum time value is 0.06, the time value that occurs most frequently is 0.08, and the average is 0.081. In a similar manner values are determined for the other three elements of the study. The number of times that the element occurs in the study is recorded in the column marked "Occurrence per Cycle."

STUDY NO. 8765	OBSERVATION SHEET														

ELEMENTS — UPPER LINE: SUBTRACTED TIME — LOWER LINE: READING

ELEMENTS	1	2	3	4	5	6	7	8	9	10	11	12	13	14	15
1. Fill core box with 3 handfuls of sand. Press sand down each time.	.09	.09	.09	.09	.08	.08	.10	.07	.08	.08	.09	.07	.08	.09	.06

												MIN. TIME	AV. TIME	SELECTED TIME	OCC. PER CYCLE	RATING	NORMAL TIME
.07	.10	.08	.08	.08	.08	.07	.08	.08	.08	.07	.07	.08	.09	.09	.06	.081	.081	1	115	.093

Figure 205 Part of observation sheet for operation "Make Core for Crank Frame." The minimum time, average time, selected time, rating factor, and normal time for one element are shown. See Fig. 203 for complete study.

The normal times are then calculated in the following way:

$$\text{Normal time} = \text{selected time} \times \frac{\text{rating in percent}}{100}$$

For element 1 (Fig 205) the normal time is determined in the following manner:

Selected time $= 0.081$ minute
Rating factor $= 115\%$
Normal time $= 0.081 \times \dfrac{115}{100} = 0.093$ minute

Time Study Summary

After the normal time values are calculated for each element, a summary is made on the back of the observation sheet in the space provided. A fatigue and personal allowance is determined for each element and recorded in the appropriate column. Twelve percent is allowed for the first and fourth elements, and 15 percent for the second and third elements. These allowances are obtained from a table similar to the one shown in Fig. 202. No other allowances are made.

The standard time is determined for each element in the following manner:

$$\text{Standard time} = \text{normal time} \times \frac{100}{100 - \text{allowance in percent}}$$

For element 1 this is:

$$\text{Standard time} = 0.093 \times \frac{100}{100 - 12} = 0.093 \times \frac{100}{88} = 0.106 \text{ minute}$$

In a like manner the standard time is determined for each of the four elements (Fig. 206). Then these are added together to give the standard time for the cycle. Because one piece is produced per cycle, the standard time per piece is the same as the standard time per cycle.

	SUMMARY					
NO.	ELEMENTS	NORMAL TIME	FAT'G & PERS'L ALLOW.	OTHER ALLOW.	TOTAL ALLOW.	STD. TIME
1.	Fill core box with 3 handfuls of sand. Press sand down each time.	.093	12	—	12	.106
2.	Press sand down with one towel stroke. Strike off with one towel stroke.	.074	15	—	15	.087
3.	Get and place plate on core box, turn over, rap, and remove box.	.170	15	—	15	.200
4.	Carry plate with core 4 feet. Dispose on oven truck.	.040	12	—	12	.046
						.439

Figure 206 Part of observation sheet for "Make Core for Crank Frame." The normal time, allowances, and the standard time for each element are shown. See Fig. 203 for complete study.

A helper supplies the core maker with core sand and plates and provides empty core-oven trucks; therefore no time for this work is included in the standard. Had this work been part of the core maker's job, it would have been timed and included as additional elements in the operation.

Stop-Watch Time Study of an Assembling and Cementing Operation

Figures 207 and 208 show the observation sheet for an assembling and cementing operation in a rubber-footware plant. Figure 209 shows the Computation Sheet, and Fig. 210 the Piece-Work Rate Sheet.

Left- and Right-Hand Operation Description

Many time study problems are created because the method used in performing the operation has not been recorded on the observation sheet in sufficient detail. One aid in solving this problem is to make a left- and right-hand description of each element

OBSERVATION SHEET

DEPARTMENT	Shoe Room	DATE	
FOREMAN	W.M. Wilson	OPERATOR	Betty Walker
OPERATION	Assemble and cement heel plugs on swing boot insoles	OBSERVER	R.J. Parson

NO.	ELEMENTS	UNITS PER ELEMENT	1	2	3	4	5	6	7	8	9	10	11	12	TOTAL TIME	NO. OF OBS'NS	AVERAGE TIME	READING OCCUR. MOST FREQUENTLY	MINIMUM TIME	REPRESENTATIVE TIME	RATING	NORMAL TIME
1.	Get supply of heel plugs	20 Pr.	.06	.07	.10	.07	.08	.08	.07	.08	.09	.10	.08	.09	1.49	18	.083	.08	.06	.083	100	.083
2.	Get supply of insoles	20 Pr.	.10 / .12	.08 / .15	.09 / .13	.08 / .12	.09	.08	.13	.14	.13	.15	.13	.13	1.99	15	.133	.13	.10	.133	100	.133
3.	Get, loosen, and lay out insoles in 15 piles	7½ Pr.	.41 / .43	.43 / .44	.42	.40	.44	.43	.42	.43	.45	.44	.45	.43	6.02	14	.430	.43	.40	.430	110	.473
4.	Get, pick, and spot heel plugs on insole	½ Pr.	.06 / .05 / .07 / .05	.05 / .05 / .08 / .05	.05 / .07 / .06 / .06	.06 / .05 / .05	.06 / .05 / .05	.05 / .05 / .05	.05 / .07 / .05	.05 / .05 / .06	.05 / .06 / .05	.05 / .05 / .05	.06 / .06 / .06	.05 / .05	2.15	39	.056	.05	.04	.056	100	.056
5.	Get brush of cement, cement, and aside brush	7½ Pr.	.24 / .24	.24 / .23	.23 / .25	.23 / .24	.22 / .23	.22 / .23	.22 / .24	.23 / .22	.22 / .24	.26 / .23	.23 / .24	.23 / .23	4.62	20	.231	.23	.18	.231	95	.219
6.	Stack completed work	30	.26	.24	.25 / .26	.24	.25	.23	.23	.25					3.88	16	.242	.24	.18	.242	100	.242
7.	Mark size on stack	30	.04	.04	.04 / .05	.04	.04	.06	.04	.05	.04	.04	.05	.04	1.02	23	.044	.04	.02	.044	100	.044
8.	Aside completed work	30	.08 / .10	.07 / .08	.08 / .09	.10 / .08	.09	.09	.08	.06	.08	.08	.05	.08	1.33	16	.083	.08	.06	.083	100	.083
9.	Get cement supply	2000	1.14	1.20	1.27	1.16	1.23								6.00	5	1.20	1.20	1.14	1.20	100	1.200
10.	Empty and clean cement pan	2000	1.23	1.11	1.18	1.20									4.72	4	1.18	1.18	1.02	1.18	100	1.180
11.	Clean up work place and cover work	2000	1.90	1.95	2.11	1.83									7.79	4	1.948	1.948	1.83	1.948	100	1.948
12.	Record production	120	(From standard data)																			.070

INFREQUENT ELEMENTS	OCCURANCE	TIME	RATING	NORM. TIME

REMARKS

STOP	10:24
START	11:06
ELAPSED	
NO. UNITS	
UNITS PER HOUR	

TS 103

Figure 207 Front of observation sheet—stop-watch time study of assembling and cementing operation, made by the repetitive method.

315

EQUIPMENT USED

Work Bench

Pan of Cement and Brush

PART DRAWING

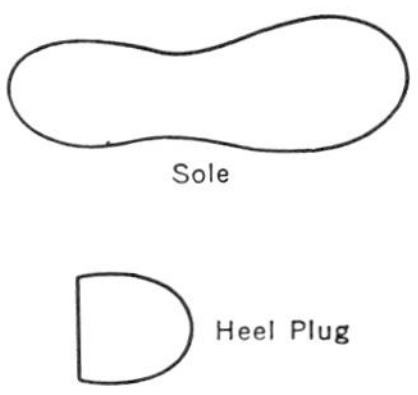

Sole

Heel Plug

DISPOSITION OF COMPLETED WORK: Onto Truck with Shelves (T431)

MATERIALS AND SUPPLIES

DESCRIPTION	PAIRS PER UNIT	SOURCE	SUPPLIED BY	HOW SUPPLIED
Cement # CT 1031		Tank	Operator	

SKETCH OF WORKPLACE   SCALE: $\frac{1}{2}'' = 1'$

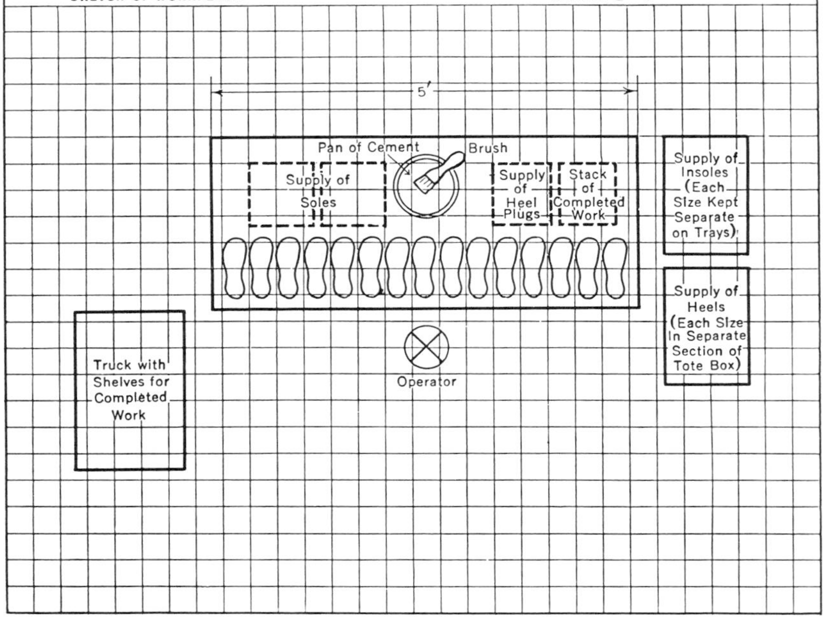

5'

Pan of Cement   Brush

Supply of Soles

Supply of Heel Plugs

Stack of Completed Work

Supply of Insoles (Each Size Kept Separate on Trays)

Supply of Heels (Each Size In Separate Section of Tote Box)

Truck with Shelves for Completed Work

Operator

Figure 208 Back of observation sheet—assembling and cementing operation.

316

COMPUTATION SHEET

OPERATION Assemble and Cement Heel Plugs on Swing Boot Insoles

DEPARTMENT Shoe Room _____ DATE _____

NO.	ELEMENTS	NORMAL TIME PER ELE-MENT	UNITS PER ELE-MEMT (Pr.)	OCCUR. OF ELE-MEMT PER 100 Pr.	NORMAL TIME PER 100 Pr.
1	Get Supply of Heel Plugs	.083	20	5	.415
2	Get Supply of Insoles	.133	20	5	.665
3	Get, Loosen, Layout Insoles in 15 Piles	.473	7½	13⅓	6.292
4	Get, Pick, and Spot Heel Plugs on Insoles	.056	½	200	11.200
5	Get Brush of Cement, Cement, and Aside Brush	.219	7½	13⅓	2.919
6	Stack Completed Work	.242	30	3⅓	.807
7	Mark Size on Stack	.044	30	3⅓	.147
8	Aside Completed Work	.083	30	3⅓	.276
9	Get Cement Supply	1.200	2000	.05	.060
10	Empty and Clean Cement Pan	1.180	2000	.05	.059
11	Clean Up Work Place and Cover Work	1.948	2000	.05	.098
12	Record Production	.07	120	.83	.058

(A) TOTAL NORMAL TIME IN MINUTES _____ 22.996

(B) ALLOWANCES (10%) IN MINUTES _____ 2.299

(C) TOTAL STANDARD TIME PER 100 Pr. (A + B = C) _____ 25.3

(D) DAY WORK HOURLY PRODUCTION _____ 237 Pr.

TS104

Figure 209 Computation sheet for assembling and cementing operation.

PIECE-WORK RATE SHEET

DEPARTMENT Shoe Room
OPERATION Assemble and cement heel plugs on insoles
TYPE SHOE Womens', misses', and child's swing boots
Womens', misses', and child's all-weather boots

DATE EFFECTIVE

JOB NUMBER 16-16 DAY WORK
16-15 PIECE WORK

DAY WORK RATE	OPERATION	DAY WORK HOURLY PROD.	PIECE WORK RATE PER 100 PAIRS
$7.50	Assemble and cement heel plugs on insoles	237 Pr.	$3.17

APPROVED J. S. Fuller SUPT.

APPROVED Earl Stone HEAD OF TIME STUDY

TS 106

Figure 210 Piece-work rate sheet for assembling and cementing operation.

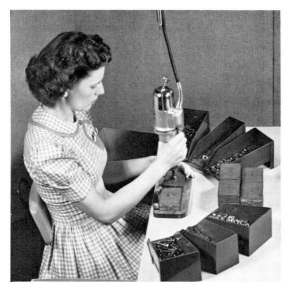

Figure 211 Layout of work place for assembly of cast-iron plates. Power wrench is suspended above the fixture.

of the operation. It may take the form of a record of each motion of each hand (Figs. 80 and 92), or it may consist of a record of get, place, use, hold, dispose, and wait for each hand. Figure 212 contains such a description of the element of a cast-iron plate assembly (Fig. 211). This left- and right-hand description would be attached to the observation sheet, and the time study would be made in the usual way.

As more time study analysts are trained in micromotion study and in the use of predetermined time data, there is certain to be greater use of the left- and right-hand operation description. This more complete description of the operation will make for a better time study.

Production Studies

Although a motion and time study may have been made with care and the instruction sheet may have been prepared and given to the operator, there is sometimes a complaint that the operator is unable to perform the task in the time called for on the instruction sheet. If, after a preliminary check, it appears that the inability to do the task in the time set is not the fault of the operator, it is essential that a new study be made to check the original time study. This new study, sometimes called a production study, covers a longer period of time than the original study—sometimes as long as a day or two. Figure 213 shows one production study summary.

The inability of the operator to perform the task in the time specified may be due to any one or a combination of the following causes: conditions of material, tools, or equipment are different from those existing at the time the original study was made; there has been a change in method, layout or working conditions; operator has not had sufficient experience on the job or is unsuited to the work; or the time study itself contained errors. The production study should be made in such detail as to permit the checking of elemental times.

Although every effort should be made to prevent errors in setting the original time standard, it is essential that the management be willing at all times to rectify errors or to demonstrate the correctness of the time standard. The workers must have confidence in the standards and in the people who set them.

Work Sampling Studies

Work sampling is being used to an increasing extent to supplement or replace the production study. As will be explained more fully in Chapter 30, work sampling is often a better and more economical method of getting facts than all-day time study.

Recording and Filing

When a time study is to be made of a series of similar operations, it is desirable to define carefully each of the elements in order that standard data for each element may finally be determined. A master form is prepared, and the essential data from

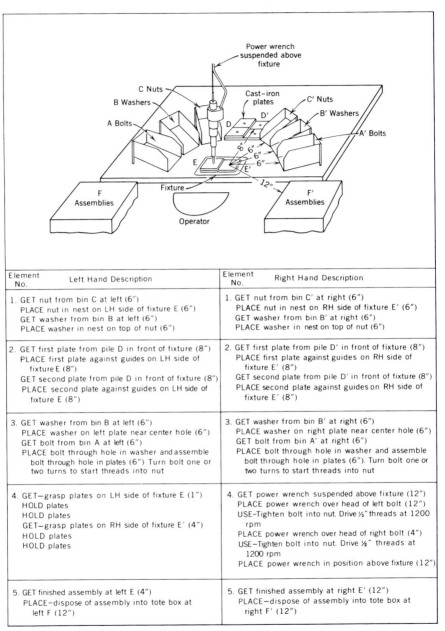

Element No.	Left Hand Description	Element No.	Right Hand Description
1.	GET nut from bin C at left (6″) PLACE nut in nest on LH side of fixture E (6″) GET washer from bin B at left (6″) PLACE washer in nest on top of nut (6″)	1.	GET nut from bin C′ at right (6″) PLACE nut in nest on RH side of fixture E′ (6″) GET washer from bin B′ at right (6″) PLACE washer in nest on top of nut (6″)
2.	GET first plate from pile D in front of fixture (8″) PLACE first plate against guides on LH side of fixture E (8″) GET second plate from pile D in front of fixture (8″) PLACE second plate against guides on LH side of fixture E (8″)	2.	GET first plate from pile D′ in front of fixture (8″) PLACE first plate against guides on RH side of fixture E′ (8″) GET second plate from pile D′ in front of fixture (8″) PLACE second plate against guides on RH side of fixture E′ (8″)
3.	GET washer from bin B at left (6″) PLACE washer on left plate near center hole (6″) GET bolt from bin A at left (6″) PLACE bolt through hole in washer and assemble bolt through hole in plates (6″) Turn bolt one or two turns to start threads into nut	3.	GET washer from bin B′ at right (6″) PLACE washer on right plate near center hole (6″) GET bolt from bin A′ at right (6″) PLACE bolt through hole in washer and assemble bolt through hole in plates (6″). Turn bolt one or two turns to start threads into nut
4.	GET—grasp plates on LH side of fixture E (1″) HOLD plates HOLD plates GET—grasp plates on RH side of fixture E′ (4″) HOLD plates HOLD plates	4.	GET power wrench suspended above fixture (12″) PLACE power wrench over head of left bolt (12″) USE-Tighten bolt into nut. Drive ½″ threads at 1200 rpm PLACE power wrench over head of right bolt (4″) USE-Tighten bolt into nut. Drive ½″ threads at 1200 rpm PLACE power wrench in position above fixture (12″)
5.	GET finished assembly at left E (4″) PLACE—dispose of assembly into tote box at left F (12″)	5.	GET finished assembly at right E′ (12″) PLACE—dispose of assembly into tote box at right F′ (12″)

Figure 212 Left- and right-hand operation described for the assembly of cast-iron plates.

320

PRODUCTION STUDY SUMMARY

OPERATION	Mold Steering Gear Housing
	OP. NO. M-27
PART NAME	Steering Gear Housing
MACH. NAME ——	
LOCATION Foundry	
TIME STARTED 7:00 A.M.	
TIME STOPPED 11:30 A.M.	

KEY	ACTIVITY	MIN.	%
	Productive Time	219.1	81.1
	Personal Time	25.1	9.3
	Get Ready and Clean Up	23.8	8.8
	Unnecessary Idle Time	1.8	.7
	Idle Time Beyond Control of Op.	.2	.1
	Total	270.0	100

PART NO. VT-179A

MACH. NO. ——

DATE

CHARTED BY L.M.K.

Figure 213 Production study summary of a foundry operation covering a 4½-hour period.

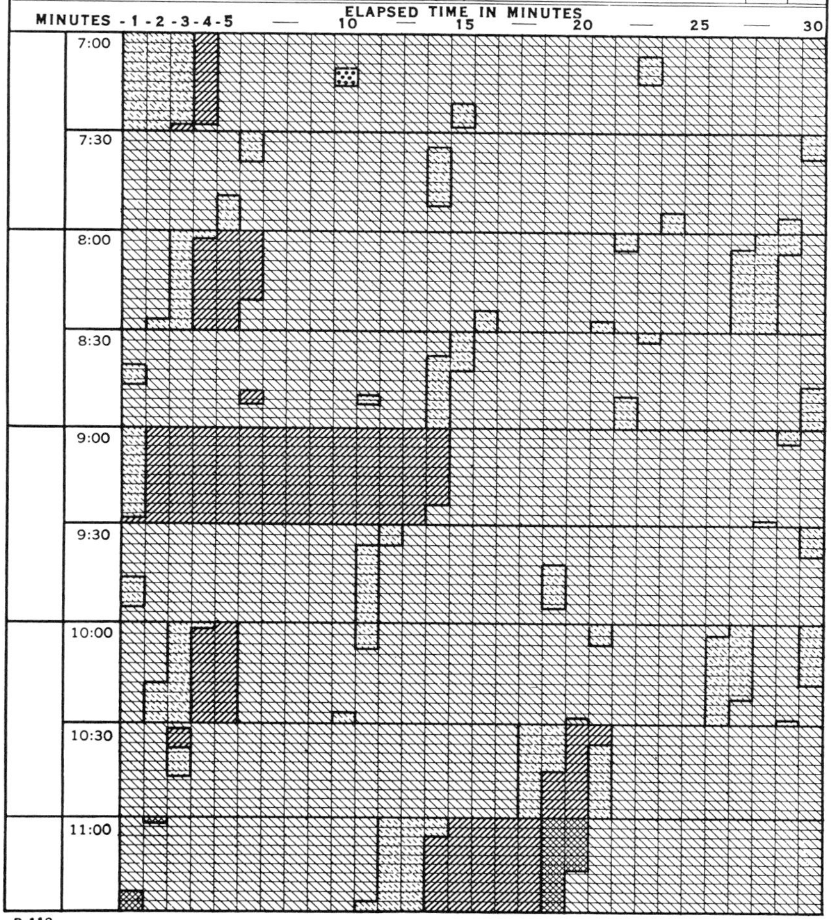

B 118

321

each time study are recorded on this sheet. After sufficient data have been accumulated, they will be used for establishing standard data and formulas for determining time standards as described in Chapters 23 and 24.

Time studies, together with other data and information concerning the operation, should be filed in such a way that they may be readily located when needed. Cross-indexing is often worthwhile.

Guaranteed Time Standard

The time standard should be guaranteed against change unless there has been a change in method, materials, tools, equipment, layout, or working conditions, or when there has been a clerical error or a mistake in the calculation of the standard.

When a time standard is set for a job, it is understood that the operator will perform the operation exactly as specified in the standard practice or on the instruction sheet. If the operation is not performed in this manner, the time standard is not valid. However, so long as the operator does the job in the prescribed manner, the company guarantees that the time standard will not be changed. The company should adhere to this policy so completely that every operator will feel free to work at whatever pace he or she chooses. Operators should have no fear that the time standard for the job will be reduced if they "earn too much" under a wage incentive system.

Methods Change

When there is a change in method, materials, tooling, or other factors affecting the time of the operation, the job should be restudied and a new time standard should be established. If an operator suggests a change which reduces the operation time, improves the quality, or makes the job safer, he or she may be compensated immediately for the suggestion. If the company has a suggestion system, the operator should be rewarded through the regular channels. When the new standard for the improved job has been established, the operator should find it just as easy to earn the accustomed incentive premium or bonus as before the method was improved. A change in method should not be used as an excuse to reduce a time standard. If management expects to get and maintain the cooperation of its employees, it must make certain that employees gain and do not lose as a result of their suggestions.

Auditing of Methods, Time Standards, and Wage Incentive Plans

Auditing is a procedure to determine how well standard policies and techniques are being followed. Ordinarily the audit report would include a statement of variations from standard practice, an evaluation of these variations, and recommendations for changes and corrections. The design of a work measurement and wage incentive plan should provide for a periodic audit. A wage incentive program is based upon carefully established policies and procedures, and unless these procedures are followed precisely, the plan may soon become unfair to management or to the employees, depending upon the nature of the error. In most cases the error favors the employee, and management consequently stands to gain most by thorough auditing procedures. If a wage incentive plan is not carefully maintained, the earnings of some employees may get out of line, that is, may become too high as compared with those of other employees. This inequity is undesirable both to management and to the employees. Management wants to be certain that year in and year out its standards will be maintained, and the employees who are on incentive want to be assured that the plan will continue on a fair and sound basis. A good auditing program can contribute much to achieving these ends.

One company has managed its work measurement and wage incentive program so well that the average performance index of some 9000 employees who are on incentive has not varied more than plus or minus 3 percent in a period of 25 years. The average performance index is computed every 3 months, by operators, by departments, by divisions, and is plotted company-wide. A distribution curve (Fig. 214) showing the performance index of workers on incentive by departments, and superimposed on this the average performance index for all incentive employees for the past 10 years. This company places great emphasis on auditing, and uses the most experienced and most competent industrial engineers for conducting their audits.

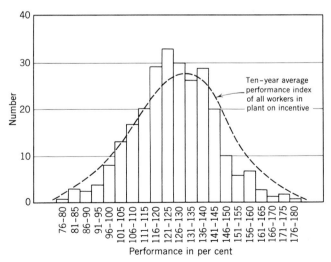

Figure 214 Distribution of performance index of 237 workers on incentive in Department 24 during 3-month period ending March 31. Superimposed is a distribution curve of the 10-year performance index of all workers in the plant on incentive.

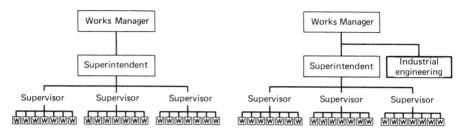

Figure 215 Organization charts: *A*, typical line organization; *B*, line and staff organization, showing typical staff department.

Time Study as a Staff Activity

The time study department is a staff department and not a line or operating agency (Fig. 215). It is important that every industrial engineer keep this fact fixed firmly in mind. Because a staff department must work through the supervisory groups, it is important that the line personnel understand the principles, techniques, and methods of the time study department. Supervisors should be so well acquainted with the time study that they can explain to an operator in the department how a time study is made, what elements are included in the operation, and exactly how the time standard for an operation is determined. The supervisor should be able to do this without having to call on the time study department for help. In unusual situations, of course, the supervisor may have to ask the time study department for additional information, or in some cases it might be wise for the time study analyst to supplement the information given to the operators by the supervisor.

Sometimes it is helpful to draw a parallel between two unrelated activities in order to clarify a situation. Guy J. Bates of General Motors has used the following analogy. When the number of rejects in a manufacturing department suddenly increases and the operator of the machine states that the cause is an inspection gauge that is out of adjustment, the supervisor will ordinarily examine the gauge to see if anything is obviously wrong, and will measure some parts to make certain the operator is using the gauge properly. If no cause for the difficulty can be found, the supervisor may call the head of the inspection department and have the gauge checked. The supervisor may be present while the check is being made, but the supervisor will expect the chief inspector to make any measurements that seem necessary to determine whether the excessive number of rejects is due to a faulty gauge.

So with time study work—just as the inspector and the tool department build, service, and check all gauges and inspection devices, so the time study department sets all time standards and maintains them. If an operator complains that the time standard is too low and that a premium cannot be earned, the supervisor will be expected to check the operation against the instruction sheet to see whether the operation is being performed according to the prescribed method. This involves checking the materials, speeds, and feeds of the machine, and other job conditions. If, after checking these things, the supervisor is unable to find a cause for the apparent error in the standard, he or she will request that a time study analyst be sent to check the standard. The supervisor may or may not remain with the time study analyst while the check study is being made, but will certainly follow in detail the checking procedure and will know the cause of the difficulty and the means that are finally used to correct the situation.

As for all staff functions in the plant, it is necessary to have a careful balance between the duties of the industrial engineering department and line departments. Although the time study department is definitely responsible for establishing and maintaining time standards in a plant, the industrial engineer works through the supervisor and does not replace him.

23

DETERMINING TIME STANDARDS FROM STANDARD DATA AND FORMULAS

Many time studies are made of a single operation, with little or no thought that the data taken will be of value on any other operation. Some kinds of work, however, have certain elements that are alike. For example, in a given class of machine-tool work all elements may be virtually alike except for the machine time or the cutting time. The same jig used for drilling the ¼-inch hole in the end of the shaft (Fig. 184) might also be used for drilling many other sizes of shafts. If the length and the diameter of the shafts fall within a limited range, handling time for drilling all shafts would be practically constant, and the only variable in the operation would be the time required to drill the hole, which would vary with its diameter and depth. Other operations using jigs similar to this one would have certain elements in common, such as "tighten set screw" or "lower drill to work."

Where motion and time studies are to be made of many different operations of a similar class of work, such as that on sensitive drill presses, lathes, and gear hobbers, it is best to consider the entire class of work as a unit, working out such improvements in methods as seem advisable, and standardizing all factors for the entire class of work. When time studies are begun on this work, the elements should be selected in a way that will make it possible eventually to construct tables of standard time data that may be applied to all elements likely to appear continually in that particular class of work.

Use of Time Values for Constant Elements

The data shown in Tables 18 to 20 were obtained from a sufficient number of time studies of representative kinds of work to guarantee their reliability. With such data available in the time study department, it is possible to set time standards for the handling elements of any job on a sensitive drill falling within the classes listed in Tables 19 and 20. These data do not give the time required to drill the hole in the piece; consequently this information must be obtained by means of a time study of this element.

Assuming that Tables 18, 19, and 20 were available and that it was necessary to determine the standard time to drill the ¼-inch hole in the end of the shaft (Fig. 184), the procedure would be as follows:

Chuck and remove piece (from Table 19)	0.50
(Class B, work held by set screw)	
Machine manipulation (from Table 20)	0.07
(Class A, drilling, one drill and no bushing)	

DRILL ¼-INCH HOLE
(stop-watch data obtained as in Fig. 184)   0.54

Total normal time per piece	1.11
5% allowance	0.06
Total standard time per piece	1.17 minutes

Setup time (from Table 18) = 15.00 minutes

The value of standard data such as those illustrated is evident. They reduce the number of time studies needed, shorten the time required to set the standard, and tend to bring greater accuracy and consistency in time standards for a given class of work.

The next step in this direction is the preparation of formulas which will make it possible to calculate quickly time values for the machine elements. Thus, with standard data for the handling elements and calculated time values for the machine elements, it is possible to determine the time standard for a given operation without making a time study. By using this procedure the time standard can readily be determined in advance of the actual production of the part. In this case a detailed drawing of the part to be made and the operation sheet or the route sheet should be supplied to the time study department in advance.

Determining Time Standards for Variables

On many kinds of machine-tool work the time for manipulating the machine and for chucking and removing the piece is likely to remain constant for each element, provided the size and shape of the piece are within reasonably close limits. The time for making the cut is the variable. The machine time can often be calculated, particularly when positive power feeds are used. For example, in milling-machine work

Table 18.   Time-Setting Data for Sensitive Drills
Setup Time

Description of Work	Time, Minutes
1. Small work held in jig which can be handled very easily by hand	15.00
2. Small work held in vise	15.00
3. Small work held to table by one or two straps	15.00
4. Small work held in jig having a number of drilled, tapped, and reamed holes	30.00
5. Small work held in jig and jig held in vise	30.00
6. Work of medium size held by one or two straps	30.00
7. Work of medium size prevented from turning on table by a stop in T-slot	15.00
8. Work of circular type such as washers, collars, bushings, and sleeves held to table by a draw bolt through center	15.00

Table 19. Elemental Time Data for Sensitive Drills
Chucking and Removing Time

Classes, work held in jig:
- *A*. Held by thumb screw
- *B*. Held by set screw
- *C*. Held by thumb and set screw
- *D*. Held by cover strap and thumb screw
- *E*. Held by cover strap and set screw
- *F*. Held by cover strap, thumb screw, and set screw

	Time, Hundredths of a Minute					
Elements	*A*	*B*	*C*	*D*	*E*	*F*
1. Pick up piece and place in jig	12	12	12	12	12	12
2. Swing cover strap and tighten lock screw	..	..	..	10	10	10
3. Tighten thumb screw	08	..	08	08	..	08
4. Tighten set screw	..	12	12	..	12	12
5. Loosen set screw	..	06	06	..	06	06
6. Loosen thumb screw	05	..	05	05	..	05
7. Swing cover strap back and loosen lock screw	..	..	..	08	08	08
8. Remove piece from jig	08	08	08	08	08	08
9. Blow out chips	12	12	12	12	12	12
Total	45	50	63	63	68	81

Note. Add 0.32 minute when jig is strapped to table. Add 0.07 minute for each additional thumb screw. Add 0.08 minute for each additional set screw.

Table 20. Elemental Time Data for Sensitive Drills
Machine Manipulation Time

Classes:
- *A*. Drilling, one drill and no bushing
- *B*. Drilling, placing and removing bushing
- *C*. Drilling, placing and removing drill
- *D*. Drilling, placing and removing drill and bushing

	Time, Hundredths of a Minute			
Elements	*A*	*B*	*C*	*D*
1. Place bushing in jig	..	06	..	06
2. Place drill in chuck	..	..	04	04
3. Advance drill to work	04	04	04	04
4. Raise drill from hole	03	03	03	03
5. Remove bushing from jig	..	05	..	05
6. Remove drill from chuck	..	..	03	03
Total	07	18	14	25

Note. Add 0.15 minute when quick-change chuck is not used (cases *B* and *C*). Add 0.06 minute for advancing work to next spindle. Add 0.05 minute when reamer is oiled before entering hole.

with power feed, if the feed of the table in inches per revolution of the cutter is known, and if the speed of the cutter in revolutions per minute is known, it is a simple arithmetical problem to find the time required to mill a piece of a given length. Allowances must be added to the length of the piece for the approach and for the overtravel of the cutter; however, they can also be calculated easily. In a similar manner, if a shaft of a given length is chucked in a lathe and if the speed and the feed are known, it is easy to calculate the length of time required to make a cut across the piece. Therefore, on machine tool work the handling time (a constant) plus the machine time (a variable) plus allowances will equal the standard time for the performance of a given operation.

SETTING TIME STANDARDS FOR MILLING SQUARE OR HEXAGON ON BOLTS, SCREWS, OR SHAFTS

With the aid of the following four tables it is possible to determine the time standard for setting up a milling machine and for milling a square or hexagon on the end of bolts, screws, or shafts. The data in Tables 21 and 22 were determined from stop-watch time studies. A sufficient number of representative jobs were studied to give reliable data. Tables 23 and 24 were compiled to facilitate the determination of the time standard for a given operation. Typical examples at the bottom of these two tables show how they are used.

There are two methods of milling squares and hexagons: (1) using a single mill, which requires a separate cut for each side (use Table 23), and (2) using a gang mill, which cuts two sides at a time (use Table 24).

Computation of Data for Table 23—Milling by Use of 6-Lip Mill

This milling operation is performed with a single milling cutter; hence four cuts are required to mill a square and six cuts to mill a hexagon. The dimension B (see sketches in Tables 23 and 24) is given as the turned diameter of the shaft rather than the width of the face to be cut, for the reason that detailed drawings (Fig. 216) are dimensioned in that manner. Because the side of a square is equal to 0.7071 times the diameter of the circumscribed circle, and because the side of a hexagon is equal to the radius of the circumscribed circle, it is easy to make the conversion.

When a single mill is used, the cut is made across the face, and the time for the cut varies as B and is independent of the dimension A, provided it falls within the scope of the data, that is, within ⅝ inch to 1¾ inch. The total handling time (HT) plus the total cutting time (M) plus the allowances equal the total time for the operation.

The handling time is composed of machine manipulation time and chucking and removing time as shown in Table 22. The cutting time can be calculated from the formula

$$M = \frac{(L + OT)N}{F}$$

where M = cutting time in minutes
$\quad L$ = length of cut in inches
$\qquad$ (a) $\quad L = 0.707 \times B$ for square
$\qquad$ (b) $\quad L = 0.5 \times B$ for hexagon
$\quad OT$ = overtravel = ½ diameter of mill in inches

Table 21. Time-Setting Data for Milling Machines
Setup Time—Machine Class 36

1. Base Setup Times—Minutes

	Work Sizes		
Type	Small	Medium	Large
A. Strapped to table or angle plate (4 straps)	25	25	25
B. Held in vise	25	25	25
C. Held in 2 vises	..	30	30
D. Vise with false jaws	35	35	35
E. Held in fixture	35	45	60
F. Held in dividing head chuck	35	35	..
G. Held in dividing head and tail stock	45	45	..

2. Additional Parts Used—Time to Be Added to Base Setup Time

	Part Sizes		
Part	Small	Medium	Large
H. Each additional strap	5	5	5
J. Angle plate	10	15	15
K. Gang mills			
(1) fractional limits	10	10	10
(2) decimal limits	15	15	15
L. False table	10	15	20
M. Round table—hand feed	10	20	20
N. Round table—power feed	20	30	30
P. High-speed head	..	40	..
Q. Universal head	..	60	..

Table 22. Elemental Time Data for Milling Square or Hexagon on Bolts, Screws, or Shafts

Machine Class 36—Milling Table 1A

1. *Setup time*—Complete—See setup table
   Change size—End mill   —10 min.
   Gang mills—20 min.

2. *Specifications*—
   A. Method of chucking—1—3-jaw chuck (small screws and bolts)
   2—Held on centers (shafts)
   3—Thread arbor in dividing head (small pieces with thread on or in end)
   B. Cutters—1—6-lip mill
   2—Gang mills (6-in. stagger tooth—side milling cutters)
   C. Length of flat   —⅝ in.–1¾ in.
   D. Size of sq. or hex.—½ in.–1⅝ in.
   E. Number of cuts   —1 per side
   F. Material   —SAE2315
   G. Indexing   —Use rapid index plate wherever possible

3. *Operation Time.*—Machine manipulation and chucking time

Time in Minutes

Elements	Speed r.p.m.	Method of Chucking									
		1				2		3			
		Square		Hex.		Sq.	Hex.	Square		Hex.	
		214	58	214	58	214	214	214	58	214	58
	Type of Mill	6-Lip Mill	Gang Mill	6-Lip Mill	Gang Mill	6-Lip Mill	6-Lip Mill	6-Lip Mill	Gang Mill	6-Lip Mill	Gang Mill
1. Stop machine .		0.04	0.04	0.04	0.04	0.04	0.04	0.04	0.04	0.04	0.04
2. Loosen dog in holder		..	..	..	..	0.08	0.08	..	..	..	..
3. Loosen center .		..	..	..	..	0.08	0.08	..	..	..	..
4. Loosen work ..		0.04	0.04	0.04	0.04	..	..	0.08	0.08	0.08	0.08
5. Remove work .		0.06	0.06	0.06	0.06	0.10	0.10	0.08	0.08	0.08	0.08
6. Remove dog ..		..	..	..	..	0.08	0.08	..	..	..	..
7. Place dog		..	..	..	..	0.08	0.08	..	..	..	..
8. Clear chips ...		..	..	..	..	0.05	0.05	0.08	0.08	0.08	0.08
9. Place piece ...		0.08	0.08	0.08	0.08	0.08	0.08	0.12	0.12	0.12	0.12
10. Tighten		0.12	0.12	0.12	0.12	0.18	0.18	0.10	0.10	0.10	0.10
11. Start machine .		0.02	0.02	0.02	0.02	0.02	0.02	0.02	0.02	0.02	0.02
12. Advance to cut		0.04	0.06	0.04	0.06	0.04	0.04	0.04	0.06	0.04	0.06
13. Change depth .		*	*	*	*	*	*	*	*	*	*
14. Mill	2⅞ † or 3⅝	M	M	M	M	M	M	M	M	M	M
15. Index ‡		0.15	0.05	0.25	0.10	0.15	0.25	0.15	0.05	0.25	0.10
16. Return table ..		0.05	0.07	0.05	0.07	0.05	0.05	0.05	0.07	0.05	0.07
TOTALS ...		0.60	0.54	0.70	0.59	1.03	1.13	0.76	0.70	0.86	0.75

* Allow 0.08 when necessary.

† Feed in inches per minute—depending upon finish required.

‡ Above time is for rapid indexing. (Double indexing time when using precision crank.)

$M = \text{Cutting time} = \dfrac{(L+OT) \times \text{No. cuts}}{\text{Feed}}$ Base time $= H.T. + M$

Standard time = Base time + Allowances

331

N = number of cuts per piece

   (*a*) $N = 4$ for a square

   (*b*) $N = 6$ for a hexagon

F = table feed in inches per minute

   (*a*)   for fine finish use 2⅞ inches

   (*b*)   for ordinary finish use 3⅝ inches

EXAMPLE   Assume that the shaft at the top of Table 23 has these dimensions: $A = 1\frac{3}{4}$ inches; $B = 1$ inch. Ordinary finish (feed = 3⅝ inches per minute); mill square with 1¾-inch diameter, 6-lip mill; piece held in a 3-jaw chuck.

The handling time (*HT*) is obtained from Table 22, under method of chucking 1, square, 6-lip mill, and is 0.60 minute.

The cutting time is calculated from the formula.

$$M = \frac{(0.707 + 0.875)4}{3.625} = \frac{6.328}{3.625} = 1.748 \qquad \begin{aligned} L &= 0.707 \times 1 = 0.707 \\ OT &= \tfrac{1}{2} \text{ of } 1\tfrac{3}{4} = \tfrac{7}{8} = 0.875 \\ N &= 4 \end{aligned}$$

$$\begin{aligned} HT &= 0.60 \qquad\qquad\quad F = 3.625 \\ M &= 1.748 \end{aligned}$$

$$\begin{aligned} \text{Total normal time} &= 2.348 \\ 5\% \text{ allowance} &= 0.117 \end{aligned}$$

Total standard time = 2.465, use 2.5 minutes

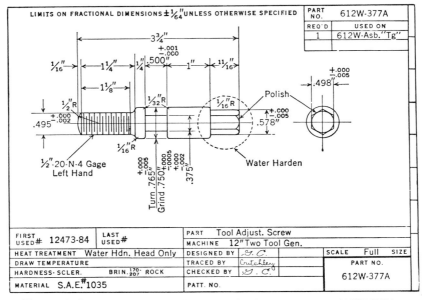

Figure 216 Detail drawing of a tool adjusting screw, part 612W-377A.

Now with reference to Table 23, since a single cutter is used and since A lies between the limits given, this table applies. Reading under symbol 8-D, the standard time equals 2.5 minutes, which checks with that calculated above.

Table 23. Time-Setting Table for Milling Square and Hexagon on Bolts, Screws, and Shafts

Machine Class 36—Milling Table 1B

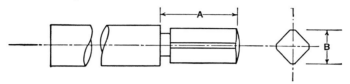

Case 1—Using a 6-Lip Mill (See Table 1C for Gang Mills)
Time per Piece in Minutes

Symbol	A (See Sketch Above)	B (See Sketch Above)	3-Jaw Chuck				On Centers				On Thread Arbor in Div. Head			
			Square		Hex.		Square		Hex.		Square		Hex.	
			Feed 2⅞	Feed 3⅝	Feed 2⅞	Feed 3⅝	Feed 2⅞	Feed 3⅝	Feed 2⅞	Feed 3⅝	Feed 2⅞	Feed 3⅝	Feed 2⅞	Feed 3⅝
			C	D	E	F	G	H	J	K	L	M	N	O
1		½	2.4	2.1	3.2	2.7	2.9	2.5	3.7	3.2	2.6	2.3	3.4	2.9
2		9/16	2.5	2.1	3.3	2.8	3.0	2.6	3.7	3.2	2.7	2.3	3.5	2.9
3		⅝	2.6	2.1	3.3	2.8	3.0	2.6	3.8	3.3	2.8	2.4	3.5	3.0
4		11/16	2.6	2.2	3.5	2.9	3.1	2.7	3.9	3.4	2.8	2.4	3.6	3.1
5		¾	2.7	2.3	3.5	3.0	3.2	2.8	4.0	3.4	2.9	2.5	3.7	3.1
6	⅝ in. to 1¾ in.	13/16	2.8	2.3	3.6	3.0	3.3	2.8	4.1	3.5	3.0	2.5	3.8	3.2
7		⅞	2.8	2.4	3.6	3.1	3.3	2.8	4.1	3.6	3.0	2.6	3.9	3.3
8		1	3.0	2.5	3.8	3.2	3.4	3.0	4.2	3.6	3.1	2.7	4.1	3.3
9		1⅛	3.1	2.6	4.0	3.3	3.5	3.0	4.4	3.7	3.3	2.8	4.2	3.4
10		1¼	3.2	2.7	4.1	3.4	3.7	3.2	4.5	3.9	3.4	2.9	4.3	3.6
11		1⅜	3.3	2.8	4.2	3.5	3.8	3.3	4.7	4.0	3.5	3.0	4.4	3.7
12		1½	3.5	2.9	4.4	3.6	4.0	3.4	4.8	4.1	3.7	3.1	4.5	3.8
13		1⅝	3.6	3.0	4.5	3.7	4.1	3.5	5.0	4.2	3.8	3.2	4.7	3.9

1. Values in this table vary as B, hence see that A falls within limits ⅝ in. to 1¾ in. before using data.
2. These time standards are based on:
   (*a*) Length of travel $= B +$ overtravel
   (*b*) Handling time from Table 1A
   (*c*) Allowance of 5 percent
3. Examples for reading above table:
   (*a*) Let B = ⅝ in., A = 1 in., Square head shaft, held on centers, 6-lip mill, 3⅝ in. feed. Since A lies between limits given this table applies. Read from table under 3-H, standard time = 2.6 min. per piece.
   (*b*) Let B = 1¼ in., A = 1½ in., Hexagon head bolt, held on thread arbor in div. head, 6-lip mill, 2⅞ in. feed. Since A lies between limits given this table applies. Read from table under 10-N, standard time = 4.3 min. per piece.

333

Computation of Data for Table 24—Milling by Use of Gang Mill

This milling operation is performed with a gang milling cutter; hence two sides are cut at one time, two cuts being required for a square and three cuts for a hexagon. The direction of travel of the mill in making the cut is from the end toward the shoulder; hence the time for the cut varies as A and is independent of B, provided it falls within the scope of the data, that is, provided the diameter of the shaft is between ½ inch and 1⅝ inches.

The total standard time for the operation is equal to the handling time (HT) plus the cutting time (M) plus the allowances. The handling time is taken directly from Table 22, and the cutting time can be calculated from the formula

$$M = \frac{(L + OT)N}{F}$$

where M = cutting time in minutes
$\quad L$ = length of cut = A
$\quad OT$ = overtravel—since the direction of travel of the gang mill is from the end to the shoulder, no overtravel is allowed.
$\quad N$ = number of cuts per piece
$\qquad$ (a) $N = 2$ for a square
$\qquad$ (b) $N = 3$ for a hexagon
$\quad F$ = table feed in inches per minute

EXAMPLE   The operation is that of milling the hexagon on the tool adjusting screw shown in Fig. 216. The following information is taken from the drawing (Fig. 216) and from the operation sheet (not shown): $A = {}^{11}/_{16}$ inch, $B = 0.578$ inch. Ordinary finish, 3⅝ inches per minute feed, 7-inch gang mill, piece held in 3-jaw chuck.

Handling time from Table 22 = 0.59 minute.
Cutting time is calculated from the formula.

$$M = \frac{(0.6875 + 0)3}{3.625} = 0.569 \text{ minute} \qquad \begin{aligned} L &= {}^{11}/_{16} = 0.6875 \\ OT &= 0 \\ N &= 3 \\ F &= 3⅝ = 3.625 \end{aligned}$$

Therefore the total time for the operation is

$$HT = 0.59$$
$$M = \underline{0.569}$$
$$\text{Total normal time} = 1.159$$
$$5\% \text{ allowance} = \underline{0.058}$$
$$\text{Total standard time} = 1.217, \text{ use } 1.25 \text{ minutes}$$

Now with reference to Table 24, since a gang mill is used and since B lies between the limits given, this table applies. Reading under symbol 2-F, the standard time equals 1.25 minutes, which checks with that calculated above.

Table 24. Time-Setting Table for Milling Square and Hexagon on Bolts, Screws, and Shafts

Machine Class 36—Milling Table 1C

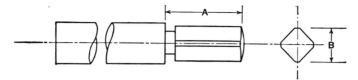

Case 2—Using Gang Mills (See 1B for 6-Lip Mill)
Time per Piece in Minutes

Symbol	A (See Sketch Above)	B (See Sketch Above)	3-Jaw Chuck				On Thread Arbor in Div. Head			
			Square		Hex.		Square		Hex.	
			Feed 2⅞	Feed 3⅝	Feed 2⅞	Feed 3⅝	Feed 2⅞	Feed 3⅝	Feed 2⅞	Feed 3⅝
			C	D	E	F	G	H	J	K
1	⅝		1.05	0.95	1.35	1.2	1.15	1.10	1.5	1.4
2	¹¹/₁₆		1.10	1.0	1.40	1.25	1.25	1.15	1.6	1.4
3	¾		1.15	1.05	1.5	1.25	1.35	1.20	1.7	1.5
4	¹³/₁₆		1.20	1.05	1.6	1.30	1.35	1.25	1.7	1.5
5	⅞		1.20	1.10	1.6	1.35	1.40	1.25	1.8	1.6
6	¹⁵/₁₆	½ in. to 1⅝ in.	1.25	1.15	1.7	1.45	1.45	1.30	1.8	1.7
7	1		1.35	1.20	1.8	1.50	1.50	1.35	1.9	1.7
8	1¹/₁₆		1.35	1.20	1.9	1.5	1.6	1.35	2.0	1.8
9	1⅛		1.40	1.25	1.9	1.6	1.6	1.40	2.1	1.8
10	1³/₁₆		1.45	1.30	2.0	1.7	1.7	1.45	2.2	1.9
11	1¼		1.50	1.30	2.1	1.8	1.7	1.5	2.2	2.0
12	1⅜		1.60	1.40	2.2	1.9	1.8	1.6	2.4	2.1
13	1½		1.7	1.45	2.3	2.0	1.9	1.6	2.5	2.2
14	1⅝		1.8	1.6	2.5	2.1	2.0	1.7	2.6	2.3
15	1¾		1.9	1.6	2.6	2.2	2.1	1.8	2.7	2.4

1. Values in this table vary as *A*, hence see that *B* falls within limits ½ in. to 1⅝ in. before using data.
2. These time standards are based on:
    (*a*) Length of travel = *A*
    (*b*) Handling time from Table 1*A*
    (*c*) Allowance of 5 percent
3. Examples for reading above table:
    (*a*) Let *A* = 1 in., *B* = 1³/₁₆ in., Square head bolt, held in chuck, gang mill, 3⅝ in. feed. Since *B* lies between limits given this table applies. Read from table under 7–*D* standard time = 1.20 min. per piece.
    (*b*) Let *A* = ¹¹/₁₆ in., *B* = 0.578 in., Hexagon head adjusting screw, held in chuck, gang mill, 3⅝ in. feed. Since *B* lies between limits given this table applies. Read from table under 2–*F*, standard time = 1.25 min. per piece.

24

USE OF STANDARD DATA AND FORMULAS FOR GEAR HOBBING

The following example of the use of standard data and formulas for setting time standards for gear hobbing demonstrates how the principles already explained may be applied to rather complicated work. The data and procedure given here have been in constant use in a well-known machine-tool plant for a number of years and serve their purpose well.

Although the data apply to the cutting of both straight and helical spur gears, only those pertaining to cutting straight spur gears will be given here. These data are applicable to straight spur gears varying from 6 to 32 diametral pitch, of steel or cast iron, and with round or spline bore. Barber-Coleman hobbers, such as that shown in Fig. 217, are used. The lot sizes of the gear blanks are small.

The following explanations concerning Tables 25, 26, and 27 may make them more easily understood.

Table 25. Handling Time—Machine Manipulation

This time for machine manipulation will depend upon the method used in cutting the gears. Three different methods are shown for spur gears. The time required to chuck and remove the gear (Table 26) is independent of the method of cutting.

Table 26. Handling Time—Chucking and Removing

The data show that the time needed to chuck and remove the gears varies with the different types of mounting.

Table 27. Approach Allowance

The approach allowance required for hobbing is determined in the same manner as for milling. It is affected by the diameter of the hob and the depth of the cut. The ⅛-inch allowance for finish hobbing is sufficient for clearance at the beginning and at the end of the cut.

Cutting Time Formula

$$M = \frac{N \times L}{F \times S \times H}$$

where M = cutting time in minutes
N = number of teeth

Figure 217   Barber-Colman gear hobber.

L = total length of cut (length of face plus approach allowance)
F = feed in inches per revolution of work
S = speed of hob in revolutions per minute
H = lead of hob
    (*a*) single = 1
    (*b*) double = 2

Hobbing is a continuous cutting action from the start to the finish of the travel of the hob across the entire gear face. One revolution of the work advances the hob a distance equal to the feed.

Table 25. Handling Time—Straight Spur Gears, Barber-Colman Hobber

Machine Manipulation

(Time in minutes)

Operation	Spur Gears			Helical Gears	
	Reg. Hob 1 Cut	Reg. Hob 2 Cuts	Rough and Finish Comb. Hob.	1 Cut	2 Cuts
1. Advance carriage	0.08	0.08	0.08	0.25	0.25
2. Unlock hob	. .	. .	0.04	. .	. .
3. Move to rough side of hob	. .	. .	0.15	. .	. .
4. Lock hob	. .	. .	0.04	. .	. .
5. Change gears	. .	. .	0.05	. .	. .
6. Start machine	0.02	0.02	0.02	0.02	0.02
7. Cut	T	T	T	T	T
8. Loosen over-arm nuts (2)	0.04	0.04	. .	0.04	0.04
9. Loosen upright nuts (4)	0.06	0.06	. .	0.06	0.06
10. Raise piece	0.03	. .	. .	0.03	0.03
11. Back carriage	0.07	0.07	. .	0.25	0.25
12. Lower piece to depth	. .	0.08	. .	. .	0.08
13. Tighten upright nuts (4)	0.08	0.08	. .	0.08	0.08
14. Tighten over-arm nuts (2)	0.06	0.06	. .	0.06	0.06
15. Advance carriage	. .	0.08	. .	. .	. .
16. Unlock hob	. .	. .	0.04	. .	. .
17. Turn to finish side of hob	. .	. .	0.15	. .	. .
18. Set hob	. .	. .	0.25	. .	. .
19. Lock hob	. .	. .	0.04	. .	. .
20. Change gears	. .	. .	0.05	. .	. .
21. Start machine	. .	0.02	0.02	. .	0.02
22. Cut	. .	T	T	. .	T
23. Loosen over-arm nuts (2)	. .	0.04	. .	. .	0.04
24. Loosen upright nuts (4)	. .	0.06	. .	. .	0.06
25. Raise piece	. .	0.03	. .	. .	0.03
26. Back carriage	. .	0.07	0.07	. .	0.25
27. Tighten upright nuts (4)	. .	0.08	. .	. .	0.08
28. Tighten over-arm nuts (2)	. .	0.06	. .	. .	0.06
Standard time	0.44	0.93	1.00	0.79	1.41

T = cutting time in minutes

Note: Allow 0.55 minute to set hob in alignment with keyway when required.

338

Table 26. Handling Time—Straight Spur Gears,
Barber-Colman Hobber

Chucking and Removing

	Time, minutes	
Operations	A	B
1. Place blanks	0.05N	0.05N
2. Place washers and arbor nut	0.23	. .
3. Oil center	0.10	0.10
4. Advance tailstock	0.03	0.03
5. Lock tailstock	0.02	0.02
6. Tighten center	0.04	0.04
7. Tighten arbor nut	0.10	. .
8. Place washer and lock washer	. .	0.08
9. Tighten draw rod	. .	0.10
10. Loosen arbor nut	0.06	. .
11. Loosen draw rod	. .	0.06
12. Unlock tailstock	0.02	0.02
13. Back tailstock	0.03	0.03
14. Remove lock washer and washers	. .	0.06
15. Remove arbor nut and washer	0.12	. .
16. Remove gears	0.09	0.09
Standard time	0.84 + 0.05N	0.63 + 0.05N

A = nut-locked arbor. Use nut-locked arbor for arbor diameters up to $1^5/_{16}$ inches.
B = draw arbor. Use draw arbor for arbor diameters $^{15}/_{16}$ in. and larger.
N = numbers of pieces per chucking.
Note: Allow 0.20 minute to insert key when keys on blanks must be aligned with teeth.

$$\frac{N \text{ (number of teeth)}}{H \text{ (lead of hob)}} = \text{revolutions of hob per revolution of work} \qquad (1)$$

$$\frac{\left[\begin{array}{c} N/H \text{ (revolutions of hob per} \\ \text{revolution of work} \end{array}\right]}{S \text{ (speed of hob in rpm)}} = \text{time in minutes per revolution of work} \qquad (2)$$

Since

$$\frac{L \text{ (total length of face)}}{\left[\begin{array}{c} F \text{ (feed in inches per} \\ \text{revolution of work)} \end{array}\right]} = \text{number of revolutions of work required} \qquad (3)$$

then

$$M = \frac{N/H}{S} \times \frac{L}{F} = \frac{N \times L}{F \times S \times H} \qquad (4)$$

Table 27. Approach Allowance

Diam. Pitch	Full Depth	Outside Diameter of Cutter																
		2"	2¼"	2½"	2¾"	3"	3¼"	3½"	3¾"	4"	4¼"	4½"	4¾"	5"	5¼"	5½"	5¾"	6"
20	0.108	0.46	0.48	0.51	0.54	0.56	0.59	0.61	0.63	0.65	0.67							
16	0.135	0.50	0.54	0.56	0.60	0.62	0.65	0.67	0.70	0.73	0.74	0.78						
15	0.144	0.52	0.55	0.58	0.61	0.64	0.67	0.70	0.72	0.75	0.77	0.79	0.81					
14	0.154	0.53	0.57	0.60	0.63	0.66	0.69	0.72	0.74	0.76	0.79	0.81	0.84	0.85				
13	0.166	0.55	0.59	0.62	0.66	0.69	0.72	0.75	0.77	0.80	0.82	0.85	0.87	0.90	0.92			
12	0.180	0.57	0.59	0.65	0.68	0.71	0.74	0.77	0.80	0.83	0.86	0.88	0.91	0.93	0.96	0.99		
11	0.196	0.59	0.64	0.67	0.71	0.74	0.77	0.81	0.84	0.86	0.89	0.92	0.95	0.98	1.00	1.03	1.05	
10	0.216	0.62	0.66	0.70	0.74	0.78	0.81	0.85	0.87	0.90	0.94	0.95	0.99	1.02	1.04	1.06	1.09	1.12
9	0.240	0.65	0.70	0.74	0.78	0.82	0.85	0.89	0.92	0.95	0.98	1.01	1.04	1.07	1.10	1.12	1.15	1.17
8	0.270	0.68	0.73	0.78	0.82	0.86	0.90	0.93	0.97	1.00	1.04	1.07	1.10	1.13	1.16	1.19	1.22	1.25
7	0.308	0.72	0.77	0.82	0.86	0.90	0.95	0.98	1.03	1.06	1.10	1.14	1.17	1.19	1.23	1.25	1.30	1.32
6	0.360	0.76	0.82	0.88	0.93	0.97	1.02	1.06	1.11	1.15	1.19	1.22	1.26	1.29	1.33	1.36	1.39	1.43
5	0.432	0.82	0.89	0.95	1.00	1.05	1.10	1.15	1.20	1.24	1.28	1.32	1.37	1.40	1.44	1.48	1.51	1.55
4	0.540		0.96	1.03	1.09	1.15	1.21	1.26	1.32	1.37	1.41	1.47	1.51	1.55	1.60	1.64	1.71	1.72
3	0.720			1.05	1.21	1.28	1.35	1.42	1.48	1.54	1.59	1.65	1.70	1.76	1.80	1.86	1.90	1.95
2½	0.863				1.27	1.36	1.44	1.51	1.55	1.64	1.71	1.77	1.83	1.89	1.95	2.00	2.06	2.11
2	1.079					1.44	1.53	1.62	1.70	1.78	1.85	1.93	1.99	2.06	2.12	2.18	2.25	2.31
1¾	1.232						1.58	1.68	1.77	1.86	1.94	2.01	2.08	2.16	2.23	2.30	2.36	2.43
1½	1.438							1.72	1.83	1.92	2.01	2.10	2.19	2.27	2.32	2.42	2.50	2.57
1¼	1.726								1.87	1.99	2.10	2.19	2.29	2.30	2.47	2.50	2.64	2.72
1	2.157									1.99	2.13	2.26	2.37	2.48	2.59	2.70	2.79	2.89

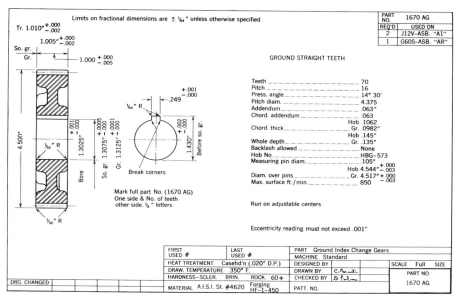

Figure 218 Detail drawing of a ground index change gear.

Table 28. Speed and Feed Table—Method of Cutting

Diam. Pitch	Cutter Speed, feet per minute	Speed of Hob, rpm	Feed, inch per rev.	Method of Cutting
Finished hobbed gears				
6–7	90	103	0.050	2 cuts, reg. single-lead hob
8–20	100	139	0.050	2 cuts, reg. single-lead hob
20–32 incl.	115	174	0.036	1 cut, reg. single-lead hob
Hobbing ground tooth-spur gears				
16	150	204	0.050	1 cut, 2-lead hob
20	160	204	0.050	1 cut, 2-lead hob
32	170	240	0.045	1 cut, 2-lead hob
Hobbing ground tooth helicals				
8	130	139	0.040	2 cuts, 2-lead hob
10	120	150	0.040	1 cut, 2-lead hob
12	110	150	0.040	1 cut, 2-lead hob
24	100	150	0.040	1 cut, 2-lead hob

EXAMPLE   In order to show how the data and the formula are applied, the time required to hob a spur gear will be determined. It will be assumed that an order has been received for 24 index change gears as shown in Fig. 218. The procedure is as follows.

1. The following data are taken from the drawing of the gear, Fig. 218: length of face, 1.005 inches; diametral pitch (D.P.), 16; number of teeth (N), 70; diameter of bore, 1.3125 inches; material, 4620; hob HBG 573, ground plain spur gear.
2. Method of cutting, from Table 28. Hobbing ground-tooth spur gears, 16 D.P.—take one cut, 2-lead hob.
3. Setup time, from Table 29. Setup time, 35.0 minutes.
4. Number of gears per chucking, from Table 30. Bore diameter $1^5/_{16}$ to $1^9/_{16}$ inches; usable length of arbor, 6 inches; 1-inch face; nut-locked arbor—6 gears per chucking.
5. Outside diameter of hob, from Table 31. Hob HBG 573, 2.50 inches.
6. Speed of hob, from Table 28. Hobbing ground-tooth spur gears, 16 D.P.—204 r.p.m.
7. Feed, from Table 28. Hobbing ground-tooth spur gears, 16 D.P.—0.050 inch per revolution of work.
8. Approach allowance, from Table 27. Diametral pitch, 16; outside diameter of hob, 2.50 inches—0.56 inch.
9. Calculation of cutting time, from formula:

$$M = \frac{N \times L}{F \times S \times H}$$

$$N = 70$$
$$L = (6 \times 1.005) + 0.56$$
$$F = 0.050$$
$$S = 204$$
$$H = 2$$

$$M = \frac{70 \times (6.030 + 0.56)}{0.050 \times 204 \times 2} = 22.61 \text{ minutes}$$

10. Determination of total handling time:

Machine manipulation, from Table 25, column 1 (spur gear, regular hob, 1 cut)	0.44
Chucking and removing, from Table 26, nut-locked arbor A, 0.84 + (6 × 0.05)	1.14
Total handling time	1.58 minutes

11. Determination of total standard time:

Total handling time, 6 gears	1.58
Total cutting time, 6 gears	22.61
Total normal time, 6 gears	24.19 minutes
Allowances	
5% of handling time	0.08
5% of cutting, up to 20 minutes	1.00
Total standard time, 6 gears	25.27 minutes
Total standard time, 1 gear	4.21 minutes

Table 29. Setup Time—Straight Spur Gears,
Barber-Colman Hobber

Machines: 183, 315, 531, 906, 908

Operations	Time, minutes
1. Get drawing and ring clock	2.0
2. Remove hob	1.0
3. Remove arbor	1.0
4. Obtain hob and arbor	3.0
5. Place hob	3.0
6. Set angle	1.0
7. Place arbor	2.0
8. Indicate arbor	2.0
9. Change index gears	3.0
10. Change speed gears	1.0
11. Change feed gears	3.0
12. Check all gearing	2.0
13. Measure piece for size and set for depth	2.0
14. Check index and size	7.0
15. Set stops	1.0
Standard setup time	
Splines	35.0
Spur gears	35.0
Helical gears	40.0
Standard time—change hob	10.0

Table 30. Number of Gears per Chucking

Bore Diameter, inches	Usable Length of Arbor, inches
$1^5/_{16}$–$1^9/_{16}$	6
$^3/_4$–$1^5/_{16}$	3
$^1/_2$–$^3/_4$	$1^1/_2$

Table 31. Hob List

Hob Number	Diam. Pitch	Hand	Outside Diameter, inches	Press. Angle, degrees PA	Lead
HB708	5	R	$3^1/_2$	$14^1/_2$	S
HB550	5	R	4	20	S
HB710	6	R	$3^1/_4$	$14^1/_2$	S
HB734	6	L	$3^1/_4$	20	S
HB542	7	R	3	$14^1/_2$	S
HBS592	8	R	$3^1/_2$	20	2
HBS593	8	L	$3^1/_2$	20	2
HB712A	8	R	3	$14^1/_2$	S
HB737A	8	L	3	$14^1/_2$	S
HB713	9	R	3	$14^1/_2$	S
HBS586	10	R	3	20	2
HBS587	10	L	3	20	2
HBS590	10	R	$2^3/_4$	20	S
HBS591	10	L	$2^3/_4$	20	S
HB526	11	R	$2^3/_4$	$14^1/_2$	S
HB744	12	R	$2^3/_4$	20	S
HB745	12	R	3	20	2
HB605	12	R	$2^3/_4$	$14^1/_2$	2
HB606	12	L	$2^3/_4$	$14^1/_2$	2
HB571	13	L	$2^3/_4$	20	S
HB716	14	R	$2^1/_2$	$14^1/_2$	S
HBG573	16	R	$2^1/_2$	$14^1/_2$	2
HBS597	16	R	$2^3/_4$	20	2
HB742	16	R	$2^1/_2$	$14^1/_2$	S
HB580	20	R	$2^1/_2$	20	2
HB721	24	R	$2^1/_2$	$14^1/_2$	2
HB746	24	L	$2^1/_2$	$14^1/_2$	2
HBS608	30	R	$2^3/_4$	20	S
HB579	32	R	$2^3/_4$	20	2
HB701	48	R	$1^7/_8$	$14^1/_2$	S

25

COMPUTER AIDED TIME STUDY

The making of a stop-watch time study requires an analyst with special skill, training, and experience. Moreover, concentration and alertness are necessary while the study is being made. The computations required to reduce the stop-watch readings and to determine the time standard are tedious and time consuming. Computerized or electronic time study is an economical replacement for stop-watch time study in many kinds of work.

Computerized Time Study

A small, general purpose, hand-held data collector with integrated circuit memory and built-in timer is available. This unit, called Datamyte, has a keyboard, a display,

Figure 219 Datamyte data collector.

Figure 220 Datamyte keyboard and display.

a clock, and contains a rechargeable battery which permits 8 hours of data collection (Fig. 219).[1] It does no calculations, but merely collects and stores data. The unit may be connected to the computer or terminal by a simple cable. The computer makes the calculations and summarizations. The unit may be used for short-cycle or long-cycle time study, work sampling, downtime studies, production studies, and other event recording.

If a time study is to be made, the observation sheet is prepared in the usual way. Instead of a stop watch the electronic collector becomes the timer. The machine records the data as well as the time. A consecutive code number is used for each element of the operation. At the start of the time study the "ENTER" key is depressed (Fig. 220). At the end of the first element the "ENTER" key is again depressed and at that instant the time, to the nearest 0.01 minute, is recorded. Elements are timed and recorded continuously. Codes for repetitive (cyclic) work elements, repetitive (noncyclic) elements, foreign, delay, and abnormal elements can be preassigned code letters and numbers or they can be made up during the study. The data are transmitted to the computer for reduction and summarization.

Taking a time study using the Datamyte is very simple, requiring little training and experience. Of course, performance rating requires the same skill as that needed for stop-watch time study or for performance rating in a work sampling study.

A computer program is available on commercial time-share. With this program time study data are processed quickly and a four-section report is produced.

---

[1] Reproduced by permission of Royal Dossett, Electro General Corporation.

1. *Observations:* All occurrences of all elements.
2. *Distributions:* Numerical histogram for each work element.
3. *Deletions:* Summary of foreign, noncyclic and abnormal work elements. These elements are summarized separately.
4. *Summary:* Summary of work elements.

Performance rating can be handled in three different ways: (1) each observation, (2) periodically, or (3) at the end of the study. Single studies up to 99 elements and 2000 observations are possible.

Making the Time Study

The procedure for making a time study[2] using the Datamyte consists of three parts:

1. *Record* the time-study data by depressing the "NUMERIC" keys to record the element being observed, and the "ENTER" key at the end of the element to record the clock-time. The element number and clock-time are recorded instantly in a solid-state memory, in a computer readable format.
2. *Transmit* the recorded data to the time-sharing computer.
3. *Process* the data by running the time-study computer program.

The procedure for making a time study can be described more easily by means of a simple example.

The operation to be timed is "Form 1.00 inch bend in copper tube." The tube is $^5/_{16}$-inch outside diameter by 6.00 inches long. The bending fixture is anchored to the front edge of the work bench. The operation is divided into two regular repetitive (cyclic) elements: (1) "Pick up and position tube." The left hand reaches approximately 6 inches to the left to pick up one tube from the bench and places it in the fixture. The right hand locks the block clamp and the bending block. (2) "Bend and remove tube." The right hand grasps the handle of the bending fixture, pulls it forward thus forming one 1.00 inch bend. The left hand unlocks the block clamp and the bending block while the right hand returns the bending handle to its original position. The left hand removes the tube and tosses it into the tote pan. There is also an auxiliary (noncyclic) element: "Pick up a handful of tubes from the tote pan and position them next to the fixture" abbreviated to "Stock work station." The operator picks up tubes from the bench and places them next to the fixture as needed.

The Datamyte Time Study

The data collector is made ready for use and the heading for the time study, such as date, study number, and time of day, are keyed in. The listing of the Datamyte information as actually transmitted to the computer will be used in the explanation

---

[2] Reproduced by permission of Soter (Art) Liberty, Chrysler Corporation.

L TSDATA
#FILE (PG3100J)TSDATA ON CTSS

100 2	(a)	2	KEY IN THE NUMBER OF ELEMENTS PER CYCLE THEN STROKE "CR–LF" KEY.
110 1	(b)	1	KEY IN THE NUMBER OF PIECES PER CYCLE THEN STROKE "CR–LF".
120 ,00000	(c)	,0	DEPRESS THE "ENTER" KEY TO START THE CLOCK (RECORDS TIME 0.00).
130 H1,00006	(d)	H1, 06	THIS STUDY BEGAN WITH A NON–CYCLIC ELEMENT (STOCK THE WORX–STATION).
140 1,00010	(e)	1, 10	
150 2,00017	(f)	2, 17	NON–CYCLIC ELEMENTS ARE DENOTED BY AN ELEMENT NUMBER PRECEEDED BY A LETTER (F, G OR H).
160 1,00021	(g)	1, 21	
170 2,00026	(h)	2, 26	ELEMENT NUMBER (KEY IN 1 FOR ELEMENT 1).
180 1,00030	(i)	1, 30	
190 2,00034	(j)	2, 34	CLOCK–TIME (0.10 MINUTES) AT THE TERMINATION OF ELEMENT 1. STROKE THE "ENTER" KEY AT THE END OF THE ELEMENT TO RECORD THE TIME.
200 1,00041	(k)	1, 41	
210 2,00045	(l)	2, 45	
220 1,00049	(m)	1, 49	CYCLIC ELEMENTS ARE DENOTED BY NUMBERS.
230 2,00054	(n)	2, 54	
240 1,00059	(o)	1, 59	
250 2,00063	(p)	2, 63	
260 1,00068	(q)	1, 68	
270 2,00073	(r)	2, 73	FOREIGN ELEMENT (A FUMBLE OCCURRED AND WAS INCLUDED IN ELEMENT 1'S TIME).
280 1F,00083	(s)	1F, 83	
290 2,00087	(t)	2, 87	
300 1,00091	(u)	1, 91	FOREIGN ELEMENTS ARE RECORDED BY KEYING THE ELEMENT NUMBER IN WHICH THEY OCCUR FOLLOWED BY A LETTER (F,G OR H)
630 2,00251	(v)	2, 251	
640 1,00257	(w)	1, 257	
650 2,00261	(x)	2, 261	
660 H1,00269	(y)	H1, 269	
670 1,00274		1, 274	
680 2,00278		2, 278	
690 1,00285		1, 285	
700 2,00289		2, 289	
710 1,00295		1, 295	
720 2,00299		2, 299	
730 100	(z)	100	KEY IN RATING FACTOR FOR ELEMENT 1 (100). THEN STROKE "CR–LF" KEY.
740 100	(Z)	100	KEY IN RATING FACTOR FOR ELEMENT 2 (100). THEN STROKE "CR–LF" KEY.
#			

Figure 221 Stream of data as recorded by Datamyte: *A*, listing of the information as it is actually transmitted to the computer; *B*, abbreviated and annotated information from the column of data on the left.

348

(Fig. 221 A). This information is abbreviated and annotated form is shown in Fig. 221 B.

Stream of Data as Recorded by Datamyte

(a) [3] Key in the number of elements per cycle, in this case 2. Then stroke the "CR-LF" key. (Fig. 221 B)

(b) Key in the number of pieces per cycle, in this study, 1. Then stroke "CR-LF".

(c) Depress the "ENTER" key to start the clock. ",0" is recorded. Time is measured in 0.01 minute.

(d) Key in H1 for the noncyclic element "Stock work station." Noncyclic elements are denoted by an element number preceeded by a letter (F, G, or H). Stroke "ENTER" at the end of the element to record time. The reading shows H1,06 which means that the time for the noncyclic element "Stock work station" is 0.06 minute $(0.06 - 0.00 = 0.06)$. Note that 0.06 does not appear in Fig. 222.

(e) Key in 1 for element 1. Then stroke "ENTER" at the end of element 1 to record the time for this element. The clock time is ,10. The time for element 1 is 0.04 minute $(0.10 - 0.06 = 0.04)$.

(f) Key in 2 for element 2. Then stroke "ENTER" at the end of element 2. The difference between the two readings is the time for element 2. That is 0.07 minute $(0.17–0.10 = 0.07)$.

(s) Foreign element. A fumble occurs and is included in element 1's time. Key in 1F to denote the fumble. Then at the end of the element stroke "ENTER". A foreign element is recorded by keying in the element number in which it occurs followed by a letter (F, G, or H).

(y) Key in H1 for the repetitive noncyclic element "Stock work station." This is the second time during the study that this element has occurred. The time for this element is 0.08 minute. $(2.69 - 2.61 = 0.08)$. Note that 0.08 does not appear in Fig. 222.

(z) Key in rating factor for element 1 (100). Then stroke "CR-LF."

(Z) Key in rating factor for element 2 (100). Then stroke "CR-LF."

Note that the clock-time is recorded *only* when the "ENTER" key has been depressed.

Time Study Summary

The results of the time study are summarized in Fig. 222 and Fig. 223. These two pages are copies of the computer print-out.

---

[3] The letters in parentheses correspond to the letters in Fig. 221 B.

Computer Print-out of Data Shown in Fig. 222

Figure 222 shows the accumulated time and the cycle time for each of the 29 consecutive cycles and the subtracted time for each reading. The time for the two noncyclic elements "Stock work station" are not shown in Fig. 222. The one foreign element (fumble) is included in element 1's time and is shown in Fig. 222. The continuous method of timing was used and the total length of the study was 2.99 minutes.

TIME STUDY DATA FILE NAME: TSDATA

OPER. 50 FORM (1) 1.0 RAD. BEND

CYCLE NO.

ELEM	1	2	3	4	5	6	7	8	9	10
	.04	.04	.04	.07	.04	.05	.05	.10	.04	.05
1	H1							1F		
	.10	.21	.30	.41	.49.	.59	.68	.83	.91	1.01
	.07	.05	.04	.04	.05	.04	.05	.04	.05	.04
2										
	.17	.26	.34	.45	.54	.63	.73	.87	.96	1.05

CYCLE NO.

ELEM	11	12	13	14	15	16	17	18	19	20
	.04	.05	.05	.06	.05	.05	.07	.05	.06	.04
1										
	1.09	1.18	1.28	1.38	1.47	1.57	1.69	1.78	1.89	1.98
	.04	.05	.04	.04	.05	.05	.04	.05	.05	.05
2										
	1.13	1.23	1.32	1.42	1.52	1.62	1.73	1.83	1.94	2.03

CYCLE NO.

ELEM	21	22	23	24	25	26	27	28	29	30
	.07	.04	.05	.04	.05	.06	.05	.07	.06	.00
1							H1			
	2.10	2.18	2.28	2.37	2.47	2.57	2.74	2.85	2.95	.00
	.04	.05	.05	.05	.04	.04	.04	.04	.04	.00
2										
	2.14	2.23	2.33	2.42	2.51	2.61	2.78	2.89	2.99	.00

Figure 222 Computer printout of time study data recorded by Datamyte.

Computer Print-out of Data Shown in Fig. 223

A. Element Time Distribution. The frequency distribution of occurrences for each of the two elements.

B. Summary of Elements. The *normal* time is the average time multiplied by the element rating factor and divided by 100 ($0.0511 \times 100/100 = 0.0511$). For element 1 this is 0.0511 minute. The *allowed time in minutes per piece* is the normal time divided by the number of pieces produced per cycle. Because only one piece is made at a time, the normal time and the allowed time are the same. The allowed time for the first element is 0.0511 minute and the total allowed time for the two regular elements of the operation is 0.0966 minute.

The two columns at the extreme right are headed *needed minimum cycles*. The first of these columns shows the number of readings needed for results that are ±5 percent accurate 87.5 percent of the time. They are 19 for the first element and 24 for the second element. The next column shows the number of readings needed for results that are ±5 percent accurate 95 percent of the time. They are 33 for element 1 and 41 for element 2.[4]

C. Summary of Foreign Elements. There is one fumble of 0.10 minute duration. This fumble is included in element 1's time.

D. Summary of Noncyclic Elements. The noncyclic element "Stock work station" occurs at fairly regular intervals during the day. During this time study this element occurred twice with the frequency in this study being once in 26 cycles. The prorated time for this element is 0.0027 minute per piece ($0.700 \div 26 = 0.0027$).

E. Reconciliation of Elapsed Time. This is designed to present an accounting for all time between the start of the study and the end of the study. The total elapsed time is 2.99 minutes.

F. Summary—Minutes per Piece. The total elemental time is 0.0993 minute. A personal allowance of 0.0052 minute is added to give the standard time in minutes per piece of 0.1045.

G. Net Production in Pieces per Hour. The standard time per piece converted into pieces per hour is 574.16.

---

[4] This time study is presented in abbreviated form in order to simplify the explanation and to save space. At least 41 cycles should have been timed.

A. ELEMENTAL TIME DISTRIBUTION

ELEMENT NUMBER : 1

TIME	FREQ	PERCENT	CUM %
.04	9	32.14	32.14
.05	11	39.29	71.43
.06	4	14.29	85.71
.07	4	14.29	100.00

ELEMENT NUMBER : 2

TIME	FREQ	PERCENT	CUM %
.04	15	51.72	51.72
.05	13	44.83	96.55
.07	1	3.45	100.00

B. SUMMARY OF ELEMENTS

ELEM NO	NO OF CYCLES	TOTAL TIME	AVE TIME	ELEM RATING	NORMAL TIME	ALLOWED MIN/PC	MIN (87.5%)	NEEDED CYCLES (95%)
1	PICK UP AND POSITION STOCK							
	28	1.43	.0511	100	.0511	.0511	19	33
2	BEND AND REMOVE STOCK							
	29	1.32	.0455	100	.0455	.0455	24	41
	TOTAL				.0966	.0966		

C. SUMMARY OF FOREIGN ELEMENTS

FORG CODE	OCCURS IN EL#	NO. OF TIMES	TOTAL TIME
1F	1	1	.10

D. SUMMARY OF NON-CYCLIC ELEMENTS

N/C CODE	OCCURS IN EL#	NO OF TIMES	TOTAL TIME	AVE TIME	ELEM AVE	N/C AVE	OBSER FREQ	PRORATE MIN/PC	ELEM RATING	ALLOWED MIN/PC
H1	PICK UP TUBES FROM TOTE PAN									
	1	2	.14	.0700	.0000	.0700	1/26	.0027	100	.0027

E. RECONCILIATION OF ELAPSED TIME:

SUM OF ALLOWED TIMES	2.75
SUM OF NON-CYCLIC TIMES	.14
SUM OF FOREIGN ELEMENTS	.10
SUM OF STRIKE-OUT TIMES	.00
TOTAL ELAPSED TIME	2.99

F. SUMMARY—MINUTES PER PIECE:

TOTAL CYCLIC ELEMENTS	.0966
TOTAL NON-CYCLIC ELEMENTS	.0027
TOTAL ELEMENTAL TIME	.0993
PERSONAL ALLOWANCE	.0052
OTHER AUTH. SHIFT ALLOWANCES	.0000
STANDARD MINUTES PER PIECE	.1045

G. NET PRODUCTION PER HOUR: 574.16

Figure 223 Computer printout of: *A*, Elemental time distribution; *B*, summary of elements *C*, summary of foreign elements; *D*, summary of noncyclic elements; *E*, reconciliation of elapsed time; *F*, summary—minutes per piece; *G*, net production in pieces per hour.

352

Summary of Electronic Time Study

The analyst, using an electronic data collector, can make a time study more accurately and more quickly than by stop-watch time study for many kinds of work. However, the greatest benefits result from having the computer perform the computations and clerical work after the time study is completed on the production floor.

The computer deletes noncyclic, abnormal, and foreign elements and processes them separately. It determines the average time for each regular element and for each noncyclic element and applies the appropriate rating factor, thus obtaining the normal time for each element. It compiles the total normal time, adds the allowances, and calculates the total standard time in minutes per piece. The computer prints out the detailed time study data showing the continuous reading and the subtracted time for each element. It makes an elemental time distribution for each element in the study and shows the number of readings needed for a given degree of accuracy. This is all done quickly, accurately, and economically. The time required to transmit the data from the data collector to the computer and to obtain the print-out depends upon the available computer facilities and the length and nature of the time study. The print-out shown in Fig. 222 and Fig. 223 was made under ideal conditions and required approximately 5 minutes.

26

COMPUTERIZED MACHINE AND EQUIPMENT DOWNTIME MONITORING AND REPORTING

Capital investment in machines and equipment is increasing, and as the equipment becomes more complex and costly the need to control downtime assumes greater importance. Downtime studies can aid in improving productivity, in reducing costs, and in increasing the number of units of product produced per dollar capital invested. Some common causes of machine and equipment downtime are:

1. Unanticipated equipment breakdown, machine failure.
2. Normal machine maintenance. Downtime for replacement of worn or broken tools, or for machine adjustments.
3. Preventive maintenance. Regularly scheduled downtime for repairs.
4. Start-up delays. Bringing equipment up to full operating capacity at the start of the day.

Some of the downtime noted above might be considered necessary or desirable but zero downtime should be the ideal, and every minute of downtime should represent an opportunity for increasing productivity.

Manual recording and summarization of downtime data may be done by the operator or by the analyst. Stop-watch time study, work sampling, the time-lapse camera, video camera, paper disc or paper tape recorder, or odometer-type counters are all available and all of these are being used. Each has a place in controlling downtime. Also computerized downtime recording is available, and it has the capacity to handle downtime problems of any magnitude. Minicomputers may monitor one or many machines and can print out the results. Each machine and each piece of equipment has its unique need for downtime monitoring. In general, the potential benefits from a study of downtime are proportional to the capital investment and to the downtime-proneness of the equipment. There are situations, however, where yield, waste, quality of product, or safety of the operator or of the equipment itself may be the controlling factors. The type of study should be suited to the problem. Work sampling is one of the simplest methods of obtaining downtime information. The computer is at the other end of the scale. However, cost limits the number of places where the computer should be used.

Automatic Downtime Recording

The Datamyte data collector already described provides a simple and economical means for recording and analyzing data and printing downtime reports.[1] This unit

[1] Reproduced by permission of Royal Dossett, Electro General Corporation.

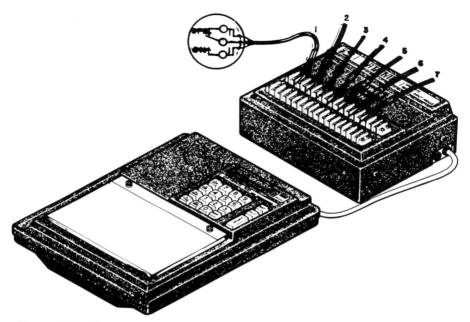

Figure 224   Datamyte and remote input module for automatic downtime recording.

together with a remote input module is shown in Fig. 224. Either mechanical or solid state switch contacts are connected to the Datamyte via the remote input module. The switch or relay is connected to a component such as a motor drive for a machine or a conveyor motor which is "on" during uptime and "off" during downtime. The Datamyte records all "on" and "off" time to the nearest 0.01 minute.

Various types of delays can be identified by code number and they may be entered manually on the keyboard by the operator. The data recording unit and the remote input module may be housed in a locked enclosure. An opening in the cover permits access to the Datamyte keyboard and the remote module if delay codes are to be entered. Machines to be monitered are connected to the remote module by three-wire cables. Figure 224 shows the arrangement for monitoring seven machines. The machines can be located 1000 feet away but the Datamyte should be placed in a location that is convenient for the operator who will enter the delay codes. A permanent installation of the equipment may be made or it can be mounted on a cart and moved about as needed. Data may be transmitted to the computer daily, weekly, or whenever convenient. Figure 225 shows a daily downtime report. The daily data summary is saved in a computer file (named RFAB in this example) permitting summary by the day, week, month, or by the shift for the year-to-date, one month, one week, one day's data.

```
EXECUTE RDATA
SAVE TO?   RFAB

RFAB
```

—————————————————————DOWNTIME SUMMARY————————————————————

YEAR	WEEK	MONTH	DAY	SHIFT							
78	(12)	03	20	−1							

CODE	%DN	DCR	AVE	HOURS	1	2	3	4	5	6	7
67	40.3	1	2.333	2.333	2.333						
41	38.2	3	.737	2.210		1.367		.526		.317	
33	17.8	2	.517	1.033		.250				.783	
15	3.7	2	.108	.215			.144	.071			
DOWNTIME HOURS				5.791	2.333	1.617	.144	.597	.000	1.100	.000
TOTAL HOURS				56.000	8.000	8.000	8.000	8.000	8.000	8.000	8.000
DOWNTIME %				10.4	29.2	20.2	1.8	7.5	0.0	13.9	0.0

(12) 03 20 −1 indicate week 12, March 20, shift 1

Figure 225 Daily downtime summary.

An Example: Monitoring Downtime of Complex Transfer Machines in the Automobile Industry[2]

Transfer machines are widely used in the automobile industry and the control of downtime is an important factor in their operation. It is important because downtime is always high with such equipment and the cost of a transfer line can run into millions of dollars. One automobile manufacturer wanted to monitor downtime of several transfer lines in a transmission plant. Figure 226 shows a schematic diagram of a typical transfer line and Fig. 227 is a diagram of one transfer line for machining aluminum transmission cases. This line, using the most advanced technology, has 75 stations and each station performs machining operations or probing (inspection) operations. The machining operations performed are chamfering, reaming, facing, spot-facing, drilling, and tapping. This line has the capacity to perform 538 distinct operations. The cycle is approximately 25 seconds and failure to cycle is considered the beginning of downtime. The transfer line is a palletized system; that is, the work-piece is first placed accurately on a large rigid metal pallet which is transferred from station to station.

The direct labor consists of the five people required to operate the line. There are two machine operators ("panel-man" and "unloader"), two inspectors, and one job-setter for each transfer line. The jobsetter is the skilled technician.

---

[2] Reproduced by permission of Leo E. Hanifin, Doctoral dissertation "Increasing Transfer Line Productivity Utilizing Systems Simulation," University of Detroit, 1975.

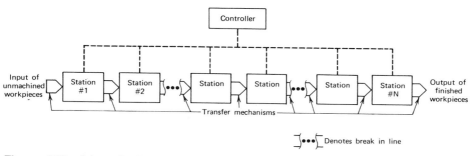

Figure 226   Schematic diagram of a typical transfer line. Each station performs 1 to 20 specific functions such as drilling, boring, or probing. All transfer mechanisms operate simultaneously.

The unmachined castings are received from the adjacent casting plant and enter the qualifier (Fig. 227 A). There they are checked for critical dimensions. Locating holes are drilled and the cases are prepared for the automated system. From there they are moved by conveyor to the transfer line load point (Fig. 227 B). At the load point the operator places the case on the pallet and it is clamped there. The case, clamped rigidly to the pallet, proceeds through the machining stations. Following the machining, the case is unloaded from the machine (Fig. 227 C) and the pallet is returned by conveyor to the load point. The case is finally inspected and is either rejected or sent on to the assembly area by conveyor.

The Datamyte and a custom-built relay module are employed on this transfer line. Repetitive machine cycles may be fed to the "auto-log electronics" (Fig. 228.) The jobsetter enters the delay codes and counts. At the beginning of each shift all transfer signals are logged for 3 minutes to record actual cycle time. The Datamyte is removed from the enclosure daily and taken to a computer terminal where the data are transmitted to a computer.

Some Results of Downtime Monitoring

Information obtained from downtime studies may include:

1. Report of frequency and duration of machine downtime in minutes per occurrance, in percent of shift, and in distribution of downtime by time of day (Figs. 229 and 230).
2. Type of maintenance craft required for repairs.
3. Cost of downtime in dollars per machine per shift.
4. Record of rejects, scrap, waste, and yield.
5. Data for balancing production lines and assembly lines.

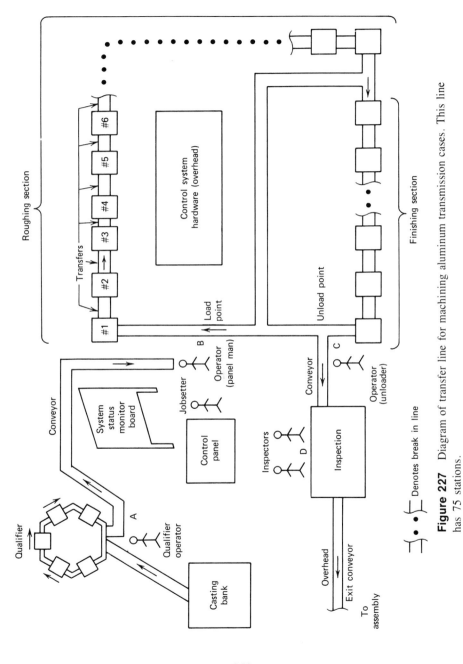

Figure 227 Diagram of transfer line for machining aluminum transmission cases. This line has 75 stations.

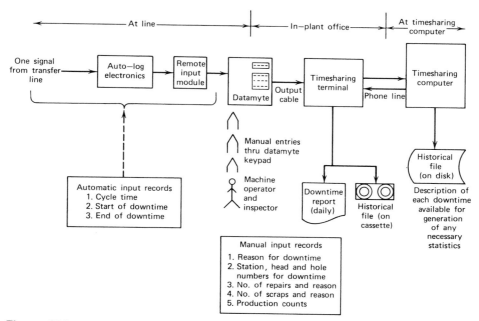

Figure 228 Downtime monitoring system. (Courtesy of Soter (Art) Liberty, L. P. Bulat and Leo E. Hanifin, Chrysler Corporation.)

DOWNTIME SUMMARY TOP (15) BY CODE 10/10/
LINE 5
SHIFT 2

STA. NO.	CODE HOLE/ FACE	CAUSE CODE	DESCRIPTION	DN TIME MIN.SEC	NO OF DOWNS	% TOT DN TIME
31-1	0	134	NO FULL DEPTH	33.31	1	10.10
17-2	86	302	SPDL TRBL	33.31	1	10.10
1-1	0	310	SHUTTLE TRBL	23.24	1	7.05
99-0	0	310	SHUTTLE TRBL	23.24	1	7.05
13-2	64	100	BROKEN DRILL	12.29	1	3.76
11-2	55	100	BROKEN DRILL	11.25	1	3.44
16-1	0	108	FALSE PROBE	6.35	2	1.99
35-2	0	134	NO FULL DEPTH	2.13	1	0.67
28-6	0	108	FALSE PROBE	1.29	1	0.45
99-0	0	106	CHANGEOVER	0.54	1	0.27
			(ALL UNACCOUNTED)	182.56	13	55.11
				331.57	24	100.00

Figure 229 Downtime summary for transfer line number 5, second shift, October 10.

Downtime Distribution by Hour of Day

Machine Number : 10

Hour	Breakdown Occurrences			Downtime	
	Freq.	Percent	Cum. %	Avg Min Down	Percent
7.00– 8.00 A.M.	26	22.41	22.41	25.94	10.96
8.00– 9.00 A.M.	18	15.52	37.93	28.42	12.01
9.00–10.00 A.M.	12	10.34	48.28	20.73	8.76
10.00–11.00 A.M.	10	8.62	56.90	23.50	9.93
11.00–12.00 A.M.	11	9.48	66.38	35.11	14.83
12.00– 1.00 P.M.	13	11.21	77.59	34.00	14.36
1.00– 2.00 P.M.	14	12.07	89.66	30.25	12.78
2.00– 3.00 P.M.	12	10.34	100.00	38.75	16.37
TOTAL	116			236.69	

Figure 230 Computer printout of downtime distribution by hour of the day. (Courtesy of Soter (Art) Liberty, J. P. Bulat and Leo E. Hanifin, Chrysler Corporation.)

6. Information for evaluation of the relationship between equipment speed and downtime. Determination of the optimum operating speed.
7. Data to be used as the basis for overhaul, rebuilding, or replacement of machines and equipment.
8. Determination of tool life.
9. Basic information for a wage incentive plan or a bonus plan.

27

PREDETERMINED TIME SYSTEMS: THE WORK-FACTOR SYSTEM

A time standard for a job or an operation may be established by time study, by work sampling, or by the use of predetermined times. A predetermined time system consists of a set of time data and a systematic procedure which analyses and subdivides any manual operation of human task into motions, body movements, or other elements or human performance, and assigns to each the appropriate time value. Each system of time data was originally developed from extensive studies of all aspects of human performance through measurement, evaluation, and validation procedures. One part of this procedure was the determination of the level of performance produced by the standards established from the predetermined time system in relation to standard performance.

Some Factors To Be Considered in Using a Predetermined Time System

The application of a predetermined time system requires that the operation being measured be divided into basic motions as called for by the particular system being used. Each system has its own specific rules and procedures which must be followed exactly.

At the time a predetermined system is first adopted by a company the level of performance as represented by the time standards produced by the system should be determined and adjustments made, if necessary, in order to match the company performance level. This is a one-time adjustment, because no further consideration need be given to performance rating.

Most predetermined time systems do not include allowances so these are added as they would be in a time study.

Predetermined time systems can be classified as to accuracy level, time required for application, and the extent of method description. The original systems were designed for general use and they can be applied to most industrial operations. In addition, numerous specialized systems are now available. Some are simplified versions designed for use on longer operations. They permit faster application and produce less accurate results. Others are functional systems intended for clerical work, machine work, or work with very small tools under magnification.

Although predetermined time systems have been used to a limited extent for many years, their application has increased as the different systems available become more numerous and as people have reached a better understanding of the advantages and limitations of such systems.

Perhaps the major advantage of a predetermined time system in comparison with time study is that such a system makes it possible to predetermine the standard time for a job or activity if the motion pattern is known. One can determine in advance how long it will take to perform an operation in the shop, merely by examining a drawing of the work place layout and a description of the method. Similarly, an accurate evaluation can be made of several different work method designs or different tool designs. Considerable use also has been made of predetermined time data for establishing standard data for various classes of machines and equipment, thus expediting the actual setting of time standards for jobs to be performed on such equipment. The use of standard data often results in greater consistency in time standards.

The main uses of predetermined time systems may be divided into the following two classes:

Work Methods

1. Improving existing methods.
2. Evaluating proposed methods in advance of actual production.
3. Evaluating suggested designs of tools, jigs, and equipment.
4. Aiding in the design of the product.
5. Training members of the staff to become motion-minded.
6. Aiding in training operators.

Work Measurement

1. Establishing time standards.
2. Compilation of standard data and formulas for specific classes of work.
3. Checking standards established by time study.
4. Auditing time standards.
5. Estimating labor costs.
6. Balancing production lines.

It is important that predetermined time systems be applied only by capable and well-trained people. The statement often is made that such systems are superior to time study because judgment is not required on the part of the analyst in evaluating the pace of the operator being studied. This, of course, is true. There are, however, numerous points in applying predetermined time data at which judgment of the analyst does come into play. Thorough training in the use of a particular system of predetermined time data is needed in order to minimize such judgment factors. If several people in a department are establishing time standards by such data, it is especially important that they all be trained to use the data in the same way insofar as possible.

Nine predetermined time systems are shown in Fig. 231, and two of these systems are described here. A number of well-designed systems now in use are not included in Fig. 231 because they are modifications of other systems or because information about them has not been published. All systems, however, have much in common. New systems are being developed and those in use are being modified and expanded.[1]

The First Predetermined Time System

A. B. Segur developed the first predetermined time system, which he called Methods-Time-Analysis (MTA).[2] He worked with Gilbreth during World War I using micromotion analysis of films made of skilled factory workers in a program to develop methods for training blind and other handicapped workers. By 1924 Segur had perfected his system and made it available on a consulting basis. His data were never published nor was any evidence to support his data made available to the public. His system was very detailed and required a high degree of skill and training on the part of the analysts applying it. However, it produced accurate and consistent time standards.

Little or no published information pertaining to predetermined times was available in the early days. Some of the first systematic research in this field took place at the Industrial Engineering Laboratory at the University of Iowa in the 1930s and 1940s. Specific research projects were carefully designed and conducted in the laboratory. A full description of the methods and procedures used, the data obtained, and the results and conclusions were published.[3]

---

[1] Chester L. Brisley, "Comparison of Predetermined Time Systems," *Proceedings Fall Industrial Engineering Conference, 1978,* American Institute of Industrial Engineers, Norcross, GA., pp. 13–21. Also, *Forty-Second Annual IMS Clinic Proceedings,* Industrial Management Society, Chicago, Ill., pp. 8–24, 1978.

[2] A. B. Segur, "Motion-Time-Analysis," *Industrial Engineering Handbook,* H. B. Maynard (editor), McGraw-Hill, New York, pp. 4–101 to 4–118, 1956.

[3] Ralph M. Barnes, "An Investigation of Some Hand Motions Used in Factory Work," *University of Iowa Studies in Engineering, Bulletin* 6, 1936. Ralph M. Barnes and Marvin E. Mundel, "Studies of Hand Motions and Rhythm Appearing in Factory Work," *Bulletin* 12; "A Study of Hand Motions Used in Small Assembly Work," *Bulletin* 16; "A Study of Simultaneous Symmetrical Hand Motions," *Bulletin* 17, 1939. Ralph M. Barnes, M. E. Mundel, and John M. MacKenzie, "Studies of One- and Two-Handed Work," *Bulletin* 21, 1940. Ralph M. Barnes, James S. Perkins, and J. M. Juran, "A Study of the Effect of Practice on the Elements of a Factory Operation," *University of Iowa Studies in Engineering, Bulletin* 22, 1940.

Name of System	First Applied Date	First Publication Describing System
Motion-Time Analysis (MTA)	1924	Data not published, but information concerning MTA published in *Motion-Time Analysis Bulletin*, a publication of A. B. Segur & Co.
Body Member Movements	1938	*Applied Time and Motion Study* by W. G. Holmes, Ronald Press Co., New York, 1938
Motion-Time Data for Assembly Work (Get and Place)	1938	*Motion and Time Study*, 2nd ed., by Ralph M. Barnes, John Wiley & Sons, New York, 1940, Chs. 22 and 23
The Work-Factor System	1938	"Motion-Time Standards" by J. H. Quick, W. J. Shea, and R. E. Koehler, *Factory Management and Maintenance*, Vol. 103, No. 5, pp. 97–108, May, 1945
Elemental Time Standard for Basic Manual Work	1942	"Establishing Time Values by Elementary Motion Analysis" by M. G. Schaefer, *Proceedings Tenth Time and Motion Study Clinic*, IMS, Chicago, pp. 21–27, November, 1946
Methods-Time Measurement (MTM)	1948	*Methods-Time Measurement* by H. B. Maynard, G. J. Stegemerten, and J. L. Schwab, McGraw-Hill Book Co., New York, 1948
Basic Motion Timestudy (BMT)	1950	Manuals by J. D. Woods & Gordon, Ltd., Toronto, Canada, 1950
Dimensional Motion Times (DMT)	1952	"New Motion Time Method Defined" by H. C. Geppinger, *Iron Age*, Vol. 171, No. 2, pp. 106–108, January 8, 1953
Predetermined Human Work Times	1952	"A System of Predetermined Human Work Times" by Irwin P. Lazarus, Ph.D. thesis, Purdue University, 1952

Figure 231 Summary of facts concerning various systems of predetermined data.

Publication Containing Information about System	How Data Were Originally Obtained	System Developed by
"Motion-Time-Analysis" by A. B. Segur, in *Industrial Engineering Handbook*, H. B. Maynard, editor, McGraw-Hill Book Co., New York, pp. 4-101 to 4-118, 1956	Motion pictures, micromotion analysis, kymograph	A. B. Segur
Applied Time and Motion Study by W. G. Holmes, Ronald Press Co., New York, 1938	Not known	W. G. Holmes
Motion and Time Study: Design and Measurement of Work, 6th ed., by Ralph M. Barnes, John Wiley & Sons, New York, 1968, Ch. 30	Time study, motion pictures of factory operations, laboratory studies	Harold Engstrom and H. C. Geppinger of Bridgeport Plant of General Electric Co.
Work-Factor Time Standards, by Joseph H. Quick, James H. Duncan, and James A. Malcolm, Jr., McGraw-Hill Book Co., New York, 1962 *Ready Work-Factor Time Standards*, by J. A. Malcolm, Jr. et al., Haddonfield, N. J., 1966. See footnote p. 366.	Time study, motion pictures of factory operations, study of motions with stroboscopic light unit	J. H. Quick W. J. Shea R. E. Koehler
"Establishing Time Values by Elementary Motions" by M. G. Schaefer, *Proceedings Tenth Time and Motion Study Clinic*, IMS, Chicago, November, 1946. Also "Development and Use of Time Values for Elemental Motions" by M. G. Schaefer, *Proceedings Second Time Study and Methods Conference*, SAM-ASME, New York, April, 1947	Kymograph studies, motion pictures of industrial operations, and electric time-recorder studies (time measured to 0.0001 minute)	Western Electric Co.
Methods-Time Measurement by H. B. Maynard, G. J. Stegemerten, and J. L. Schwab, McGraw-Hill Book Co., New York, 1948 See footnote p. 376.	Time study, motion pictures of factory operations	H. B. Maynard G. J. Stegemerten J. L. Schwab
Basic Motion Timestudy by G. B. Bailey and Ralph Presgrave, McGraw-Hill Book Co., New York, 1958	Laboratory studies	Ralph Presgrave G. B. Bailey J. A. Lowden
Dimensional Motion Times by H. C. Geppinger, John Wiley & Sons, New York, 1955	Time study, motion pictures, laboratory studies	H. C. Geppinger
"Synthesized Standards from Basic Motion Times," *Handbook of Industrial Engineering and Management*, W. G. Ireson and E. L. Grant, editors, Prentice-Hall, Englewood Cliffs, N. J., pp. 373–378, 1955	Motion pictures of factory operations	Irwin P. Lazarus

THE WORK-FACTOR SYSTEM

The Work-Factor system[4] was one of the first predetermined time systems to have wide general use. The first actual shop application was made in 1938, and the time values were first published[5] in 1945. The first system developed was the Detailed System, which has been enlarged to include the following:

1. Detailed Work-Factor.
2. Ready Work-Factor (1969).
3. Abbreviated (Using Form A) 1951.
4. Abbreviated (Using Form B) 1951.
5. Brief Work-Factor (1977).
6. Detailed Mento-Factor (1960).

With the exception of Detailed Mento-Factor, all others are based on the Detailed Work-Factor System.

This system makes it possible to determine the Work-Factor Time[6] for manual tasks by the use of predetermined time data. First, a detailed analysis of each task is made, based on the identification of the four major variables of work and the use of Work-Factors as a unit of measure. Then the proper standard time from the table of motion-time values is applied to each motion. The total may then be increased by personal, fatigue, and delay allowances.

A basic motion is defined as that motion which involves the least amount of difficulty or precision for any given distance and body member combination; for example, tossing a bolt into a box. Work-Factor is a unit used as the index of additional time required over and above the basic time when motions are performed involving the following variables: (1) manual control, (2) weight or resistance.

Four Major Variables

According to the Work-Factor system there are four major variables which affect the time to perform manual motions: (1) body member used, identified by exact definition; (2) distance moved, measured in inches; (3) manual control required, measured in Work-Factors, defined or dimensional; and (4) weight or resistance involved, measured in pounds, converted to Work-Factors.

---

[4] Reproduced with permission from *Work-Factor Time Standards,* by Joseph H. Quick, James H. Duncan, and James A. Malcolm, Jr., McGraw-Hill, New York, 1962. Also see "The Work-Factor System," by Joseph H. Quick, James H. Duncan, and James A. Malcolm, Jr., *Industrial Engineering Handbook,* 3rd ed., Harold B. Maynard (editor), McGraw-Hill, New York, 1971, pp. 5–65 to 5–101.

[5] J. H. Quick, W. J. Shea, and R. E. Koehler, "Motion-Time Standards," *Factory Management and Maintenance,* Vol. 103, No. 5, pp. 97–108, May, 1945.

[6] Work-Factor Time includes no allowances in the elemental time tables, and represents the work pace of the average experienced operator, performing with good skill and good effort.

Body Member. Work-Factor recognizes six definite body members and provides motion times for each: finger or hand, arm, forearm swivel, trunk, foot, and leg. Time values for these body members are shown in Table 32.

Distance. All distances except those with a change in direction are measured as a straight line between the starting and stopping points of the motion are described by the body member. The point at which the distance should be measured for the various body members is shown in Table 32.

Manual Control. The following classification of the types and degrees of control reflects the difficulty involved: Definite Stop Work-Factor, Directional Control Work-Factor (Steer), Care Work-Factor (Precaution), and Change of Direction Work-Factor.

Weight or Resistance. The effect of weight on time varies with (1) the body member used, and (2) the sex of the operator. The two variables, distance and body member, are measured in terms of inches and the member used, respectively. They are not modified or affected by Work-Factors.

To facilitate an understanding of the Work-Factor principle, the Work-Factor can be considered as merely a means of describing the motion according to the amount of control or weight (or resistance) involved in its performance.

Because the value of a Work-Factor in terms of time has been established in tabular form, it remains only for the analyst to become familiar with the specific dimensions and rules necessary to determine the number of Work-Factors involved in a given motion. Because the simplest or basic motion involves no Work-Factors, it is apparent that, as complexities are introduced to a motion, they add Work-Factors and consequently time.

The Work-Factor Motion-Time Table

The Work-Factor motion-time table (Table 32) provides elemental times for the Detailed Work-Factor System with Detailed Work-Factor motion-time values in tabular form. They are so arranged that, when a motion has been identified according to the four major variables, the correct time value can be selected quickly.

Standard Elements of Work

Work-Factor recognizes the following standard elements of work:

1. Transport (Reach and Move) (TRP).
2. Grasp (GR).
3. Pre-position (PP).
4. Assemble (ASY).

Table 32. Work-Factor* Motion-Time Table for Detailed Analysis

(Time in ten-thousandths of a minute)

Distance Moved	Basic	Work Factors				Distance Moved	Basic	Work Factors			
		1	2	3	4			1	2	3	4
(A) Arm—Measured at Knuckles						(L) Leg—Measured at Ankle					
1″	18	26	34	40	46	1″	21	30	39	46	53
2″	20	29	37	44	50	2″	23	33	42	51	58
3″	22	32	41	50	57	3″	26	37	48	57	65
4″	26	38	48	58	66	4″	30	43	55	66	76
5″	29	43	55	65	75	5″	34	49	63	75	86
6″	32	47	60	72	83	6″	37	54	69	83	95
7″	35	51	65	78	90	7″	40	59	75	90	103
8″	38	54	70	84	96	8″	43	63	80	96	110
9″	40	58	74	89	102	9″	46	66	85	102	117
10″	42	61	78	93	107	10″	48	70	89	107	123
11″	44	63	81	98	112	11″	50	72	94	112	129
12″	46	65	85	102	117	12″	52	75	97	117	134
13″	47	67	88	105	121	13″	54	77	101	121	139
14″	49	69	90	109	125	14″	56	80	103	125	144
15″	51	71	92	113	129	15″	58	82	106	130	149
16″	52	73	94	115	133	16″	60	84	108	133	153
17″	54	75	96	118	137	17″	62	86	111	135	158
18″	55	76	98	120	140	18″	63	88	113	137	161
19″	56	78	100	122	142	19″	65	90	115	140	164
20″	58	80	102	124	144	20″	67	92	117	142	166
22″	61	83	106	128	148	22″	70	96	121	147	171
24″	63	86	109	131	152	24″	73	99	126	151	175
26″	66	90	113	135	156	26″	75	103	130	155	179
28″	68	93	116	139	159	28″	78	107	134	159	183
30″	70	96	119	142	163	30″	81	110	137	163	187
35″	76	103	128	151	171	35″	87	118	147	173	197
40″	81	109	135	159	179	40″	93	126	155	182	206
Weight Male in Lbs. Fem.	*2* *1*	*7* *3½*	*13* *6½*	*20* *10*	*UP* *UP*	*Weight Male in Lbs. Fem.*	*8* *4*	*42* *21*	*UP* *UP*	*—* *—*	*—* *—*

368

(T) Trunk—Measured at Shoulder					
1″	26	38	49	58	67
2″	29	42	53	64	73
3″	32	47	60	72	82
4″	38	55	70	84	96
5″	43	62	79	95	109
6″	47	68	87	105	120
7″	51	74	95	114	130
8″	54	79	101	121	139
9″	58	84	107	128	147
10″	61	88	113	135	155
11″	63	91	118	141	162
12″	66	94	123	147	169
13″	68	97	127	153	175
14″	71	100	130	158	182
15″	73	103	133	163	188
16″	75	105	136	167	193
17″	78	108	139	170	199
18″	80	111	142	173	203
19″	82	113	145	176	206
20″	84	116	148	179	209
Weight Male	*11*	*58*	*UP*	*—*	*—*
in Lbs. Fem.	*5½*	*29*	*UP*	*—*	*—*

(F, H) Finger-Hand—Measured at Finger Tip					
1″	16	23	29	35	40
2″	17	25	32	38	44
3″	19	28	36	43	49
4″	23	33	42	50	58
Weight Male	*⅔*	*2½*	*4*	*UP*	*—*
in Lbs. Fem.	*⅓*	*1¼*	*4*	*UP*	*—*

(FT) Foot—Measured at Toe					
1″	20	29	37	44	51
2″	22	32	40	48	55
3″	24	35	45	55	63
4″	29	41	53	64	73
Weight Male	*5*	*22*	*UP*	*—*	*—*
in Lbs. Fem.	*2½*	*11*	*UP*	*—*	*—*

(FS) Forearm Swivel—Measured at Knuckles					
45°	17	22	28	32	37
90°	23	30	37	43	49
135°	28	36	44	52	58
180°	31	40	49	57	65
Torque Male	*3*	*13*	*UP*	*—*	*—*
Lbs. Ins. Fem.	*1½*	*6½*	*UP*	*—*	*—*

Work-Factor Symbols
W—Weight or Resistance
S—Directional Control
(Steer)
P—Care (Precaution)
U—Change Direction
D—Definite Stop

Walking Time			
30″ Paces			
Type	1	2	Over 2
General	Analyze from Table	260	120 + 80/Pace
Restricted		300	120 + 100/Pace

Add 100 for 120°–180° Turn at Start or Finish

Up Steps (8″ Rise–10″ Flat)	126
Down Steps	100

Visual Inspection

Focus	20
Inspect	30/Point
React	20

Head Turn 45° 40, 90° 60

1 Time Unit =
.006 Second
.0001 Minute
.00000167 Hour

*Work-Factor is a registered trade mark of the Work-Factor Company. All tables reproduced by permission of the Work-Factory Company, which holds the copyright.

369

Table 33. Work-Factor Grasp Table

Size (Major dimension or length)		Solids & Brackets Thickness (over 3/64" .0469")		Thin Flat Objects Thickness (less than 1/64" 0–.0156")		Thin Flat Objects Thickness (1/64 to 3/64" .0156"–.0469")		Cylinders and Regular Cross Sectioned Solids Diameter 0–.0625" (1/16")	.0626"–.125" (1/8")	.1251"–.1875" (3/16")	.1876"–.5000" (1/2")		.5001" & up (over 1/2")		Add for Entangled Nested or Slippery Objects*
		Blind —Simo	Visual —Simo	Blind —Simo	Visual —Simo	Blind —Simo	Visual —Simo	Blind —Simo	Blind —Simo	Blind —Simo	Blind —Simo	Visual —Simo	Blind —Simo	Visual —Simo	—Simo
.0000"–.0625"	1/16" & less	120 172	B B	— —	— —	131 189	B B	S S	S S	S S	S S	S S	S S	S S	17 26
.0626"–.1250"	over 1/16" to 1/8"	79 111	B B	108 154	B B	85 120	B B	85 120	S S	S S	S S	S S	S S	S S	12 18
.1251"–.1875"	over 1/8" to 3/16"	64 88	B B	102 145	B B	74 103	B B	79 111	74 103	S S	S S	S S	S S	S S	12 18
.1876"–.2500"	over 3/16" to 1/4"	48 64	B B	72 100	B B	56 76	B B	79 111	68 94	64 88	S S	S S	S S	S S	8 12
.2501"–.5000"	over 1/4" to 1/2"	40 52	B B	64 88	B B	48 64	B B	62 85	56 76	56 76	44 58	B B	40 52	S S	8 12
.5001"–1.0000"	over 1/2" to 1"	40 52	32 40	64 88	60 82	48 64	44 58	62 85	56 76	48 64	48 64	44 58	40 52	32 40	8 12
1.0001"–4.0000"	over 1" to 4"	37 48	20 22	53 72	36 46	45 60	28 34	56 76	48 64	40 52	40 52	36 46	37 48	20 22	8 12
4.0001" & up	over 4"	46 61	20 22	70 97	44 58	62 85	36 46	56 76	48 64	40 52	40 52	36 46	37 48	20 22	9 14

B = Use Blind column since visual grasp offers no advantage. S = Use Solid Table.

* Add the indicated allowances when objects: (a) are entangled (not requiring two hands to separate); (b) are nested together because of shape or film; (c) are slippery (as from oil or polished surface). When objects both entangle and are slippery, or both nest and are slippery, use double the value in the table.

Note: Special grasp conditions should be analyzed in detail.

Table 33. (Continued)

Distance Between Targets

Distance Between Targets	Percent Addition to Alignments	Method of Alignment
0– .99"	Neg.	Simo
1– 1.99"	10%	Simo
2– 2.99"	30%	Simo
3– 4.99"	50%	Simo
5– 6.99"	70%	Simo
7–14.99"	Align 1st, Insert 1st, Align 2nd (1) Insert 2nd.	
15" & up	Align 1st, Insert 1st, Focus and Inspect, Align 2nd (1), Insert 2nd.	

(1) If connected, treat 2nd Assembly as open target with no upright.

Blind Targets

Percent Addition to Alignments

Distance from Target to Visible Area	Permanent (Blind at all times)	Temporary (Blind during assembly)
.0– .49"	20%	0%
.5– .99"	30%	10%
1.0– 1.99"	40%	20%
2.0– 2.99"	70%	30%
3.0– 4.99"	130%	50%
5.0– 6.99"	250%	70%
7.0–10.00"	380%	120%

Gripping Distance

Distance from Gripping Point to Alignment Point	Percent Addition to Alignments	Length of Upright Motion
0– 1.99"	Neg.	1"
2– 2.99"	10%	1"
3– 4.99"	20%	2"
5– 6.99"	30%	2"
7– 9.99"	40%	3"
10–14.99"	60%	5"
15–19.99"	80%	6"
20" & up	100%	7" & up

General Rules for Assembly

1. When required add W and P Work Factors to all Assembly Motions according to rules for Transports.
2. Reduce number of Alignments by 50% when hand is rigidly supported.
3. Where Gripping Distance, Two Targets and Blind Targets are involved, add each percentage to Original Alignment. Don't pyramid percentages.
4. Alignments for Surface Assembly are taken from .224 column and are A1SD Motions.
5. Index is F1S, A1S or FS45°S.

Table 34. Work-Factor Assembly Table

Target Diameter	Average No. of Alignments (A1S Motions)					
	Closed Targets					
	Ratio of Plug Dia. ÷ Target Dia.					
	To .224	.225 to .289	.290 to .414	.415 to .899	.900 to .934	.935 to 1.000
.875" & up	(D*) 18	(D*) 18	(D*) 18	(¼) 25	(¼†) 51	(¼‡) 59
.625" to 874"	(D*) 18	(D*) 18	(SD*) 18	(¼) 25	(¼†) 51	(¼‡) 59
.375" to .624"	(SD*) 18	(SD*) 18	(¼) 25	(½) 31	(½†) 57	(½‡) 65
.225" to .374"	(½) 31	(1) 44	(1) 44	(1½) 57	(1½†) 83	(1½‡) 91
.175" to .224"	(1) 44	(1) 44	(1) 44	(1½) 57	(1½†) 83	(1½‡) 91
.125" to .174"	(1) 44	(1¼) 51	(1½) 57	(1½) 57	(1½†) 83	(1½‡) 91
.075" to .124"	(2½) 83	(2½) 83	(2½) 83	(2½) 83	(2½†) 109	(2½‡) 117
.025" to .074"	(3) 96	(3) 96	(3) 96	(3) 96	(3†) 122	(3‡) 130

Target Diameter	Average No. of Alignments (A1S Motions)					
	Open Targets					
	Ratio of Plug Dia. ÷ Target Dia.					
	To .224	.225 to .289	.290 to .414	.415 to .899	.900 to .934	.935 to 1.000
.875" & up	(D*) 18	(D*) 18	(D*) 18	(D*) 18	(¼†) 51	(¼‡) 59
.625" to 874"	(D*) 18	(D*) 18	(D*) 18	(SD*) 18	(¼†) 51	(¼‡) 59
.375" to .624"	(SD*) 18	(SD*) 18	(SD*) 18	(½) 31	(½†) 57	(½‡) 65
.225" to .374"	(¼) 25	(½) 31	(½) 31	(¾) 38	(¾†) 64	(¾‡) 72
.175" to .224"	(½) 31	(½) 31	(½) 31	(¾) 38	(¾†) 64	(¾‡) 72
.125" to .174"	(¾) 38	(1) 44	(1) 44	(1) 44	(1†) 70	(1‡) 78
.075" to .124"	(1¼) 51	(1¼) 51	(1¼) 51	(1¼) 51	(1¼†) 77	(1¼‡) 85
.025" to .074"	(1½) 57	(1½) 57	(1½) 57	(1½) 57	(1½†) 83	(1½‡) 91

*Letters indicate Work Factors in move preceding Assembly.

†Requires A(X)S Upright for all ratios of .900 and greater. (Table value includes A1S Upright.)

‡Requires A(Y)S Upright and A(Z)P Insert for all ratios of .935 and greater. (Table value includes A1S Upright and A1P Insert.)

5. Use (Manual, Process, or Machine Time) (US).
6. Disassemble (DSY).
7. Mental Process (MP).
8. Release (RL).

Work-Factor Notation

The symbols employed for the body members and Work-Factors are shown in Fig. 232.

Body Members	Symbol	Work–Factors (written in this sequence)	Symbol
Finger	F	Weight or Resistance	W
Hand	H	Directional Control (Steer)	S
Arm	A	Care (Precaution)	P
Forearm Swivel	FS	Change Direction	U
Trunk	T	Definite Stop	D
Foot	FT		
Leg	L		
Head Turn	HT		

Figure 232   Symbols for body members and Work-Factors.

Recording the Analysis

Symbols are used for recording a motion analysis. The body member is indicated first; the distance moved, second; and the Work-Factors, third. For example:

Description of Motion	Motion Analysis	Time, Minutes
1. Toss small part aside 10 inches (Basic Motion)	A10	0.0042
2. Reach 20 inches to bolt in bin (Definite Stop Motion)	A20D	0.0080
3. Move 4-pound brick 30 inches from pile to place on worktable (Weight, Definite Stop Motion)	A30WD	0.0119

EXAMPLE   The analysis of motions required to get pen from holder, mark X on paper, replace pen in holder, and return hand to paper is shown in Fig. 233. The penholder is located about 12 inches from the center of the writing area.

Ready, Abbreviated, Brief, and Detailed Mento Work-Factor Systems

Time standards may be established by any one of the following five Work-Factor systems: Detailed, Ready, Abbreviated, Brief, and Detailed Mento-Factor. The Detailed

	Detailed Work-Factor Analysis		
Element Number	Element Description	Motion Analysis	Work-Factor Time Units
1	Reach to pen (12 inches)	A12D	65
2	Grasp pen	1/2 Fl	8
3	Move to paper (12 inches)	A12D	65
4	Position pen on paper	F1SD	29
5	Make 1st stroke of X	F1D	23
6	Position pen for 2nd stroke	F1D	23
7	Make 2nd stroke of X	F1D	23
8	Move pen to holder (12 inches)	A12SD	85
9	Align pen to holder	1/4 VA1S	7
10	Insert pen in holder	F1P	23
11	Release pen	1/2 Fl	8
12	Move arm to paper (12 inches)	A12D	65
	Total time units		424

Figure 233 Example of Detailed Work-Factor analysis of an operation being performed by one hand. Note the decimal point and zeros in the "Work-Factor Time Units" column are omitted for simplification in writing the analysis. 424 Time Units equals 0.0424 minute.

system has been described in the preceding paragraphs. There are some situations where one cannot justify the use of the Detailed Work-Factor system. Long-cycle operations are in this category as are studies made for cost estimating.

Ready System. This system is based on appropriate averages of the Detailed data and enables the analyst to apply the data more quickly. When the Ready System is applied to operations to which it is suited, it is expected to provide time values which allow 0 to 5 percent more time than those resulting from Detailed study. The Ready Time Unit is 0.001 (recorded as 1), thus simplifying the making of analyses.

Ready Work-Factor is the most widely used of the Work-Factor systems. For this reason it is available in three presentations:

1. The Ready Work-Factor Manual for class teaching and use.
2. The Wocom Computer Ready Work-Factor Program.
3. The Ready Work-Factor Manual Programmed for Self-Instruction.

Abbreviated Systems. The abbreviated systems were developed to fill a need for a very simple system of predetermined time standards. They provide a rapid measurement procedure, inasmuch as they make use of special time study forms which contain the time data. This makes it unnecessary to refer to a separate table of time values. The abbreviated Time Unit is 0.005 (recorded as 5) minute rather than the 0.0001 minute used in the Detailed and Mento Systems. When correctly applied to appropriate types of work, the accuracy of the Abbreviated systems is expected to average ± 12 percent of the Detailed system.

Brief System. The Brief System is relatively new and like the Abbreviated Systems uses a Time Unit of 0.005 minute (recorded as 5). It was developed to make the format conform with the Detailed, and with the Ready Systems.

Detailed Mento-Factor System. This is a very complete system for measuring mental processes used for beneficial work such as inspection, proofreading, composing, color matching, calculations, and virtually any repetitive or semirepetitive and predominantly mental operation. The method of applying Mento-Factor is the same as for the Detailed System.

The Wocom Group. This refers to a series of computer programs which have been developed for use on the General Electric Time Share System. The automated program follows the same procedure as that used by the manual method. The computerized program for establishing the standards is more accurate and requires about one-third of the time needed in using the manual method.

The Modules now in the computer are: Detailed Work-Factor, Ready Work-Factor, Mento-Factor, A Revision Program to keep standard data up-to-date, Learning Curves (not training), Automatic Line Balancing, and Multiple Regression Formulae.

28

PREDETERMINED TIME SYSTEMS: METHODS-TIME MEASUREMENT

The Methods-Time Measurement (MTM) system[1] of predetermined time standards was developed from motion picture studies of industrial operation, and the time standards were first published in 1948. This system is defined as a procedure which analyzes any manual operation or method into the basic motions required to perform it, and assigns to each motion a predetermined time standard which is determined by the nature of the motion and the conditions under which it is made.[2]

Beginning in 1963 the first new member of the MTM system called General Purpose Data (MTM-GPD) was introduced and at that time MTM-1 was used to designate the original basic MTM system. Today, the family of systems includes MTM-1, MTM-GPD, MTM-2, MTM-3, MTM-V, MTM-M, MTM-C, and 4M DATA.

MTM-1

Tables 35 though 48 give the motion-time data for each basic element. The unit of time used in these tables is one hundred-thousandth of an hour (0.00001 hour), and is referred to as one time-measurement unit (TMU). Thus, one TMU equals 0.0006 minute.

Reach

Reach is the basic element used when the predominant purpose is to move the hand or finger to a destination. The time for making a reach varies with the following factors: (1) condition (nature of destination), (2) length of the motion, and (3) type of reach.

Classes of Reach

There are five classes of reach (Table 35). The time to perform a reach is affected by the nature of the object toward which the reach is made.

---

[1] Reproduced with permission of the MTM Association for Standards and Research.

[2] Harold B. Maynard, G. J. Stegemerten, and John L. Schwab, *Methods-Time Measurement,* McGraw-Hill, New York, 1948. William Antis, John M. Honeycutt, Jr., and Edward N. Koch, *The Basic Motions of MTM, 4th ed.,* The Maynard Foundation, Naples, Fla., 1973. Delmar W. Karger and Franklin H. Bayha, *Engineered Work Measurement,* 3rd ed., Industrial Press, New York, 1977. Karl Eady, ''Today's International MTM Systems—Decision Criteria for Their Use,'' *Proceedings AIIE Spring Annual Conference,* American Institute of Industrial Engineers, Norcross, Ga., 1977.

Table 35. Reach—R

Distance Moved Inches	Time TMU				Hand in Motion		Case and Description
	A	B	C or D	E	A	B	
¾ or less	2.0	2.0	2.0	2.0	1.6	1.6	A Reach to object in fixed location, or to object in other hand or on which other hand rests.
1	2.5	2.5	3.6	2.4	2.3	2.3	
2	4.0	4.0	5.9	3.8	3.5	2.7	
3	5.3	5.3	7.3	5.3	4.5	3.6	B Reach to single object in location which may vary slightly from cycle to cycle.
4	6.1	6.4	8.4	6.8	4.9	4.3	
5	6.5	7.8	9.4	7.4	5.3	5.0	
6	7.0	8.6	10.1	8.0	5.7	5.7	
7	7.4	9.3	10.8	8.7	6.1	6.5	
8	7.9	10.1	11.5	9.3	6.5	7.2	C Reach to object jumbled with other objects in a group so that search and select occur.
9	8.3	10.8	12.2	9.9	6.9	7.9	
10	8.7	11.5	12.9	10.5	7.3	8.6	
12	9.6	12.9	14.2	11.8	8.1	10.1	
14	10.5	14.4	15.6	13.0	8.9	11.5	
16	11.4	15.8	17.0	14.2	9.7	12.9	D Reach to a very small object or where accurate grasp is required.
18	12.3	17.2	18.4	15.5	10.5	14.4	
20	13.1	18.6	19.8	16.7	11.3	15.8	
22	14.0	20.1	21.2	18.0	12.1	17.3	
24	14.9	21.5	22.5	19.2	12.9	18.8	E Reach to indefinite location to get hand in position for body balance or next motion or out of way.
26	15.8	22.9	23.9	20.4	13.7	20.2	
28	16.7	24.4	25.3	21.7	14.5	21.7	
30	17.5	25.8	26.7	22.9	15.3	23.2	
Additional	0.4	0.7	0.7	0.6			TMU per inch over 30 inches

All MTM data tables copyrighted by the MTM Association. (Tables courtesy MTM Association)

Case A reach: to object in fixed location, or to object in other hand, or on which other hand rests.

Case B reach: to object whose general location is known. Location may vary slightly from cycle to cycle.

Case C reach: to objects jumbled with other objects in group.

Case D reach: to very small object or where accurate grasp is required.

Case E reach: to indefinite location to get hand into position for body balance, or next move, or out of the way.

The *length* of a motion is the true path, not just the straight-line distance between the two terminal points.

There are three *types* of reach to be considered: (1) hand is not moving at beginning and at end of reach, (2) hand is moving at either beginning or end of reach, and (3) hand is in motion at both beginning and end of reach.

Move

Move is the basic element used when the predominant purpose is to transport an object to a destination. There are three classes of moves:

Case A move: object to other hand or against stop.
Case B move: object to approximate or indefinite location.
Case C move: object to exact location.

The time for move is affected by the following variables: (1) condition (nature of destination), (2) length of the motion, (3) type of move, and (4) weight factor, static and dynamic.

The time for move is affected by its *length,* in a manner similar to reach. The three *types* of moves are the same as those described for reach. Additional time is needed when an object is moved or a force is applied (above 2.5 pounds), as indicated in Table 36.

Turn

Turn is the motion employed to turn the hand, either empty or loaded, by a movement that rotates the hand, wrist, and forearm about the long axis of the forearm. The time for a turn depends on two variables: (1) degrees turned, and (2) weight factor, as indicated in Table 37.

Apply Pressure

Table 38 presents the time values for apply pressure. It provided full cycle time or developments by the components as related to other motions.

Table 36. Move—M

Distance Moved Inches	Time TMU				Wt. Allowance			Case and Description
	A	B	C	Hand In Motion B	Wt. (lb.) Up to	Dynamic Factor	Static Constant TMU	
¾ or less	2.0	2.0	2.0	1.7				
1	2.5	2.9	3.4	2.3	2.5	1.00	0	
2	3.6	4.6	5.2	2.9				A Move object to other hand or against stop.
3	4.9	5.7	6.7	3.6	7.5	1.06	2.2	
4	6.1	6.9	8.0	4.3				
5	7.3	8.0	9.2	5.0	12.5	1.11	3.9	
6	8.1	8.9	10.3	5.7				
7	8.9	9.7	11.1	6.5	17.5	1.17	5.6	
8	9.7	10.6	11.8	7.2				
9	10.5	11.5	12.7	7.9	22.5	1.22	7.4	B Move object to approximate or indefinite loca-tion.
10	11.3	12.2	13.5	8.6				
12	12.9	13.4	15.2	10.0	27.5	1.28	9.1	
14	14.4	14.6	16.9	11.4				
16	16.0	15.8	18.7	12.8	32.5	1.33	10.8	
18	17.6	17.0	20.4	14.2				
20	19.2	18.2	22.1	15.6	37.5	1.39	12.5	
22	20.8	19.4	23.8	17.0				
24	22.4	20.6	25.5	18.4	42.5	1.44	14.3	C Move object to exact location.
26	24.0	21.8	27.3	19.8				
28	25.5	23.1	29.0	21.2	47.5	1.50	16.0	
30	27.1	24.3	30.7	22.7				
Additional	0.8	0.6	0.85		TMU per inch over 30 inches			

Table 37. Turn—T

	Time TMU for Degrees Turned										
Weight	30°	45°	60°	75°	90°	105°	120°	135°	150°	165°	180°
Small—0 to 2 Pounds	2.8	3.5	4.1	4.8	5.4	6.1	6.8	7.4	8.1	8.7	9.4
Medium—2.1 to 10 Pounds	4.4	5.5	6.5	7.5	8.5	9.6	10.6	11.6	12.7	13.7	14.8
Large—10.1 to 35 Pounds	8.4	10.5	12.3	14.4	16.2	18.3	20.4	22.2	24.3	26.1	28.2

Table 38. Apply Pressure—AP

Full Cycle			Components		
Symbol	TMU	Description	Symbol	TMU	Description
APA	10.6	AF + DM + RLF	AF	3.4	Apply Force
			DM	4.2	Dwell, Minimum
APB	16.2	APA + G2	RLF	3.0	Release Force

Grasp

Grasp is the basic element employed when the predominant purpose is to secure sufficient control of one or more objects with the fingers or hand to permit the performance of the next required basic element. The classes of grasps, with a description of each type and the time values for each, are given in Table 39.

Position

Position is the basic element employed to align, orient, and engage one object with another object, where the motions used are so minor that they do not justify classification as other basic elements. The time for position is affected by (1) class of fit, (2) symmetry, and (3) ease of handling, as shown in Table 40. Recent research presents the position data with tolerances and measured depth of insertion. This is supplementary data in Table 40—Position.

Release

Release is the basic element to relinquish control of an object by the fingers or hand (Table 41). The two classifications of release are (1) normal release, simple opening of fingers; and (2) contact release, the release begins and is completed at the instant the following reach begins (no time allowed).

Table 39. Grasp—G

Type of Grasp	Case	Time TMU	Description	
Pick-up	1A	2.0	Any size object by itself, easily grasped	
	1B	3.5	Object very small or lying close against a flat surface	
	1C1	7.3	Diameter larger than ½"	Interference with Grasp on bottom and one side of nearly cylindrical object.
	1C2	8.7	Diameter ¼" to ½"	
	1C3	10.8	Diameter less than ¼"	
Regrasp	2	5.6	Change grasp without relinquishing control	
Transfer	3	5.6	Control transferred from one hand to the other.	
Select	4A	7.3	Larger than 1" x 1" x 1"	Object jumbled with other objects so that search and select occur.
	4B	9.1	¼" x ¼" x ⅛" to 1" x 1" x 1"	
	4C	12.9	Smaller than ¼" x ¼" x ⅛"	
Contact	5	0	Contact, Sliding, or Hook Grasp.	

Table 40. Position*—P

Class of Fit		Symmetry	Easy to Handle	Difficult to Handle
1—Loose	No pressure required	S	5.6	11.2
		SS	9.1	14.7
		NS	10.4	16.0
2—Close	Light pressure required	S	16.2	21.8
		SS	19.7	25.3
		NS	21.0	26.6
3—Exact	Heavy pressure required	S	43.0	48.6
		SS	46.5	52.1
		NS	47.8	53.4
Supplementary Rule for Surface Alignment				
P1SE per alignment: $>^1/_{16} \leqslant \frac{1}{4}''$		P2SE per alignment: $\leqslant ^1/_{16}''$		

*Distance moved to engage—1" or less.

381

Table 41. Release—RL

Case	Time TMU	Description
1	2.0	Normal release performed by opening fingers as independent motion.
2	0	Contact Release

Disengage

Disengage is the basic element used to break contact between one object and another. It includes an involuntary movement resulting from the sudden ending of resistance. The time for disengage is affected by the following three variables: (1) class of fit, (2) ease of handling, and (3) care of handling (Table 42).

Table 42. Disengage—D

Class of Fit	Height of Recoil	Easy to Handle	Difficult to Handle
1—Loose—Very slight effort, blends with subsequent move.	Up to 1"	4.0	5.7
2—Close—Normal effort, slight recoil.	Over 1" to 5"	7.5	11.8
3—Tight—Considerable effort, hand recoils markedly.	Over 5" to 12"	22.9	34.7

Eye Times

In most work, time for moving and focusing the eye is not a limiting factor and consequently does not affect the time for the operation. When the eyes do direct the hands or body movements, however, eye times must be considered. There are two types of eye time, eye focus time and eye travel time.

Eye focus time is the time required to focus the eyes on an object and look at it

Table 43. Eye Travel and Eye Focus—ET and EF

Eye Travel Time $= 15.2 \times \dfrac{T}{D}$ TMU, with a maximum value of 20 TMU.

> where $T =$ the distance between points from and to which the eye travels.
> $D =$ the perpendicular distance from the eye to the line of travel T.

Eye Focus Time $= 7.3$ TMU.

Supplementary Information

—Area of Normal Vision = Circle 4" in Diameter 16" from Eyes
—Reading Formula $= 5.05$ N Where N = The Number of Words.

long enough to determine certain readily distinguishable characteristics within the area which may be seen without shifting the eyes.

Eye travel time is affected by the distance between points from and to which the eye travels, and the perpendicular distance from the eye to the line of travel, as indicated in Table 43.

Body, Leg, and Foot Motions

The body, leg, and foot motions are described in Table 44, and the time values are also shown in this table.

Table 44. Body, Leg, and Foot Motions

Type		Symbol	TMU	Distance	Description
Leg–Foot Motion		FM	8.5	To 4″	Hinged at ankle.
		FMP	19.1	To 4″	With heavy pressure.
		LM__	7.1	To 6″	Hinged at knee or hip in any direction.
			1.2	Ea. add'l inch	
Horizontal Motion	Side Step	SS__C1	*	<12″	Use Reach or Move time when less than 12″. Complete when leading leg contacts floor.
			17.0	12″	
			0.6	Ea. add'l inch	
		SS__C2	34.1	12″	Lagging leg must contact floor before next motion can be made.
			1.1	Ea. add'l inch	
	Turn Body	TBC1	18.6	—	Complete when leading leg contacts floor.
		TBC2	37.2	—	Lagging leg must contact floor before next motion can be made.
	Walk	W__FT	5.3	Per Foot	Unobstructed.
		W__P	15.0	Per Pace	Unobstructed.
		W__PO	17.0	Per Pace	When obstructed or with weight.
Vertical Motion		SIT	34.7	—	From standing position.
		STD	43.4	—	From sitting position.
		B,S,KOK	29.0	—	Bend, Stoop, Kneel on One Knee.
		AB,AS,AKOK	31.9	—	Arise from Bend, Stoop, Kneel on One Knee.
		KBK	69.4	—	Kneel on Both Knees.
		AKBK	76.7	—	Arise from Kneel on Both Knees.

Limiting Motions

In performing most industrial operations, it is desirable to have more than one body member in motion at a time. Usually the most effective method of performing an operation can be approached when two or more body members are in motion at the same time. If two or more motions are combined or overlapped, all can be performed in the time required to perform the one demanding the greatest amount of time, or the limiting motion. When two motions are performed at the same time by the body member, they are called *combined motions*. When the two motions are performed by different body members, they are called *simultaneous motions*. Table 45 is a guide to limiting motions, although it does not apply in every case.

Conventions for Recording MTM

It has been found convenient to develop a code for referring to the various classes of motions. It would be awkward, for example, to have to refer to a "Case B reach 10 inches long with hand in motion at the end" in so many words every time a motion of that sort was encountered. Therefore, for convenience, this is coded as R10Bm. Table 46 gives the coding for all types of motions.

Table 45.   Simultaneous Motions

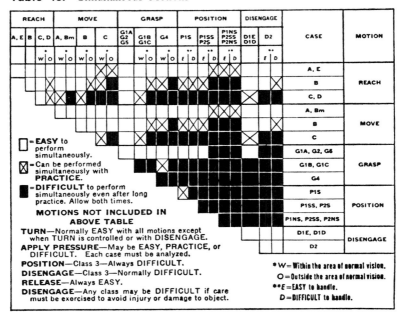

Table 46. Conventions for Recording MTM

Table	Example	Significance
35	R8C	Reach, 8 inches, Case C
	R12Am	Reach, 12 inches, Case A, hand in motion at end.
36	M6A	Move, 6 inches, Case A, object weighs less than 2.5 pounds
	mM10C	Move, 10 inches, Case C, hand in motion at the beginning, object less than 2.5 pounds
	M16B15	Move, 16 inches, Case B, object weighs 15 pounds
37	T30	Turn hand empty 30 degrees
	T90L	Turn object weighing more than 10 pounds 90 degrees
38	APB	Apply pressure, includes regrasp
39	G1A	Grasp, Case G1A
40	P1NSD	Position, Class 1 fit, nonsymmetrical part, difficult to handle
41	RL1	Release, Case 1
42	D2E	Disengage, Class 2 fit, easy to handle
43	EF	Eye focus
	ET14/10	Eye travel between points 14″ apart where line of travel is 10″ from eyes
44	FM	Foot motion
	SS16C1	Sidestep, 16 inches, Case 1
	TBC1	Turn body, Case
	W4P	Walk four paces

When these symbols are recorded, they are written down in such a way as to indicate the hand making the motions, the sequence, and the time values.

LH	TMU	RH
R12C	14.2	
G4A	7.3	
M10A	11.3	
G3	5.6	G3
	5.2	M2C
	5.6	P1SE
	2.0	RL1
Total	51.2	

This indicates that the following motions take place. The left hand makes a 12-inch Case C reach followed by a G4A to pick up an object. The left hand then moves the object back to the other hand. A transfer grasp puts the object in the right hand, which then moves it 2 inches to an exact location, positions it, and releases it.

EXAMPLE The analysis shown in Fig. 234 includes the motions required in order to dispose of one part and obtain the next in a given layout.

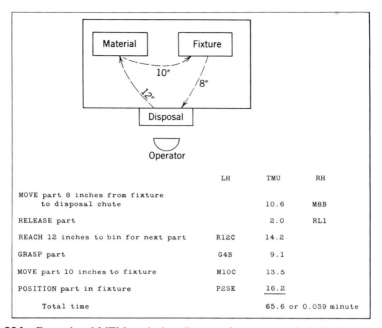

	LH	TMU	RH
MOVE part 8 inches from fixture to disposal chute		10.6	M8B
RELEASE part		2.0	RL1
REACH 12 inches to bin for next part	R12C	14.2	
GRASP part	G4B	9.1	
MOVE part 10 inches to fixture	M10C	13.5	
POSITION part in fixture	P2SE	16.2	
Total time		65.6 or 0.039 minute	

Figure 234 Example of MTM analysis—dispose of one part and obtain the next. Machine operation time not shown.

MTM-2

Of the family of MTM predetermined time systems MTM-1 is the most accurate, provides the most detailed methods description, but requires the longest time for analysis.

MTM-2 was developed by constructing motion combinations from basic motions of MTM-1. It has a smaller number of distance ranges and fewer cases of control than MTM-1. Although the analysis can be made more quickly than with MTM-1, accuracy and method description are not as great. MTM-2 is suitable for work that is not highly repetitive and for elements that are not less than 1 minute long. The system consists of nine categories of manual motions:

	Motion	*Symbol*			*Motion*	*Symbol*
1.	Get	G		6.	Crank	C
2.	Put	P		7.	Step	S
3.	Apply Pressure	A		8.	Foot Motion	F
4.	Regrasp	R		9.	Bend and Arise	B
5.	Eye Action	E				

Get and Put are the only two variable categories and only 37 time standards appear on the MTM-2 data card (Table 47).

Get

Definition. Get—reaching with hand or fingers to an object, grasping object, and subsequently releasing it.

Get has three variables:

1. The case of get (action employed): GA—no grasping motion; GB—closing fingers to gain control; GC—complex grasping.
2. The distance reached 2, 6, 12, 18, and over 18 inches.
3. Weight of object, or its resistance to motion Get Weight: GW-1 TMU per 2 lb.

Put

Definition. Put—moving an object to a destination with the hand or fingers.

Put has three variables:

1. The case of put is affected by the number of "correcting" motions or no correction required: PA—continuous smooth motion; PB—one correction; and PC—more than one correction.
2. The distance moved (same as for Get).
3. Weight of object, or its resistance to motion (same as for Get).

Put Weight: PW-1 TMU per 10 lb.

Accuracy. The combination system and application decision is such that MTM-2 analyses are within ±5 percent with 95 percent confidence level from MTM-1 with cycles of 1 minute or more. Speed of analysis with MTM-2 is twice as fast as with MTM-1.

Table 47. MTM-2

Range	Code	GA	GB	GC	PA	PB	PC
Up to 2″	-2	3	7	14	3	10	21
Over 2″–6″	-6	6	10	19	6	15	26
Over 6″–12″	-12	9	14	23	11	19	30
Over 12″–18″	-18	13	18	27	15	24	36
Over 18″	-32	17	23	32	20	30	41
		GW 1-per 2 lb.			PW 1-per 10 lb.		
		A	R	E	C	S	F	B
		14	6	7	15	18	9	61

MTM-3

MTM-3 is the simplest of the MTM systems and is intended for use with long-cycle short-run operations. The MTM-3 system consists of four categories of motions:

	Motion	Symbol
1.	Handle	H
2.	Transport	T
3.	Step and Foot Motion	SF
4.	Bend and Arise	B

Of these, the two motions HANDLE and TRANSPORT have variable categories and only ten time standards appear on the MTM-3 data card (Table 48).

Table 48. MTM-3

Range	Code	HA	HB	TA	TB
Up to 6″	-6	18	34	7	21
Over 6″	-32	34	48	16	29
		SF	18	B	61

Handle and Transport

Definition. Handle—gaining control of an object and placing it in a new location.

Transport—placing an object in a new location when the hand already has control of the object.

Handle and *Transport* variables:

1. Case—HA or TA—no correcting motions needed.
   HB or TB—correcting motions are necessary.
2. The distance the object is moved—up to 6 inches or over 6 inches.

The two additional categories are SF, which combine the Step and Foot categories; and B, Bend and Arise.

Speed of analysis with MTM-3 is seven times as fast as with MTM-1 and three times as fast as with MTM-2.

Limitations. MTM-3 should not be used for analyzing manual motions with a frequency higher than 10 or a sequence of eye movements. In such cases MTM-2 or MTM-1 should be used.

Precise rules for the general application of MTM-2 and MTM-3 have been established. A thorough understanding of these rules is necessary to use these data properly.

MTM-3 has been computerized and utilizes a data collection instrument and desk-top computer. Other MTM systems are presently being computerized.

OTHER MTM SYSTEMS

MTM-GPD (General Purpose Data) has been derived from MTM-1 time values for basic data. This is a "building block process" for development of standard data.

MTM-V is designed for use with machine tool operations including such items as setting machine tools, handling tools and work pieces, measuring and gaging, operating the machine, and cleaning work pieces and equipment.

MTM-M is a second level functional system of original data designed for the analysis and measurement of manual assembly work performed under stereoscopic magnification of 5 to 30 power.

MTM-C is a two-level data system synthesized from MTM-1 and is used for clerical related work. Its use includes desk top operations and such tasks as filing, typing, keypunching, and data entry.

4D DATA (Micro-Matic Methods and Measurement) is a computer-aided means of applying MTM-1. The computer takes over much of the work of the analyst and assists in standard data development, recalling elements, and mass changing standards.

29

STANDARD DATA FROM PREDETERMINED TIMES—COMPUTER AIDED WAGE INCENTIVE APPLICATION

Standard data is a form of work measurement that consists of time values for specific elements of work. The manual part of a task is broken down into groups of hand motions or body movemnts that can be precisely defined and that are applied only in connection with a particular machine or a specific operation. The elemental time values usually take the form of tables, formulas, or graphs. Elemental time values for establishing standard data had been determined by stop-watch time study until predetermined time systems became available. Predetermined times have some important advantages over time study but the detailed motion analysis is very time consuming. However, through a simple plan for combining motions into "elemental building blocks" and the further combination of these data, Deere and Company has developed a system of "Operational Data" which they have used successfully over a period of years.[1] Some 700 different sets of data have been developed covering 250 separate manufacturing processes. The areas covered by these data include foundry, forge shop, punching, forming, shearing, machining, welding, heat treating, painting, assembly, warehousing and shipping, and other miscellaneous processes. Eighty percent of all incentive standards in their domestic plants are established by their Operational Data. Fifty percent of all factory employees are paid on an incentive basis.

OPERATIONAL DATA AS DEVELOPED AND USED BY DEERE AND COMPANY

Deere and Company is a manufacturer of farm equipment, industrial equipment, and consumer products which consist of lawn and garden equipment, snowblowers, and snowmobiles. It has 11 factories in this country and a worldwide employment exceeding 55,000 people. The first official piece rates were established in 1904, and this system of wage incentives was used until 1955 when the company replaced piece rates with a standard hour wage incentive plan.

---

[1] Reproduced by permission of Deere and Company. Also, Harvey J. Teadwald, "Modern Wage Administration," Robert E. Trunnell, Jr., "Computerized Standard Data," and Robert D. Mays, "Planning and Operations Processing," *Proceedings Thirty-Ninth Annual IMS Clinic,* Industrial Management Society, Chicago, November 1975, pp. 55–81.

Deere factories produce a broad line of products and each product may have many different variations and sizes. Most products are large with many parts, and several operations are required to produce each part. The farm equipment industry is much like the automobile industry in that models are changed and new models are added annually. Thus, there are many new time standards to be established each year. Last year over 300,000 new time standards were established in the domestic plants and the number is increasing by 5 percent per year.

When employees were paid on a piece-work basis the piece rates were determined by stop-watch time study. Also, time study was used for setting time standards when the standard hour incentive plan was installed. In the late 1940s Deere was one of the first companies to use predetermined times. They were also early users of work sampling and made some use of standard data. As the number of time standards to be established increased it was evident that the use of standard data was the most satisfactory solution to their work measurement problems. They developed a system using predetermined times as the basis for establishing standard data, or Operational Data, as they call it. Their system will be described here.

Summary of Operational Data Development Steps

The Deere plan consists of four parts or steps:

1. Predetermined time system
   Micromotion time
2. Basic Data
   Combination of predetermined times for motions
3. Universal Data
   A combination of blocks of Basic Data
4. Operational Data
   Time values for elements for a specific type of operation

Basic Data and Universal Data

The building blocks shown in Figure 235 are based on the fact that most elements of manual work consist of:

A. REACH
B. BODY TRAVEL — either a *reach* or a *body travel* to an object
C. GAIN CONTROL — the *gain control* of the object
D. MOVE
E. BODY TRAVEL — either a *move* or *body travel* with the object
F. RELINQUISH CONTROL — usually a relinquish control of the object
G. *DISENGAGE* — in addition, after gaining control of an object there might or might not be a *disengage*
H. *POSITION* — also, there might or might not be a *position*

Table 49. Universal Data for Part Handling Element—Body Travel to the Part and Body Travel with the Part. The Variables Are "Body Travel Distance in Feet" and "Maximum Weight of Part in Pounds"

AA11 Part to Fixture from Container
Body Travel to Part—Body Travel with Part

Casting and Forging Handling

Maximum Distance of Body Travel to Part in Feet	\ Maximum Distance of Body Travel with Part in Feet → 1	2	3	4	5	6	7	8	9	10
1	1	2	3	4	5	6	7	8	9	10
2		1	2	3	4	5	6	7	8	9
3			1	2	3	4	5	6	7	8
4				1	2	3	4	5	6	7
5					1	2	3	4	5	6
6						1	2	3	4	5
7							1	2	3	4
8								1	2	3
9									1	2
10										1

Maximum Weight of Part in Pounds							Std. Min. Per Occ.
2.0							.066
7.0	5.0						.069
10.0	5.0						.072
12.5	9.0	4.0					.076
14.5	12.0	8.5					.079
17.0	14.0	11.0	6.0				.083
18.5	16.0	14.5	10.0	6.5	5.0		.087
20.5	18.0	16.0	13.0	10.0	5.0		.091
22.0	20.0	18.0	16.5	13.0	10.0	5.0	.096

24.0	22.0	20.0	18.5	15.5	13.0	9.5	4.5												.100
26.0	24.0	22.5	20.5	18.0	16.0	12.5	10.0	5.5											.105
28.0	26.0	24.0	22.5	20.0	18.0	16.0	13.5	10.0	6.0										.110
30.0	28.0	26.0	24.0	22.0	20.5	18.5	16.0	13.5	10.0	7.5									.115
32.5	30.0	28.0	26.0	24.0	22.0	20.0	18.0	16.0	13.5	11.0	7.0	2.0							.120
35.0	32.5	30.5	28.0	26.0	24.0	22.5	21.0	19.0	16.0	14.5	11.0	7.0	3.0						.126
36.0	35.0	33.0	31.5	29.0	26.5	24.5	23.0	21.5	19.0	18.0	15.0	12.5	9.5	5.0					.132
38.0	36.5	35.0	34.5	32.5	29.0	27.0	25.0	24.0	21.5	20.5	18.0	15.5	13.0	10.0	6.0				.138
40.0	38.0	37.0	36.0	35.5	31.5	30.0	28.0	26.5	24.5	23.0	21.0	19.0	17.0	15.0	12.0	9.0	5.0		.145
41.5	39.5	38.5	37.0	36.5	33.5	34.0	30.0	29.0	27.0	25.5	23.0	21.0	19.5	17.5	15.0	12.5	9.0	5.0	.151
45.5	42.5	40.5	38.5	37.5	36.0	36.0	33.0	32.0	30.0	28.0	26.0	24.0	22.5	21.0	19.0	17.0	14.0	11.5	.159
51.0	46.0	43.0	40.0	39.0	38.5	37.0	35.5	34.0	32.0	30.0	28.5	27.0	25.0	23.0	21.5	20.0	17.5	15.0	.166
57.5	53.0	49.0	44.5	41.0	41.0	38.5	38.0	36.5	35.0	33.0	31.5	29.5	27.5	26.0	24.5	23.0	21.0	19.0	.174
63.0	59.0	55.0	50.5	47.5	44.5	40.0	40.0	39.0	37.0	35.5	34.0	32.5	30.5	29.0	27.5	25.5	24.0	22.0	.182
70.0	66.0	61.0	57.0	54.5	50.0	46.0	44.5	42.0	40.0	38.5	37.0	35.5	34.0	32.5	31.0	29.0	27.0	25.0	.191
75.0	75.0	68.0	64.0	60.0	56.0	52.5	48.5	45.0	43.0	41.0	39.5	38.0	37.0	35.5	34.0	32.0	30.0	28.5	.200
		75.0	69.5	65.5	62.0	58.5	55.0	51.0	48.0	44.5	42.5	40.5	39.0	38.0	37.0	35.0	33.5	32.0	.209
			75.0	75.0	69.0	65.0	61.5	57.5	54.5	50.5	47.0	44.0	42.0	40.5	39.0	38.0	37.0	35.0	.219
					75.0	75.0	68.0	64.5	61.0	57.0	54.0	50.0	47.0	44.0	42.0	41.0	39.0	38.0	.229
							75.0	71.0	67.5	64.0	60.0	57.0	53.5	50.0	47.0	44.5	42.5	40.5	.240
									75.0	70.5	67.5	64.0	60.0	57.0	53.5	50.5	48.0	44.5	.251
											75.0	71.5	67.5	64.0	61.0	58.0	55.0	51.0	.263
												75.0	75.0	71.0	67.5	65.0	61.0	58.0	.275
														75.0	75.0	75.0	68.0	65.0	.288
																	75.0	75.0	.302

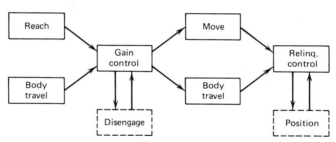

Figure 235　Basic elements of work. Building block concept for developing "Basic Data" and "Universal Data."

All of the blocks shown in Figure 235 were the building blocks that were used for parts handling elements, and basic data were determined for each of these blocks. The next step was to combine the time values that are shown in the solid line blocks into the various combinations in which they might actually be performed, thus forming the Universal Data for the parts handling elements. The basic disengage values and the position values were also used as universals.

Table 49 is an example of a Universal Data time table for a casting part handling element, that is, for the element "body travel to the part and body travel with the part." Similar data tables are available for parts handling for bar stock and sheet metal, as well as data for machine manipulation, clamping and unclamping, gaging, and other similar operations. This table also takes into consideration the variable of the weight of the casting handled. The table covers all combinations of distances to the part and distances with the part, to and including 10 feet, and covers casting weights up to and including 75 pounds.

Table 50.　Universal Data for Positioning Part in Fixture. The Variables are "The Number of Positions" and "Maximum Weight of Part in Pounds"

John Deere Data						
Position Casting in Fixture						
Max. Wt. of Part in Lbs.						No. of Positions
0–15	75					None
	0–10	45	75			Single
			0–10	56	75	Multiple
.003	.010	.015	.020	.030	.040	
Std. Mins. Per Occ.						

Table 50 contains the Universal Data for the element "position casting in fixture." Fixtures are classified into three basic types:

1. Those that require no positioning.
2. Those that require a single positioning.
3. Those that require multiple positioning.

The weight of the part is also incorporated in this table. Thus, Table 50 shows the "Standard Minutes per Occurrence" for the various types of positioning and for various part weights.

The procedure for constructing an Operational Data time table will be described. Assume that Operational Data for the element "part to fixture from skid" for a specific machine or battery of similar machines is to be established. The layout of the workplace requires 3 feet of body travel to the part and 4 feet of body travel with the part. The weight of the part ranges from 2 to75 pounds.

The horizontal and vertical dotted lines in Table 49 are used to facilitate the explanation. The horizontal line extends from "3" feet on the left "Maximum distance of body travel to part in feet" to "4" feet located under "Maximum distance of body travel with part in feet" at the top. The vertical dotted lines extends down to "5.0," which is the "Maximum weight of part in pounds." The time corresponding to the 3-foot body travel to the part and the 4-foot body travel with the part when the weight of the part is 5 pounds is .091 minute per occurrence as shown in the vertical column on the right. The time values range from .091 to .229 minute for weights varying from 5 to 75 pounds.

Table 51 shows how the times from two universals are combined. The time values shown in the left-hand column "Reference Line" are taken from the Table 49 column "Standard Minutes per Occurrence;" that is, .091 to .229. The upper portion of the table is the positioning table (Table 50) with the time values varying from .003 to .040 minute. By adding together the data in these two reference lines the data in the body of the table are obtained. For example, .091 plus .003 gives .094, the first value shown in the table. Just below it is .096 plus .003, which gives .099. This illustrates the procedure that is used to construct an Operational Data table from the two Universal Data tables. Table 52 is the completed Operational Data time table with the reference lines removed. This table provides data for establishing the time standards for the part handling element "Body travel to the part on the skid, pick up part and carry it to the fixture and position it in the fixture if positioning is called for." The fixed elements are "Three feet of body travel to the part" and "Four feet of body travel with the part." The variables that this table can accommodate are the "Number of positions" and the "Weight of the part."

Operational Data time tables include personal and fatigue allowances. Most machines and work places in Deere plants would have more or less fixed locations for skids for parts to be machined and for skids containing finished parts. Thus, a battery of similar machines such as drill presses or lathes would have identical layouts and

Table 51. Table Showing How the Universal Data for the Part Handling (Table 49) is Combined with the Universal Data for the Positioning Part (Table 50). The Left-Hand Column Time Data Are Added to the Positioning Time Data at the Upper Part of the Table to Give the Operational Data for the Element ''Part to Fixture from Skid''

		John Deere Data						
A26 Part to Jig or Fixture From Skid Element Ends: Release of Part								
		Max. Wt. of Part in Lbs.						No. of Positions
		0–15	75					None
Max. Wt. of Pt. in Lbs.	Ref. Line		0–10	45	75			Single
					0–10	56	75	Multiple
		.003	.010	.015	.020	.030	.040	Ref. Line
5.0 10.0 13.0	.091 .096 .100	.094 .099	.101 .106	.106 .111	.111	.121	.131	
16.0 18.0 20.5	.105 .110 .115							
22.0 24.0 26.5	.120 .126 .132							
29.0 31.5 33.5	.138 .145 .151							
36.0 38.5 41.0	.159 .166 .174							
44.5 50.0 56.0	.182 .191 .200							
62.0 69.0 75.0	.209 .219 .229							
		Std. Mins. Per Occ.						

Table 52. Operational Data Time Table for Element "Part to Fixture from Skid." The Variables are "Maximum Weight of Part" and "Number of Positions"

John Deere Data
Drill Press

Skids: 25% Waist

A26   Part to Jig or Fixture From
Skid Preceded by Place in Skid

Element Ends: Release of Part

Max. Wt. of Part in Lbs.						No. of Positions
0–15	75					None
	0–10	45	75			Single
			0–10	56	75	Multiple
Max. Wt. of Part in Lbs.						
5.0	.094	.101	.106	.111	.121	.131
10.0	.099	.106	.111	.116	.126	.136
13.0	.103	.110	.115	.120	.130	.140
16.0	.108	.115	.120	.125	.135	.145
18.0	.113	.120	.125	.130	.140	.150
20.5	.118	.125	.130	.135	.145	.155
22.0	.123	.130	.135	.140	.150	.160
24.0	.129	.136	.141	.146	.156	.166
26.5	.135	.142	.147	.152	.162	.172
29.0	.141	.148	.153	.158	.168	.178
31.5	.148	.155	.160	.165	.175	.185
33.5	.154	.161	.166	.171	.181	.191
36.0	.162	.169	.174	.179	.189	.199
38.5	.169	.176	.181	.186	.196	.206
41.0	.177	.184	.189	.194	.204	.214
44.5	.185	.192	.197	.202	.212	.222
50.0	.194	.201	.206	.211	.221	.231
56.0	.203	.210	.216	.220	.230	.240
62.0	.212	.219	.224	.229	.239	.249
69.0	.222	.229	.234	.239	.249	.259
75.0	.232	.239	.244	.249	.259	.269

Std. Mins. Per Occ.

397

one table (such as Table 52) would serve all of these machines insofar as determining the time for this element is concerned.

Methods Reference Tables

One of the important advantages of standard data is the ability to predetermine time standards. To do this, however, it is necessary to know exactly how the operation will be performed. Deere has developed (a) Methods Reference Tables, which are an integral part of their operational standard data for determining the economical method for an operation, and (b) Mechanical Data Sheets, which contain the economical mechanical method for each operation. Standard data makes it possible to apply time values to all possible manual methods of performing the range of operations covered by the Operational Data. Thus, it is possible to determine which method is most economical. Table 53 is an example of one part of the standard data for bar shears. This table contains variables similar to those that appear in the standard data time tables except that the answers from this table represent a method rather than a time value.

This table is used to determine the number of bars that will be cut at the same time. The variables are the width and the thickness of the bars. If the bar is 2 inches

Table 53. The Number of Bars Cut at a Time

Flat, Square and Plate

Max. Width of Bar in Inches	Maximum Thickness of Bar in Inches				
$1/2$ $3/4$ 1	$5/16$ $1/4$ $3/16$	$1/2$ $3/4$ $7/16$	1		
$1\,1/4$ $1\,1/2$ $1\,3/4$		$7/16$ $3/8$	1 $7/8$ $1/2$	$1\,1/4$ 1 1	$1\,3/4$ $1\,3/4$
2 $2\,1/4$ $2\,1/2$			$1/2$	1 $5/8$ $5/8$	$1\,3/4$ $1\,3/4$ $1\,3/4$
$2\,3/4$ 3 $3\,1/2$				$5/8$ $5/8$ $1/2$	$1\,3/4$ $1\,3/4$ $1\,3/4$
4 Over 4				$3/8$	$1\,3/4$ $1\,3/4$
	5	4	3	2	1
	Number of Bars Cut at a Time				

JOB DETAIL AND STANDARD SHEET	FACTORY	PART NUMBER	OPERATION NO	PAGE
O·1627C·STOCK·1·78 PRINTED IN U.S.A	JD HARVESTER WKS	H 87257	50	1

DEPT. NO.	MACHINE NO.	OPERATION DESCRIPTION		STD. CODE	LABOR GRADE
325	32588	MILL 2 WOODRUFF KEYWAY(S) IN LINE, FILE (2) KEYWAY(S)		25	6

	DATE	STARTING DIMENSIONS		T.O. HOURS	
29 AUG		1.360 RND. X 41.00 JDM 1045CD 17.37#			

CODE	ELEMENTAL DESCRIPTION	D/R/X	OCC/CYCLE	STD. MIN/CYCLE
A2131	PART FROM FIXTURE AND PLACE ON MACHINE TABLE	D	1/1	0.048
M18 G29o	BRUSH CHIPS FROM V BLOCKS,END STOP AND/OR LOCATOR-WALK BETWEEN AS NECESSARY	D	1/1	0.130
A2135	PART TO FIXTURE FROM MACHINE TABLE PRECEDED BY WORK AT MACHINE	D	1/1	0.057
B35	ENGAGE LOCATOR PIN	D	1/1	0.024
E1228	PUSH BUTTON TO MAGNETIZE	D	1/1	0.014
B10	CLOSE STAR KNOB	D	1/1	0.040
E1229	PUSH BUTTON TO START CYCLE	D	1/1	0.006
	HEAD TO AND/OR TRAVERSE TABLE TO-MILL KEYWAYS MT=0.331	MT	1/1	X.XXX
	C.6884 INCHES LONG			
MC3-4	FILE (2) KEYWAYS	R	1/1	0.138
M12	BLOW OFF KEYWAYS IN FINISHED PART	R	1/1	0.070
A1780	STOCK ASIDE PART(S) TO SKID DROP	R	1/ 1	0.073
A2143	STOCK UP PART(S) TO MACHINE	R	1/ 1	0.075
F26	GAGE WITH WIDTH & DEPTH GAGE	R	1/10	0.022
F51	GAGE WITH STEEL TAPE OR SCALE 4 POINTS	R	1/100	0.004
A118	TALLY COUNT	R	1/10	0.004
	HEAD TO AND/OR TABLE TRAVERSE OUT-MAGNET OFF DURING MT=0.163	MT		
B10	OPEN STAR KNOB	D	1/1	0.040
B35	DISENGAGE LOCATOR PIN	D	1/1	0.024
CL	CHANGE LOADS	D		0.007
	IDA			0.261
	A.C.T.S. = 1.450			

THE APPROVED METHOD IS AS SHOWN ON THIS FORM AND NO CHANGE IN METHOD MAY BE MADE BY THE EMPLOYEE WITHOUT SECURING APPROVAL OF THE COMPANY AS INDICATED BY THE ISSUANCE OF A REVISION.

W A F	PCS/CYCLE	TOTAL STD MIN/CYCLE
	1	1.037

REMARKS:
REASON FOR CHANGE * METHOD CHANGE

STANDARD HOURS/100PCS
1.8000

Figure 236   Job detail and standard sheet.

wide and ½-inch thick, the method is to cut three bars at one time. The Job Detail and Standards Sheet is the form that contains a complete description of the manual part of the operation (Fig. 236).

Mechanical Data Sheets

In addition to predetermining the preferred manual method it is necessary to predetermine and specify the correct method pertaining to the mechanical aspects of the operation. This is done by the Process and Tool Engineering Department at the time the routing is prepared for each part. All of the necessary information is recorded on a form which is called the Mechanical Data Sheet (Fig. 237). The basic function of this data sheet is to provide specific instructions for performing the preplanned method. It serves the same purpose for the mechanical part of the operation that the Job Detail and Standard Sheet does for the manual part of the operation. The Mechanical Data Sheet includes the machine tool, the tooling, equipment, jigs, fixture, gages, templates, speeds, feeds, machine time, and all other information related to the mechanical aspects of the operation.

Date (Orig) 4 JUNE	By SONCARTY		Mach. No.	Part No. H-89450
Date (Rev.) 31 MAR	By AERN	Decision 82239	Mach. Code 33029	Oper. No. 10
Revision REVISED TO SUPPLEMENT OF 23 MAR				
Mach. JCL ATL			Part Name SHAFT - INPUT	

Coolant Yes [X] No [ ] Type _____

Air Pressure _____

Mat'l H-89451 FORGING

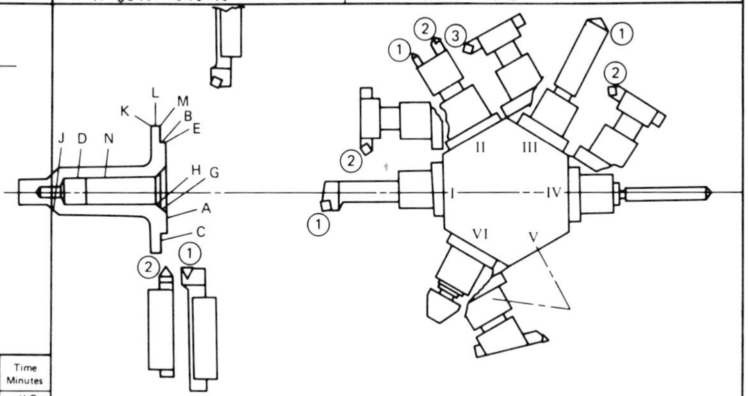

Tool Position	Speed rpm	Feed ipr–ipm	Travel Inches	Time Element Description	Time Minutes	Operation Description	Tool Position	Life Pieces	Tool or Gage JDH Number	Tool or Gage Description	Tot. Qty.
I	380	75	400		46				508685	CHUCK JAWS	1/SET
RCS	380	57	250		40						
FCS	380	30	112		30					TNMG-432E (C-91) INSERT	3
II	70	5	48		96				N34C-26-6	PTFNR-16-4 INSERT HLDR	1
III	165	20	150		75	FACE C TO RGH FORM B	FCS ①	370		A-3058 TOOL BLOCK	3
IV	540	45	164		36	CHAMFER K	FCS ①	350	N34C-26-4	TNMG-322 (C-91) INSERT	1
V	760	70	20		05				96563	TE-10-3C INSERT HOLDER	1
VI	83	15	41		27					A-3058 TOOL BLOCK	1
				R+¢NX	55	FACE A	RCS	210	N33-15-1	SNG 433(C-91) INSERT	1
									045160	KSFR-164C INSERT HLDR	1
										A-3058 TOOL BLOCK	1

TOTAL MACHINE TIME, MINUTES 4 10

M-4943   NOTE: The approved method is as shown on this form and no change in method may be made by the employee without securing approval of the company as indicated by the issuance of a revision.

Figure 237 Mechanical data sheet.

Figure 237 is an example of a Mechanical Data Sheet for a semiautomatic lathe operation. The top of the sheet shows the heading information, such as the part number, operation number, and machine code. The upper right-hand side shows the part and the surfaces to be machined as well as the turret and the location of the tools. The lower left-hand side shows the tool positions, the speeds, feeds, travel in inches, and the machine time. The lower right-hand area lists the operations, tools, and gages. In addition to providing the information required for presetting time standards the Mechanical Data Sheet also serves as instructions for the operator, as an aid in training new operators, and as documentation of the approved method.

Example of Use of Operational Data for Drilling

Assume the problem is to determine the time for the operation "Drill one ½-inch hole in cast iron bracket #721." The information needed for determining the time for a drilling operation ordinarily would be obtained from (a) drawing of the part, (b) Job Detail and Standard Sheet, and (c) Mechanical Data Sheet. However, the information needed is given below.

DRILL HOLE IN CAST IRON BRACKET

Operation:	Drill hole 0.500-inch diameter, depth of hole 1.50 inches, blind hole
Part:	Cast iron bracket #721—weight 10 pounds
Machine:	Single spindle drill with power feed
Fixture:	Single position

Elements

1. Get casting from skid and place in fixture — Three-foot body travel to skid (*C* to *A* in Fig. 238). Four foot body travel with casting to fixture (A to B)

2. Drill ½-inch hole in casting. Single position fixture — Drill speed 400 RPM, feed 0.025 inches per revolution of drill

3. Remove casting from fixture and dispose onto skid — Four-foot body travel with casting to skid (*B* to *C*)

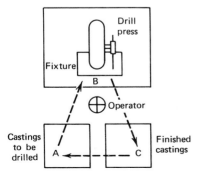

Figure 238 Layout of work place—single spindle drill.

Table 54. Operational Data Time Table for 3-Foot Body Travel to Part and 4-Foot Body Travel with Part

Max. Wt. of Part in Lbs.	Max. Wt. of Part in Lbs.					No. of Positions
	0–15	75				None
		0–10	45	75		Single
				0–10	56	75	Multiple
5.0	.094	.101	.106	.111	.121	.131	
10.0	.099	.106	.111	.116	.126	.136	
13.0	.103	.110	.115	.120	.130	.140	
16.0	.106	.115	.120	.125	.135	.145	
18.0	.113	.120	.125	.130	.140	.150	
20.5	.118	.125	.130	.135	.145	.155	
22.0	.123	.130	.135	.140	.150	.160	
24.0	.129	.136	.141	.146	.156	.166	
26.5	.135	.142	.147	.152	.162	.172	
29.0	.141	.146	.153	.158	.168	.178	
31.5	.148	.155	.160	.165	.175	.185	
33.5	.154	.161	.166	.171	.181	.191	
36.0	.162	.169	.174	.179	.189	.199	
38.5	.169	.176	.181	.186	.196	.206	
41.0	.177	.184	.189	.194	.204	.214	
44.5	.185	.192	.197	.202	.212	.222	
50.0	.194	.201	.206	.211	.221	.231	
56.0	.203	.210	.216	.220	.230	.240	
62.0	.212	.219	.224	.229	.239	.249	
69.0	.222	.229	.234	.239	.249	.259	
75.0	.232	.239	.244	.249	.259	.269	

Std. Min. Per Occ.

Formula for Calculating Drill Time. The time to drill a hole on a drill press with a power feed can be calculated when the speed and feed of the drill are known.

$$D = \frac{L}{F \times R}$$

D—Cutting time in minutes

F—Feed of drill in inches per revolution of drill

L—Total length the drill must travel[2]

R—Speed of drill in revolutions per minute

[2] When a hole is drilled completely through a flat piece of material using a fluted drill, the lead of the drill must be added to the length of the hole to obtain the total travel of the drill. In the case of a blind hole such as this one the total length of the drill travel is the same as the length of the hole. For information about the length of the lead for different drill diameters see a Machinist's Handbook.

SOLUTION. The time for handling elements 1 and 3 can be obtained from Operational Data Tables 54 and 55 and the drilling time can be calculated using the formula above.

Table 55. Operational Data Time Table: Part from Fixture and Place on Skid. Companion Element = 12-inch Reach to Part and 4-Foot Body Travel with Part

Max. Wt. of Part in Lb.	Std. Min. Per Occ.	Max. Wt. of Part in Lb.	Std. Min. Per Occ.
2.0	.058	25.5	.097
6.0	.061	27.5	.102
10.0	.064	30.0	.106
11.5	.066	33.0	.111
14.0	.069	37.5	.116
15.5	.072	42.5	.121
17.0	.075	48.5	.126
18.5	.078	55.0	.132
20.0	.082	60.0	.138
21.0	.085	65.5	.144
23.0	.089	71.0	.151
24.0	.093	75.0	.157

Elements

1. Get casting from skid and place in fixture   0.106
   (Weight of casting 10 pounds, single position in fixture, 3-foot body travel to part, 4-foot body travel with part)
   Use Table 54 Column 1 and Column 3

2. Drill ½-inch hole in cast iron bracket #721   0.150
   (Depth of hole 1.50 inches—blind hole, speed of drill 400 rpm, feed 0.025-inch per revolution)

$$D = \frac{L}{F \times R} = \frac{1.50}{0.025 \times 400} = 0.150$$

3. Remove casting from fixture and dispose onto skid   0.064
   (12-inch reach for part and 4-foot body travel with part).
   Use Table 55.
                                                                        _____
                                                    Total time   0.320

The time for the operation "Drill Hole in Cast Iron Bracket" is 0.320 minute per piece. This time includes personal and fatigue allowances since such allowances are included in the tables. Allowances covering the drilling element and possibly delay allowances might also be added. Since this example is intended to illustrate the use of the Operational Data time tables, the matter of allowances will not be dealt with here.

Computerized Standard Data

The availability of systems of standard data and mechanical data makes it possible to predetermine time standards as has just been demonstrated. This is done easily and quickly by the analyst referring to the values in the time tables and tabulating and adding applicable time values, thus obtaining the standard time for the operation. However, the work of the analyst can be performed by a computer.

During the past 12 years Deere has been using the computer to establish time standards as the basis for their incentive wage payment plan. At the present time 50 different types of operations are covered by their computer systems. These include machine shop, foundry, and forge shop operations. In fact, 45 percent of all their incentive standards are set by the computer.

The primary objective of the computerized standard data is to be able to preset incentive standards accurately and consistently prior to the first production run. The sequence of operations performed by the computer to establish time standards is as follows:

1. It selects the most economical method.
2. It selects the elements that are necessary for performing the most economical method.
3. It computes the standard time for each one of the elements.
4. It computes the time standard for the operation.
5. It prints a Job Detail and Standards Sheet that shows the elements in proper sequence, the time for each element, the total standard time in minutes per cycle, and the incentive standard in hours per 100 pieces.

Standard Data and Wage Incentives

Although standard data has many uses it is the heart of the Deere wage incentive plan. For an equitable wage incentive system to survive it must satisfy stringent requirements. The administration and control of such a system is one of management's most difficult tasks. Deere spent four years in the design and development phases of their Standard Hour Plan and in the preparation for the changeover from the piece-work system. They have successfully used their incentive plan for over 20 years.

At the time the standard hour plan was introduced their Senior Vice President in Charge of Manufacturing issued a formal statement on the incentive system to all factory managers. This was done to make sure that there would be no misunderstanding about how the incentive standards were to be established and how the plan was to be administered. This statement has served as a guide during the intervening years. The main points in the statement are given below.

1. All incentive standards will be established in the same consistent and accurate manner, whether to cover permanent conditions or special conditions for a limited period.
2. Any change made in design, equipment, material specifications, or manufacturing methods affecting an operation will be simultaneously reflected in either a revision or withdrawal of the incentive standard.
3. The Industrial Engineering Department will prepare a job detail card[3] containing all pertinent data on which the incentive standard was established. This card will be kept at the machine or work location during the time the operation is being performed.
4. An effective methods audit program will be established. This will consist of a careful and thorough comparison of the method shown on the job detail card with the method used by the operator.
5. Employees' time slips will be audited periodically to insure that proper practices are being followed.
6. A determined effort will be made to obtain the highest practical level of incentive coverage.
7. Incentive standards complaints will be promptly and thoroughly investigated and corrective action will be taken to insure that these complaints do not become written grievances.
8. A determined effort will be made to obtain the highest practical degree of standard data coverage.

---

[3] The "job detail card" has been replaced by the Job Detail Standard Sheet and the Mechanical Data Sheet.

WORK SAMPLING

Work sampling was first used by L. H. C. Tippett[1] in the British textile industry, and it was introduced into this country under the name of "ratio delay" in 1940. Work sampling is a fact-finding tool. In many cases, needed information about men or machines can be obtained in less time and at lower cost by this method than by other means.

Work sampling has three main uses: (1) *activity and delay sampling*—to measure the activities and delays of workers or machines—for example, to determine the percentage of the day that a person is working and the percentage that he or she is not working;[2] (2) *performance sampling*—to measure working time and nonworking time of a person on a manual task, and to establish a performance index or performance level for the person during his or her working time;[3] (3) *work measurement*—under certain circumstances, to measure a manual task, that is, to establish a time standard for an operation.

Work sampling is based upon the laws of probability. A sample taken at random from a large group tends to have the same pattern of distribution as the large group or universe. If the sample is large enough, the characteristics of the sample will differ but little from the characteristics of the group. *Sample* is the term used for this small number, and *population* or *universe* is the term used for the large group. Obtaining and analyzing only a part of the universe is known as *sampling*.

Simple Example of Work Sampling

The determination of the percentage of the working day that the operator or machine is working or idle is based on the theory that the percentage *number* of observations recording the worker or machine as idle is a reliable measure of the percentage *time* that the operation is in the delay state. The accuracy of the result is a function of the number of observations taken.

Briefly, the work sampling procedure in its simplest form consists of making observations at random intervals of one or more operators or machines and noting

[1] L. H. C. Tippett, "Statistical Methods in Textile Research. Uses of the Binominal and Poisson Distributions. A Snap-Reading Method of Making Time Studies of Machines and Operatives in Factory Surveys," *Shirley Institute Memoirs*, Vol. 13, pp. 35–93, November, 1934. Also, *Journal of the Textile Institute Transactions*, Vol. 26, pp. 51–55, 75, February, 1935.

[2] D. S. Correll and Ralph M. Barnes, "Industrial Application of the Ratio-Delay Method," *Advanced Management*, Vol. 15, No. 8 and No. 9, August and September, 1950.

[3] Ralph M. Barnes and Robert B. Andrews, "Performance Sampling in Work Measurement," *Journal of Industrial Engineering*, Vol. 6, No. 6, November–December, 1955.

whether they are working or idle. If the operator is working, he or she is given a tally mark under "working"; if idle, the worker is given a tally mark under "idle." The percentage of the day that the worker is idle is the ratio of the number of idle tally marks to the total number of idle and working tally marks.

In Fig. 239 there are 36 working observations and 4 idle observations, or a total of 40 observations. In this example the percentage of idle time is $4 \div 40 \times 100 = 10\%$. Working time is $36 \div 40 \times 100\% = 90\%$. If this study covered one operator for an 8-hour day, the results would indicate that the operator was idle 10 percent or 48 minutes of the day ($480 \times 0.10 = 48$), and was working 90 percent or 432 minutes of the day ($480 \times 0.90 = 432$).

State	Tally	Total
Working	⊞ ⊞ ⊞ ⊞ ⊞ ⊞ ⊞ |	36
Idle	||||	4

Figure 239 Tally of working time and idle time.

Explaining Work Sampling

Managers, supervisors, and operators should be familiar with the methods, procedures, and tools of the industrial engineer. The basic concepts of probability and random sampling should be understood before such studies are undertaken. Short training sessions which include demonstrations and which enable the participants to try work sampling for themselves are effective.

Figure 240 Work sampling demonstration panel.

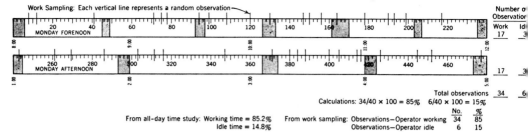

Calculations: 34/40 × 100 = 85%   6/40 × 100 = 15%

Total observations   34   6

	No.	%
From all-day time study: Working time = 85.2%	From work sampling: Observations—Operator working	34	85
Idle time = 14.8%	Observations—Operator idle	6	15

Figure 241 Simple work sampling study. Results of random observations shown on the bars represent one working day.

DEMONSTRATION OF THE WORK SAMPLING METHOD

The bars below represent to scale the 240 minutes of the forenoon and the afternoon for five working days-Monday through Friday-a full 40-hour (2400-minute) week. The results of a continuous time study of one operator for one week are shown. White = working time; black = idle time.

The total actual *working* time for the week from time study = 2035 minutes. The total *idle* time for the week from time study = 365 minutes.

$$\text{Percentage working time} = 2035/2400 \times 100 = 84.8\%$$
$$\text{Percentage idle time} = 365/2400 \times 100 = 15.2\%$$

Now see how you can obtain similar information by the use of random sampling. You can make your own random observations by following the instructions on Fig. 243.

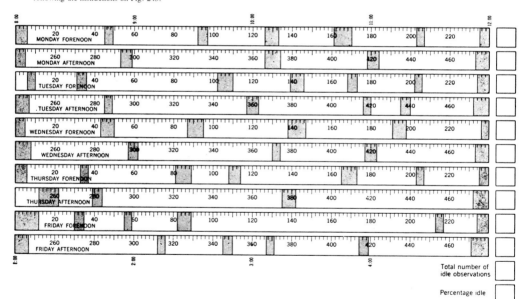

Total number of idle observations

Percentage idle

RESULTS

Count the number of times your marks intersect the black portion of the bars and post this number in the box at the end of the line. Then add the number of idle observations and divide this total by 200. This gives you the percentage of the week that the operator was idle by the random sampling procedure. Now compare your answer with the actual idle percentage of 15.2 percent, which was originally obtained by time study.

Figure 242 Demonstration of the work sampling method. Working time and idle time for one operator for five consecutive working days.

408

Figure 240 shows a panel with 480 blocks representing the 480 minutes of an 8-hour day arranged across the bottom of the board. The white blocks represent working time, and the colored blocks idle time. By drawing numbers from a hat or by the use of a random number table, it is possible to simulate a work sampling study.

Figure 241 shows the working time and idle time of one operator for one day as obtained from a continuous time study. The complete record is shown graphically by the two bars. The top bar is for the forenoon, the lower bar for the afternoon. White indicates working time and black indicates idle time. The results of the all-day time study show that the operator worked 85.2 percent of the day and was idle 14.8 percent of the day.

Now suppose we obtain similar information by means of work sampling instead of by time study. We might take 480 small pieces of paper and number them from 1 to 480 to represent the 480 minutes in the eight-hour day. These slips of paper might be placed in a hat and mixed thoroughly. Then a number might be drawn and a mark placed on the bar at the time corresponding to the number on the slip of paper. Note that 40 such ''random observations'' have been made and recorded on the two bars in Fig. 241. Those marks that fall on the white bars represent observations of the operator while working, and those marks that fall on the black bars represent observations of the operator while idle. There were a total of 6 idle observations during the day. Therefore 6 divided by 40, multiplied by 100, equals 15 percent. This then is the percentage of the day during which the operator was idle as determined by work sampling. This result corresponds closely to the 14.8 percent idle time as determined by time study.

Figure 242 shows the results of an all-day time study made of the operator during five consecutive 8-hour working days. Working time and idle time are shown as previously described. It is suggested that you determine the percentage of idle time and working time for this operator for the week using the random sampling method—just follow the instructions given in Figs. 242 and 243. The results can then be compared with the data obtained from the all-day time study for the week, as shown in Fig. 242.

Random sampling requires that there be no bias in the sampling process. Each part comprising the universe must have as much chance of being drawn as any other. It is important that the concept of randomness be understood and carefully followed in work sampling studies.[4]

The Normal Distribution Curve

The normal distribution curve is typical of the kind of frequency distribution which is of importance in work sampling because it represents graphically the probability of

---

[4] There is evidence to show that the intervals may be regular if the activity or process being observed is random. See Harold Davis, ''A Mathematical Evaluation of a Work Sampling Technique,'' *Naval Research Logistics Quarterly,* Vol. 2, No. 1 and 2, pp. 11–117, March–June, 1955.

the occurrence of certain chance phenomena. The normal curve is significant because of the relationship of the area under the curve between ordinates at various distances on either side of the mean ordinant. In the curve on the left in Fig. 244, the shaded area represents 1 sigma, or one standard deviation on either side of the mean ordinate *A*. This area will always be 68.27 percent of the total area under the curve. The area at 2 sigma equals 95.45 percent, and the area at 3 sigma equals 99.73 percent of the total area.

Confidence Level

At the outset it is necessary to decide what level of confidence is desired in the final work sampling results. The most common confidence interval is 95 percent. The area under the curve at 2 sigma or two standard deviations is 95.45 percent, which, if rounded off, gives 95 percent. This means that the probability is that 95 percent of the time the random observations will represent the facts, and 5 percent of the time they will not. One sigma would give a confidence interval of 68 percent (68.27 percent rounded off to 68 percent). This means that the data obtained by random sampling has a 68 percent chance of representing the facts, and that it will be in error 32 percent of the time.

Make a photocopy of Fig. 242 and Fig. 243. Superimpose Fig. 243 over Fig. 242 and place a sheet of carbon paper between them. Draw *at random* 20 vertical marks across each of the ten lines shown above. Do not space the marks at regular intervals—space them haphazardly along the entire length of the line. These marks represent 20 random observations made of the operator during the forenoon and the afternoon. Now turn to bottom of Fig. 242.

Figure 243   Demonstration of work sampling method—work sheet.

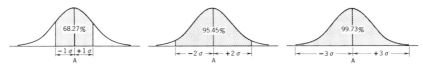

Figure 244 Areas under the normal curves.

The formula for determining the sample size for a confidence level of 68 percent or 1 sigma is

$$Sp = \sqrt{\frac{p(1-p)}{N}}$$

where S = desired relative accuracy
p = percentage expressed as a decimal
N = number of random observations (sample size)

Accuracy of Work Sampling Measurement

The accuracy of work sampling results deserves more than passing consideration, for when we determine the degree of accuracy desired, we are in effect determining the number of observations required. The number of observations, of course, affects the time and cost of making the study. The purpose of the work sampling study will suggest the degree of accuracy of the results desired, but there may be considerable latitude in specifying accuracy.

In designing the work sampling study the analyst will size up the entire situation. He will want results that will be satisfactory from an accuracy viewpoint and at the same time will not require an unreasonably large number of observations. Fortunately, in a work sampling study the analyst can determine in advance the number of observations needed for a given degree of accuracy.

One of the things the analyst will consider, consciously or unconsciously, is the inherent variability of the men, machines, or processes being measured. A department that is operating week in and week out with a steady volume of output, with raw material of uniform quality, low labor turnover, and good supervision, presents an ideal subject for work sampling.

For many kinds of measurement an accuracy of ±5 percent is considered satisfactory. This is sometimes referred to as the standard error of the percentage. For the following illustrations we will assume that a confidence level of 95 percent and an accuracy of ±5 percent are satisfactory. Also assuming that the binomial distribution is used as the basis for determining the error, then the formula for determining the number of observations required is

$$Sp = 2\sqrt{\frac{p(1-p)}{N}} \qquad (1)$$

where S = desired relative accuracy

   p = percentage occurrence of an activity or delay being measured, expressed as a percentage of the total number of observations or as a decimal, that is, $15\% = 0.15$

   N = total number of random observations (sample size)

Even if the desired accuracy is known, there are still two unknowns in the equation: p, the percentage occurrence, and N, the total number of observations. In order to find N, p is generally assumed or estimated by a preliminary study.

EXAMPLE   Suppose we want to determine the percentage of idle time of the automatic screw machines in a department by work sampling. Further, assume that a confidence level of 95 percent and an accuracy of ±5 percent have been decided upon. We want to know how many random observations will be needed to give us the desired results. Before we can use equation 1 it is necessary to estimate the value of p. In other words, a trial study would be made of the screw machines to get a first estimate as to the percentage of idle time.

Suppose that a total of 100 observations were made, and in this preliminary study 25 observations showed the machines to be idle. The percentage of idle time would be 25 percent ($25 \div 100 \times 100 = 25\%$).

We are now ready to calculate N. Where $p = 25\% = 0.25$, and $S = \pm 5\% = \pm 0.05$,

$$Sp = 2\sqrt{\frac{P(1-p)}{N}}$$

$$0.05p = 2\sqrt{\frac{p(1-p)}{N}}$$

$$0.0025p^2 = 4\left[\frac{p(1-p)}{N}\right] = \frac{4p(1-p)}{N}$$

$$N = \frac{4p(1-p)}{0.0025p^2} = \frac{4(1-p)}{0.0025p} = \frac{1600(1-p)}{p}$$

$$= \frac{1600(1-0.25)}{0.25} = 4800$$

Table 56 or the alignment chart in Fig. 245 could be used instead of the formula to determine the number of observations.

After the work sampling study is under way and 500 observations have been made, a new calculation might be made in order to check our original value for N. Assume that the results were as follows:

Observations of machines working	350
Observations of machines idle	150
Total observations	500

   $150 \div 500 \times 100 = 30\%$ idle time

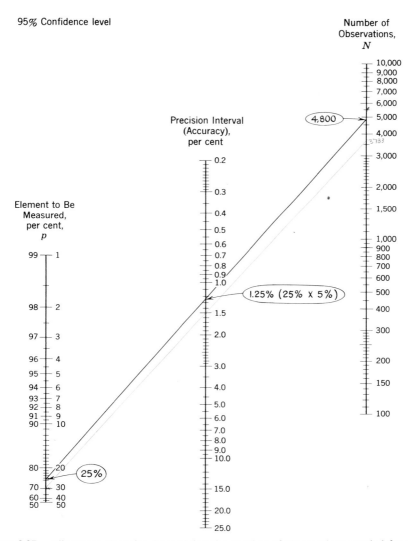

Figure 245 Alignment chart for determining the number of observations needed for a given degree of accuracy and value of p, 95% confidence level. (Courtesy Johns-Manville Corporation.)

413

Table 56. Table for Determining the Number of Observations for a Given Degree of Accuracy and Value of p, 95% Confidence Level

Percent of Total Time Occupied by Activity or Delay, p	Degree of Accuracy									
	± 1	± 2	± 3	± 4	± 5	± 6	± 7	± 8	± 9	± 10
1	3,960,000	990,000	440,000	247,500	158,400	110,000	80,800	61,900	48,900	39,600
2	1,960,000	490,000	217,800	122,500	78,400	54,400	40,000	30,600	24,200	19,600
3	1,293,300	323,300	143,700	80,800	51,700	35,900	26,400	20,200	16,000	12,900
4	960,000	240,000	106,700	60,000	38,400	26,700	19,600	15,000	11,900	9,600
5	760,000	190,000	84,400	47,500	30,400	21,100	15,500	11,900	9,390	7,600
6	626,700	156,700	69,600	39,200	25,100	17,400	12,800	9,790	7,740	6,270
7	531,400	132,900	59,000	33,200	21,300	14,800	10,800	8,300	6,560	5,310
8	460,000	115,000	51,100	28,800	18,400	12,800	9,380	7,190	5,680	4,600
9	404,400	101,100	44,900	25,300	16,200	11,200	8,250	6,320	5,000	4,040
10	360,000	90,000	40,000	22,500	14,400	10,000	7,340	5,630	4,450	3,600
11	323,600	80,900	36,000	20,200	12,900	8,990	6,600	5,060	4,000	3,240
12	293,300	73,300	32,600	18,300	11,700	8,150	5,980	4,580	3,620	2,930
13	267,700	66,900	29,700	16,700	10,700	7,440	5,460	4,180	3,310	2,680
14	245,700	61,400	27,300	15,400	9,830	6,830	5,010	3,840	3,040	2,460
15	226,700	56,700	25,200	14,200	9,070	6,300	4,620	3,540	2,800	2,270
16	210,000	52,500	23,300	13,100	8,400	5,830	4,280	3,280	2,590	2,100
17	195,300	48,800	21,700	12,200	7,810	5,420	3,980	3,050	2,410	1,950
18	182,200	45,600	20,200	11,400	7,290	5,060	3,720	2,850	2,250	1,820
19	170,500	42,600	18,900	10,700	6,820	4,740	3,480	2,660	2,110	1,710
20	160,000	40,000	17,800	10,000	6,400	4,440	3,260	2,500	1,980	1,600
21	150,500	37,600	16,700	9,400	6,020	4,180	3,070	2,350	1,860	1,510
22	141,800	35,500	15,800	8,860	5,670	3,940	2,890	2,220	1,750	1,420
23	133,900	33,500	14,900	8,370	5,360	3,720	2,730	2,090	1,650	1,340
24	126,700	31,700	14,100	7,920	5,070	3,520	2,580	1,980	1,560	1,270
25	120,000	30,000	13,300	7,500	4,800	3,330	2,450	1,880	1,480	1,200
26	113,800	28,500	12,600	7,120	4,550	3,160	2,320	1,780	1,410	1,140
27	108,100	27,000	12,000	6,760	4,330	3,000	2,210	1,690	1,340	1,080
28	102,900	25,700	11,400	6,430	4,110	2,860	2,100	1,610	1,270	1,030
29	97,900	24,500	10,900	6,120	3,920	2,720	2,000	1,530	1,210	980
30	93,300	23,300	10,400	5,830	3,730	2,590	1,900	1,460	1,150	935
31	89,000	22,300	9,890	5,570	3,560	2,470	1,820	1,390	1,100	890
32	85,000	21,300	9,440	5,310	3,400	2,360	1,730	1,330	1,050	850
33	81,200	20,300	9,000	5,080	3,250	2,260	1,660	1,270	1,000	810
34	77,600	19,400	8,630	4,850	3,110	2,160	1,580	1,210	960	775
35	74,300	18,600	8,250	4,640	2,970	2,060	1,520	1,160	915	745
36	71,100	17,800	7,900	4,440	2,840	1,980	1,450	1,110	880	710
37	68,100	17,000	7,570	4,260	2,720	1,890	1,400	1,060	840	680
38	65,300	16,300	7,250	4,080	2,610	1,810	1,330	1,020	805	655
39	62,600	15,600	6,950	3,910	2,500	1,740	1,280	980	775	625
40	60,000	15,000	6,670	3,750	2,400	1,670	1,220	940	740	600
41	57,600	14,400	6,400	3,600	2,300	1,600	1,170	900	710	575
42	55,200	13,800	6,140	3,450	2,210	1,530	1,130	865	680	550
43	53,000	13,300	5,890	3,310	2,120	1,470	1,080	830	655	530
44	50,900	12,700	5,660	3,180	2,040	1,410	1,040	795	630	510
45	48,900	12,200	5,430	3,060	1,960	1,360	1,000	765	605	490
46	47,000	11,700	5,220	2,940	1,880	1,300	960	735	580	470
47	45,100	11,300	5,010	2,820	1,800	1,250	920	705	555	450
48	43,300	10,800	4,810	2,710	1,730	1,200	885	675	535	435
49	41,600	10,400	4,630	2,600	1,670	1,160	850	650	515	415
50	40,000	10,000	4,440	2,500	1,600	1,110	815	625	495	400

Table 56. *(Continued)*

Percent of Total Time Occupied by Activity or Delay, p	Degree of Accuracy									
	±1	±2	±3	±4	±5	±6	±7	±8	±9	±10
51	38,430	9,610	4,270	2,400	1,540	1,070	785	600	475	385
52	36,920	9,230	4,100	2,310	1,480	1,030	755	575	455	370
53	35,470	8,870	9,860	2,220	1,420	985	725	555	435	355
54	34,070	8,520	3,790	2,130	1,360	945	695	530	420	340
55	32,730	8,180	3,640	2,050	1,310	910	670	510	405	325
56	31,430	7,860	3,490	1,960	1,260	870	640	490	390	315
57	30,180	7,550	3,350	1,890	1,210	840	615	470	375	300
58	28,970	7,240	3,220	1,810	1,160	805	590	450	360	290
59	27,800	6,950	3,090	1,740	1,110	770	565	435	345	280
60	26,670	6,670	2,960	1,670	1,070	740	545	415	330	265
61	25,570	6,390	2,840	1,600	1,020	710	520	400	315	255
62	24,520	6,130	2,720	1,530	980	680	500	385	305	245
63	23,490	5,870	2,610	1,470	940	650	480	365	290	235
64	22,500	5,630	2,500	1,410	900	625	460	350	275	225
65	21,540	5,390	2,390	1,350	860	600	440	335	265	215
66	20,610	5,150	2,290	1,290	825	570	420	320	255	205
67	19,700	4,925	2,190	1,230	790	545	400	305	245	195
68	18,820	4,705	2,090	1,180	750	520	385	295	230	190
69	17,970	4,490	2,000	1,120	720	500	365	280	220	180
70	17,140	4,285	1,900	1,070	685	475	350	265	210	170
71	16,340	4,085	1,815	1,020	655	455	335	255	200	165
72	15,560	3,890	1,730	970	620	430	315	245	190	155
73	14,790	3,700	1,640	925	590	410	300	230	180	145
74	14,050	3,510	1,560	880	560	390	285	220	175	140
75	13,330	3,330	1,480	835	535	370	270	210	165	135
76	12,630	3,160	1,400	790	505	350	255	195	155	125
77	11,950	2,990	1,330	745	480	330	245	185	145	120
78	11,280	2,820	1,253	705	450	315	230	175	140	110
79	10,630	2,660	1,180	665	425	295	215	165	130	105
80	10,000	2,500	1,110	625	400	275	205	155	125	100
81	9,380	2,345	1,040	585	375	260	190	145	115	94
82	8,780	2,195	975	550	350	245	180	135	110	88
83	8,190	2,050	910	510	325	225	165	130	100	82
84	7,620	1,905	845	475	305	210	155	120	94	76
85	7,060	1,765	785	440	280	195	145	110	87	71
86	6,510	1,630	725	405	260	180	130	100	80	65
87	5,980	1,495	665	375	240	165	120	93	74	60
88	5,450	1,360	605	340	220	150	110	85	67	55
89	4,940	1,235	550	310	200	135	100	77	61	49
90	4,440	1,110	495	280	175	125	90	69	55	44
91	3,960	990	440	250	160	110	80	62	49	40
92	3,480	870	385	220	140	96	70	54	43	35
93	3,010	750	335	190	120	83	61	47	37	30
94	2,550	640	285	160	100	71	52	40	31	26
95	2,110	525	234	130	85	59	43	33	26	21
96	1,670	420	185	105	67	46	34	26	21	17
97	1,240	310	140	78	50	34	25	19	15	12
98	815	205	91	51	33	23	17	13	10	8
99	405	100	45	25	16	11	8	6	5	4

This new information would enable us to recalculate the number of observations needed.
Now $p = 30\% = 0.30$.

$$0.05(0.30) = 2 \sqrt{\frac{0.30(1 - 0.30)}{N}} \quad \text{or } N = \frac{0.84}{0.000225} = 3733$$

As will be explained later, it is advisable to recalculate N at regular intervals, perhaps at the end of each day, in order to better evaluate the progress of the study. The control chart may also be used as explained later in this chapter.

Determination of Accuracy for a Given Number of Observations

After the study is completed, a calculation is made to determine whether the results are within the desired accuracy. This can be done by calculating S in the formula instead of N as was previously done.

Assume that the final results of the study were as follows:

Observations of machines working	2600
Observations of machines idle	1400
Total observations	4000

Then $p = 1400 \div 4000 \times 100 = 35\% = 0.35$

$$Sp = 2 \sqrt{\frac{p(1-p)}{N}}$$

$$0.35S = 2 \sqrt{\frac{0.35(1 - 0.35)}{4000}} = 2 \sqrt{\frac{0.35 \times 0.65}{4000}} = 2 \sqrt{\frac{0.2275}{4000}}$$

$$S = \pm \frac{0.01508}{0.35} = \pm 0.043 = \pm 4.3\%$$

Because ± 4.3 percent is below the ± 5 percent required accuracy, the number of observations is sufficient.

In this case the statement could be made that we are 95 percent confident that the automatic screw machines were idle 35 percent of the time. The accuracy or standard error of ± 4.3 percent means that the results were correct within ± 4.3 percent of 35 percent ($\pm 4.3\% \times 35\% = \pm 1.5\%$), or the true value was between 33.5 percent and 36.5 percent. The 95 percent confidence level means that the probability is that in 95 cases out of 100 the above results will represent the facts.

Table 57 could be used instead of the formula for determining the degree of accuracy.

Table 57. Table for Determining the Degree of Accuracy for a Given Number of Observations and Value of p, 95% Confidence Level

Percent of Total Time Occupied by Activity or Delay, p	Number of Observations														
	10,000	9,000	8,000	7,000	6,000	5,000	4,000	3,000	2,000	1,000	900	800	700	600	500
1	±19.9	±21.0	±22.3	±23.8	±25.7	±28.1	±31.5	±36.3	±44.5	±62.9	±66.3	±70.4	±75.2	±81.3	±89.0
2	14.0	14.8	15.7	16.7	18.1	19.8	22.1	25.6	31.3	44.3	46.7	49.5	52.9	57.2	62.6
3	11.4	12.0	12.7	13.6	14.7	16.1	18.0	20.7	25.4	35.9	37.9	40.2	43.0	46.5	50.8
4	9.8	10.3	11.0	11.7	12.7	13.9	15.5	17.9	21.9	31.0	32.7	34.6	37.0	40.0	43.8
5	8.7	9.2	9.8	10.4	11.3	12.3	13.8	15.9	19.5	27.6	29.1	30.8	33.0	35.6	39.0
6	7.9	8.3	8.9	9.5	10.2	11.2	12.5	14.5	17.7	25.0	26.4	28.0	29.9	32.3	35.4
7	7.3	7.7	8.2	8.7	9.4	10.3	11.5	13.3	16.3	23.1	24.3	25.8	27.6	29.8	32.6
8	6.8	7.2	7.6	8.1	8.8	9.6	10.7	12.4	15.2	21.5	22.6	24.0	25.6	27.7	30.3
9	6.4	6.7	7.1	7.6	8.2	9.0	10.1	11.6	14.2	20.1	21.2	22.5	24.0	26.0	28.4
10	6.0	6.3	6.7	7.2	7.6	8.5	9.5	11.0	13.4	19.0	20.0	21.2	22.7	24.5	26.8
11	5.7	6.0	6.4	6.8	7.3	8.1	9.0	10.4	12.7	18.0	19.0	20.1	21.5	23.2	25.4
12	5.4	5.7	6.1	6.5	7.0	7.7	8.6	9.9	12.1	17.1	18.1	19.2	20.5	22.1	24.2
13	5.2	5.5	5.8	6.2	6.7	7.3	8.2	9.5	11.6	16.4	17.3	18.3	19.6	21.1	23.1
14	5.0	5.2	5.5	5.9	6.4	7.0	7.8	9.1	11.1	15.7	16.5	17.5	18.7	20.2	22.2
15	4.8	5.0	5.3	5.7	6.2	6.7	7.5	8.7	10.6	15.1	15.9	16.8	18.0	19.4	21.3
16	4.6	4.8	5.1	5.5	5.9	6.5	7.3	8.4	10.3	14.5	15.3	16.2	17.3	18.7	20.5
17	4.4	4.7	4.9	5.3	5.7	6.3	7.0	8.1	9.9	14.0	14.7	15.6	16.7	18.0	19.8
18	4.3	4.5	4.8	5.1	5.5	6.0	6.8	7.8	9.5	13.5	14.2	15.1	16.1	17.4	19.1
19	4.1	4.4	4.6	4.9	5.3	5.8	6.5	7.5	9.2	13.1	13.8	14.6	15.6	16.9	18.5
20	4.0	4.2	4.5	4.8	5.2	5.7	6.3	7.3	8.9	12.7	13.3	14.1	15.1	16.3	17.9
21	3.9	4.1	4.3	4.6	5.0	5.5	6.1	7.1	8.7	12.3	12.9	13.7	14.6	15.8	17.4
22	3.8	4.0	4.2	4.5	4.9	5.3	6.0	6.9	8.4	11.9	12.6	13.3	14.2	15.4	16.8
23	3.7	3.9	4.1	4.4	4.7	5.2	5.8	6.7	8.2	11.6	12.2	12.9	13.8	14.9	16.4
24	3.6	3.8	4.0	4.3	4.6	5.0	5.6	6.5	8.0	11.3	11.9	12.6	13.5	14.5	15.9
25	3.5	3.7	3.9	4.1	4.5	4.9	5.5	6.3	7.8	11.0	11.6	12.3	13.1	14.1	15.5
26	3.4	3.6	3.8	4.0	4.4	4.8	5.3	6.2	7.5	10.7	11.2	11.9	12.8	13.8	15.1
27	3.3	3.5	3.7	3.9	4.2	4.7	5.2	6.0	7.4	10.4	11.0	11.6	12.4	13.4	14.7
28	3.2	3.4	3.6	3.8	4.1	4.5	5.1	5.9	7.2	10.1	10.7	11.3	12.1	13.1	14.4
29	3.1	3.3	3.5	3.7	4.0	4.4	5.0	5.7	7.0	9.9	10.4	11.1	11.8	12.8	14.0
30	3.05	3.2	3.4	3.65	3.9	4.3	4.8	5.6	6.8	9.7	10.2	10.8	11.6	12.5	13.7
31	3.00	3.1	3.3	3.60	3.85	4.2	4.7	5.5	6.7	9.4	9.9	10.6	11.3	12.2	13.4
32	2.90	3.05	3.25	3.50	3.75	4.1	4.6	5.3	6.5	9.2	9.7	10.3	11.0	11.9	13.0
33	2.85	3.00	3.20	3.40	3.70	4.0	4.5	5.2	6.4	9.0	9.5	10.1	10.8	11.6	12.7
34	2.80	2.90	3.10	3.30	3.60	3.9	4.4	5.1	6.2	8.8	9.3	9.9	10.5	11.4	12.5
35	2.70	2.85	3.05	3.25	3.50	3.85	4.3	5.0	6.1	8.6	9.1	9.6	10.3	11.1	12.2

417

Table 57. (*Continued*)

| Percent of Total Time Occupied by Activity or Delay, p | \multicolumn{15}{c}{Number of Observations} |
	10,000	9,000	8,000	7,000	6,000	5,000	4,000	3,000	2,000	1,000	900	800	700	600	500
36	2.65	2.80	3.00	3.20	3.45	3.75	4.2	4.9	6.0	8.4	8.9	9.4	10.1	10.9	11.9
37	2.60	2.75	2.90	3.10	3.35	3.7	4.1	4.8	5.8	8.3	8.7	9.2	9.9	10.7	11.7
38	2.55	2.70	2.85	3.05	3.30	3.6	4.0	4.7	5.7	8.1	8.6	9.0	9.7	10.4	11.4
39	2.50	2.65	2.80	3.00	3.25	3.55	3.95	4.6	5.6	7.9	8.3	8.8	9.5	10.2	11.2
40	2.45	2.60	2.75	2.90	3.15	3.45	3.85	4.5	5.5	7.8	8.2	8.7	9.3	10.0	11.0
41	2.40	2.55	2.70	2.85	3.10	3.40	3.80	4.4	5.4	7.6	8.0	8.5	9.1	9.8	10.7
42	2.35	2.50	2.65	2.80	3.05	3.30	3.70	4.3	5.3	7.4	7.8	8.3	8.9	9.6	10.5
43	2.30	2.45	2.60	2.75	2.95	3.25	3.65	4.2	5.2	7.3	7.7	8.1	8.7	9.4	10.3
44	2.25	2.40	2.50	2.70	2.90	3.20	3.55	4.1	5.0	7.1	7.5	8.0	8.5	9.2	10.1
45	2.20	2.35	2.45	2.65	2.85	3.15	3.50	4.05	4.95	7.0	7.4	7.8	8.4	9.0	9.9
46	2.15	2.30	2.40	2.60	2.80	3.05	3.40	3.95	4.85	6.9	7.2	7.7	8.2	8.8	9.7
47	2.10	2.25	2.35	2.55	2.75	3.00	3.35	3.85	4.75	6.7	7.1	7.5	8.0	8.7	9.5
48	2.10	2.20	2.30	2.50	2.70	2.95	3.30	3.80	4.65	6.6	6.9	7.4	7.9	8.5	9.3
49	2.05	2.15	2.30	2.45	2.65	2.90	3.20	3.70	4.55	6.5	6.8	7.2	7.7	8.4	9.1
50	2.00	2.10	2.25	2.40	2.60	2.85	3.15	3.65	4.45	6.3	6.7	7.1	7.6	8.2	8.9
51	1.96	2.06	2.19	2.34	2.53	2.77	3.10	3.58	4.38	6.20	6.53	6.93	7.41	8.00	8.76
52	1.92	2.02	2.15	2.29	2.48	2.71	3.04	3.51	4.29	6.07	6.40	6.79	7.26	7.84	8.59
53	1.88	1.98	2.10	2.25	2.43	2.66	2.97	3.43	4.20	5.95	6.27	6.65	7.11	7.68	8.41
54	1.84	1.94	2.06	2.20	2.38	2.60	2.91	3.36	4.11	5.82	6.13	6.51	6.95	7.51	8.23
55	1.81	1.91	2.02	2.16	2.34	2.56	2.86	3.30	4.05	5.72	6.03	6.40	6.84	7.39	8.09
56	1.77	1.87	1.98	2.12	2.29	2.50	2.80	3.23	3.96	5.60	5.90	6.26	6.69	7.23	7.92
57	1.73	1.82	1.93	2.07	2.23	2.45	2.74	3.16	3.87	5.47	5.77	6.12	6.54	7.06	7.74
58	1.70	1.79	1.90	2.03	2.19	2.40	2.69	3.10	3.80	5.38	5.67	6.01	6.43	6.94	7.60
59	1.66	1.75	1.86	1.98	2.14	2.35	2.62	3.03	3.71	5.25	5.53	5.87	6.27	6.78	7.42
60	1.63	1.72	1.82	1.95	2.10	2.30	2.58	2.98	3.64	5.15	5.43	5.76	6.16	6.65	7.29
61	1.59	1.68	1.78	1.90	2.05	2.25	2.51	2.90	3.56	5.03	5.30	5.62	6.01	6.49	7.11
62	1.57	1.65	1.76	1.88	2.01	2.22	2.48	2.87	3.51	4.96	5.23	5.55	5.93	6.41	7.02
63	1.53	1.61	1.71	1.83	1.98	2.16	2.42	2.79	3.42	4.84	5.10	5.41	5.78	6.25	6.84
64	1.50	1.58	1.68	1.79	1.94	2.12	2.37	2.74	3.35	4.74	5.00	5.30	5.67	6.12	6.71
65	1.47	1.55	1.64	1.76	1.90	2.08	2.32	2.68	3.29	4.65	4.90	5.20	5.56	6.00	6.57

66	1.44	1.52	1.61	1.72	1.86	2.04	2.28	2.63	3.22	4.55	4.80	5.09	5.44	5.88	6.44
67	1.40	1.48	1.57	1.67	1.81	1.98	2.21	2.56	3.13	4.43	4.67	4.95	5.29	5.72	6.26
68	1.37	1.44	1.53	1.64	1.77	1.94	2.17	2.50	3.06	4.33	4.57	4.84	5.18	5.59	6.13
69	1.34	1.41	1.50	1.60	1.73	1.89	2.12	2.45	3.00	4.24	4.47	4.74	5.06	5.47	5.99
70	1.31	1.38	1.46	1.57	1.69	1.85	2.07	2.39	2.93	4.14	4.37	4.63	4.95	5.35	5.86
71	1.28	1.35	1.43	1.53	1.65	1.81	2.02	2.34	2.86	4.05	4.27	4.53	4.85	5.26	5.72
72	1.24	1.31	1.39	1.48	1.60	1.75	1.96	2.26	2.77	3.92	4.13	4.38	4.69	5.06	5.55
73	1.21	1.28	1.35	1.45	1.56	1.71	1.91	2.21	2.71	3.83	4.03	4.28	4.57	4.94	5.41
74	1.18	1.24	1.32	1.41	1.52	1.67	1.87	2.15	2.64	3.73	3.93	4.17	4.46	4.82	5.28
75	1.15	1.21	1.29	1.37	1.48	1.63	1.82	2.10	2.57	3.64	3.83	4.07	4.35	4.69	5.14
76	1.12	1.18	1.25	1.34	1.45	1.58	1.77	2.04	2.50	3.54	3.73	3.96	4.23	4.57	5.01
77	1.09	1.15	1.22	1.30	1.41	1.54	1.72	1.99	2.44	3.45	3.63	3.85	4.12	4.45	4.87
78	1.06	1.12	1.19	1.27	1.37	1.50	1.68	1.94	2.37	3.35	3.53	3.75	4.01	4.33	4.74
79	1.03	1.09	1.15	1.23	1.33	1.46	1.63	1.88	2.30	3.26	3.43	3.64	3.89	4.21	4.61
80	1.00	1.05	1.12	1.20	1.29	1.41	1.58	1.83	2.24	3.16	3.33	3.54	3.78	4.08	4.47
81	0.97	1.02	1.08	1.16	1.25	1.37	1.53	1.77	2.17	3.07	3.23	3.43	3.67	3.96	4.34
82	0.94	0.99	1.05	1.12	1.21	1.33	1.49	1.72	2.10	2.97	3.13	3.32	3.55	3.84	4.20
83	0.90	0.95	1.01	1.08	1.16	1.27	1.42	1.64	2.01	2.85	3.00	3.18	3.40	3.67	4.02
84	0.87	0.92	0.97	1.04	1.12	1.23	1.38	1.59	1.95	2.75	2.90	3.08	3.29	3.55	3.89
85	0.84	0.89	0.94	1.00	1.08	1.19	1.33	1.53	1.88	2.66	2.80	2.97	3.17	3.43	3.76
86	0.81	0.85	0.91	0.97	1.05	1.15	1.28	1.48	1.81	2.56	2.70	2.86	3.06	3.31	3.62
87	0.77	0.81	0.86	0.92	0.99	1.09	1.22	1.41	1.72	2.43	2.57	2.72	2.91	3.14	3.44
88	0.74	0.78	0.83	0.88	0.96	1.05	1.17	1.35	1.65	2.34	2.47	2.62	2.80	3.02	3.31
89	0.70	0.74	0.78	0.84	0.90	0.99	1.10	1.28	1.57	2.21	2.33	2.47	2.65	2.86	3.13
90	0.67	0.71	0.75	0.80	0.86	0.95	1.06	1.22	1.50	2.12	2.23	2.37	2.53	2.74	3.00
91	0.63	0.66	0.70	0.75	0.81	0.89	1.00	1.15	1.41	1.99	2.10	2.22	2.38	2.57	2.82
92	0.59	0.62	0.66	0.71	0.76	0.83	0.93	1.08	1.32	1.87	1.97	2.09	2.23	2.41	2.64
93	0.55	0.58	0.61	0.66	0.71	0.78	0.87	1.00	1.23	1.74	1.83	1.94	2.08	2.25	2.46
94	0.50	0.53	0.56	0.60	0.65	0.71	0.79	0.91	1.12	1.58	1.67	1.77	1.89	2.04	2.24
95	0.46	0.48	0.51	0.55	0.59	0.65	0.73	0.84	1.03	1.45	1.53	1.63	1.74	1.88	2.06
96	0.41	0.43	0.46	0.49	0.53	0.58	0.65	0.75	0.92	1.30	1.37	1.45	1.55	1.67	1.83
97	0.35	0.37	0.39	0.42	0.45	0.49	0.55	0.64	0.83	1.10	1.17	1.24	1.32	1.43	1.57
98	0.28	0.30	0.31	0.33	0.36	0.40	0.44	0.51	0.63	0.88	0.93	0.99	1.06	1.14	1.25
99	0.20	0.21	0.23	0.24	0.26	0.28	0.32	0.37	0.45	0.63	0.67	0.71	0.79	0.82	0.89

Absolute Error or Desired Absolute Accuracy

Table 58 shows the number of observations required for the different values of p where the confidence level is 95 percent and the desired degree of accuracy is ± 5 percent. The table shows at a glance the relationship between the value of p and the number of observations required. When p is 1 percent, 158,400 observations are needed, whereas only 1600 are required when p is 50 percent. The absolute error in the first case is ± 5 percent of 1 percent, or ± 0.05 percent. In the second case the absolute error is ± 5 percent of 50 percent, or ± 2.5 percent. There is little reason to require an absolute error of ± 0.05 percent in one instance and to be satisfied with an error of ± 2.5 percent in another. Perhaps an absolute error of 2.5 percent or 3 percent or possibly 3.5 percent represents a compromise which is acceptable for many kinds of work sampling.[5]

Table 58. Relationship between Value of p and Number of Observations

Percent of occurrence time, p	1	2	3	4	5	10	15	20	25	30	40	50
Number of observations, N	158,400	78,400	51,700	38,400	30,400	14,400	9,070	6,400	4,800	3,730	2,400	1,600

A sample size of 158,000 observations, for example, for a work sampling study is simply not realistic. However, this discussion will serve to explain why the formula for standard error may be modified when values of p are small. An understanding of the meaning of absolute error will aid the analyst in designing the work sampling study to be made in a given situation.

Table 59 shows the number of observations required for a given value of p and a given *desired absolute accuracy,* at 95 percent confidence level. Table 60 is used for determining the absolute degree of accuracy for a given number of observations and value of p, at 95 percent confidence level.

Control Charts

Control charts have found extensive use in quality control practice. Inspection data obtained at random and plotted on the control chart show graphically whether or not the process is in control.

In a similar manner the control chart in work sampling enables the analyst to plot the daily or the cumulative results of the sampling study. If a plotted point falls outside the control limits, this is likely to indicate that some unusual or abnormal condition may have been present during that part of the study. The 3-sigma limit is ordi-

[5] A. J. Rowe, "The Work Sampling Technique," *Transactions of ASME,* pp. 331–334, February, 1954.

narily used in determining the upper and lower control limits. This means that there are only three chances in 1000 that a point will fall outside the limits owing to a chance cause. It can be safely assumed that when a point falls outside the limits there is a reason for it. For example, a minor fire in one part of a factory building might disrupt production in the adjoining departments, and the sampling data taken in these areas during the day might therefore show excessive idle time on the part of the operators studied. This would be an assignable cause for the data being out of control for that particular day. Since this is an unusual occurrence, the data taken during the day of the fire would not be used, and the results of the study would be determined from the remainder of the data. To satisfy the requirements as to the number of observations, it probably would be necessary to extend the study an extra day.

The results of a work sampling study of the idle time of the operator of a large press are shown in Fig. 246. One-hundred observations were made each day for a period of 12 consecutive working days. The data indicate that the operator was idle for as little as 6 percent of the day on December 9, and as much as 23 percent on December 13.

Figure 246 shows the formula for computing the upper and lower control limits, which are +19 percent and +1 percent respectively, and the control chart for the data. The results of the study for December 13 were out of control for an "assignable cause"—this was the day of the fire in a neighboring department. The alignment chart in Fig. 247 could also be used for computing the upper and lower control limits.

The control chart is also useful in determining the length of a work sampling study. The chart in Fig. 248 shows that the percentage of "semitractor trucks available" is beginning to level off around 800 observations. This indicates that a sufficient number of observations have been taken. However, to make certain that the final results are within the desired accuracy the necessary checks should be made, as explained earlier.

Use of Random Number Tables

Work sampling, to be statistically acceptable, requires that each individual moment have an equal opportunity of being chosen. In other words, the observations must be random, unbiased, and independent. The use of a table of random numbers is perhaps the best method of ensuring that the sample is random. The table will serve, first of all, to determine the time of day that an observation should be made. It may also be used to indicate the order in which the operators should be observed, or the specific location in the department or plant where a reading should be taken.

In Table 61 the first number is 950622. The first digit of this number might indicate the hour, and the second and third digits the minutes. Thus, 950 would indicate 9.50, or 9:30 o'clock. The second half of this number, 622, might be read as 6.22, or approximately 6:13 o'clock. Since this plant operates only during the periods

Table 59. Table for Determining the Number of Observations for a Given Absolute Error or Absolute Degree of Accuracy and Value of p, 95% Confidence Level

Percent of Total Time Occupied by Activity or Delay, p	Absolute Error (%)					
	±1.0	±1.5	±2.0	±2.5	±3.0	±3.5
1	396	176	99	63	44	32
2	784	348	196	125	87	64
3	1,164	517	291	186	129	95
4	1,536	683	384	246	171	125
5	1,900	844	475	304	211	155
6	2,256	1,003	564	361	251	184
7	2,604	1,157	651	417	289	213
8	2,944	1,308	736	471	327	240
9	3,276	1,456	819	524	364	267
10	3,600	1,600	900	576	400	294
11	3,916	1,740	979	627	435	320
12	4,224	1,877	1,056	676	469	344
13	4,524	2,011	1,131	724	503	369
14	4,816	2,140	1,204	771	535	393
15	5,100	2,267	1,275	816	567	416
16	5,376	2,389	1,344	860	597	439
17	5,644	2,508	1,411	903	627	461
18	5,904	2,624	1,476	945	656	482
19	6,156	2,736	1,539	985	684	502
20	6,400	2,844	1,600	1,024	711	522
21	6,636	2,949	1,659	1,062	737	542
22	6,864	3,050	1,716	1,098	763	560

Percent of Total Time Occupied by Activity or Delay, p	Absolute Error (%)					
	±1.0	±1.5	±2.0	±2.5	±3.0	±3.5
51	9,996	4,442	2,499	1,599	1,110	816
52	9,984	4,437	2,496	1,597	1,109	815
53	9,964	4,428	2,491	1,594	1,107	813
54	9,936	4,416	2,484	1,590	1,104	811
55	9,900	4,400	2,475	1,584	1,099	808
56	9,856	4,380	2,464	1,577	1,095	804
57	9,804	4,357	2,451	1,569	1,089	800
58	9,744	4,330	2,436	1,559	1,083	795
59	9,676	4,300	2,419	1,548	1,075	790
60	9,600	4,266	2,400	1,536	1,067	784
61	9,516	4,229	2,379	1,523	1,057	777
62	9,424	4,188	2,356	1,508	1,047	769
63	9,324	4,144	2,331	1,492	1,036	761
64	9,216	4,096	2,304	1,475	1,024	753
65	9,100	4,044	2,275	1,456	1,011	743
66	8,976	3,989	2,244	1,436	997	733
67	8,844	3,931	2,211	1,415	983	722
68	8,704	3,868	2,176	1,393	967	710
69	8,556	3,803	2,139	1,369	951	698
70	8,400	3,733	2,100	1,344	933	686
71	8,236	3,660	2,059	1,318	915	672
72	8,064	3,584	2,016	1,290	896	658

n						
23	578	787	1,133	1,771	3,148	7,084
24	596	811	1,167	1,824	3,243	7,296
25	612	833	1,200	1,875	3,333	7,500
26	628	855	1,231	1,924	3,420	7,696
27	644	876	1,261	1,971	3,504	7,884
28	658	896	1,290	2,016	3,584	8,064
29	672	915	1,318	2,059	3,660	8,236
30	686	933	1,344	2,100	3,733	8,400
31	698	951	1,369	2,139	3,803	8,556
32	710	967	1,393	2,176	3,868	8,704
33	722	983	1,415	2,211	3,931	8,844
34	733	997	1,436	2,244	3,989	8,976
35	743	1,011	1,456	2,275	4,044	9,100
36	753	1,024	1,475	2,304	4,096	9,216
37	761	1,036	1,492	2,331	4,144	9,324
38	769	1,047	1,508	2,356	4,188	9,424
39	777	1,057	1,523	2,379	4,229	9,516
40	784	1,067	1,536	2,400	4,266	9,600
41	790	1,075	1,548	2,419	4,300	9,676
42	795	1,083	1,559	2,436	4,330	9,744
43	800	1,089	1,569	2,451	4,357	9,804
44	804	1,095	1,577	2,464	4,380	9,856
45	808	1,099	1,584	2,475	4,400	9,900
46	811	1,104	1,590	2,484	4,416	9,936
47	813	1,107	1,594	2,491	4,428	9,964
48	815	1,109	1,597	2,496	4,437	9,984
49	816	1,110	1,599	2,499	4,442	9,996
50	816	1,111	1,600	2,500	4,444	10,000

n						
73	644	876	1,261	1,971	3,504	7,884
74	628	855	1,231	1,924	3,420	7,696
75	612	833	1,200	1,875	3,333	7,500
76	596	811	1,167	1,824	3,243	7,296
77	578	787	1,133	1,771	3,148	7,084
78	560	763	1,098	1,716	3,050	6,864
79	542	737	1,062	1,659	2,949	6,636
80	522	711	1,024	1,600	2,844	6,400
81	502	684	985	1,539	2,736	6,156
82	482	656	945	1,476	2,624	5,904
83	461	627	903	1,411	2,508	5,644
84	439	597	860	1,344	2,389	5,376
85	416	567	816	1,275	2,267	5,100
86	393	535	771	1,204	2,140	4,816
87	369	503	724	1,131	2,011	4,524
88	344	469	676	1,056	1,877	4,224
89	320	435	627	979	1,740	3,916
90	294	400	576	900	1,600	3,600
91	267	364	524	819	1,456	3,276
92	240	327	471	736	1,308	2,944
93	213	289	417	651	1,157	2,604
94	184	251	361	564	1,003	2,256
95	155	211	304	475	844	1,900
96	125	171	246	384	683	1,536
97	95	129	186	291	517	1,164
98	64	87	125	196	348	784
99	32	44	63	99	176	396

Table 60. Table for Determining the Absolute Error or Absolute Degree of Accuracy (%) for a Given Number of Observations and Value of p, 95% Confidence Level

Percent of Total Time Occupied by Activity or Delay, p	Number of Observations									
	10,000	9,000	8,000	7,000	6,000	5,000	4,000	3,000	2,000	1,000
1	±0.20	±0.21	±0.22	±0.24	±0.26	±0.28	±0.30	±0.36	±0.44	±0.63
3	0.34	0.36	0.38	0.41	0.44	0.48	0.54	0.62	0.76	1.08
5	0.44	0.46	0.49	0.52	0.56	0.62	0.69	0.79	0.97	1.38
7	0.51	0.54	0.57	0.61	0.66	0.72	0.81	0.93	1.14	1.61
10	0.60	0.63	0.67	0.72	0.77	0.85	0.95	1.10	1.34	1.89
15	0.71	0.75	0.79	0.85	0.92	1.00	1.12	1.29	1.59	2.26
20	0.80	0.84	0.89	0.96	1.03	1.13	1.26	1.46	1.79	2.53
25	0.86	0.91	0.96	1.04	1.11	1.22	1.36	1.57	1.92	2.74
30	0.91	0.96	1.01	1.09	1.17	1.29	1.44	1.66	2.03	2.89
35	0.95	1.00	1.06	1.14	1.23	1.34	1.50	1.73	2.12	3.02
40	0.97	1.02	1.08	1.17	1.25	1.37	1.53	1.77	2.17	3.09
45	0.99	1.04	1.10	1.19	1.28	1.39	1.57	1.80	2.21	3.13
50	1.00	1.06	1.11	1.20	1.29	1.41	1.58	1.82	2.24	3.16
	900	800	700	600	500	400	300	200	100	
1	±0.66	±0.70	±0.75	±0.81	±0.89	±1.00	±1.15	±1.41	±1.99	
3	1.13	1.21	1.29	1.39	1.52	1.71	1.97	2.41	3.41	
5	1.45	1.54	1.65	1.78	1.95	2.18	2.52	3.08	4.36	
7	1.70	1.80	1.93	2.08	2.28	2.55	2.94	3.61	5.10	
10	1.99	2.12	2.27	2.45	2.68	3.00	3.46	4.24	6.00	
15	2.38	2.52	2.70	2.90	3.19	3.57	4.12	5.05	7.14	
20	2.67	2.83	3.02	3.27	3.58	4.00	4.62	5.66	8.00	
25	2.89	3.06	3.27	3.54	3.87	4.33	4.99	6.12	8.66	
30	3.06	3.24	3.46	3.74	4.10	4.58	5.29	6.48	9.17	
35	3.18	3.37	3.60	3.90	4.27	4.77	5.51	6.75	9.54	
40	3.26	3.46	3.70	3.99	4.38	4.90	5.65	6.92	9.80	
45	3.30	3.50	3.74	4.04	4.43	4.95	5.71	7.00	9.91	
50	3.33	3.54	3.78	4.08	4.47	5.00	5.77	7.07	10.00	

Table 61. Table of Random Numbers

950622	220985	742942	783807	907093	989408	037183
133869	362686	485453	194660	687432	674192	695066
899093	785915	610163	414101	171067	096124	978142
269577	163214	211559	168942	326355	358421	268787
947189	069133	356141	679380	866478	595132	347104

Date of Study	Total Number of Observations	Number of Observations "Operator Idle"	Per Cent of Day "Operator Idle"
12-5	100	9	9
12-6	100	10	10
12-7	100	12	12
12-8	100	8	8
12-9	100	6	6
12-12	100	9	9
12-13	100	23	23
12-14	100	9	9
12-15	100	8	8
12-16	100	9	9
12-19	100	9	9
12-20	100	8	8
	1200	120	

The formula for determining the control limits for p is:

Control limits for $p = p \pm 3 \sqrt{\dfrac{p(1-p)}{n}}$

N = total number of observations = 1200

n = number of daily observations = $\dfrac{\text{total number of observations}}{\text{number of days studied}} = \dfrac{1200}{12} = 100$

$p = \dfrac{\text{number of "operator idle" observations}}{\text{total number of observations}} = \dfrac{120}{1200} = 0.10$

Control limits for $p = 0.10 \pm 3 \sqrt{\dfrac{0.10 \times 0.90}{100}}$

$= 0.10 \pm 3 \sqrt{0.0009} = 0.10 \pm 0.09$

$= +0.19$ and $+0.01 = +19\%$ and $+1\%$

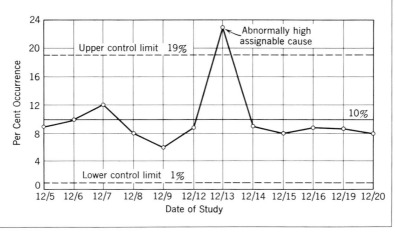

Figure 246 Control chart.

Three standard deviations

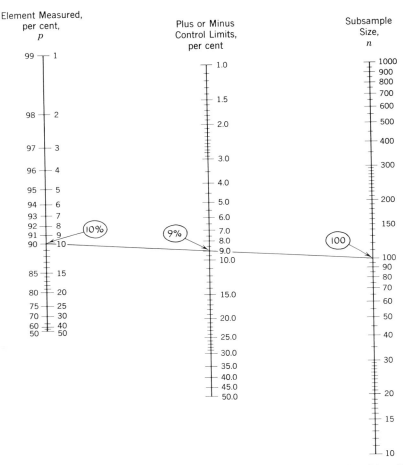

Figure 247　Alignment chart for determining control limits. (Courtesy Johns-Manville Corporation.)

8:00 A.M. to 12:00 and 1:00 P.M. to 5:00 P.M., this number would be discarded because it falls outside the working period. The next number, 133, would indicate that an observation should be made at 1.33, or approximately 1:20 o'clock. In a similar manner, random times would be selected as required for the particular study. If 50 observations are to be made per day, then 50 numbers would be obtained from the table of random numbers and each placed on a card. These cards, arranged in order

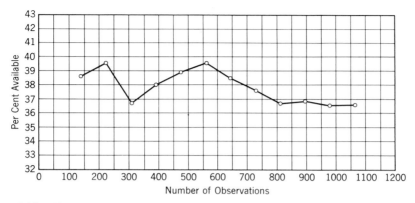

Figure 248   Chart showing the variation in the availability of trucks during a work sampling study, by days.

from the start of the shift to the end of the shift, would provide the schedule to be followed by the analyst in making the observations. Observations usually are not made during the lunch period or during regularly scheduled rest periods.

Ordinarily the observer would start the trip through the department or plant at a different place each time. The location for starting could also be selected by using the random number table. The number 9506 might indicate that this trip start at 9:30 A.M., and that it begin with Department 6. The observer also might change direction and path of travel in going from department to department, in order to achieve a greater degree of randomness.

Since it is important that a plan of random sampling be followed, it is desirable that it be as simple as possible. The table of random sampling times (Table 62) was devised from a table of random numbers. This table lists 25 chronological random sampling times for each of 14 eight-hour work days. The figures which appear in the columns are easily translated into actual clock times. They represent the hours and minutes after the start of the work shift. For example, assuming that the working period begins at 8:00 A.M., the first sampling time of the first column, 0:05, would be interpreted as 8:05 A.M. Similarly, the last sampling time of the same column, 7:25, would represent $8:00 + 7:25 = 15:25$, or 3:25 P.M.

By the proper use of this table, a list of random times of any desired length can be obtained. If 25 or less sampling times are planned for a day, one column will be sufficient. After the column selected has been translated into clock times, those times falling in scheduled rest and lunch periods are eliminated. If the number of sampling times remaining is greater than planned, the numbers in parentheses to the left of certain times are used to reduce the list to the desired number. These auxiliary numbers indicate the order in which the times were originally selected from the random number table. In order to maintain the randomness of the list, numbers should be

Table 62. Table of Random Sampling Times

1	2	3	4	5	6	7
(19)0:05	0:20	0:10	0:15	(18)0:05	(23)0:10	0:15
0:20	(18)0:50	(16)0:35	0:25	0:25	0:25	(21)0:20
0:55	(24)1:20	0:55	(16)1:20	0:45	(21)0:30	(16)0:35
(22)1:10	(21)1:45	(24)1:00	1:40	1:05	0:40	(15)0:50
(20)1:20	1:55	1:10	1:55	(21)1:50	1:10	1:00
(24)1:35	2:00	1:45	2:00	(20)2:10	1:20	1:25
2:30	2:30	(19)2:00	2:30	2:20	1:30	(23)1:40
3:05	2:40	2:05	(15)2:50	2:30	2:25	(22)1:50
(16)3:10	3:10	(21)2:45	3:10	(19)2:35	2:35	1:55
(25)3:15	(23)3:30	2:50	(18)3:30	(17)2:50	2:40	2:45
3:25	(22)3:40	(22)3:00	3:45	(23)3:00	(24)2:55	(25)3:05
(21)3:45	3:50	3:20	3:50	(16)3:10	(19)3:05	3:50
4:00	4:05	3:30	4:30	3:40	3:15	(19)4:00
4:10	(16)4:15	(20)4:40	(20)4:40	(24)3:45	(17)3:25	4:25
(18)4:35	(17)4:20	4:45	5:10	(15)4:30	(15)3:30	(18)4:45
4:55	(19)4:25	4:55	5:20	5:00	3:40	(20)5:00
5:00	4:30	5:00	(17)5:30	5:45	(16)3:50	5:10
(15)5:05	(15)4:35	(18)5:55	(25)5:45	(22)5:50	4:00	(24)5:15
(17)5:35	5:20	(25)6:00	(19)5:50	5:55	4:15	6:20
5:55	5:35	6:05	(21)6:15	6:00	4:25	6:25
(23)6:20	6:15	(23)6:35	6:20	6:35	(18)4:35	6:50
6:45	(20)6:40	(15)6:40	(24)6:25	6:45	(22)5:40	6:55
6:50	(25)6:45	7:10	6:50	(25)7:00	(25)6:45	7:15
7:10	7:10	7:35	7:30	7:45	6:55	7:40
7:25	7:35	(17)7:50	7:55	7:55	(20)7:35	(17)7:45

8	9	10	11	12	13	14
(17)0:05	0:25	0:05	(25)0:05	(22)0:10	(25)0:10	0:10
(18)0:20	0:30	0:15	(18)0:15	0:20	0:15	(17)0:15
(15)1:05	0:40	0:40	0:20	0:30	1:10	0:20
1:25	(24)0:45	1:30	0:25	1:30	(21)1:30	(22)0:25
1:30	1:00	1:45	0:55	(19)1:45	1:40	(24)0:50
2:05	(18)1:10	(21)2:20	1:20	1:50	1:45	(18)1:25
2:25	(17)1:25	2:25	1:35	2:25	(16)2:05	1:35
(24)2:40	1:40	(22)3:10	1:55	(25)2:35	2:40	(23)2:10
(16)3:00	2:15	(20)3:40	(17)2:10	(17)3:05	(19)2:45	(20)2:15
3:20	2:20	(15)3:50	2:30	3:10	2:55	2:40
4:25	2:30	4:15	2:45	3:50	(22)3:40	2:55
4:45	(15)2:40	(24)4:20	(21)2:50	3:55	3:45	3:35
4:50	2:45	4:30	(22)2:55	4:05	(18)3:50	(21)3:40
(25)4:55	(21)3:05	(25)4:40	(15)3:00	4:10	(24)4:05	4:35
5:05	(16)3:30	4:55	(16)3:30	4:50	(20)4:25	(16)4:45
5:15	3:35	5:00	3:35	(21)5:10	4:55	(19)5:05
5:50	4:00	5:15	(23)3:45	(16)5:25	5:15	5:10
5:55	4:15	(19)5:20	4:05	(15)5:30	5:45	5:50
(22)6:00	(23)4:50	5:25	5:00	(24)6:00	(15)6:20	6:05
(20)6:10	(20)5:45	(23)6:05	(19)5:40	6:05	6:25	6:20
(19)6:20	(22)5:50	(17)6:45	(24)5:50	6:15	(17)6:30	7:05
6:35	6:25	(18)7:15	6:25	6:30	6:35	7:10
(23)7:10	(19)6:50	7:25	7:20	(18)6:50	(23)7:35	7:20
7:15	(25)7:05	7:35	7:40	(23)6:55	7:50	(25)7:50
(21)7:30	7:30	(16)7:55	(20)7:50	(20)7:25		(15)7:55

eliminated from the list in reverse order to their selection. Thus, if only 20 sampling trips were planned from column 1, times designated as (25), (24), (23), (22), and (21), which would be 3:15, 1:35, 6:20, 1:10, and 3:45 respectively, would be omitted.

Should more than 25 trips be desired in any one day, two or more columns may be combined and duplications eliminated. The same procedure as outlined above can then be applied to achieve the desired number of sampling trips. Different columns or combinations of columns should be used for planning the sampling trips for different days.

PROCEDURE FOR MAKING A WORK SAMPLING STUDY

The procedure for planning and organizing a work sampling study will now be described, and in the latter part of this chapter an explanation is given of the procedure to be followed for measuring work by sampling.

Steps in Making the Study

The following steps are usually required in making a work sampling study.

1. Define the problem.
   A. State the main objectives or purposes of the project or problem.
   B. Describe in detail each element to be measured.
2. Obtain the approval of the supervisor of the department in which the work sampling study is to be made. Make certain that the operators to be studied and the other people in the department understand the purpose of the study—obtain their cooperation.
3. Determine the desired accuracy of the final results. This may be stated as the standard error of a percentage or desired accuracy, or as the absolute error or desired absolute accuracy. The confidence level should also be stated.
4. Make a preliminary estimate of the percentage occurrence of the activity or delay to be measured. This may be based on past experience; however, it is usually preferable to make a one-day or two-day preliminary work sampling study.
5. Design the study.
   A. Determine the number of observations to be made.
   B. Determine the number of observers needed. Select and instruct these people.
   C. Determine the number of days or shifts needed for the study.
   D. Make detailed plans for taking the observations, such as the time and the route to be followed by the observer.
   E. Design the observation form.
6. Make the observations according to the plan. Analyze and summarize the data.
   A. Make the observations and record the data.
   B. Summarize the data at the end of each day.

   C.　Determine the control limits.
   D.　Plot the data on the control chart at the end of each day.
7.　Check the accuracy or precision of the data at the end of the study.
8.　Prepare the report and state conclusions. Make recommendations if such are called for.

Purpose of Study

Ordinarily a work sampling study would be undertaken only upon request from a line or staff department supervisor or manager. In many organizations the industrial engineering department or the methods and standards department would be asked to make the study. Unless the study requires the rating of operator performance and the establishment of time standards, it would not be necessary to use trained analysts or industrial engineers to make it. In fact, supervisors themselves often make work sampling studies.

The objectives of the proposed study should be worked out following the initial request. A full statement of the purpose should be prepared, so that the study can be properly designed. The analyst should try to visualize in detail what the final report of the study will contain. This will aid in determining the degree of accuracy required and the length of the period over which the study should be made.

Elements to Be Measured

The purpose of the study will indicate how the activities and delays should be broken down. When over-all information is needed, a few elements may be satisfactory. In other situations a finer breakdown may be called for, and consequently each element will represent a smaller percentage of the whole. This calls for more observations, and so increases the cost of making the study. If a work sampling study is being made to aid in reducing nonworking time and increasing output per man-hour, the elements should be such that they will reveal delays within the control of the operator, such as late starting and early quitting. The elements should also reveal delays within the control of management, such as shortage of materials or machine down for repair or adjustment. If a work sampling study is being made to establish time standards, the unit of measure is considered first, as in a time study. The units produced must permit easy and positive count.

Irrespective of the purpose of the study or the nature of the breakdown, each element to be measured must be carefully defined so that there can be no mistake in identifying it. A carefully prepared written definition is desirable.

Design of Observation Form

In most cases a new observation form will be designed for each work sampling study. Many of these forms, however, will follow a similar pattern. One of the purposes of the preliminary study is to determine just what information is to be obtained, and this, of course, will form the basis for the design of the observation sheet. The form should be simple and should be arranged to facilitate recording and summarizing data, and yet should contain sufficient space to record all information that may be needed to prepare the final report of the study. When the work sampling study is used for establishing time standards, the form will include essentially all the information that would appear on a time study observation sheet.

The Motion Picture Camera for Work Sampling Studies

The motion picture camera can be used satisfactorily for some kinds of work sampling studies. The camera and timer shown in Fig. 249 permit pictures to be made at random intervals. The observation times can be preset by the placement of the small metal clips around the circumference of the timer dial. A random number table may be used in locating the clips. The timer can also be set to take pictures at *regular* intervals during the day if this is desired. The electric motor-driven timer operates the synchronous motor, which drives the camera at 1000 frames per minute. A separate device on the timer permits the camera "run time" to be set for intervals of 2 to 30 seconds each. The camera run time, or the length of the observation time, would be preset on the timer and maintained throughout the study. Since pictures are taken at a speed of 1000 frames per minute, when the film is projected at this same speed a performance rating of the operator can be made from the film.

A motor drive or a solenoid-operated drive can be attached to the camera to take pictures at 60 or 100 frames per minute or at other speeds. A single frame or a few frames can be exposed at random intervals or at regular intervals during the day. For many kinds of work such a film record permits the satisfactory analysis of activities and delays of operators or machines. With a time-lapse camera drive, all necessary data can be obtained from the film, and a relatively small footage of film is needed for an entire day's record.

Electronic Equipment for Work Sampling Studies

For some kinds of work one of the best ways of making a work sampling study is by the use of an electronic data collector (Fig. 219). Codes can be used for working elements and for the various categories of nonworking elements. A performance rating may be entered for each observation of a working element. The data can be transmitted to the computer at the end of the day or week and quickly reduced and summarized. The computer report might show the percentage of the day or week during which the employees in a department were working, their average performance index, and also the percentage of time during which they were not working. The nonworking time could be subdivided into as many categories as desired.

The video camera and recorder can be used much as the motion picture camera is used in making work sampling studies. The equipment is portable and the pictures are immediately available.

Figure 249 Motion picture camera with synchronous motor drive and timer set to actuate the camera at random intervals during an 8-hour day.

Performance Sampling

Performance sampling is the process during which the analyst makes a rating of the operator's performance or speed at the time of the observation. This rating in percent is recorded on the data sheet the same as in making a time study. Had the analyst made a performance sampling study such as the example shown in Fig. 239, the observation sheet would have shown 36 performance rating figures in percents for the 36 "working" observations and 4 tally marks for the 4 "idle" observations. The average of the 36 ratings would represent the average performance of this operator for the period covered by the study. Eastman Kodak at Kodak Park was one of the first companies to use performance sampling[6] and we were among the first to suggest its use.[7] Later we determined the statistical validity of this process.[8]

Continuous Performance Sampling

In most organizations labor cost control is of special importance. The usual method is to establish time standards for specific operations and then obtain a count of the number of units finished each day. Thus, the number of standard minutes earned can be compared with the number of minutes actually worked and a performance index can be determined for each worker and for the department. This plan of labor control is widely used and is very effective in many situations. However, much work does not lend itself to direct measurement. The cycles may be long and varied, methods may not be standardized, and it is often difficult to obtain a count of the units of work completed. Much indirect factory labor falls into this category. In such situations it is possible to obtain some control of labor costs by the use of work sampling. Continuous performance sampling can be carried on—that is, observations can be made of all workers in a department at random during the entire week or month and the results can be computed for this period. This procedure, repeated week after week, provides management with information concerning the work force such as:

1. Percentage of time working.
2. Percentage of time out of department.
3. Percentage of time idle.
4. Average performance index while working.
5. Labor effectiveness factor (Item 1 × Item 4).

This information can be compiled weekly or monthly, and can be posted in a central chart room with copies made for the supervisors and for other members of management.

Productivity Sampling at Boeing

The Boeing Wichita Company, Division of The Boeing Company, has used performance sampling for many years and at the present time their program, called Productivity Sampling, covers approximately 3000 people in 120 shops.[9]

[6] George H. Gustat, "Incentives for Indirect Labor," *Proceedings Fifth Industrial Engineering Institute,* University of California, Los Angeles-Berkeley, CA, 1953, pp. 80–86.
[7] D. S. Correll and Ralph M. Barnes, "Industrial Application of the Ratio-Delay Method," *Advanced Management,* Vol. 15, No. 8 and No. 9, August and September, 1950.
[8] Ralph M. Barnes and Robert B. Andrews, "Performance Sampling in Work Measurement," *Journal of Industrial Engineering,* Vol. 6, No. 6, November–December, 1955.
[9] Reproduced by permission of The Boeing Wichita Company.

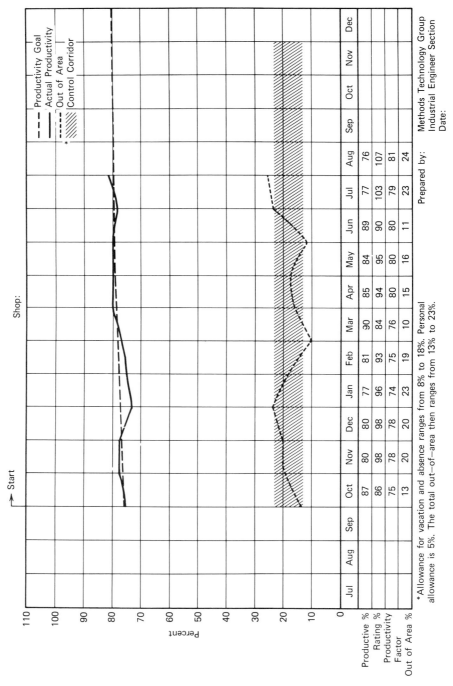

Figure 250 Monthly productivity sampling report—data obtained by continuous performance sampling—by Boeing at Wichita.

434

The objectives of productivity sampling at Boeing are to increase productivity and reduce costs in the shops. The studies pinpoint areas for improvement and reveal specific problems. The program is designed to measure activities in designated areas or production units and makes no reference to the activities of specific individuals. Shop management is motivated to set goals for increasing productivity, and continuous sampling measures management's success in reaching these goals. The data obtained help to improve work crew balance, to identify layout and systems problems and to improve communications between administrative supervisors. The supervisor is aided in identifying and solving administrative problems, discovering areas for self-improvement, and evaluating employees' performance.

Observations are made by trained people at random times through the work period on a continuing basis. The following categories are used for the employees: (1) working (productive), (2) nonworking (nonproductive) (3) rating, and (4) out of area. When the employee is observed working, a performance rating is made and recorded. The productivity factor = (productive or working time) × (rating factor).

First-line supervisors are also observed and three categories are used: (1) supervisory—in area actively observing, training and instructing employees. (2) administrative—doing paperwork, talking on phone, talking to engineers, inspectors, maintenance people, and others, (3) out of area.

Two or three members of the Methods Technology Group devote their full time to the program, and in addition each shop superintendent provides one shop supervisor who joins the group. These people are given special training and work on this assignment for five weeks. Most supervisors and general supervisors consider this assignment a good opportunity to get acquainted with the rest of the shops and supervisors and to compare, evaluate, and improve their own supervisory approach.

Each supervisor prepares a productivity goal for his department. The General Supervisor reviews his or her supervisors' goals and passes them on to Methods Technology. This Group plots the goals on the supervisors' charts. The Group also combines the data for the General Supervisor and the Superintendent charts. The sampling data are summarized and reports are compiled on a monthly basis. Some of the information is transferred to the Productivity Graph by shops (Fig. 250). A composite of the reports of several shops is sent to the general supervisor and to the superintendent.

Figure 250 is an example of a Productivity Sampling Report for one shop. For the month of October the people in this shop worked an average of 87 percent of the time and had an average performance rating of 86 percent, which gave a Productivity Factor of 75 ($87 \times 86 = 75$). Out of area amounted to 13 percent for the month. The solid black line on the chart indicates the productivity factor and the light dotted line shows out of area percentage.

Work Sampling Applied to Nonmanufacturing Activities

Banks, hospitals, restaurants, airlines, and department stores are among those organizations that use work sampling to determine daily and hourly personnel requirements and for cost control.

Work sampling studies are successfully made of supervisors, draftsmen, engineers, and technical personnel. One large and expanding company that constructs its own factories and warehouses regularly makes work sampling measurements of the activities of all construction personnel, such as welders, pipe fitters, and carpenters.

DETERMINING TIME STANDARDS BY WORK SAMPLING

Sampling can be used for measuring work as well as for measuring delays, idle time, and performance. On short-cycle repetitive operations, however, time study, standard data, or predetermined time data would usually be preferred for establishing time standards. Sampling can be used profitably for measuring long-cycle operations, work where people are employed in groups, and activities that do not lend themselves to time study.

It is possible to determine by work sampling the percentage of the day that a person is idle and the percentage of the day that he is working, as well as the average performance index or speed at which he worked during the working portion of the day. For example, assume that John Jones works an 8-hour day as a drill-press operator. A work sampling study might show that he was idle 15 percent of the day or 72 minutes ($480 \times 0.15 = 72$), and that he worked the remainder of the day, or 408 minutes, at an average performance index of 110 percent. If the record shows that he turned out 420 pieces of acceptable quality during the day, the standard time for the operation he performed could be computed as shown in Fig. 251. The assumption is made that the allowances for this drill-press operation would be taken from the company time study manual.

In establishing a time standard, the same rigorous analyses would be required of work sampling as of time study. The method of performing the operation would be standardized and a detailed written description prepared. Quality standards would be required, as well as assurance from the supervisor that the job was running the way it should. During the study the analyst would make an instantaneous observation as to whether the operator was working or idle, and when the operator was working, the analyst would rate his speed and note whether he was performing a regular part of the cycle of work. Information would be obtained as to the starting time and quitting time, and the total number of parts of acceptable quality finished during the day. The sampling study would measure with a preassigned degree of accuracy the percentage of the 8-hour day that the operator was working on the regular drill-press operation, and his average performance index or speed for the working portion of the day.

Information	Source of Data	Data for One Day
Total time expended by operator (working time and idle time)	Time cards	480 min.
Number of parts produced	Inspection Department	420 pieces
Working time in per cent	Work sampling	85%
Idle time in per cent	Work sampling	15%
Average performance index	Work sampling	110%
Total allowances	Company time-study manual	15%

$$\text{Standard time per piece} = \frac{\left(\substack{\text{Total time}\\\text{in minutes}}\right) \times \left(\substack{\text{Working time}\\\text{in per cent}}\right) \times \left(\substack{\text{Performance index}\\\text{in per cent}}\right)}{\text{Total number of pieces produced}} + \text{Allowances}$$

$$= \left(\frac{480 \times 0.85 \times 1.10}{420}\right) \times \left(\frac{100}{100 - 15}\right) = 1.26 \text{ minutes}$$

Figure 251 Data sheet and computation of standard time.

Establishing Time Standard for an Assembly Operation

The following case illustrates how a time standard was established on a mechanical subassembly operation by work sampling.

Ten operators regularly performed this job, and all ten were studied during a 3-day period. Each day 240 observations were made, making a total of 720 observations. Of this number the analyst found the ten operators working 711 times, and the performance index was noted and recorded for each of the 711 observations. Nine times during the 3-day period, the analyst observed the operators idle.

As the summary of the results of the study shows (Fig. 253), the total time expended by the operators, including working time and idle time, was 13,650 minutes. The working time was 98.7 percent ($711 \div 720 \times 100 = 98.7\%$). The remainder, or 1.3 percent, was idle time. The number of minutes of working time was 13,473 ($13,650 \times 98.7 = 13,473$). During this time the ten operators turned out 16,314 subassemblies of acceptable quality. The average performance index of this group was 123.6 percent. Figure 252 shows a summary of the performance index for the 711 observations, and the way in which the average performance index was determined. The computations showing how the standard time was determined for this operation are given at the bottom of Fig. 253.

DAILY SUMMARY					Computation of Average Performance Index
Performance Index	April 1	April 2	April 5	Total	
100	3	6	1	10	100 × 10 = 1,000
105	13	22	9	44	105 × 44 = 4,620
110	32	21	24	77	110 × 77 = 8,470
115	48	45	17	110	115 × 110 = 12,650
120	47	49	39	135	120 × 135 = 16,200
125	27	28	56	111	125 × 111 = 13,875
130	26	13	22	61	130 × 61 = 7,930
135	15	8	11	34	135 × 34 = 4,590
140	14	15	22	51	140 × 51 = 7,140
145	8	20	27	55	145 × 55 = 7,975
150	2	10	11	23	150 × 23 = 3,450
					711 87,900
"Working" Observations	235	237	239	711	$\frac{87,900}{711}$ = 123.6
"Idle" Observations	5	3	1	9	
Total Observations	240	240	240	720	

Figure 252 Daily summary and computation sheet.

Information	Source of Data	Data for Three-Day Period
Total time expended by operator (working time and idle time)	Time cards	13,650 min.
Number of parts produced	Inspection Department	16,314 pieces
Working time in per cent	Work sampling	98.7%
Idle time in per cent	Work sampling	1.3%
Average performance index	Work sampling	123.6%
Total allowances	Company time-study manual	15%

$$\text{Standard time per piece} = \frac{\left(\substack{\text{Total time} \\ \text{in minutes}}\right) \times \left(\substack{\text{Working time} \\ \text{in per cent}}\right) \times \left(\substack{\text{Performance index} \\ \text{in per cent}}\right)}{\text{Total number of pieces produced}} + \text{Allowances}$$

$$\left(\frac{13,650 \times 0.987 \times 1.236}{16.314}\right) \times \left(\frac{100}{100 - 15}\right) = 1.20 \text{ minutes}$$

Figure 253 Data sheet and computation of standard time.

438

Some Advantages and Disadvantages of Work Sampling in Comparison with Time Study

Advantages

1. Many operations or activities which are impractical or costly to measure by time study can readily be measured by work sampling.
2. A simultaneous work sampling study of several operators or machines may be made by a single observer. Ordinarily an analyst is needed for each operator or machine when continuous time studies are made.
3. It usually requires fewer man-hours and costs less to make a work sampling study than it does to make a continuous time study. The cost may be as little as 5 to 50 percent of the cost of continuous time study.
4. Observations may be taken over a period of days or weeks, thus decreasing the chance of day-to-day or week-to-week variations affecting the results.
5. It is not necessary to use trained time study analysts as observers for work sampling studies unless performance sampling is required. If a time standard or a performance index is to be established, however, then an experienced time study analyst must be used.
6. A work sampling study may be interrupted at any time without affecting the results.
7. Work sampling measurements may be made with a preassigned degree of reliability. Thus, the results are more meaningful to those not conversant with the methods used in collecting the information.
8. With work sampling the analyst makes an instantaneous observation of the operator at random intervals during the working day, thus making prolonged time studies unnecessary.
9. Work sampling studies are less fatiguing and less tedious to make on the part of the observer.
10. Work sampling studies are preferred to continuous time studies by the operators being studied. Some people do not like to be observed continuously for long periods of time.
11. A stop watch is not needed for work sampling studies. If an electronic data collector is used the results are shown on a computer printout.

Disadvantages

1. Ordinarily work sampling is not economical for studying a single operator or machine, or for studying operators or machines located over wide areas. The observer spends too much time walking to and from the work place or walking from one work place to another. Also, time study, standard data, or predetermined time data are preferred for establishing time standards for short-cycle repetitive operations.

2. Time study permits a finer breakdown of activities and delays than is possible with work sampling. Work sampling cannot provide as much detailed information as one can get from time study.
3. The operator may change his or her work pattern upon sight of the observer. If this occurs, the results of such a work sampling study may be of little value.
4. A work sampling study made of a group obviously presents average results, and there is no information as to the magnitude of the individual differences.
5. Management and workers may not understand statistical work sampling as readily as they do time study.
6. In certain kinds of work sampling studies, no record is made of the method used by the operator. Therefore, an entirely new study must be made when a method change occurs in any element.
7. There is a tendency on the part of some observers to minimize the importance of following the fundamental principles of work sampling, such as the proper sample size for a given degree of accuracy, randomness in making the observations, instantaneous observation at the preassigned location, and careful definition of the elements or subdivisions of work or delay before the study is started.

31

MEASURING WORK BY
PHYSIOLOGICAL METHODS

Over the years many people have sought an objective method of measuring physical work. Frederick W. Taylor saw the great need for work measurement and created stop-watch time study to perform this function. In developing the time study technique, he experimented with the concept of horsepower (that is, foot-pounds of work per minute) as a measure of work but found this approach to be unsatisfactory.

Around the turn of the century, physiologists demonstrated the validity of using rate of oxygen consumption as the basis for measuring energy expenditure. Later studies showed that change in heart rate was also a reliable measure of physical activity. Extensive human energy expenditure studies have been carried on in various parts of the world. Studies have been made to gain new knowledge about human performance, to better understand the behavior of champion athletes, and to aid the physically handicapped.

Interest in work physiology is increasing partly because a more objective method of measuring physical work is needed and also because better equipment has become available for measuring oxygen consumption and heart rate. Sufficient evidence is now available to show that physiological measurement can supplement present work measurement techniques for some kinds of physical tasks.

Physical work results in changes in oxygen consumption, heart rate, pulmonary ventilation, body temperature, and lactic acid concentration in the blood. Although some of these factors are only slightly affected by muscular activity, there is a linear correlation between heart rate, oxygen consumption, and total ventilation, and the physical work performed by an individual. Of these three, the first two—heart rate and oxygen consumption—are the most widely used for measuring the physiological cost of human work.

The performance of physical work requires the use of groups of muscles. Some muscles are needed to maintain the body posture while others perform the task. Davis and Miller[1] have classified physical effort tasks into three types: (1) *full body work* which utilizes the large muscle groups usually involving two-thirds or three-fourths of the body's total muscles, (2) *localized muscular work* which requires less expenditure of energy because fewer muscle groups are used to perform the task, and (3) *static muscular work* during which the muscles are used to exert a force but no mechanical work is done. Static work requires the contraction of muscle groups and

---

[1] H. L. Davis and C. I. Miller, "Human Productivity and Work Design," *Industrial Engineering Handbook,* 3rd ed., Harold B. Mayanard (ed.), McGraw-Hill, New York, 1971, pp. 7–76.

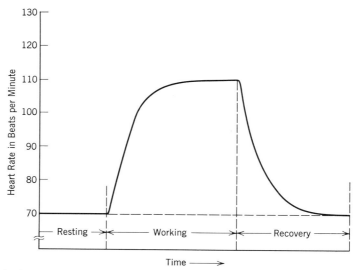

Figure 254 Heart rate in beats per minute before, during, and after physical work.

can be very demanding. The physiological cost of performing a task, then, is affected by the number and type of muscles involved, either to move a member of the body or to control antagonist contraction.

When a person is at rest, heart rate and the rate of oxygen consumption are at a fairly steady level. Then when the person does muscular work, that is, when he changes from a "resting level" to a "working level," both the heart rate and the oxygen consumption increase. When work ends, recovery begins, and the heart rate and oxygen consumption return to the original resting level.

Heart Rate Measurement

The resting heart rate of the individual shown in Fig. 254 was 70 beats per minute. When he started to work, his pulse rate increased rapidly to 110 beats per minute and leveled off during the working period. When he stopped working, his heart rate dropped off and finally returned to the original resting level. The increase in heart rate during work may be used as an index of the physiological cost of the job. Also the rate of recovery immediately after work stops can be utilized in some cases in evaluating physiological cost. The *total* physiological cost of a task consists not only of the energy expenditure during work but also the energy expenditure above the resting rate during the recovery period, that is, until recovery is complete.

Each time the heart beats, a small electric potential is generated. By placing electrodes on either side of the chest, this potential can be picked up and transmitted by

Figure 255 Apparatus for measuring heart beat and oxygen consumption. *A*, transmitter for telemetering heart beats; *B*, respirometer for measuring volume of exhaled air; *C*, rubber football bladder for collecting random sample of exhaled air.

wire or by radio transmitter to a receiver (Fig. 255). There the individual heart beats can be counted directly, or by means of a cardiotachometer the impulsives can be converted into heart rate, that is, heart beats per minute. These data can be recorded continuously on ruled graph paper by a milliampere recorder. The graph is in effect a curve similar to the one shown in Fig. 254.

Heart beat signals can also be obtained by means of an ear lobe unit. This apparatus consists of a photo duodiode placed behind the ear and illuminated by a light source mounted on the other side of the ear. The opacity of the ear lobe changes as the blood surges through the ear with each heart beat. The impulse created by each heart beat can be transmitted by wire or by radio transmitter and recorded as described above.

Information concerning rate of recovery also can be obtained simply by using a stethoscope and stop watch. Studies made at the Harvard Fatigue Laboratory showed that heart rate data obtained in this manner are reliable and easy to secure. The procedure consists of obtaining the total number of heart beats during the second half-minute after work stops. Then the number of heart beats is taken during the second half-minute of the second minute, and the second half-minute of the third minute, after work stops. Such data make it possible to compare the rate of recovery during different working conditions. For example, Fig. 263 shows such information for a person working under conditions of high temperature and humidity wearing (*A*) ordinary clothes and (*B, C*) a ventilated suit.

Portable Heart Rate Recorder

A compact, lightweight, two-lead heart rate recorder which records signals up to 26 hours can be worn by the worker.[2] The unit has a synchronous motor drive, integrated circuitry, and a rechargable battery pack. An event marker button, when depressed by the worker, records an event mark on the tape for precise time/event correlation.

An automatic tape scanning system, called Electrocardioscanner, permits the recordings to be played back at real time recorded speed, or at rapid speeds of 30, 60, or 120 times real time. All tape scanning, summarization, and real time documentation is automatic. Heart rate is shown as a trend line on an oscilloscope and is automatically printed on a summary trend chart. Automatic real time write-out of worker-noted events is made, and each chart is stamped with the exact real time. Heart rate is recorded over a range of 0 to 250 beats per minute.

Measuring Oxygen Consumption

Change in the rate of oxygen consumption from the resting level to the working level is also a measure of the physiological cost of the work done. A person extracts oxygen from the air breathed. In order to measure the oxygen consumed per unit of time, it is necessary to measure the volume of air exhaled and the oxygen content of this air. Oxygen consumption may be defined as the volume of oxygen expressed in liters per minute which the individual extracts from the air inhaled. A common method of obtaining this information is by means of a portable respirometer, such as the one shown in Fig. 255. This is a light weight (5½ pounds) gas meter which can be worn on the back. The person is equipped with a mask and a 1-inch rubber tube which carries the exhaled air from the mask to the respirometer. The respirometer indicates directly the volume of exhaled air in liters. A sample of the exhaled air is drawn off at random intervals into a rubber football bladder, and an analysis of its content is made. This permits a comparison of the oxygen content of the sample of expired air with that of the air in the room.

A curve showing the energy expenditure before, during, and after physical work would look much like the curve for heart rate in Fig. 254. In the case of a worker handling 10-pound cartons in the shipping room at the rate of 12 cartons per minute, the resting rate for one study was 1.2 calories (abbreviation for kilocalories) per minute. When he started to work, his energy expenditure increased rapidly to 5.0 calories per minute and then returned to the resting level when he stopped work. Thus, both heart rate and oxygen consumption can be used to measure physical work.

---

[2] Reproduced by permission of Del Mar Avionics.

Figure 256 The Beckman Metabolic Measurement Cart is a data processing system. The subject provides exhaled air through a mouthpiece and flexible tube connected to the cart. The cart stores the data, monitors the input, then calculates the answers—measuring oxygen consumption, carbon dioxide, and expired air.

Total Metabolic Measurement System

Although the respirometer described above is still widely used, a total measurement system is available which has integrated transducing, sample handling, and data processing components providing printed results. Figure 256 shows the Beckman Metabolic Measurement Cart designed for making measurements of oxygen consumption, carbon dioxide, expired volume, and other related information.[3] The subject provides exhaled air through a mouthpiece and a flexible tube connected to the cart. The cart is a data processing system as well as a system of transducers and a sample-handling system. A program card inserted in the unit controls its operation. The card is read and the functions of the Metabolic Measurement Cart are defined for the test to be performed. The keyboard is used to enter data about the subject. The processor then controls the timing, sets the correct operating conditions, interrogates the analyzers and transducers, stores the data, monitors the input, and then calculates and prints the answers. It repeats this as often as every 30 seconds.

Individual Differences

There is a great difference in the ability of individuals to perform muscular work. Studies were made of a group of 2000 healthy college students, which included men

[3] Reproduced by permission of Beckman Instruments, Inc.

of low physical efficiency as well as varsity athletes. The results of this study show that the capacity to withstand the stress of hard physical work was ten times as great in the fit as in the unfit.

Even in a more restricted and highly selected group of varsity and junior varsity trained athletes, the best men were able to perform hard physical work twice as efficiently as their less fit colleagues. These results emphasize, quantitatively, the well-known fact that men vary markedly as far as their physical capacity is concerned; and that, even in trained and selected groups, wide variations are found in the physiological price that individuals have to pay to accomplish a given task.

The physical capacity of the individual is the result of numerous factors such as the innate potential of physiological mechanisms, age, health and nutritional status, sex, specific fitness for a given job and for given environmental conditions. These factors exist in any industrial population, and similar differences have been found among workers.[4]

Practice—Fitness for Job

There is evidence to show that a well-trained male worker who is physically fit and suited to his job might be expected to expend approximately 5 calories per minute, or 2400 calories per 8-hour day, on his job.[5] The physiological cost to this same man as a beginner on the same job would be greater if he attempted to produce the same number of units of product per day. Practice enables the worker to do a job with a lower expenditure of energy. Moreover, the better trained the worker is, the sooner the heart rate will return to the resting level after he stops work. Figure 257 shows the effect of training on heart rate for a standard task. The top curve shows the heart rate for the person pedaling a bicycle ergometer for 20 minutes with a heavy workload. The other curves show heart rate after 22 days, 56 days, and 84 days of training.[6] On the initial ride the heart rate increased to 175 beats per minute; after 84 days of practice it did not exceed 143 beats per minute. Also the recovery rate was much more rapid for the trained person.

Physiological Cost of Walking

Studies of energy expenditure in walking have been made by many different investigators. Results of these studies[7] indicate that for speeds of 2 to 4 miles per hour energy expended in calories per minute is linearly proportional to the speed of walking in miles per hour. Assuming a metabolic cost at the resting state (zero point on the abscissa of Fig. 258) to be 1.2 calories per minute, then the relationship can be expressed by the equation

---

[4] Lucien Brouha, "Physiological Approach to Problems of Work Measurement," *Proceedings Ninth Industrial Engineering Institute,* University of California, Los Angeles-Berkeley, p. 13, 1957.

[5] For the average female worker this would be 4 calories per minute.

[6] Lucien Brouha, *Physiology in Industry,* Pergamon Press, New York, p. 30, 1960.

[7] R. Passmore and J. V. G. A. Durnin, "Human Energy Expenditure," *Physiological Reviews,* Vol. 35, No. 4, p. 806, October, 1955.

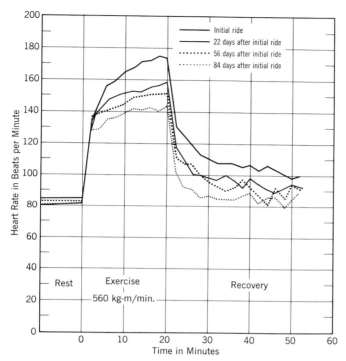

Figure 257 Effect of training on heart rate for a standard amount of exercise: pedaling a bicycle ergometer for 20 minutes with a heavy work load. Training was achieved by riding the bicycle 4 days a week with the same work load.

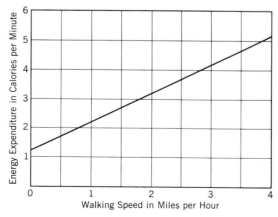

Figure 258 Curve showing relationship between energy expenditure in calories per minute and speed of walking in miles per hour.

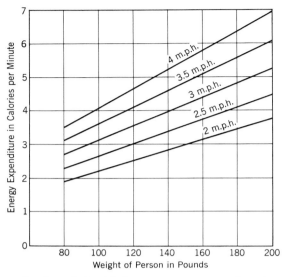

Figure 259 Curves showing relationship between energy expenditure in calories per minute, speed of walking in miles per hour, and body weight in pounds.

$$C = 1.0V + 1.2$$

where C equals energy expenditure in calories per minute, and V equals the walking speed in miles per hour. As the curve (Fig. 258) shows, the energy expended while walking at 3 miles per hour is 4.2 calories per minute.

However, energy expenditure is also proportional to body weight. One study of 50 persons walking at 3 miles per hour led to the equation

$$C = 0.047W + 1.02$$

where W is the weight of the person in kilograms. The curves in Fig. 259 have been drawn from the data developed from this study. The energy expenditure for a person weighing 150 pounds and walking 3 miles per hour would be 4.2 calories per minute, whereas for a 200-pound person it would be 5.3 calories per minute.

Use of Physiological Measurements in Work Methods Design

When a new plant and its production facilities are being designed or purchased, management is often confronted with the problem of whether a person can physically perform a particular operation, or how best to organize the work for each person when a group is needed to do the job, or how much rest will be required by a worker performing a specific task. The objective is to design the work method so that the operator can perform the task 8 hours per day, 5 days per week, without undue fatigue. Physiological measurements of the worker on the actual job or on a simulated operation can provide useful information pertaining to such problems.

A Specific Case—Power Shear Operation

An example is given here of the use of physiological measurements for the evaluation of the physical requirements for operating a power shear for cutting photographic paper. A power shear is commonly used in paper manufacturing and in the printing and photographic industries to cut large sheets of paper into smaller sizes. The operation consists of stacking the paper onto a pile or lift several inches high and cutting it by a power-operated knife at the back of the shear. Eastman Kodak Company was considering the purchase of a new power shear larger than any it was then using.[8] The company wanted to know whether a person could operate this new machine manually or whether a completely mechanized feeding and unloading device would be required. This special equipment would cost approximately $20,000 and would place certain constraints on the flexibility of the new power shear.

Physiological studies using changes in oxygen consumption and heart rate were conducted to make the evaluation. A mock-up of the new power shear and work place was constructed, and the operation of the new machine was simulated. The operation of the new power shear would consist of moving lifts of paper stock from a pallet located on a levelator onto the bed of the machine. Each lift was 52 inches by 43 inches by 1 inch in size and weighed approximately 45 pounds. Five lifts were transferred from the pallet to the machine to form a total lift 5 inches high and weighing 225 pounds. An air table was used as the bed of the machine, thus greatly reducing the effort required to move the paper. The paper was trimmed and two cuts were made. These cuts were then transferred to another pallet located on a levelator at the other side of the machine bed. The cycle was then repeated.

The man selected for the study was an experienced power-shear operator. On the day before the actual study, the operator was asked to do some standard lifting tasks and to perform a treadmill operation. Oxygen consumption and heart rate data were obtained. The results of these tests showed the responses of this operator to be well within the range of a group of other factory workers who had been studied in the past. On the day of the study the operator performed the simulated task for 3½ hours. He was paced by signals from a tape recorder which gave a uniform cycle time of 4.65 minutes. The results of the study are shown in Table 63.

Since the average energy expenditure of 4.25 calories per minute and a heart rate of 109 beats per minute were well within the accepted range of 5.00 and 100 to 125 respectively, it was decided that the new square cutter could be purchased and that

[8] H. L. Davis and C. I. Miller, "Work Physiology as an Aid to Job Design," *Thirteenth Annual Conference Proceedings,* American Institute of Industrial Engineers, Norcross, GA, pp. 281–286.

Table 63. Energy Expenditure and Heart Rate for Operator While Working on Simulated Power-Shear Operation

	Average	Minimum	Maximum
Energy expenditure in calories per minute	4.25	4.00	5.00
Heart rate in beats per minute	109	92	118

the mechanized feeding and unloading device would not be needed. This study gave the company assurance that the operation of the new machine would not place unreasonable stress on the operator. The power shear was purchased and installed (Fig. 260), and actual experience was almost identical with that forecast by the simulation study.

ESTABLISHING TIME STANDARDS BY PHYSIOLOGICAL METHODS

Time standards established by time study, standard data, or by predetermined time data are generally set so that the average qualified, well-trained, and experienced operator working on a manual task against the time standard can produce at a level of approximately 125 percent day-in and day-out when employed in a plant where wage incentives are used. It is expected that approximately 96 percent of the working pop-

Figure 260   Power shear for square-cutting photographic paper.

Table 64. Change in Energy Expenditure and Heart Rate for Three Operators in the Shipping Room, Working at Three Different Speeds

	Energy Expenditure in Calories per Minute			Heart Rate in Beats per Minute		
Cartons Handled Per Minute	6	9	12	6	9	12
Operator						
Jones	3.2	3.9	5.0	87	93	99
Brown	3.5	4.4	5.5	88	92	98
Smith	2.8	3.7	4.9	89	98	105

ulation can meet or exceed the standard (Fig. 199). It is known that some people can attain the 100 percent performance level much more easily than others. As a result, some people regularly work at a level of 150 or 160 percent, whereas others using the same expenditure of energy may attain a level of only 110 or 115 percent. Time standards are set for the *task,* that is, for a specific and carefully defined job.

To illustrate this point, let us consider three men, Jones, Brown, and Smith, who performed a carton-handling operation[9] in the shipping room (Fig. 255). This job consisted of the operator standing in front of a worktable 34 inches high, and lifting a 10-pound carton from a conveyor on his left up 10 inches to the table, stamping the shipping address on the carton, and disposing of it onto a conveyor located 10 inches above the table. Each man worked at three different speeds, handling cartons at the rate of 6 per minute, 9 per minute, and 12 per minute. Speeds were established by the use of signals from a tape recorder. The energy expenditure in calories per minute and the change in heart rate in beats per minute are shown in Table 64 and Fig. 261. Although the heart rate of the three men is not greatly different at any given working speed, there is some difference in energy expenditure as measured by calories per minute. At the slow speed of 6 cartons per minute, Jones expended 3.2 calories per minute, Brown 3.5, and Smith 2.8. At the high speed of 12 cartons per minute, the energy expenditure was 5.0, 5.5, and 4.9 calories, respectively.

Physiological measurements can be used to compare the energy cost on a job for which there is a satisfactory time standard, with a similar operation on which there is no standard, but the comparison should be made for the same person. For example, if handling 10-pound cartons at the rate of 12 cartons per minute under the conditions described above was considered normal performance,[10] and if the energy cost for Jones was 5 calories per minute, the answer to the question of what the time standard should be for handling 15-pound cartons under the same conditions might be obtained

---

[9] Study made by Ralph M. Barnes, Robert B. Andrews, James I. Williams, and B. J. Hamilton.
[10] This is a hypothetical case.

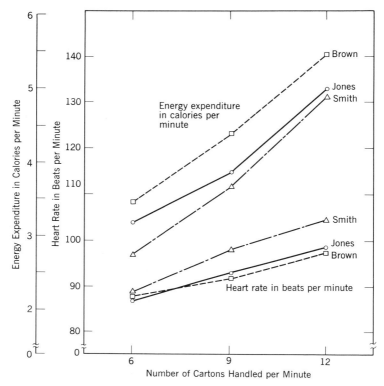

Figure 261 Curves showing change in energy expenditure and heart rate for the three operators in the shipping room, working at three different speeds.

by having Jones handle 15-pound cartons at various speeds, and then selecting the speed that gave an energy cost of 5 calories per minute. Thus, the energy cost of the two jobs would be similar, and the time standard, that is, the number of 15-pound cartons handled per minute, could be determined.

Dr. Lucien Brouha has compiled a classification of work loads in terms of physiological reactions[11] as shown in Table 65. Table 66 shows energy expenditure data for a number of different tasks. This information is taken from research reports of many different investigators as compiled by Passmore and Durnin.[12]

To summarize, the results of research and experience in industry support the fol-

[11] Lucien Brouha, *Physiology in Industry*, Pergamon Press, New York, 1960, p. 87.
[12] R. Passmore and J. V. G. A. Durnin, "Human Energy Expenditure," *Physiological Reviews*, Vol. 35, No. 4, pp. 816–834, October, 1955.

Table 65. Classification of Work Loads in Terms of Physiological Reactions

Work Load	Oxygen Consumption in Liters per Minute	Energy Expenditure in Calories per Minute	Heart Rate During Work in Beats per Minute
Light	0.5–1.0	2.5– 5.0	60–100
Moderate	1.0–1.5	5.0– 7.5	100–125
Heavy	1.5–2.0	7.5–10.0	125–150
Very heavy	2.0–2.5	10.0–12.5	150–175

Table 66. Energy Expenditure Table

Type of Operation	Energy Cost in Calories per Minute
Sitting—idle	1.2
Watch and clock repair	1.6
Clerical work—sitting	1.65
Light assembly work	1.8
Draftsman	1.8
Clerical work—standing	1.90
Tailor hand sewing	2.0
Hand compositor	2.2
Tailor machine sewing	2.6
Sheet metal work	3.0
Punch-press operator	3.8
Tailor pressing suit	4.3
Trimming battery plates	4.4
Straightening lead contact bars	4.6
Pushing wheelbarrow at 2.8 miles per hour with 125-pound load on fairly smooth surface	5.0
Shoveling 18 pounds of sand through a distance of 3 feet with 1.5-foot lift at 12 throws per minute	5.4
Unloading battery boxes from oven	6.8
Pushing wheelbarrow at 2.8 miles per hour with 330-pound load on fairly smooth surface	7.0
Shoveling 18-pound load through a distance of 3 feet with lift up to 3 feet at 12 throws per minute	7.5
Digging ditch in clay soil	8.5
Tending furnace in steel mill	10.2

lowing statements as to the acceptable physiological cost of full body muscular work over an 8-hour day:

For the average male worker a maximum average energy expenditure of 5 calories per minute—a maximum average heart rate of 115 to 120 beats per minute.

For the average female worker a maximum average energy expenditure of 4 calories per minute—a maximum average heart rate of 115 to 120 beats per minute.[13] Data are not available for older workers.

[13] The *heart rate* criteria should be used for measuring hot environment. Oxygen consumption does not change appreciably with change in temperature.

32

FATIGUE

Since one of the main objectives of motion and time study is to reduce fatigue and to make the work as easy and satisfying for the individual as possible, it is desirable at this time to examine the nature of fatigue.

PHENOMENA ASSOCIATED WITH FATIGUE

The term *fatigue* has various meanings, depending upon the point of view that is taken in considering the subject. Fatigue in industry refers to three related phenomena: (1) a feeling of tiredness; (2) a physiological change in the body (the nerves and muscles fail to function as well or as fast as is normal because of chemical changes in the body resulting from work); and (3) a diminished capacity for doing work.

Feeling of Tiredness

A feeling of tiredness is commonly associated with long periods of work. It is subjective in nature, and consequently the extent of tiredness cannot be determined by an observer. Tiredness may be localized in some particular muscle, or it may be a general sensation of weariness.

This feeling of fatigue acts as a protective device in preventing exhaustion, but there is often no direct correlation with physiological fatigue that manifests itself in decreased ability to do work. A person may feel tired and yet may work as efficiently as ever, or may feel normal and yet may be actually working at a low rate because of physiological fatigue. Therefore, the feeling of tiredness does not seem to be a valid basis for judging the effect of work on the individual.

Physiological Changes Resulting from Work

From the physiological point of view the human body may be thought of as a machine [1] which consumes fuel and gives out useful energy. The principal mechanisms of the body that are involved are (1) the circulatory system, (2) the digestive system, (3) the muscular system, (4) the nervous system, and (5) the respiratory system. Continuous physical work affects these mechanisms both separately and collectively.

Fatigue is the result of an accumulation of waste products in the muscles and in the blood stream, which reduces the capacity of the muscles to act. Very possible the

[1] A. V. Hill, *Living Machinery,* Harcourt Brace and Co., New York.

nerve fiber terminals and the central nervous system may also be affected by work, thereby causing a person to slow down when tired. Muscular movements are accompanied by chemical reactions which require food for their activities. This food is furnished as *glycogen,* a starchlike substance which is carried in the blood stream and is readily converted into sugar. When the muscle contracts, the gycogen is changed into lactic acid, a waste product that tends to restrict the continued activity of the muscle. In the recovery phase of muscular action, oxygen is used to change most of the lactic acid back to glycogen, thus enabling the muscles to continue moving. The supply of oxygen and the temperature affect the speed of recovery. If the rate of work is not strenuous, the muscle is able to maintain a satisfactory balance. Excessive lactic acid does not accumulate and the muscle does not go into "oxygen debt," both of which diminish the capacity of the muscle to act.

An athlete running the mile might be used as an example of individual exerting himself to the utmost. He is using the supply of fuel and oxygen at a rapid rate, and therefore will require time for recuperation, that is, time to bring his muscles back to equilibrium.

Effects of Physical Environment on the Worker

The physiological cost of doing work is affected by environmental factors, such as temperature, humidity, air movement, and atmospheric contamination. A person has certain energy requirements just to maintain bodily functions; when he does physical work, his energy requirements increase. If the resting environment and the working environment are changed—for example, if the temperature is increased from 70 to 90° F—then the energy cost increases at both the resting level and the working level. Change in heart rate appears to be the best means of measuring the effects of such environmental factors. Figure 262 shows the heart rate and oxygen consumption before, during, and after a standard exercise was performed under two conditions of dry-bulb temperature and relative humidity. In this study six men pedaled a bicycle ergometer at two different speeds.[2] The men worked for 30 minutes at a medium work load and then for a 4-minute period at a heavy load. The environmental conditions were as follows:

Normal room temperature: 72° F. and 50 percent relative humidity
Hot wet: 90° F. and 82 percent relative humidity

The curves show that an immediate increase in heart rate and oxygen consumption occurs as exercise begins. As the moderate work at room temperature progresses there is a slight increase of the heart rate, but the oxygen consumption remains at a steady level. As soon as the work load becomes heavy, both heart rate and oxygen

---

[2] Lucien Brouha, "Physiological Approach to Problems of Work Measurement," *Proceedings Ninth Industrial Engineering Institute,* University of California, Los Angeles-Berkeley, p. 13, 1957.

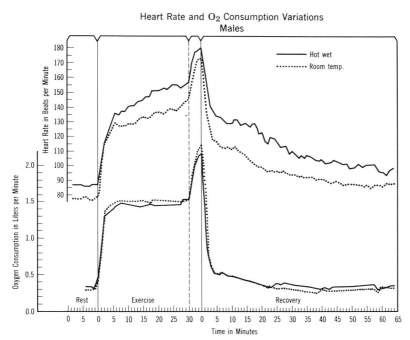

Heart Rate and O$_2$ Consumption Variations
Males

Figure 262   Heart rate and oxygen consumption during rest, during exercise at two different work loads, and during recovery. These experiments were performed in two different environments.

consumption increase immediately and continue to increase until the exercise ends. During the recovery period the oxygen consumption returns to the resting level after 35 minutes; whereas the heart rate diminishes less rapidly and is still well above the resting level after 65 minutes of recovery.

For any job in which the physiological expenditure is great enough to produce significant changes in heart rate, the heart rate recovery curves will determine the physiological cost of the job and will permit evaluation of any modification that is made in attempting to reduce stress and fatigue. For example, in a job where men had to skim impurities from the surface of a liquid with a long and heavy ladle, the tanks were situated at such a height above the floor that the operation had to be performed at shoulder level. Average reactions were high, reaching 160 beats per minute for the first pulse recorded 1 minute after skimming one tank. Special platforms were built so that men could operate slightly above waist level. The average heart rate recorded 1 minute after the operation dropped to 112 beats per minute, indicating a drastic reduction in the "physiological work" necessary to perform the job.[3]

[3] Lucien Brouha, "Fatigue—Measuring and Reducing It," *Advanced Management,* Vol. 19, No. 1, p. 13, January 1954.

The following is a procedure for evaluating the effect of physical environment upon the operation of a drop hammer in a forge shop.[4] Heart rate and oxygen consumption data were obtained from the operator performing his regular job in the factory. The same operator then was asked to operate a bicycle ergometer which had been moved into the factory and placed beside the drop hammer. The worker operated the ergometer at a load that produced approximately the same heart rate and oxygen consumption as were present when he was working on his regular job. The ergometer was then moved into the laboratory, where the temperature was maintained at 70° F. and the relative humidity at 50 percent, and the operator worked at the same speed as in the factory. His heart rate and oxygen consumption in the laboratory were obtained. The difference was a measure of the effects of the shop environment, that is, high temperature, humidity, smoke, and fumes.

Effect of Protective Clothing on Pulse Rate

Although industry is striving to reduce fatigue and improve working conditions, there are still some heavy jobs that have to be performed under conditions of high temperature and humidity. Brouha's studies show that pulse rate can be used as a measure of the effectiveness of special clothing to protect the worker from heat and noxious fumes.[5]

Figure 263 shows the effect of a ventilated suit on the heart rate. The curve at the top shows the average reaction in 45 operations without the ventilated suit. The pulse rate was 127 beats per minute at the end of the first minute, 115 at the end of the second, and 109 at the end of the third. The second curve gives the results for operators working with suits inflated with air at room temperature, 90° F. The pulse rate was 111 beats per minute at the end of the first minute, 101 at the end of the second, and 96 at the end of the third. The bottom curve shows the results for operators with the suit inflated with air cooled to 70°. In this case the pulse rates were 92, 85, and 81 at the end of the first, second, and third minutes respectively.

Decrease in Output an Indication of Fatigue

Some people believe that the most practical and useful index of fatigue is its effect upon the quantity and the quality of the individual's work; that fatigue can be measured in terms of reduced output resulting from work. However, one cannot say definitely that a reduction in output results from fatigue. That a person turns out less work during the last hour of the day may, of course, be due to the fact that he is tired. It may also be due to the fact that he has lost interest in the job, or that he is

---

[4] F. H. Bonjer, Netherlands Institute for Preventive Medicine, Leyden, Holland.
[5] Lucien Brouha, "Fatigue—Measuring and Reducing It," *Advanced Management,* Vol. 19, No. 1, p. 9, January 1954.

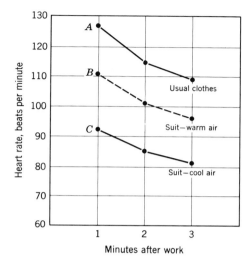

Figure 263 Average heart rate recovery curves of workers performing the same operation in a magnesium plant: *A*, usual working clothes; *B*, suit ventilated with air at 90° F.; *C*, suit ventilated with air at 70° F.

worried about some personal problem, or simply that he believes he has already done a day's work.

The amount of work done per unit of time may be shown by means of a production curve, sometimes called an output curve or a work curve. It is possible that the production curve for *very heavy* manual work might take the shape shown in Fig. 264. Some people interpret this curve in the following way. The upward slope of the curve indicates a "warming up" period in the morning. This is followed by an increase in output until the middle of the morning, when a falling off in production occurs, possibly because of the fatigue of the worker. The curve for the afternoon is

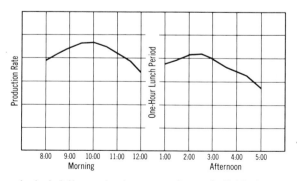

Figure 264 Hypothetical daily production curve for an individual engaged in very heavy physical work.

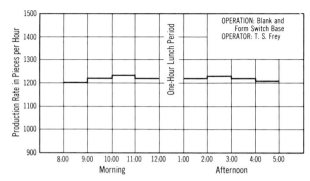

Figure 265 Production curve for blanking and forming switch base on Bliss press.

similar in shape to that for the forenoon, except that it falls off more rapidly toward the end of the day.

Much work in industry today is light and requires little physical exertion on the part of the operator. The production curve shown in Fig. 265 seems to be typical for such work, there being a fairly uniform output throughout the day. The operator has such a reserve of energy and the physical requirements of the task are so small that it is entirely possible for the operator to maintain a steady output for the entire day. In fact, it is not uncommon to find an operator actually increasing speed during the last hour of the day when a delay has existed earlier in the day causing him to fall behind, or when a rush job has been put into production.

FACTORS AFFECTING DEGREE OF FATIGUE

Many factors affect the amount of work that an individual will do in a day and the extent of the physical fatigue that will result from this work. With a given set of working conditions and equipment, the amount of work done in a day will depend upon the ability of the worker and the speed at which he or she works. This latter factor depends directly upon the individual's inclination or the "will to work," which itself is affected by many things. The fatigue resulting from a given level of activity will depend upon such factors as (1) hours of work, that is, the length of the working day and the weekly working hours; (2) the number, location, and length of rest periods; (3) working conditions, such as lighting, heating, ventilation, and noise; and (4) the work itself.

Hours of Work

The findings of the Health of Munition Workers Committee organized in Great Britain in 1915 gave impetus to the movement for decreasing the length of the working day. At that time the 12- to 15-hour day was common. The reports of this committee and of many other investigations made since that time indicate the economy of shorter working hours. There is evidence to show that on most work, except for operations whose output depends mainly upon the speed of the machine, reduction of the length of the working day to 8 hours has resulted in an increase in hourly and daily output.

The 10-hour day and 4-day week, the 7-hour day and 5-day week, as well as the staggered starting time of the conventional 8-hour day are now being tried. Permanent part-time employees are common; two people may split a full-time job and determine their own work schedule. In some areas where there is a shortage of labor and where some employees do not want to work a full week they are asked to indicate a week in advance which days they wish to work. The desires of our work force are changing, and flexibility in arranging hours of work is becoming a requirement for some employers.

There is an increase in the machines and facilities that must operate 24 hours per day 7 days per week, and more workers are now employed on the second and third shifts. One investigation showed that one-third of the employees cannot adjust to the night shift, and many dislike the rotation plan because of its effect on their health and personal lives. Instead of the usual work schedule which calls for one week on the day shift, the next week on the 4 P.M. to midnight shift, and the third week midnight to 8 A.M., a plan called the rapid rotation is being tried with some success. Instead of working a full week on each shift, the rapid rotation plan calls for two days on each shift with two days off at the end of six days. The objective in all cases is to find a plan that will result in high productivity, low cost, and greatest satisfaction for the employees.

Rest Periods

When a person performs heavy physical work, it is necessary to stop and rest at intervals during the working day. If heavy work is done under conditions of high temperature and humidity, then the worker experiences still greater stress and consequently needs more time to recuperate. On such jobs the worker will rest a considerable part of the day whether "official" rest periods are allowed by management or not. Vernon found that on *heavy work* men rested one-half to one-fourth of the working time.[6] Taylor, in his classic experiment of handling pig iron, increased the output from 12½ to 47 tons per day mainly by requiring that the workmen rest 57 percent of the time and work but 43 percent of the time.[7] It should be noted that these examples

---

[6] H. M. Vernon et al., "Rest Pauses in Heavy and Moderately Heavy Industrial Work," Industrial Fatigue Research Board, *Report* 41, p. 20.

[7] F. W. Taylor, *The Principles of Scientific Management*, Harper & Bros., New York, 1911, p. 57.

are taken from *heavy work* and that much work in industry today is light and requires little physical exertion on the part of the operator.

As previously explained, a person can work with an energy expenditure up to 5 calories per minute over an 8-hour day without going into "oxygen debt." On a task that does not tax a person beyond this level, no rest period would be needed. If the work is more demanding physically, or if the temperature and humidity are high and the energy expenditure exceeds 5 calories per minute, then rest periods should be introduced. Each person has a certain "physiological capital" upon which he or she can draw.

Some work is intermittent in nature. For example, the operator may perform the physically demanding task of loading the machine, then while it is making the cut, the operator may gauge the previous piece, which requires little effort. Thus, energy peaks may exceed the 5 calories per minute level at intervals throughout the day and still not overload the operator. The low energy parts of the job permit the operator to recover from the more demanding peaks. Müller[8] has suggested that the average person might be considered to have an energy reserve of 25 calories. If a worker uses 7 calories per minute, he would draw on his reserve at the rate of $(7 - 5 = 2)$ 2 calories per minute and would use his reserve in approximately 12 minutes. Once the 25 calories reserve is used the work period should not begin until the resting level has been reached. Although this may not be precise it does provide a method for determining the length and frequency of rest and work periods.

In many kinds of work, both heavy and light, rest periods are desirable for the following reasons: (1) rest periods increase the amount of work done in a day, (2) the workers like the rest periods, (3) rest periods decrease the variability in the rate of working and tend to encourage the operator to maintain a level of performance nearer his or her maximum output, (4) rest periods reduce physical fatigue, and (5) rest periods reduce the amount of personal time taken during the working hours. Rest periods are particularly effective in heavy manual work, in operations that require close attention and concentration, such as fine inspection work, and in work that is highly repetitive and monotonous. Rest periods are usually placed in the middle of the morning and the middle of the afternoon, and range in length from 5 to 15 minutes. The proper number of rest periods, the spacing, and the proper length of each will depend upon the nature of the work and can be determined most satisfactorily by experiment or by physiological measurement. In general, several short rest periods are better than fewer long ones. When a person must work under hot, humid conditions, the rate of recovery will be much more rapid if he or she can rest in a cool, air-conditioned rest room. Where several people work as a group, the rotation of jobs at frequent intervals may serve to reduce the total physiological cost per person in that different sets of muscles may be brought into use with a change in the job.

---

[8] E. A. Müller, "The Physiological Basis of Rest Pauses in Heavy Work," *Quarterly Journal of Experimental Physiology,* Vol. 38, No. 4, 1953.

Where rest periods are needed, tests show that definite rest periods sanctioned by the management have a greater recuperative effect than those which must be taken surreptitiously. Whether the rest is in the form of "soldiering" or whether it is enforced because of lack of materials, such hit or miss rests may have as little as one-fifth the value of prescribed rests in relieving fatigue according to one study.

When workers are paid by the hour, when their work is not measured, and when they are employed to perform tasks on which they can set their own pace, workers can rest when they wish and are free to adjust their working time and their resting time to suit their own needs. However, when an operation is measured and the worker is given an opportunity to earn a wage incentive, a time standard is established for the job, and this time standard contains an allowance for personal needs (personal allowance) and an allowance for rest or recuperation (fatigue allowance). Each company has its own method for determining fatigue allowances, and among older well-established companies these data have been obtained by trial and error over a period of many years. There is a real need for a more systematic method of determining fatigue allowances, and physiological measurements are contributing to the solution of this problem.

Lighting, Heating, and Ventilation

Lighting, heating, and ventilation have a definite effect upon the physical comfort, mental attitude, output, and fatigue of the worker. Working conditions should be so adjusted as to make the shop and office a comfortable place in which to work. The requirements for proper illumination, heating, and ventilation are well understood, and equipment that will supply comfortable physical conditions for work is available.

Of these three factors, illumination is perhaps most inadequately provided. Where the work is of such a nature that visual perception is required for its satisfactory performance, the output is often increased when adequate illumination is provided. Inspection operations such as those described on pages 213 to 219 are examples of work of this nature.

Noise and Vibration

Noise and vibration are annoying, they are undesirable, and should be reduced or eliminated insofar as possible. Stamping, cutting, and presswork are often segregated in one part of the factory so that the remainder of the plant may be kept relatively free of noise. Where large numbers of employees are affected and where the work requires a high degree of concentration or attention, it may be desirable to reduce the noise by covering the ceilings and walls with acoustic board, as is done in many places. Some companies are completely enclosing noisy equipment such as automatic punch presses with solid walls of sound-absorbing materials. The walls are designed so that they can be opened up for servicing and adjusting the equipment.

Effect of Mental Attitude on Fatigue

Fatigue is by no means simple and easily defined. Researchers have pointed out many different aspects of this phenomenon. A carefully conducted study, lasting over a period of several years, of fatigue of factory operators on regular production work at the Western Electric Company showed that the mental attitude of the workers was by far the most important factor governing their efficiency.

Specific conclusions [9] relating to this point are:

(1)   The amount of sleep has a slight but significant effect upon individual performance.

(2)   A distinct relationship is apparent between the emotional status or home conditions of the girls and their performance.

(3)   Total daily productivity is increased by rest periods, and not decreased.

(4)   Outside influences tend to create either a buoyant or a depressed spirit, which is reflected in production.

(5)   The mental attitude of the operator toward the supervisor and working and home conditions is probably the biggest single factor governing the employee's efficiency. [10]

[9] G. A. Pennock, "Industrial Research at Hawthorne, an Experimental Investigation of Rest Periods, Working Conditions, and Other Influences," *Personnel Journal,* Vol. 8, No. 5, p. 311.

[10] See Chapter 39 "Motivation and Work."

33

HUMAN FACTORS

Human factors is a system concerned with the relationship between human beings, machines, and the work environment. The object is to obtain the optimum balance between the human capabilities and the demands of the task. Human factors directs its attention largely to complex systems, and places greater emphasis on the results of research and less on past experience and empirical information in solving problems. When documented research data are not available, studies are made to obtain the necessary information. The diverse and complex nature of problems encountered by the human factors group in many organizations calls for an interdisciplinary approach and may require skills from a variety of professions such as psychology, sociology, biology, physiology, and engineering. McCormick[1] approaches the definition of human factors in three stages, as follows:

- The central *focus* of human factors relates to the consideration of human beings in the design of the man-made objects, facilities, and environments that people "use" in the various aspects of their lives.
- The *objectives* of human factors in the design of these man-made objects, facilities, and environments are twofold, as follows: (1) to enhance the *functional effectiveness* with which people can use them; and (2) to maintain or enhance certain desirable *human values* in the process (e.g., health, safety, and satisfaction); this second objective is essentially one of human welfare.
- The central *approach* of human factors is the systemic application of relevant information about human characteristics and behavior to the design of the man-made objects, facilities, and environments that people use.

The worker-machine relationship is the central core of human factors. The worker and the machine may perform similar functions. Both have certain capabilities and limitations. The worker-machine system, like any system, has an objective or purpose, and consists of inputs and outputs: raw material is processed, books are printed, a hole is drilled in a bar of steel.

A person ordinarily does three things (Fig. 266) in performing any task:

1. Receives information—through the sense organs: eyes, ears, touch, etc.
2. Makes decisions—acts on the information obtained and on the basis of his or her own knowledge.
3. Takes action—action resulting from the decision that has been made. The action

[1] Ernest J. McCormick, *Human Factors in Engineering and Design,* 4th ed., McGraw-Hill, New York, 1976, p. 4. Reproduced by permission.

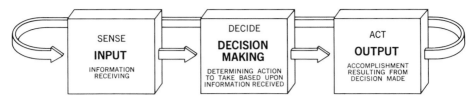

Figure 266   The basic control cycle consists of three parts: sense, decide, and act.

may be purely physical, such as operating a machine, or it may involve communication, such as giving oral or written instructions.

Men and machines both have sensors. The machine senses by mechanical, chemical, or electrical means. Decision making or information processing by machine occurs through the use of computers, electrical circuits, or mechanical means. The action function is the accomplishment or the output resulting from the decisions made. Both men and machines may store information and there is usually feedback. The division of work between men and machines is generally determined by economic considerations although many other factors enter the picture. McCormick[2] makes the following generalizations about the relative capabilities of human beings and of machines.

Humans are generally *better* in their abilities to:

• Sense very low levels of certain kinds of stimuli: visual, auditory, tactual, olfactory, and taste.

• Detect stimuli against high-"noise"-level background, such as blips on cathode-ray-tube (CRT) displays with poor reception.

• Recognize patterns of complex stimuli which may vary from situation to situation, such as objects in aerial photographs and speech sounds.

• Sense unusual and unexpected events in the environment.

• Store (remember) large amounts of information over long periods of time (better for remembering principles and strategies than masses of detailed information).

• Retrieve pertinent information from storage (recall), frequently retrieving many related items of information; but reliability of recall is low.

• Draw upon varied experience in making decisions; adapt decisions to situational requirements; act in emergencies. (Does not require previous "programming" for all situations.)

• Select alternative modes of operation, if certain modes fail.

• Reason inductively, generalizing from observations.

• Apply principles to solutions of varied problems.

• Make subjective estimates and evaluations.

• Develop entirely new solutions.

[2] Ernest J. McCormick, *Human Factors in Engineering and Design,* 4th ed., McGraw-Hill, New York. 1976. pp. 461–462. Reproduced by permission.

- Concentrate on most important activities, when overload conditions require.
- Adapt physical response (within reason) to variations in operational requirements.

Machines are generally *better* in their abilities to:

- Sense stimuli that are outside man's normal range of sensitivity, such as x-rays, radar wavelengths, and ultrasonic vibrations.
- Apply deductive reasoning, such as recognizing stimuli as belonging to a general class (but the characteristics of the class need to be specified).
- Monitor for prespecified events, especially when infrequent (but machines cannot improvise in case of unanticipated types of events).
- Store coded information quickly and in substantial quantity (for example, large sets of numerical values can be stored very quickly).
- Retrieve coded information quickly and accurately when specifically requested (although specific instructions need to be provided on the type of information that is to be recalled).
- Process quantitative information following specified programs.
- Make rapid and consistent responses to input signals.
- Perform repetitive activities reliably.
- Exert considerable physical force in a highly controlled manner.
- Maintain performance over extended periods of time (machines typically do not "fatigue" as rapidly as humans).
- Count or measure physical quantities.
- Perform several programmed activities simultaneously.
- Maintain efficient operations under conditions of heavy load (men have relatively limited channel capacity).
- Maintain efficient operations under distractions.

The number of people working in the human factors field grew rapidly during World War II. A most important contribution of this group was the solving of complex man-machine problems such as assisting in the design of aircraft cockpits, fire-control systems, sonar devices, and ship and submarine control systems. In some cases military equipment had not been designed for effective human use—failures occurred, human errors were made, and planes and ships were lost because people operating the equipment were unable to perform their functions—the designer had not taken into consideration human capabilities.

Human factors groups continue to be used in military and space systems design but increasingly these groups play an important part in business and industry.

Human Factors at Eastman Kodak Company

For some 20 years imaginative and important work in human factors has been under way at the Eastman Kodak Company.[3] Harry L. Davis and other people in the industrial engineering department at Kodak Park had become concerned about the need for more quantitative methods of measuring physical work, and in 1959 steps were

[3] Reproduced by permission of the Eastman Kodak Company.

taken to enter this field. The next year Davis and Charles I. Miller, a physician in the industrial medicine department, organized the human factors section and began a systematic study of the physical capabilities of workers. This section remained in the industrial engineering division for a number of years but as the size and scope expanded it became a corporate function as a part of the Health, Safety, and Human Factors Laboratory.[4] It now numbers 22 people representing the disciplines of medicine, physiology, engineering, and psychology. It is organized into three subdivisions: product, plant, and research. The company also has human factors support at its Tennessee Eastman Company and the Kodak Colorado Division.

The laboratory is concerned with the human factor of manufacturing system design, physical capacity evaluation, and the many problems and opportunities which industry faces as a result of the Occupational Safety and Health Act (OSHA), Equal Employment Opportunity (EEO), and Consumer Product Safety Commission (CPSC). Also for some years the human factors group has been heavily involved in the design of new products and in the redesign of old ones. A member of the human factors group serves on the design committee for new products, and consulting service is also provided on redesign work.

Some of the early studies dealt with the measurement of fairly heavy jobs to determine whether employees were under too great physical stress. Volunteers from the factory performed such tasks as walking and running on the treadmill, and measurements of oxygen consumption and heart rate were made. Also, similar measurements were made of simulated factory operations and actual factory jobs. Thousands of workers and jobs have been studied and some valuable guidelines have been developed for men and for women. For example, in a specific case a decision can be made concerning the suitability of the job. If the task is too strenuous, the employee can be given easier work or perhaps the job itself can be changed.

Other areas that have received intensive study are vision and illumination, inspection work including inspection on conveyor belts, workplace design, rotation plan for shift work, and complex jobs involving both physical effort and mental demands. The laboratory is committed to fitting jobs to people, to reducing undue strain, and to helping people work better.

Kodak is an example of a private industry successfully operating a Human Factors Laboratory in addition to a large Industrial Engineering Division, which has an outstanding record covering some 65 years. The two organizations complement each other and both contribute to the company's success.

Human Factors Engineering at Lockhead

The Space Systems Division of Lockhead Missiles and Space Company (LMSC) is acknowledged as a leader in the development of advanced unmanned earth satellites

---

[4] The Health, Safety, and Human Factors Laboratory consists of the following sections: Clinical Chemistry, Biochemistry, Industrial Hygiene, Human Factors, Occupational Health Services, Toxicology, and Technical Safety Research.

and spacecraft.[5] Human Factors Engineering is important in unmanned spacecraft activities because people have significant roles in these systems. Lockheed also develops and manufactures a very broad range of other products and systems in addition to unmanned spacecraft. These systems involve human operators, controllers, and maintainers. In the final analysis, virtually all of the products and systems manufactured by the Space Systems Division involve human interfaces with the material elements of the system—the hardware, facilities, computer programs, and the procedures by which personnel operate, maintain, and support the system.

As the largest interdisciplinary group of its type within Lockheed Corporation, Space Systems Division Human Factors Engineering is also called upon to support programs in LMSC's Advanced Systems Division and Missile Systems Division, and to assist other Lockheed corporate divisions, such as the Lockheed-Georgia, Lockheed-California, and Lockheed Electronics companies. In addition, the Human Factors Engineering group performs research, analytical design support, and simulation studies under contract for various government agencies and civilian companies as a part of Space Systems Division's effort to maintain a continuing high level of professional expertise in its various technology disciplines.

Definition of Human Factors Engineering at Lockheed

"Human Factors Engineering is a comprehensive, interdisciplinary technical field that has as its objective the integration of scientific knowledge about human characteristics, capabilities, and limitations into the development of products and systems of all kinds. Within the parameters established by system equipment, facility, and software requirements, the Human Factors Engineering program for a new system will be designed to improve, and to optimize wherever possible, all man/machine interfaces in order to achieve the required personnel performance during system operation, maintenance, and control."

"Typically, the technical scope and level of effort in Human Factors Engineering is tailored to the size, complexity, type of system being developed, degree of man's involvement as a system component, and technical risks associated with advancements in the state-of-the-art that may be required. In those new systems where past information and experience are inadequate to permit anticipation of all of the variables that may affect human performance, simulation studies are performed to develop insights into the areas of potential technical and economic risk."

A FULL SCALE STUDY OF COMPLEX WELDING OPERATIONS

Some kinds of work may require precise hand movements, foot-actuated controls, constrained body and head position, use of the eyes, and a large degree of concentration. When such work involves a sizable number of people on a job of long duration, a full-scale study of each aspect of the operation is called for.

The following is an example of such a situation and an excellent illustration of the way the Human Factors Engineering Group, Missile Systems Division of the Lock-

---

[5] Reproduced by permission of the Lockheed Missiles & Space Company, Inc., Space Systems Division.

heed Missiles and Space Company analyzed the task, identified the problems, and employed appropriate methods to solve the problems.[6] A high degree of imagination and ingenuity brought about a successful solution.

Application of Human Engineering Principles and Techniques in the Design of Electronic Production Equipment

Approximately 40 women worked at tables welding grids, slabs, and modules (Fig. 267). The grids varied in size from 2 to 3 inches square and were inscribed with the exact location of the circuit to be produced. The grid wires were welded at the designated locations on the grid and the wires were trimmed. As many as 60 welds and trims were required on a single grid. A ten-power microscope was used by the operator. The welding was done by placing the joint to be welded between a fixed and a movable electrode. The operator depressed a foot pedal which closed the movable electrode and performed the weld. The operators were provided with diagrams and written instructions including voltage, pressures, and pulse duration of welds. Pushbuttons enabled the operator to control these parameters. In succeeding operations grids were assembled into slabs and welded, and then the slabs were further assembled into modules.

The microscope and the weld unit were mounted directly on the table top. A standard drafting lamp provided lighting. The employees compalined of fatigue and back pains and in addition the manipulation of the foot pedal seemed to cause leg pains. Despite hourly break periods the task was extremely demanding.

When the decision was made to improve the job, the Human Engineering Group[7] carefully studied all aspects of the operation. The employees were consulted individually and in groups. Lockheed at that time had a worker motivation plan called *Team* which encouraged employee participation and involvement in work design and methods improvement. The *Team* program was under the direction of the Human Engineering Group.

A drawing (Fig. 268) was made showing the female figure relative to the work place, which included dimensions required to accommodate the range of operators who would be performing the tasks. A proposed work place design consisted of four tables around a center frame forming an island 8 feet in diameter (Fig. 269). This design was reviewed by Manufacturing Engineering and Production Management and they recommended that work on the project be continued. Design details were developed and a foam rubber mockup was constructed. This aided greatly in arriving at such details as the shape of the individual table top, location of arm rests, position of the pushbutton control box, position of the microscope, weld unit, and storage

[6] Milton Rosenthal, "Application of Human Engineering Principles and Techniques in the Design of Electronic Production Equipment," *Human Factors*, Vol. 15, No. 2, pp. 137–148, April 1973. By permission of The Human Factors Society, Inc.

[7] Later renamed Human Factors Engineering Group.

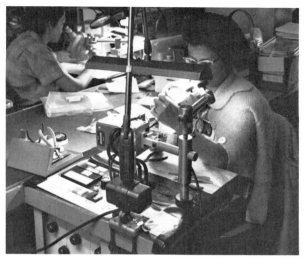

Figure 267 Weld work place before modification.

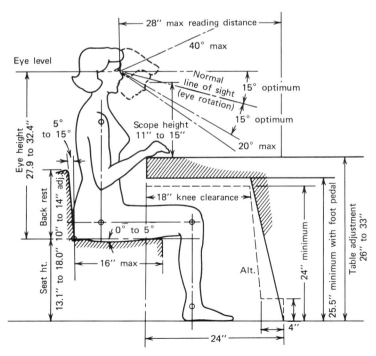

Figure 268 Operator and work place dimensions.

471

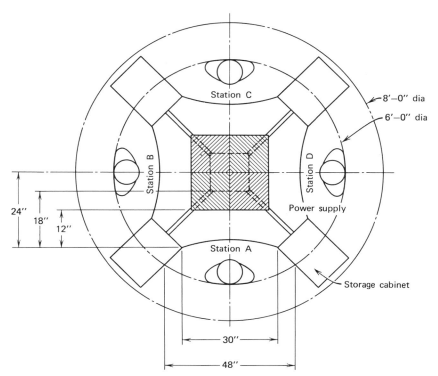

Figure 269 Four-station island layout.

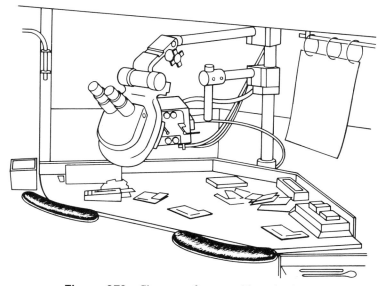

Figure 270 Close-up of new weld work place.

472

drawers. Also, matters such as the mechanism for adjusting the height of the table top and the exact design of the foot pedal were worked out.

A prototype of the unit was built by Lockheed's metal and woodworking development shops and was placed in the working area. Four employees performed the weld and trim operation for a period of six weeks. Workers were rotated in order to get their ideas and suggestions. As deficiencies in the work place were identified changes were immediately made. Different lighting techniques were tried, and an indirect lighting fixture was designed and installed on the prototype. After the operators were satisfied with the work place and after the improvement in output was demonstrated, management approved the construction of the new design to replace the existing tables (Fig. 270). Forty-eight stations or 12 islands were built and installed.

The contoured table top was made of plastic covered plywood with the sides and back raised about an inch. Elbow rests were made of foam rubber and covered with soft plastic material. Identical cutouts were located on both sides of the table top, one for the pushbutton controls and the other for a container that could be used for wire clippings. The control box and the container were removable and could be interchanged to accomodate the handedness of an individual operator. Curtains were placed between work stations to prevent wire clippings from striking other operators. Specification sheets and instructional material were hung from a rod placed at the right of the operator.

Figure 271 Layout of new weld work stations.

The operator could adjust the height of the work place using a wrench on a screw-type mechanism. The microscope and weld unit were mounted on a vertical post and could be easily adjusted by the operator (Fig. 271). The foot pedal was redesigned to reduce leg strain. Information received through the *Team* program revealed that there were wide differences in the light intensity preferred. A fluorescent fixture with push-button control provided an intensity of 150 ft candles on the work surface, which was found to be adequate. Because of the individual differences in the amount of light desired an auxiliary high-intensity gooseneck lamp capable of being focused on the work was available for the operator. Medium blue as a background color was found to cause the wires to show up most clearly and to minimize eye strain.

Tools and material storage cabinets were conveniently located beside the operator so she could use them without moving from her work position. There was space for four tote boxes, and for two drawers in which to store required tools. The cabinet also contained a cutting board which could be pulled out for use. A chair which the operator could adjust for height and which had a sloping back rest was used. The chair was equipped with casters to provide an opportunity for the operator to move the chair toward or away from the work table.

Results

The operators felt that a vast improvement in the work environment had been made. They took pride in their individual work stations. Innovations such as background music and color schemes were introduced. There was a significant increase in output and a marked decline in error rate.

Human Factors Research—Anthropometric Data

Much work in the field of human factors has consisted of carefully controlled research experiments supported by various military and governmental agencies and by private industry. The literature in this field is in the form of detailed research reports and abstracts of research studies which have been assembled into logical and systematic presentations, particularly manuals and handbooks. These provide a ready reference for such groups as equipment and product designers, industrial stylists, work methods designers, and engineers.[8]

[8] Ernest J. McCormick, *Human Factors in Engineering and Design,* 4th ed., McGraw-Hill, New York, 1976. E. Grandjean, *Fitting the Task to the Man,* Taylor & Francis Ltd., London, 1969. Harold P. Van Cott and Robert G. Kinkade (eds.), *Human Engineering Guide to Equipment Design,* (Revised edition), 1972, Department of Defence, Superintendent of Documents, U.S. Government Printing Office, Washington, D.C. T. R. Tichauer, *The Biomechanical Basis of Erognomics,* John Wiley, New York, 1978. Wesley E. Woodson, *Human Engineering Guide for Equipment Designers,* University of California Press, Berkeley-Los Angeles, CA, 1964.

The following are examples of anthropometric data.[9] Figure 272 and 273 contain such data for the standing adult male and female, accommodating 95 percent of the U.S. adult population. Figure 274 shows basic display data and Fig. 275 basic control data.

The information shown on the drawings[9] in Figs. 272–275 was developed after many years of research by Henry Dreyfuss and his associates.

[9] Charts reproduced by permission from *The Measure of Man,* by Henry Dreyfuss, published by Whitney Library of Design, New York, 1960.

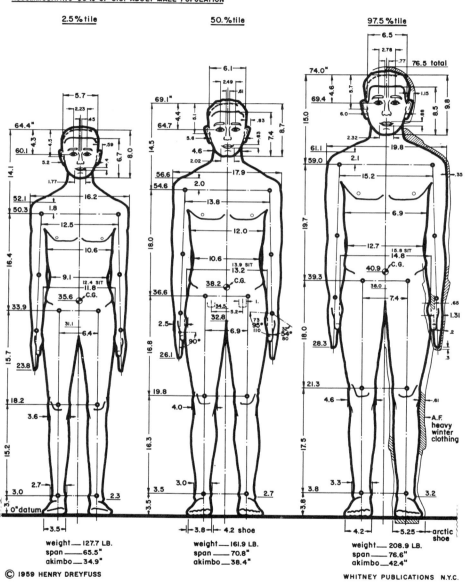

Figure 272 Human dimensions of the standing adult male. (Chart from *The Measure of Man* by Henry Dreyfuss, published by Whitney Library of Design, New York.)

476

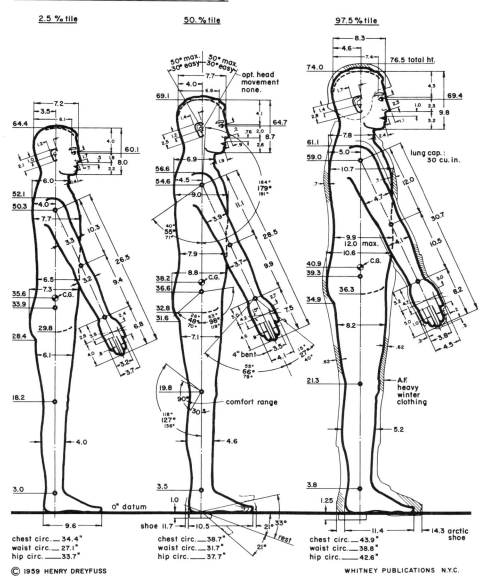

2.5 % tile

50. % tile

97.5 % tile

chest circ.__ 34.4"
waist circ.__ 27.1"
hip circ.____ 33.7"

shoe 11.7

chest circ.__ 38.7"
waist circ.__ 31.7"
hip circ.____ 37.7"

chest circ.__ 43.9"
waist circ.__ 38.8"
hip circ.____ 42.6"

© 1959 HENRY DREYFUSS

WHITNEY PUBLICATIONS N.Y.C.

477

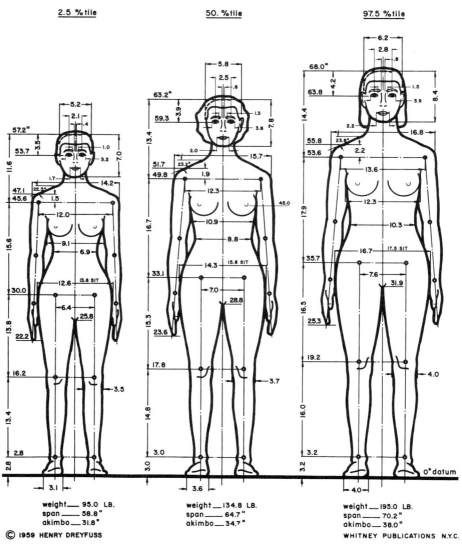

Figure 273 Human dimensions of the standing adult female. (Chart from *The Measure of Man* by Henry Dreyfuss, published by Whitney Library of Design, New York.)

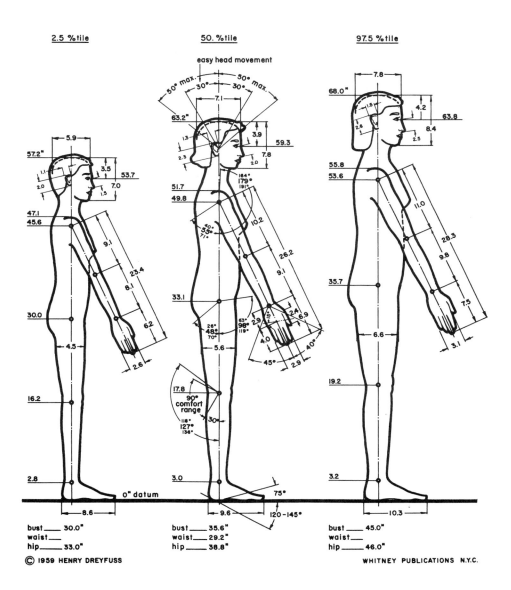

2.5 %tile

50. %tile

97.5 %tile

easy head movement

bust _____ 30.0"
waist _____
hip _____ 33.0"

bust _____ 35.6"
waist _____ 29.2"
hip _____ 38.8"

bust _____ 45.0"
waist _____
hip _____ 46.0"

WHITNEY PUBLICATIONS N.Y.C.

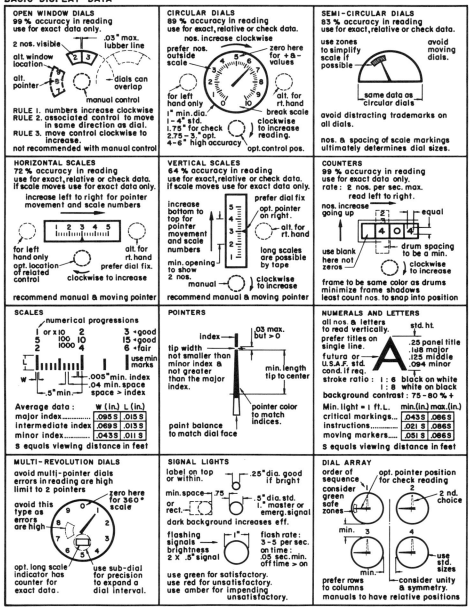

Figure 274 Basic display data. (From *The Measure of Man* by Henry Dreyfuss, published by Whitney Library of Design, New York.)

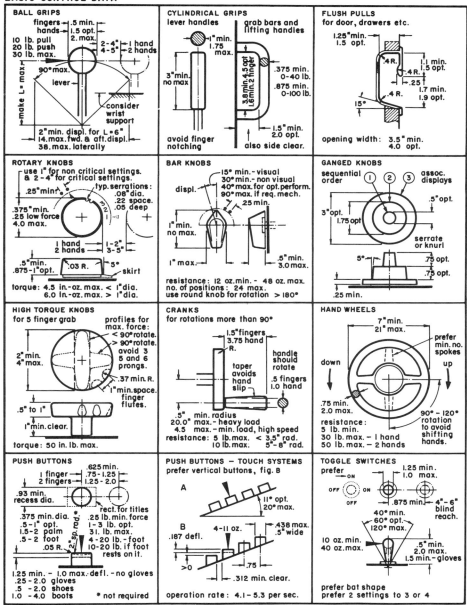

© 1960 HENRY DREYFUSS   WHITNEY PUBLICATIONS N.Y.C.

Figure 275 Basic control data. (From *The Measure of Man* by Henry Dreyfuss, published by Whitney Library of Design, New York.)

34

WAGE PAYMENT—THE RELATION OF MOTION AND TIME STUDY TO WAGE INCENTIVES

WAGE PAYMENT

Each company, plant, or group has its own management philosophy and its own plan or organization and operation. This includes the way it deals with the people in its organization—managers, supervisors, and hourly employees. The productivity and effectiveness of the organization is closely related to the motivation of the people in it. Here we are concerned mainly with hourly employees and the ways of paying them for their services. There are many different management styles and numerous wage payment plans. Each company should determine its own policy concerning employee motivation and financial compensation to fit its own needs and mode of operation. We shall describe here some of the basic plans of wage payment, and in later chapters present other ways of motivating people.

Wage Incentives

People are motivated to work for many different reasons and they are paid for their work in different ways. Two of the most common are (1) for the time they work, that is, by the hour, by the day, month or year, and (2) for the work they accomplish or produce, that is, by the piece, by the ton, or by the number of *standard minutes* or *standard hours* they produce per day.

Daywork

When employees are paid for time worked, the wage rate may be determined by job evaluation, by the established rate structure of the company, or by collective bargaining. Ordinarily there is a wage rate for each class of work and there may be a range which permits some variation in payment within each class. The payment for time recognizes and compensates employees for their performance and productivity in a general way by adjusting the base wage as the business prospers and as profits increase. Wages are also increased to compensate for the cost of living.

Piecework

Piecework is one of the oldest forms of wage payment. It is simple, direct, and easy to understand. Money payments are made to the worker in direct proportion to his or her output. However, the plan involves both the time needed to perform a task and the base wage of the worker. Therefore, the piece rate must be changed each time there is a change in the base wage rate. Moreover, if the piece rate is to be equitable, the "time per piece" on which the piece rate is based must be determined by work measurement and the job method and conditions must be standardized and recorded. A guaranteed base wage is a part of the piecework plan today and there are also federal laws which require a minimum hourly wage.

Standard Hour Plan

The standard hour plan or the 100 percent incentive plan is the most widely used financial wage incentive plan in this country. For each 1 percent performance over standard the employee is rewarded by 1 percent payment over base wage. This pay plan is similar to the piecework plan in that the employee receives 100 percent of the premium earned and the base wage is guaranteed. Standards are expressed in time per unit produced and at the end of the day the standard hours produced are multiplied by the hourly base rate to give the total earnings for the day. A performance index or productivity factor can be determined by dividing the standard hours produced by the number of hours worked during the day and multiplying by 100. In most cases time standards for a job as established by work measurement are expressed in minutes per unit produced and then converted into hours at the time the wage calculations are made.

The advantages of the standard hour plan over the piecework plan are that standards are expressed in time per unit produced rather than in money. The mixing of pieces produced and hourly wages to give a piece rate is eliminated. Piece rates must be changed when there is a change in base wages, whereas time standards are guaranteed against change unless there is a change in methods, tools, or other conditions of the job. Also, the ever changing piece rates due to wage rate adjustment can be confusing to the employee.

Measured Daywork

Measured daywork in its present form is not a wage incentive plan; the employee's base wage is guaranteed irrespective of his or her performance level. Work is measured, standards are applied to each job, and a performance index for each individual employee is calculated just as for a wage incentive plan. This information may be used by management for control purposes exclusively, or the performance index for each person might be posted in the department. In the latter case it serves to let each person know how well he or she is performing and perhaps may provide some motivation, but there is no direct incentive payment involved. In either case the details of the plan would be explained and discussed with the employees before it is installed.

Measured daywork serves a useful purpose for managers and supervisors because they can make more objective decisions based on factual information about the performance of the employees and equipment on a daily basis. To be successful a measured daywork plan must be designed and maintained with the same care as would a financial wage incentive plan. When measured daywork first came into use in the 1930s, the base wage was tied to the performance index of the individual and adjustments in the hourly wage rate were made at 3-month intervals. This part of the plan was abandoned, however, because of problems in lowering the wage rates when the performance index dropped.

Early Use of Time Study and Wage Incentives

Time study was originally designed to measure work and in turn the time standards determined by time study were used as the basis for wage incentives. Before the advent of time study employees were either paid by the hour, by piece rate, or by some form of bonus or premium plan which was based on estimates or past records. Often these incentive plans were not sufficiently accurate to be equitable to either the employee or the employer. As a result, rates often were cut, production count was padded, quality suffered, and thus many of these incentive plans failed. Fortunately, this is mostly in the past.

Well-designed and well-maintained wage incentive plans have been used successfully for many years and surveys indicate that 40 to 50 percent of the manufacturing industry in this country have wage incentive applications.[1] Of those using wage incentives, 60 percent use the standard hour plan.

THE RELATION OF MOTION AND TIME STUDY TO WAGE INCENTIVES

Effects of Motion and Time Study and Wage Incentive Applications on the Worker

The two phases of motion and time study that concern the worker most are (1) improving the method of doing work, and (2) setting a time standard as the basis for a wage incentive. These two functions affect the operator in distinctly different ways. Both tend to reduce unit labor cost to the employer, mainly by decreasing the labor hours required; consequently, both tend to displace labor on a given operation. That is, if windows in the factory and office buildings can be washed in half the time formerly taken, through the use of a well-designed method and a wage incentive, then only half as many window washers will be required on the payroll of the company as would otherwise be employed. In this respect motion and time study falls into the category with tools and machinery which reduce labor costs because of their greater efficiency.

---

[1] Robert S. Rice in collaboration with Patton Consultants, Inc. and the American Institute of Industrial Engineers, "Survey of Work Measurement and Wage Incentives," *Industrial Engineering*, Vol. 9, No. 7, pp. 18–31.

The manufacturing industry has a continuous record of producing more with fewer labor hours. It has been fully demonstrated that in the long run every one benefits from increased productivity.[2] Each organization should see that such general benefits are obtained without asking anyone to work inordinately hard or without creating unemployment, even temporarily. Some companies guarantee their employees that no one will be laid off as the result of the introduction of new machines, processes, or methods, or because of the installation of a wage incentive system.

By the improvement of methods alone, the work is often made sufficiently easy so that with the same expenditure of energy the operator is able to produce more units per day. Thus, through the use of duplicate bins and the simple fixture for the assembling of the bolt and washers described in Chapter 15, the operator was able to do a half more work in the same time. This phase of motion and time study enables the operator to do more work without asking that he or she use more energy.

In contrast, the second phase of motion and time study, that of setting a time standard to be used with a wage incentive, reduces man-hours by offering to pay the operator more wages to do more work in a given period of time. To earn this extra compensation the operator produces more, mainly through the elimination of idle time, through greater concentration on the job, and through greater expenditure of energy.

Perhaps an example is the best way to show the whole picture. This case will indicate not only how these two phases of motion and time study affect the employee through increase in earnings, but also how they affect the employer through a decrease in the direct-labor cost of the product. It will be assumed that no increase in wages is given to the operator when improvements in methods alone are made.

The operation is assembling a work-rest bracket for a bench grinder. The data in Fig. 276 show a 40 percent saving in time from an improvement in the method of assembling the bracket. The operator worked without incentive in both Case I and Case II; that is, he was paid a flat hourly rate irrespective of the output. He exerted approximately the same physical effort and gave approximately the same mental attention in both cases. However, in Case I he made 720 assemblies per day, whereas in Case II he made 1200 assemblies per day. This increase in output resulted not from working faster, but from a better arrangement of the work place and from the use of a special fixture which enabled the operator to use his hands to better advantage. He could do more work in the same time and with the same expenditure of energy because he

---

[2] The current agreement between General Motors Corporation and the UAW contains an improvement factor clause which states

"The improvement factor provided herein recognizes that a continuing improvement in the standard of living of employees depends upon technological progress, better tools, methods, processes and equipment, and a cooperative attitude on the part of all parties in such progress. It further recognizes the principle that to produce more with the same amount of human effort is a sound economic and social objective."

On the assumption that an increase in productivity will bring lower costs, the contract states that each employee is to receive an improvement factor increase in hourly wage rate.

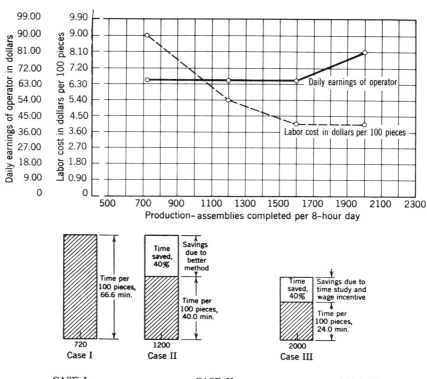

CASE I

Method. Assemble one piece at a time. Left hand holds bracket while right hand assembles parts. Method poor.

Supervision. Poor.

Operator Performance. Poor.
Method of Wage Payment. Day work. Hourly rate = $8.10 Daily earnings of operator = $64.80.

Average Production, taken from past records = 720 pieces for an 8-hour day. Average time per 100 pieces = 66.6 minutes.

Average Labor Cost per 100 pieces = $9.00

CASE II

Method. Assemble two pieces at one time, using special fixture. Method good.

Supervision. Poor.

Operator Performance. Poor.

Method of Wage Payment. Day work. Hourly rate = $8.10. Daily earnings of operator = $64.80.

Average production, taken from past records = 1200 per 8-hour day. Average time per 100 pieces = 40.0 minutes.

Average Labor Cost per 100 pieces = $5.40

CASE III

Method. Assemble two pieces at one time, using special fixture. Method good.

Supervision. Good.

Operator Performance. Good. Operator now on incentive.

Method of Wage Payment. Straight piece rate with guaranteed minimum rate of $8.10 per hour. Standard time per 100 pieces set by time study = 30.0 minutes. Piece rate per 100 pieces = $4.05. Standard output per day = 1600 pieces. Average number of pieces actually produced per day by this operator = 2000. Average daily earnings of this operator = $81.00

Average Labor Cost per 100 pieces = $4.05

OPERATION: Assemble work-rest bracket for bench grinder
OPERATOR: H.G. Meyers
BASE WAGE: $8.10 per hour—8-hour day—40-hour week
WAGE-INCENTIVE PLAN: Straight piece rate

Figure 276 The relation to motion and time study to wage incentives.

could assemble a bracket with fewer motions, with no tiring holding of parts, and with an easy rhythm which was not possible in Case I.

In Case III a time standard was set by means of a stop-watch time study and a piece rate was established for the operation. The operator now had the opportunity of earning more than his guaranteed base wage of $64.80 per day. In fact, he was easily able to do 25 percent more work than the standard, and in return for this extra performance, he earned $81.00 per day.

The increased output resulting from the application of the piece rate came because the operator "worked harder" than he did in Case II. That is, he worked more consistently through the day, eliminated idle time, took less personal time, and perhaps visited less frequently with neighbors. He started work on time and worked until quitting time, concentrating on the work he was doing during the entire day. Although it is likely that the operator used approximately the same motions in completing a cycle in Case III as in Case II, it is certain that he used more effort in Case III than in Case II. The incentive of greater pay for greater output was responsible for this. It is also likely that the operator was more fatigued at the end of the day in Case III than in Case II.

It is therefore apparent that greater output through improved methods ordinarily causes the operator no increase in fatigue. In fact, the improved method is usually easier, more satisfying, and less fatiguing than the original one. On the other hand, the application of a wage incentive usually encourages the operator to work harder. The extent of the operator's exertion will depend upon his own inclination and his fitness for the job. With straight piece rate or with a 100 percent premium plan of wage payment, the reward is in direct proportion to the output. The operator sets his or her own pace.

For the employer the application of motion study reduced the direct labor cost 40 percent, and the application of the piece rate reduced it another 25 percent. The direct-labor cost per 100 pieces in Case I was $9.00, in Case II $5.40, and in Case III $4.05. This is shown graphically by the curve at the top of Fig. 276.

Ways in Which Motion and Time Study and Wage Incentives Increase Output

The question is frequently raised as to why there is often such a great difference between the output of a person paid on a day-work basis without production standards established for the job and the output of the same person after time standards have been set and an incentive system of wage payment is used.

There are three main reasons why motion and time study and a wage incentive installation may bring greater daily output among direct labor.

1. Improved work methods enable the operator to produce more with the same effort. In some organizations it is the practice to improve methods before beginning the work measurement. Even if this procedure is not followed, it is still possible

that some improvement in methods will result from preliminary work incident to work measurement.

In some plants, particularly those with poor supervision, we may find work done in a hit-or-miss manner, with inadequate planning, lack of standardization, and little or no idea of what a day's work should be. In such plants, materials that vary from standard may force operators to work at a slow pace or to perform extra operations which may result in low output per hour. Delays may be caused by machines and equipment not being kept in good repair. Lack of work, delay in sharpening tools, and inadequate supervision may cause idleness on the part of the operator. Time study would reveal such inefficiencies, and a wage incentive system would require that they be corrected. Standardization of materials, methods, tools, equipment, and working conditions *must always precede* the installation of a wage incentive system. This is management's responsibility.

2.   If all employees know what a standard day's work is and if they are paid a bonus for work produced above the standard, they will in most cases on their own accord eliminate waste time within their control, such as late starting, early quitting, and unnecessary idleness during the day. Moreover, they will put pressure on management to eliminate causes of idle time beyond their control, such as shortage of material, machine breakdowns, and delays in sharpening tools.

Some people prefer to work during some or all of the time allowed for personal needs and fatigue. When there are no fixed rest periods, workers are paid for the output which they produce during this time. It should be pointed out that fatigue allowances are intended to permit the operator to relax and recuperate during the working day, and it is expected that most workers will take time out for this purpose. However, some workers do not seem to need such time for rest and prefer to work straight through the day with only the noon hour off.

3.   Since the work standard is set so that qualified operators can easily exceed it and thus earn additional compensation, the wage incentive serves to encourage workers to increase their speed and thus turn out more work per hour than they would normally.

Nearly every person finds that he or she can exceed the hourly output defined as "normal performance," and the average output of a group of qualified operators working on incentives usually exceeds normal by 15 to 45 percent.

Work measurement establishes the correct time standard, and the wage incentive system serves to pay workers for the extra output they produce beyond the standard. The effort that an employee chooses to exert at a given time or on any particular day is entirely a personal matter with him. Each person is guaranteed his hourly rate of pay irrespective of his output.

A Motion and Time Study and Wage Incentive Application

The demand for a new product often exceeds that predicted for it, and in order to satisfy the demand an extra shift is used or additional machines are purchased, with little or no change being made in the production methods. Eventually, however, a more careful analysis of each operation will be made, and some organizations make such an analysis at the time they put the work on incentive. The following case gives a day-by-day record of steps that were taken and the results that were obtained on one job. The operation was a rather complicated assembly, involving some gaging and adjustment. The job had been running for one week on day work, and the average output of the operator was around 22 pieces per hour (Fig. 277).

A new method was suggested by the supervisor, and a special fixture was made and installed at the end of the working day on April 16. This new fixture and the new work-place layout enabled the operator to make the assemblies faster than formerly, but the socket wrench gave trouble. The operator liked the new layout but complained that the socket on the power wrench was too small for the nuts. Production dropped to 16 pieces per hour, mainly because of trouble with the wrench. After work on April 17, the supervisor tried to have the socket made larger, but the next day the operator still had some trouble. A new socket was ordered. Production, however, jumped to 32 pieces per hour on April 18. On the morning of April 22 a new socket was installed on the power wrench which made it easier to use, and this increased output to 36 pieces per hour. The output gradually increased to around 40 pieces per hour. The operator was somewhat amazed at the amount of work he was

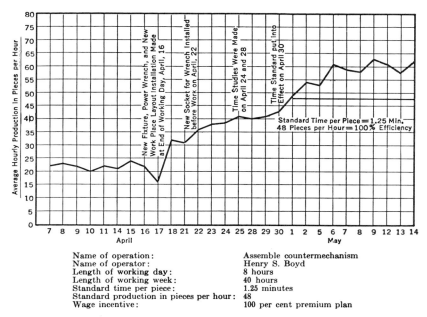

Name of operation: Assemble countermechanism
Name of operator: Henry S. Boyd
Length of working day: 8 hours
Length of working week: 40 hours
Standard time per piece: 1.25 minutes
Standard production in pieces per hour: 48
Wage incentive: 100 per cent premium plan

Figure 277 Production curve showing the effects of the installation of wage incentives. Output is expressed in pieces per hour.

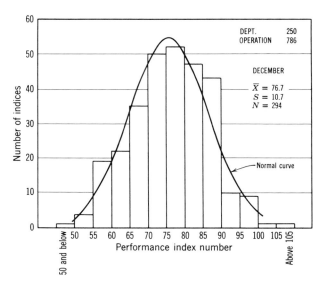

Figure 278   Distribution curve of daily performance index for the workers in the final assembly department for the month of December, the period just before the wage incentive plan was put into effect. The average performance index was 76.7%.

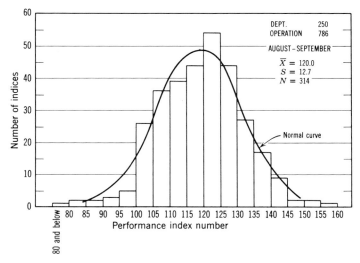

Figure 279   Distribution curve of daily performance index for the workers in the final assembly department after the wage incentive plan had been in effect for approximately 8 months. The average performance index was 120%.

490

turning out each day. A time study was made of the job on April 24 and April 28. The standard was set at 48 pieces per hour, and the new standard was put into effect on April 30. The next day the average hourly production was 49 pieces per hour, and the following day it went up to 54 pieces. Production for this operation stabilized at around 58 to 60 pieces per hour, which represents an efficiency of 120 to 125 percent. At this level of production the operator earned a bonus of 20 to 25 percent, or 20 to 25 percent more money than it was possible for him to earn before the installation of the wage incentive.

Distribution of Operator Performance Index before and after Wage Incentive Application

Some interesting data on operator performance were obtained from a lock manufacturing company at the time it was installing a wage incentive plan.[3] After the methods and conditions had been standardized and the time standards were established, it became necessary to delay the actual application of the incentive plan for several months. During this period, production records were kept and the daily performance index for each operator was calculated just as though a wage incentive were being paid, but the workers were paid their regular day rate only. Figure 278 shows the distribution curve for the 294 workers in the final assembly department during the month of December, the period just before the wage incentive plan was put into effect. The average performance index for this group was 76.7 percent. Figure 279 shows the distribution curve for the same department after the wage incentive plan had been in effect for approximately 8 months. Now the average performance index has increased to 120 percent, but the general shape of the distribution curve is not greatly different from that shown in Fig. 278.

---

[3] Donald C. Demangate, "Statistical Evaluation of Worker Productivity," *Proceedings Sixth Industrial Engineering Institute,* University of California, Los Angeles-Berkeley, pp. 89–91.

35

MULTI-FACTOR WAGE INCENTIVE PLANS
EVALUATING AND CONTROLLING FACTORS
OTHER THAN LABOR

In some industries labor costs are small in comparison with operating costs of machines and process equipment. Similarly, in some departments in a factory more can be saved by controlling quality and scrap and by increasing material utilization than by increasing labor effectiveness. For example, the loss to the company from one hour down time of a paper-making machine or a large coating machine may be greater than the wages paid to the operators of the equipment for an entire shift. The ideal incentive plan for the operators of costly machines and process equipment might be a multi-factor plan. For example, a plan might be designed to include such factors as square feet of material processed, percentage of product of acceptable quality produced, and utilization of material (Fig. 280). As industry becomes more highly mechanized, greater attention will be paid to those factors that make for low operating costs of the equipment. The goal will be lower unit cost of the end product rather than low direct labor costs alone.

Performance or Utilization Index for Factors Other Than Labor

It is possible to measure the effectiveness of each of the major factors affecting the cost of a manufactured product. Machine and equipment utilization and material utilization are of special concern in many organizations. An index number can be provided to indiciate performance, that is its effectiveness or utilization. Although the measurement may not be done with the same precision as that for direct labor it can serve a useful purpose. For example, a daily or hourly report of machine downtime by causes can provide managers and operators with information needed for better control and can aid in correcting difficulties and in reducing downtime.

The two factors in the equation for determining the equipment utilization index are (1) the output, or the number of good pieces produced per day, and (2) the maximum capacity of the equipment, or the total number of pieces that could be produced per day. The capacity might be determined from experience or from the specifications provided by the equipment manufacturer. An 8-hour day or a 24-hour day would be used depending upon conditions in a particular plant. If the equipment is capable of 24-hour operation, then this figure should be used. For the bottle filling operation shown in Fig. 280 the equipment utilization index would be:

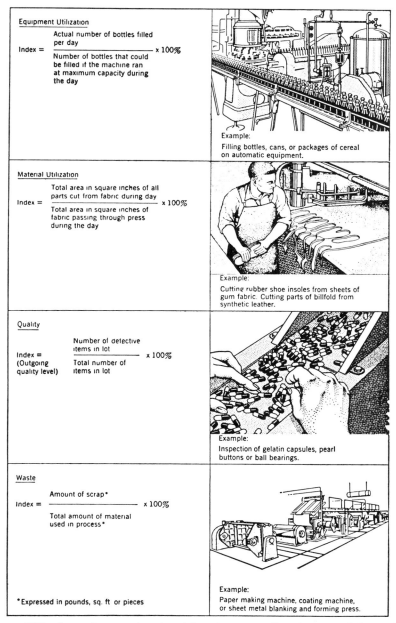

Figure 280 Some factors other than labor that may affect the cost of the product.

$$\text{Equipment Utilization Index} = \frac{\text{Actual number of bottles filled during day}}{\begin{array}{l}\text{Number of bottles that could be filled if}\\ \text{the machine ran at maximum capacity}\\ \text{during the day}\end{array}} \times 100$$

Material utilization index would be the ratio of the amount of material that is actually contained in the finished product to the amount of material that enters the production floor each day. Or the utilization index could be determined for one or all of the parts of the product. For example, in the manufacture of tennis shoes the utilization index for the insoles cut from sheets of gum fabric as shown in Fig. 280 would be:

$$\text{Material Utilization Index} = \frac{\begin{array}{l}\text{Total area in square inches of all parts cut}\\ \text{from fabric during day}\end{array}}{\begin{array}{l}\text{Total area in square inches of fabric passing}\\ \text{through the press during the day}\end{array}} \times 100$$

In a similar manner ratios can be determined for other cost factors.

A Machine Utilization Development Group under the auspices of the Industrial Engineering Coordinationg Committee at General Motors developed a plan for measuring and reporting machine utilization.[1] Their plan consists of three factors: actual utilization, standard cost utilization or planned utilization, and machine utilization efficiency. Their plan is the result of careful study involving many plants and staff groups. It is universal in scope and it was designed for use throughout the corporation.

Manual and Machine-Controlled Operations

An operation such as turning the outside diameter of a gear blank on an engine lathe consists of two parts: the loading and unloading of the machine, during which the operator works, and the cutting time (machine-controlled elements), during which the machine works and the operator is idle. The objective is to provide an incentive that will result in the maximum utilization of both the operator and the machine. If the lathe is a relatively inexpensive one and if the proportion of the cycle that the operator is forced to remain idle is relatively small, the usual type of measurement and financial incentive will give satisfactory results. If the machine is an expensive one to operate (high overhead rate) and the machine-paced portion of the cycle is large, the situation requires different treatment.

[1] John D. Lorenz and Anthony A. Mehle, "Measuring Machine Utilization", *Industrial Engineering*, Vol 11, No. 2, pp. 44-47, February, 1979.

The kind and amount of incentive that must be provided to persuade the operator to keep the equipment operating is a matter that must be worked out for each individual case. We can use time study and the other measurement tools for determining the labor content of an operation, but the weight that should go to other factors, such as equipment utilization, quality, and yield, can be determined only in a more or less arbitrary manner.

For example, the operation of sorting gelatin capsules consists of removing the defective capsules (called scag) as the capsules pass in front of the inspector on a power-driven transparent belt drawn across an illuminated inspection table. It is possible to determine by time study what the standard time should be to sort 1000 capsules of a given size and color with a given percentage of defects. Time study will be of little value, however, in determining the weight that should be given to other factors in a multi-factor incentive plan that might be used on such an operation. There is no way to determine what extra alertness or attention is needed on the part of the operator to keep defective capsules from getting in with the good capsules, or to prevent good capsules from getting in with the scag. Therefore, in a case such as this the weight given to these two factors might be based on the importance of each factor to the company costwise. A defective capsule among good capsules could cause delay in the process of filling the capsules with powder. In addition, certain kinds of defective capsules may not be detected until after the capsule has been filled, with the result that both the capsule and its contents have to be scrapped. In the case of the good capsule among the scag, the only loss is the value of the empty capsule itself.

As manufacturing processes become more highly mechanized and as process equipment becomes more complex and costly, it seems certain that there will be an increasing number of opportunities for management to reduce costs by evaluating and controlling factors other than labor. In many cases it will be impossible to measure the effort, attention, or alertness that will be required on the part of the operator to produce the desired results. Often the plan will have to be designed through trial and error and in an empirical or arbitrary manner. The conditions that permit the measurement and incentive compensation of an operator on manually controlled activities will not apply.

Perhaps the most common illustration of this is the policy of dealing with machine-paced work. It is true, of course, that working time interspersed with waiting time caused by machine-controlled elements permits the operator to work at a faster pace when he does work, inasmuch as he is able to rest while the machine works. However, the procedure for determining the "incentive opportunity" that should be allowed for the machine-paced part of the job is an arbitrary one. Such factors as the following must be considered:

1. Lowest cost of end product—including overhead and material as well as direct labor cost.

Per Cent of Cycle During Which Operator Did Manual Work	Hours on Manual Work	Base Earnings, Manual Work	Premium Earned, Manual Work	Hours on Machine-Controlled Work	Base Earnings, Machine-Controlled Work	Total Earnings for Eight-Hour Day
A. 100% Manual (0% Machine controlled) 100%	100% × 8 = 8	8 × $7.20 = 57.60	$57.60 × 25% = $14.40	0	0	$57.60 + $14.40 = $72.00
B. 60% Manual (40% Machine controlled) 60% 40%	60% × 8 = 4.8	4.8 × $7.20 = $34.56	$34.56 × 25% = $8.64	40% × 8 = 3.2	3.2 × $7.20 = $23.04	$34.56 + $8.64 + $23.04 = $66.24
C. 20% Manual (80% Machine controlled) 20% 80%	20% × 8 = 1.6	1.6 × $7.20 = $11.52	$11.52 × 25% = $2.88	80% × 8 = 6.4	6.4 × $7.20 = $46.08	11.52 + 2.88 + $46.08 = $60.48
D. 0% Manual (100% Machine controlled) 100%	0	0	0	100% × 8 = 8	8 × $7.20 = $57.60	$57.60

Operation: Turn outside diameter of gear blank on lathe. When power feed is used no attention is required on part of operator during cut.
Length of work day = 8 hours. Hourly base rate = $7.20
Average effectiveness or performance index on manual work performed by the operator = 125%.

Figure 281   The effects of a machine-paced operation on the earnings of the operator.

2. Sufficient incentive to encourage the worker to produce at a pace above standard and to fully utilize the machine.
3. Earning opportunities that are in line with other jobs in the plant.

The effect of machine control on the earnings of an operator is illustrated in Fig. 281. The operation is turning the outside diameter of a gear blank on a lathe. In condition A the operation is 100 percent manual, and consequently the operator has an opportunity to earn incentive during the entire cycle. In condition B 40 percent of the cycle is machine paced. The operator is idle (while the machine works), and consequently has no incentive opportunity during this time. If the operator works at a 125 percent performance index during the manual part of the operation and if he is guaranteed his base hourly rate, his earnings are shown in the column at the extreme right in Fig. 281. It is obvious that in case B there is not a full incentive to encourage the operator to keep the equipment in operation, in case C he has only a small incentive opportunity, and in case D no incentive opportunity is provided.

Innumerable plans are in use to provide incentives for the operator in situations such as B, C, and D. Some plans provide a flat incentive opportunity during machine-paced portions of the cycle, from 10 or 15 percent to as high as 25 or 30 percent. Other plans provide a graduated incentive based upon the percentage of the cycle that is controlled by the machine. However, if the operator referred to in Fig. 281 were paid a 25 percent bonus on the machine-controlled portion of the job, and if his average performance index for the day on the manually paced portion of the job were 125 percent, then in cases A, B, C, and D in Fig. 281 the operator would receive the same earnings in each case. He would earn 125 percent of his base wage, or $72 ($8 × $7.20 × 1.25 = $72).

The points in favor of providing an incentive opportunity during machine-paced parts of an operation are: (1) it encourages the operator to increase his or her productivity and the productivity of the machine (where this is possible); (2) it provides incentive earnings that are more nearly in line with those of other employees working on incentives. There are two principal arguments against providing such an incentive opportunity. (1) The operator is doing no physical work during the machine-paced part of the cycle; some would say that he should receive his guaranteed hourly rate only—the same amount that he would receive if he were a day-work employee. The fundamental concept of a wage incentive plan for direct labor on manual tasks has been stated as follows: "The worker receives extra pay for extra effort—for extra output that is produced above standard. If there is no extra work produced, then the worker should not receive extra pay." (2) If a worker earns a premium or bonus on the machine-paced part of his job, during which he exerts no physical effort, he may feel that he must work harder to earn the same bonus when he is employed on a job that is entirely manual, and that this is unfair.

It should be emphasized again that the manner of handling the machine-paced part of the cycle is out of the realm of work measurement. Rather, a systematic and carefully thought-out company policy should be established and followed for the evaluation, control, and payment of all factors that affect cost and that are within the control of the operator.

MULTI-FACTOR INCENTIVE PLAN FOR THE MANUFACTURE OF CORRUGATED FIBERBOARD

Corrugated fiberboard is made on a corrugating machine (Fig. 282) consisting of several separate units placed in line or tandem. This integrated unit makes the corrugated fiberboard by feeding mill rolls of paper into the wet end of the machine (right side of Fig. 282), through the various units, and into the cutoff machine, which automatically cuts the board to the desired lengths and widths and stacks the cut sheets on a table. This machine can make corrugated board up to 85 inches wide and will operate satisfactorily on certain kinds of board at a speed up to 700 feet per minute. The machine is operated by a crew of five, consisting of an operator and an assistant operator at the wet end of the machine, and a knife man and two off-bearers at the dry end of the machine.

With a machine as expensive to operate as this one (overhead around $200 per hour) it is desirable to produce as much corrugated board of acceptable quality as possible. Also, because of the value of the paper (approximately $2500 worth of paper is fed through the machine per hour), it is important that scrap and waste be kept as low as possible. The two factors, machine speed and waste, are both within the control of the crew. In order to encourage the five members of the crew to operate

Figure 282   Machine for making corrugated fiberboard.

the machine as efficiently as possible, a two-factor wage incentive plan was designed and put into effect. The following is the description of the plan.

Factor I—Lineal Feet of Corrugated Board Produced

The number of lineal feet of corrugated board produced by the machine during the day or shift is determined by multiplying the number of sheets of board produced by the length of each sheet in feet. The standard time in hours per 1000 lineal feet of board produced is shown in Table 67. These time standards were determined by time study. The total lineal feet (in thousands) of board produced by the crew during the day multiplied by the standard time in hours per 1000 lineal feet gives the total standard hours produced by the crew insofar as this factor is concerned.

Factor I = total lineal feet (in thousands) × standard hours per 1,000 lineal feet

Table 67.   Standard Time in Hours per Lineal Feet of Corrugated Board Produced

Board Combination		Standard Time, Hours per 1,000 Lineal Feet
33–9–33		.043
42–9–33	125 lb. test	.043
42–9–42		.043
69–9–42		.053
69–9–69	275 lb. test	.053
42–9–69		.053
76–38–76	350 lb. test	.070

Factor II—Waste Produced

All paper fed into the machine either becomes corrugated board of acceptable quality or is classified as waste. Waste may result from paper scrapped in threading the machine at the start of a shift, corrugated board of unacceptable quality detected and discarded at the dry end of the machine, or defective board found and discarded in

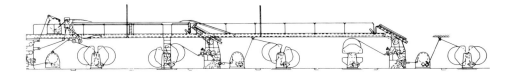

subsequent operations, such as printing, cutting, and stitching. All waste is delivered to the baling room, where it is segregated, weighed, baled, and then shipped to the paper mill. Thus the total amount of waste in pounds produced during the day can be accurately determined.

It is impossible to operate a corrugating machine without producing some waste. Studies show that 2 percent waste can be considered "standard," and a table (Table 68) was worked out showing the relationship between waste in percent and standard

Table 68. Waste Standards

Percent Waste	Standard Hours Added	Percent Waste	Standard Hours Subtracted
1.00	.193	2.00	.000
1.05	.183	2.05	.010
1.10	.175	2.10	.020
1.15	.165	2.15	.030
1.20	.155	2.20	.040
1.25	.145	2.25	.048
1.30	.135	2.30	.058
1.35	.127	2.35	.067
1.40	.117	2.40	.077
1.45	.107	2.45	.087
1.50	.097	2.50	.097
1.55	.087	2.55	.107
1.60	.077	2.60	.117
1.65	.067	2.65	.127
1.70	.058	2.70	.135
1.75	.048	2.75	.145
1.80	.040	2.80	.155
1.85	.030	2.85	.165
1.90	.020	2.90	.175
1.95	.010	2.95	.183
2.00	.000	3.00	.193

When the percent waste is below 2%, the corresponding standard hours are added to Factor I (standard hours earned from lineal feet of corrugated board produced). When the percent waste is above 2%, the corresponding standard hours are subtracted from Factor I.

hours. As the table shows, if the crew kept their waste at 2 percent of the total weight of corrugated board produced during the day, it was considered satisfactory performance. If they could do better, that is, if they could keep the waste below 2 percent, then standard hours as indicated in the table would be added to any incentive hours they might have earned from Factor I. If they produced more than 2 percent waste, the standard hours shown in the table would be subtracted from the incentive hours earned from Factor I. The percentage of waste was determined in the following way:

1. $\text{Percent waste} = \dfrac{\text{total pounds waste produced per day}}{\text{total pounds board produced per day}}$

2. The standard hours corresponding to percent waste is obtained from Table 68.

3. Factor II = standard hours (Table 68) × number of hours worked on standard

EXAMPLE Assume that an order has been received for 500,000 cartons that will require sheets 21 × 60 inches in size, of ordinary double-faced corrugated fiberboard, 125-pound test. Since the machine will produce board up to 85 inches wide, four widths of 21 inches each can be cut from 85-inch rolls, so this width will be used.

On January 16 the five-man crew worked an 8-hour day on the above order. Their record for the day was as follows.

Factor I—Corrugated Board Produced

(a) Total run: Total number of lineal feet of corrugated board produced during the day. Footage obtained from counter on cutoff unit at the dry end of machine (40,685 sheets × 5 feet each = 203,425 lineal feet) ...... 203,425 lineal feet

(b) Width of board = 84 inches

(c) Total production of board in square feet = $\dfrac{203,425 \times 84}{12}$ ...... 1,423,975 square feet

(d) Weight of board = 98 pounds per 1,000 square feet

(e) Weight of dry run = $\dfrac{1,423,975 \times 98}{1,000}$ ...... 139,550 pounds

(f) Time standard for 125-pound combination = 0.043 hour per 1,000 lineal feet (Table 67)

(g) Standard hours produced during 8-hour day = $\dfrac{203,425 \times 0.043}{1,000}$ ...... 8.75 standard hours

Factor II—Waste Produced

(a) Pounds of waste produced during day. Weight obtained from baler operator, who bales and weighs all waste from each corrugated fiberboard machine ...... 1,824 pounds

(b)   Percent waste $= \dfrac{1,824}{139,550}$ 1.30%

(c)   Standard hours (Table 68). For percent waste of 1.30%, the corresponding standard hours is 0.135

(d)   Since the crew worked 8 hours during the day on a job for which there was a time standard, then 0.135×8 1.08 standard hours

This extra 1.08 standard hours was earned because the members of the crew were able to operate during the day with less than the standard amount of waste.

Summary of Bonus Computations

Factor I—Hours earned because of corrugated board produced   8.75
Factor II—Hours earned because of low waste   1.08
Time allowed for setup in the morning (standard make-ready time),
    from special table of allowances   0.07

      Total standard hours earned   9.90

Bonus or premium hours $= 9.90 - 8 = 1.90$

Efficiency factor for day $= \dfrac{9.90}{8} = 1.24\%$

This means that each member of the five-man crew will be paid an incentive or premium based upon the efficiency of the crew. In other words, each person will be paid for 9.90 standard hours produced instead of the 8 hours which he or she actually worked. The earnings for the individual members of the crew for the day are listed in Table 69.

Table 69.   Daily Earnings of Individual Crew Members

Crew Member	Hourly Base Rate	Standard Hours Earned	Total Earnings for Day
Operator	8.65	9.90	85.64
Roll shafter	7.47	9.90	73.95
Knife man	8.54	9.90	84.55
Off-bearer	7.05	9.90	69.80

MULTI-FACTOR INCENTIVE PLAN FOR TRANSFER MACHINE OPERATION

At The Maytag Company the standard hour wage incentive plan is extensively and successfully used for predominantly manual work.[2] More recently on highly mechan-

[2] This material reproduced by permission of The Maytag Company.

ized and automated jobs a new approach to incentive design has been to pay incentive premiums based on machine utilization and other cost factors which operators can influence significantly. Incentive pay is not based on how hard operators work. In many installations the work content of the operator's job decreases when the productivity is the highest. The degree of operator control must be measurable for a cost factor to be included in the incentive plan, and it must permit accurate evaluation of operator performance without requiring excessive administrative attention.

Transfer Line for Machining Operations

A typical application of the multi-factor incentive plan will be described here. The Buhr transfer line for machining the two major aluminum parts for the gear case of an automatic clothes washer and for the assembly of two bushings and three stud shafts is shown in Fig. 283. These parts are shown in Fig. 284. The machine has 11 separate transfer stations, 65 cutting tools, five hopper feeders for the shafts and bushings, and an in-line wash booth (Fig. 285). One gear housing and one top cover are mounted on a transfer pallet and are machined together (Fig. 286). The bushings and pins are inserted and pressed into place at stations 9 and 10 (Fig. 285). Two workers are needed to operate the machine. One operator loads and unloads the two parts (the parts are automatically clamped and unclamped) and performs the necessary inspection. A second operator checks the finished parts for porosity in a separate machine and places them on the conveyor. He also pre-sets tools and patrols the transfer machine to correct conditions that might otherwise cause machine downtime or quality defects. Both operators work together to make tool changes and adjustments, or to correct minor problems causing machine stoppages.

Designing the Incentive Pay Plan

At the time the Buhr transfer line went into operation the development of an incentive pay plan was undertaken. The incentive design objectives were to maintain a high level of quality and to achieve an optimum balance between machine utilization and indirect costs such as tool usage and tool change. This approach required predicting the normal operating characteristics of the machine after the equipment development phase was completed. Because the parts were run previously on incentive using standard machine tools, quality results and other operating data were available. These, together with the transfer machine design specifications, provided a good starting point for predicting normal operating results.

The quality premium was designed to provide variable payments ranging from 0 to 7 percent for 14 specified levels of defective parts produced, with an expected average premium of 5 percent. The remainder of the incentive pay was based on machine utilization as measured by the number of pieces produced.

The incentive pay plan for the Buhr line contains two factors:

1. Machine utilization—based on number of pieces produced.
2. Quality—based on defective parts.

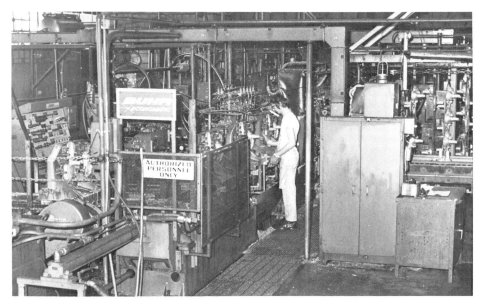

Figure 283 Transfer line for machining two major parts for the gear case of an automatic clothes washer. The operator is at the load-unload station. The two major parts are delivered and removed by conveyor at the right.

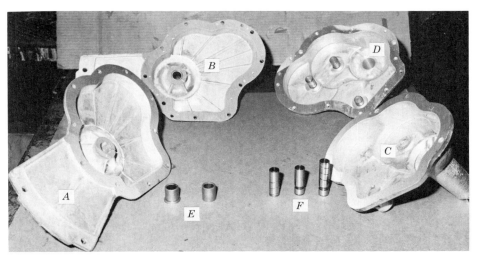

Figure 284 Parts for gear case: *A*, Unmachined gear housing; *B*, machined gear housing; *C*, unmachined top cover; *D*, machined top cover with bushing and stud shafts assembled; *E*, bushings, *F*, stud shafts.

503

Left hand stations / **Right hand stations** (Stations #1–#6)

Station	Left — Cover	Left — Housing	Right — Cover	Right — Housing
#1	Unclamp	Idle		Idle
#2	Idle	Idle	Load and unload	
#3	Clamp		Idle	Idle
#4	Drill angle hole	Idle	Semi–fin. hol. mill O.D.	Fice & che. I.D. of stem
#5	Core Dr. (1) hole Drill (2) holes	Core Dr. (1) hole Drill (10) holes	Fin. hol. mill th'd. O.D. Fin. face & chf. hub	Semi–fin. bore (8) holes
#6	Idle	Sportface & ct's ink (3) bosses Ct bore hub bot. Drill (2) holes	Fin. groove O.D. Thread hub	Tap–(10) holes

Left hand stations / **Right hand stations** (Stations #7–#11)

Station	Left — Cover	Left — Housing	Right — Cover	Right — Housing
#7	Bore & ct sink for bottom bushing	Semi–fin. bore center hole, (8) stud shaft holes (2) dowel pin holes	Bore & ct sink stem for upper bushing	Idle
#8	Idle	Idle	Idle	Fin. bore (1) center hole (3) stud shaft holes (2) dowel pin holes
#9	Press bush into bottom of cover	Press stud shaft into housing	Part back–up	Part back–up
#10	Part back up	Press (2) stud shafts into housing	Press bushing in top of cover	Part back–up
#11	Fin. bore bot. bush. Bore (2) dowel pin holes	Idle	Fin. bore & face upper bush. Hol. mill O.D. of stem	Idle

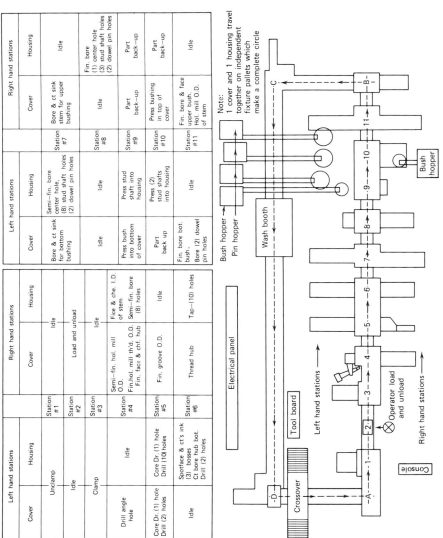

Console | Crossover | Electrical panel | Tool board | Left hand stations → | Operator load and unload | Right hand stations → | Bush hopper → | Pin hopper → | Wash booth | Bush hopper

Note:
1 cover and 1 housing travel together on independent fixture pallets which make a complete circle

Figure 285 Schematic diagram of the transfer machine. The chart at the top shows the operations performed at each of the 11 stations.

504

Figure 286   Machine operator shown loading a transfer pallet.

Establishing the anticipated machine utilization, or production capacity, required incorporating in the standard the time for all necessary interferences to continuous operation of the machine. Those interruptions included in the standard were:

1. Machine startup and shutdown.
2. Tool changes, including:
   a. Metered, where groups of tools are changed at specified but different frequencies. Production from each group of tools is recorded on the operator's control panel and reset at each change.
   b. Nonmetered, where guides are established for frequency of changing groups of tools, but where actual determination of the change frequency is left largely to the judgment of the operators.
   c. Unscheduled, where some malfunction may result in an unplanned tool change.
3. Tool adjustments, for which guides are established for adjustment frequencies for particular tools or groups of tools, but where the operators make the actual determination of when adjustments are necessary.

Tool change and adjustment frequencies were established by industrial engineers and tool engineers to provide an optimum balance between tool costs and machine utilization. However, because operators receive incentive payment for both quality and machine utilization, they are also motivated to achieve an optimum balance.

4. Malfunctions of feeders and presses for the two bushings and three stud shafts.
5. Miscellaneous minor delays. These were defined as less than 30 minutes in length and were included in the standard based on average frequency of occurrence and length of time.
6. Miscellaneous major delays. Delays in excess of 30 minutes, for which the first 30 minutes are included in the operator's incentive assignment time and the remainder paid at the off-standard base rate.

Both the minor and major delays were incorporated in the standard in such a way as to motivate operators to prevent or minimize those interruptions. The structuring also prevented substantial erosion of incentive earnings if major problems, beyond the operators' control, were encountered.

Other work, such as loading and unloading parts, visual and dimensional inspection, monitoring the machine, and other similar activities are done during the machine cycle.

The written job instructions are extensive. They are directed primarily toward identifying expected end results rather than detailed descriptions of manual work methods, and in specifying those things that are particularly important for obtaining high quality and optimum costs.

Administration of the Plan

Incentive payment is calculated on a shift basis. The shift calculation can cause wide ranges in daily premiums because of variation in machine operation. A weekly calculation would level these variations, but operators have preferred the shift calculations and have accepted the daily variations in earnings.

Data must be maintained on all interruptions to continuous operation of the machine. These data are needed to identify abnormal operating conditions so that prompt, corrective action can be taken, and to provide information for changes that might require revisions in the standard. Much of the data on time and frequency of tool change, and normal and abnormal delays are recorded by the operators on special forms. To identify longer-range trends in operating conditions, weekly graphs are maintained showing the frequency and average time for all classes of machine interruptions for which time is provided in the standard.

The labor standard is adjusted whenever changes in job conditions occur, such as changes in part design, material, or tooling that substantially affect the standard. Every six months the most recent three months and last 20 shift data for all time elements included in the standard are reviewed. Adjustments of elemental times and the labor standard are then made, if needed. Changes, if any, are thoroughly reviewed with the operators and union representatives.

Results

Multi-factor incentive applications similar to that described for the Buhr transfer machine have been used for other highly mechanized installations where direct labor is not the most substantial cost consideration. Those installations represent a significant change in approach to work measurement and incentives for supervisors, operators, and union representatives who were accustomed to standards based solely on manual work content. Incentive application models were constructed and simulated incentive results were reviewed to provide an understanding of the incentive opportunity and variations in day-to-day earnings. A six-month trial period was established, after which either management or the union could reject the plan. During that period the operators were guaranteed their hourly rates.

The Buhr transfer line was the first one placed on incentive. This plan provided operator earnings comparable with those attained on jobs where the standard hour plan was used. It also resulted in substantially higher productivity, improved quality, and lower overall operating costs than could be expected had the plan not been installed. Subsequent multi-factor installations have been readily accepted and have experienced equal success.

For complex, mechanized installations there is generally an equipment and tooling refinement period, sometimes lasting several months, before optimum production capabilities are achieved. All multi-factor incentive installations, following the initial use on the Buhr line, included a preliminary incentive application which requires periodic increases in production volume until the anticipated machine capacity is attained. The permanent standard is not established until that development period has been completed. Operators appreciate the early incentive opportunity during the equipment development phase, and the company obtains a progressive, predictable improvement in productivity and costs.

To date, multi-factor incentives have been applied only to mechanized equipment installations at Maytag. However, the principle of paying incentive premiums for specified measurable end results that are economically important and which can be influenced by operators, can also be applied to other work situations.

EXTENT TO WHICH MOTION AND TIME STUDY MAY BE PROFITABLY USED

At the very outset the cost of a motion and time study application should be considered together with the expected return. If an operation is being considered for improvement, the extent to which the several steps in the problem-solving process will be carried out will depend upon the potential benefits. The problem definition, analysis, and search for possible solutions will be handled in a cursory manner if the operation is a temporary one or if the volume is small or the potential savings insignificant. On the other hand, an exhaustive study might be justified on a job involving many workers, costly materials, and expensive equipment.

If time standards are to be established on an operation and used as the basis for wage incentives, then no short cuts can be permitted on the work measurement phase of motion and time study. The use of work measurement techniques is in a different category from methods design—management must be prepared to guarantee time standards against change, and also a fully documented standard practice is required.

Motion and Time Study Techniques

There are many combinations of the various techniques that may be used, and each of them has been described in the preceding chapters. It seems convenient to list in tabular form (Table 70) five combinations that are frequently used in motion and time study applications. They range from the most complete, Type A, on the left, to the simplest, Types D and E, on the right.

Four principal factors determine the combination of motion and time study techniques to be used. They are:

1. The extensiveness of the job, that is, the average number of man-hours per day or per year used on the work.
2. The anticipated life of the job.
3. Labor considerations of the operation, such as:
   (a) The hourly wage rate.
   (b) The ratio of handling time to machine time.
   (c) Special qualifications of the employee required, unusual working conditions, labor union requirements, etc.
4. The capital investment in the buildings, machines, tools, and equipment required for the job.

Table 70. Combinations of Motion and Time Study Techniques

Type	A	B	C	D	E
Methods Design					

Finding the preferred method—the most economical way considering
  a. Methods
  b. Materials
  c. Tools and equipment
  d. Working conditions
	Process analysis
	Full micromotion study of operation
	Application of motion economy principles
		Process analysis
		Motion study Detailed analysis by therbligs
		Application of motion economy principles
			Process analysis
			Motion study Detailed analysis of elements
			Application of motion economy principles
				. . . .
				Motion study Cursory analysis
				Application of motion economy principles
					. . . .
					Motion study Cursory analysis
					Application of motion economy principles

Standardizing the:
  a. Methods
  b. Materials
  c. Tools and equipment
  d. Working conditions
	Standardization of the operation	Standardization of the operation	Standardization of the operation	Standardization of the operation	Standardization of the operation

Written standard practice	Written standard practice Instruction sheet Motion picture record of improved method	Written standard practice Instruction sheet	Written standard practice or Instruction sheet	Written standard practice or Instruction sheet	Written standard practice or Instruction sheet (standardized for each class of work)
Work Measurement					

Determining the time standard	1. Time study
	2. Micromotion study
	3. Standard time data
	  a. Certain therbligs
	  b. Certain elements
	4. Standard data
	5. Predetermined time data
	6. Formulas
	7. Work sampling
		1. Time study
		2. . . . .
		3. Standard time data
		  a. Certain therbligs
		  b. Certain elements
		4. Standard data
		5. Predetermined time data
		6. Formulas
		7. Work sampling
			1. Time study
			2. . . . .
			3. . . . .
			4. . . . .
			5. . . . .
			6. . . . .
			7. . . . .
				1. Time study
				2. . . . .
				3. . . . .
				4. . . . .
				5. . . . .
				6. . . . .
				7. . . . .
					1. . . . .
					2. . . . .
					3. . . . .
					4. Standard data
					5. Predetermined time data
					6. Formulas
					7. Work sampling

Training the operator	In separate training department or At work place Motion pictures Videotape Instruction sheets	In separate training department or At work place . . . . Instruction sheets	. . . . At work place Instruction sheets	. . . . At work place Instruction sheets	. . . . At work place . . . . Instruction sheets (standardized for each class of work)
Applying the wage incentive	This is not a part of motion and time study but often accompanies it.				

An Example of the Most Refined Use of Motion and Time Study

The Type A study would include an analysis of the process and the construction of a chart of the entire manufacturing process of which the operation under consideration is a part. It would require a full micromotion study and the application of the principles of motion economy, which would include consideration of the most economical use of materials, tools, and equipment, and provisions for satisfactory working conditions. After the preferred method of doing the work had been found, it would be standardized and a standard practice record would be prepared. The Type A study might also involve the making of motion pictures of the old and of the improved method. A time standard would then be set by means of time study, or from data taken from the micromotion study, or from predetermined time data or standard data already available. The Type A study would also provide for the training of the operator, either in a separate training department or at the work place, with the aid of motion pictures and instruction sheets. This might be followed by the application of a wage incentive to the job.

An example will be given to show where a Type A study would be used. The job is a semiautomatic lathe operation. The data for this operation, tabulated under the four headings listed above, would appear as follows:

1. More than 100 people are employed on this operation. They work an 8-hour day and a 40-hour week, which amounts to approximately 200,000 man-hours per year.
2. The job is a permanent one. This operation has been performed for some years, and it is expected that it will be continued indefinitely.
3. Female labor is used.
   a. The basic hourly wage is the going rate in the community. A 100 percent premium plan of wage payment is used. Standards are set by time study, and the hourly wage is guaranteed.
   b. Each cycle requires 0.25 minute, of which approximately 60 percent is handling time and 40 percent machine time.
   c. Because special skill is required to perform this operation, each new operator is given 6 weeks of training in a separate training department. Working conditions are normal.
4. The special semiautomatic lathe, fully equipped, costs approximately $10,000 when new.

It is apparent that this operation has great potential savings. The fact that 100 people are employed on this single operation, producing more than 50 million units annually, would at once indicate a Type A study.

An Example of the Simplest Use of Motion and Time Study

On the other extreme are the Type D and the Type E motion and time studies. These are alike except that the Type E is used where an entire class of work has been previously standardized and where only sufficient analysis need be made to determine into what subdivision a given operation falls. The Type D study would be made on operations of short duration and with little prospect for improvements. This study would involve only a cursory analysis and a very general application of the principles of motion economy, a written standard practice, a time standard set by a stop-watch time study, and an instruction sheet prepared to aid in training the operator.

A Type D study would be used on the following job. The operation is drilling and counterboring a small bracket on a sensitive drill press. The job requires the time of one person for 10 days per month. The operation is expected to last for 6 months, when the model will be changed. In this case a cursory analysis would include a check of the drill speeds, the arrangement of the tote boxes, location of the jig and air hose, and other similar factors. Only a few hours would be required for the analysis and for the execution of the recommended changes.

The time required for making this Type D study would be short and the cost would be small, whereas months might be required for a study of the semiautomatic lathe operation and considerable expense would be involved.

Type A and B studies are used either for individual jobs or for classes of similar work; Type C and D studies are used primarily for individual jobs. In some plants there are many short operations of similar nature which in themselves would warrant only a Type D study, but when considered together as a class would justify a Type A or B study.

The Type E study is used for individual jobs within classes or families, for jobs of a similar nature, and for work already standardized. This type would largely involve the selection of necessary information from standard data on file. Chapter 24 gives an example of such a class of work, that is, hobbing teeth on straight spur gears. The methods, tools, equipment, and working conditions have been standardized. By means of standard time data, perdetermined time data, and formulas, it is possible to determine time standards synthetically for such work. Instruction sheets are prepared by filling in the necessary machine time (see italics in Fig 293) on standard forms.

Operating Cost and Capital Cost.

Mechanization and automation tend to reduce labor costs but often call for an increase in capital invested in machines and equipment. Therefore in the evaluation of alternatives consideration must be given to both these costs. The following example shows how this may be done.

A Specific Case—Distribution Center

When a new warehouse and distribution center for Eastman Kodak Company was being considered, a "steering committee consisting of personnel on a high management level was appointed to study the problem. They in turn established subcommittees composed of production and staff personnel who examined our existing facilities and considered the alternative possibilities. These committees (1) determined that a real problem did exist and that the need for *new* facilities was valid; (2) they recommended a unit load handling system as being most promising for such facilities; (3) they established the over-all space requirements for the new center, its location, and the general shape thereof; and (4) they evaluated the economies involved."[1]

The following five handling methods were considered for the new distribution center: (1) fork truck, (2) conveyor, (3) tractor train, (4) dragline, and (5) combination of tractor train and dragline. Investigations showed that the final selection of handling equipment should be made from these three alternatives: (A) tractor train and dragline, (B) dragline only, and (C) tractor only.

In making the final evaluation, consideration was given to three factors:

1. Total capital invested in handling equipment.
2. Annual cost to operate the handling equipment.
3. Annual depreciation on equipment.

Table 71.   Capital Investment in Equipment

Equipment	A Tractor Train and Dragline	B Dragline Only	C Tractor Train Only
Tugs	$ 9,200	—	$16,500
Trucks	53,700	$52,500	52,500
Dragline conveyor	28,900	28,900	—
Electrical installation	750	600	380
Total	$92,640	$82,000	$69,380
Less sale of present equipment	—	−4,650	—
Net capital investment	$92,640	$77,350	$69,380

As shown in Table 71, the tractor train and dragline combination had the highest capital investment of $92,640, as against $69,380 for the tractor train system. However, the tractor train and dragline combination gave the lowest annual operating cost (Table 72). This was $63,300, including depreciation, as against $71,100 for the tractor train. After weighing the two factors of capital investment and operating cost, and considering some intangible factors, the decision was made to install the tractor train and dragline combination.

[1] R. C. Bryant, S. A. Wahl, and R. D. Willits, "Tractor Train or Dragline Conveyor?" *Modern Materials Handling,* Vol. 6, No. 9, pp. 54–57.

COST — REDUCTION REPORT

DESCRIPTION OF ITEM INVOLVED   **FILE** 11-B

    DEPT. Finished Stock & Shipping   **DEPT. NO.** 64   **DATE**

    OPERATION Marking with name and address of consignee.   **PRODUCT** Cartons to be shipped

    OBJECT OF ANALYSIS To determine possible savings through stamping instead of stenciling.

COMPARISON

PRESENT METHOD	PROPOSED METHOD
MACHINE	**MACHINE**
TOOLS Fountain stencil brush and pre-cut stencil.	**TOOLS** Rubber stamp and stamp pad.
DESCRIPTION Stencils are prepared in advance and kept on file for all major consignees, and name and address is stenciled on each carton.	**DESCRIPTION** Rubber stamps would be made up for all major consignees, and name and address is stamped on each carton.

COST OF OPERATIONS INVOLVED	$ PER	COST OF OPERATIONS INVOLVED	$ PER
LABOR	carton	**LABOR**	carton
0.16 minute per carton		0.05 minute per carton	
@ $6.00 per man-hour	$0.0160	@ $6.00 per man-hour	0.0050
MATERIALS		**MATERIALS**	
MISC.		**MISC.**	
TOTAL OF ABOVE ITEMS	0.0160	**TOTAL OF ABOVE ITEMS**	0.0050

ESTIMATE OF SAVING

    SAVING WITH PROPOSED CHANGE ($ 0.0160 −$ 0.0050) **EQUALS $** 0.0110 **PER** carton

    PROBABLE YEARLY REQUIREMENTS, 1,250,000 cartons   **ESTIMATED BY** Sales Dept.

    ESTIMATED SAVINGS PER YEAR (BASED ON 1,250,000 **PER YEAR)** ——————————— $ 13,750.00

                              PROBABLE SAVINGS PER YEAR — $ 13,000.00

ESTIMATED COST OF CHANGE			
DESIGN	**$**	**EST. BY**	**LESS TOTAL COST OF CHANGE** —————— $ 1,000.00
EQUIPMENT	$1,000.00	" "	**NET SAVINGS FIRST YEAR** ————— $ 12,000.00
INSTALLATION	$	" "	**NEW METHOD WOULD PAY FOR ITSELF IN.** ____1____
	$	" "	**MONTHS.**
	$	" "	**NOTE:** 100 rubber stamps required a $10.00 each.
TOTAL COST			**SUGGESTED BY** John Ryan
OF CHANGE	$1,000.00		**REPORT PREPARED BY** T. A. Wilson

CC TO	ATTACHED ARE		DATE		DATE
	1 SHEETS DRAWINGS	FIRST CONSIDERED		EXPEN. APPR.	
	SHEETS PRINTS	INVSTGN. STARTED		INSTALLED	
	2 SHEETS DETAILS	REPT. SUBMITTED		FINAL REPT.	

Figure 287 Cost-reduction report.

Table 72. Comparative Annual Operating Costs, Including Depreciation on Equipment

Cost Items	A Tractor Train and Dragline	B Dragline Only	C Tractor Train Only
Labor cost—operating personnel	$43,350	$54,800	$57,600
Depreciation on equipment	9,440	8,180	7,790
Space differentials	7,000	0	3,000
Maintenance	3,010	2,800	2,500
Power consumption	500	420	210
Total	$63,300	$66,200	$71,100
Annual cost differentials	0	2,900	7,800

Cost-Reduction Report

It is essential that an estimate be made of the expected savings resulting from improvements in methods before they are made, and also that a report be made after the project is finished and in effect.

The cost-reduction report shown in Fig. 287 may be used for presenting proposed changes to management, and also for reporting the savings from new methods after they are installed.

Unit operation times for the old and new methods are based on time studies or on over-all production rates, whichever gives the more representative results for the particular project. Labor costs are based on the average base rate for the particular project. Labor costs are based on the average base rate for the particular job, plus the average bonus for the department and a percentage to cover compensation insurance, federal pension, old-age insurance, and other costs that are directly related to labor cost.

Calculated savings do not include fixed overhead costs such as supervision and machine burden, since the annual expenditure for these items would not necessarily be lessened by reducing the labor requirements of a particular job. If a proposed change would increase machine capacity, and if the additional capacity might forestall having to buy more equipment, this fact would be brought out in a note attached to the cost-reduction report.

37

MOTION AND TIME STUDY TRAINING PROGRAMS—DELIBERATE CHANGE

The work of the motion and time study department in some organizations is not as successful as it should be because members of the organization do not understand how such studies are made and consequently do not give this department the support and cooperation it needs. This lack of understanding may extend from the president of the company to the supervisors and the workers in the plant.

One of the best ways to overcome such difficulties is to acquaint all members of the organization with motion and time study methods and procedures through well-organized and carefully conducted training programs. Some typical programs of this kind are described here.

MOTION STUDY TRAINING PROGRAMS

Before any job can be started, someone must plan it and set it up. This preliminary work includes determining the steps to be followed in doing the work, selecting the tools and equipment to be used, and training the operator.

When the production of a given article is large, staff engineers usually work out the details and aid the supervisors in putting the job into production. Much work is not highly repetitive, however, and an operator may do several different jobs during the course of a day or a week. In such cases the supervisor usually decides how the job is to be done, lays out the work place, selects the tools and equipment, and instructs the operator. For this reason it is desirable that people in immediate charge of operations know the fundamentals of good work design. Even when the production of the article is expected to be large and when industrial engineers are assigned to work out the manufacturing methods, the supervisors usually play an important part in aiding the engineers to develop the procedures to be followed. Here, too, it is desirable for the supervisor to have a working knowledge of the industrial engineer's techniques which pertain to work methods design.

In the final analysis, however, it is the operator who does the job. It is the operator who uses the tools and equipment selected by the supervisor or the engineer, and who employs the methods suggested by him. Therefore it is logical that the operator should understand those methods and techniques which will enable him to do his job in the easiest and most efficient manner.

It has been demonstrated many times that both supervisors and operators can profitably design work methods. Here, the supervisor should take the initiative in improving job methods. When this is done, the operator may be expected to absorb this knowledge more quickly either through instruction from the supervisor or through a formal training course.

Training programs designed to present the procedures and techniques of the industrial engineer to top executives, supervisors, and operators provide an effective means of promoting better work methods in any organization. A methods design and methods improvement training program, to be most effective, should be developed to meet the needs of the particular group to receive the training.

A Preview of the Program

A work methods design program, like any other important activity in an organization, must be understood and fully supported by top management if it is to be successful. In fact, every executive, manager, and supervisor must be acquainted with the philosophy, purposes, and objectives of the program and must understand the principles and approaches used in developing better work methods. For this reason it is essential that a preview of or introduction to the program be given to top management.

As has been indicated, the program must be worked out to fit the particular needs of the organization, and the preview given at the very outset should reflect the type of program which will follow.

The Program

In many cases it has been found profitable to present the program to industrial engineers, supervisors, process engineers, tool and jig designers, mechanical engineers, group leaders, and key operators. A program 30 to 40 hours long is quite common. Perhaps greatest success is obtained when the program is given in one continuous period of approximately 2 weeks. The forenoons may be devoted to conference room discussions and demonstrations, and the afternoons to working on projects or problems. A combination shop and laboratory is needed if project work is included in the program. If it does not seem feasible to present the entire program in one continuous session, the material may be given in a series of 1-, 2-, or 3-hour sessions held once or twice a week as conditions seem to indicate.

Training at the Armstrong Cork Company

The Company, founded in 1860, employs more than 24,000 people in 59 manufacturing facilities worldwide. Training has played an important part in the growth and success of the company and training in industrial engineering has been especially effective. The company is well-managed and has had a staff of well-trained industrial engineers at the corporate level and in each of the large plants for many years. Industrial engineering training has included programs for developing improved methods and for increasing productivity.

For example, an Industrial Engineering Center was established at the main plant in

1945 and at the same time a Methods Development Program was inaugurated. The purposes were to give greater emphasis to this phase of industrial engineering in the company, to standardize the techniques and procedures among all plants and personnel of the organization, and to lay groundwork for a Methods Development Program for production supervisors that later would be conducted in each plant.

Industrial engineers, process engineers, mechanical engineers, and top management representatives from various plants came to the Industrial Engineering Center in groups of 10 to 15 for 2 weeks' training, consisting of conferences and project work. At the completion of this program a shorter series of conferences for production supervisors was held in each plant. This program was designed to fit the needs of the particular plant in which it was presented. An important feature of these conferences was the project work which each supervisor did in his or her own department. The methods and techniques presented in the conferences were applied to specific problems by the supervisors. The industrial engineers in the plant as well as the conference leaders were able to assist the participants when they needed help with their projects.

When the company established the Industrial Engineering Center, the Methods Development Program was designed as the first part of a long-range training program in the field of industrial engineering. Over the years this program has been successfully carried out.

At the present time the corporate industrial engineering staff has underway a Productivity Improvement Seminar for manufacturing supervisors. The emphasis is on methods and the plan is to include all plants.

New industrial engineers usually join the company as a group early in the summer and begin their training with a month's indoctrination. The program includes such areas as methods engineering with in-plant methods projects, cost reduction programs, work measurement, pace rating, incentive management, and facilities planning. Some 15 additional areas of industrial engineering are also a part of this program.

Fifty Years of Training in Motion Study, Time Study, and Predetermined Times

For 50 years the General Electric Company at the Fort Wayne plants has maintained a training program in motion study, time study, and predetermined times. From the outset this company realized the importance of training members of its supervisory personnel and staff people in these techniques.

In 1928 representatives from the various plants of the General Electric Company were sent to Schenectady, where training in motion study was given. This training included both classroom instruction and the application of the principles in the laboratory and factory. These representatives, after thorough training, returned to their respective plants and proceeded to carry out training programs of their own.

L. P. Persing of the Fort Wayne works attended the first Schenectady course, and he returned to Fort Wayne with great enthusiasm and with an original and unique idea. Instead of offering training in motion study only to industrial engineers and staff people, his plan was to condense the three-month Schenectady course and offer this shorter program to all first line foremen and supervisors. As a part of the program, each supervisor would have the opportunity of applying the principles to specific jobs in his own department, and the operators working on the jobs would be consulted and encouraged to contribute their ideas to finding better work methods. Also, the supervisor would pass his knowledge of motion study on to his workers.

Persing started by acquainting management with the content of his proposed program and the way he planned to conduct it. Courses were then held for staff people in the manufacturing division. The first class of planning and time study engineers was held in January 1929. During a 3-year period the following classes were conducted:[1]

3	Classes of planning and time study engineers (beginners)	27
4	Classes of planning and time study engineers (advanced)	61
16	Classes of general foremen, foremen, assistant foremen, leading operators	268
2	Classes of special tool and machine designers	27
3	Classes of leading operators, expert workers, and personnel workers (women)	42
1	Class of plant construction engineers	22
1	Class of expert workers (assemblers)	16
30	Total number of classes Total number of persons trained	463

During the period in which the training was being carried on, new methods were devised by the application of motion study principles. In all, 96 jobs were studied and the methods revised. The new methods brought about an average reduction in time of 40%, and the tools and equipment necessary to put the improved methods into effect cost 7.4% of the total savings.

Figure 288 shows part of the original motion study laboratory which Persing developed for use in his program.

Resistance to change has always been a common problem. There has been some opposition to the use of motion and time study since the time of Taylor and Gilbreth. Supervisors as well as operators often oppose change, and considerable time and effort may be required to gain acceptance of new ideas even though they are desirable and profitable.

Persing created a new approach, by giving the managers, supervisors, and operators the tools and techniques of the industrial engineer and by organizing things so that they, themselves, could suggest changes. A supervisor who originates the idea for a better method in his or her department is motivated to see that the change is made instead of resisting it. Persing also provided specific ways for recognizing the

[1] L. P. Persing, "Motion Study—The Teacher," *Factory and Industrial Management,* Vol. 83, No. 9, pp. 337–340, September, 1932.

Figure 288 The original motion study laboratory at the Fort Wayne works of the General Electric Co. (Courtesy of General Electric Co.)

people who introduced improvements. For example, a monthly magazine called *The Better Way*, containing descriptions of completed projects with pictures of the persons involved, was circulated throughout the plant. Motion pictures of the old method and the new method were shown in the department during the noon hour and the people involved could take the film and projector home overnight to show to family and friends.

The results of the Persing innovations were phenomenal in producing lower costs, higher quality, and better relations between the industrial engineers and other staff people and the line personnel. Credit is due Persing for his early contributions to participative management.

Over the years at General Electric the use of time study and predetermined times has increased. During a 3-year period the following classes were conducted at the Fort Wayne works and its branch plants.

18	Classes in motion study and predetermined time values for methods planners, time standards men, and foreman (32 periods of 1½ hours each, biweekly)	211
1	Class in motion study and predetermined time values for methods planners and design engineers (32 periods of 1½ hours each, biweekly)	9
1	Class in motion study and predetermined time values for methods planners, tool planners, and foreman (32 periods of 1½ hours each, biweekly)	10

1	Class in motion study and predetermined time values for product design engineers (36 periods of 2 hours each, biweekly)	7
1	Class in motion study and predetermined time values for methods planners, design engineers, and design draftsmen (20 periods of 2 hours each, biweekly)	11
3	Classes in motion study and predetermined time values for foremen and general foreman (20 periods of 2 hours each, biweekly)	24
2	Classes in time study for time standards men (24 periods of 2 hours each, biweekly)	16
2	Classes in motion study for apprentice toolmakers—students (20 periods of 1½ hours each, biweekly)	24
36	Classes in motion study and predetermined time values for process and equipment planners; time standards analyst; foremen; supervisors of cost, production, purchasing; tool designers; and design engineers (30 periods of 1½ hours each, biweekly)	432
65	Total number of classes Total number of persons trained	744

Persing, in supplying the above information, made the following statement:

Thousands of profitable projects have been worked out by members of these classes in connection with our motion study and predetermined time value training programs during this period. Moreover, this type of training has promoted a better understanding in our manufacturing organization and has made the work of all groups more effective.

Corporate Program

In the late 1940s and early 1950s General Electric industrial engineers developed a predetermined time system called Motion Time Survey (MTS). This system is used not only to establish time standards but it is wisely used by the analyst to evaluate in detail the method of performing the work. In the early 1950s a training course was established at the corporate level for training instructors in MTS and in Methods Analysis and Improvement. These instructors returned to their respective locations and trained others. The pyramiding effect has resulted in the training of more than 45,000 General Electric employees worldwide in MTS and closely related subjects. This training continues under Corporate Industrial Engineering Consulting.

Methods Change Program

The Procter and Gamble Company is a large and successful organization with worldwide operations. It has been a pioneer in many areas, having introduced profit sharing in 1885 and guaranteed annual employment in 1923. Its industrial engineering program in the early days was mainly concerned with work measurement, wage incentives, and cost control. During the 1930s the company had placed special emphasis on improving performance in its plants and had achieved considerable success.[2]

---

[2] Richard A. Forberg, "Administration of the Industrial Engineering Activity," *Proceedings Twelfth Industrial Engineering Institute,* University of California, Los Angeles-Berkeley, pp. 22–30. Also see Richard A. Forberg, "Effective Control of the Industrial Engineering Function," *Proceedings Management*

However, by the early 1940s the rate had diminished considerably, and it became apparent that if the rate of cost reduction was to be maintained at an acceptable level, major emphasis on methods change would be necessary. Since it is essential to sell major changes in management practice from the top down, the methods program was begun by giving manufacturing management appreciation sessions in the concepts and techniques of work simplification. Then a special course was conducted for methods engineers—men who were college graduates with 1 to 5 years of company experience. After completion of the 1-week training course, these men returned to their respective plants to begin work as methods specialists.

1. *Specialist.* During the period 1946–1949, trained methods engineers served as specialists on methods improvement and worked more or less independently. As projects were completed and put into effect, the results were summarized in short reports. The savings during this period amounted to approximately $700 per year per member of factory management. The program was considered a success, and additional persons were trained and the program was extended to more plants.

2. *Coordinator.* However, it became apparent that this organizational approach had some limitations. By 1950 the position of the methods engineer had changed from specialist to coordinator. Formerly, the engineer had suggested the changes, and the foreman had not participated actively. He was inclined to take the suggested changes as criticism. Now the engineer spent approximately two-thirds of his time helping the factory supervisors on their projects and the other one-third of his time working on special factory projects as an individual. Each member of plant management had several selected costs to be reduced. He worked on these himself and requested help from the methods engineer as required. The methods engineer also conducted training courses at his plant for the line organization and other staff people. With the active participation of plant management, the rate of savings per member of management[3] had increased to $2300 per year by 1950. As the program grew and expanded, a bimonthly bulletin was published to promote the reapplication of successful methods changes in the other plants and to summarize achievements of the program. The company wanted all plant management, both line and staff, to participate in the plan.

3. *Methods Teams Formed.* In the beginning, any project that seemed to have savings potential was selected for study. Some of these had been small, but it was important that the men work on projects that interested them. Small successes gave them confidence to carry out savings projects regularly.

Engineering Conference, SAM-ASME, pp. 217–219, April, 1957; Arthur Spinanger, "Increasing Profits Through Deliberate Methods Change," *Proceedings Seventeenth Industrial Engineering Institute,* University of California, Los Angeles-Berkeley, pp. 33–37. This material reproduced by permission of the Procter and Gamble Company.

[3] Example: If the annual savings in this plant amounted to $230,000 and if there were a total of 100 members of management (all line and staff management people in the plant), the savings per member of management would be $2300. (230,000 ÷ 100 = $2300.)

The plants experimented with various organizational approaches. One plant, for example, organized management into teams of four to eight people. Study of operations by groups tended to build a backlog of better projects. These projects were then ranked according to estimates of effort and potential savings, with consideration for the rate of return on any capital required. About this time the company developed "the elimination approach." This approach is applied to any cost, operation, machine, or piece of equipment by identifying the basic cause for the cost. It is an approach that asks the question, "If it were not for what basic cause, this cost could be eliminated." When this questioning shows that there is no basic cause, or that the basic cause can be eliminated, then the cost is eliminated. The process of identifying basic causes is most successful when done by a group of people. These groups were referred to as methods teams. In addition to increasing the annual savings rate to $3000 per member of management, the team approach had other values. Opportunities for recognition of good work were increased. Individuals who found it difficult to show results were aided and stimulated by the example of the more successful people on the team. There was a friendly rivalry for first place in plant standing between teams. Display boards and intraplant newsletters showed team standings.

4. *Team-Goal Approach.* Another plant experimented with a different approach. Since they were a high-cost plant they were motivated to take a total approach to cost reduction. Previously, plants had usually only concerned themselves with costs under their control. This plant began to consider all of the product costs such as materials, inbound and outbound freight, insurance and taxes, as well as the direct operating expenses. A goal of $500,000 was established for the year which represented over $5000 per member of management. With the participation of the Buying and Traffic Departments and with considerable plant effort the goal was achieved. The company-wide savings for 1954 amounted to approximately $4000 per member of management.

5. *All-Plant Team Goals.* The experience of this plant indicated that the cost-reduction program should be company-wide, and that all costs should be challenged. The central industrial engineering staff analyzed the strengths and weaknesses of the separate plant programs and recommended the most successful of these to the other plants. Thus the team-goal approach was extended to all plants. Teams committed themselves to a dollar methods change goal and then worked as a team to attain it. A periodic report showing comparison of results of the program in each plant was circulated, which further increased the desire to make a good showing.

Richard A. Forberg, while Director of Industrial Engineering for Procter and Gamble, made the following statement [4] concerning the program:

Early in the program, plants tended to think that they had "skimmed the cream." The easy projects had all been picked off. Next year would be harder, they thought; consequently a

[4] Richard A. Forberg, "Administration of the Industrial Engineering Activity," *Proceedings Twelfth Industrial Engineering Institute,* University of California, Los Angeles-Berkeley, p. 27, 1960.

lower goal was in order. We had to sell some people on the reasonableness of a higher goal each year.

Higher goals were reasonable because of increased experience at cost reduction. The growth in business was another factor. Getting the less active team members to do more offered real potential for increased savings.

Although we had concluded that the goal setting process should be democratic, some guides were useful. The teams were encouraged to compare themselves with others on a dollars saved per member of management basis. Comparisons were also made in terms of goal as a percent of operating expense and as a percent of product value. The desire of plant management groups to show up well in all-plant comparisons was a strong factor in motivating teams to choose goals which required their best efforts for attainment.

6. *Program Extended to Other Parts of the Business*. From 1965 to 1975 the methods change program was extended to technical staff groups and to nonmanufacturing functions.

7. *Company Wide Divisional Programs Established*. In 1975 conclusive evidence of successful results in one international division of the company was presented to general management. Top management decided to formally extend the methods change program to all divisions of the company. Currently, all divisions of the company have a coordinator assigned and a carefully organized methods change program that includes setting annual dollar goals, reporting quarterly results, and providing positive recognition. Program results are formally reported to the Administrative Committee of the company annually.

DELIBERATE METHODS CHANGE

The Procter and Gamble Company has developed a number of original and unique approaches that have proved effective in reducing costs, improving quality, and increasing profits. One of these is the principle of deliberate methods change.[5] In the highly competitive industry in which it operates, Procter and Gamble must exert great effort to make a profit and maintain its place in the field. It expects to obtain this profit by giving value to the customer and by making quality products the customer wants.

Philosophy of Deliberate Methods Change

Management has fully accepted the principle of deliberate methods change. Deliberate methods change is quite different from improvement. Improvement means performing a method more effectively. Change means developing and using a new method. When an operation is perfectly done there is no more opportunity for improvement. However, there is still a potential for savings by making a deliberate change.

[5] Arthur Spinanger, "Increasing Profits Through Deliberate Methods Change," *Proceedings Seventeenth Industrial Engineering Institute*, University of California, Los Angeles-Berkeley, pp. 33–37, 1965. This material reproduced with the permission of the Procter and Gamble Company.

At Procter and Gamble, as a first step, no attempt is made to improve the operation. The reason for this is that if an examination is made of a well-run department with good methods, the conclusion is soon reached that nothing can be done or needs to be done, and so the same decision is made for all of the other departments, for the manager of each department feels that his or her department is well run. As a result, costs are not reduced and profits are not increased because no changes are made. Instead, the question is asked of well-run operations, "How can we change them?" The present operations may be perfect, but the company cannot continue doing them that way any longer. They must be changed and continued to be changed. Of course each change must be for the better.

The following principles form the basis for the deliberate change approach to profit improvement.

1. Perfection is no barrier to change.
2. Every dollar of cost must contribute its fair share of the profits.
3. The savings potential is the full existing cost.
4. Never consider any item of cost necessary.

The following examples from Procter and Gamble illustrate these four principles.

1. *Perfection is no Barrier to Change. Cheer,* one of the company's products was shipped in containers consisting of one layer of six cartons with a support sheet in the middle. This was considered to be correctly designed and was performing perfectly, and no consideration was given to changing it. However, a packing department manager, acting on the principle that perfection is no barrier to change, suggested that another way of packing the cartons in the container would be in two layers of three cartons each. After testing this idea it was found that the support sheet could be eliminated and less cardboard would be used in the container resulting in savings of over $100,000 annually for all brands.

2. *Every Dollar of Cost Should Contribute its Fair Share of the Profits.* The second principle means that no dollars are spent unless there is a possibility of making a profit. An illustration to test this point might be, "How much profit does the company make on a storage tank?" A natural reaction to this question might be "You really can't expect a storage tank to make a profit by itself. A tank is a part of the process equipment needed to manufacture a product or material for a product." Yet the profit question was asked, and attractive profits to the company resulted.

The company's Quincy, Massachusetts plant formerly received liquid lye from a supplier that was located in the Great Lakes district of the United States. This particular company made lye during the summer and shipped it by barge down to New York City harbor for storage and distribution. These barge shipments terminated when the Great Lakes system and the canal system of the Hudson River froze over in the winter. During this period of the year they ship lye from New York City by tank car to customers. In fact, the Quincy plant received all of its lye by tank car from

New York City. The question was raised as to why this lye should be shipped all the way down to New York City by barge and then back to Quincy by the higher-costing tank-car method. With barge unloading facilities checked out as feasible, the buying department and traffic department asked the lye supplier if he could deliver the chemical directly to Quincy by barge. The supplier was pleased with this proposal because it would simplify his method of delivering the lye. Furthermore, the supplier said that they could pay the Quincy plant rent on the tanks because they now pay rent to the owners of the New York City tank field. In addition, they said that Quincy need not pay the cost of this lye until it was actually sent to its first point of use. As a result, Quincy now rents these tanks and has, in effect, reduced working capital. This same approach was followed at the company's New York City plant. They had surplus tanks and, upon checking around with users of tanks, they found a company anxious to rent them. Thus, the New York City plant is now renting some of their tanks.

If one accepts the principle "Every dollar of cost should contribute its fair share of the profits," it tends to lead to the recognition of savings opportunities of this type.

3. *The Savings Potential is the Full Existing Cost.* As an example, *Drene* shampoo used to be packaged in a carton with a liner. Application of the elimination approach led to the elimination of the liner first, and then the carton as well. The company found that the attractive product sold better without a carton than with a carton.

4. *Never Consider Any Item of Cost Necessary.* The company used to handle its case goods on wood pallets with fork trucks.[6] This operation was quite satisfactory. However, because tens of thousands of wood pallets costing $3 to $5 each were used, the company set out to deliberately change the method and eliminate the costly wood pallets. The next step was to develop a paper pallet costing 50¢ to 70¢ along with a Pul Pac type of truck. Then the clamp truck was designed which permits the company to handle 90 percent of its cases *without any pallets*. An annual savings of $500,000 has resulted.

Experience shows that the deliberate change program functions best in a favorable atmosphere. Small groups take the initiative in selecting problems which they want to study and in establishing their own goals.

Recognition

A successful methods change program depends upon positive recognition. The approaches to recognition generally fall into the following categories.

Methods Program Kickoff Meeting
Methods Goal Victory Celebrations
Team Status Bulletin Board

[6] See page 245.

Monthly Methods Change Newsletter
Plant and Team Rotating Trophies
Small personal awards of recognition to members of a successful team
Letters of commendation

The plants have been very ingenious in devising ways to recognize successful methods change achievements. One plant, for example, conducted a methods saving contest and awarded stamps for completed projects. This contest was a takeoff on commercial trading-stamp plans. The plant printed its own stamps, stamp books, and prize catalogues. However, the savings exceeded expectations, the supply of stamps was exhausted, and vouchers had to be issued for the additional stamps earned. A victory celebration banquet was held at which stamps could be redeemed for modest prizes or exchanged for bingo cards in the hope of improving one's lot. The important point is that the recipients were recognized publicly and were made to feel important because their contribution was important.

Summary

The key points in organizing a methods change program based on Procter and Gamble's experience are the following ones.

1. Form methods teams

a. Organize the program so that each manager can spend part—possibly 5 percent of the time working on deliberate changes as a member of a methods team or a profit team.

b. The teams should survey all of the dollars in the area. There was a time when most cost-reduction thinking was related primarily to labor costs. All costs should be challenged.

c. All management people should join in the program because cost reduction is possible wherever dollars are spent. No group should be above participating in cost reduction.

d. The responsibility for the success of the program should fall on the line organization.

2. Establish dollar goals

a. Challenging goals should be established. Procter and Gamble's experience indicates a need for building the goals democratically, starting with first-line supervision. Comparisons providing competition among plants and functional groups are a real incentive to achievement.

b. A capable person, such as a methods engineer, should be assigned to give the program continuing assistance and coordination that leads to meeting the goals. The coordinator will help with ideas, work on reports, obtain information from other technical organizations, and keep the record of achievement.

c. It is necessary to fight the delusion that cost reduction is "cream skimming"—that next year's goal will be harder to make because of success this year.

The point should be emphasized that every dollar of cost is a dollar of potential savings. Past success points the way to ever greater profit increase through deliberate change.

3. Provide positive recognition

a. People like to be recognized in the presence of their associates. They want to be a member of a winning team. Procter and Gamble has found that when sincerely done it is almost impossible to overdo proper recognition.

Results

Figure 289 shows the entire record of savings of the methods change program. The savings per member of management was $400 in 1946 and slightly over $43,000 in

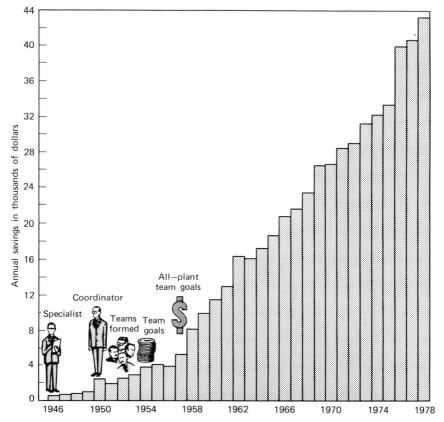

Figure 289   Annual savings per member of management resulting from the methods change program.

1977–1978.[7] The program produces one of the company's most attractive payouts. Since 1946 when the program started, the rate of return—using first-year savings only—has been around 1000 percent. In other words, $10 of profit is returned for every $1 spent. Some of the key events during the past that have caused the growth of the program to exceed the growth of the business are these:

1946–1949	Trained methods engineers served as specialists
1950	Coordinators appointed in manufacturing plants
1952	Methods teams formed in manufacturing plants
1954	Team goals established
1957	All-plant team goals established
1965–1975	Program extended to other parts of the business
1975	Company-wide divisional programs established

The Procter and Gamble program has a strong commitment of the top executives to the goals of the effort and this is communicated to all employees around the world.

Motion Study Training for Employees

Although motion study training programs for supervisors have been most common, there is increasing use of such programs for factory and office employees. A company-wide work simplification training program was inaugurated by the Maytag Company in 1949, and as a part of this program all factory workers have received 2½ hours of training in this field from the Industrial Engineering Department. The training program is tied in with the company's "Employee Idea Plan." This is a form of suggestion system whereby an employee is paid 50 percent of the first 6 months' net savings resulting from an idea which he has submitted. Cash awards up to a maximum of $5000 are given to hourly employees for ideas they suggest that result in cost reduction. The training in work simplification is designed to aid and encourage the employees to think of and submit ideas that will reduce costs to the company. Last year 93 percent of the employees submitted one or more ideas.

Since the Employee Idea Plan was started in 1949, a total of 93,817 ideas have been submitted and 31,815 have been installed, resulting in first-year savings to the company of $6,918,698. The total amount of awards paid to employees for suggestions during this period was $1,581,387.

The Maytag Idea Plan has been recognized by the National Association of Suggestion Systems for best overall Excellence of Performance. It is the sixth time in seven years that the Maytag Plan has won the top award in its employment category.

The supervisors at Maytag also submit ideas for methods improvement and cost reduction. Since the supervisors' work simplification program was started in 1949,

---

[7] To illustrate, if a company had 1000 members of management and made a similar savings of $43,000 per member of management, the total savings for the year from the methods change program would amount to $43 million.

44,549 ideas have been submitted and 21,391 were installed, resulting in a first-year cost reduction to the company of $38,301,195. Since cost reduction is a regular part of the supervisor's job, no awards are made for their ideas.

The idea plans are a systematic way of increasing productivity through suggestions provided by production and management employees. Since 1949 the combined first-year savings have amounted to approximately $45.2 million.

Organization Patterns for the Use of Motion and Time Study

Ways in which motion and time study is used may be classified into the following three patterns:

Pattern A. (Fig. 3) Taylor and Gilbreth and the people who followed them worked largely as *specialists* providing services to the operating or line organization.

Pattern B. The basic concept exemplified by the pioneering work of Persing at General Electric represented a drastic change in the use of motion study. He provided training in motion study and the problem-solving process to the *line supervisors* which enabled them to improve operations in their own departments. The General Electric Company was one of the first organizations to give motion study training to large numbers of its staff, and A. H. Mogensen was one of the first consultants to advocate this practice.[8]

Pattern C. The third organization pattern is the one that encourages the *workers themselves* in teams or groups to participate in the design of their own jobs. The non-management workers receive training in motion and time study and the problem-solving process, perform management functions, learn new skills, assume greater responsibility, and receive higher pay. This will be described in greater detail beginning with Chapter 39.

TIME STUDY AND WORK MEASUREMENT TRAINING PROGRAMS

People with a knowledge of even the elementary principles of motion study and methods design are usually able to make valuable suggestions for improving methods, and consequently the training of supervisors and operators in this field can be justified on this basis. However, only a qualified person, who is thoroughly trained in the fundamentals of time study and has served an "apprenticeship" under an experienced time study analyst, should be permitted to set time standards. People with only a superficial knowledge of time study should not attempt to do this work.

---

[8] For information on work simplification see "Work Simplification—A Program of Continuous Improvement," by Allan H. Mogensen, *Industrial Engineering Handbook,* 3rd ed., Harold B. Maynard (editor), McGraw-Hill Book Co., New York, 1971, pp. 13–18 to 13–26; "Work Simplification," by Herbert F. Goodwin, *Production Handbook,* 3rd ed., Gordon B. Carson, Harold A. Bolz, and Hewitt H. Young (eds.), Ronald Press, New York, 1972, pp. 14–1 to 14–33.

Time Study Training Programs for Top Executives, Managers, and Supervisors

A time study training program designed for top executives, managers, and supervisors is not intended to train them to make time studies. Rather, it is the purpose of such a training program to acquaint these people with the methods and procedures of time study so that they can assist the time study department in doing a better job. The main reasons why these groups should know how time studies are made may be listed as follows.

1. The planning and control department will better understand the importance of a smooth flow of parts and materials of the proper specifications to the processing departments.
2. The maintenance department will realize the importance of keeping all equipment in good repair, with the result that there will be a minimum of interruptions in the operation of equipment.
3. The inspection department will specify and maintain a definite standard of quality for each product. If quality standards change at frequent intervals, time standards cannot be used satisfactorily.
4. All branches of management will be on the alert to report to the time study department any changes in methods, tools, equipment, or other factors affecting the operations on incentives.
5. All members of management will understand the importance of keeping an accurate record of work done and applying the correct time standard (or piece rate) for each job completed.
6. All members of the organization will understand the procedure of rating operator speed, and will know the meaning of normal performance.
7. The supervisor will have the operation to be timed running smoothly before requesting that a time study be made.

A Specific Case

A successful time study training program for top management and supervisors was conducted in a midwestern plant. Since it is perhaps typical of such programs in medium-size manufacturing plants, the program is described here in some detail. This plant has a well-organized industrial engineering department, and the piece rate plan of wage incentives is used.

Size of organization: One plant with approximately 1000 factor employees, 60 percent of whom are women.

Product: Complete line of rubber footwear.

Wage payment plan: (a) Hourly base rates established by job evaluation. (b) Time standards set by time study. (c) Straight piecework, with normal performance equal to 100 percent efficiency. At this point the hourly day-work rate is guaranteed.

Groups receiving training:

Group 1—Top executives.[9]

Group 2—All foremen: two groups, 7 persons in each group.

Group 3—All supervisors: three groups, 5 persons in each group.

Note: Junior members of the following departments also received this training: time study, production planning and control, and payroll.

The sessions were approximately 1½ hours in length, and they were held on consecutive days. The same material was presented to all three groups. All three sessions for Group 1 were completed before the Group 2 conferences were started, and sessions for the second group were completed before the Group 3 conferences were started. All conferences were held during the working day, either in the forenoon or in the early afternoon. Meetings were held in the plant conference room, with ample space and facilities for showing motion pictures and displaying charts.

The factory manager was present through all sessions of Group 1, and introduced the program to each of the other groups. He was also present at the conclusion of each session of Groups 2 and 3, and made certain that each supervisor received complete and satisfactory answers to all his questions. In fact, the factory manager was familiar with every phase of time study and was fully convinced that all members of the organization should understand the detailed procedures. He encouraged the supervisors to raise questions on any points that were not perfectly clear to them.

The conferences were conducted mainly by the head of the industrial engineering department, with the assistance of the factory manager. An outline of the conference follows.

First Session.. (1) Statement of the purpose of the conferences by the factory manager. Statement of benefits the company expects to receive from the conferences and the benefits the people attending the conferences should receive. General outline of the material to be covered in the conferences, by the head of the industrial engineering department.

(2) Showing of a 30-minute motion picture film presenting the complete time study procedure. This film showed step by step just how a time study is made, including the calculation of the final time standard.

(3) Discussion of the company time study manual. This manual was read section by section, and each section was carefully explained by means of specific illustrations.

Second Session. Continuation of discussion of the time study manual. An actual job from the plant was brought into the conference room and demonstrated to the group. The time study of this job (Fig. 207) which had previously been made had been

[9] The top executive group included the factory manager, superintendent, chief chemist, chief engineer, head of production planning and control, head of cost accounting and payroll office, chief designer, head of purchasing department, and their assistants.

transferred to a large wall chart 4 feet by 8 feet in size, and to a computation sheet 4 feet by 8 feet in size (Fig. 209). These charts were hung in the front of the conference room. Each item on the time study sheet and on the computation sheet was explained to the group. This explanation led to the final establishment of the time standard for the job, and then to the determination of the piece rate for it. Finally, an explanation was made as to how the piece rate was put into effect.

Third Session. The first part of this session was devoted to a definition of "normal operator performance" as it pertained to this plant. Then the group was shown the introductory reel of the Unit I Work Measurement Film. After this each person rated ten different walking speeds and a film of several different factory operations. There was a general discussion of the meaning of "100 percent performance." The importance of the supervisors being able to evaluate operator speed accurately was emphasized.

There was a discussion of the relationship between the earnings of operators and their efficiencies above and below 100 percent performance. The number of people who might be expected to attain efficiencies in the range of 125 to 150 percent of normal was also discussed. The importance of accurately reporting work done was emphasized.

The entire time study procedure was reviewed in light of just how it affected the supervisor in the particular group. There was a question and discussion period, with both the factory manager and the head of the industrial engineering department participating.

After the conferences for the three groups had been completed, the factory manager and the head of industrial engineering held a 2-hour conference with the president of the union and the shop steward. The same material, in somewhat condensed form, was presented to these people. This session was followed by several discussion periods.

Follow-up. This series of three conferences was followed each month with a 1-hour conference for Groups 2 and 3, at which time a review of current problems pertaining to time standards and wages was made and each person was given the opportunity to make ratings of motion picture films of factory operations for which known standards were available. Actual factory operations were also rated.

This company owns its own motion picture camera, projector, screen, and auxiliary equipment for making and showing 16-mm. films.

Time Study Training for Industrial Engineers from Several Plants of the Same Organization

Even though time study analysts may be doing accurate and consistent work in a given plant, if a company operates several plants, it is good policy to standardize the work measurement procedure for all plants. This is especially desirable if identical operations are performed in two or more plants, if time study analysts are frequently transferred from one plant to another, if labor cost comparisons are made between plants, and if company-wide standard data are to be developed and used most effectively.

There is merit in having time study procedures so standardized and time study analysts so trained that if all time study analysts in all plants of a company were simultaneously to time the same operation independently they would establish essentially the same time standard for the job. Because the standardization of time study procedure and the training of time study analysts in this procedure are of growing importance, an actual case will be presented to show how a group of time study analysts were trained in one organization.

A Specific Case

The following case illustrates what may be accomplished through a systematic attempt to improve work measurement procedures. The company referred to here has five plants in four different midwestern states and employs a total of some 10,000 people. The company has been in business many years and has used time study in all plants for a long time. Before the inauguration of the Time Study Conferences, each plant had its own time study procedure and there was almost no exchange of information in this area between the plants. As might be expected, the time study methods differed, not all the time study forms used were alike, and there was considerable variation in time standards for identical jobs performed in the several plants.

Top management had received complaints from plant managers and from union officers about the variation in time standards, and a survey of time study procedures in all plants confirmed this point. Management decided to develop and standardize time study procedures that would best serve its needs, and a plan was inaugurated to have the time study analysts themselves, under the guidance of an able executive of the company, solve their own problems. The plan took the form of 2-day Time Study Conferences, which were held at approximately 2-month intervals.

The first conference was attended by the chief industrial engineer and two or three of his assistants from each of the five plants. Work measurement procedures used in each plant were described and criticized. Everyday operating problems were presented by each person and discussed. The group agreed that they should work toward a standardized work measurement procedure, and that they should adopt the best time study practices available. A new time study form was designed, and the problem of performance rating was considered.

At succeeding conferences, the following subjects were discussed: methods of timing, the determination and application of allowances, waiting time, the development of a performance rating procedure for the company, all-day time studies, a "methods development program" for training supervisors in all plants, the development of standard data for common operations in all plants, and other related subjects.

The rating of walking, of dealing cards, and of films of factory operations was a part of each conference. Also, during conferences 3 to 7, several actual factory operations were timed. Each time study analyst independently made a time study of each operation. The analyst was given ample time to work up his data and to determine the time standard in the same way he ordinarily did this in his own plant. The completed time studies were immediately submitted to the chairman of the conference, and a summary was prepared similar to that shown in Fig. 290. The time studies were then returned to the time study analysts for use in the discussion which followed.

After all time study data were tabulated, the conference leader read off the values for each of the seven items, without mentioning from whose time study the values had been taken. Then there was a general discussion of the variations and the probable reason for them. After the discussion of a particular study was completed, the original time studies were turned in to the conference leader. Later these studies were reproduced and bound together, and a copy of the complete set of time studies was given each person for his file.

Several factors contributed to the success of the program described above. Among them the following seem to be the most important.

1. Top management was in complete sympathy with the program and was determined that the company should make use of the best time study techniques and practices.
2. A capable man (the assistant to the vice-president in charge of production) was selected to direct the program. It was his belief that time study analysts from all plants should assist in working out the details of the program, rather than that the program should be developed in the main office. He felt that the training each man would receive in the process of developing the new time study procedure would be very valuable.
3. Each time study analyst was made to see the merits of having a standardized work measurement procedure for all plants, and each man contributed to the development of a workable system. At the suggestion of the time study analysts themselves, the program was expanded to include such things as determination of allowances, analysis of down time, development of a "methods improvement program for supervisors," and the determination of standard data for use in all plants.
4. The plant managers and other executives in the organization were interested in the details of the program and kept informed as to the progress that was being made. The president and the vice-president of the company on several occasions attended the Time Study Conferences and took part in them.
5. A bound volume of proceedings, prepared after each time study conference, served as a progress report. A copy went to the vice-president in charge of

RESULT SHEET

Operation: Chain Idler Assembly for Combine

Information from Time Study	Industrial Engineer Who Made Study									Aver-age
	A	B	C	D	E	F	G	H	I	
1. Number of elements	9	7	9	10	9	8	11	8	13	9
2. Performance rating factor	110	105	105	105	100	105	110	110	110	107
3. Personal allowance in per cent	5	3	3	3	5	5	5	5	3	4
4. Delay allowance in per cent	2	2	3	2	2	2	2	2	2	2
5. Fatigue allowance in per cent	2	4	2	5	5	2	3	4	3	3
6. Total allowances in per cent	9	9	8	10	12	9	10	11	8	10
7. Total standard time in minutes	1.08	.98	1.04	1.02	1.00	1.04	1.06	1.06	1.03	1.03

Operation: Chain Idler Assembly for Combine

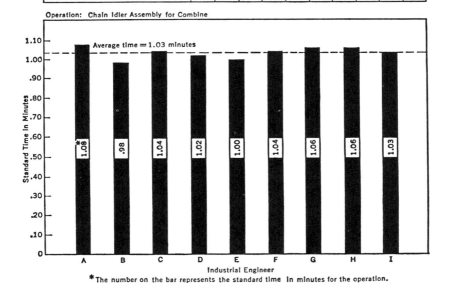

*The number on the bar represents the standard time in minutes for the operation.

Figure 290 Table and chart showing the results of a simultaneous time study made by nine different industrial engineers from five different plants.

production and to other executives, as well as to each time study analyst. A reproduction of every time study made during the conference (but without the time study analyst's name) was included in the volume, as well as summary sheets similar to Fig. 290. These reports were successfully used by the management in discussing with the union the ability of time study analysts to determine accurate, consistent, and fair standards.

Results of a Simultaneous Time Study Made by a Group of Time Study Analysts

There has been much speculation about the variation that would be found in time standards set by a group of time study analysts if they were to study the same operation at the same time.

As a part of each Time Study Conference already referred to, the time study analyst made time studies of actual factory operations. An experienced operator performed the job, and each time study analyst made his time study in his accustomed way. Figure 290 shows the summary of one of the best studies made by this group at the seventh Time Study Conference. Assembling a chain idler for a combine was the operation studied. Time study analyst B set a low time standard of 0.98 minute, and A set a high standard of 1.08 minutes on this job. The average of the nine time study analysts was 1.03 minutes. B was 5 percent lower and A was 5 percent higher than the average of the group. All time standards fell within ±5 percent of the average for the group. Although it seems certain that these men will further improve their ability to set accurate and consistent time standards with more practice and experience, it might be added that their record, as shown in Fig. 290, is perhaps as good as will be found among time study analysts in general. These men worked in five different plants, and only two men had seen the operation before they studied it.

It should also be noted that the average performance rating factor for the nine men was 107 percent, with E using the lowest factor of 100 percent, and A, G, H, and I using the highest factor of 110 percent. E was 7 percent low, and A, G, H, and I were 3 percent high.

The total allowances varied from a low of 8 percent to a high of 12 percent, with an average of 10 percent.

Training in Rating Operator Performance

Practice in the rating of walking and the rating of dealing cards serves to show the importance of performance rating in time study work. Such rating studies may well be included in all time study training programs. These studies are also excellent for training beginning time study analysts and for improving the rating ability of experienced industrial engineers. The rating of walking and dealing cards is so widely used in industry that suggestions for making rating studies of these two activities are given on pages 654 to 658.

Rating of other simple operations, such as filling a pinboard (Figs. 81 and 82), tossing blocks, and assembling small parts, is also recommended. A motion picture film of an actual factory operation may be formed into a continuous loop and projected at constant speed for rating purposes. Considerable use is being made of such film loops for practice in rating and for time study training purposes. Time studies can be made of operations on the screen, and standards can be established. Some companies have a library of such films to use for training purposes and to serve as standards on their important operations.

Effect of Practice on Accuracy of Rating

In order to measure the variations in ratings made by experienced time study analysts over a long period, Eli Lilly and Company repeated the walking study and the card-dealing study each week for a period of 4 months. The results shown in Figs. 291 and 292 are as follows: for walking, the systematic error was reduced from -13.7 to -2.3, and the mean deviation from 7.6 to 2.4; for card dealing, the systematic error was reduced from $+1.8$ to $+0.8$, and the mean deviation from 6.2 to 2.4.

The following general statements can be made concerning training in performance rating.

1. An individual's accuracy and consistency in performance rating can be improved through proper training.
2. An individual can rate more accurately on performances that are close to normal. There is some tendency to rate too high on slow working speeds and too low on working speeds that are considerably above normal.
3. On simple work (free and unrestricted motions) a person can rate a motion picture film of an operation about as accurately as the operation itself.

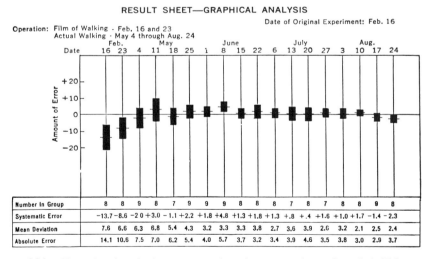

Figure 291 Chart showing the improvement in rating over a 4-month period. This group of time-study analysts rated a film of walking on February 16 and on February 23, and then rated actual walking during the remainder of the period. Study made by Methods and Standards Department, Eli Lilly & Co.

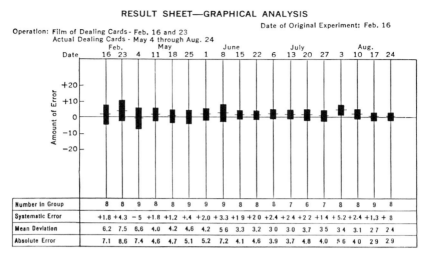

Figure 292   Chart showing the improvement in rating over a 4-month period. This group of time-study analysts rated a film of card dealing on February 16 and on February 23, and then rated actual card dealing during the remainder of the period. Study made by Methods and Standards Department, Eli Lilly & Co.

4. Motion picture films serve a valuable purpose for training individuals in performance rating. They may also be used to assist in acquainting management and nonmanagement people with work measurement techniques. A library of films showing operators working at normal tempo, and at known speeds above and below normal, can serve as standards or bench marks for time study work in a plant.

5. Periodic time study conferences or clinics within a company, at which all phases of time study practices are discussed, are needed to keep a time study department functioning well. Practice in making simultaneous time studies of actual factory jobs should be a part of such conferences.

TRAINING THE OPERATOR—
EFFECT OF PRACTICE

It is not the purpose here to discuss the broad field of employee training, but rather to present some specific methods that have been found useful in training operators to do a particular job. Although such training is usually given by the supervisory force, the motion and time study analyst or a special instructor may handle this work.

We often have pictured for us large groups of workers performing identical routine operations over long periods, but this is not the typical situation even in large plants. Not only does the worker normally perform many different operations in the course of a month, but also, with constant changes in methods, with improvements in materials, and with the rapid introduction of new models, there are many new jobs which the operator must learn. The worker today, more than ever before, must be able to do a variety of work, which tends to increase the amount of training required in industry.

Training Methods on Simple Operations

The best method for doing a given task is of little value unless the operator does the work in the proper manner. Where one or a very few persons are employed on a given job and where the work is relatively simple, the ordinary instruction sheet forms an excellent guide for training the operator. Also, on semiskilled work where the worker is familiar with the operation of the machine but needs instructions for the performance of particular operations, the simple instruction sheet is satisfactory. The example shown in Fig. 293 gives a written description of the elements required for turning the gear blank, and the drawing at the top of the sheet shows the exact location of the tools and of the parts to be machined. The time value for each element is also included, as well as the total standard time for the operation.

Where the work is entirely manual, instructions prepared on the order of the operation chart shown in Fig. 68 are of value in that they indicate exactly what hand motions are required and show the layout of the work place.

Another case is taken from a chocolate factory. When a new box or a new assortment of chocolates is to be packed, the pattern is determined and the operators are required to pack by this pattern. The customary procedure was to send a sample package to the supervisor, along with the order for packing. Sometimes the first order was a rush one, and a number of operators were put on packing at once. Before the operators could begin work, the supervisor had to pack a sample box for each of them, often having the workers standing around waiting while this was being done.

Customer Amer. Tool Co.

Part Name Spur gear   Case D

Part No. 1073 A–F

Operation Name Drill, rough one side and ¾ of outside diameter

Operation No. 5 TR.

Dept. 11   Machine class, 58   Machine name, Jones & Lamson

Made by S. R. K.   Approved by S. M.   Date   Mat'l SAE2315

Tool layout

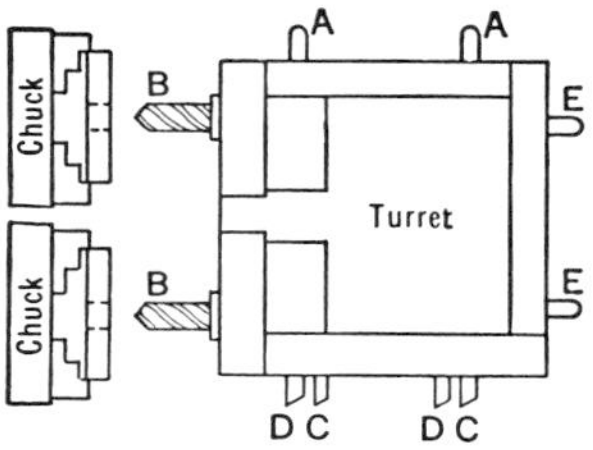

Set-up Time:

New set-up   60.00

Change of size   30.00

No.	Procedure	Tools—jigs, etc.	Speed Setting	Speed Ft. min.	Feed Setting	Feed In./rev.	Base time
1	Pick up and chuck 2 pieces..........	....					0.12
2	Start machine and true up (if necessary).....						0.10
3	Change speed.........						0.03
4	Adv. turret and throw in feed..........						0.06
5	ROUGH OUTSIDE DIAMETER (¾).........	A. ¾×1¼ in. tools........		70	71	0.014	2.32
6	Back turret and index...						0.07
7	Advance turret, set headstock, throw in feed and change speed.						0.12
8	DRILL..........	B. 1 3⁄16 in. drills........		60	71	0.014	0.58
9	Back turret and index..						0.07
10	Advance turret and lock						0.08
11	Advance headstock, change speed and throw in feed.....						0.08
12	ROUGH FACE 1 SIDE....	C. ¾×1¼ in. tools........		70	71	0.014	1.65
13	ROUGH FACE HUB.....	D. ¾×1¼ in. tools........		30	71	0.014	....
14	Unlock, back and index turret..........						0.07
15	Advance turret and set head stock.........						0.09
16	CHAMFER INSIDE FLANGE	E. ¾×1¼ in. Form tools		70	Hand		0.10
17	Advance head stock....						0.06
18	CHAMFER HUB.....	E. ¾×1¼ in. Form tools		30	Hand		0.10
19	Back turret and index..						0.07
20	Set head stock........						0.12
21	Stop machine.........						0.03
22	Loosen and remove 2 pieces..........						0.10
	Total handling time for two pieces..........						1.47
	Total machine time for two pieces..........						4.55
	Total base time for two pieces..........						6.02
	Total base time for one piece..........						3.01
	Allowances 10 per cent..						0.30
	Standard time in minutes per piece..........						3.31

Figure 293   Instruction sheet for turret lathe operation.

½ Lb. BLUE RIBBON BOX (Flange) List No. 4623–12

Cups	Unit No.	Name	Cups	Unit No.	Name
Round	203	Raspberry Cup	Round	376	Caramelized Brazil
"	204	Apricot Cup	"	392	Croquante Whirl
"	221	Strawberry Creme	"	393	Vanilla Caramel
"	275	Coffee Creme	"	394	Marzipan Sandwich
"	371	Orange Marzipan	"	396	Tosca Pate

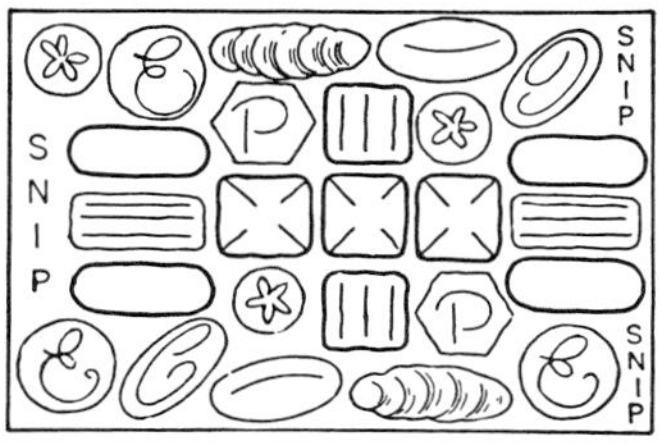

Heavy lines
= Foil Covered
Units

Make weight with Accommodation Units, one less than weight of last Chocolate.
If Light Add: 1 Croquante Whirl, 1 Apricot Cup.
If Heavy Take Out: 1 Apricot Cup.

	No.		Patt. No.	Paper No.
Linings (Center) (Emb. E. Foil)	1	$13, \frac{3}{8} \times 6, \frac{7}{8}$	Shaped	8795
" (Ends)	2	$4, \frac{7}{8} \times 2, \frac{15}{16}$	3226	8796
Top-Pad	1	$6, \frac{13}{16} \times 4, \frac{13}{16}$	....	4990
" Stock No. 04990— To be cleared first				
Cups (Round)	25	....	....	3569
Wrap	1	$14, \frac{13}{16} \times 11, \frac{1}{8}$	2716	142
Wrap fastened on bottom with Gloy, ends folded and fastened on bottom with Gloy.				
Printed Identification Key	1	$8, \frac{3}{4} \times 6, \frac{7}{8}$	....	5070

Snip—Brown.
Filled on Printed Identification.
Tear-off Price Seal (Stk. No. 2878) on wrap, top-left.

Foil (Stock No. 8666) Blue and Silver E. Design—to be used when Stk. No. 08666 is cleared.

FOILS

Stock No. 08666—Blue Printing on Silver.

Width of Reel 3″ for Tosca Pate, Marzipan Sandwich and Strawberry Creme.

Symbol No. F. 136.
Outer No. R. 976—Packed ¼ dozen.
Outer tied String—Single.

First packing to be sent to Inspection Office.

New Lines Office

Issued to Inspection Office from New Lines Office.

Figure 294 Instruction sheet for packing chocolates.

541

The use of an instruction sheet similar to that shown in Fig. 294, prepared in advance, has not only saved the operators waiting time but has also enabled them to bring their packing speed up to standard in a very short time.

Pictorial Instruction Sheets

The use of still pictures in connection with written instructions, as shown in Figs. 295 and 296, has proved very effective in supplementing the efforts of the instructor in training operators in a rubber footwear plant[1] and a glass plant. After glass bottles are made, they must be inspected for defects. The handling and inspection of bottles require considerable time to learn, and there is a knack to doing the job. The instruction sheet shown in Fig. 296 was developed by the Training Department of the Armstrong Cork Company to show the key points. It is supplemented by a motion picture showing an experienced operator inspecting bottles. Several different sizes and shapes of bottles are included, and some slow-motion shots illustrate the position of the hands and fingers in grasping and turning the bottles.

It seems that much of the skill required in doing some kinds of manual work centers around the exact way certain motions are performed, particularly grasp, hold, position, and pre-position. It appears that the transport and use motions require less attention and are more easily taught. In other words, it is more useful to show the operator how to take hold of the object before moving it, and how to position it before releasing it, than it is to show the actual transportation or movement of the object.

Another example of the usefulness of still pictures is given in Figs. 124 and 125, showing how the operator grasps the bone and how she positions it at the beginning of the creasing motion in folding paper.

Training Assembly Operators

The following is a detailed description of the procedure that was followed in training a group of ten operators to perform a short-cycle assembly operation. This operation consisted of placing four small parts together, using both hands and the eyes. Figure 297 is a drawing of the finished mechanism assembly. The new operation was a combination of two old operations, which will be referred to as the superseded operations. Figure 298 shows the arrangement of the work place. The only special equipment needed was a steel plate containing a small V-block to hold the lead carrier while it was placed in the stem of the assembly.

The improved method, which saved over 13,000 man-hours of direct labor per year, was developed by L. F. Youde. He describes[2] the training procedure which he used in the following way:

---

[1] A. Williams, "Teach It with Pictures," *Factory Management and Maintenance,* Vol. 94, No. 12, pp. 50–51.
[2] L. F. Youde, "A Study of the Training Time for Two Repetitive Operations," thesis, University of Iowa.

OPERATION: Lacing
TYPES: L.T.T.—S.U.
DETAIL: 1 Spindle
MACHINE: Ensign
CODE: No. 52

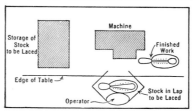

Sketch of Layout

 Get next upper like this, first finger of left hand between eyelet edges.

 Lift upper from stack with left hand, inserting second, third, and fourth fingers in top of shoe. Insert first finger of left hand between eyelet edges.

 Line up eyelet edges by moving hands in opposite directions and closing eyelet edges together.

 Get top end of eyelet edges between thumb and first finger of right hand. Move first finger of left hand out from between eyelet edges and grasp edges like this.

 Position fifth eyelet over spindle.

 Pull upper down onto spindle.

 Press down pedal to start machine and move fingers to this position.

 Hold upper while being laced. As spindle is automatically removed, upper is moved up and slightly to right while machine ties knot and cuts thread. Laced upper is finished in this position.

 Move finished upper to a position over stack of finished uppers.

 Place finished upper on stack.

Repeat Cycle.

Figure 295 Pictorial instruction sheet for lacing tennis shoes.

543

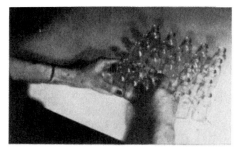

1. Pick up bottles (2 rows of 3).

   Grasp 6 bottles (2 in left hand, 4 in right hand). Hold thumbs toward you and fingers away from you.

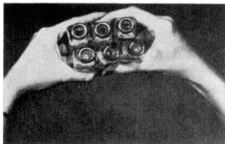

2. Inspect necks.

   Tilt necks slightly so that the light will show defects.

3. Separate bottles.

   Separate bottles so that the left hand holds 2 and the right hand 4.

4. Turn left wrist to left with palm of hand up. At the same time move the left thumb toward the left so that the top bottle falls into place to the left of the bottom bottle. This places 2 bottles in the palm ready for inspection. Use the left thumb as a stop.

Figure 296 Pictorial instruction sheet for inspection of bottles (1-ounce French squares). (Courtesy Armstrong Cork Company.)

544

5. Lower upper left bottle in right hand to the fingers of left hand. To do this, tilt both hands slightly to the left, raise the right thumb, and let bottle slide to tips of fingers of left hand. (Keep hands together so that tips of fingers are touching. This prevents bottles from falling.)

6. Lower upper right bottle to palm of right hand. Slide right thumb to the right, pushing bottle into place to right of all bottles.

7. Line up bottles on tips of fingers and shift bottles toward right thumb as a guide. (Keep bottles tight together to shift more easily.)

8. To inspect sides, roll bottles one-fourth turn. Four bottles are in the right hand, the fifth bottle is on the tips of the fingers just ready to fall. With the left thumb turn the left bottle one-fourth turn to the left.
Hold the thumb as a guide.
Tilt both hands to left so that bottles roll one-fourth turn, one at a time.

9. Repeat steps 7 and 8 so that you can inspect the other side of the bottles.

10. Inspect bases and pack neck down in cartons. Keep all bottles tight together between thumbs, inspect bases, and slide between partitions. Make sure that carton is filled with bottles.

Figure 297 Mechanism assembly.

After the V-block was made for the new operation, the motion study analyst proceeded to perform the new operation for approximately four hours in the methods laboratory. This trial run was made for the following reasons: (1) To test the equipment and eliminate any "bugs" that were present. This is important, as equipment should be fully tested before an operator is placed in training on the job. (2) To check the movements and establish a time standard for the operation from predetermined data. (3) To make certain that the motion study analyst who was to act as the trainer was able to perform the new operation with the correct movements.

The procedure described below was used to train the first operator on the new job.

(1) The new operation was shown and explained in general terms to the operator. Since she had been working on one of the superseded operations, she was told that her old job was being combined with another job so as to make a more efficient operation. Also, that the change was part of the regular methods improvement program. Other operations in her department that had been improved were pointed out to her as examples of the program. Because this operator had been on one of the superseded operations, it was not necessary to describe to her where the assembly was used.

Figure 298 Mechanism assembly operation—arrangement of work place.

(2)   The operator was told what the time standard was on the new operation and that after a period of training she would be placed on piecework.

(3)   With the operator standing slightly to his left and rear, the trainer demonstrated the new operation as follows:

(*a*)   For 20 cycles the trainer performed the operation quite rapidly in order to give the operator an over-all picture of the new job.

(*b*)   For 20 cycles the trainer performed quite slowly in order to give the operator a picture of the "gets" and "places" and the hand that performed them.

(*c*)   For 10 cycles the trainer explained and performed slowly each of the "gets" and "places" in the operation. The explanation consisted of telling the operator where the eyes were used, which fingers were used in getting different parts, and how the parts were placed together. In running 10 cycles, each explanation was repeated 10 times. This repetition helped the operator retain more of the instructions than if only one cycle had been explained.

(4)   The operator was seated at the work place and she was asked to perform the operation slowly the first day or two. She was told that at first the output was not important—that it was more important that she learn the correct methods, and that the speed would come naturally later.

(5)   The operator was then told to go ahead and start performing the operation. The operator's performance as to the correct movements was checked as follows:

(*a*)   The trainer watched the operator for her first ten minutes on the job to be sure she had the right idea and to correct any very bad errors.

(*b*)   The operator was allowed to run one hour to get the feel of the operation and its parts.

(*c*)   During the remainder of the operator's first day on the job, the trainer checked her once every hour to change any incorrect movements before they became a habit.

(*d*)   During the second and third days, the trainer checked the operator once every two hours.

(*e*)   For the remainder of the time until the operator reached standard time and was placed on piecework, the trainer checked twice a day. The amount of checking varied among the different operators trained on the new operation. Figure 299 shows the learning curve for the first operator on this job.

The other operators were trained in exactly the same way as the first one, except that their training was done on the production floor instead of in the methods laboratory.

Training Methods on Complex Operations

Some operations are complex in nature, and the operator may require considerable skill to perform them satisfactorily. A much longer training period is ordinarily required for this type of work than for simpler operations.

Where a sizable group of employees is engaged in such work, there is an opportunity for a more elaborate training program. Some companies find it profitable under such conditions to establish a vestibule training school or a separate training department apart from the regular production departments.

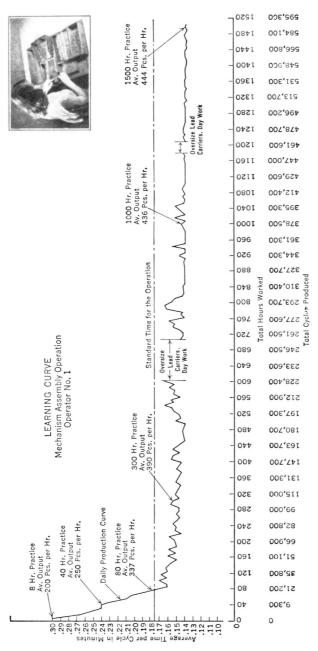

Figure 299 Learning curve for mechanism assembly operation. The average hourly output for the first day was 200 pieces. After 500,000 cycles of practice, output increased to 444 pieces per hour.

548

With over 100 operators on the semiautomatic lathe operation described in Chapter 36, the company established a special school for training new operators for this work. Whereas it formerly took 6 months to train these operators, the time was reduced to 6 to 8 weeks.

To cite another case[3] of group training on complex operations, Persing of the Fort Wayne works of the General Electric Company supervised the training of 200 new operators hired for a rush job of assembling large numbers of extremely delicate parts required in the manufacture of electric meters.

The entire assembly process was broken down into small assemblies, which were studied to determine the best way of making these subassemblies. Where special trays, fixtures, and combination tools were required, they were built, and the correct layout of the work place was arranged. One operator was trained by the instructor, and after becoming proficient in the new method, motion pictures were made of the operation to use in the training of the other operators.

It was found practical to train 18 operators at one time. The training of this group was carried out in the following way. Eighteen duplicate sets of trays and tools were installed in exactly the same way on tables in the motion study laboratory. All the operators were seated at these tables, facing the motion picture screen at the front of the room. A general explanation of the operation was made, and instructions were given in the care that should be exercised in handling the parts so that the finish would not be marred or intricate and delicate parts damaged during the assembly operation. The motion pictures of the operation were then projected several times on the screen, both forward and backward and at reduced speed, so that the new operators could see the correct way of doing the work. With the projector running very slowly, the instructor pointed out the correct way of grasping, carrying, positioning the parts, and performing each of the other motions of the cycle. There were two instructors: one operated the projector and explained the motions, and the other, an experienced operator, gave individual instruction and inspected the work for the group.

With the ordinary method of using an experienced operator to train one or two new workers on the production floor, the experienced operator produced but 40 to 50 percent of the normal output. Also this method of training required an exceedingly long training period. Using the new method, two instructors trained 18 new operators in a separate room where there was no interference with the regular manufacturing operations. At the end of one week of training, the 18 operators were transferred to the production floor, properly trained for their task. This was but one third of the time required for training new operators by the old method.

Persing gives the following reasons why the company prefers to train the operators in a separate room:

---

[3] L. P. Persing, "Motion Study—The Teacher," *Factory and Industrial Management,* Vol. 82, No. 9, pp. 337–340, September, 1932.

(1) We could get 100 percent attention. There was not the confusion and noise of other activities to distract the operator's attention, such as you have on the average manufacturing floor.

(2) The operator does not get as nervous when trained in a separate room. There are not a lot of other workers watching the instructor teach the new cycle of motions, which in general are a great deal different from those they have seen before, and the layout of the trays is a curiosity.

(3) When any problem came up that was of interest to all the operators, you could get their attention at once and explain how to overcome or correct the fault.

(4) As the operators on this particular operation were to be taught the cycle of motions by watching the experienced operator assemble the register on the moving picture screen, it was necessary that the room be in semidarkness.

The Colonial Radio Corporation was one of the first radio manufacturers to successfully operate a school for training new assembly operators. At the time of employment all operators were given 2 to 3 days' training in a separate room, under the supervision of a competent instructor.

The classroom contained assembly benches with jigs, fixtures, hand tools, and the necessary parts and bins to handle such typical factory operations as screwdriver work, assembly and benchwork with pliers, and soldering operations. Groups of 8 to 12, and never more than 15, were trained at a time. The operators were paid their regular hourly base wage during the training period. At the beginning of the training period a simple explanation of the purpose of the course was given to the group. Extracts from this explanation are given below:

As you are probably aware, the purpose of this class is to teach a better way of performing some of our more common assembly operations, which involve such familiar parts as nuts, screws, lock washers, wires, condensers, resistors, etc.

All of us realize the fact that certain ways of doing a thing are better than others. It has been established that there is a best way of performing any given act, and we have also made the discovery, which most of you have probably known all along, that the best way is almost invariably also the easiest way. Haven't you found this to be the case in your experience?

Just as you in your home attempt to find the best way of performing your household duties, so in industry we attempt to find the best way of doing the things required of us.

It has been established that at least 25 percent of the motions used by the average employee in the average factory operations are wasted motions. These wasted motions are needless motions which contribute only one thing as far as the operator or the operation is concerned, and that is fatigue.

Naturally you may ask—"What is the purpose of finding the best and easiest way of performing operations in the plant?" This can be stated briefly as follows:

"It is the desire on the part of Colonial to build a better radio set at a lower cost without, however, requiring the expenditure of any more physical effort on the part of those of us directly engaged in building them."

All of you realize the amount of work we have in our plant depends on the number of radio sets the Sales Organization of the Colonial Radio Company can sell. When you and I, and millions of other consumers, decide to buy a radio set, or any other merchandise, we always attempt to get the best product we can for the money we want to spend, and, if the best radio set we can buy for a given sum of money happens to be a Colonial radio, we will buy it. In other words, the welfare of the Colonial Radio Corporation and, coincidentally in a large measure, all of us, depends on the ability of Colonial to build at least as good a set as any other manufacturer at the same or at a lower price.

After the above explanation has been made and any questions by members of the class have been discussed, the group is given a simple assembly operation to perform. An explanation is given of what the finished job must be like, and then each person is allowed to do the task in any way that she wishes. Each operator is given a timer and pencil and paper to record the time for making ten assemblies. The operator continues to do this task for an hour, recording the time for each set of ten assemblies.

Then an assembly fixture and improved bins are given to the operator. The proper arrangement of the work place is made, and the operator is carefully instructed in the proper method of doing the work. An explanation is also given of the principles of motion economy employed, and why the new method is easier, faster, and safer than the old one.

After the operator understands how to do the task in the proper way, she again works for an hour or so, timing herself for groups of ten pieces and recording the time as before. The fact that the improved method saves time is obvious to her, since she has set her own pace and read and recorded her own time. She is well aware that motion study is not a "speed-up," but that it enables her to do more work with less fatigue.

After the new operator has worked on a simple assembly operation, she is given other jobs that are typical of those she will see in the factory, some of which she may work on after the training period is over.

Although the main purpose of the school is to train new operators in the principles of motion economy, Colonial has found that the school also serves another very important function. It shows the employees, in a most convincing manner, that improving methods of doing work is for their benefit as well as for the company's, and that actually the best way from a motion study angle is invariably the least fatiguing way and the most satisfactory way in every respect for the operator.

Incidentally, it requires approximately 50 percent less time for an operator who has been through the training school to attain standard performance than for new operators going directly onto the production floor without the traning. During a 2-year period more than 700 persons were trained in the manner described above.

Audio-Visual Instruction for Operators on Complex Long-Cycle Operations

Audio-visual instructions provide one solution to the problem of training operators on long-cycle operations. The assembly of some electronic components may take as long

Figure 300 Standard work bench equipped with 35-mm color slide projector and magnetic tape player which provide the operator with visual and oral instructions. (Courtesy of Hughes Aircraft Company.)

as an hour or more, and it is not feasible to break the operations into small subassemblies. In such cases, detailed instruction in the form of 35-mm color slides which are shown on a translucent screen directly in front of the operator and oral instructions from a tape player are provided. The operator controls the speed of the audiovisual instructions by a foot-operated switch. It is reported that on complex, long-cycle work this form of operator instruction reduces labor costs and improves the reliability and quality of the product (Fig. 300).

Training to Reduce Anxiety Among New Employees

A study made in a large manufacturing department at Texas Instruments Incorporated led to a plan for reducing causes of anxiety among new employees.[4] The unique indoctrination and training program that they developed resulted in the following gains:

1. Training time was shortened by one half.
2. Training costs were lowered to one third of their previous levels.
3. Absenteeism and tardiness dropped to one half of the previous normal.
4. Waste and rejects were reduced to one fifth of their previous levels.
5. Costs were cut as much as 15 percent to 30 percent.

Earlier studies and the analysis of 135 individual interviews with 405 operators made by the department manager indicated that new employees had many anxieties associated with lack of job competence during the early days of employment. The following facts were revealed: "Anxiety interfered with the training process. "New employee initiation" practices by fellow workers intensified anxiety. Turnover of newly hired employees was caused primarily by anxiety. The new operators were reluctant to discuss problems with their supervisors."

It was well known that anxiety dropped as competence was achieved. The question was then asked, "Is it possible to accelerate achievement to the competence level by reducing anxiety at a faster rate?" A study was designed to obtain factual information bearing on this question. The setting for the study was a rapidly growing department employing over 1400 people spread throughout three shifts. The department manufactured integrated circuits (microminiature circuitry units). The subjects of the study were women operators who collectively performed approximately 1850 different operations. Approximately 57 percent of the operators worked with microscopes, and all jobs placed a premium on visual acuity, eye-hand coordination, and mechanical aptitude. Training was a continuous activity in this department—training new people hired for expansion and replacement purposes and retraining transferees and the technologically displaced. Figure 301 shows the learning curve for the ball bonders and is fairly typical of production operations in the department.

The ball bonders required approximately three months to reach what was termed the "competence" level. (The competence level is the stage at which assemblers can independently manufacture the product, but have not yet achieved the speed and accuracy ultimately expected of them to reach the labor standards set by industrial engineering. The competence level is about 85 percent of labor standards; a position about 115 percent of standard is termed the "mastery" level.)

A group of 10 girls hired for bonding work in the second shift was chosen as the first experimental group. A control group was selected from the first and third shifts.

---

[4]E. R. Gomersall and M. Scott Myers, "Breakthrough in On-The-Job Training," *Harvard Business Review,* Vol. 44, No. 4, pp. 62–72, July–August, 1966.

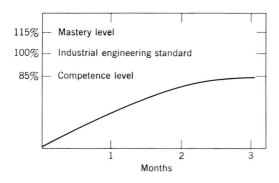

Figure 301 Learning curve for ball bonders.

Conventional Indoctrination

The control group was given the usual first-day orientation, which consisted of a 2-hour briefing on hours of work, parking, insurance, work rules, and employee services. This session included warnings of the consequences of failure to conform to organization expectations, and tended to raise rather than reduce anxieties. However, this was not intended as a threat.

Following this orientation, it was customary for a bonder to be introduced to her supervisor, who gave her further orientation and job instruction. Unfortunately, the supervisor's familiarity with the operations had desensitized him to the technological gap between them, and the following might be typical of what the operator heard him say:

Alice, I would like you to take the sixth yellow chair on this assembly line, which is in front of bonding machine #14. On the left side of your machine you will find a wiring diagram indicating where you should bond your units. On the right-hand side of your machine you will find a carrying tray full of 14-lead packages. Pick up the headers, one at a time, using your 3-C tweezers and place them on the hot substrate below the capillary head. Grasp the cam actuator on the right-hand side of the machine and lower the hot capillary over the first bonding pad indicated by the diagram. Ball bond to the pad and, by moving the hot substrate, loop the wire to the pin indicated by the diagram. Stitch bond to this lead, raise the capillary, and check for pigtails. When you have completed all leads, put the unit back in the carrying tray.

Your training operator will be around to help you with other details. Do you have any questions?

Overwhelmed by these instructions and not wishing to offend this polite and friendly supervisor or look stupid by teling him she did not understand anything he said, the operator would go to her work station and try to learn by watching the operators on either side of her. But they, in pursuit of operating goals, had little time to assist her. Needless to say, her anxieties were increased, and her learning ability was impaired. And the longer she remained unproductive, the more reluctant she was to disclose her frustration to her supervisor, and the more difficult her job became.

Experimental Approach

The experimental group participated in a special one-day program designed to overcome anxieties not eliminated by the usual process of job orientation. Following the two-hour orientation by members of the Personnel Department, they were taken directly to a conference room. They were told that there would be no work the first day; that they should relax, sit back, and use the time to get acquainted with the organization and each other; and that they should ask questions. Throughout this one-day anxiety-reduction session, questions were encouraged and answered. This orientation emphasized four points:

1. *"Your opportunity to succeed is very good."* Company records disclosed that 99.6 percent of all persons hired or transferred into this job were eventually successful in terms of their ability to learn the necessary skills. Trainees were shown learning curves illustrating the gradual buildup of competence over the learning period. They were told five or six times during the day that all members of this group could expect to be successful on the job.

2. *"Disregard 'hall talk.' "* Trainees were told of the hazing game that old employees played—scaring newcomers with exaggerated allegations about work rules, standards, disciplinary actions, and other job factors—to make the job as frightening to the newcomers as it had been for them. To prevent these distortions by peers, the trainees were given facts about both the good and the bad aspects of the job and exactly what was expected of them.

The basis for "hall talk" rumors was explained. For example, rumor stated that more than one half of the people who terminated had been fired for poor performance. The interviews mentioned earlier disclosed the fact that supervisors themselves unintentionally caused this rumor by intimating to operators that voluntary terminations (marriage, pregnancy, leaving town) were really performance terminations. Many supervisors felt this was a good negative incentive to pull up the low performers.

3. *"Take the initiative in communication."* The new operators were told of the natural reluctance of many supervisors to be talkative and that it was easier for the supervisor to do his job if they asked him questions. They were told that supervisors realized that trainees needed continuous instruction at first, that they would not understand technical terminology for a while, that they were expected to ask questions, and that supervisors would not consider them dumb for asking questions.

4. *"Get to know your supervisor."* The personality of the supervisor was described in detail. The absolute truth was the rule. A description might reveal that—the supervisor is strict, but friendly; his hobby is fishing and ham radio operation; he tends to be shy sometimes, but he really likes to talk to you if you want to; he would like you to check with him before you go on a personal break, just so he knows where you are.

Following this special day-long orientation session, members of the experimental group were introduced to their supervisor and their training operators in accordance with standard practice. Training commenced as usual, and eventually all operators went on production.

Results

The attitude and learning rate of the two groups was different from the beginning. By the end of four weeks the experimental group was significantly outperforming the control group—excelling in production and job attendance as well as in learning time. The one-month performance levels of the experimental and control groups were as follows:

	Experimental Group	Control Group
Units per hour	93	27
Absentee rate	0.5%	2.5%
Times tardy	2	8
Training hours required	225	381

Figure 302 shows the comparison of the learning curves for the two groups for the first eight weeks. The people at Texas Instruments believe that the area between the experimental curve and the control curve represents the learning time lag caused by anxiety.

When the experimental study began to show significant results, the anxiety-reduction process was used on additional groups. More than 200 people were employed in experimental and control groups for assembling, welding, and inspection operations. The performance curves for these groups are shown in Fig. 303. It should be noted that the third week's methods change in the inspection department depressed the per-

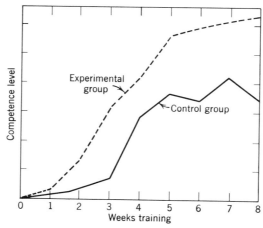

Figure 302 Learning curves of experimental and control groups.

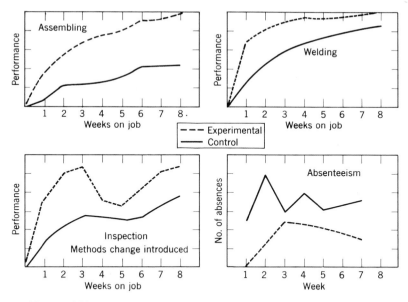

Figure 303 Further comparisons of experimental and control groups.

formance of the experimental group more than that of the control group, but the experimental group recovered more rapidly.

The motivated assemblers in the integrated circuits group without methods improvement exceeded the labor standards by approximately 15 percent to achieve the "mastery level" in two to three months (Fig. 304), whereas the control groups took about five months. The area between the experimental group and the control group curves in Fig. 304 represents an improvement in the performance of approximately

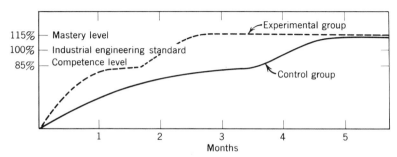

Figure 304 Mastery attainment by experimental and control groups.

50 percent. This was equal to a net first-year savings of at least $50,000 for 100 new employees. Considering reduced turnover, absenteeism, and training time, it was estimated that there was an additional savings of $35,000.

Another benefit was noted. The new trainees with less anxiety gradually influenced the performance of the work groups they joined. The older employees were inspired by the greater confidence of the trainees. Also, the higher performance of the new members established a new reference point for stimulating the natural competitiveness that existed among members of the work group. There was also a definite improvement in quality, and inspection labor costs were lowered by 30 percent.

Training Center for Coal Miners

The United States Steel Corporation, the nation's sixth largest coal producer, has opened a training center for coal miners near Waynesberg, PA, not far from the company's new Cumberland Coal Mine.[5] This mine will produce three million tons of bituminous coal a year. The training center resembles a warehouse, but inside is a simulated coal mine (Fig. 305). As one, wearing a miner's cap lamp, moves along the entryways and crosscuts, one sees a continuous mining machine, a shuttle car, a ram car, and other pieces of mining equipment. In one of the "make-believe" roof-supported pillars a doorway opens into a fully equipped classroom.

The above-ground simulated mine is adjacent to the main classroom building— both a part of the company's regional training center. The center is equipped to train new employees and experienced miners. There is a staff of full-time instructors and also front-line foremen teaching part-time. The curriculum covers eight basic areas: orientation, skills training, maintenance training, supervisory development, coal preparation and surface training, emergency medical training, retraining and skills upgrading, and certification.

The orientation program, for example, gives the beginner, a person who has never worked inside a mine, a concentrated three-week course in all aspects of safety and underground mining techniques. One-third of the instruction is conducted in the classroom and the balance of the training takes place in the simulated mine (Fig. 306 and 307) where the students get the feel of actual underground coal mining.

Orientation subjects include: accident prevention, general mine safety, first aid, ventilation, mine mapping, roof and rib control, health and sanitation, track laying, directing mine air flow, conveyor usage, fire fighting, mine equipment introduction, emergency procedures, and underground communications.

Retraining, skill updating and various motivational subjects for experienced miners are also a part of the center's curriculum. Available courses include both basic and advanced equipment maintenance, surface operations, crew training, mine rescue, and underground equipment operations.

---

[5] "USS Opens Training Center for Coal Miners," *US Steel News,* Vol. 42, No. 4, pp. 12–15, April, 1977. Reproduced by permission of the United States Steel Corporation.

A separate training program for foremen covers subjects dealing with leadership and motivational skills, human relations, safety, emergency procedures, mining law, and labor relations. In later phases of the program, the foremen trainees serve as instructors of a class often composed of the crew they will be working with underground.

The regional training center also offers an Emergency Medical Technicians (EMT) program. The completion of the course entitles the students to certification by the state of Pennsylvania as Emergency Medical Technicians.

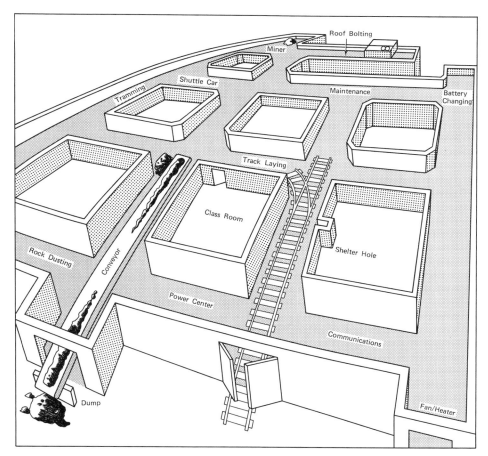

Figure 305   Floor plan of the simulated mine in the United States Steel's regional coal miner training center.

Figure 306 Two students receiving instruction in roof bolting. This section of the fully operative mine permits actual drilling and bolt setting, utilizing concrete cores mounted in the roof.

Figure 307 An instructor and two students discuss the controls of a continuous coal mining machine, one of the training aids used inside the simulated mine.

EFFECT OF PRACTICE

If a person can perform a manual task at all, with practice he or she can reduce the time required per cycle. The shape of the learning curve will be affected by the nature of the work and by the traits, abilities, and attitude of the individual performing the task.

Figure 299 shows the learning curve for an operator assembling a mechanical pencil mechanism.[6] The operator on her first day of work averaged 200 assemblies per hour. After 11 days of practice she turned out 343 assemblies per hour, which was standard performance. Since the piecework plan of wage payment was used in this plant, this operator earned a bonus for all work produced above the standard of 343 pieces per hour. Although the operator was producing 444 pieces per hour after 1500 hours of practice, it is apparent that the greatest increase in production took place during the first few weeks of work on the job. At the end of the first week the operator had increased her output 25 percent over that of the first day, and at the end of 2 weeks she had increased it 68 percent over that of the first day. After 38 weeks of practice, the total increase amounted to 122 percent. Of this increase, over half took place during the first 2 weeks of practice.

Figure 308   Punch-press operation—arrangement of work place.

[6] L. F. Youde, op. cit.

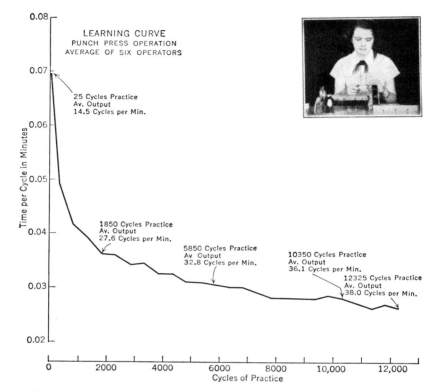

Figure 309 Learning curve for punch-press operation. The average output without practice was 14.5 pieces per minute. This increased to 38 pieces per minute after 12,325 cycles of practice.

Figure 309 shows the average learning curve for six operators performing a fairly complicated punch-press job (Fig. 308) involving the use of both hands and one foot. The output increased 75 percent after 1350 cycles of practice, and doubled at the end of 3350 cycles of practice.

Figure 310 shows the learning curve for a very simple operation, filling a pinboard with 30 pins, using the two-handed method (Fig. 82). Here the output increased very rapidly because of the simplicity of this operation.

A number of studies[7] have been made of typical factory operations to determine

[7] Harold T. Amrine, "The Effect of Practice on Various Elements Used in Screwdriver Work," *Journal of Applied Psychology,* Vol. 26, No. 2, pp. 197–209, and J. V. Balch, "A Study of Symmetrical and Asymmetrical Simultaneous Hand Motions in Three Planes," *Motion and Time Study Applications,* Section 14, pp. 70–72.

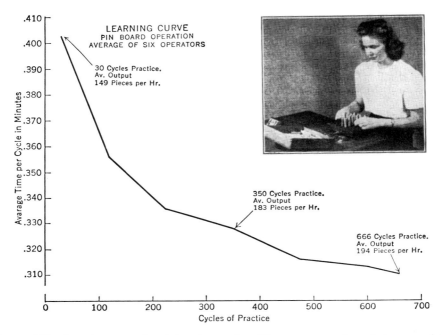

Figure 310 Learning curve for pinboard operation. The average number of pieces per hour without practice was 149. This increased to 194 pieces per hour after 666 cycles of practice.

the effect of practice on the fundamental hand motions. On one job, for example, although there was a reduction in time of 40 percent after 3000 cycles of practice for the operation as a whole, the reduction in time for the transport loaded motion was 15 percent, whereas the reduction in time for the position was 55 percent.

In another investigation[8] an attempt was made to determine through micromotion anlysis the difference between the way the operator performed the job without experience and the way she performed it after she had become proficient. Motion pictures were made of the operator as a beginner and then at intervals during the learning period until she reached a high level of proficiency. Figure 311 shows the results of this study. The upper line *A* is the actual learning curve, whereas the lower line *B* is the learning curve with the fumbles, delays, and hesitations removed. This study shows that in this case two-thirds of the increase in output during the learning period can be attributed to the elimination of fumbles, delays, and hesitations on the part of the operator, and one-third perhaps to faster hand motions.

[8] Ralph M. Barnes, James S. Perkins, and J. M. Juran, "A Study of the Effect of Practice on the Elements of a Factory Operation," *University of Iowa Studies in Engineering, Bulletin* 22, p. 67.

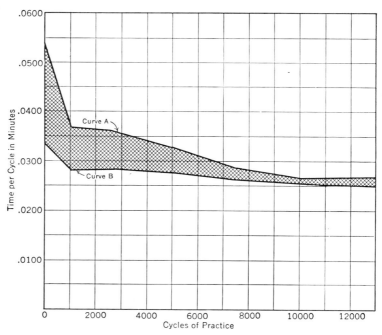

Figure 311   Curves showing effects of fumbles and delays. Curve A is based on data including all fumbles and delays. Curve B is based on the same studies but excluding fumbles and delays.

The following is an analysis of the differences of the two learning curves:

Cycle time at the outset	0.052 minute
Cycle time at the finish	0.027 minute
Improvement	0.025 minute

The improved performance can be traced to the following overlapping causes:

Reduction in fumbles and delays	0.017 minute
Faster performance	0.008 minute
Total	0.025 minute

There is evidence to show that the beginner does not use the same method that he or she will use after becoming proficient in performing the job. This difference in method is the biggest single factor affecting the cycle time for the job during the learning period.

Lost Time

The studies just referred to were made in the laboratory, and the conditions there are not always identical with those in the factory. Other studies seem to show that there is considerable difference between the average time per piece as determined by time study and the average time per piece as determined by dividing the number of minutes worked during the day by the number of pieces completed during the day. Figure 312 shows such information.[9] The upper curve A is a record of the total daily output, whereas the lower curve B is the actual time per piece as determined by a time study made of 50 cycles at the end of the day. This shows that as a beginner the operator "loses more time" per day than she does after she has had some practice.

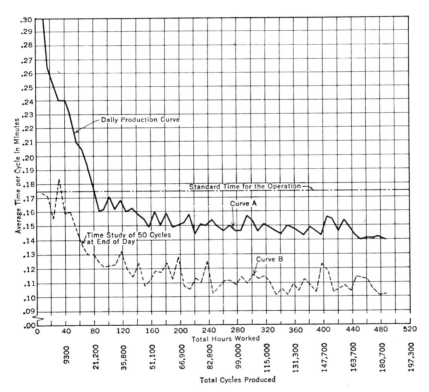

Figure 312 Learning curves for mechanism assembly operation. Curve A is a record of the total daily output. Curve B is the actual time per piece as determined by a time study made of 50 cycles at the end of the day.

[9] L. F. Youde, *op. cit.*

If the operator is given proper instruction, the learning period can be reduced, thus lowering unit labor cost to the employer and giving the operator greater satisfaction on his job. In time study work, emphasis is always placed on standardizing the method before setting a time standard for the job. The discussion and the learning curves in this chapter would indicate that time standards should not be established from time studies made of inexperienced operators. Experienced time study analysts know this only too well.

Time for Experienced Operators to Learn Another Job

Figure 313 shows the average weekly performance index of three operators in a washing machine factory for the period January 3 to April 25. During the month of January these three operators were working at a very high level, averaging 143, 150, and 154 percent efficiency. At the end of January the operations they were working on were discontinued, and they were transferred to other work. It became necessary for them to learn a new job, and almost three weeks was required to bring their performance index up to the standard of 100 percent, and a much longer period to reach the same level of efficiency at which they had been working before the change in jobs.

At the time these men were transferred to the new job, they stated that in their opinion the time standard on the new operation was too low—that they could not make the same performance index as they had in the past. The effect of practice was carefully explained to these operators, and they were persuaded to apply themselves

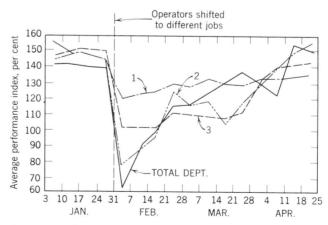

Figure 313 Average performance index of three operators in a factory. A change in the design of the product eliminated their job on January 31. They immediately started on new work.

to the new job as they had done in the past. Figure 313 shows the progress made by these three operators in regaining their high performance level.[10]

Learner's Progress Record

When a vacancy occurs or when a new job is established, it is management's desire to select a person for the work who has the traits and qualities that will enable him or her to succeed on the job and to get personal satisfaction from it. It is also management's responsibility to train the worker so that he or she reaches standard performance in as short a period of time as possible. In order to have definite knowledge of the progress that a learner should make on a given job, some companies have made extensive studies of learning curves for various types of work, and have prepared "normal learning curves" for their operations. The following procedure illustrates how such curves may be used.

A Specific Case

The purpose of the "learner's progress record" is to compare the learner's progress with the average performance of normal learners. This record serves also as a guide to the supervisor and the instructor as to the necessary items to be included in the training of each learner. The normal learning curve is shown[11] in Fig. 314 and the "learner's progress record card" in Figs. 315 and 316. It should be emphasized that the normal learning curve developed by this company is only a rough indication of

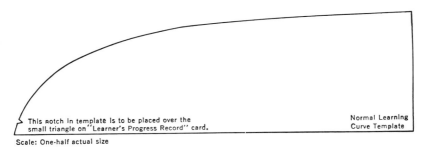

Scale: One-half actual size

Figure 314 Normal learning-curve template (plastic). The shape of this curve has been determined from studies of hundreds of different operations made by this company over a period of years.

[10] J. F. Biggane, "Time Study Training for Supervision and Union," *Proceedings Fourth Industrial Engineering Institute,* University of California, Los Angeles-Berkeley, p. 12.

[11] The shape of the curve in Fig. 315 is different from the learning curves on the preceding pages because the vertical scale for Fig. 315 is "Performance in Percent," whereas that of the preceding curves is "Time per Cycle in Minutes."

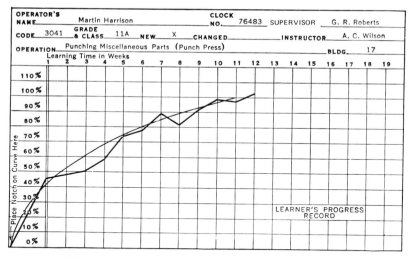

Figure 315 Learner's progress record—front of card.

C-4 OPERATOR'S RECORD					QUALITY: E-EXCELLENT G-GOOD F-FAIR P-POOR		
					ATTITUDE: Very good. Operator	INSTRUCTOR'S CHECK	
STARTING DATE: December 3, 1947					wants to learn the job.	TOOLS REQUIRED X	
RECORD WEEKLY						INTRODUCTION X	
QUALITY RATING ————————→						QUALITY X	
EFFICIENCY PERCENTAGE ————→						SAFETY AND HOUSEKEEPING X	
F	F	G		G	COMMENTS:	COOPERATION X	
45	48	50		58	At end of second week:	FAIRNESS X	
G	G	G		E	Operator seems slow in	RATES OF PRODUCTION X	
74	79	89		83	learning job.	ALLOWED PERSONAL TIME X	
E	E	E		E	At end of fourth week:		
92	98	98		103	Operator is still slow.		
					He thinks he can handle		
					the job.	FOREMAN'S CHECK	
					At end of sixth week:	WAGE PAYMENT PLAN X	
					Operator is progressing	POSSIBLE ADVANCEMENT X	
					satisfactorily.	SAFETY X	
						QUALITY X	
					SIGNATURE	CONTINUALLY STRESS	
					INSTRUCTOR'S SIGNATURE	SAFETY AND QUALITY X	

Figure 316 Learner's progress record—back of card.

the expected output at intervals during the learning period. This curve is not sufficiently accurate for use as the basis for a wage incentive for learners.

The new employee or the employee who is assigned to a new job is turned over to an instructor, who is also a skilled operator. This instructor, together with the supervisor of the department, is responsible for the learner's progress on the job. At the time the learner begins work, the progress record card (Figs. 315 and 316) is filled out and the learning curve is constructed for the job in the following way. The normal curve (Fig. 314), a template cut from a sheet of transparent plastic, is used for all training periods. The curve is placed with the notch in the lower left-hand corner of the card (Fig. 315). The top of the template intersects the 100 percent horizontal line at the point of intersection of the vertical line designating the number of weeks of training required for that labor grade. A line is drawn which follows the contour of the template, and this line represents the learning curve for the job in question. The card is retained by the supervisor or instructor until the learner becomes proficient on the job (reaches 100 percent) or changes jobs.

Each week the progress of the learner is recorded on the back of the card (Fig. 316) in two ways. The performance index is computed and recorded in the appropriate box, and a letter designating the quality of the work done by the learner is inserted above and to the left of the performance index. At the same time this information is recorded on the back of the card, a point representing the index is plotted on the front, and a straight line is drawn connecting the zero point on the curve with the performance at the end of the first week. In a similar manner the performance is recorded and plotted each week, and the quality of the work is indicated on the back of the card. The learning curve is shown to operators when they first begin work on the job, and its meaning and purpose are discussed with them in detail. Then each week, after the learners' performance has been posted on the card, the instructor or the supervisor goes over his accomplishment with each learner. They discuss all of the items listed on the back of the card, such as quality, safety, and good housekeeping. Each item is checked after it has been thoroughly explained to the learners.

The instructor records the attitude of the learner toward the job. Notes are also recorded concerning the learner's progress and any irregularities that may have occurred during the period. After the operator reaches standard performance (100 percent), the progress record card is sent to the supervisor of training, where it is permanently filed with other records of the employee.

The procedure described above has proved to be a very effective method of keeping the employee, as well as the supervisor, informed each week as to the progress being made. In cases where an operator proves to be unsuited to the work and his or her output consistently falls below the expected production, it is possible to transfer this person to other work without excessive loss of time.

MOTIVATION AND WORK

Many changes have taken place in the way goods and services have been produced over the years. Prior to the industrial revolution, skilled work was done by craftsmen who provided the skill and who, aided by relative simple tools, produced the entire product, such as a pair of shoes, a wood carving, or a suit of clothes. The craftsmen worked for wages, sold their products directly to the consumer or to a middleman for a fixed price, or perhaps were vassals of a landowner and paid their keep in labor instead of money. Some craftsmen worked in factories and were often paid on a piece-rate basis.

The Industrial Revolution

During the latter part of the eighteenth century a revolution took place in production methods and work organization. The basic change was the transfer of the skill of the worker to the machine. For a given operation, the more skill that was transferred to the machine, the less skill was required by the worker. Semiautomatic machines, which eventually came into use, needed only an unskilled person to feed material to the machine and remove the finished part and, in the case of automatic machines, no operator was needed. Transfer of skill, however, is not directly related to division of labor, the factory system, or the use of power in industry. In fact, factories existed from ancient times up to the time of the industrial revolution. Craftsmen worked under one roof, there was some division of labor, and waterpower was available in some factories. However, it was the concept of transfer of skill that revolutionized production methods—first in Great Britain in spinning and weaving, and then the idea spread rapidly into many other areas and into other parts of the world. Factories were equipped with steam power-driven machines, since Watt's steam engine had been perfected and put into use about this time. In many cases each machine was designed to perform a single operation, and unskilled men, women, and even children were employed to operate them. Often this consisted of merely placing the material in the machine, forming or processing the part, and then removing the finished piece from the machine. The new system resulted in an enormous increase in industrial production, lower unit cost, lower selling price of manufactured products, increased consumption, and increased demand for people to work in the factories.

For over 100 years, from around 1775 to the latter part of the nineteenth century, emphasis was placed on the invention and development of new products, the improvement of machine tools and manufacturing processes, and the expansion of the manufacturing industries. The number of industrial workers increased greatly, but more thought and effort were given to expanding and improving the physical aspects of production than to the welfare of the industrial workers.

Scientific Management

During the latter part of the nineteenth century, scientific management appeared on the scene and had a profound influence on the industrial world. Taylor, Gantt, the Gilbreths, and other pioneers used the scientific approach in work organization and work design, and their methods resulted in further increases in productivity and still lower production costs along with increased wages for the worker. Under scientific management, thorough study and experimentation were used to determine the most economical production process and the best method for doing each job. The worker was selected and trained to do the task in the prescribed manner and was paid according to his or her output. Piece rates had been used from early times as a method of compensation, and some form of wage incentives became an integral part of the new management system. Because of the spectacular results of scientific management, there was greater demand for people to install this system in industry than there were qualified people available. Unfortunately, incompetent and unscrupulous "engineers" and consultants entered the picture. This, together with deliberate "rate cutting" by some managers brought about many unsatisfactory applications and some failures and along with this was the opposition of some workers and labor unions to scientific management. It required many years to overcome the ill effects of the "efficiency expert" and to bring about an improvement in the situation. New and better methods and techniques were developed, colleges and universities provided trained people in increasing numbers, and management performed its functions in a more satisfactory manner. Confidence was restored in the overall system of scientific management, including payment of wages based on results where such systems were practical.

With industrial growth and increased productivity, there was a gradual increase in benefits provided for factory workers in addition to the bonus paid for high productivity—such as better lighting, heating, and ventilation, lunch rooms and food service, and company recreation facilities and training programs. Although scientific management as proposed by Taylor and his associates was broad in scope and applied to management as well as to labor, the applications during the period 1885 to the 1930s too often amounted to the measurement of labor and the use of wage incentive systems as a means of increasing productivity and reducing costs. In fact, many people believed that incentive pay was a highly satisfactory motivator for factory workers.

The Hawthorne Experiment

An investigation was started in 1927 at the Hawthorne works of the Western Electric Company that was destined to point the way to a new and different approach to motivating people at work. The Hawthorne experiment was dramatic in revealing some of the things that bring job satisfaction to the workers, resulting in increased productivity, improvement in quality, and lower absenteeism.[1] Originally, an investigation was undertaken at Hawthorne to determine the effect of varying the intensity of illumination on the production of the workers in the factory. However, the results showed that regardless of whether the lighting was brighter, dimmer, or constant, production increased. This led to a new and more carefully designed study to investigate rest periods and the length of the working day. Special steps were taken to keep all factors constant except the one being studied. This investigation ran from 1927 to 1932, a period of five years. In one phase of the study five skilled young women were selected from a large group of relay assemblers and began working in a separate test room adjacent to the main relay assembly department in the factory. The relays weighed a few ounces, consisted of 40 or 50 parts, and required approximately one minute to assemble. The whole experiment was discussed with the workers, and their cooperation was sought. The results of this study were startling. Output increased at every step along the way. The length of the rest periods and the length of the working day were of minor importance to the workers compared with the motivation they received from their new environment. From the moment they started work in the test room they were the center of attention. Continuous records were kept of their production, of the quality of the incoming materials and purchased parts, and the quality of the finished product. Even their conversation was monitored and recorded. They no longer had the feeling that they were just a small part of a large assembly department, subjected to the routine orders and instructions from management. They responded by increasing their output beyond anything that had been expected.

The following statements are taken from a report of the Hawthorne experiment.[2]

There has been a continual upward trend in output which has been independent of the changes in rest pauses. This upward trend has continued too long to be ascribed to an initial stimulus from the novelty of starting a special study.

The reduction of muscular fatigue has not been the primary factor in increasing output. Cumulative fatigue is not present. . . .

There has been an important increase in contentment among the girls working under test-room conditions.

There has been a decrease in absences of about 80 percent among the girls since entering the test-room group. Test-room operators have had approximately one-third as many sick absences as the regular department during the last six months.

---

[1] T. N. Whitehead, *Leadership in a Free Society,* Harvard University Press, Cambridge, Mass., 1937; T. N. Whitehead, *The Industrial Worker,* Two Volumes, Harvard University Press, Cambridge, Mass., 1938; F. J. Roethlisberger and W. J. Dickson, *Management and the Worker,* Harvard University Press, Cambridge, Mass., 1940; Henry A. Landsberger, *Hawthorne Revisited,* Cornell University, Ithaca, N.Y., 1958; Eugene L. Cass and Frederick G. Zimmer (editors), *Man and Work in Society,* Van Nostrand Reinhold, New York, 1975.

[2] From a privately published report by the Division of Industrial Research to officers of the Western Electric Company, May 11, 1929, pp. 34–131. Reproduced in Elton Mayo, *The Human Problems of an Industrial Civilization,* Viking Press, New York, 1960, pp. 65–67.

Observations of operators in the relay assembly test room indicate that their health is being maintained or improved and that they are working within their capacity. . . .

Important factors in the production of a better mental attitude and greater enjoyment of work have been the greater freedom, less strict supervision and the opportunity to vary from a fixed pace without reprimand from a gang boss.

The operators have no clear idea as to why they are able to produce more in the test room; but as shown in the replies to questionnaires . . . there is the feeling that better output is in some way related to the distinctly pleasanter, freer, and happier working conditions.

Hierarchy of Human Needs

The Hawthorne studies had an important impact on industry. The results emphasized human relations and worker's needs. Questions continued to be raised about ways of motivating employees.

Abraham Maslow's theory of human needs contributed to a better understanding of human motivation.[3] He stated that human needs exist on different levels—there is a hierarchy of importance. At the lowest level is the basic need for *survival*—air, food, shelter, and when these are satisfied, they no longer are motivators. The next level is the need for *security,* safety, protection against danger, and deprivation. With these needs satisfied, *social needs* become important motivators. These needs are for group acceptance, friendship, and belonging. Above the social needs are the *egoistic needs*—for self-esteem, self-respect, self-confidence, and recognition, for deserved respect of one's fellows. Finally, at the highest level discussed by Maslow are the human needs for self-fulfillment, for realizing one's own potential, and for being creative. When one need is satisfied, another need arises. A satisfied need is soon forgotten and the next higher level of needs then can become the motivator.

Theory X and Theory Y

Douglas McGregor's contribution centered around his views concerning assumptions about human behavior and managerial decisions and actions based on these assumptions.[4] He used Theory X to refer to those assumptions that guide the traditional manager: the average human being has an inherent dislike for work and will avoid it if possible. He or she must be controlled, coerced, and prefers to be directed. The average human being wishes to avoid responsibility, has little ambition, and wants security above all.

McGregor concluded that the research coming from social science indicated that these assumptions were largely false and he used Theory Y to refer to the following generalizations: The expenditure of physical and mental effort in work is as natural as play or rest, and people will exercise self-direction and self-control in carrying out

---

[3] Abraham H. Maslow, "A Theory of Human Motivation," *Psychological Review,* Vol. 50, No. 4, pp. 370–396, July, 1943; *Motivation and Personality,* Harper & Row, New York, 1970.

[4] Douglas McGregor, *The Human Side of Enterprise,* McGraw-Hill, New York, 1960.

objectives to which they are committed. The average person will not only accept responsibility but will seek it if properly motivated. Human beings are capable of exercising a high degree of imagination, ingenuity, and creativity in the solution of problems which are important to them. Most people do not use their full potential.

Motivation-Maintenance Theory

Although scientific management was well entrenched in American industry, there were an increasing number of people who objected to certain practices such as excessive job specialization, monotonous short-cycle repetitive operations, machine-paced jobs, and the use of piece rates and other forms of wage incentives as motivators. Also, changes in business and industry were taking place at a more rapid rate. Methods, tools, machines, and equipment—in fact, many aspects of the employee's job were affected, and some people resented these changes and the way they were made.

Over the years many investigators have conducted studies to learn more about the whole subject of work organization, social systems, work design, group dynamics, and the motivation to work. Most of the studies contributed new knowledge and advanced our understanding of human behavior in the work environment. Because the motivation-maintenance theory has been well validated and successfully applied, it will be described here.

The results of an investigation of job attitudes made by Frederick Herzberg have been very useful in identifying and better understanding specific factors that affect the motivation of people.[5] Moreover, his motivation-maintenance theory is supported by over 30 replications or variations of his original study designed to test the validity of the theory.[6] Business and industry to an increasing extent are studying and testing this theory and a number of organizations are successfully using it. The plan here is to present a statement of Herzberg's findings on motivation and then to describe some actual industrial applications.

An analysis of earlier research led Herzberg to observe that there are some things that workers like about their jobs and there are some things they dislike—some factors are "satisfiers" and some are "dissatisfiers." His investigation was designed to test the concept that humans have two sets of needs: their needs as an animal to avoid pain or unpleasant situations and their needs as humans to grow psychologically—their need for self-actualization in their work.

Some 200 engineers and accountants who worked for 11 different Pittsburgh firms were carefully interviewed. Each person was asked to recall an event that had occurred at work and that had either resulted in a substantial improvement in his job satisfaction or had led to marked reduction in job satisfaction. The interviewer was

[5] Frederick Herzberg, B. Mausner, and B. B. Snyderman, *The Motivation to Work,* 2nd ed., John Wiley, New York, 1959.

[6] Frederick Herzberg, "Work and the Nature of Man," World Publishing, New York, 1966, pp. 92–167.

looking for an event or series of events or objective happenings that took place during the time in which feelings about the job were exceptionally good or exceptionally bad. The results of the interviews are shown in Fig. 317. The objective events that the engineers and accountants disclosed were classified as to satisfiers and dissatisfiers. The length of each box indicates the frequency with which this factor appeared in the events presented, and the width of the box indicates the time during which the good or bad job attitude lasted. A short duration of attitude change ordinarily lasted less than two weeks, whereas a long duration of attitude change may have lasted for some years.

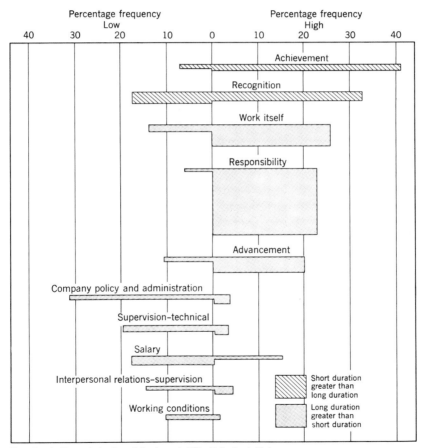

Reproduced with permission from F. Herzberg et al. The Motivation to Work.
John Wiley and Sons, New York, 1959

Figure 317 Comparison of satisfiers and dissatisfiers.

There were five factors that strongly determined job satisfaction—these motivators were achievement, recognition, work itself, responsibility, and advancement. The maintenance or hygiene factors—the potential dissatisfiers—were company policy and administration, supervision, salary, interpersonal relations, and working conditions.

The motivators all have to do with the job—opportunity to undertake a difficult assignment; freedom to use imagination and ingenuity in doing the job; encouragement to learn new skills, to be promoted, and to earn more money as recognition for achievement. All of these things encouraged the people to be more productive, and brought more satisfaction and good feeling about the job. On the other hand, the maintenance factors had no positive effect but served mainly to provide a satisfactory environment for the motivators. The maintenance factors do not influence workers to increase their productivity or do their jobs well. However, they can be dissatisfiers. Unsatisfactory supervision, inadequate pay, or poor working conditions can bring about a substantial negative attitude. This is an important point. Human relations programs, supervisory training, recreation facilities, wages, and the long list of fringe benefits do not serve as motivators. If these maintenance factors are reasonably well satisfied, the setting is right for the motivators to operate.

Man has long understood and used motivators in industry; however, it seems that few managers fully recognize the sharp differentiation between motivators and maintenance factors, which recent research has revealed. This new knowledge now makes the manager's job easier. A manager can more intelligently organize the operations in order to maximize the satisfiers and minimize the dissatisfiers.

James F. Lincoln, who founded the Lincoln Electric Company in 1895, understood how to motivate the members of his organization.[7] Over his lifetime he employed most of the satisfiers referred to above. His objective was to assist his people in their striving for self-realization. He states "No man wants to be just a cog in a wheel. The most insistent incentive is the development of self respect and the respect of others. Earnings that are the reward for outstanding performance, progress, and responsibility are signs that he is a man among men. The worker must feel that he is part of a worthwhile project and that the project succeeded because his ability was needed in it. Money alone will not do the job." The last sentence is of special interest inasmuch as the Lincoln Electric employees are among the highest paid people in the world. Last year the average year-end bonus was $17,809 per person. This is in addition to a base wage equal to or greater than the community rate plus incentive earnings.

[7] James F. Lincoln, *Incentive Management*, The Lincoln Electric Company, Cleveland, Ohio, 1951; James F. Lincoln, *A New Approach to Industrial Economics*, Devin-Adair, New York, 1961.

Study of Motivation at Texas Instruments

Texas Instruments Incorporated made a six-year study of motivation in their Dallas divisions.[8] Their research procedure was similar to that used in the Herzberg Pittsburgh study. Texas Instruments wanted to see whether the motivation-maintenance theory could be validly applied to their own workers. Two hundred and eighty-two subjects were selected at random from a list of representative employees distributed almost equally over five job categories of scientist, engineer, and manufacturing supervisor, and hourly paid technician and assembler. Of the 282 subjects, 52 were female hourly assemblers.

Each subject was interviewed by a competent personnel administrator beginning by explaining the general purpose of the study and the nature of the information required. Then, following Herzberg's interview pattern, the interviewer asked:

Think of a time when you felt exceptionally good or exceptionally bad about your job, either your present job or any other job you have had. This can be either "long-range" or the "short-range" kind of situation, as I have described it. Tell me what happened.

After the employee had described a sequence of events that he felt good about ("favorable"), he was asked to tell of a different time when he felt the opposite ("unfavorable") or vice versa. A total of 715 sequences was obtained from the 282 interviews. Each of the sequences was classified "favorable" or "unfavorable" and as "long-range" (strong feelings lasting more than two months) or "short-range" (strong feelings lasting less than two months). Sample favorable and unfavorable responses to interview questions are given below.

MANUFACTURING SUPERVISOR—FAVORABLE

I was asked to take over a job which was thought to be impossible. We didn't think Texas Instruments could ship what had been promised. I was told half would be acceptable, but we shipped the entire order! They had confidence in me to think I could do the job. I am happier when under pressure.

MANUFACTURING SUPERVISOR—UNFAVORABLE

I disagreed with my supervisor. We were discussing how many of a unit to manufacture, and I told him I thought we shouldn't make too many. He said, "I didn't ask for your opinion . . . we'll do what I want." I was shocked as I didn't realize he had this kind of personality. It put me in bad with my supervisor and I resented it because he didn't consider my opinion important.

HOURLY MALE TECHNICIAN—FAVORABLE

I was given a bigger responsibility though no change in job grade. I have a better job, more interesting and one that fits in better with my education. I still feel good about it. I'm working harder because it was different from my routine. I am happier . . . feel better about my job.

[8] M. Scott Myers, "Who Are Your Motivated Workers?" *Harvard Business Review,* Vol. 42, No. 1, pp. 73–88.

HOURLY MALE TECHNICIAN—UNFAVORABLE

I was working on a project and thought I had a real good solution. A professional in the group but not on my project tore down my project bit by bit in front of those I worked with. He made disparaging remarks. I was unhappy with the man and unhappy with myself. I thought I had solved it when I hadn't. My boss smoothed it over and made me feel better. I stayed away from the others for a week.

Results

Fourteen first-level factors were identified by the interviewer and the head of the project. Figure 318 shows the factors and the number of sequences grouped under each factor. *Achievement* was the largest category, accounting for 33 percent of the sequences. Also *achievement* is comprised of almost twice as many favorable responses as unfavorable ones. On the other hand, *company policy and administration* (the employee's perception of company organization, goals, policies, procedures, practices, or rules) account for more than four times as many unfavorable as favorable responses.

Personality Differences. . . . the potency of any of the job factors mentioned, as a motivator or dissatisfier, is not solely a function of the nature of the factor itself. It is also related to the personality of the individual.

For most individuals, the greatest satisfaction and the strongest motivation are derived from *achievement, responsibility, growth, advancement, work itself,* and *earned recognition.* People like this, whom Herzberg terms "motivation seekers," are motivated primarily by the nature of the task and have high tolerance for poor environmental factors.

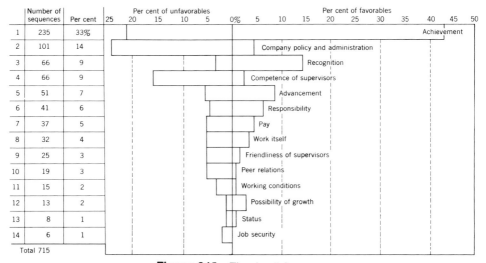

Figure 318   First-level factors.

"Maintenance seekers," on the other hand, are motivated primarily by the nature of their environment and tend to avoid motivation opportunities. They are chronically preoccupied and dissatisfied with maintenance factors surrounding the job, such as pay, supplemental benefits, supervision, working conditions, status, job security, company policy and administration and fellow employees. Maintenance seekers realize little satisfaction from accomplishment and express cynicism regarding the positive virtues of work and life in general. By contrast, motivation seekers realize great satisfaction from accomplishment and have positive feelings toward work and life in general.

Maintenance seekers show little interest in kind and quality of work, may succeed on the job through sheer talent, but seldom profit professionally from experience. Motivation seekers enjoy work, strive for quality, tend to overachieve, and benefit professionally from experience. . . .

Although an individual's orientation as a motivation seeker or a maintenance seeker is fairly permanent, it can be influenced by the characteristics of his various roles. For example, maintenance seekers in an environment of achievement, responsibility, growth, and earned recognition tend to behave like and acquire the values of motivation seekers. On the other hand, the absence of motivators causes many motivation seekers to behave like maintenance seekers, and to become preoccupied with the maintenance factors in their environment.

Conclusions

The study clearly shows that the fulfillment of both motivation and maintenance needs is required for effective job performance. Moreover, the study points out that the factors in the work situation which motivate employees are different from the factors that dissatisfy employees. Figure 319 shows motivational needs to include growth, achievement, responsibility, recognition, and the job itself, and are satisfied through the media grouped in the inner circle. Motivational factors focus on the individual and his or her achievement of personal and company goals. Maintenance needs are satisfied through media listed in the outer circle under the headings of economic, security, orientation, status, social, and physical (Fig. 319). The study shows that maintenance factors have very little motivational value. If an environment is provided in which motivational need can be satisfied, the maintenance factors have relatively little influence either as satisfiers or dissatisfiers. An abundance of fringe benefits and actions, which overrate maintenance needs, are no substitute for a work environment rich in opportunities for satisfying motivational needs. The conclusions of the study were concisely stated as follows.

What motivates employees to work effectively? A challenging job which allows a feeling of achievement, responsibility, growth, advancement, enjoyment of work itself, and earned recognition.

What dissatisfies workers? Mostly factors which are peripheral to the job—work rules, lighting, coffee breaks, titles, seniority rights, wages, fringe benefits, and the like.

When do workers become dissatisfied? When opportunities for meaningful achievement are eliminated and they become sensitized to their environment and begin to find fault.

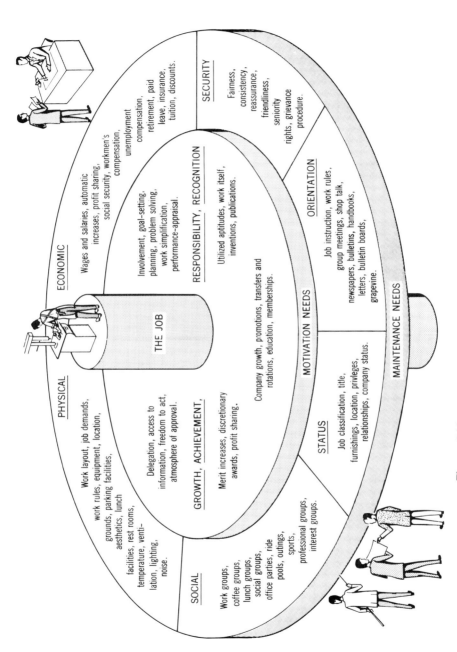

Figure 319 Employee needs—motivation and maintenance.

MOTIVATION NEEDS

ECONOMIC
Wages and salaries, automatic increases, profit sharing, social security, workmen's compensation, unemployment compensation, retirement, paid leave, insurance, tuition, discounts.

SECURITY
Fairness, consistency, reassurance, friendliness, seniority rights, grievance procedure.

PHYSICAL
Work layout, job demands, equipment, location, work rules, parking facilities, grounds, lunch facilities, rest rooms, aesthetics, venti-lation, lighting, temperature, noise.

RESPONSIBILITY, RECOGNITION
Utilized aptitudes, work itself, inventions, publications.

GROWTH, ACHIEVEMENT,
Delegation, access to information, freedom to act, atmosphere of approval.

Involvement, goal-setting, planning, problem solving, work simplification, performance-appraisal.

Company growth, promotions, transfers and rotations, education, memberships.

Merit increases, discretionary awards, profit sharing.

THE JOB

ORIENTATION
Job instruction, work rules, group meetings, shop talk, newspapers, bulletins, handbooks, letters, bulletin boards, grapevine.

STATUS
Job classification, title, furnishings, location, privileges, relationships, company status.

SOCIAL
Work groups, coffee groups, lunch groups, social groups, office parties, ride pools, outings, sports, professional groups, interest groups.

MAINTENANCE NEEDS

580

Statement by the President of Texas Instruments

At the 1967 annual meeting of stockholders of Texas Instruments Incorporated, President Mark Shepherd, Jr. made the following statement.

. . . by far our greatest opportunity for improved performance at Texas Instruments lies in the area of increasing human effectiveness. It is our goal that the work of every person be made as meaningful as possible to the individual, and that their individual career goals and the corporate goals for growth and development are compatible.

This means that the people at Texas Instruments not only must understand what they are expected to do in a specific job assignment, but that they must have the opportunity to plan the job or influence the planning that goes into it, and that they must themselves be concerned with the measurement or evaluation of how well the job is performed.

This kind of participation in planning and managing work is being multiplied now in many operations throughout Texas Instruments. We feel that a significant step has been made in finding ways to help increase our total human effectiveness. In turn, this will enhance our ability to set and achieve our personal and our institutional goals.

Texas Instruments continues to consider this philosophy important in its operations. During the period from 1967 when Mr. Shepherd made his statement until the present Texas Instruments' annual sales have more than tripled and profits have increased more than 500 percent.

The back cover of the 1966 Annual Report of Texas Instruments Incorporated contained the statements and pictures shown in Fig. 320.

Creating change—through increased human effectiveness. Technical innovation leads to useful new products and services to fill the needs of society. Innovation in how people plan and manage their own work can lead to greater realization of their individual potential. This idea to elevate jobs to more than the routine performance of set tasks is taking on real meaning among a growing percentage of men and women of Texas Instruments. These examples illustrate how the people of Texas Instruments contributed to their own and to the company's success in 1966.

Planning together, this group worked out ways to reduce time to produce radar from 130 to as low as 36 hours per system.

An operator in Germanium transistor test group wrote a training manual from the operator's viewpoint that stepped up job knowledge and effectiveness of her entire assembly and test section.

Figure 320 Excerpts from Annual Report of Texas Instruments.

40

JOB ENLARGEMENT
A MANUFACTURING SYSTEM DESIGNED FOR PEOPLE—VOLVO
IMPROVING THE QUALITY OF WORK LIFE AT GENERAL MOTORS

Many different approaches have been used to reduce monotony and give more meaning to industrial work. Job enlargement is one method that has become of increasing importance. Before presenting a case for job enlargement, however, perhaps a statement should be made explaining why we have highly repetitive operations and assembly line work.

Division of labor has been practiced for many centuries, but the present high degree of job specialization has evolved since the time of the Industrial Revolution. Adam Smith, the Scottish economist enumerated in *The Wealth of Nations* (1776) the advantages of division of labor which enabled "one man to do the work of many": (1) the development of a high degree of skill and dexterity, (2) the saving of time normally lost in changing from one kind of work to another, and (3) the invention of machines and tools that normally occurs when workers perform repetitive tasks. Charles Babbage was an English mathematician with interests in economics and manufacturing. Babbage discussed at length division of labor in his book, *On the Economy of Machinery and Manufacturers* (1832), and added a fourth important advantage: Dividing the task into short operations requiring varying degrees of skill allows wages to be paid for each operation in proportion to its difficulty. Babbage used as an example the manufacture of common straight pins. The process he described consisted of a sequence of seven operations (Table 73): (1) drawing wire, (2) straightening the wire, (3) pointing, (4) twisting and cutting the heads, (5) heading, (6) tinning or whitening (similar to modern plating), and (7) papering (placing pins in papers). As the table shows daily earnings ranged from a low of 6 pence for straightening to a high of 6 shillings for tinning. Babbage emphasized the several advantages of division of labor including that of permitting the employer to purchase just the amount of skill needed.

The constant drive to subdivide work has occurred because of the increase in labor effectiveness and the lower unit production costs resulting from such practice.

Table 73. Analysis of Processes and Manufacturing Costs in Pin Making English Manufacture. Pins, *"Elevens,"* 5,546 weigh one pound; *"one dozen,"* 6,932 pins weigh twenty ounces, and require six ounces of paper.

Name of the Process	Workmen	Time for Making 1 lb of Pins, *hours*	Cost of Making 1 lb of Pins, *pence*	Workman Earns per Day, *s. d.*		Price of Making Each Part of a Single Pin, in Millionths of a Penny
1. Drawing wire (§170.)	Man	.3636	1.2500	3	3	225
2. Straightening the wire	Woman	.3000	.2840	1	0	51
(§171.)	Girl	.3000	.1420	0	6	26
3. Pointing (§172.)	Man	.3000	1.7750	5	3	319
4. Twisting and cutting	Boy	.0400	.0147	0	4½	3
the heads (§173.)	Man	.0400	.2103	5	4½	38
5. Heading (§174.)	Woman	4.0000	5.0000	1	3	901
6. Tinning, or whitening	Man	.1071	.6666	6	0	121
(§175.)	Woman	.1071	.3333	3	0	60
7. Papering (§176.)	Woman	2.1314	3.1973	1	6	576
		7.6892	12.8732			2320

Number of persons employed: men, 4; women, 4; children, 2; total, 10.
Reproduced from *The Economy of Machinery and Manufactures,* 1832.

Specialization of work can be carried out with (*a*) the operation entirely within the control of the worker, or (*b*) the work paced, such as operations on an automobile assembly line. The following advantages are often given for such specialized and paced work:

1. Management can be assured of meeting production schedules, because there is a steady flow of finished products coming off the conveyor line.
2. The conveyor forces service departments and parts-supply lines to perform their functions properly; otherwise, the conveyor line would stop.
3. No one operator can work ahead of others, thus accumulating work-in-process. It is the finished part or product coming off the conveyor that is desired, not parts in various stages of completion.
4. Work performed on conveyors makes efficient use of floor space. Often overhead auxiliary supply conveyors can be employed to bring parts to the operator, thus making unnecessary the storage of parts at the assembly line.

The statements listed above have been validated[1] in thousands of factories throughout the world, and there are many situations today in which labor effectiveness can be increased and unit costs and total costs reduced by division of labor. In some cases, however, specialization has been carried too far. Benefits resulting from job enlargement may outweigh those resulting from division of labor.

Jobs may be enlarged horizontally *or* vertically, or horizontally *and* vertically.[2] If a job is expanded so that it includes a greater number or a greater variety of operations, it is enlarged horizontally. Horizontal job enlargement is intended to counteract oversimplification and to give the worker an opportunity to perform a "whole natural unit of work." Vertical job enlargement involves operators in planning, organization, and inspection, as well as the performance of their work. Vertical job enlargement brings most of the motivators into play. Jobs can also be individual or group. There is evidence to show that job enlargement—horizontal or vertical, individual or group—results in improved performance and greater job satisfaction. Job enlargement may be part of a management system that more completely involves the worker in solving production problems and in setting goals.

Job Enlargement at IBM Corporation

The term *job enlargement* was first used at the International Business Machines Corporation to identify a program that was inaugurated at the suggestion of the president of the company. The president believed that the job should be enriched by making it more interesting, more varied, and more significant; that a person employed on a meaningful job would be motivated to do more and better work and would receive greater satisfaction from the job.

Walker[3] made a study of job enlargement at IBM and reported it in 1950. The plan was first introduced in a general machine shop in 1943. Several hundred people were employed as operators of the basic machine tools such as lathes, drill presses, broaching machines, milling machines, and grinders. Their work consisted mainly of placing the part in the machine and removing the piece after the cutting tool or drill had performed the machine operation. The operators needed very little skill and could be trained to do the work in a relatively short time. A specially trained setup person prepared the machine for each new job, tools were ground in a central tool room, and

---

[1] By the use of assembly-line methods, Henry Ford reduced the time to assemble a car from 12 hours and 28 minutes (September, 1913) to 1 hour and 33 minutes (April 30, 1914). This is one of the first and most spectacular uses of the assembly line. Horace L. Arnold and Fay L. Faurote, *Ford Methods and the Ford Shops,* The Engineering Magazine Co., New York, 1915.

[2] E. R. Gomersall and M. Scott Myers, "Breakthrough in On-The-Job Training," *Harvard Business Review,* Vol. 44, No. 4, p. 63, July–August, 1966.

[3] Charles R. Walker, "The Problem of the Repetitive Job," *Harvard Business Review,* Vol. 28, No. 3, pp. 54–58, May 1950.

finished parts were checked by inspectors. Although many of the operators had been on this work for years and had acquired the skill to set up the machine and check the work, they were not permitted to do so because this was considered an inefficient method of operating the department.

Under the new plan each operator was taught how to set up his machine for each new job from the blueprints provided. He sharpened some of his tools and inspected his own work. By 1950 all setup men had been completely eliminated and inspectors were used only when an operator asked for an inspection double check. The installation of the plan resulted in the displacement of all of the setup men and most of the inspectors, inasmuch as the operators had learned the skills of these men. In line with company policy, no one lost his job or suffered a reduction in pay. Since the company's business was expanding, it was not difficult to solve this problem. For example, of the 35 displaced setup men, 21 became operators without loss in pay, 12 were promoted to other jobs within the company, all but one with increases in pay, and two men voluntarily left the company.

Results

The main outlay entailed in installing the new plan consisted of the cost of training the operators in the new skills and the higher wage that they received because they were now qualified for a higher rank under the company job evaluation plan. Also there was the cost of additional inspection equipment which was provided. These outlays were more than offset by lower costs and other benefits.

1. Better product quality resulted—there were fewer defects and less scrap. Management attributed this to "greater responsibility taken by the individual operator for the quality of his work."
2. Less idle time of both operators and machines resulted because inherently it was simpler for operators to set up and check their own work than it was to call a setup man and an inspector to do this. Records showed that the cost of setting up and inspecting was reduced 95 percent.
3. Management stated that job enlargement "enriched the job for the worker." It introduced variety, interest, pride, and responsibility which had not been present before. Because of their higher skill, the men now received higher pay for their work.

Job Enlargement at The Maytag Company

The Maytag Company has had many years of successful experience in changing from predominantly conveyor-paced operations for major subassemblies to bench type work design, where each operator is responsible for the complete assembly and its quality. Job enlargement principles have also been incorporated in other work designs including management jobs.[4] From their experience and results of academic research of job enlargement installations at Maytag,[5] the people at Maytag summarize the more important results that have been characteristic of these installations as follows:

1. Quality has improved.
2. Labor costs are lower.
3. A large majority of operators came to prefer job enlargement in a relatively short time.
4. Problems inherent in paced groups have been largely eliminated. For example, realignment of each operator's job content is no longer necessary whenever production levels change, resulting in less training, higher productivity, fewer changes in production standards, reduction in grievances, and so on.
5. Equipment and installation costs have been recovered by tangible savings in an average of about two years.
6. Space requirements for enlarged jobs of the type described here are comparable to that required for powered conveyor-line assembly.

Assembly of Water Pump for Automatic Washer

The assembly of the water pump for the automatic washer is an early example of the application of job enlargement concepts. The paced conveyor system with several operators performing a highly repetitive portion of the total assembly was replaced by individual work stations where each operator assembles and tests the entire component.

Original System of Group Assembly of Pump

The water pump for the automatic washing machine consisted of 26 parts, was 7 inches in diameter, and weighed 1½ pounds. It was previously assembled by a group of from five to seven operators, depending upon the production level. This included one person for relief, repair, and stock-up. The cycle time for the various levels ranged from 0.33 minutes to 0.44 minutes per pump, depending upon the number of operators in the group. The pump was assembled on a combination bench and power-driven slat conveyor. The first operator, working at a bench, performed the first operation by assembling five parts of the pump housing. The next operator assembled eight parts to the housing. He worked on two housings at one time, completing half of his operation at the bench; then he transferred the two pumps to the conveyor

---

[4] Paul A. Stewart, "Job Enlargement," Monogram Series No. 3, University of Iowa, Iowa City, 1967; Irwin A. Rose, "Increasing Productivity Through Job Enlargement," *Proceedings Fifteenth Industrial Engineering Institute,* University of California, Los Angeles-Berkeley, 1963.

[5] E. H. Conant and M. D. Kilbridge, "An Interdisciplinary Analysis of Job Enlargement: Technology, Costs, and Behavioral Implications," *Industrial and Labor Relations Review,* Vol. 18, No. 3, pp. 377–395, April 1965. These cases reproduced by permission of The Maytag Company.

where he finished his operation. The third operator worked entirely on the moving conveyor, assembling five parts on each pump and positioning seven screws in every other pump. The last operator positioned seven screws in the remaining pumps and drove the screws in all pumps. He removed the completed assembly and tested it for leaks. Rejects were set aside to be repaired and acceptable pumps were placed in a container and moved to the main assembly department. The operators in this group were paid under the company wage incentive system.

Enlarged Job—New One-Man Assembly Operation

A new method was to be designed that would permit one operator to have complete responsibility for assembling and testing the pump and at a lower assembly cost. Improvements in material handling and housekeeping were also desired. Studies indicated that three operators working at three individual benches or workplace areas could do the work previously done by the four operators and the one relief person. The main technical problem was to design efficient material handling to and from the three benches.

Figure 321 One-man pump assembly and test station. Partial view of double assembly fixture at left center, with run-in and leak test fixture at right.

Figure 321 shows one of the enlarged work places. It provides a compact arrangement of the fixtures, tools, materials, and testing equipment for the finished assembly. The assembly operation starts at the point of delivery of the pump housing at the extreme left (outside of picture). Most of the work is done in the double fixture at the left. After the unit is assembled, it is given run-in and leak tests in the fixtures in the right foreground. The completed assembly is then placed in a container for deliv-

Table 74. Assembly of Water Pump for Automatic Washer

Item	Original System: Group Assembly	Present System: Enlarged Job
Quality	The system results in sharing responsibility for quality with several other operators. The operator tends to lose identification of his or her work with the quality of the total assembly. The paced conveyor allows the operator little time to correct personal mistakes or solve problems caused by variations in the quality of material. When a new operator joins the group, there is a special problem created in maintaining quality.	The operator assembles a complete unit and tests it immediately, resulting in maximum personal identification with the quality of the total unit. This system permits operators to correct their own mistakes; and if any parts are defective, this is known immediately and no additional assemblies will be produced until satisfactory parts are available. The present system brought about a reduction in defective pumps from 5% to less than one half of 1%.
Productivity Imbalance of work	It is impossible to establish an equal amount of work for each operator on a conveyor line. Therefore, certain idle time or waiting time is inherent in this type of system. On the pump assembly, imbalance averaged about 5% of the total labor cost.	When the individual works alone, there is no imbalance among operators.
Effects of new operators and changes in production schedules on output	When a new operator is assigned to work on a conveyor, the output of the entire group is limited to the output of the new operator, or there is the added cost of a "helper" who might be assigned to assist the new operator. When a new production schedule is put into effect, it is necessary to rebalance the conveyor line and reorganize the work for each individual on the line.	No rebalancing of work for changes in production schedules is required. New operators are influenced to quickly attain higher output by exposure to the successful experiences of other operators performing exactly the same work.

Table 74. *(Continued)*

Item	Original System: Group Assembly	Present System: Enlarged Job
Operator training	Whenever the production schedule is changed, operators are either added to or removed from the conveyor and the task of each person is changed. Therefore, retraining is necessary.	It is necessary to train a new operator only when the production schedule increases, or when the method has been changed.
Time standards	Wage incentives are used in this plant; therefore, whenever the line is rebalanced, it is necessary to make a restudy and determine a new time standard for the revised method.	New time standards are required only when there is a change in method, which would be less frequent than mere changes in the production schedule.
Maintenance costs	Considerable maintenance is encountered on highly mechanized equipment. Moreover, greater down time may be expected. The original cost of the unit is high.	There is practically no maintenance cost. The fixtures and other equipment are very simple. The total cost is less than $1,500 per unit.
Material handling	Inconvenient location of containers and tote boxes increases stock-up time. The paced conveyor prevents the operator from stocking parts, unless the system is shut down.	Major parts are delivered by conveyors and chutes directly to the work place. Less time is required for stocking small parts, and the need for a separate material handler is eliminated.
Cost reduction		Reduction of both direct and indirect labor costs were substantial. Reduction of both rework and scrap also contributed to reduced costs.

ery to the final assembly line. The double-station assembly and testing fixtures were designed to permit the use of simultaneous motions for the major part of the operation. Conveyors bring tote pans of components close to the assembly position, and the container for the finished assemblies is located directly adjacent to the water-testing tank. A comparison of the important characteristics of the original group assembly method with the new enlarged job is given in Table 74.

To summarize, several manufacturing problems identified with conveyorized groups were eliminated by the newer work design. Of major importance to supervision was the greater stability of production when changes were made in schedules, or when new operators were assigned. It was no longer necessary to retrain all the operators in the group when a production schedule was revised. No rebalancing of the work of the group was required. When a new operator is now assigned, the production of the other operators is not affected, and shop supervision can more accurately predict the production which can be attained. Since Maytag has a wage incentive system, the operators were pleased that their incentive pay was not dependent upon the capabilities or performance of other members of the group. The normal earnings now equal or exceed the performance under the group method. Turnover from job bidding has been substantially reduced, and grievances have been largely eliminated.

A MANUFACTURING SYSTEM DESIGNED FOR PEOPLE—VOLVO

A revolutionary new automobile assembly plant was built by Volvo at Kalmar, Sweden under the direction of Pehr G. Gyllenhammar, its president.[6] With imagination, ingenuity, and bold determination a new system was developed which replaced the traditional conveyor line with independent self-propelled carriers on which the car assembly took place (Fig. 322). The carrier, a low steel platform, was slightly larger than the car and moved over the factory floor directed by an electronic system through cables imbedded in the floor. The central computer controlled the movement of the carriers through the plant but it could be overridden by the employees at any time.

Also there was a drastic change in the plan of organization and operation of the new plant. The employees were more fully involved. Teams were formed and assumed the responsibility for completing major units of the car. The teams as a whole determined job assignments, work schedules, rest periods, and inspected their own work.

Background

Volvo is a stockholder-owned, Swedish manufacturer of cars, trucks, busses, and other products. It has been in business since 1927 and now has 65,000 employees. At first groups of skilled craftsmen worked on a single car until it was finished. A foreman directed the operations and the management problems were relatively simple.

Over the years the company prospered and new plants were built. During the 1950s and 1960s factories became heavily mechanized with continuous moving conveyor lines and short work cycles. Industrial engineers played an important part in many aspects of the expansion that took place. The company introduced a predeter-

---

[6] Pehr G. Gyllenhammar, *People at Work*, Addison-Wesley, Reading, Mass., 1977; "How Volvo Adapts Work to People," *Harvard Business Review*, Vol. 55, No. 4, pp. 102–113, July–August 1977; Rolf Lindholm and Jan-Peder Norstedt, *The Volvo Report*, Swedish Employers' Confederation, Stockholm, Sweden, 1975. By permission of Volvo.

Figure 322 Computer controlled self-propelled carriers move along the floor at Volvo. The carrier at the left shows a car turned on its side so that work can be conveniently performed on the bottom of the car.

mined time system from the United States in 1953, and it became the main means for establishing time standards for planning and for other purposes; it is still in use. The work of the industrial engineers became extremely sophisticated and they also participated heavily in the creation of new forms of work organization.

In 1969 the company encountered serious labor problems. Labor turnover reached 52 percent and absenteeism was high. Although worker participation on a relatively small scale had been undertaken in some plants there were wildcat strikes and general employee dissatisfaction. As early as 1954 the first Work Council composed of representatives of employees and managers was organized. Job rotation and job enlargement was introduced in 1964. Steps were taken to increase consultation with employees and to make plants lighter, quieter, and more attractive places to work. During these years business continued to increase and profits were high. There was a shortage of Swedish labor and foreign workers were being employed.

In 1971 worker unrest was at a peak and it was evident that drastic changes had to be made. A new assembly plant of conventional design was about to be built in Kalmar. However because of the critical situation the design was changed completely.

The Kalmar Factory

The factory at Kalmar consisted of four interlocking hexagons (Fig. 323) which gave each work group its own work area with an outside wall and large windows overlooking the countryside. Three of the hexagons were two-story and the other one-story. The plant was designed to accommodate 25 working groups of approximately 20 people each, a total of 500 factory employees. Each team had its own building entrance and its own nonworking area consisting of carpeted rooms for a pantry, stove, and refrigerator. In addition, each set of two groups shared showers, bathrooms, saunas, change rooms, and lockers.

The materials were stored in the middle of the building. The production process flowed around the outside area of the building and each team occupied its own section, giving it a small factory atmosphere. There was room for six carriers in each working area with additional space in the buffer zone for three more carriers. The carriers were controlled and checked in three ways: from a central computer, from a computer terminal located in each group area, and through controls located on each carrier and which could be actuated by the worker.

The noise level was kept below 65 decibels in most of the production area by using sound absorbing walls, partitions, and ceilings. The maximum of 80–85 decibels was confined to a few special areas.

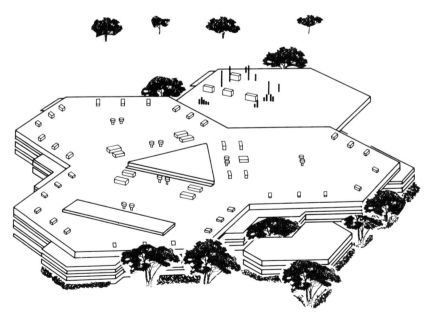

Figure 323 Volvo factory at Kalmar. The hexagon shaped building permits teams to have their own work areas along outside walls.

Figure 324 High-level carriers enable the operator to work in a comfortable position.

The teams could divide the work in any way that they wished. In some cases each person did a different job as the carrier progressed through the work area, somewhat like the traditional assembly conveyor except that the team controlled the speed of the carrier and the carrier stopped while the work was being performed. In other cases sub-groups of two or three people worked on a carrier and when they completed their job, the carrier moved on to the next group. Low-level carriers were used for most of the assembly work (Fig. 322). The carrier had equipment which could turn the car through 90 degrees so that work could be conveniently performed on the bottom of the car. A high-level carrier was also available which raised the lower parts of the car so that the employee could assume a normal working position (Fig. 324). Each carrier had rechargeable batteries so it could be moved anywhere in the plant.[7]

There was a foreman for each two or three working groups who served as consultant and teacher on production problems. About the only control was that the group must accomplish the agreed upon number of finished units per day. If the team filled the buffer zone, an employee might double-check his or her work, ask another person

[7] Carriers supported by an "air cushion" are being used in a new truck plant in Eskilstuna and in some other plants. A carrier with a load of several tons can easily be moved with light pressure of the hand on the carrier.

for instructions about the job, or stop for coffee and relaxation. Each group worked on a particular product such as the exhaust system or wheel and brake units and assumed the responsibility for meeting all requirements.

Quality Reporting

Approximately every third work station was a special inspection station, and these areas, later in the assembly, had rolling-road equipment where the cars were test driven and the computer flashed inspection information on the closed-circuit TV screens at work stations if there were problems. The computer also stored information as to how similar problems were solved before. There was a printout for each car as it left the factory. This was a record of the results of all inspections and tests made during the manufacturing process. In addition, the computer followed the car through the entire assembly process. Special instructions were printed out for each work station where special parts or components were to be used.

Redesign of the Car and the Process

It was necessary to redesign some parts of the car in order to accommodate the team method. The electric wiring assembly is one place where such changes were made. Changes were also made in the manufacturing process to make the tasks less fatiguing and to eliminate heavy, hot, disagreeable jobs by using advanced mechanization and automation.

In the Torslanda plant the entire upholstery process was radically changed because the work was producing excessive wrist, arm, shoulder, and back fatigue. Job rotation was first tried and produced some relief. Then with the introduction of new equipment there was a sharp drop in the aches and pains. The extent of job rotation increased and jobs were enlarged so that the group assumed the responsibility for planning all of its own work. The group obtained the assembly requirements from the teleprinter and then determined individual assignments. Moreover, the group was responsible for getting the upholstery material of the correct kind and color to go with the particular car for which it was intended. After a short training period, the upholstery group took over the quality inspection of incoming upholstery material, replacing four inspectors. Each employee learned to perform more of the jobs and understood the entire process. Team spirit and morale increased and absenteeism and employment turnover decreased drastically.

At Olofstrom, the pressed steel and welded body component plant, the ultimate solution to the problem of noisy, monotonous, and difficult jobs at one work station was to automate the entire task. In the case of 18 press lines, some were automated and others were equipped with magazine feeds which reduced the number of employees by half.

Results

The Kalmar design and plan of organization was successful from the beginning. It was clearly demonstrated that the carrier was a satisfactory substitute for the traditional assembly line. The work became more meaningful. Employees had an opportunity to work in groups; they were able to rotate jobs and vary their paces. Each person could learn more jobs, thus acquire greater skills, and make greater contributions. The large majority of workers wanted to assume responsibility for the quality of the product. Increasingly the teams assumed management functions. There was increased cooperation—one person helped another. The arrangement of the working and nonworking areas seemed to draw the members together. There was increased group loyalty to the company, to the product, and to the component they made. Absenteeism and employee turnover were greatly reduced. Cost and production targets were met. The quality of the Kalmar products was as good as the quality levels from other Volvo plants although final adjustments took more time than was anticipated. Also, productivity at Kalmar was equal to that of any other comparable plant.

The Volvo plan is presented here as an illustration of work organization designed to reduce the high degree of specialization and to eliminate entirely the assembly conveyor line in an industry that thus far has found no substitute for the traditional methods. For Volvo their plan seems to be a successful venture. Many conditions in Sweden are different from those in this country and there is some evidence to indicate that such a plan might not be competitive with our methods of automobile manufacture.[8] The Volvo plan has created much interest throughout the world and a full evaluation will certainly be made.

IMPROVING THE QUALITY OF WORK LIFE AT GENERAL MOTORS

In response to the rapid change in the attitudes, values, and expectations of people at work, General Motors has committed itself to improving the quality of work life as a corporate philosophy.[9] This involves providing people with the opportunity to participate more fully in the decision-making process and to influence organizational goals and results. Human resources are better utilized and the lives of the workers are enriched.

"General Motors is pursuing a course of action that is based on the belief that the process of maintaining a work environment that contributes to personal dignity and self-respect is simply one dimension of the process of organizational effectivenes

---

[8] Warren C. Haick, "Volvo; Costly Solution to Assembly Line Blues," *Forty-Second Annual IMS ge- Proceedings*, 1978, Industrial Management Society, Chicago, Ill., pp. 199–204; also, *Industrial ment*, Vol. 21, No. 1, pp. 9–20 and Vol. 21, No. 2, pp. 17–26, 1979.

[9] Reproduced by permission of the General Motors Corporation.

This belief has found support in a long series of studies and projects which have led to a concerted effort in General Motors to enhance the quality of work life." [10]

Basic Principles of the Quality of Work Life Effort at General Motors

1. Develop a broad and flexible understanding of how organizations function, change, and develop.
2. Start where the organization is, not where people think it is.
3. Use measurement/research as a source of information and as a developmental strategy.
4. Involve in the developmental process those who are most likely to be affected by any significant changes.
5. Ability to influence decisions and the decision-making process must be an integral of the involvement process.
6. Resources must be provided to support developmental strategies and to ensure their continuity.

In attempting to provide a higher quality of work life for all of its people GM employs a highly flexible approach which provides each organization, whether a work group or an entire division, the opportunity to institute its own quality of work improvement activities. There is no rigid or formal program that must be followed by every group.

The Beginning of the Quality of Work Life Activities at General Motors

The General Motors-United Auto Workers (UAW) National Committee to Improve the Quality of Work Life was established by agreement between GM and the UAW during the 1973 labor contract negotiations. Two officers of the union represented UAW and the Vice President in charge of the Industrial Relations Staff and the Vice President in charge of the Personnel Administration and Development Staff represented GM. The GM-UAW National Committee is not a substitute for collective bargaining. It is a formal system apart from collective bargaining to enable management and the union to cooperate in developing mutual objectives pertaining to the quality of work life of represented employees.

Measuring the Quality of Work Life

comprehensive survey for measuring the quality of work life at GM was developed by the Organizational Research and Development Department. This survey is capable of measuring 16 areas or dimensions of the quality of work life. The combined

10 "State,
Economic General Motors Corporation on the Changing Work Environment" submitted to the Joint
e of the Congress of the United States, Washington, D.C., June 28, 1978.

assessment of these areas can then give an accurate picture of the total quality. The survey form contains 90 items and uses a five-point scale to record employee responses. There are 11 additional items for recording such information as length of service, sex, educational level, salary level, and type of work performed. Space has been provided so that local units can include up to 20 additional items.

Each GM organization that uses the survey receives the following results:

1. Results from each item on the questionnaire.
2. A separate score or index for each of the 16 dimensions.
3. An overall quality of work index.
4. Comparison with corporate norms.

Although the report includes overall results of the organization and of each major function, the unit may request additional results for departments within the major functions, and further analyses of the data by salary level, sex, and so on.

The initial use of the survey gives the organization a benchmark of the level of quality of work life. Additional surveys can be used to monitor this level. When used periodically by an organization, the survey provides management:

1. An evaluation of specific quality of work life improvement efforts.
2. Measurement of the impact of management actions on the quality of work life in the organization.
3. Early warning of problems before they reach a critical stage.

The GM Organizational Research and Development Department initiated a training program for the plant and division survey coordinators who are responsible for managing the survey process in their organizations. Additional training is also given the survey coordinators to help them conduct a post-survey action planning process in their organizations. This places heavy emphasis on employee involvement in identifying specific problems and implementing solutions for improving the quality of work life. GM considers the Quality of Work Life Survey an essential part of the process of providing people the opportunity to assume more effective roles in their organizations.

Results

Quality of work life projects, large and small, involving management people and hourly employees in many locations are now underway. One of the projects mentioned most often is the one at the GM Assembly Division plant in Tarrytown, New York. In the late 1960s and early 1970s this plant was a trouble spot, with low morale, absenteeism, grievances, and discipline problems, and there was an atmosphere of hostility between management and the local union. Production was low, costs were high, and quality poor.

At this point a major layout change was planned prior to the model start-up for

1973. The local managers, supervisors, and engineers decided to ask the hourly employees to help with the new layout and work place arrangements. The proposed drawings and diagrams were discussed in detail and constructive suggestions were received. Communications between management, the union, and the employees improved. As a result the new model start-up was the best the plant ever had.

The Tarrytown management and the union formalized their relationship on quality of work life, patterned after the GM-UAW National plan, and the process has continued to develop. Today the project includes special training for employees in team problem-solving, communications, and related subjects. The program is available to all employees and 95 percent want to become involved. Both management and employees are pleased with the results of the quality of work life process. Grievances are down—fewer than 70 compared with 700 in 1970. There has not been a strike or work stoppage since the program started. "The plant's performance has improved dramatically. Today, the Tarrytown plant is one of the best performing plants in the General Motors Assembly Division. This fact is not only important to the Corporation, it is equally important to the employes whose accomplishments have made it possible." [11]

[11] Ibid.

41

EVOLUTION OF MEASUREMENT, INCENTIVES AND DESIGN OF WORK AT KODAK PARK

The events described in this chapter deal with the largest of the Eastman Kodak Company [1] plants, the Kodak Park Division, which is located in Rochester, New York.[2] It employs about 28,000 people, is almost 7 miles long, and includes 195 major manufacturing buildings with 21 million square feet of floor area on about 2000 acres of land. Kodak Park is virtually a city within a city, with its own power plants, cafeterias, laundry, and other needed services. The men and women of Kodak Park produce some 650 types of film—including roll film, sheet film, and motion picture film—325 types of photographic paper, more than 1000 types of photographic chemicals, 40 types of photographic plates, and some 6000 synthetic organic chemicals.

Early Measurement and Incentives at Kodak Park

In 1914 an industrial engineering department was organized and initially spent much of its time measuring work and installing and maintaining wage-incentive plans for direct labor. After a few years, a uniform plan of wage incentives for direct and indirect labor was established, which proved to be effective. Originally, the system was mainly a 100 percent premium plan with individual and group incentives and a guaranteed base wage. However, the process-type operations, of which there were many, did not lend themselves to individual incentives, and they were covered by multifactor incentive plans.

The plant maintained its standards and incentive systems during World War II, but, following the war, faced new challenges as technological improvements developed. The problem of providing satisfactory incentive opportunity on process-type operations, mechanized jobs, and indirect labor became more difficult. The history of measurement on these jobs has been one of continuing change and improvement.

Experience gained over the years indicated that, although money was a powerful

---

[1] For 100 years the Eastman Kodak Company has been known for the excellence of its products and the productivity of its operations. During the last 10 years, for example, prices paid by Kodak for raw materials increased at the average rate of 10 percent a year. Hourly pay rose at the rate of 8 percent. Over the same interval, Kodak selling prices increased by a more modest 3½ percent a year. During the past 10 years, Kodak productivity, as measured by output versus the input of hours worked, has improved twice as fast as productivity in all of U.S. manufacturing industry. For last year the rate of improvement at Kodak was about four times the national average. *Data from Kodak Annual and Quarterly Reports.*

[2] Appreciation is expressed to Eastman Kodak Company, Kodak Park Division, and, in particular, to James A. Richardson, for the information on which this chapter is based.

stimulator, people gave outstanding effort to their jobs for other reasons as well. This led the engineers to examine the field more closely in order to determine whether these other reasons could be more formally and consistently added to all measurement systems.

By 1959, the Industrial Engineering Division began studies to determine whether or not work could be made more meaningful from the standpoint of both the individual and the industry. A senior member of the Industrial Engineering Division and one of the company psychologists began the study. This included a systematic examination of the literature in the area of motivation, group dynamics, management systems, and related fields. Published results of research were studied, visits were made to colleges and universities and other organizations where research projects were underway, and discussions were held with leaders in the field. During 1959 and 1960 the senior industrial engineer and the psychologist held discussions with management at various levels to consider such matters as more precise definitions of goals, different ways of stimulating further interest in meeting the company goals, ways of creating an environment for introducing change, and organizing things so that the individual's goals and the company's goals would be more nearly the same. Also, during this period a seminar was held for industrial engineering supervisors.

Because of the growing interest in the subject, the senior industrial engineer prepared a document called a "Working Theory." This amounted to a digest of the research written in simple language. This working theory presentation was made to the supervision[3] in one of the large manufacturing departments on an experimental basis. Several other industrial engineers joined the senior industrial engineer and, working together, a plan was developed. It was referred to as the Individual Rate—Performance Premium Payment Plan.

Basic Concepts of the Individual Rate—Performance Premium Payment Plan

This plan embodied a stable pay plan for nonmanagement personnel and replaced the wage-incentive plans in most areas. It was not a rigid system nor a standardized program. In fact, no two applications were alike and the way in which applications were made varied. It implied a different way of looking at work and suggested a different way of planning, organizing, and operating resources of men, materials, and facilities. It provided uniformity of earnings free from the day-to-day fluctuations that often occur in conventional wage-incentive plans. It tried to establish an environment that made it possible to bring company goals and individual goals closer together, aiming at better performance. The purpose was to provide information leading to improved efficiency and reduced costs—a plan that facilitated changes and promoted

---

[3] "Supervision" refers to the division superintendent, assistant superintendent, department head, foreman, and first-line supervisor.

the design of more meaningful work. The following statements further amplify the intents of the plan.

1. Management and nonmanagement people, through discussion and consultation, develop a better understanding of department goals and individual goals.
2. Each person has greater opportunity for self-direction. Fewer detailed instructions are necessary, and decisions are made at the lowest practical level. Once the goals are fully understood and accepted, each person has greater freedom to use his or her initiative in determining the way the task will be done to achieve the goals.
3. In this plan, as in all other operations of the company, each person is recognized as an individual. Individual performance is important in day-to-day work and for future progress. It is assumed that each person wants to do his best and wants to be considered for advancement in accordance with performance and as the opportunity arises.
4. Management and nonmanagement people understand that the continual development and introduction of new and improved methods and processes are necessary to the successful conduct of the business, and only by utilizing these improvements can the company continue to provide employment at good wages. Under this plan, management and nonmanagement people become intimately acquainted with the analysis and design techniques and the problem-solving approach of the industrial engineer, and learn to apply these techniques as a part of their day's work. Each person has talents for innovation and creativity, and welcomes the opportunity to use these talents.
5. Job security has long been recognized as an essential part of any plan that calls for the full cooperation of all members of the organization, and this plan continues this policy. In a dynamic organization change will occur, work methods will be modified, machines and processes will be automated, and jobs eliminated. Nevertheless, before such improvements are made, careful attention is given to any possible effect upon the individuals concerned. Through this longstanding policy, the company adopts changes essential to its growth and at the same time endeavors to avoid hardship to individuals involved.
6. The concepts of the plan are different from those traditionally found in use in manufacturing industries, and a longer period of time is needed to develop full understanding among all those concerned. A change in thinking on the part of the people takes place. Experience shows that from 9 to 18 months are required before the changeover to the plan could be put into effect with assurance of success.

The plan is most successful when the members of management of a division understand the plan, realize its potential, and initiate studies essential to an installation.

The industrial engineer plays an important part in all of the installations. Capable and experienced industrial engineers are thoroughly grounded in the features of the new plan and therefore can contribute to its success.

Procedure

The first few installations of the plan were started because the department supervisors believed they would help them to operate more effectively. They recognized that the plan was new and that some aspects of it probably would have to be modified with experience.

Possible Steps in Making an Installation

The following is a list of the steps that might be used in making an installation.

1. Background and work sessions. Discussions between management and industrial engineers.
2. Briefing sessions with nonmanagement people by the department head and industrial engineer.
3. Development of a timetable and more detailed plans for the installation.
4. Individual discussions with each person in the department.
5. Group discussions and individual discussions between management and nonmanagement people.
6. Presentation of the pay stability features.
7. Putting the plan into effect.

One early example of the new plan:

SCRAP COLLECTION—AN APPLICATION OF THE NEW PLAN

Discussions were started with the superintendent and supervision of the Scrap Collection Department with the idea of bringing truck drivers and their helpers into the plan. Several manufacturing departments were successfully using the plan, and it seemed to be a good time to study a different type of activity. The department head and supervision were very receptive to the idea, and full discussions took place between the industrial engineer and division supervision and then the truck driver-helper group.

Some years earlier a study had been made of all phases of scrap collection by the Industrial Engineering Division in cooperation with the department head and the supervisors. Truck routes were revised, schedules were changed, and methods of handling scrap were improved, resulting in a reduction in the number of trucks, drivers, and helpers needed in the department. The work was measured and the performance index and incentive pay for the truckers was based on the number of loads of scrap delivered to the incinerator and the paper bailers, which were located in a remote part of Kodak Park property. The Scrap Collection Department seemed to be operating in a satisfactory manner, the truckers' earnings were good, the scrap was being taken care of properly, and supervision was satisfied with the quality of the work. Although costs had been reduced substantially when the original study was made, supervision still felt that the scrap collection costs were too high. The people disliked the method of keeping records of the number of truckloads of scrap moved per day and often complained about it. A checker located near the incinerator and paper bailers inspected and recorded each truckload of scrap delivered. The truckers felt that this inspection and record-keeping was a form of policing, and they objected to it.

In line with the plan, the truckers came into the conference room in small groups, and supervision and the industrial engineer discussed the objectives of the new plan. They were told that when the plan was put into effect, each trucker would receive his base pay plus a 15 percent premium or his "average earnings during the previous three-month period," whichever was greater. There would be no day-to-day fluctuations in earnings, which sometimes occurred under the incentive plan. In line with this approach, the checker would not be needed, and a record no longer would be kept of the truckloads of scrap moved per day. The point was made that supervision and truckers, with the assistance of the industrial engineer, would work toward determining the goals of the Scrap Collection Department and determine how best to achieve these goals. Also, it was indicated that supervision was seeking ways of decreasing the cost of scrap collection, and that an attempt would be made to find some acceptable method of measuring the effectiveness of scrap collection. Individual discussions were then held with each person. These discussions lasted from one to two hours, and a summary report was produced covering all information obtained. Each trucker was asked what he thought the goals or purposes of the Scrap Collection Department were and how best to achieve these goals. Supervision also was looking for suggestions to improve the operation of the department, ideas for better equipment, better methods and ways to reduce costs and to make the job better for the truckers. After the discussions had been completed, more meetings were held between supervision and the truckers and, gradually, valuable ideas emerged. For example, there was uniform agreement that the purpose of the Scrap Collection Department was to "keep Kodak Park clean" and that the number of truckloads of scrap handled per day was not necessarily a true index or measure of the objective. In fact, the truckers revealed that some days when scrap output was low, they had to load their trucks with empty boxes, throw some loose scrap over them, and haul them to the paper bailer in order to earn their customary premium.

Once the new plan went into effect, and the truckers realized that they really were on the plan and that their assistance was needed by supervision to reduce costs, they responded in a positive way. On the average, the number of trips per day was reduced by 25 percent. One driver suggested that he did not need a helper in the forenoons and that this person could be used on other work. Another driver stated that he would need a helper only occasionally and, if he could get a person when necessary, this would be satisfactory. A driver who worked on the night shift and who had a helper stated that he did not need the helper. Moreover, he said he had time and could move the empty four-wheel scrap containers from his truck onto the loading platform and into the factory building, thus making it unnecessary for the material handlers to interrupt their own work to do this job.

After further study and consultation, supervision, the truckers, and the industrial engineer worked out a rather simple system of determining a performance index based on tonnage of scrap moved per month. This was calculated on a monthly basis and seemed to be directly related to the goal of "keeping Kodak Park clean." If plantwide production increased or decreased, or if new manufacturing processes were put into operation, the index number would reflect the load on the trucks and on the truckers.

The department head and the supervisor spent some time each day driving over the Kodak Park area—around the buildings and warehouses in order to appraise special problems that might occur in their efforts to "keep Kodak Park clean." An old factory building might be demolished to make room for a new one, a roadway might be relocated, a new sewer line might be installed, or outside contractors might create special problems. The department head and the supervisor, as a part of their job, were well aware of the activities of each trucker. In fact, the department head had at one time been a truck driver in the Scrap Collection Department. There was excellent communication between the truckers and the supervisor and when a special problem developed involving other departments or activities, the truckers knew that their supervisor would be on the job to effect a solution that would be in the best interest of the company, and they felt assured that they would not be affected adversely whatever the outcome of the situation might be. They had experienced satisfaction in working out countless problems together with supervision, and their jobs had become more meaningful because they had a part in designing them. They were recognized for their ability to perform an important and necessary function in the Kodak Park facility.

As the summary in Table 75 shows, the plan assisted supervision in making it possible for 4 helpers to do the work of 17. One new truck was added to the fleet to handle scrap. In line with company policy, the helpers who were no longer needed in this department were transferred to other jobs.

The changes described in this example were made during the early 1960s. Over the subsequent five years nearly every department in Kodak Park which had been on conventional incentives was converted to a similar wage payment configuration. The general approach remained the same but differed in detail to accommodate a wide variety of operations.

During the 1970s, the early emphasis on conversion of Wage Payment Systems diminished and further refinements and developments are continuing in the approaches to:

Table 75. Summary of the Number of Truckers and Helpers in the Scrap Collection Department Before and After the Installation of the New Plan

Kind of Scrap—Type of Truck	Before		After	
	Trucks and Drivers	Helpers	Trucks and Drivers	Helpers
1. General scrap dump trucks	8	8	8	2
2. General trash and scrap—bucket handling type trucks	3	0	3	0
3. Incinerator scrap "packer" type trucks	3	6	4	2
4. Bailer scrap "stake" and covered trucks	3	3	3	0
	17	17	18	4
Totals	34		22	

- Employee participation in determining job methods and goals
- Redesigning the work to provide for greater employee responsibility
- Establishment of more meaningful goals and appropriate performance feedback systems

The essence of these subsequent developments is:

Employee Participation

More positive and structured approaches to employee participation have been developed and used. These have taken several forms. In some cases, regular reviews of production schedule attainment and standard cost performance are routinely held, coupled with periodic reviews of and the re-establishment of new objectives.

Where operations have lent themselves to teamwork, small teams of interdependent people have been formed and encouraged to work in a multi-skill environment where most individuals are cross trained to do all tasks. In many cases formal team building sessions are held with teams of employees away from the job site to build teamwork skills.

Designing/Redesigning Work

Early attempts to enlarge and enrich individual jobs proved marginally successful. It was learned that individual job-by-job enlargement was an unsatisfactory strategy. Rather, collections of jobs making up production systems were redesigned, usually into team configurations. This approach acknowledged the strong interdependence of jobs in work systems and allowed more alternatives for enrichment. At the same time it made work redesign more of a long-range task to be included with major technology changes and not to be approached in a piecemeal fashion.

Currently it is recognized that Work Design/Redesign is a major task requiring simultaneous consideration of three sets of variables,

- the technological
- the Human Factors
- the Social/Motivational

and the current development focus in Work Systems Design is to make such simultaneous consideration practical and useful.

Establishment of Goals and Supporting Performance Feedback Systems

The trend away from traditional incentive systems highlighted that the goals or standards established to facilitate an incentive system were often counterproductive in motivating people to achieve organizational objectives. A set of criteria is now used to evaluate the "goal structures."

Comprehensiveness—Traditional work-measured incentive standards emphasized output quantity to the exclusion of other objectives. Current practice is to consider quantity, quality, service, cost, safety, improvement, absence, individual development, all as legitimate objectives, worthy of building into the goal structure unique to the job situation.

Establishment Process—When at all possible, some participative process which permits participant input to the review and setting of goals is encouraged to build commitment.

Integration—Goals are rarely independent but usually are hierarchically arranged in some structure. Congruence of goals, both horizontally with sequential operations and vertically within the organizational structure, promotes higher levels of optimization and less internal conflict.

Face Validity—Typically, traditional measures have often dealt with abstractions such as "percentages of effectiveness," "point hours," and similar forms of scorekeeping. Insofar as possible current practice is to deal in measures that are as tangible, visible, and real as possible.

Performance Feedback

Closely related to but often obscured by goals themselves is the matter of performance feedback. Recent experience, rooted in theories of the psychology of learning, demonstrates the power of the design of good performance feedback which stress the following:

Basic Principle. Behaviors followed by positive consequences tend to increase in frequency. Behaviors followed by neutral or negative consequences tend to decrease in frequency.

Key ingredients in implementing this principle to induce good performance are:

- as stated before, clear goals, in terms of outputs, which are understandable, measurable
- feedback which is immediate, simple, objective, if possible maintained by the performer, portrayed as trends, permanent, and positive
- consequences to the individual which stress the positive for good performance; initially continuous, later intermittent

At present it continues to appear that evolutionary changes will stress for the future:

- employee participation in the management of work itself
- design/redesign of work to increase responsibility
- establishment of meaningful goals and appropriate performance feedback systems

As always these will continue to be done in an overall industrial relations environment which recognizes the unique worth of the individual and promotes teamwork and collaboration.

42

MOTOROLA PARTICIPATIVE MANAGEMENT PROGRAM

Motorola Inc., with 36 plants in this country and abroad, is successfully using a Participative Management Program (PMP) which the company has developed over a period of years.[1] The philosophy and the basic features have been carefully thought out and the present program has evolved as the result of experience in a number of plants. The program is uniform in design and yet sufficiently flexible to be adapted to the unique characteristics of each operational organization.

The plan requires a change in the "culture of managing employees," which includes greater participation by the employees in goal setting and greater awareness and involvement of employees in achieving the business goals. The employees are involved in the decision-making process and in the day-to-day activities of the group or team of which they are a part. The plan also provides an opportunity for the employee to earn a bonus. The program, designed to enable the work force to increase productivity, provides for the sharing of benefits. Both the employees and the company share in the net reduction of those costs over which the employees have direct control.

The Participative Management Program introduces a new philosophy of management—changing from Theory X to Theory Y.[2] Employees make more decisions as they perform their jobs. Managers and supervisors seek to provide more avenues for cooperation and openness and more information about the operation of the business. Questions and recommendations from the employees are sought, discussed, and acted upon. A period of months is required for the "change in culture" to occur. During this time many forms of training take place. Each person on the team is learning about the total operation and controllable areas of cost.

THE INCENTIVE BONUS

The employees receive a bonus for exceeding valid goals for the six elements: (1) current cost, (2) delivery, (3) quality assurance, (4) housekeeping and safety, (5) inventory, and (6) cost improvement. (Fig. 325). The group can earn bonus percentage points by exceeding the standards and targets for the three elements "current cost," "quality assurance," and "cost improvement." At the same time it is expected that the group will meet the targets for the remaining three elements. If these targets are

---

[1] Reproduced by permission of Motorola Inc.
[2] See page 573.

Program Measurement Definitions

Elements	Bonus %	Measurement Factors
1. Current Cost	+24%–17% Max.	Measurement of costs related to producing a product for a customer
2. Delivery	Unlimited Neg.	Measurement of product scheduled and delivered to a customer
3. Quality Assurance	±5% Max.	Measurement of product delivered, returns and in process
4. Housekeeping and Safety	−1% Max.	Maintenance of a clean and safe manufacturing facility
5. Inventory	Unlimited Neg.	Raw stock, work in process, and finished goods

6. Cost Improvement [1]
  (A) Pre-Program
   (or "Going-in"
   Phase Only)
	+6% Max.	Only those elements of current cost for which there are standards

(B) During Program	+12% Max.	All goals such as input material, material yielded, labor, margin, quality, etc.

[1] The cost improvement element provides an incentive for reducing costs. This element is divided into two parts: (a) *Pre-program* (during the period that the PMP installation is being made.) This includes current cost (labor, material yield) for which there are standards. The maximum bonus is 6%. (b) *Program* (after the PMP installation is in effect). This includes all defined positive goals such as input material, material yield, labor, quality, etc. Also improvements in methods, tooling, equipment, and processes which are the result of actions by group employees. The maximum bonus is 12 percent.

$$\begin{pmatrix} \text{Cost improvement} \\ \text{in percent} \end{pmatrix} = \frac{\begin{pmatrix} \text{Current cost} \\ \text{target in dollars} \end{pmatrix} - \begin{pmatrix} \text{Revised current cost} \\ \text{target in dollars} \end{pmatrix}}{(\text{Current cost target in dollars})} \times 100$$

Figure 325 Participative Management Program measurement definitions.

not met, negative percentage points will be subtracted from the earned points. However, employees will never earn less than their base wage. There is a ceiling of 24 percent on "current cost" and 12 percent on "cost improvement." The maximum employee bonus is 36 percent.

OBJECTIVES AND GOALS OF THE PARTICIPATIVE MANAGEMENT PROGRAM

1. Provide the best value and service to customers. Improve the company's competitive position in the marketplace by lowering costs and improving quality, delivery and customer service.

2. Give the greatest job security, equity, and opportunity for employees consistent with their desires and abilities.
3. Improve the performance of the employee-manager organizational unit. Foster better employee relations.
4. Increase the level of business knowledge and involvement and improve communications between management and employees.
5. Share cost savings equitably with direct labor and indirect labor employees and the company.
6. Deliver the best returns to the stockholders.

THE PARTICIPATIVE MANAGEMENT PROGRAM

Managers and supervisors throughout the company are familiar with the philosophy, goals, and purposes of PMP and know about the changes that occur in operating procedures and the benefits that result when the program is introduced in a plant. Although the managers in each plant now using the plan, worked out the details of the program themselves, they have drawn on the experience of other plants and obtained help from the corporate officers and staff. Corporate industrial engineering and plant industrial engineering have contributed greatly to the design and implementation of PMP. For example, the "Motorola Semiconductor Group Participative Management Program Manual," which was prepared by the people in this plant for their own use, could serve as a handbook for other Motorola plants where consideration is being given to a PMP installation.

INTRODUCING THE PLAN

When the decision is made to install the Participative Management Program in a plant, steering committees at several different levels are formed to implement the introduction of the program. This introduction includes (1) Planning, (2) Make-Ready (including the Dry-Run), and (3) Start-Up.

PLANNING PHASE

During the planning phase a Business Center Operations Steering Committee is organized and regular meetings are held as needed. The objectives of the committee itself are determined and then the PMP group and sub-groups are defined and organized. For example, the Rectifier PMP Business Center Operations Steering Committee decided that there would be three PMP product groups within the Business Center. These were (1) Industrial Rectifiers, (2) Commercial Rectifiers, and (3) Wafer Processing. Other steps taken by this Steering Committee were:

1. Develop a practical make-ready phase time table.
2. Determine the critical support items required and factor them into the make-ready plan.

3. Determine performance measurement criteria for current cost, delivery, quality assurance, housekeeping and safety, inventory, and cost improvement.
4. Determine existing problem areas that should be factored into the make-ready plan with provisions for their correction.
5. Recommend improvement possibilities that might be included in the make-ready plan.

MAKE-READY PHASE (INCLUDING DRY-RUN)

The following steps are now taken to activate the make-ready plan:

1. Training sessions are scheduled for all management and supervisory personnel in the group.
2. The Production Steering Committee's appropriate subcommittees collect performance measurement data to establish valid measurement standards for the six key elements (Fig. 325).
3. Group managers and supervisors make a thorough presentation of the PMP to all of the group employees. This should take place 3 to 6 months prior to the actual full-scale program installation. A complete briefing is also given just before the start-up phase.
4. The "I Recommend"[3] program is organized and put into effect.
5. The Business Center Operations Steering Committee makes a final review of the foregoing make-ready steps and obtains the Division Steering Committee's approval of the standards and the dry-run data prior to the actual start-up.

START-UP PHASE

After the final approval for start-up is obtained from the Division Steering Committee the manager of the Business Center Operations group takes the following steps:

1. The manager or supervisor of the production group meets with the employees to discuss the start-up and redefines the PMP objectives and goals. The employees are reminded of the factors which govern their performance measurements.
2. The standards and targets as originally explained during the make-ready phase are fully discussed again. Examples of Dry-Run performance measurement data are shown to illustrate how a bonus can be earned.
3. The performance of other PMP groups is described and examples are given to show the areas in which groups similar to theirs have earned bonus payments.

---

[3] The "I Recommend" program is designed to encourage the flow of ideas between employees and management. A bulletin board located in an area accessible to all employees in the group is available for anyone to post ideas. Blank forms which may or may not be signed are placed there. The bottom part of the form provides space for the answers. Prompt and accurate answers to each question or suggestion are posted within 72 hours, and the name of the person who will work on the solution and the date appear on it. Thus all employees have visible evidence of the two-way communication that is taking place.

The manager explains the relationship between the targets and standards of measurement and the bonus payments, noting that the payments are awarded for exceeding the standards. The results of a one-month history of the group's actual performance against the standards is given to the employees. If they would have earned a bonus, they are told the amount; if not, opportunities for improvement are discussed.

Calculation of Pay

The employees in the group are kept informed at all times as to their performance on each element included in the bonus plan. A weekly performance report or cost sheet is posted each week on a special board in the area. The group is small enough so that cause and effect can easily be seen by the group members. The bonus percent is the same for all members of the group and is based on base pay, hours worked, and the bonus percentage for a given month. The bonus is available by the middle of the following month and a separate bonus check is given to each employee by his or her supervisor. At that time the supervisor and the employee talk over the details of the previous month's record, including those elements that contribute to the bonus and those that may have had a negative effect. The example below shows how the pay is calculated.

Example of Bonus Payment

Robert Jones, an operator in Department 17, worked during a four-week month. His base wage is $5.50 per hour or $880.00 per month $(4 \times 40 \times 5.50 = \$880.00)$.

Base wage for the month	$880.00
Monthly bonus percentage	12.1%
Monthly bonus earnings	106.48 $(880.00 \times 0.121 = 106.48)$
Total monthly earnings	986.48 $(880.00 + 106.48 = 986.48)$

Results

The Participative Management Program has resulted in increased productivity and in reduction of unit costs. There has been improvement in delivery, quality, housekeeping and safety, and inventory. Bonuses have been paid to the employees regularly; there have been other benefits such as a reduction in turnover and an increase in morale and enthusiasm on the part of the employees.

In one division, for example, inventory was cut in half. The employees ferreted out raw materials, work in process, and finished goods that had for one reason or another been stored on the production floor, under benches, in aisles, and on loading docks. Action was taken either to use the items, reprocess them, or reject them.

The loss of precious metals in the plating department of one plant seemed to be an insoluble problem. Production supervision had made every effort to correct the situation. The quality assurance and industrial engineering staff had made repeated studies and the accounting group became involved, but despite their combined efforts losses were running around 20 percent.

Small electronic components were being plated with chrome, nickel, silver, platinum, and gold. The cost of gold ingots alone for the plating operation amounted to $1 million a month. With the participation program under way the employees in the department set out to study the problem, and in less than three months the losses had been reduced to zero. When the plating process was designed and the equipment installed, provision had been made for the security of the precious metals and the recovery of scrap and unused material of every kind, including dust and chemical solutions. However, some of the recovery equipment was being bypassed, plating solutions went down the drain, dust filters were defective, and losses were occurring in numerous other places. The employees in the department together with management and staff people located the problems and solved them with the result of large dollar savings. Additional benefits were the improvement in the quality of the finished product and an increase in output.

43

THE LAKEVIEW PLAN

The ABC Company produces a wide variety of consumer products in 15 plants located in various parts of the country. Although the industry is highly competitive, ABC has been a leader for many years. New factories are built as needed to provide for the increasing demands for the company's products. Over the years there has been much discussion concerning the size and organization of an ideal plant and, in 1961, a committee was formed to study this matter and to assist with the design of a new factory scheduled to be built the following year. The committee consisted of the Director of Industrial Engineering, the Chief Engineer, the Manager of Manufacturing, and the Director of Industrial Relations. The city of Lakeview, with a population of 50,000 was selected for the location of the plant. The plant was designed to manufacture 10 different kinds of consumer products.

In 1927 the ABC Company organized an industrial engineering department and installed work measurement and wage incentives in all of its plants. Over the years the functions of the industrial engineering division were enlarged and expanded. Industrial engineering has had a continuous record of outstanding leadership and has contributed in a very important way to the profits of the company. The company still maintains a highly successful system of wage incentives and cost control in its manufacturing plants.

During the period 1958 to 1961 the Director of the Industrial Engineering Division, some members of his staff, and other members of management began studying and discussing among themselves the whole matter of more precise definition of plant goals, different ways of motivating operators and managers to meet the company goals, ways of creating an environment for introducing change, and organizing things so that the worker's goals and the company goals would be more nearly the same. Over a period of several years these people became well acquainted with the research in the whole area of motivation. Therefore, in 1961 when the committee proposed that the Lakeview plant follow a radically different plan of organization from that used in the other plants, the members of management were knowledgeable in this area.

In February 1961, a company division manager with long experience was given charge of the Lakeview plant design. Working with the planning committee and new plant management, he created a design for the Lakeview plant that incorporated the best equipment and processes in the industry. Construction of the plant was completed in January 1963, and approximately 165 people were employed by the end of the first year of operation.

The warehouse and shipping department had been constructed first, and were put into operation as a distribution center for company products about six months before the manufacturing plant was completed. A carefully designed program of selecting and training workers was started in October 1962. No nonmanagement people were transferred from other company plants to Lakeview.

Development of a Philosophy of Management

One of the objectives at Lakeview was to introduce unique methods of work organization and management systems in order to establish relationships and to create an environment in which fewer orders and instructions would be given and people would have greater opportunity for self-direction. Another objective was to bring the company's goals and the individual's goals as close together as possible. This was referred to as "a common objective approach." Many of the ideas now in effect evolved during the plant design and construction period, and some were added or modified after the plant went into operation in 1963.

At Lakeview the people were given greater freedom to make decisions. There was greater opportunity for self-direction. Provision was made for effective communications. The importance of teamwork was emphasized. The goals of the company were carefully explained to all management and nonmanagement people, and discussions were frequently held to consider this and other aspects of the Lakeview operations. Each person was considered a unique individual. It was taken for granted that he was mature, intelligent, and honest, that he wanted a meaningful job, that he would improve his skills on the job, that he wanted to work to his full capacity, and that he would assume responsibility. Furthermore, it was assumed that when he did his job well, he would be recognized by his fellow workers and by his supervisor, and that he wanted to be in line for a better job because of his success in this present work. At Lakeview, management and nonmanagement people worked together to define problems, to develop solutions, and to appraise results. When a failure occurred, there was opportunity to determine just what went wrong and to try again. In the early days of operation at the Lakeview plant, the phrase "every man his own manager" evolved.

Department Organization

Each department is self-contained and is operated with a minimum of direction from above. The decisions are made at the lowest possible level. The department operates as a team with definite daily and weekly goals, but with great freedom as to how they will organize their facilities and personnel to meet the goals. In the conference room, wall charts show goals that the people have set for themselves and their progress toward achieving them.

Packing Department

For example, the packing-line mechanic might relieve the line operator for short periods; the people in the department might help decide which lines to run, determine packing-line speeds, and decide how to handle the situation in case of a major breakdown. The operators and mechanics on the packing lines worked out a way to stagger their lunch and break periods in order to keep the packing line operating the entire eight-hour shift and thus to produce more product. They figured out how they could do this and came to the supervisor requesting permission to try it out.

With 10 different products and 12 different package sizes being produced it is necessary to make changeovers at frequent intervals. There is a difference in the capacity, reliability, and flexibility of the various packing lines and also a difference in the time required to clean the equipment when a different product is to be packaged or when the package size is changed. With all the members of management and nonmanagement working together as a team, they have an opportunity to use their combined ingenuity, imagination, and effort to maximize the utilization of the equipment. They are challenged to make the changeovers as quickly as possible, to anticipate equipment failures, to reduce the possibility of shutting down the lines because of lack of product or packaging materials, and to maintain a high level of quality. Preventive maintenance is a part of every machinist's and operator's job. Operators may carry tools and make minor adjustments and repairs. They also work on a rotating basis to do line cleanup at night, since this is important to the efficient operation of the department. If the cartons are in especially good condition and if the packing line is well adjusted, the operators increase the line speed, thus increasing the output of the packing line for the shift. Recently, when all six packing lines broke all previous production records, the department manager provided free coffee and doughnuts for the department. It is not unusual for an individual or the people in a production unit to be recognized in some special way.

Communications

The Lakeview plan requires a high level of communication. Each department has a well-appointed conference room where the manager or supervisor can talk with his people in the right kind of environment. Department managers hold regular meetings with their people. Subjects discussed range from the consideration of department-operating problems to economics, business forecasts, civic responsibilities, comparative wage rates, fringe benefits, and companywide business-operating problems. The department manager has a private discussion with each of his or her people at least every six months. This provides an opportunity for the manager to discuss the employee's progress and for the employee to make suggestions or discuss things that are on his or her mind.

Indirect Labor

It has been possible to reduce the amount of indirect labor at Lakeview. Janitor service for locker rooms and offices is contracted out. The plant opened with 11 office and clerical people, which is less than one-third the number in the best of other similar plants. For example, the cashier handles payroll, weekly and monthly effectiveness pay calculations, first aid, sale of safety shoes, and the payment of bills. The administration of the salary and the effectiveness pay plan is so simple that it requires only one-half the time of the cashier and one-half the time of the one plant industrial engineer. Line management is responsible for setting correct measures for the effectiveness pay plan in their department. The plant industrial engineer is responsible for the overall pay plan, for measure maintenance, and for pay calculations. This engineer advises and consults, trains, guides, and helps the department managers to make decisions for setting correct measures in their departments.

Training

Great care has been used in selecting and training management and nonmanagement people. As a result the plant is staffed with outstanding, young, cooperative, enthusiastic, hard-working people, many of whom have those qualities that bring rapid promotion. Some operators and machinists perform certain management functions. They gain authority through their knowledge and make decisions because of their know-how. At the present time, approximately 50 percent of the plant supervisors have been promoted to this position from the operator position. The ages of these people range between 22 and 45, with half of the group under 25 years old. College graduates go almost immediately into supervisory positions. At the present time, 6 are in this position, and 11 more are department managers. One of these people moved into this position after but one year as a supervisor and another after two years' experience. Promotion is not based on seniority or on effort expended, but rather on results.

During a three-year period some 80 operators, machinists, and clerks received formal training in methods and work simplification. The course, with 10 or 12 in a group, was taught by the department managers and the group managers with staff managers serving as coordinators. A project engineer, safety and training specialist, and the accounting manager served as coordinators. The course was held two hours per day for a 10-day period. In addition, each participant completed at least one methods-improvement project. The payout for this training came quickly in actual methods savings made by the people on their jobs. Also they learn to think like managers in selecting, evaluating, and installing changes, and better understand that improvement is part of everybody's job.

Managers and supervisors make certain that each person joining the organization fully understands that the Lakeview method of operation is possible only because the company can supply the customer with products of uniformly high quality at low cost, delivered to the customer in good condition when he wants them. Another program was completed in which members of the organization in groups of three or four spent two weeks learning about the various functions of the business such as purchasing, quality standards determination and control, distribution, and costs. Each member of management, including the plant manager, discussed his or her duties, responsibilities, and typical day-to-day decisions with these people. This broadened the outlook of the people at Lakeview, resulting in their greater interest and enthusiasm, and provided wider opportunities for their contribution to the success of the business—that is, higher output, better quality, lower costs, and more profits. This brought greater satisfaction and greater financial returns to the people.

Superior Performance from Superior People

The absence of time clocks, the introduction of unlocked tool rooms and storerooms, and then in 1966 the advent of the weekly salary provide evidence that the people at Lakeview are trusted. However, this is not a philanthropic organization. Goals are high, quality standards must be maintained, and delivery schedules are rigid. There is a big job to be done everyday. Each person works with his mind as well as with his hands, and only the best qualified can survive at Lakeview. This is a place for superior people who do a superior job and who are highly rewarded. Although the financial rewards are excellent, the great motivator seems to be the opportunity to be a member of the unique and dynamic Lakeview organization, knowing that each person's very best creative efforts are wanted and needed, joining with others in using imagination and ingenuity in achieving worthwhile goals, and being employed by a company where every person is important and is recognized and rewarded for his accomplishments.

Results

In the early years of the plant's operation the results could be summarized as follows:

1. The Lakeview plant produced more product than the factory and equipment were designed to produce.
2. The start-up was more rapid and less costly than was customary for such a plant.
3. The productivity per man-hour was equal to or greater than that of any other plant in the company making similar products, and it increased steadily as the people gained experience.
4. The quality was equal to or better than that of other plants.

Although the original plant has been enlarged the philosophy of management and the organizational system remain essentially the same today. The Lakeview plant continues to achieve the high level of results that was evident in the early years and remains a leader when compared with other company plants producing similar products.

The company continues to be highly pleased with the plant's operation and the people at Lakeview are enthusiastic about the results. They look forward to new and exciting opportunities ahead.

THE LAKEVIEW EFFECTIVENESS PAY PLAN

The effectiveness pay plan consists of a base salary plus extra compensation in the form of a monthly cash payment when superior results are achieved.

Salary

It is the policy of the company to maintain a base pay that is equal to or higher than the average pay of similar companies in the community. A wage survey is made at frequent intervals and base wage adjustments are made as necessary. Although there have never been time clocks at Lakeview, wages were paid for time worked until June 1966 when a weekly salary plan was introduced. Now, qualified management and nonmanagement people alike are paid a salary. The new employee is paid only for the hours he works for the first three months or until he is qualified for the weekly salary. Each qualified person receives his full weekly salary even when absent, provided that there is a good reason for his absence and provided that he is not absent more than four days in any week. All nonmanagement employees are positioned in the salary structure into six broad-range technical levels. Positioning at the appropriate level is based on the breadth and depth of demonstrated skills and job responsibilities. Movement within the level is related to time assuming satisfactory performance. The overall salary philosophy is supportive of employee growth and development.

Effectiveness Pay

The effectiveness pay plan provides up to 30 percent compensation in addition to the base salary for group accomplishments in the areas of cost reduction, cost control, and quality achievements depending upon the plant performance. These areas or categories are divided into several factors, each of which is weighted according to its contribution to the profitableness of the Lakeview operations.

Effectiveness pay takes the form of a separate monthly check, which is given to each person by his supervisor. This pay is not considered to be a wage incentive in the usual sense. However, it is a constant reminder that superior performance results in higher pay. It is not easy to reach the maximum bonus of 30 percent. The plan is designed to eliminate month to month fluctuation in pay inasmuch as some of the factors in the plan are based on running averages of from 4 to 12 months. The effectiveness pay together with the base salary provide a total compensation for each person that is proper for a superior job. It is somewhat higher than could be earned elsewhere in the community. Everyone at Lakeview except the plant manager participates in the pay plan on the same basis.

The following criteria were followed in designing the effectiveness pay plan.

1. The application of the pay plan must be in harmony with other important factors affecting motivation, such as respect, fairness, challenge, opportunity, goal setting, and self-realization.
2. Measurement is made of results, not of effort expended.
3. Emphasis is placed on change, which is considered a basic responsibility of all.
4. Management and nonmanagement people are on the same percentage basis of measurement.
5. People of different skills or pay classification, who have common objectives, should be on the same basis of performance measurement (mechanics and operators in the same department, for example).
6. Each combination of measures used to determine effectiveness pay attempts to balance opposing needs. This includes balancing between end results (as they might be seen in the end product) and partial results strongly influenced by the participant. There is an attempt to attain a balance between long-range importance and early feedback of results.

EFFECTIVENESS PAY CALCULATIONS

Lakeview Plant—Month of May

The package-filling department (Department 3) will be used to illustrate how the effectiveness pay plan functions. The department is equipped with high-speed packing lines similar to the one shown in Fig. 326. The product is fed into the filling head of the packing lines from bins located on the floor above. The finished product is either stacked into unit loads from the end of the case-sealing machines by hand or by an automatic stacking machine, and is removed by a clamp truck.

The procedure required to determine the effectiveness factor and the effectiveness pay will be described briefly. The three areas or categories included in the plan are (1) cost reduction, (2) cost control, and (3) quality. The Plant Summary Statement for the month of May is shown in Fig. 327.

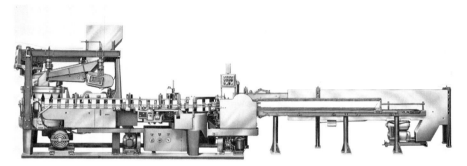

Figure 326　Typical high-speed packing line.

EFFECTIVENESS PAY PROGRAM

Lakeview Plant Summary Statement for Month of May

	Department 1 Product Manufacturing		Department 2 Package Filling		Department 3 Package Filling		Department 4 Warehouse		Department 5 Shipping		Plant Staff	
	Per cent	E.F.	Per cent	E.F.	Per cent	E.F.	Per cent	E.F.	Per cent	E.F.	Per cent	E.F.
1. COST REDUCTION												
Plant methods	10	.96	10	.96	10	.96	10	.96	10	.96	10	.96
Plant target reduction	10	.86	10	.86	10	.86	10	.86	10	.86	20	.86
Department target reduction	10	.78	10	.91	10	1.09	10	.96	10	.82		
2. COST CONTROL												
Plant product system	20	.94	25	.94	25	.94	30	.94	25	.94	55	.94
Department operations	20	.87	30	.88	30	.98	30	1.09	25	1.04		
3. QUALITY												
Plant product system	10	1.00	05	1.00	05	1.00	05	1.00	05	1.00	15	1.00
Department production	20	1.00	10	.86	10	.89	05	.84	05	.84		
Department control									10	.75		
WEIGHTED AVERAGE E.F.	100	.922	100	.908	100	.959	100	.979	100	.926	100	.935
EFFECTIVENESS PAY PER CENT		22.2		20.8		25.9		27.9		22.6		23.5

Figure 327 Lakeview plant summary statement for month of May.

621

1. Cost reduction

a.   Plant Methods
b.   Plant Target Reduction
c.   Department Target Reduction

At the Lakeview plant, the management and nonmanagement people consider cost reduction a regular part of their job. The effectiveness pay program (EPP) is designed to recognize and reward these people for success in this area. Cost reduction is divided into three categories: (*a*) Plant Methods, (*b*) Plant Target Reduction, and (*c*) Department Target Reduction.

Plant Methods. Each year a target is established for cost reduction through better plant methods. For the current calendar year the target is $30,000 per budgeted member of management. This is the same for all plants in the company. Because the Lakeview plant has 30 budgeted members of management, the total target or expected reduction in costs for the current year is $900,000 ($30,000 × 30 = $900,000). An "Effectiveness Factor" (E.F.) or results factor is computed each month, and it is based upon the relationship of the target to the actual reduction in costs for the month. The effectiveness factor for the month of May is combined with the E.F. for the preceding 11 months to obtain a running 12-month average. As Fig. 327 shows, this E.F. was .96. This refers to *plant* methods and applies to management and non-management people in all departments.

Example. If a certain raw material could be purchased in larger containers resulting in lower freight costs and lower handling costs, this saving would fall under the "Cost Reduction-Plant Methods" category.

Plant Target Reduction. This factor is intended to encourage management and non-management people to make improvements and to revise the targets and bring them in line with improvements in costs that have been made. The targets cover the controllable items of manufacturing expense such as management and nonmanagement salaries, mechanical labor, employee benefits, repair materials and expenses, contract services such as guard and janitorial people, telephones, utilities, etc. Not included are taxes, insurance, depreciation, and expenses in connection with new equipment installations.

The improvement or cost reduction is the actual reduction in costs of the controllable items made during the month of May. The effectiveness factors for the Plant Target Reduction and the Department Target Reduction are determined by taking a 12 month running average of target reduction for the plant (or department) in dollars and comparing it with the budgeted dollars for the controllable items for the same 12 month period. There is a separate effectiveness factor for each department. The plant E.F. is the weighted average of the effectiveness factor of all departments plus the general plant overhead. As Fig. 327 shows, the Department 3 Plant Target Reduction Effectiveness Factor was .86 and the Department Target Reduction E.F. was 1.09.

Examples. The purchase and use of an automatic floor-scrubbing machine, which reduces the target from two men to one man, illustrates both a plant methods change and a plant and department target reduction.

Alertness and teamwork on the part of the managers, operators, and mechanics resulting in increased output of the automatic filling and casing machines is another illustration of a change in plant and department target reduction.

2. Cost control

a. Plant Product System
b. Department Operations

Cost control is concerned with the cost of all direct and indirect labor, repairs and expenses, utilities, losses, and rework. Taxes, depreciation, and insurance are not considered.

Targets or standards for direct labor are determined by conventional work measurement methods. Budgets are used for indirect labor such as clerks, machinists, and managers—also for repairs and expenses, utilities, losses, and rework. The dominant factor in cost control is manufacturing efficiency. The effectiveness factor for the department is determined by comparing the actual costs with the budgeted or target costs. The calculations are made weekly and are accumulated for one month. The effectiveness factor for the month of May for Department 3 was .98 and for the plant it was .94 (Fig. 327).

3. Quality

Quality standards are stated in percent of the product not meeting specifications and they are established for each department.

Examples

Product-Manufacturing Department—Department 1. Finished product quality index is based upon variation from specifications.

Package-Filling Department—Department 3. Quality index is affected by variation from specified weight of product in the package and volume or density of product in the package.

Warehouse and Shipping—Departments 4 and 5. Quality index is based on the percent of the product that must be scrapped or reworked due to improper handling.

The effectiveness factor for quality is calculated as a six-month running average. For the month of May the Quality-Plant Product System E.F. was 1.00, and for Department 3 it was .89 (Fig. 327).

The total weighted average effectiveness factor for Department 3 for May was .959 which is equivalent to 25.9 percent effectiveness pay. Thus all management and non-management people in Department 3 earned additional pay based on this effectiveness factor of 25.9 percent. A check for 25.9 percent of each person's base salary for May was given to him in person by his supervisor. Ordinarily this payment is made around the 20th of the following month—in this case, by the 20th of June.

Example. John Smith, an operator in Department 3, worked during the entire month of May. His base salary is $330 per week or $1430.00 for the month of May.

$$\frac{330.00 \times 52}{12} = 1,430.00$$

Effectiveness Pay =	$1,430.00 \times 25.9\% = \$370.37$
Base salary for month of May	1,430.00
Effectiveness Pay	370.37
Total earnings for May	$1,800.37

The effectiveness pay percentage for Department 1 was 22.2 percent, for Department 2, 20.8 percent, for Department 4, 27.9 percent, for Department 5, 22.6 percent, and for the staff personnel (all group managers and laboratory, engineering, office, industrial relations, and cost accounting people) it was 23.5 percent.

WAGE INCENTIVE MANUAL

The Maytag Company has prepared a *Wage Incentive Manual*, which they use in connection with a time study training program given to all foremen and supervisors. This manual also serves as a handbook of methods and procedures pertaining to time study and wage incentives. The first six pages and the last three pages from this manual are reproduced here.

THE MAYTAG COMPANY
EXECUTIVE OFFICES
NEWTON, IOWA

TO: MAYTAG MANAGEMENT

Over the years since the Maytag Wage Incentive Plan was introduced in 1946, the benefits to our employees, our customers, and our Company, have become increasingly evident. Our employees have attained higher wages than would have otherwise been possible. Our customers have been able to buy Maytag products at the lowest cost.

This has been due in great part to the high level of productivity resulting from the installation of the best manufacturing methods, and exertion of the best skill and productive effort by our employees. With such productivity and competitive costs, our Company has grown to provide new jobs and new opportunities for each of us.

The future success of our organization, and therefore your success, is to a large degree dependent upon the continuing improvement of methods, and of effort and skills.

You, a Maytag Supervisor, have a great responsibility for the success of one of the best tools of productivity, -- the Wage Incentive Plan. Your thorough understanding and enthusiastic support of the principles, application and administration of the Incentive Plan, can help assure the many benefits to our employees, our customers, and our Company.

This Manual has been prepared to assist you in the application and administration of the Incentive System in your Department. I urge you to become thoroughly familiar with the material in the Manual. I am sure that such knowledge will enable you to take an active part in the Wage Incentive program with self assurance and confidence. In turn this should lead to matter-of-fact acceptance, and provide a firm basis for our future establishment of even better methods and lower costs.

The **MAYTAG**
STANDARD HOUR INCENTIVE PLAN
is designed to help you in . . . . .

YOUR JOB
of **PROPERLY**
UTILIZING

raw materials

equipment

supplies

and most importantly, of managing

people

to **BUILD**
BETTER PRODUCTS
at **LOWER COSTS**

the following pages explain the
MAYTAG WAGE INCENTIVE PLAN

wage
incentives

The Maytag Wage Incentive Plan, which is based on thorough analyzation of each job, establishing the best method of performing the work, training the operator to use the best method, and proper application of Labor Standards, provides many benefits to our Employees, our Customers, and our Company

The **PURPOSES OF WAGE INCENTIVES** include:

- **Increasing employee's earnings.**
- **Establishing the most economical manufacturing costs.**
- **Providing greater utilization of machines and equipment.**
- **Scheduling production.**
- **Planning changes in manufacturing methods, and estimating costs.**
- **Budgeting and controlling costs.**

Although wage incentives require determining the necessary time to perform a job and result in extra pay for extra effort and skill of the operator, the job study which must be made before a Labor Standard can be established requires analyzing the job to PROVIDE:

- The most effective **EQUIPMENT.**
- The proper **MATERIALS.**
- The most effective **TOOLING.**
- The best manual **METHOD.**
- The best **FLOW OF MATERIALS.**
- Proper **WORKING CONDITIONS.**
- Adequate **SAFETY CONTROLS.**
- Adequate **QUALITY CONTROLS.**
- Proper **SELECTION AND TRAINING OF THE OPERATOR.**

627

wage incentives

wage incentives.....
make your job easier

1. **Careful study of jobs results in better and simpler methods of doing the work.** Industrial Engineering and other staff departments will assist you in developing good work methods. These methods must be developed before a labor standard is determined.

2. **Your employees will work more efficiently.** You are assured of producing according to schedule because your workers will want to exceed the standard in order to increase their pay. Your job of supervising becomes easier when the workers are so motivated.

3. **The detailed job instructions on the labor standard sheet helps you train the worker how to do the job.** The job instructions are written to provide a detailed description of the method, which will result in quality production and will reflect safe operating practices.

4. **Labor Standards help you plan your production.** When you know how many pieces per hour can be produced on a job, it is easy to determine how many men and machines you will need on the job to produce a specified number of units in a certain period of time. Also, materials needed for the job can be scheduled into your department systematically.

5. **Your labor turnover is reduced.** You do not have so many new workers to train because high earnings influence your experienced workers to stay at Maytag.

The help which wage incentives will provide you depends upon your knowledge of the Incentive Plan, your participation in establishing standards, and your proper administration of the incentive program in your department.

Labor Standards are the basis of the Maytag Wage Incentive Plan

successful application of Labor Standards depends on . .

1. Development of the **Best Practical Method.**

2. **Training the Workers** to do the job using the best practical method.

3. **Accurate Measurement** of the manual work and machine time by means of job study, considering method, effort, most economical equipment operation, and application of proper allowances.

4. **Participation by the Employee** in changes affecting his job, and his thorough understanding of the Labor Standard.

5. **Follow Up** after Labor Standards are issued to assure proper application, acceptance and adequate performance by the employee, and to keep the standards up-to-date.

In order to establish Labor Standards promptly and accurately, let's follow through, step by step, the procedure for wage incentive application.

629

Steps to be taken in determining and maintaining a Labor Standard

prepare the job
The foreman, with cooperation of staff departments, prepares the job for study by the Industrial Engineering Department.

request the Labor Standard
The foreman requests the Industrial Engineering Department to study the operation.

study the operation
The industrial engineer studies the operation after checking the details of the job with the foreman and the operator.

compute the Labor Standard
The industrial engineer computes the labor standard.

apply the Labor Standard
The industrial engineer writes up the "Labor Standard Sheet," including detailed job instructions, and after necessary approvals, issues it to the shop. The labor standard is then thoroughly explained to all operators, and any questions which they may have are answered.

follow-up the Labor Standard
Both foreman and industrial engineer observe the job closely on initial application of labor standard to be sure of operator acceptance and adequate performance, and periodically thereafter to assure that the job is being performed in accordance with the requirements of the "Labor Standard Sheet."

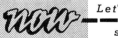 *Let's consider these steps in detail*

administration
of the
WAGE INCENTIVE
PLAN

During the time since the Maytag Wage Incentive Plan was introduced, its benefits to our employees, our customers and our Company have become increasingly evident. New and better manufacturing methods and increasing skill and productive effort of our employees has made it possible for our customers to buy quality products at the lowest prices. With the increased productivity, for which the wage incentive program has played an important part, and wider distribution of our products, our company has grown to provide new job opportunities and greater security.

As a Maytag Supervisor you have a great responsibility for the success of the Wage Incentive Plan. Only with your thorough understanding and active participation in the application and administration of wage incentives can the many benefits to our employees, customers and company continue.

Your responsibilities for proper administration of the Wage Incentive Plan require:

1. **A thorough knowledge of Maytag Wage Incentive Plan.**

2. **Active participation in the incentive program.**

3. **Proper application of wage incentives.**

4. **Adequate communication with employees.**

5. **Proper administration of the incentive sections of the Labor Agreement.**

▷ KNOWLEDGE of the MAYTAG WAGE INCENTIVE PLAN

This manual has been prepared to help you in understanding the purposes of wage incentives and the procedures for establishing the best methods and applying labor standards. A thorough understanding of this material and the incentive sections of the Labor Agreement should provide you the knowledge to take an active part in the wage incentive program with self assurance and confidence.

administration of the
Wage Incentive Plan
(CONTINUED)

2 PARTICIPATION in the INCENTIVE PROGRAM

Although the industrial engineers have had the specialized training for determining the best job methods, for measuring work and applying and administering wage incentives, the success of the wage incentive program is largely dependent on your active participation and skill in handling your many responsibilities in establishing labor standards and for the administration of incentives in your area.

This manual explains most of your responsibilities from preparing the job for study through the follow-up of labor standards and administration of the incentive plan. With adequate knowledge of these responsibilities, active participation in the incentive program and proper utilization of the assistance of industrial engineering and other staff departments, you will find that the many advantages of wage incentives can be obtained with a minimum of problems.

3 PROPER APPLICATION of WAGE INCENTIVES

It is the Company's policy to provide fair and equitable labor standards and apply them to jobs which, in the opinion of the Company, can properly be placed on incentive. With such a policy, labor standards should be applied to as many jobs as practical. However, for various reasons it is not always practical to establish standards for all operations. IT MUST ALWAYS BE REMEMBERED THAT THE FUNDAMENTAL CONCEPT OF WAGE INCENTIVES IS BASED ON EXTRA PAY FOR EXTRA EFFORT. Some operations, because of machine or process control, include substantial observation time and therefore do not provide an opportunity for extra effort. For such operations labor standards should not be used merely as a device to increase the operator's pay, but you should provide the additional work necessary, by combination of operations or the addition of other required work, in order to make the application of a labor standard practical. When new operations are first started in production, tooling or equipment problems often make it impossible to immediately establish a standard. Adequate pre-planning can often eliminate such problems, but if adverse conditions do exist they should be immediately corrected so that a standard can be established and the operator provided an opportunity for incentive earnings. If you question the advisability of applying a standard, it is always a good idea to confer with the industrial engineer. He may have suggestions which will be helpful in preparing the job for standard more quickly.

Preliminary Estimates play an import part in the wage incentive program. They are designed to be used until a labor standard can be established for new operations, or where major changes are made on existing operations and time allowances or disallowances are not applied. A P.E. provides the operator an opportunity to attain higher earnings and usually results in higher production than if the job were run on daywork. In order to attain these advantages you should arrange to have the P.E. established before the operator is assigned to the job. For most operations the P.E. can be established in advance of production if the industrial engineer is provided information on the job conditions, and the machine feeds and speeds or cycle times are known. A P.E. is intended to be a temporary method of incentive payment and should be replaced by a labor standard within 40 hours of operation of the job, or sooner if possible.

632

The most important responsibility which you, as the shop supervisor, have for proper application of wage incentives is to see that your operators are not compensated by standards inapplicable to the job because of changes in the manual method or job conditions. Remember, this responsibility requires that you frequently check each operation to determine if it is running exactly the same as when the standard was established and if it is not, to immediately report the changes to the Industrial Engineering Department so that the standard can be properly revised.

4 COMMUNICATION with EMPLOYEES

Often many of the problems encountered in the application of wage incentives result from misunderstandings among employees, shop supervisors and industrial engineers, which could have been eliminated through better communications. Incentive employees should know how labor standards are established and how the wage incentive plan operates. Naturally, they look to their supervisors for such information. Sometimes, because of the technical implication of their questions, it may be necessary for you to ask the industrial engineer to assist in the answer. Whatever may be required, it is important that you provide your incentive employees the answers to any legitimate questions that they may have concerning wage incentives. With such an approach much of the so-called "mystery" of wage incentives, and many of your problems, can be eliminated.

The Employee Attitude Survey conducted by the University of Michigan showed conclusively that the employees were most satisfied with the incentive system when they saw their foremen doing a good job of explaining wage incentives and the reasons for changes that affected their jobs. It is important to the employees that their foremen do a good job of communications.

It is equally important that you do not, through careless remarks, give your employees an improper impression of wage incentives. For example, if you ever say to an employee, or otherwise give him the impression that you believe a standard is "too tight," you are making a generalized conclusion that has little meaning to anyone, and can be interpreted as criticism of the Company's incentive program. Any such generalized criticism can soon lead employees to believe that they are being unfairly treated. On the other hand, specific criticism of a labor standard can be helpful. If, for example, you say, "This standard does not provide for the increase in the machine-cycle time and will be checked for any necessary change in the standard," you are properly carrying out your responsibility for keeping standards current. Remember, you will be criticized for negative, generalized remarks, but you will be doing your job if you make constructive criticisms intended to correct specific errors.

5 ADMINISTRATION of the LABOR AGREEMENT

The incentive provisions of the Labor Agreement provide the employees assurance of fair treatment in the application and administration of the wage incentive program, and also provides the requirements for a sound wage incentive plan that will continue to provide the many benefits to the employees, our customers and our Company. Your knowledge and proper application of these contractual requirements can have a great affect on the continuing success of the Maytag Wage Incentive Plan.

METRIC SYSTEM CONVERSION TABLES

U.S. Units to Metric Units	Metric Units to U.S. Units

LENGTH

1 inch = 2.54 centimeters	1 centimeter = 0.394 inch
1 inch = 0.0254 meter	1 meter = 39.37 inches
1 foot = 0.3048 meter	1 meter = 3.281 feet
1 yard = 0.914 meter	1 meter = 1.093 yards
1 mile = 1.609 kilometers	1 kilometer = 0.621 mile

AREA

1 square inch = 6.45 square centimeters	1 square centimeter = 0.155 square inch
1 square foot = 0.092 square meter	1 square meter = 10.764 square feet
1 square yard = 0.836 square meter	1 square meter = 1.196 square yards
1 square mile = 2.59 square kilometers	1 square kilometer = 0.386 square mile
1 acre = 0.405 hectare	1 hectare = 2.471 acres

VOLUME

1 cubic inch = 16.387 cubic centimeters	1 cubic centimeter = 0.061 cubic inch
1 cubic foot = 0.028 cubic meter	1 cubic meter = 35.314 cubic feet
1 cubic yard = 0.764 cubic meter	1 cubic meter = 1.308 cubic yards
1 gallon = 3.785 liters	1 liter = 0.264 gallon

WEIGHT OR MASS

1 ounce (dry) = 28.35 grams	1 gram = 0.035 ounce
1 pound = 0.453 kilogram	1 kilogram = 2.204 pounds
1 pound = 0.000454 metric ton	1 metric ton = 2,204.6 pounds
1 short ton = 0.907 metric ton	1 metric ton = 1.1023 short tons

TEMPERATURE

$$°\text{Fahrenheit} = \frac{(°\text{Celsius})9}{5} + 32 \qquad °\text{Celsius} = \frac{(°\text{Fahrenheit} - 32)5}{9}$$

PROBLEMS

CHAPTER 1

1. How might an increase in productivity of a business affect (*a*) employees, (*b*) stockholders, (*c*) consumers? What might be the effects where not-for-profit organizations are concerned?

2. Present data for the past ten years showing the following information for a manufacturing company: selling price index of its products, hourly wages, number of people employed, and U.S. consumer price index.

3. Discuss the importance of productivity among the factors affecting the total wealth of our country as used in the following statement:

The *total* wealth that any people can create is governed primarily by two factors: (1) the natural resources of the country that they inhabit, and (2) the tools and methods of production, mental and physical, that they possess for developing these resources.

4. State some of the reasons for the record of high productivity at (*a*) Eli Lilly and Company, and (*b*) Texas Instruments, Inc.

5. Name some organizations in this country that are primarily concerned with increasing productivity, and state the nature of their activities. Describe the services provided by one of these organizations.

CHAPTER 2

6. Define motion and time study according to (*a*) Taylor, and (*b*) Gilbreth.

7. Explain fully the meaning of the phrases "most economical way of doing work," "determining the ideal method," "designing the preferred work method."

8. Draw an organization chart of a typical manufacturing company and show the location of the motion and time study function.

9. State the factors that might be used to evaluate the performance of motion and time study and wage incentives in an organization.

10. Name some of the activities administered by the industrial engineering department in a typical manufacturing organization.

CHAPTER 3

11. Summarize Taylor's investigation of (*a*) handling pig iron, (*b*) cutting metals, (*c*) shoveling, and (*d*) his plan of functional foremanship.

12. State the major differences between motion and time study practices and wage incentive applications today and those used by Taylor.

13. Name and evaluate some of the chief criticisms of Taylor's work.

14. Summarize Gilbreth's (*a*) investigation of bricklaying, (*b*) his work at the New England Butt Company, and (*c*) his use of motion pictures.

15. What were Mrs. Gilbreth's unique qualifications that enabled her to make contributions in this field?

16. Summarize the major contributions of Henry L. Gantt, Carl G. Barth, and Harrington Emerson to scientific management.

CHAPTER 4

17. Formulate any one of the following problems: (*a*) protect your home against burglars, (*b*) devise a substitute for the use of real coins in a self-serve laundry, and (*c*) add a garage to a house that now has none. In stating the problem include what is known, what is unknown, and what is desired.

18. Describe the concept of lateral thinking as stated by Edward de Bono.

19. Develop specifications or requirements for the ideal (*a*) pogo stick, (*b*) water skis, (*c*) wheelbarrow for use by the homeowner, and (*d*) egg crate for transportation and storage of eggs from the processing plant to the market and on to the consumers' refrigerator.

20. What are the essential requirements for a successful brainstorming session?

21. Discuss the following statement by Niccolo Machiavelli: "There is nothing more difficult to take in hand, more perilous to conduct, or more uncertain in its success, than to take the lead in the introduction of a new order of things."

CHAPTERS 5, 6 and 7

22. Determine in outline form the planning, preproduction and the production phases for (*a*) manufacturing bubble gum, or (*b*) establishing a dry-cleaning plant.

23. Visit a factory and develop the *ideal* process and operator methods for one product.

24. Construct a process chart and flow diagram for: (*a*) making coffee in an electric coffee maker, (*b*) mailing an insured package at the post office, (*c*) installing an antenna on top of the house.

25. You have volunteered to help a young peoples' club make 5000 toy ships which will be sold as a means of raising money. The ships (Fig. 328) are made of wood and are to have no paint or other finish.

(*a*) Design the jigs and fixtures needed to manufacture the three parts and to make the assembly of these parts. Assume that ordinary power-driven woodworking tools are available. The assembly is performed by forcing the dowel (stack) through the hole in the cabin and into the hull. Friction holds the parts together. Material for the stack will be supplied in the form of dowels ½ inch in diameter, in 3-foot lengths; pine strips for the cabin, ¾″ × ¾″ × 10′ long; and pine strips for the ship hull, ¾″ × 2¾″ × 10′ long. All exposed surfaces of all parts are to be sanded, and all sharp edges are to be lightly sanded.

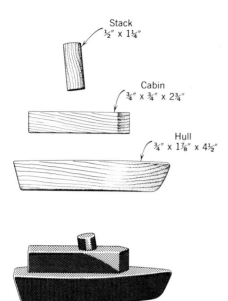

Stack
½" x 1¼"

Cabin
¾" x ¾" x 2¾"

Hull
¾" x 1⅞" x 4½"

Figure 328   Parts and assembly of toy ship.

The method you develop now will be reexamined later to see if improvements can be made.

(*b*)   Construct an operation sheet for the manufacture of each of the three parts of the toy ship, and for the assembly of the parts.

(*c*)   Construct a process chart and flow diagram.

CHAPTER 8

26.   Draw a man and machine chart showing one man (the operator) operating two semiautomatic lathes. The cycle consists of *load machine,* ¾ minute; *machine part,* 1½ minutes (the machine stops at the end of cut); and *unload machine,* ½ minute. The two machines are alike, and each completes the machining operation and stops automatically. The man and machine chart is to show the operator starting the machines in the morning with both machines empty, and continues until each machine has completed two cycles; that is, until it has machined two pieces. The man and machine chart should have one column for the man, and a column each for machine No. 1 and machine No. 2.

27.   The electric toaster shown in Fig. 329 is hand-operated, each side being operated independently of the other. A spring holds each side of the toaster shut, and each side must be held open in order to insert bread. In toasting three slices of bread in the above toaster, what method would you recommend to obtain the best equipment utilization—that is, the very shortest over-all time? Assume that the toaster is hot and ready to toast bread.

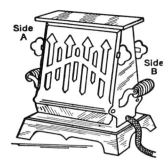

Figure 329 Electric toaster.

The following are the elemental times necessary to perform the operations. Assume that both hands can perform their tasks with the same degree of efficiency.

Place slice of bread in either side of toaster	3 seconds
Toast either side of bread	30 seconds
Turn slice of bread on either side of toaster	1 second
Remove toast from either side of toaster	3 seconds

Make a man and machine chart of this operation.

28. Make a man and machine chart showing the activities of the customer, the filling station attendant, the car, and the gasoline pump for the operation ''Fill tank with gas and check under hood.'' Use actual data.

29. One-hundred thousand studs ½″ × 2½″ are manufactured each year for use in airplane motors. These studs must be accurately machined, and after they are threaded, all burrs must be removed. This is now done by brushing each end of the stud by rotating it by hand against a buffing wheel, as shown in Fig. 330. Develop a better method for performing this operation.

30. Make a man and machine chart of the truck and of each member of the crew for a trash pick-up operation for one block on your street. Use actual data.

CHAPTER 9

31. Make a left- and right-hand operation chart for each of the following: (a) unlocking the door to your car, and (b) checking the pressure in your tires using the gauge located in the glove compartment.

32. Design the most economical method for assembling the rope clip (page 101). Assume that there is sufficient production to keep two operators employed 40 hours per week on this job during the next year. Make a left- and right-hand operation chart of your proposed method.

33. Make a left- and right-hand operation chart for opening several different designs of soft-drink and beer cans and bottles.

Figure 330 Brushing studs for airplane engines—old method.

CHAPTERS 10, 11, and 12

34.   Prepare a list of teaching aids and procedures that would facilitate learning the 17 fundamental hand motions and understanding good motion patterns.

35.   Illustrate each of the 17 therbligs by means of an operation with which you are familiar.

36.   Obtain information about 8-mm and 16-mm motion picture cameras and video cameras. Show in tabular form the special features and uses of each, under the headings of micromotion study and memomotion study.

37.   Make a motion picture at normal speed of: (a) assembling a ½″ pipe union, (b) drilling a ¼″ hole in an iron plate, and (c) spray painting a small object.

38.   Make a motion picture at 60 frames and at 100 frames per minute of operations such as: (a) a crew pouring a cement sidewalk, and (b) excavation of the foundation for a large building, showing the operation of a power shovel and line of trucks hauling dirt away.

CHAPTERS 13 and 14

39.   Prepare an analysis sheet of the following operations. List the therbligs for each hand, omitting the time values. (a) Placing a sheet of paper on a bulletin board using two thumb tacks, (b) removing cubes from ice tray, and (c) replacing battery in radio.

40.   Analyze the film of the operations in Problem 37 and record the data on an analysis sheet similar to that shown on page 146.

41. Make a simo chart of the operations in Problem 37. Use a form similar to the one shown on page 147.

42. Determine the time required to fill the pinboard shown in Fig. 82 under each of the following conditions: (a) pins with bullet nose down are inserted into bevel holes in the board, using simultaneous motions of the two hands, and (b) pins with square end down are inserted into holes without bevel, using simultaneous motions of the two hands.

43. Make an analysis of the spray painting operation in Problem 37 (c) and determine the percentage of the time the operator is spraying the object being sprayed and the time the gun is on but is missing the object.

CHAPTERS 15, 16, and 17

Determine the most economical method of performing the operations described below. Prepare an instruction sheet of the proposed method, showing the motions of the two hands. Include a layout of the work place.

44. Assembling two cast iron plates, $\frac{1}{2}'' \times 2\frac{1}{2}'' \times 3\frac{1}{2}''$ as shown in Fig. 336. The order size is 10,000.

45. Assembling the four parts of a connector for thin wall conduit. The order size is 50,000.

46. Reexamine your solution of Problem 25. Can any of the principles of motion economy be applied?

47. An order has been received for 10,000 toy pigs similar to the one shown in Fig. 331. These pigs are to be made of wood and are to be delivered without paint or other finish.

(a) Design any jigs or fixtures needed to manufacture the parts and to make the assembly of the parts. Assume that ordinary power-driven woodworking tools are available. The snout, head, and body are held together by quick-drying glue. The glue is applied and the parts are pressed together by hand and allowed to dry. No clamps are used. Material for the snout, head, and body is clear white pine. The snout and head are $\frac{1}{4}''$ thick and the body is $\frac{7}{16}''$ thick. Material for the legs is $\frac{3}{16}''$ diameter dowels. Staggered holes are drilled in the lower edge of the body for the four legs. A No. 55 size drill is used for drilling a hole in the top edge of the body for a screw eye. A No. 37 size drill is used for the holes in the head and snout. All exposed surfaces are sanded including the sharp edges of the parts.

b) Construct an operation sheet for making each of the parts of the toy pig and for the assembly of the parts.

48. Design an electric motor driven concrete mixer of a wheelbarrow type for use by the homeowner. The mixer must be lightweight and capable of being placed in a station wagon.

49. The XYZ Company manufactures two models of bathroom scales, deluxe and standard. They are identical except the deluxe model has more chrome and a dial of different design. Both are made in four colors.

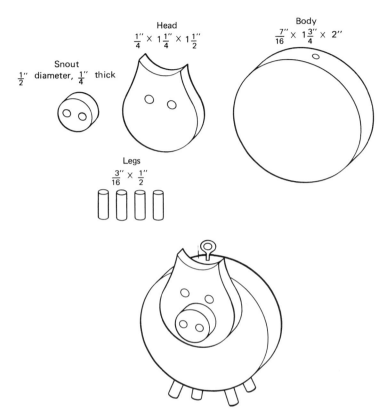

Figure 331 Parts and assembly of toy pig (Design by Anne Gaw).

Design a better method of inspecting scales (*a*) with the present volume of 12 scales per minute, and (*b*) with a proposed increased output of 24 scales per minute. The scales are now inspected by a person who steps onto each scale as it passes by on a conveyor moving at the rate of 12 feet per minute. The scales are spaced 1 foot apart on the conveyor. The inspector observes the dial and if the scale indicates his correct weight within ±¼ pound, he steps off the scale and it moves on to the packing and shipping department. If the scale shows his weight to be too high or too low, he pushes the scale off the conveyor with his foot onto an adjoining surface. The defective scales are adjusted or repaired and again placed on the conveyor for inspection.
50.   Design a folding or collapsible ladder for use on the second floor of a two-story dwelling as a means of exit in case of fire.

CHAPTER 18

51.   Visit a factory or office where automatic or semiautomatic equipment has been installed during the past few years. Obtain facts concerning the following: (*a*) the extent to which the manual part of the operation had been improved before it was mechanized; (*b*) the number of different kinds or makes of equipment considered before the purchase was made; (*c*) the method of evaluation of (1) production or output per hour, (2) unit cost of product, (3) cost of maintenance of equipment, and (4) obsolescence cost or depreciation of equipment; (*d*) the kind of information given to employees before, during, and after installation of equipment and the manner in which this information was given; (*e*) if equipment has been installed long enough, the immediate and long-range effect of the introduction of the new equipment on employment in the department and in the plant.

52.   Obtain information for a specific manufactured product from a trade association, showing the annual (*a*) output per man-hour, (*b*) hourly base wages of the workers, (*c*) unit labor cost, and (*d*) the total unit factory cost of the product over the past ten years.

53.   Make a study of the conventional check-out operation in a supermarket and compare it with an electronic scanning system.

54.   A manufacturer using automated processes for high volume standardized products often lacks the flexibility to adapt quickly to new or modified products. Discuss.

CHAPTER 19

55.   Prepare a written standard practice for Problems 44 and 45.

56.   Assume that a foreign organization has obtained the rights to duplicate the lipstick manufacturing process described in Chapter 5. Outline the information that this company would need.

CHAPTERS 20, 21, and 22

Make a stop-watch time study of the following operations. Use the "average" method of selecting the time, and include allowances. Make an instruction sheet for the operation.

57.   Assembling small parts such as those in Problems 44 and 45.

58.   Drilling a hole in a small piece held in a jig.

59.   Turning a piece in a lathe.

60.   Milling a piece strapped to the table.

61.   Time 10 cycles of any of the operations referred to above. Using Table 13, determine the number of readings required for each element of the time study. Use 5 percent precision and 95 percent confidence level.

62.   Time 32 cycles of the operation referred to above. Using the curves in Fig. 190, determine the number of readings required for each element.

63.   From the alignment chart in Fig. 193 determine the number of readings required for each element of the study in Problem 62.

64. Draw a control chart for each element of the study in Problem 62.

65. The time study shown below was made of the operation "assemble and rivet flanges to hub of metal spool." This operation consisted of two elements as follows:

Element 1—Assemble Flanges to Hub

Pick up hub in right hand, flange in left hand. Position hub to flange and place assembly over pin on fixture. Pick up second flange and position to hub with both hands. Remove assembly and dispose to turntable.

.14	.15	.14	.20*	.15	.20	.18	.17	.19	.18	.14	.17
.19	.13	.15	.17	.17	.19*	.14	.17	.18	.16	.14	.16
.13	.19	.14	.13	.14	.17	.12	.13	.14	.18*	.14	

*Flange sticking.

Element 2—Rivet

Reach to spool on turntable with right hand as left removes and disposes spool to chute. Pick up spool with right hand and move to left hand. Grasp with left hand. Positions on hammer with both hands and rivet with foot-controlled riveting machine.

.09	.06	.06	.06	.05	.07	.06	.09	.07	.07	.06	.07
.07	.07	.07	.08	.07	.07	.07	.07	.07	.07	.07	.06
.06	.07	.06	.07	.06	.07	.07	.07				

Use the alignment chart in Fig. 193 to determine the number of observations required for each element of this study—desired precision ±5 percent, confidence level 95 percent.

66. Make a pinboard and pins according to the drawing shown in Fig. 332 and try the experiment described below.

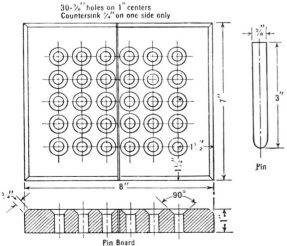

Figure 332 Details for making pinboard and pins.

(a)   Determine the time required to fill the 30 holes in the board with 30 pins under each of the three conditions indicated in Fig. 333. Time ten consecutive cycles and take the average.

(b)   Determine the number of pinboards that could be filled in an 8-hour day under each of the three conditions. Assume that an operator could maintain the pace used in the experiment and that no fatigue or delay allowances were made.

(c)   Calculate in percentage how much more time was required to fill the pinboard under condition *B* and *A;* under condition *C* than *A*.

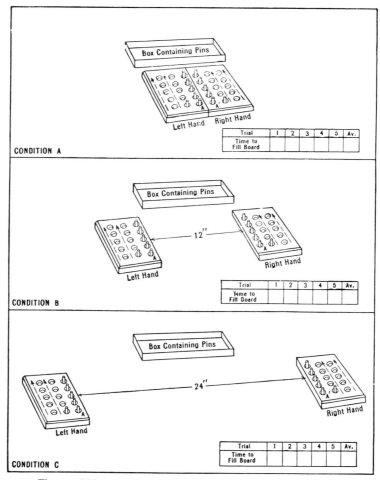

Figure 333   Arrangement of work place for pinboard study.

(*d*) Compute the total distance in feet through which the two hands would move in filling 1000 pinboards under each of the three conditions.

(*e*) Calculate in percentage how much farther the hands would move under condition *B* than *A;* under condition *C* than *A.*

67. Make a study of three or more different types of self-service retail grocery store check-out counters found in your community. Decide on a "standard" or "average" order size. For each of the different types of checkout counter, determine the time for the following: (1) remove articles from cart and place them on counter or belt, (2) ring up, (3) take money, (4) make change, (5) position bag, (6) bag merchandise, and (7) other work.

(*a*) Determine the production in orders per hour for: (1) one person working on the check-out counter, (2) two persons.

(*b*) Using the prevailing hourly wage rate for these people in the community, determine the cost in cents per order for each of the conditions in (*a*).

68. Determine the actual walking speed for men and women. Measure off 50 feet on a smooth, level sidewalk. Then from a point where you can see clearly this 50-foot section of sidewalk, with a decimal-minute stop watch determine the time required by individuals to walk this 50-foot distance. Obtain data on people walking singly rather than in groups. Also make the following classifications of your data: first, men and women; second, three age groups—15 to 18, 18 to 50, over 50; and then under each of these age groups further subdivide the people as to height—short, medium, and tall. The data might be recorded on the form shown in Fig. 334.

69. Determine the standard time by use of time study for each operation in Problem 25. Determine the total direct labor cost for manufacturing the toy ship using prevailing wage rates in your community for this type of work. Obtain the total factory cost using prevailing material costs and an overhead or burden rate of 100 percent of the direct labor cost.

70. Determine the total factory cost for manufacturing the toy pigs in Problem 47.

Men ☐ Women ☐ Place				Date		Temperature		Humidity	
Age 15 to 18			Age 18 to 50			Age over 50			
Short	Medium	Tall	Short	Medium	Tall	Short	Medium	Tall	

Figure 334 Data form for Problem 68.

CHAPTERS 23 and 24

71. Determine the standard time for drilling the part shown on the sketch at the bottom of the observation sheet (Fig. 184) if the piece is 1.750 inches in diameter and the actual drilling time is 0.94 minute. Use time-setting tables for the sensitive drill.

72. Determine the time required to mill the hexagon, using a gang mill, on part 612W-377A (Fig. 216) if the dimension A (length of the hexagon) is 1.125 inches and all other dimensions are as shown.

73. Calculate time for cutting teeth on index change gear similar to part 1670 AG (Fig. 218) if length of face is 1.150 inches; diametral pitch (D.P.), 16; number of teeth (N), 60; diameter of bore, 1.250 inches; material, 4620; hob HBG 573. Ground-tooth spur gear. Size of order 50 gears.

CHAPTERS 25 and 26

74. The mastery of stop-watch time study requires practice, coaching from an experienced analyst, and on-the-job training. Which parts of time study are most difficult to learn?

75. The use of an electronic data collector simplifies the making of a time study. State what parts of time study are eliminated by the use of the data collector and the computer. What new elements are introduced with computer-aided time study? One of the most important parts of time study still must be performed using either the stop watch or the data collector. What is it?

76. In what ways does monitoring and measuring downtime aid in increasing productivity of machines and equipment?

77. List the common devices that are in use for monitoring downtime. State one place where each device might be used advantageously.

CHAPTERS 27 and 28

78. Using the Work-Factor System determine the time required to perform the motion sequence "get pen from holder, mark X on paper, replace pen in holder, and return hand to paper (Fig. 233)" when the penholder is located 5, 10, 15, and 20 inches from the center of the writing area.

79. Using Methods-Time Measurement determine the time required to perform the motions in disposing of one part and obtaining the next in the layout shown in Fig. 234 with the distances doubled, that is 16", 20", and 24".

80. Make a comparison of predetermined time data and stop-watch time study as methods for establishing time standards for use as the basis of a wage incentive plan for direct factory labor on short-cycle repetitive operations.

81. The apparatus shown in Fig. 335 is used by the Maytag Company for demonstration purposes in connection with training programs in motion and time study. Using any one of the systems of predetermined time data, determine the time

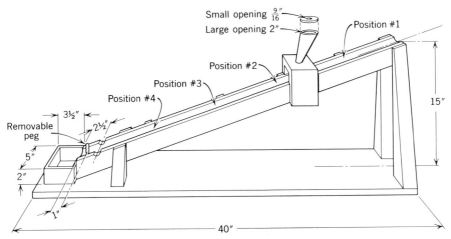

Figure 335 Demonstration unit—time required for hand motions.

required per cycle to obtain one pin and place it in the hopper. Pins may be placed in the hopper either end down. Present your results in tabular form.

There are four positions of the hopper along the chute. Distance of center of hopper from grasp point: position 1—30 inches; position 2—24 inches; position 3—18 inches; and position 4—12 inches. Size of pin is ⅜" × 3", bullet nose on one end and square on the other. For each of the four distances (a) get pin from box and place in large (2") disposal opening, and (b) get pin from box and place in small (⁹/₁₆") disposal opening.

82.   Study three different predetermined time systems and determine the time required to perform some simple, short-cycle, manual operation using each system. For each system evaluate (a) the completeness of the method description, and (b) the ease of determining the time standard.

83.   Using any predetermined time system, determine the standard time required to "assemble two cast iron plates, two washers, bolt, and nut," as shown in Fig. 336. The arrangement of the work place is shown in Fig. 337.

84.   Determine the standard time for assembling the two cast-iron plates using the method and duplicate fixture shown in Fig. 211 and 212.

CHAPTER 29

85.   Standard data have had wide use over many years. State reasons for the continued use of this method of work measurement.

86.   What are the advantages of using predetermined time data as the basis for establishing standard data over stop-watch time study?

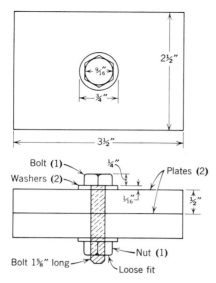

Figure 336 Plate assembly.

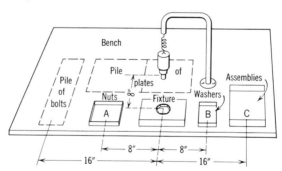

Figure 337 Arrangement of the work place for the plate assembly.

87. Why do companies using individual wage incentives for direct labor place such great emphasis on the way the time standards are to be established and the way the standards and the incentive plan are to be administered?

88. Determine the handling time and the drilling time for the operation "drill hole in cast iron bracket" (Fig. 238). All conditions remain the same as described in the example except the casting weighs 20 pounds instead of 10.

CHAPTER 30

89. Make a work sampling study of one department in a factory or office to determine the working time and idle time of each piece of equipment.

90.   Work sampling is to be used to measure the down time of a group of presses. A preliminary study shows that the down time is likely to be around 30 percent. Determine the number of observations required for this study, for a 95 percent confidence level and a desired accuracy of ±5 percent. Use the formula in solving this problem.

91.   By means of work sampling determine the working time, and the average performance index of a group of people performing some nonrepetitive activity.

92.   *Time* [1] magazine reported that a city councilman made the record of activities of a seven-man crew of electrical maintenance workers shown in Fig. 338. The councilman, believing the operation of the City Electrical Department was inefficient, followed the crew for an entire day to get this information. Using the random sampling technique, determine the percentage of nonworking time for the crew shown in Fig. 338.

93.   One company occasionally asks the supervisors of maintenance crews to make what is called a "period study." In making a period study, the supervisor observes a group of two, three, or four men working together on a job. The supervisor observes the members of the crew for 10 or 15 consecutive 5-minute periods, and records on a simple data sheet whether each member of the crew is working or idle more than half of each 5-minute period. For example, if man No. 1 worked more than 2½ minutes during a 5-minute period, the supervisor would place a tally mark for this man under "working"; if the man was idle more than 2½ minutes during the 5-minute period, he would receive a tally marked under "idle." The supervisor tries to determine from observation (he does not use a watch) whether each member of the crew worked more than half of each 5-minute period. The percentage of the total study period that each member of the crew is working and is idle is determined in the same way as for a regular work sampling study. The main purposes of the period study are to encourage the supervisor to really look at the activities of each member of a crew, and to better determine the proper crew size.

Make an investigation to compare this type of period study with the conventional work sampling study and with a continuous time study of some activity similar to maintenance work, involving two or three crew members.

94.   Make a performance sampling study of the employees in one department of a factory for a period of a week.

95.   What can be done to convince employees unfamiliar with statistical procedures that work sampling can be used to measure working time and nonworking time of people and machines?

96.   Time study, predetermined time systems, and standard data may be used as the basis for determining the average performance index of the employees in a department. Continuous performance sampling may also be used for this same purpose. Compare the two.

[1] "Let There Be Light," *Time*, Vol. 60, No. 26, p. 15.

Time / Event	Elapsed Minutes	Men Working	Man-Minutes of Work	Per Cent Non-Productive Time
8:30 a.m.: Starting time.				
8:34 a.m.: First maintenance truck leaves city garage with two men aboard.	70	2	140	71
9:40 a.m.: Truck stops at 2020 West Cullerton. One man apparently siphons gas from truck into gas can and puts it in another car.	17	0	0	100
9:57 a.m.: Truck proceeds to Maplewood & Flournoy, meets five men, who drive up in own cars.	5	2	10	71
10:02 a.m.: Two men put ladder against pole. Others do nothing.	3	2	6	71
10:05 a.m.: One man ascends pole to attach rope at top. Others do nothing.	18	1	18	86
10:23 a.m.: One man starts painting base of pole. Man on pole erects pulley arrangement to enable him to get can of paint to top of pole without carrying it.	6	2	12	71
10:29 a.m.: Three men go to other car and drive off. Only one man working.	18	1	18	86
10:47 a.m.: Three men come back in their car.	7	1	7	86
10:54 a.m.: Cars and truck leave.	31	2	62	71
11:25 a.m.: New location, School & Ravenswood.	1	2	2	71
11:26 a.m.: Equipment unloaded. One man digging, others watching.	19	1	19	86
11:45 a.m.: Six off for lunch. Go to tavern nearby.	15	1	15	86
12:00 a.m.: Last man to lunch.	24	0	0	100
30 MINUTE LUNCH PERIOD				
12:54 p.m.: Six men return from tavern and one resumes digging.	9	1	9	86
1:03 p.m.: One man ascends pole and detaches electric wire. One man digs.	5	2	10	71
1:08 p.m.: One descends pole.	29	1	29	86
1:37 p.m.: Two men working to remove pole.	12	2	24	71
1:49 p.m.: Two men remove pole, using pulley; put in new pole.	13	2	26	71
2:02 p.m.: Two men tamp dirt.	2	2	4	71
2:04 p.m.: Two men go to tavern.	11	0	0	100
2:15 p.m.: One man on top of pole, attaching wire.	6	1	6	86
2:21 p.m.: One man on top of pole, one painting base of pole.	4	2	8	71
2:25 p.m.: Man on pole working, others in truck.	15	1	15	86
2:40 p.m.: One man painting pole—three in tavern—three in truck.	8	1	0	86
2:48 p.m.: Man descends pole, puts ladder back in truck. Nobody working.	4	1	4	86
2:52 p.m.: Another man leaves for tavern; no one working.	2	0	0	100
2:54 p.m.: Last three men leave for tavern. All seven men in tavern now. Truck unattended though motor is running, as it has been all day.	18	0	0	100
3:12 p.m.: Mass exodus from tavern.	7	0	0	100
3:19 p.m.: Truck drives off. Other men get in cars and leave.	71	2	142	71
4:30 p.m.: Quitting time.	480		594	81%

Figure 338 All-day study made by a city councilman showed 81% nonproductive time for the members of a seven-man crew of electrical maintenance workers. (Reproduced by permission, from *Time*, Vol. 60, No. 26, p. 15.)

650

CHAPTERS 31, 32, and 33

97.   Determine the physiological cost of walking, using heart rate in beats per minute before and after walking on a smooth level surface at four different speeds.

(*a*)   Have a male subject sit in chair for 5 minutes. Record his heart rate in beats per minute for a period of ½ minute.

(*b*)   Have subject walk 2½ miles per hour for a period of 5 minutes, then have subject sit in chair and record his heart rate in beats per minute for the second half of the first minute, the second half of the second minute, and the second half of the third minute after walking ends.

(*c*)   Repeat (*b*) at walking speeds of 3, 3½, and 4 miles per hour. Allow time between trials for heart rate to return to normal.

Plot curves showing "Heart rate in beats per minute" as the ordinate and "Minutes after work" as the abscissa.

98.   Determine the physiological cost of handling brick at four different speeds, using heart rate in beats per minute.

(*a*)   Have subject sit in chair for 5 minutes. Record his heart rate in beats per minute for a period of ½ minute.

(*b*)   Have subject pick up bricks one at a time from the floor and stack them on a bench 33 inches high at a speed of 16 bricks per minute. Have subject work for a period of 5 minutes, then have subject sit in chair and record his heart rate in beats per minute for the second half of the first minute, the second half of the second minute, and the second half of the third minute after work ends.

(*c*)   Repeat (*b*) at working speeds of 22, 28, and 34 bricks per minute. Allow time between trials for heart rate to return to normal.

Plot curves showing "Heart rate in beats per minute" as the ordinate, and "Minutes after work" as the abscissa.

99.   Repeat Problems 97 and 98 with female subjects.

100.   Measure the heart rate of three men and three women riding bicycles at speeds from slow to fast, varying the speed by 2 miles per hour increments. Show results in tabular and graphical form.

101.   Measure heart rate and oxygen consumption of a person climbing stairs at five different speeds. Show results in tabular form.

102.   The 10-hour day, 4-day work week is sometimes used instead of the usual 8-hour day, 5-day week. Design procedures that might be used to measure the amount of rest that would be required during the work-day on 100 percent heavy manual tasks in each situation.

103.   Study the design of the operating controls and visual displays of any one of the following: (*a*) clock radio, (*b*) kitchen stove, (*c*) small tractor, (*d*) food mixer, or (*e*) electric welder. Prepare a written report on the good and poor design features and recommend improvements.

104.   State some of the major activities performed by the Human Factors Laboratory

at Eastman Kodak Company and by Space Systems Division Human Factors Engineering at Lockheed.

105. What factors received the greatest attention in the redesign of the welding operations described in Chapter 33 in the text?

106. State the objectives of The Human Factors Society.

CHAPTERS 34 and 35

107. *Daywork* and the *standard hour plan* (100 percent incentive plan) are probably the two most commonly used wage payment plans for hourly employees in industry. State the advantages and disadvantages of each. Consider the point of view of the employer and the employee. Assume that the company is well-managed, employs approximately 1500 people on direct factory work, and that the operations are short cycle, repetitive, and operator controlled.

108. Assume that measured daywork is used in the factory mentioned above. All direct labor is measured by time study, predetermined times, or standard data, and a performance index is calculated daily for each employee and listed on the department bulletin board the next day. State the advantages and disadvantages of such a plan in comparison with unmeasured daywork. If the posting of operator performance indexes were omitted from the measured daywork plan, what would be the effects?

109. Interview five people who are now working in a factory or office. Analyze their comments on the subjects of motion and time study, and methods of wage payment.

110. A company using the piecework system of wage payment negotiated a labor contract which called for across-the-board increase in wages of 50 cents per hour for all hourly employees. The piece rates were not to be changed. The piece rate for "Drilling ½" hole in a casting, Part #Z267, Operation 5" was 18 cents per piece. (Standard time per piece = 1.50 minutes, hourly wage rate = $7.20.) Now, in addition to receiving 18 cents per piece produced, the operator will be paid 50 cents per hour worked or $4.00 for an 8-hour day. (*a*) Calculate the total earnings for an operator who completes 375 pieces during an 8-hour day, (*b*) the statement sometimes is made that an across-the-board wage increase dilutes a piece rate incentive system. Discuss, using computations based on the above data.

111. Fifty people are employed in one department on short-cycle manual operations of several different kinds. An individual wage incentive plan is used and there are no restrictions on output. Time standards are established by stop-watch time study. Thirty percent of the operators in this department regularly have performance indexes of from 175 to 200 percent (100% = normal performance). The superintendent believes these high performance indexes are due to incorrect time standards.

(*a*) State three other factors that might account for the high performance index of this group. Discuss each fully.

(*b*) What procedure might be used to determine whether the time standards are correct?

112.   Obtain the following information from a factory using wage incentives and which has operations containing machine-controlled elements.

(a)   How are the people paid for the machine-controlled part of the operation?

(b)   What plan would the company prefer to use if it were to install an entirely new work measurement and wage incentive system?

113.   (a)   Determine the total factory cost per hour to operate one unit or one battery of automatic machines.

(b)   Determine the cost per piece or per unit of product produced for each of the following: (1) direct labor, (2) indirect labor, (3) direct material, and (4) all other factory costs including overhead.

114.   The crew referred to on page 497 produced 212,650 lineal feet of fiberboard, 125-pound test, with 1.35 percent waste in one 8-hour day. Time allowed for setup in the morning was 0.07 hour. Determine the earnings for each crew member for the day, using the base hourly rate and the standard data given in the text.

115.   Study a soft-drink bottling plant and design a multi-factor incentive system that would promote high productivity, low cost, meet safety and quality standards, and also provide a bonus for the operators. Describe the methods to be used in establishing the standards and targets for each factor and state how the count or output for each factor will be obtained.

116.   What operations or functions of the transfer machine described in Chapter 35 are within the control of the operators and thus provide an incentive opportunity for them?

117.   You are the supervisor of the assembly department of a plant manufacturing electrical supplies. A program of motion and time study has been in successful operation in your department for 6 months. One of your best employees asks you if the results of this work will not mean fewer jobs and less work for the employees in the plant. How will you answer?

CHAPTER 36

118.   What factors affect the extent to which motion and time study may be profitably used?

119.   Determine the extent of a motion and time study investigation that should be made in a specific plant or office.

120.   Obtain information concerning the actual installation of a piece of production equipment. Determine the number of years required for the savings in operating costs to pay for the initial cost of the equipment. Also compute the rate of return in percent per year on the investment.

121.   Assume that an "improved method" results in doubling the output per hour of a fully automatic machine. However, there is no other use for this machine so it now stands idle half of the day. Discuss how this improvement contributes to company profits.

122.   What policies and procedures might be followed by a company in determining

"cost savings" and "increased output" so that the results will be accurate and free from bias?

CHAPTER 37

123.　State the purposes and scope of the Industrial Engineering Center established by the Armstrong Cork Company. Currently what is the nature of their training in motion and time study and wage payment?

124.　What original approach to motion study applications did Persing introduce at the Fort Wayne works of the General Electric Company? Describe their current training programs in motion and time study and related fields.

125.　State the advantages and disadvantages of conducting a methods design training program that includes project work, that is, an opportunity to work on actual operating problems. This might require the use of a laboratory or work shop.

126.　Evaluate the Procter and Gamble Methods Change Program. What aspects of the program are the greatest contributors to its success?

127.　Design a suggestion system or "Employee Idea Plan" for a small- or medium-sized manufacturing plant.

128.　The multi-plant training program for industrial engineers described in the text was based on the premise that the industrial engineers themselves could develop uniform and effective company-wide industrial engineering policies and procedures. Compare this with a plan in which the main office prepared an industrial engineering manual for company-wide use.

129.　Design a motion and time study training program for managers and supervisors for a specific plant in your locality.

130.　Make a performance rating study of walking.

Object

To obtain group practice in rating operator performance.

Equipment and materials needed.

1.　Decimal-minute stop watch, tape measure, chalk, string.
2.　Rating forms: B204 (Fig. 339).

Place

Select a room with smooth level floor, or use a smooth level sidewalk.

Procedure for conducting rating study.

(1)　Measure off 50 feet of unobstructed floor space, marking a starting and a stopping line on the floor and allowing 10 or 15 feet of additional space at either end for the operator to start and stop. Tie a string to the back of one chair and throw it loosely across the back of another chair so that the string is stretched directly above the starting line on the floor. Also place a string across two chairs at the other end of

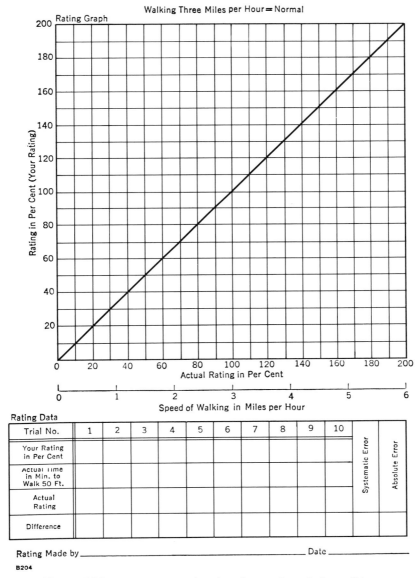

Figure 339 Performance rating data sheet and graph for walking.

655

the 50 feet. These strings are to help the operator to start the watch and read it at the proper instant.

(2) Have someone (this person will be called the operator) practice walking the 50 feet at exactly 3 miles per hour. This practice should take place before the group assembles. The operator should take 0.189 minute to walk the 50 feet. After a little practice it will not be difficult for the operator to walk the 50 feet in this time or at a speed of 3 miles per hour.

(3) Provide each person with a data sheet similar to Form B204 (Fig. 339). Have the person fill in name and date at the bottom of this form. No stop watch or clock is to be used by member of the group in this study.

(4) The operator then walks at 3 miles per hour, and the group is told that this speed represents a rating of 100 percent. Two or three trials are made at this speed. The operator times himself, and if he takes more or less than 0.189 minute to walk the 50 feet, he informs the group of that fact and immediately determines the actual speed in percent, which he gives to the group. The group, of course, makes no record of these preliminary trials.

(5) The operator then walks the 50 feet ten different times, called trials, varying his speed at random. At the end of each trial he records on his data sheet the actual time it took him to walk the 50 feet, and the corresponding rating in percent. This information ordinarily is not given to the group until all ten trials are finished, although the correct ratings may be announced immediately after each trial. The walking speeds should fall between approximately 2.5 miles per hour (85 percent of normal) and 4.5 miles per hour (150 percent of normal), inasmuch as working speeds in practice are usually within these limits.

(6) Each person watches the operator walk the 50 feet and rates him, using 100% = 3 miles per hour as normal. Each trial is recorded in percent on the first horizontal line at the bottom of Form B204.

(7) Then read the correct ratings in percent, and ask each person to copy these ratings on the third horizontal line at the bottom of Form B204.

(8) Ask each person to plot his or her ratings on the rating graph. Each person should then draw a straight line through the average position of these points.

(9) Compute the systematic error, mean deviation, and absolute error for each person and for the group.

(10) Repeat this walking experiment each week until there is no further improvement. Use the same person as the subject or "operator" throughout the experiment.

131. Make a performance rating study of dealing cards.

Object

To obtain practice in rating operator performance.

Equipment and materials needed

1. Decimal minute stop-watch, deck of cards, card table.
2. Rating forms: B205 (Fig. 340).

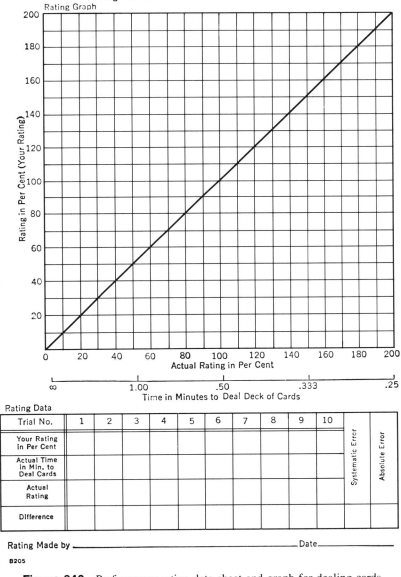

Figure 340 Performance rating data sheet and graph for dealing cards.

Place

Select a room large enough to accommodate the group of people who will participate in the study.

Procedure for conducting rating study

(1) Have someone (this person will be called the operator) practice dealing the deck of cards in four equal piles in ½ minute. Another person, called the timer, will by means of a stop watch time the operator and record the total time for dealing the deck. If the operator takes more or less than ½ minute to deal the deck, the timer informs the group of this fact and immediately determines the actual speed in percent, which he or she gives to the group. The group, of course, makes no record of the preliminary trials. The operator is seated and deals a standard deck of 52 cards in the following way. The deck is held in the left hand and the top card is positioned with the thumb and index finger of the left hand. The right hand grasps the positioned card, carries it, and tosses it onto the table. The four piles of cards are arranged on the four corners of a 1-foot square. The only requirements are that the cards shall all be face down and that each of the four piles shall be separate from the others. Care should be used to make certain that the method does not deviate from this as the speeds are varied. After a little practice, the operator can deal the cards in exactly ½ minute or at 100 percent rating.

(2) Provide each person with a data sheet similar to Form B205 (Fig. 340). Have each person fill in name and date at the bottom of this form. No stop watch or clock is to be used by members of the group in this study.

(3) The operator then deals the deck of cards in ½ minute, and the group is told that this speed represents a rating of 100 percent. Two or three trials are made at this speed.

(4) The operator then deals the deck ten different times, called trials, varying the speed at random. At the end of each trial the timer records the time and shows it to the operator, but does not give this information to the group until after all ten ratings have been made. The speeds should fall between approximately 85 percent of normal (dealing deck in 0.588 minute) and 150 percent of normal (dealing deck in 0.33 minute), inasmuch as working speeds in practice are usually within these limits.

(5) Each member of the group watches the operator deal the deck of cards and rates him or her, using $100\% = $ ½ minute as normal. Each trial is recorded in percent on the first horizontal line at the bottom of Form B205.

(6) Then read the correct ratings in percent and ask each person to copy these ratings on the third horizontal line at the bottom of Form B205.

(7) Ask each person to plot his or her ratings on the rating graph. Each person should then draw a straight line through the average position of these points.

(8) Compute the systematic error, mean deviation, and absolute error for each person and for the group.

(9) Repeat this card-dealing experiment each week until there is no further im-

provement. Use the same person as the subject or "operator" throughout the experiment, and make certain that the same method of dealing the cards is used.

CHAPTER 38

132. Discuss the advantages and the disadvantages of training the operator at the machine versus training in a separate training school.

133. Indicate the training that would be given to a new employee beginning work on operations described in Problems 44 and 45.

134. What would be the ultimate effect on the personnel of an organization of a training program in motion study and methods design for every new employee?

135. The output per hour of an operation after practice is greater than it was when the operator was a beginner. The statement might be made that the operator has becomed "skilled." State the evidence that accounts for the operator's productivity increase with practice.

136. Summarize steps necessary to reduce the time required for a new employee to reach standard performance level. How does anxiety affect learning time?

CHAPTER 39

137. Division of labor and specialization brought about increased productivity and lower costs of manufactured products. Around the turn of the century scientific management resulted in still greater productivity and further reduction in costs. Explain how scientific management accomplished this.

138. Give a resume of the results of the Hawthorne Experiment at the Western Electric Company.

139. Review and evaluate the contributions by Douglas McGregor, Abraham Maslow, and Rensis Likert.

140. State the results of Texas Instruments' replication of Frederick Herzberg's original investigation which led to his motivation-maintenance theory.

141. The Lincoln Electric Company has been using a form of participative management for many years. Describe the motivators in their plan.

CHAPTER 40

142. Study and evaluate the arguments that have been made for and against division of labor and specialization in the factory and the office.

143. What are the greatest objections to the paced assembly line from the workers' point of view?

144. Explain why the standard time for each position on an assembly line must be changed when the production schedule is changed and the number of people on the line is increased or decreased.

145. Study a situation where a paced assembly line was installed and make a comparison of each cost factor before and after the installation.

146. Make a study of the method and time required to wash a car using three different systems or degrees of mechanization. Determine the preferred system and prepare an appropriate report.

147. What event marked the beginning of General Motors' involvement in the quality of work life activities as a corporate policy?

148. Describe General Motors' plan for measuring the quality of work life in their organizations.

149. State the results of the application of the quality of work life philosophy in one of the General Motors plants.

150. How did the design and operation of Volvo's Kalmar factory differ from the design and operation of their other plants?

151. Summarize the advantages and disadvantages of the ''Volvo Plan'' in comparison with traditional automobile assembly.

CHAPTERS 41, 42, and 43

152. Summarize, in chronological order, the events or changes that have taken place at the Kodak Park facilities of Eastman Kodak Company in the areas of work measurement, work methods design, and incentives during the past 65 years.

153. What were the factors that led to the changes in the operation of the Scrap Collection Department in Kodak Park?

154. Both the Motorola plan and the Lakeview plan provide extra compensation for accomplishing stated objectives. Discuss the importance of this aspect of these plans.

155. Name and discuss those factors that you think account for the success of the participative management plan at Lakeview over such a long period of time.

156. If you were an employee, what do you think you would like most and least about (a) the Motorola Participative Management Program, and (b) the Lakeview Plan?

157. For a plan of participative management to be successful what changes must take place in the philosophy, mode of operation, and activities of management, assuming a traditional form of organization?

158. Make a critical evaluation of the current program of a company which has a formal plan for motivating its employees. If you are unable to make a first-hand study of such an organization, make your evaluation from available literature.

159. State some of the main reasons why industry is not moving at a faster rate in applying the research findings of social and behavioral scientists in the field of motivation.

BIBLIOGRAPHY

Abruzzi, Adam, *Work, Workers and Work Measurement,* Columbia University Press, New York, 1956, 318 pages.

Abruzzi, Adam, *Work Measurement,* Columbia University Press, New York, 1952, 290 pages.

Ackoff, Russell L., *Redesigning the Future,* John Wiley & Sons, New York, 1974, 260 pages.

Aitken, H. G. J., *Taylorism at Watertown Arsenal,* Harvard University Press, Cambridge, Mass., 1960, 269 pages.

Alford, L. P., *Henry Laurence Gantt,* American Society of Mechanical Engineers, New York, 1934, 315 pages.

Amar, Jules, *The Human Motor,* George Routledge & Sons, London, 1920, 470 pages.

American Society of Mechanical Engineers, ASME Standard No. 101, *Operation and Flow Process Charts,* New York, 1972. Also *Materials Handling Operation and Flow Charts,* ANSI Standard, Y 15-3-1974, American National Standard Institute, New York.

AIIE and ASME *Industrial Engineering Terminology,* American National Standard Z-94, 1972: 1, Biomechanics, 2 Cost Engineering, 3 Data Processing and Systems Design, 4 Distribution and Marketing, 5 Engineering Economy, 6 Facilities Planning, 7 Materials Processing, 8 Applied Mathematics, 9 Organization Planning and Theory, 10 Production Planning and Control, 11 Applied Psychology, 12 Work Measurement and Methods, Index, American Institute of Industrial Engineers, Norcross, Ga. or American Society of Mechanical Engineers, New York.

Anderson, N. G., *From Concept to Production,* Taylor and Francis, Ltd., London, 1975, 300 pages.

Antis, William, John M. Honeycutt, Jr., and Edward N. Koch, *The Basic Motions of MTM,* 4th ed., The Maynard Foundation, Naples, Florida, 1973.

Apple, J. M., *Plant Layout and Materials Handling,* 3rd ed., John Wiley & Sons, New York, 1977, 600 pages.

Apple, J. M., *Material Handling Systems Design,* John Wiley & Sons, New York, 1972, 656 pages.

Argyris, Chris, *Increasing Leadership Effectiveness,* John Wiley & Sons, New York, 1976, 286 pages.

Argyris, Chris, *Management and Operation Development: The Path From XA to BY,* McGraw-Hill Book Co., New York, 1971, 211 pages.

Argyris, Chris, *Organization and Innovation,* Richard D. Irwin, Homewood, Ill., 1965, 274 pages.

Argyris, Chris, *Integrating the Individual and the Organization,* John Wiley & Sons, New York, 1964, 330 pages.

Argyris, Chris, *Interpersonal Competence and Organizational Effectiveness,* The Dorsey Press, Homewood, Ill., 1962, 292 pages.

ASME, *The Frank Gilbreth Centennial,* The American Society of Mechanical Engineers, New York, 1969, 116 pages.

Babbage, Charles, *On the Economy of Machinery and Manufactures,* 4th ed., Charles Knight, Pall Mall, East, London, 1835, 408 pages.

Backman, Jules, *Wage Determination,* D. Van Nostrand Co., Princeton, N.J., 1959, 316 pages.

Bailey, G. B., and Ralph Presgrave, *Basic Motion Timestudy,* McGraw-Hill Book Co., New York, 1958, 195 pages.

Barnes, Ralph M., *Motion Study and Time Study,* Caryl Heyel (editor), *The Encyclopedia of Management,* 2nd ed., pp. 590–596, Van Nostrand Reinhold Co., New York, 1973.

Barnes, Ralph M., *Industrial Engineering Survey,* University of California, Los Angeles, 1967, 16 pages.

Barnes, Ralph M., *Motion and Time Study Problems and Porjects,* 2nd ed., John Wiley & Sons, New York, 1961, 232 pages.

Barnes, Ralph M., *Motion and Time Study Applications,* 4th ed., John Wiley & Sons, New York, 1961, 188 pages.

Barnes, Ralph M., *Work Sampling,* 2nd ed., John Wiley & Sons, New York, 1957, 283 pages.

Barnes, Ralph M., *Work Measurement Manual,* 4th ed., William C. Brown Co., Dubuque, Iowa, 1951, 297 pages.

Barnes, Ralph M., *Work Methods Training Manual,* 3rd ed., William C. Brown Co., Dubuque, Iowa, 1950, 337 pages.

Barnes, Ralph M., *Work Methods Manual,* John Wiley & Sons, New York, 1944, 136 pages.

Barnes, Ralph M., "An Investigation of Some Hand Motions Used in Factory Work," *University of Iowa Studies in Engineering, Bulletin* 6, 1936, 63 pages.

Barnes, Ralph M., *Industrial Engineering and Management,* McGraw-Hill Book Co., New York, 1931, 366 pages.

Barnes, Ralph M., and Robert B. Andrews, *Performance Sampling,* University of California, Los Angeles, 1955, 58 pages.

Barnes, Ralph M., and N. A. Englert, *Bibliography of Industrial Engineering and Management Literature,* William C. Brown Co., Dubuque, Iowa, 1946, 136 pages.

Barnes, Ralph M., and M. E. Mundel, *University of Iowa Studies in Engineering:* "Studies of Hand Motions and Rhythm Appearing in Factory Work," *Bulletin,* 12, 1938, 60 pages; "A Study of Hand Motions Used in Small Assembly

Work," *Bulletin* 16, 1939, 66 pages; "A Study of Simultaneous Symmetrical Hand Motions," *Bulletin* 17, 1939, 36 pages.

Barnes, Ralph M., M. E. Mundel, and John M. MacKenzie, "Studies of One- and Two-Handed Work," *University of Iowa Studies in Engineering, Bulletin* 21, 1940, 67 pages.

Barnes, Ralph M., J. S. Perkins, and J. M. Juran, "A Study of the Effect of Practice on the Elements of a Factory Operation," *University of Iowa Studies in Engineering, Bulletin,* 22, 1940, 95 pages.

Bedworth, David D., *Industrial Systems: Planning, Analysis, Control,* Ronald Press Co., New York, 1973, 504 pages.

Belcher, David W., *Compensation Administration,* Prentice-Hall, Englewood Cliffs, N.J.., 1974, 606 pages.

Bennis, Warren G., David E. Berlew, Edgar H. Schein, and Fred I. Steele (editors), *Interpersonal Dynamics,* 3rd ed., Dorsey Press, Homewood, Ill., 1973, 608 pages.

Bennis, Warren G., Kenneth D. Benne, and Robert Chin (editors), *The Planning of Change,* 2nd ed., Holt, Rinehart and Winston, New York, 1969, 627 pages.

Birn, S. A., R. M. Crossan, and R. W. Eastwood, *Measurement and Control of Office Work,* McGraw-Hill Book Co., New York, 1961, 318 pages.

Blake, R. R., and J. S. Mouton, *The Managerial Grid,* Gulf Publishing Co., Houston, Texas, 1964.

Brouha, Lucien, *Physiology in Industry,* Pergamon Press, New York, 1960, 145 pages.

Buffa, Elwood S., *Modern Production Management: Managing the Operations Function,* 5th ed., John Wiley & Sons, New York, 1977, 743 pages.

Buhl, Harold R., *Creative Engineering Design,* Iowa State University Press, Ames, Iowa, 1960, 195 pages.

Carroll, Phil, *How to Chart Data,* McGraw-Hill Book Co., New York, 1960, 260 pages.

Carroll, Phil, *Timestudy Fundamentals for Foremen,* 3rd ed., McGraw-Hill Book Co., New York, 1972.

Carson, Gordon B., H. A. Bolz, and H. H. Young (editors), *Production Handbook,* 3rd ed., John Wiley & Sons, New York, 1972, 1450 pages.

Cass, Eugene L., and Frederick G. Zimmer (editors), *Man and Work in Society,* Van Nostrand Reinhold Co., New York, 1975, 313 pages.

Cole, Robert E., *Work, Mobility, and Participation,* University of California Press, Berkeley-Los Angeles, Ca., 1979, 293 pages.

Connellan, Thomas K., *How to Improve Human Performance: Behaviorism in Business and Industry,* Harper & Row, New York, 1978, 185 pages.

Crossan, Richard M., and Harold W. Nance, *Master Standard Data: The Economic Approach to Work Measurement,* 2nd ed., McGraw-Hill Book Co., New York, 1972, 259 pages.

Clark, Wallace, *The Gantt Chart,* Ronald Press Co., New York, 1923, 157 pages.

Close, G. C., *Work Improvement*, John Wiley & Sons, New York, 1960, 388 pages.

Copley, F. B., *Frederick W. Taylor, Father of Scientific Management*, Vols. 1 and 2, Harper & Brothers, New York, 1923.

Dallas, Daniel B. (editor), *Tool and Manufacturing Engineering Handbook*, McGraw-Hill Book Co., New York, 1976, 2500 pages.

Damon, A., H. W. Stoudt and R. A. McFarland, *The Human Body in Equipment Design*, Harvard University Press, Cambridge, Mass., 1966, 360 pages.

Davidson, Sidney, and Ronald L. Weil (editors), *Handbook of Cost Accounting*, McGraw-Hill Book Co., New York, 1978.

Davis, Louis E., Albert B. Cherns, and Associates, *The Quality of Working Life*, two volumes, The Free Press, New York, 1975, Vol. 1—450 pages, Vol. 2—387 pages.

Davis, Louis E., and James C. Taylor (editors), *Design of Jobs*, 2nd ed., Goodyear Publishing Co., Santa Monica, Ca., 1979, 250 pages.

de Bono, Edward, *Lateral Thinking for Management*, American Management Association, New York, 1971, 225 pages.

de Bono, Edward, *The Use of Lateral Thinking*, Johanathan Cape, London, 1967, 157 pages.

De Garmo, E. Paul, *Materials and Processes in Manufacturing*, 5th ed., Macmillan Publishing Co., New York, 1979, 1076 pages.

Del Mar, Ronald, and Rodger D. Collons, *Classics in Scientific Management: A Book of Readings*, The University of Alabama Press, Mobile, Ala., 1976, 444 pages.

Dickson, W. J., and F. J. Roetlisberger, "Management and the Worker—Technical vs. Social Organization in an Industrial Plant," Graduate School of Business Administration, Division of Research, *Business Research Studies* 9, Harvard University, Boston, 1934, 17 pages.

Dreyfuss, Henry, *The Measure of Man*, Whitney Library of Design, New York, 1960.

Dreyfuss, Henry, *Designing for People*, Simon & Schuster, New York, 1955, 240 pages.

Drury, H. B., *Scientific Management; A History and Criticism*, Columbia University Press, New York, 1922, 271 pages.

Dubin, Robert (editor), *Handbook of Work, Organization, and Society*, Rand McNally, Chicago, Ill., 1976, 1068 pages.

Dudley, Norman A., *Work Measurement: Some Research Studies*, Macmillan, London, 1968, 139 pages.

Elliott, Jaques, *The Changing Culture of a Factory*, Tavistock Publications Ltd., London, 1951, 341 pages.

Emerson, H., *The Twelve Principles of Efficiency*, 5th ed., Engineering Management Co., New York, 1917, 423 pages.

Emerson, H., *Efficiency as a Basis for Operation and Wages*, Engineering Magazine Co., New York, 1912, 254 pages.

Fein, Mitchell, *Wage Incentive Plans,* Publication No. 2, American Institute of Industrial Engineers, Norcross, Ga., 1970, 42 pages.

Fein, Mitchell, *Motivation for Work,* Monograph No. 4, American Institute of Industrial Engineers, Norcross, Ga., 1974, 86 pages.

Ford, Robert N., *Motivation Through Work Itself,* American Management Association, New York, 1969, 267 pages.

Ford, Robert N., *Why Jobs Die & What to do About It,* Amacom, New York, 1979, 197 pages.

Fournies, Ferdinand F., *Coaching for Improved Work Performance,* Van Nostrand Reinhold Co., New York, 1978, 214 pages.

Francis, Richard L., and John A. White, *Facilities Layout and Location: An Analytical Approach,* Prentice-Hall, Englewood Cliffs, N.J., 1974, 468 pages.

Galbraith, Jay R., *Organization Design,* Addison-Wesley, Reading, Mass., 1977, 426 pages.

Gantt, H. L., *Work, Wages and Profits,* Engineering Management Co., New York, 1913.

Gellerman, S. W., *Motivation and Productivity,* American Management Association, New York, 1963, 304 pages.

Geppinger, H. C., *Dimensional Motion Times,* John Wiley & Sons, New York, 1955, 100 pages.

Gilbert, Thomas F., *Human Competence,* McGraw-Hill Book Co., New York, 1978, 376 pages.

Gilbreth, F. B., *Primer of Scientific Management,* D. Van Nostrand Co., Princeton, N.J., 1914, 108 pages.

Gilbreth, F. B., *Motion Study,* D. Van Nostrand Co., Princeton, N.J., 1911, 116 pages.

Gilbreth, F. B., *Bricklaying System,* Myron C. Clark Publishing Co., Chicago, 1909, 321 pages.

Gilbreth, F. B., and L. M., *Motion Study for the Handicapped,* George Routledge & Sons, London, 1920, 165 pages.

Gilbreth, F. B., and L. M., *Fatigue Study,* 2nd ed., Macmillan Co., New York, 1919, 175 pages.

Gilbreth, F. B., and L. M., *Applied Motion Study,* Sturgis & Walton Co., New York, 1917, 220 pages.

Gilbreth, Lillian M., *The Psychology of Management,* Sturgis & Walton Co., New York, 1914, 344 pages.

Gilbreth, Lillian M., and A. R. Cook, *The Foreman in Manpower Management,* McGraw-Hill Book Co., New York, 1947.

Gilbreth, Lillian M., Orpha Mae Thomas, and Eleanor Olymer, *Management in the Home,* Dodd, Mead, 1954, 241 pages.

Glaser, Edward M., *Improving the Quality of Worklife,* Human Interaction Research Institute, Los Angeles, Ca., 1975, 356 pages.

Goldmark, Josephine C., *Fatigue and Efficiency,* Charities Publication Committee,

Russell Sage Foundation, New York, 1912, 591 pages.

Gomberg, W., *A Trade Union Analysis of Time Study,* 2nd ed., Prentice-Hall, Englewood Cliffs, N.J., 1955, 318 pages.

Graham, Ben S., Jr., and Parvin S. Titus (editors), *The Amazing Oversight,* Amacom, New York, 1979, 197 pages.

Grandjean, E., *Fitting the Task to the Man,* Taylor & Francis Ltd., London, 1969, 164 pages.

Grant, E. L., W. G. Ireson, and R. S. Leavenworth, *Principles of Engineering Economy,* 6th ed., John Wiley & Sons, New York, 1976, 624 pages.

Grant, Eugene L., and Richard S. Leavenworth, *Statistical Quality Control,* 4th ed., McGraw-Hill Book Co., New York, 1972, 694 pages.

Gray, Jerry L. (editor), *The Glacier Project: Concepts & Critiques,* Crane, Russak & Co. Inc., New York, 1976, 445 pages.

Greenberg, Leo, and Don B. Chaffin, *Workers and their Tools,* Pendell Publishing Co., Midland, Mich., 1978, 143 pages.

Greene, James H., *Production and Inventory Control: Systems and Decisions,* revised ed., Richard D. Irwin, Homewood, Ill., 1974.

Griffith, John R., Walton M. Hancock, and Fred C. Munson, *Cost Controls in Hospitals,* Health Administration Press, University of Michigan, Ann Arbor, Mich., 1976, 447 pages.

Grossman, Lee, *The Change Agent,* American Management Association, New York, 1975, 168 pages.

Gyllenhammar, Pehr G., *People at Work,* Addison-Wesley, Reading, Mass., 1977, 164 pages.

Haire, Mason, *Psychology in Management,* 2nd ed., McGraw-Hill Book Co., New York, 1964, 238 pages.

Hansen, B. L., *Work Sampling for Modern Management,* Prentice-Hall, Englewood Cliffs, N.J., 1960, 263 pages.

Heiland, R. E., and W. J. Richardson, *Work Sampling,* McGraw-Hill Book Co., New York, 1957, 243 pages.

Herzberg, F., *Work and the Nature of Man,* The World Publishing Company, New York, 1966, 203 pages.

Herzberg, F., B. Mausner, and B. B. Snyderman, *The Motivation of Work,* 2nd ed., John Wiley & Sons, New York, 1959, 157 pages.

Herzberg, F., B. Mausner, R. O. Peterson, and D. F. Capwell, "Job Attitudes: Review of Research and Opinion," *Psychological Service of Pittsburgh,* Pittsburgh, Pa., 1957, 279 pages.

Heyel, Carl (editor), *The Encyclopedia of Management,* 2nd ed., Van Nostrand Reinhold Co., New York, 1973, 1161 pages.

Hill, A. V., *Living Machinery,* Harcourt Brace & Co., New York, 1927, 306 pages.

Holmes, W. G., *Applied Time and Motion Study,* revised, Ronald Press Co., New York, 1945, 383 pages.

Hoxie, R. F., *Scientific Management and Labor,* D. Appleton & Co., New York, 1915, 302 pages.

Handbook of Human Engineering Data, 2nd ed., Institute for Applied Experimental Psychology, Tufts College, Medford, Mass., 1951.

Hunt, E. E. (editor), *Scientific Management Since Taylor; a Collection of Authoritative Papers,* McGraw-Hill Book Co., New York, 1924, 263 pages.

Industrial Engineering Institute Proceedings, University of California, Los Angeles-Berkeley, annually, 1950–1965.

IMS Clinic Proceedings, Industrial Management Society, Des Plaines, Ill., annually since 1938.

Ireson, W. G., *Factory Planning and Plant Layout,* Prentice-Hall, Englewood Cliffs, N.J., 1956, 385 pages.

Ireson, W. G., and Eugene L. Grant (editors), *Handbook of Industrial Engineering and Management,* 2nd ed., Prentice-Hall, Englewood Cliffs, N.J., 1971, 907 pages.

Jenkins, David, *Job Power: Blue and White Collar Democracy,* Doubleday & Co., Garden City, N.Y., 1973, 375 pages.

Job Reform in Sweden, Swedish Employers' Confederation, Stockholm, Sweden, 1975, 131 pages.

Jones, Alan, and Peter Whittaker, *Testing Industrial Skills,* John Wiley & Sons, New York, 1975, 195 pages.

Juran, J. M., Frank M. Gryna, Jr., and R. S. Bingham, Jr. (editors), *Quality Control Handbook,* 3rd ed., McGraw-Hill Book Co., New York, 1974.

Kakar, Sudhir, *Frederick Taylor: A Study in Personality and Innovation,* The MIT Press, Cambridge, Mass., 1970, 221 pages.

Karger, Delmar W., and Franklin H. Bayha, *Engineered Work Measurement,* 3rd ed., Industrial Press Inc., New York, 1977, 811 pages.

Keeling, B. Lewis, Norman Kallaus, and John J. Neuner, *Administrative Office Management,* 7th ed., South-West Publishing Co., Cincinnati, OH, 1978, 768 pages.

Kepner, Charles H., and Benjamin B. Tregoe, *The Rational Manager,* McGraw-Hill Book Co., New York, 1965, 275 pages.

Kish, Joseph L., *Business Forms: Design and Control,* John Wiley & Sons, New York, 1971, 226 pages.

Konz, Stephen, *Work Design,* Grid Publishing, Inc., Colombus, Ohio, 1979, 592 pages.

Krick, E. V., *Methods Engineering,* John Wiley & Sons, New York, 1962, 530 pages.

Krick, E. V., *An Introduction to Engineering and Engineering Design,* 2nd ed., John Wiley & Sons, New York, 1969, 220 pages.

Kuttner, Monroe S., *Managing the Paperwork Pipeline,* John Wiley & Sons, New York, 1978, 236 pages.

Landsberger, Henry A., *Hawthorne Revisited*, Cornell University, Ithaca, N.Y., 1958, 119 pages.

Lehrer, R. N., *The Management of Improvement*, Reinhold Publishing Co., New York, 1965, 415 pages.

Lehrer, R. N., *Work Simplification*, Prentice-Hall, Englewood Cliffs, N.J., 1957, 394 pages.

Lewin, Kurt, *Resolving Social Conflict*, Harper & Row, New York, 1948, 230 pages.

Lichtner, W. O., *Time Study and Job Analysis*, Ronald Press Co., New York, 1921, 397 pages.

Likert, Rensis, *The Human Organization: Its Management and Value*, McGraw-Hill Book Co., New York, 1967, 258 pages.

Likert, Rensis, *New Patterns of Management*, McGraw-Hill Book Co., New York, 1961, 279 pages.

Lincoln, James F., *A New Approach to Industrial Economics*, The Lincoln Electric Co., Cleveland, Ohio, 1961, 166 pages.

Lincoln, James F., *Incentive Management*, Lincoln Electric Co., Cleveland, Ohio, 1951, 280 pages.

Lincoln, James F., *Lincoln's Incentive System*, McGraw-Hill Book Co., New York, 1946, 192 pages.

Lokiec, Mitchell, *Productivity and Incentives*, Bobbin Publications Inc., Columbia, S.C., 1977, 450 pages.

Lindholm, Rolf, and Jan-Peder Norstedt, *The Volvo Report*, Swedish Employers' Confederation, Stockholm, Sweden, 1975, 92 pages.

Louden, J. K., and J. W. Deegan, *Wage Incentives*, 2nd ed., John Wiley & Sons, New York, 1959, 227 pages.

Lowry, S. M., H. B. Maynard, and G. J. Stegemerten, *Time and Motion Study*, 3rd ed., McGraw-Hill Book Co., New York, 1940, 432 pages.

Luckiesh, M., *Seeing and Human Welfare*, Williams & Wilkins Co., Baltimore, 1934, 193 pages.

McCormick, Ernest J., *Job Analysis: Methods and Applications*, Amacom, New York, 1979, 371 pages.

McCormick, Ernest J., *Human Factors in Engineering and Design*, 4th ed., McGraw-Hill Book Co., New York, 1976, 491 pages.

McGregor, Douglas, *The Human Side of Enterprise*, McGraw-Hill Book Co., New York, 1960, 246 pages.

McGregor, Douglas, *The Professional Manager* (edited by Caroline McGregor and W. F. Bennis), McGraw-Hill Book Co., New York, 1967, 202 pages.

Magee, J. F., and D. M. Boodman, *Production Planning and Inventory Control*, 2nd ed., McGraw-Hill Book Co., New York, 1967, 397 pages.

Malcolm, J. A., Jr., W. J. Frost, R. E. Hannan, and W. R. Smith, *Ready Work-Factor Time Standards*, WOFAC Corporation, Haddonfield, N.J., 1966.

Marrow, A. J. (editor), *The Failure of Success,* American Management Association, New York, 1972, 339 pages.

Marrow, A. J., *Making Management Human,* McGraw-Hill Book Co., New York, 1957, 241 pages.

Marrow, A. J., D. G. Bowers, and S. E. Seashore, *Management by Participation,* Harper & Row, New York, 1967, 264 pages.

Maslow, Abraham H., *Motivation and Personality,* Harper & Row, New York, 1970, 369 pages.

Maslow, Abraham H., *Toward a Psychology of Being,* 2nd ed., Van Nostrand Co., Princeton, N.J., 1968

Maynard, H. B. (editor), *Handbook of Modern Manufacturing Management,* McGraw-Hill Book Co., New York, 1970.

Maynard, H. B. (editor), *Industrial Engineering Handbook,* 3rd ed., McGraw-Hill Book Co., New York, 1971.

Maynard, H. B., G. J. Stegemerten, and J. L. Schwab, *Methods-Time Measurement,* McGraw-Hill Book Co., New York, 1948, 292 pages.

Maynard, H. B., and G. J. Stegemerten, *Guide to Methods Improvement,* McGraw-Hill Book Co., New York, 1944, 82 pages.

Maynard, H. B., and G. J. Stegemerten, *Operation Analysis,* McGraw-Hill Book Co., New York, 1939, 298 pages.

Mayo, Elton, *The Human Problems of an Industrial Civilization,* 2nd ed., Harvard University Press, Cambridge, 1946.

Mayo, Elton, *The Social Problems of an Industrial Civilization,* Division of Research, Graduate School of Business Administration, Harvard University, Boston, 1945, 150 pages.

Meister, David, *Human Factors: Theory and Practice,* John Wiley & Sons, New York, 1971, 415 pages.

Merrick, Dwight V., *Times Studies as a Basis for Rate Setting,* Engineering Magazine Co., New York, 1920, 36b pages.

Miles, L. D., *Techniques of Value Analysis and Engineering,* McGraw-Hill Book Co., New York, 1961, 267 pages.

Miller, Richard B. (editor), *Participative Management, Quality of Worklife and Job Enrichment,* Noyes Data Corp., Park Ridge, N.J., 1977, 199 pages.

Mogensen, A. H., *Common Sense Applied to Motion and Time Study, McGraw-Hill* Book Co., New York, 1932, 228 pages.

Moore, Brian E., and T. L. Ross, *The Scanlon Way to Improved Productivity: A Practical Guide,* John Wiley & Sons, New York, 1977, 256 pages.

Morrow, R. L., *Motion Economy and Work Measurement,* Ronald Press, New York, 1957, 468 pages.

Moski, Bruno A., *The Human Side of Production Management,* Prentice-Hall, Englewood Cliffs, N.J., 1979, 288 pages.

Mudge, Arthur E., *Value Engineering: A Systematic Approach,* McGraw-Hill Book Co., New York, 1971, 286 pages.

Mundel, M. E., *Motion and Time Study,* 5th ed., Prentice-Hall, Englewood Cliffs, N.J., 1978, 750 pages.

Muther, Richard, *Systematic Layout Planning,* 2nd ed., CBI Publishing Co., Inc., Boston, Mass., 1973, 314 pages.

Muther, Richard, *Practical Plant Layout,* McGraw-Hill Book Co., New York, 1956, 384 pages.

Muther, Richard, *Production-Line Technique,* McGraw-Hill Book Co., New York, 1944, 320 pages.

Myers, M. Scott, *Every Employee a Manager,* McGraw-Hill Book Co., New York, 1970, 233 pages.

Nadler, Gerald, *Work Design: A Systems Concept,* rev. ed., Richard D. Irwin, Homewood, Ill., 1970, 816 pages.

Nadler, Gerald, *Motion and Time Study Work Simplification,* McGraw-Hill Book Co., New York, 1957.

Nanda, R., and G. L. Adler (editors), *Learning Curve Theory and Application,* American Institute of Industrial Engineers, Norcoross, Ga.

Niebel, B. W., *Motion and Time Study,* 6th ed., Richard D. Irwin, Homewood, Ill., 1976, 719 pages.

Norstedt, Jan-Peder, and Stefan Aguren, *The Saab-Scania Report,* Swedish Employers' Confederation, Stockholm, Sweden, 1977, 50 pages.

O'Brien, J. J., *Value Analysis in Design and Construction,* McGraw-Hill Book Co., New York, 1976, 301 pages.

Osborn, Alex F., *Applied Imagination,* rev. ed., Charles Scribner's Sons, New York, 1957, 379 pages.

Ostwald, Philip E., *Cost Estimating for Engineering and Management,* Prentice-Hall, Englewood Cliffs, N.J., 1974, 492 pages.

Pickett, Ronald M., and Thomas J. Triggs (editors), *Human Factors in Health Care,* D. C. Heath and Co., Lexington, Mass., 382 pages.

Porter, L. W., E. E. Lawler, and J. R. Hackman (editors), *Perspectives on Behavior in Organizations,* McGraw-Hill Book Company, New York, 1977, 485 pages.

Poulton, E. C., *Tracking Skill and Manual Control,* Academic Press, New York, 1974, 427 pages.

Prenting, Theodore O., and N. T. Thomopolos *Humanism and Technology in Assembly Line Systems,* Hayden Book Co., Rochelle Park, N.J., 1974, 404 pages.

Presgrave, Ralph, *The Dynamics of Time Study,* 2nd ed., McGraw-Hill Book Co., New York, 1945, 238 pages.

Presgrave, Ralph, and G. B. Bailey, *Basic Motion Timestudy,* McGraw-Hill Book Co., New York, 1958, 195 pages.

Pressman, Roger S. and John E. Williams, *Numerical Control and Computer-Aided Manufacturing,* John Wiley & Sons, New York, 1977, 302 pages.

Quick, J. H., J. H. Duncan, and J. A. Malcolm, Jr., *Work-Factor Time Standards,*

McGraw-Hill Book Co., New York, 1962, 458 pages.

Rice, A. K., *Productivity and Social Organization: The Ahmedabad Experiment,* Tavistock Publications Ltd., London, 1958, 298 pages.

Richardson, Wallace J., *Cost Improvement, Work Sampling, and Short Interval Scheduling,* Reston Publishing Co., Reston, Va., 1976, 228 pages.

Rock, Milton L. (editor), *Handbook of Wage and Salary Administration,* McGraw-Hill Book Co., New York, 1972.

Roebuck, J. A., H. E. Kroemer, and W. G. Thomson, *Engineering Anthropometry Methods,* John Wiley & Sons, New York, 1975, 459 pages.

Roethlisberger, F. J., *Management and Morale,* Harvard University Press, Cambridge, 1941, 194 pages.

Roethlisberger, F. J., and W. J. Dickson, *Management and the Workers,* Harvard University Press, Cambridge, 1940, 615 pages.

Rosow, J. M. (editor), *The Worker and the Job: Coping With Change,* Prentice-Hall, Englewood Cliffs, N.J., 1974, 208 pages.

Ross, Joel E., *Managing Productivity,* Prentice-Hall, Englewood Cliffs, N.J., 1977, 186 pages.

Rothenberg, Albert, and Carl R. Hausman (editors), *The Creative Question,* Duke University Press, Durham, N.C., 1976, 366 pages.

Roy, Robert H., *The Cultures of Management,* Johns Hopkins University Press, Baltimore, Md., 1977, 431 pages.

Rubinstein, Mosha F., *Patterns of Problem Solving,* Prentice-Hall, Englewood Cliffs, N.J., 1975, 544 pages.

Ruch, William A., and James C. Hershauer, *Factors Affecting Worker Productivity,* Bureau of Business & Economic Research, Arizona State University, Tempe, Arizona, 1974, 122 pages.

Rudd, Dale F., and Charles C. Watson, *Strategy of Process Engineering,* John Wiley & Sons, New York, 1968, 466 pages.

Salvendy, Gavriel, and W. Douglas Seymour, *Prediction and Development of Industrial Work Performance,* John Wiley & Sons, New York, 1973, 351 pages.

SAVE Proceedings, annually, Society of American Value Engineers, P.O. Box 210877, Dallas, TX 75211.

Schnelle, Kenneth E., *Case Analysis and Business Problem Solving,* McGraw-Hill Book Co., New York, 1967, 230 pages.

Shaw, Anne G., *An Introduction to the Theory and Application of Motion Study,* Harlequin Press, London, 1953, 37 pages.

Shaw, Anne G., *Purpose and Practice of Motion Study,* 2nd ed., Columbine Press, London, 1960, 324 pages.

Shumard, F. W., *A Primer of Time Study,* McGraw-Hill Book Co., New York, 1940, 519 pages.

Shwinger, P., *Wage Incentive Systems,* John Wiley & Sons, New York, 1975, 200 pages.

Simon, Herbert A., *The New Science of Management Decision,* rev. ed., Prentice-

Hall, Englewood Cliffs, N.J., 1977, 175 pages.

Smalley, H. E., *Hospital Industrial Engineering,* Reinhold, New York, 1966, 460 pages.

Smith, George L., *Work Measurement: A Systems Approach,* Grid Publishing, Columbus, Ohio, 1978, 123 pages.

Spriegel, William R., and C. E. Myers (editors), *The Writings of the Gilbreths,* Richard D. Irwin, Homewood, Ill., 1953, 513 pages.

Stewart, Paul A., "Job Enlargement," Monogram Series No. 3, University of Iowa, Iowa City, 1967, 64 pages.

Stivers, C. L., "Experience in Retraining on the Dvorak Keyboard," American Management Association, *Supplementary Office Management Series, No. 1,* New York, 1941, 12 pages.

Sutermeister, Robert A., *People and Productivity,* 3rd ed., McGraw-Hill Book Co., New York, 1976, 475 pages.

Sylvester, L. A., *The Handbook of Advanced Time-Motion Study,* Funk & Wagnalls Co., New York, 1950, 273 pages.

Tanner, William R. (editor), *Industrial Robots,* two volumes, Society of Manufacturing Engineers, Dearborn, Mich.

Taylor, F. W., *Scientific Management; Comprising Shop Management, Principles of Scientific Management, and Testimony before Special House Committee,* Harper & Brothers, New York, 1947.

Taylor, F. W., *The Principles of Scientific Management,* Harper & Brothers, New York, 1911, 144 pages.

Taylor, F. W., "On the Art of Cutting Metals," *Transactions of the ASME,* Vol. 28, pp. 31–350, 1907.

Taylor, F. W., *Shop Management,* Harper & Brothers, New York, 1919, 207 pages reprinted from *Transactions of the ASME,* Vol. 24, pp. 1337–1480, 1903.

Taylor Society, *Scientific Management in American Industry,* Harper & Brothers, New York, 1929, 472 pages.

Taylor, James C. et al., *The Quality of Working Life: An Annotated Bibliography,* Center for Organizational Studies, Graduate School of Management, UCLA, Los Angeles, Ca., 1972, 500 pages.

Terry, George R., *Office Management and Control,* 7th ed., Richard D. Irwin, Homewood, Ill., 1975, 791 pages.

Thompson, C. B. (editor), *Scientific Management,* Harvard University Press, Cambridge, 1914, 878 pages.

Thuesen, H. G., W. J. Fabrycky, and G. J. Thuesen, *Engineering Economy,* 5th ed., Prentice-Hall, Englewood Cliffs, N.J., 1977, 608 pages.

Tichauer, E. R., *The Biomechanical Bases of Ergonomics,* John Wiley & Sons, New York, 1978, 93 pages.

Tiffin, Joseph, and E. J. McCormick, *Industrial Psychology,* 6th ed., Prentice-Hall, Englewood Cliffs, N.J., 1974, 625 pages.

Tippett, L. H. C., *Technological Applications of Statistics,* John Wiley & Sons, New York, 1950, 184 pages.

Towne, Henry R., *The Engineer as an Economist,* ASME Transactions, American Society of Mechanical Engineers, New York, 1886.

Trist, E. L., G. W. Higgin, H. Murray, and A. B. Pollock, *Organizational Choice,* Tavistock Publications Ltd., London; 1963, 332 pages.

Tucker, Spencer A., *The Complete Machine-Hour Rate System for Cost-Estimating and Pricing,* Prnetice-Hall, Englewood Cliffs, N.J., 1975, 383 pages.

Turner, Wayne C., Joe H. Mize, and Kenneth E. Case, *Introduction to Industrial and Systems Engineering,* Prentice-Hall, Englewood Cliffs, N.J., 1978, 416 pages.

U.S. Department of Health, Education and Welfare Task Force, *Work in America,* The MIT Press, Cambridge, Mass., 1973, 262 pages.

University of California, *Proceedings of Industrial Engineering Institute,* University of California, Los Angeles-Berkeley, annually, 1950–1965.

Urwick, L. (editor), *The Golden Book of Management,* Newman Neame, London, 1956, 208 pages.

Urwick, L., and E. F. L. Brech, *The Making of Scientific Management,* Vol. 1, *Thirteen Pioneers,* Management Publications Trust, London, 1945, 196 pages.

Van Cott, Harold P., and Robert G. Kincade (editors), U.S. Department of Defense, *Human Engineering Guide to Equipment Design,* Revised edition, Superintendent of Documents, U.S. Government Printing Office, Washington, D.C., 1972.

Van Doren, H. L., *Industrial Design,* 2nd ed., McGraw-Hill Book Co., New York, 1954, 379 pages.

Vaughn, Richard C., *Introduction to Industrial Engineering,* 2nd ed., University Press, Ames, Iowa, 1977, 495 pages.

Von Fange, E. K., *Professional Creativity,* Prentice-Hall, Englewood Cliffs, N.J., 1959, 260 pages.

Vough, Clair F., with Bernard Asbell, *Productivity,* Amacom, New York, 1979, 212 pages.

Vroom, Victor H., *Work and Motivation,* John Wiley & Sons, New York, 1964, 331 pages.

Walker, C. R., and R. H. Guest, *The Man on the Assembly Line,* Harvard University Press, Cambridge, 1952, 180 pages.

Walker, C. R., R. H. Guest, and A. N. Turner, *The Foreman on the Assembly Line,* Harvard University Press, Cambridge, 1956, 197 pages.

Walker, C. R., and A. G. Walker, *Modern Technology and Civilization,* McGraw-Hill Book Co., New York, 1962, 469 pages.

Warr, Peter, *Personal Goals and Work Design,* John Wiley & Sons, New York, 1976, 264 pages.

Wechsler, David, *The Range of Human Capacities,* 2nd ed., Williams & Wilkins Co., Baltimore, 1952, 190 pages.

Weiner, J. S., and H. G. Maule (editors), *Human Factors in Work, Design and Production,* Taylor & Francis Ltd., London. In the U.S., Halsted Press, New York, 1977, 138 pages.

Whitehead, T., *Leadership in a Free Society,* Harvard University Press, Cambridge, 1947, 266 pages.

Whitehead, T., *The Industrial Worker,* Harvard University Press, Cambridge, 1938, two volumes.

Whitehouse, Geary E., *Systems Analaysis and Design Using Network Techniques,* Prentice-Hall, Englewood Cliffs, N.J., 1973, 500 pages.

Whiting, C. S., *Creative Thinking,* Reinhold Publishing Co., New York, 1958, 168 pages.

Whiting, Williams, *What's on the Worker's Mind,* Charles Scribner's, New York, 1920.

Whyte, W. F., *Men at Work,* Richard D. Irwin, Homewood, Ill., 1961, 393 pages.

Whyte, William F., *Money and Motivation: An Analysis of Incentives in Industry,* Harper & Brothers, New York, 1955, 268 pages.

Wild, R., *Work Organization: A Study of Manual Work and Mass Production,* John Wiley & Sons, New York, 1975, 226 pages.

Woodson, W. E., and D. W. Conover, *Human Engineering Guide for Equipment Designers,* 2nd ed., University of California Press, Berkeley, 1964.

Wylie, Harry L., and James Q. Harty (editors), *Office Management Handbook,* 2nd ed., John Wiley & Sons, New York, 1958, 900 pages.

Yoder, Dale, and Herbert G. Heneman (editors), *ASPA Handbook of Personnel and Industrial Relations,* The Bureau of National Affairs, Inc., Washington, D.C., 1979.

York, Lyle, *A Radical Approach to Job Enrichment,* Amacom, New York, 1976, 209 pages.

Yost, Edna, *Frank and Lillian Gilbreth: Partners for Life,* Rutgers University Press, New Brunswick, N.J., 1949, 372 pages.

Zollitsch, Herbert G., and Adolph Langsner, *Wage and Salary Administration,* South-West Publishing Co., Cincinnati, Ohio, 1970, 751 pages.

PERIODICALS

Advanced Management Journal, quarterly, Society for Advancement of Management, a division of American Management Association, 135 West 50th Street, New York, N.Y. 10020.

AIIE Transactions, quarterly, American Institute of Industrial Engineers, 25 Technology/Park, Norcross, GA 30092.

AIIE Proceedings of Annual Conference, annually since 1955, American Institute of Industrial Engineers, 25 Technology Park/Atlanta, Norcross, GA 30092.

American Machinist, monthly, McGraw-Hill, Inc., 1221 Avenue of the Americas, N.Y., 10020.

AMA Management Digest, monthly, American Management Association, 135 West 50th Street, New York, N.Y. 10020.

American Psychologist, monthly, American Psychological Association, Inc., 1200 Seventh Street, N.W., Washington, D.C. 20036.

Annals of Biomedical Engineering, quarterly, Journal of the Biomedical Engineering Society, Academic Press Inc., 111 Fifth Avenue, N.Y. 10003.

Decision Sciences, quarterly, American Institute for Decision Sciences, University Plaza, Atlanta, GA 30303.

The Engineering Economist, quarterly, a joint publication of the Engineering Economy Division of AIIE and American Society for Engineering Education, American Institute of Industrial Engineers, 25 Technology Park/Atlanta, Norcross, GA 30092.

Ergonomics, monthly, Taylor & Francis Ltd., 10–14 Macklin Street, London WC 2B 5NF.

Harvard Business Review, bimonthly, Graduate School of Business Administration, Harvard University, Boston, MA 02163.

Human Factors, bimonthly, Human Factors Society, Box 1369, Santa Monica, CA 90406.

Industrial Engineering, monthly, American Institute of Industrial Engineers, 25 Technology Park/Atlanta, Norcross, GA 30092.

Industrial Management, bimonthly, Industrial Management Society, 570 Northwest Highway, Des Plaines, Ill. 60016.

Interactions, monthly, Society of American Value Engineers, P.O. Box 210887, Dallas, TX 75211.

Interfaces—A TIMS-ORSA Journal, quarterly, The Institute of Management Sciences and The Operations Research Society of America, 146 Westminster Street, Providence, R.I. 02903.

International Journal of Production Research, bimonthly, Taylor & Francis Ltd., 10–14 Macklin Street, London WC2B 5NF.

Journal of Applied Behavioral Science, quarterly, NTL Institute for Applied Behavioral Science, P. O. Box 9155, Rosslyn Station, Arlington, VA 22209.

Journal of Applied Psychology, bimonthly, American Psychological Association, Inc., 1200 Seventeenth Street, N.W., Washington, D.C. 20036.

Journal of Biomechanical Engineering, quarterly, American Society of Mechanical Engineers, 345 East 47th Street, New York, N.Y. 10017.

Journal of Methods-Time Measurement, quarterly, MTM Association for Standards and Research, 16-01 Broadway, Fair Lawn, N.J. 07410.

Management Review, monthly, American Management Association, 135 West 50th Street, New York, N.Y. 10020.

Manufacturing Engineering, monthly, Society of Manufacturing Engineers, One SME Drive, P.O. Box 930, Dearborn, Mich. 48128.

Materials Handling Engineering, monthly, Penton/IPC Inc., 614 Superior Ave. West, Cleveland, Ohio 44113.

Mechanical Engineering, monthly, American Society of Mechanical Engineers, 345 East 47th Street, New York, N.Y. 10017.

Modern Materials Handling, monthly, Cahners Publishing Co., 221 Columbus Ave., Boston, Mass. 02116.

The Office, monthly, Office Publications, Inc., 1200 Summer Street, Stamford, Conn. 06904.

Plant Engineering, biweekly, Technical Publishing Co., Barrington, Ill. 60010.

Product Engineering, monthly, Morgan-Grampian Publishing Co., 205 East 42nd Street, New York, N.Y. 10017.

Quality Progress, monthly, American Society for Quality Control, Inc., 161 West Wisconsin Avenue, Milwaukee, Wis. 53204.

Robot Newsletter, quarterly, Robot Institute of America, 20501 Ford Road, P.O. Box 930, Dearborn, Mich. 48128.

Sloan Management Review, quarterly, Sloan Management Review Association, Massachusetts Institute of Technology, 50 Memorial Drive, Cambridge, MA 02139.

Value World, quarterly, Society of American Value Engineers, P.O. Box 210887, Dallas, TX 75211.

Work Study, monthly, Sawell Publications, Ltd., 127 Stanstead Road, London, SE23 1JE.

FOREIGN TRANSLATIONS OF BOOKS BY RALPH M. BARNES

Manual de Metodos de Trabajo. Translated by Saturnino Alvarez. Introduction by Fermin de la Sierra. Published by Aguilar, S. A. de Ediciones, Juan Bravo 38, Madrid, Spain, 1950, 161 pages.

Étude des Mouvements et des Temps, troisieme edition. Translated by le Bureau des Temps Élémentaires. Published by Les Editions d'Organization, 8 Rue Alfred de Vigny, Paris 8e, France, 1953, 560 pages.

Studio dei Movimenti e dei Tempi. Translated by Giorgio Deangeli. Published by Edizioni di Communità, Via Manzoni 12, Milan, Italy, 1955, 380 pages.

Estudio de Movimientos y Tiempos. Translated by Carlos Paz Shaw. Published by Aguilar, S. A. de Ediciones, Juan Bravo 38, Madrid, Spain, 1956, 575 pages.

Practique des Observations Instantanées. Translated by le Bureau des Temps Élémentaires. Published by Les Editions d'Organisation, 8 Rue Alfred de Vigny, Paris 8e, France, 321 pages, 1958.

Motion and Time Study, 4th ed. Translated into Japanese by Mayumi Otsubo. Published by Nikkan Kogyo Shimbun-Sha, No. 1, 1-chome Iidamachi, Chiyoda-Ku, Tokyo, Japan, 1960, 658 pages.

Études des Mouvements et des Temps, quatrieme edition. Translated by M. Maze-Sencier and le Bureau des Temps Elementaires. Published by Les Editions d'Organization, 8 Rue Alfred de Vigny, Paris 8e, France, 1960, 749 pages.

Work Sampling, 2nd ed. Translated into Japanese by Masakazu Tamai. Published by Nikkan Kogyo Shimbun-Sha, No. 1, 1-chome Iidamachi, Chiyoda-Ku, Tokyo, Japan, 348 pages, 1961.

Industrial Engineering. Translated into Japanese and published by Nippon Noritsu Kyokai, New Ohtemachi Building, 2–4, Ohtemachi, Chiyoda-Ku, Tokyo, Japan, 1961, 115 pages.

La Technica del Muestreo Aplicada a la Medida del Trabajo, translated into Spanish by Anselmo Calleja Siero, Actuario Matemático Estadistico Facultativo del Instituto Nacional de Estadística. Published by Aguilar, S. A. de Ediciones, Madrid, Spain, 1962, 301 pages.

Motion and Time Study, 4th ed., translated into Serbo-Croatian language by Dmitar Culíc-Jugoslovenska Autorska Agencija, Zegreb, Yugoslavia. Published 1964, 726 pages.

Estudo de Movimentos E de Tempos: Projeto E Medida do Trabajo, translated into Portuguese by Sérgio Luiz Oliveira Assis, José S. Guedes Azevedo and Arnaldo Pallotta. Published by Editora Edgard Blücher Ltda., Editora da Universidade de São Paulo, São Paulo, Brazil, 1966, 744 pages.

Estudio de Movimientos y Tiempos, 5th ed., translated into Spanish by Ricardo Garcia-Pelayo Alonso. Published by Aguilar, S. A. de Ediciones, Juan Bravo, 38 Madrid, Spain, 1966, 746 pages.

L'Analisi del Lavoro con il Metodo del Campionamento, translated into Italian by Olinto Praturlon, published by Etas-Kompass, S.p.A., Via Mantegna 6, Milan, Italy, 1967, 361 pages.

Estudo de Movimentos e de Tempos: Projecto e Medida do Trabalho, 6th edition, Editora Edgard Blucher Ltd., Sao Paulo, Brazil, 1977, 635 pages.

FOREIGN PUBLICATIONS IN THE ENGLISH LANGUAGE

Motion and Time Study, 4th ed., Modern Asia Edition. Published by the Charles E. Tuttle Company, 15 Edogawa-Cho, Bunkyo-ku, Tokyo, Japan, 1960, 665 pages.

Motion and Time Study: Design and Measurement of Work, International Edition, John Wiley & Sons, Inc., London, 1965, 739 pages.

Motion and Time Study, 4th ed., Modern Asia Edition, published by the Charles E. Tuttle Company, ISTIQIAL PRESS, Lahore on behalf of Printing Corporation of Pakistan Ltd., Islamabad, 1972, 665 pages. For sale and use in Pakistan.

Motion and Time Study—Design and Measurement of Work, 6th ed., Published by Mei Ya Publications, Inc., Tapiei, Taiwan, 1972, 799 pages. For sale in Taiwan only.

MOTION PICTURE FILMS

Produced by Ralph M. Barnes, Robert B. Andrews, and O. E. Patterson.

Color, Sound 16 mm

THE FOREMAN DISCOVERS MOTION STUDY, Running Time 16 minutes.
INTRODUCTION TO WORK SAMPLING, Running Time 19 minutes.
MAKING A WORK SAMPLING STUDY, Running Time 23 minutes.
ESTABLISHING WORK STANDARDS BY SAMPLING, Running Time 25 minutes.
Above films sold and rented by University of California Extension, Media Center, 2223 Fulton Street, Berkeley, California 94720.

Performance rating films produced by Ralph M. Barnes

Black and White 16 mm.

UNIT I WORK MEASUREMENT FILMS, Five Reels.
UNIT II WORK MEASUREMENT FILMS, Six Reels.
Above films rented by the International Film Bureau, Inc., 332 South Michigan Avenue, Chicago, Ill., 60604.

INDEX